Chinese-Soviet Relations
1937–1945

Chinese-Soviet Relations 1937–1945

The Diplomacy of Chinese Nationalism

JOHN W. GARVER

New York   Oxford
OXFORD UNIVERSITY PRESS
1988

Oxford University Press

Oxford   New York   Toronto
Delhi   Bombay   Calcutta   Madras   Karachi
Petaling Jaya   Singapore   Hong Kong   Tokyo
Nairobi   Dar es Salaam   Cape Town
Melbourne   Auckland

and associated companies in
Berlin   Ibadan

Copyright © 1988 by Oxford University Press, Inc.

Published by Oxford University Press, Inc.,
200 Madison Avenue, New York, New York 10016

Oxford is a registered trademark of Oxford University Press

Library of Congress Cataloging-in-Publication Data
Garver, John W.
Chinese-Soviet relations, 1937–1945.
Bibliography: p.   Includes index.
1. China—Foreign relations—Soviet Union.
2. Soviet Union—Foreign relations—China.
3. China—Politics and government—1937–1945. I. Title.
DS740.5.S65G37   1988   327.51047   88-1462
ISBN 0-19-505432-6

Printing (last digit): 9 8 7 6 5 4 3 2 1

For Penelope and Vanessa

The author wishes to thank the Committee for Scientific and Scholarly Cooperation with the U.S.A. of Taiwan's Academia Sinica and the Inter-University Program Administered by Stanford University in Taibei for a Research Fellowship during 1982–1983 which made possible the initial research for this project.

Preface

Research for this book began in 1982–1983 under the auspices of a research fellowship of Taiwan's Committee for Scientific and Scholarly Communications with the U.S.A. of Academia Sinica, and the Inter-University Program (IUP) Administered by Stanford University in Taibei. In Taibei a number of people most graciously facilitated my research, including Dr. James E. Dew, director of the IUP, Dr. Chang Chong-tung at Academia Sinica, Mr. Chen Shao-yi of the KMT Committee on Party History, Mr. Lu Shou-chang of the historical materials office at Academia Historica, Mr. Vernon Feng at the historical office of the Bureau of Investigation of the Ministry of Justice, and Lieutenant General Dunn Ju-mou of the historical compilation office of the Ministry of National Defense. Thanks are especially due to Dr. Wang Chi-wu, the vice director of Taiwan's National Science Council, who not only helped arrange my research but also made available to me the diary of his father, Dr. Wang Shijie, for the period covering the negotiation of the 1945 Chinese-Soviet treaty. On the other side of the Taiwan Strait, many people in Nanjing also helped me in my research while I was at Nanjing University as Pomona College's liaison representative in 1984. I am especially grateful to Mr. Chen Guanghua of Nanjing University's foreign affairs office, Professor Zhang Xianwen of NanDa's history department, and the staff of the Jiangsu Provincial Library. Thanks are also due to Dr. Li Tien-min, Mr. Kuo Te-chuan, Dr. Peter Kuhfus, Dr. Robert M. Slusser, Mr. Gordon Creighton, Miss Chen Li-wen, Miss Wang Yueh-min, Professor Cai Dejin, and Major General Fine Y. Fan for help at various stages.

The first draft of this book was completed while I was a visiting research associate at the Center of Chinese Studies at the University of Michigan during 1984–1985, a position for which I thank Professors Michel Oksenberg and Robert F. Dernberger. I am especially grateful to Professors Steven I. Levine, Michael H. Hunt, Lloyd E. Eastman, and Thomas E. Stolper for plowing through and criticizing an earlier, more lengthy version of the manuscript. Professors Allen S. Whiting and William C. Kirby also read respectively the chapters on Xinjiang and KMT diplomacy. Any errors of fact or interpretation which remain are, of course, my own. Finally, I wish to thank the *Political Science Quarterly* for allowing the reprint of a version of the chapter on Sino-Soviet alliance which appeared in the summer 1987 issue of that journal.

This book is written for both China specialists as well as a more general audience. In order to make it more readable for nonspecialists, discussions of academic points of interpretation and evidence are restricted to the notes. Scholars will be interested in the ways in which my interpretations of events differ from those of earlier studies, in the full evidence underlying my conclusions, in the reliability of various sources, and in the resolution of contradictions between different bodies of evidence. They will therefore wish to turn to the notes. Nonspecialists would probably find such matters tiring, and it is for them that such discussions are excluded from the main text so as to maintain the continuity of events.

A mea culpa is also appropriate regarding the inevitable criticism that by focusing on Chiang Kai-shek and his diplomacy I depict the Nationalist regime as a united state apparatus rather than the fragmented entity that it in fact was. As is well known, the Nationalist regime of the wartime period was so fragmented that in many respects it makes more sense to think of that entity as a diverse collection of bureaucratic, partisan, and regional groups joined in a loose coalition against Japan, rather than as a unified Chinese state leading a people in a struggle for national survival. Nonetheless, I believe that several considerations justify this book's perspective of the Nationalist regime as an individual decision-maker. First, in virtually all countries the locus of authority as regards "high diplomacy" (dealing with fundamental orientations toward the powers) is highly centralized. In wartime, this is even more the case. Second, the very nature of modern "sovereignty" gives a very few individuals the power to speak authoritatively for many millions. In other words, while other Chinese politicians could influence China's international relations, only Chiang Kai-shek could speak for "China." Although I have tried to consider the disunity of the Nationalist regime, and of China, when this impinged directly on Chiang's diplomacy, in a broader sense the criticism of my perspective is valid. Still, I believe that this approach has allowed me to capture the essence of Chiang's—and consequently "China's"—high diplomacy toward the Soviet Union during the war.

I have generally followed the *pinyin* style of latinization of Chinese words except for the names of individuals and organizations well known in the West by more traditional forms (e.g., the Kuomintang, Chiang Kai-shek, T.V. Soong, H.H. Kung, and V.K. Wellington Koo). References to these individuals in the titles or texts of Chinese language works are, however, in *pinyin*.

A few words are also perhaps in order about the use of the racist epithet "Jap" in direct quotes throughout the text. Some readers have questioned my retention of this racist invective in direct quotations, suggesting that I might substitute in brackets a less objectionable term. I have decided, however, to retain the original term for several reasons. First, its use is true to the historical record. Second, the racist connotations of the term convey precisely the racial undertones which I am convinced played a significant role in Chinese politics. Third, its use helps people of other times and places understand how some Chinese viewed Japan during those dark years. It conveys very well the spirit of war and hatred of that era.

Atlanta   J.W.G.
October 1987

Contents

Shortened Citations of Major Sources   xi

Chapter I
Introduction   3

Chapter II
The Sino-Soviet Alliance of 1937–1939   15

Chapter III
Revolution in China and Soviet National Security   58

Chapter IV
China and Soviet-Axis Alignment   90

Chapter V
The CCP and Soviet-Axis Alignment   123

Chapter VI
The Xinjiang Cockpit   153

Chapter VII
China and World War II   182

Chapter VIII
The CCP and World War II   237

Chapter IX
Conclusion   271

Bibliography   278

Index   295

Shortened Citations
of Major Sources

Cankao Ziliao: *Zhonggong Dangshi Cankao Ziliao* [Reference Materials on CCP History], Zhongguo Renmin Jiefangjun Zhengzhi Xueyuan Dangshi Jiaoyan-shi [Party history instructional office of the Political College of the Chinese People's Liberation Army], no date or place of publication given.

Duiwai Guanxishi, 1840–1949: *Zhongguo Jindai Duiwai Guanxishi Ziliao Xuanji, 1840–1949* (Selection of materials on China's modern foreign relations, 1840–1949), vol. 2, book 2, Shanghai: Renmin Chubanshe, 1977.

Milu: *Jiang Zongtong Milu* [Secret diary of President Chiang], Taibei: Zhongyang Ribao Chubanshe, 1978.

Waijiaoshi Ziliao (1937–1945): *Zhongguo Waijiaoshi Ziliao Xuanbian, Di San Ci (1937–1945)* [Selection of materials on China's diplomatic history, vol. 3, 1937–1945], Beijing: Waijiao Xueyuan, 1958.

Zhanshi Waijiao: *Zhonghua Minguo Zhongyao Shiliao Chubian—Dui Ri Kang Zhan Shiqi, Di San Bian, Zhanshi Waijiao, II* [Preliminary compilation of important historical materials of the Republic of China, period of the war of resistance against Japan, vol. 3, book 2], Taibei: Zhongguo Guomindang Dangshi Weiyuanhui, 1981.

Zongtong Dashi: *Zongtong Jianggong Dashi Changbian Chugao* [Preliminary extensive chronology of President Chiang], Taibei: Zhongguo Guomindang Dangshi Weiyuanhui, 1978.

FRUS: *Foreign Relations of the United States,* Washington, D.C.: U.S. Department of State. This annual series includes a number of special volumes dealing with the major wartime Allied conferences, e.g., those at Quebec, Washington, Casablanca, Cairo and Tehran, Malta and Yalta, and Potsdam. These latter, special volumes are referred to in both the notes and bibliography by the names of the conferences they deal with.

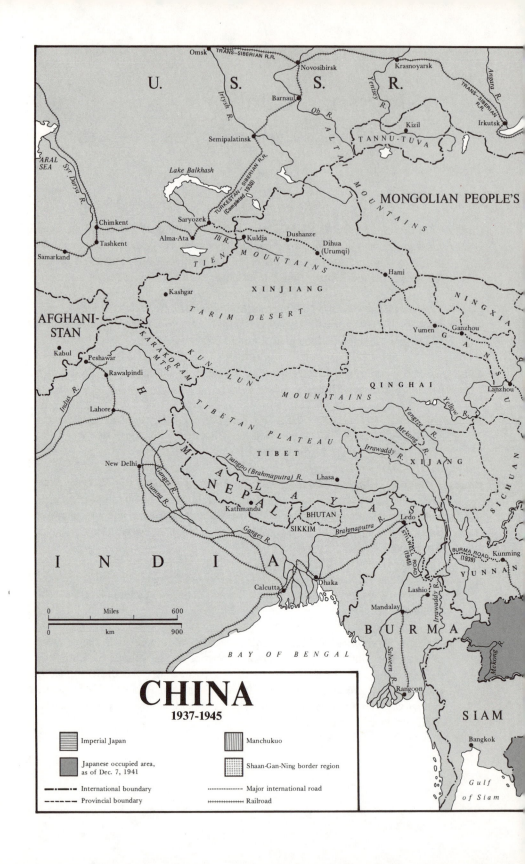

U. S. S. R.

TRANS–SIBERIAN R.R.

Omsk Novosibirsk Krasnoyarsk

Barnaul

Semipalatinsk Kizil

TANNU-TUVA

ARAL SEA

Lake Balkhash

ALTAI MOUNTAINS

MONGOLIAN PEOPLE'S

Chimkent

Saryozek

TURKESTAN-SIBERIAN R.R. (Completed 1930)

Alma-Ata Kuldja Dushanze

Tashkent Ili R. Dihua (Urumqi)

Samarkand

Hami

TIEN MOUNTAINS

NINGXIA

Kashgar

XINJIANG

AFGHANI-STAN

TARIM DESERT

Yumen Ganzhou

G   A   N

Kabul Peshawar

KARAKORAM MTS.

KUN-LUN

Rawalpindi

QINGHAI

Lanzhou

S   U

Lahore

MOUNTAINS

Yellow R.

Indus R.

TIBETAN PLATEAU

Yangtze R.

Mekong R.

SICHUAN

TIBET

Irrawaddy R.

XIJANG

New Delhi

Tsangpo (Brahmaputra) R. Lhasa

NEPAL

Ganges R.

Jumna R.

Kathmandu

BHUTAN

Ledo

Brahmaputra R.

SIKKIM

STILWELL ROAD (1945)

Ganges R.

BURMA ROAD (1939) Kunming

I   N   D   I   A

Calcutta Dhaka

Lashio

Irrawaddy R.

Y U N N A N

Mandalay

B   U   R   M   A

Salween R.

Mekong R.

BAY   OF   BENGAL

Rangoon

CHINA

1937-1945

SIAM

Bangkok

	Imperial Japan		Manchukuo
	Japanese occupied area, as of Dec. 7, 1941		Shaan-Gan-Ning border region
–·–·–	International boundary	··········	Major international road
–––––	Provincial boundary	++++++++	Railroad

Miles 0 600

km 0 900

Gulf of Siam

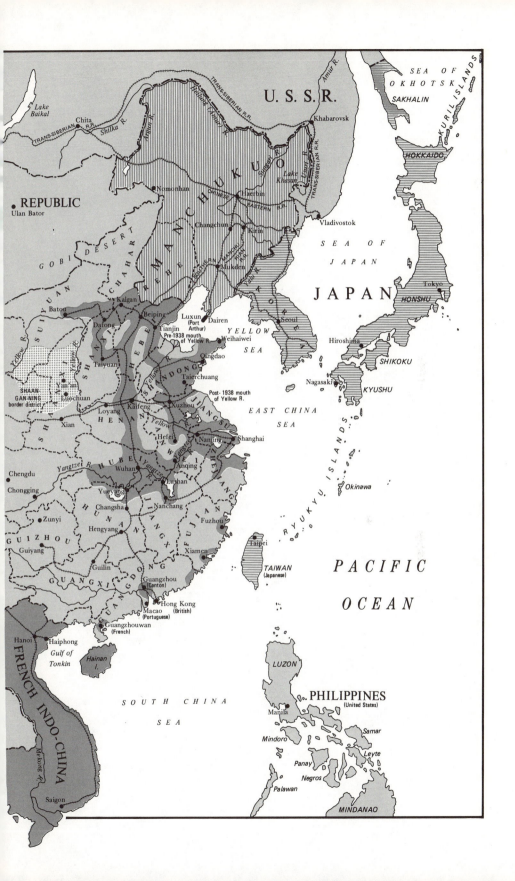

Chinese-Soviet Relations, 1937–1945

Chapter I

Introduction

The Politics of Nationalism

Our story is about the relationship between the Soviet Union and Chinese nationalism during a critical period in the latter's formation. One of the most significant aspects of the turbulent third and fourth decades of the twentieth century was the tempering of Chinese nationalism in the forge of total war. Nationalism, the synthesis of a powerful central state and an identification of the masses with that state through the medium of notions of race and ethnicity, had transformed the face of Europe a century and a half earlier. The French Revolution and the movements and wars associated with that upheaval had turned the largely passive and apathetic subjects of the early modern absolutist states into citizens actively concerned with the destiny of "their" countries. Once this transformation began and large numbers of ordinary people began routinely participating in the political process, the modern era of politics had begun.

Chinese nationalism arose in response to the virulent Western imperialism generated, in part, by this mass nationalism in the West. Over several millennia the Chinese had evolved a concept of the uniqueness of their own civilization and their central place in human history. But while conscious of their own unique ethnicity, China's ordinary people seldom identified with the state, and except during the periods of chaos between the twilight of one dynasty and the rise of a new one, they saw little reason to call for the strengthening of the state. The disruptive impact of Western imperialism on China's traditional society, however, gradually changed this. By the end of the Opium War in 1842, a few Chinese thinkers were calling for reforms to strengthen China's ability to withstand the Western onslaught. By the 1870s bitterness over the humiliation of China at the hands of the Westerners was widespread, as was the conviction that reforms were necessary to strengthen and save China. But it was not until the end of the nineteenth century that these ideas began percolating down to the masses and modern nationalism, mass nationalism, began to emerge. In this sense, the Boxer Rebellion of 1900 was China's first major nationalist movement.

By the early twentieth century, nationalist ideas were rapidly becoming the lingua franca of successful politics in China. The desire to overthrow the racially alien (at least so they were perceived) Manchus and restore Han rule was at the core of the Revolution of 1911. The alien Manchu autocracy was to be replaced by a system in which the masses of ordinary people, largely Han people, could participate via the mechanism of parliamentary democracy.

Sun Yat-sen, the foremost figure of the 1911 Revolution, is generally regarded as the father of Chinese nationalism. In the early 1920s Sun systematized his thoughts on China's struggle into his Three Principles of the People. The first of these principles was nationalism, which Sun defined as the loyalty of the Chinese race or nation—and to Sun race and nation were virtually synonymous—to the Chinese state. The purpose of the Three Principles, Sun made clear, was to secure China's National Salvation, that is, to "elevate China to an equal position among the nations . . . so that she can permanently exist in the world." But ensuring China's survival was only the first step. The second was to restore China to the position of international prominence it enjoyed throughout most of history and to which its size, antiquity, and brilliance entitled it. In the past the Chinese nation was far superior to all others. Indeed, in the 1920s it was still superior, Sun said, in terms of culture. But over the past few hundred years the European nations had excelled in science and technology while China had gradually lost its sense of nationalism. Thus, while China ought to be advancing in line with the nations of Europe and America, it faced instead the possibility of loss of its sovereignty and the eventual destruction of the Chinese race. This danger had to be averted and the Chinese nation-race restored to the international position it once held.[1]

Sun's ideas had made a great impression on the young Chiang Kai-shek in the early years of the twentieth century.[2] The May Fourth Movement developed as a result of the shabby treatment accorded China at the Versailles Peace Conference of 1919, giving nationalism a much more leftist, explicitly antiimperialist cast. By the mid-1920s nationalist movements encompassing large numbers of students, merchants, entrepreneurs, workers, and intellectuals were able effectively to challenge Western interests in China's major cities.

Nationalism was not, of course, the only Western ideology introduced into China: Marxism–Leninism was another. The form of Marxism–Leninism which originally entered China contrasted starkly with nationalism. Gradually, however, Chinese revolutionaries realized that the fusion of nationalism and Marxism–Leninism would greatly increase the appeal of the latter doctrine, and they struggled during the 1920s and 1930s to bring about such a synthesis. Ultimately it was Mao Zedong and the philosophers associated with him who successfully accomplished this amalgamation. By creating a truly distinctive Chinese Communist ideology, Mao and his lieutenants greatly enhanced the appeal of that ideology to China's intelligentsia which increasingly sought an affirmation of China's cultural independence from the West, including the Soviet Union.[3]

Mao himself came to Marxism–Leninism via nationalism. His earliest writings were permeated by an overriding concern with the possibility that the Chinese people would suffer catastrophe, lose their state, and become slaves without a country— notions encapsulated in the Chinese phrase *wang guo*. By the mid-1920s Mao was no longer primarily a nationalist; by then he was also a revolutionary. Yet throughout his life, nationalism was a key theme in Mao's thinking.[4]

Japan's seizure of Manchuria after the Mukden Incident in September 1931 and its expansion into northern China in the five years which followed, fanned nationalist passions in China. The major contestants for political power in China increasingly became political parties which tried to harness the energies of this mass nationalism through democratic-centralist organizational forms borrowed from the Soviet Union. Chief among these were the Chinese Nationalist Party or Kuomintang (KMT) and the Chinese Communist Party (CCP). As the 1930s progressed, successful politics in China increasingly meant mass nationalist politics, and a central aspect of the KMT–CCP contest became the struggle to win the status as the most sincere, genuine, and effective representative of Chinese nationalism. To win and hold political power in mid-twentieth century China, a party had to present a set of convincing symbols and programs designed to rescue the nation. It had also to harness organizationally the energies of the large numbers of ordinary people roused by these symbols and programs. This mass awakening was illustrated most graphically by the patriotic student demonstrations which erupted in December 1935 and which had a nationwide impact.[5] The Xian Incident a year later also reflected the growing strength of nationalist passions.

This mounting nationalism ultimately forced the Nationalists to suspend their anticommunist military campaigns and turn to confront Japan. It also forced the Communists to shelve their revolutionary programs—including their drive to overthrow China's National Government—and to accept a subordinate position within a united front against Japan. The political realities of the time, first and foremost the force of nationalist ideas, meant that neither party could afford to be seen as standing in the way of national unity against Japan.

These nationalist passions were then fanned to a white heat by the 1937–1945 war. The horrible brutality of Japan's armies and the very real prospect of the restoration of alien rule and the dismemberment of the Chinese nation deeply shocked Chinese of all classes. Very often ordinary Chinese were left with no alternative but resistance to Japan.[6] As military, economic, and political crises deepened, people by the tens of millions concluded that the fate of the nation demanded bold action. And as the crisis grew, three different Chinese regimes—the KMT, the CCP, and the pro-Japanese government headed by Wang Jingwei—competed for nationalist legitimacy.[7]

Both Chiang Kai-shek and Mao Zedong realized the importance of these nationalist sentiments, and each attempted to establish his party as the sole sincere and effective representative of Chinese nationalism. Indeed, a central aspect of the political contest between the Nationalists and the Communists was a struggle for nationalist legitimacy. In line with this, the propaganda of each party denigrated the nationalist credentials of the other. The KMT tarred the CCP as a Soviet puppet, a Soviet fifth column operating within China. Areas under CCP control were the Soviet equivalent of Manchukuo (the puppet regime established by the Japanese in Manchuria in 1932) or the other "special regimes" created by Japan in northern China. The CCP, on the other hand, depicted the KMT as a pliant vassal of this or that imperialist power. The class nature of the KMT was such, the Communists charged, that it was inherently incapable of leading an uncompromising struggle against the foreign imperialists plundering China. Both the Nationalists and the Communists genuinely believed the charges they leveled against their opponents. That is to say, each party was genuinely convinced of its own nationalist credentials and saw itself as the only sincere representative of the Chinese nation.

The criticism by each side of the other was constrained to a greater or lesser degree by the requirement of maintaining the united front against Japan; this political imperative reflected the strong nationalist passions of that era. Both the KMT and the CCP were aware that whichever party was perceived as creating friction in—or even worse, splitting—the united front would be seen as betraying the nation by putting narrow partisan or ideological interests above the collective good.

Both the KMT and the CCP continually attempted to expand their own power while checking the moves of the other side. Moreover, both sides justified their own offensive operations and condemned the offensive moves of their rival on nationalist grounds. The Communists proclaimed that the expansion of their armies and base areas was merely a patriotic expansion of the "anti-Japanese forces." It followed that Nationalist attempts to check Communist expansion were tantamount to treason while Communist efforts to beat back such Nationalist efforts at containment were patriotic and served the nation. The Nationalists, on the other hand, conducted military, political, and economic operations against the CCP on the grounds that such measures were necessary to prevent a Communist seizure of power which was variously described as leading either to a Brest-Litovsk type treaty with Japan or to a Soviet takeover of part or all of China. (Brest-Litovsk was the treaty between Bolshevik Russia and imperial Germany in March 1918 which took Russia out of World War I and turned over large tracts of the old Russian Empire to the German sphere of influence.) Both parties used nationalist rhetoric which resonated among the masses.

There was, of course, much more to Chinese politics during the wartime years than mere nationalism. While I would argue that the dominant political culture of those years did in fact center on nationalist themes, other factors such as regionalism, kinship, and class were also very important. Especially in the countryside, large, relatively abstract national concerns had difficulty subordinating more parochial interests. Yet even in the countryside, nationalism played a key role. One way to look at Mao Zedong's winning revolutionary strategy is that it funneled urbanites, mobilized by essentially nationalistic concerns, into the countryside to organize, educate, and lead the more parochial peasants. In Marxian terms, Mao's strategy integrated the national and class issues. Only when those two were fused was a critical mass reached; either alone would have failed.[8]

While the imperatives of China's domestic politics in the 1930s and 1940s meant that those who would rule had to speak in a nationalist idiom, the imperatives of the international system meant that they had to come to terms with the great powers hovering about China. First among these were Japan and the Soviet Union. The Soviet Union was a major factor in the KMT–CCP contest to rule China, and the Soviet policies of both Chiang and Mao cannot be understood without reference to that struggle. A major factor in Chiang's calculations regarding the Soviet Union was the nature of relations between the Chinese Communist Party and the Soviet Union. Efforts to influence these ties were often a major consideration underlying Chiang's interactions with the Soviet Union. Calculations regarding relations between the USSR and the Republic of China (ROC) also had a significant impact on Chiang's approach to the CCP. Likewise, Mao's appraisal of the Soviet Union was very much influenced by the state of relations between the Soviet Union and Republic of China. Moreover, CCP policy toward the KMT was influenced by the state of relations between the Chinese Communist Party and the Soviet Union. In other words, all these interrelationships were inextricably linked and must be considered together.

The international system within which Chiang and Mao tried to come to terms with the Soviet Union did not remain constant throughout the wartime period. Rather, the pattern of alignments among the major powers—the Soviet Union, the United States, Germany, and the British, Japanese, and French Empires—which constituted the system of international power went through four different stages between 1937 and 1945.

During the first stage there was a very general convergence between Soviet, American, British, and French policies in opposition to Germany and Japan. Berlin and Tokyo were joined in anti-Soviet cooperation under their anti-Comintern pact of November 1936, while Moscow wooed the Western democracies with proposals of collective security against the "fascist" powers. London, Paris, and Washington did not, of course, accept Moscow's collective security proposals, yet they did generally oppose German and Japanese aggression. The second international configuration came with the conclusion of the German-Soviet Nonaggression Pact of August 1939 and the Soviet-Japanese rapprochement which began about the same time. These developments brought the Soviet Union squarely into alignment with the incipient Axis bloc. The third phase began with the German attack on the Soviet Union and the prompt British and American support extended to Moscow. This Grand Alliance did not become global, did not extend to the Far East, until literally the last days of the war. Moscow's April 1945 cancellation of its 1941 Neutrality Treaty with Japan laid the basis for the Soviet declaration of war on Japan in August 1945, thereby moving the international power system into its fourth state during the compass of our study.

The Soviet policies of Chiang and Mao had to adapt to these changes in the international system. This meant that their diplomatic strategies differed from period to period. At times they found a greater degree of Soviet support for their aims; at other times they found less support or even hostility. Yet one of the constants of the wartime period was the remarkable tenacity which both Chiang and Mao showed in the pursuit of their nationalist objectives. Their policies varied, but the pursuit of those aims was indefatigable. Perhaps more than anything else, this constancy was a tribute to the intensity of the nationalist passions of wartime China and to both Chiang's and Mao's understanding that he who would rule had to satisfy those passions.

The Soviet Union and China's National Revival

Perhaps the most important way in which Chiang Kai-shek and Mao Zedong sought to win the support of the nationalist passions fanned by Japan's onslaught was by presenting a program of national revival. These programs were quite different in terms of their socioeconomic content, but both aimed at restoring China's national integrity and transforming China into a powerful, respected nation.

Chiang Kai-shek's program of national revival centered on what might be called the restoration of China's national grandeur—the creation of a united and powerful China standing among the first rank of the nations of the world. Although Chiang did not use the phrase "national grandeur," he held views similar in this regard to those of Charles de Gaulle. Like de Gaulle, Chiang sought the restoration of his "humiliated" and disgraced nation to its "rightful" place in the world. Both men sought the creation of a powerful country respected by other nations both for its might and independence and for the genius and brilliance of its civilization.

For Chiang, several elements were necessary for the restoration of China's national grandeur. The first prerequisite, Chiang believed, was internal unification. The suppression of the Communist insurgency and the assertion of effective central control over various regional warlords was the *sine qua non* of national power, social stability, and economic progress. Only a united China could be a powerful China, Chiang believed. Second, the "unequal treaties" imposed on China during the nineteenth century, which had limited China's sovereignty while disgracing its national honor, had to be canceled. Chiang viewed these treaties as a primary cause of the poverty, political disunity, and moral decay of China, and saw their termination as an essential step in China's regeneration. Third, China's lost territories were to be regathered to the fatherland. Among these were Hong Kong, Manchuria, Xinjiang, Outer Mongolia, Taiwan, Tibet, and perhaps other areas such as the Pamirs region of Central Asia, the small Himalayan states, the Ryukyu Islands, and northern Burma. Fourth, China was to win recognition as a major world power, as the full equal of other major powers. The exact form such recognition would take was uncertain in 1937, but Chiang was clear that it would ultimately be based on military might and brought about by Chinese participation in a victorious war against Japan. Throughout the 1937–1945 war Chiang considered China's participation in the peace conference as a victorious power to be a major vehicle for institutionalizing China's newly won great-power status. Finally, Chiang's program of the restoration of national grandeur entailed the military defeat of Japan. By the time he led China to war in 1937, Chiang had concluded that rising nationalist passions within China combined with continued Japanese aggression made peace impossible. He concluded that a limited military defeat of Japan was essential both to consolidate his domestic political base and to check Japan's advance. He did not imagine a defeat of Japan as total as that of 1945, but he did expect a limited military defeat which would force Japan to come to terms with China as a great power in its own right.

The achievement of much of Chiang's diplomatic program impinged on Soviet interests. Soviet Russia had led the way in 1919 by formally renouncing the special privileges it had acquired in China under the nineteenth-century treaties. This renunciation was formalized when Sino-Soviet relations were normalized in 1924.[9] The 1935 sale of the Chinese Eastern Railway to Japan, eliminated the last remnant of Russia's special rights in Manchuria. Yet vast tracts of what Chiang considered Chinese territory remained under de facto Soviet control. The most important of these were Xinjiang and Outer Mongolia. Clearly, China's regathering of these lost territories ran counter to Soviet national interests. The Soviet Union also remained concerned with the future of Manchuria. Russia and Japan had gone to war in 1904 over this vast and mineral-rich region, which was also blessed with warm-water ports precious to the Russian navy. Soviet Russia had also fought a brief war with China in 1929 to uphold its special rights in Manchuria and had relinquished those rights in 1935 only very reluctantly in order to avoid war with Japan.[10] Once Manchukuo was established it was by no means certain that Manchuria would be returned to China if and when Japan were defeated. Moscow might well decide that its interests would be best served by supporting an independent Manchuria state amenable to Soviet control.

Chiang also believed Soviet cooperation was essential to the military defeat of Japan. Chiang realized that China was militarily too weak to defeat Japan alone. China would have to win the support of other powers. In 1937 Chiang hoped that the United States and the British Empire would support China by adopting effective economic and financial sanctions against Japan. Throughout the first years of the war, Chiang's diplomats pushed assiduously for such sanctions, and in 1940 these efforts bore fruit.[11] In 1937, however, Chiang looked not primarily to Washington and London but to Moscow for military support. Russia was Japan's historic rival for influence in northeastern Asia. Moreover, Soviet-Japanese relations had followed a path of chronic crisis after 1931 and the two countries had seemingly gone to the brink of war several times in the years after the Mukden Incident in Manchuria.[12] Soviet industrial and military power also expanded rapidly in the 1930s. While the British and American governments were cutting defense spending in the misguided hope of reviving their depressed economies by balancing their budgets, Soviet power was expanding rapidly with the First and Second Five-Year Plans. Within two years of the Mukden Incident, Soviet military deployments in the Far East had quadrupled to 100,000 men. Both the power of Soviet forces in the far East and the level of Soviet-Japanese hostility were demonstrated by the clashes along the Manchurian-Siberian border which began in 1935. All of this gave Chiang hope that the Soviet Union would join China in war against Japan. Once Japan's armies were pinned down in central China, and with the United States and Britain adopting friendly and supportive positions, the Red Army, Chiang hoped, would strike the depleted Japanese forces in the north, and China and the Soviet Union would together defeat Japan's armies.

Soviet cooperation was also necessary if China was to attain the status of a recognized great power after Japan's defeat. Chiang had to consider that even as a member of a victorious coalition, China might be slighted in the postwar settlement and remain very much a junior partner. The historical lessons of the Versailles Conference, in which Germany's rights in China were transferred to Japan even though China had openly and actively supported the Allied cause, weighed heavily on Chiang's mind. To avoid a repetition of the 1919 experience, the friendly support of the major powers, especially the Soviet Union, was essential.

Finally, the suppression or at least the disarming of the CCP touched on Soviet interests because the CCP had close links to the Soviet Union. Since the founding of the Communist International (Comintern) in 1919, the foreign policy of the Soviet regime had operated through dual government-to-government and party-to-party channels. Control of the international Communist movement was an extremely important mechanism of Soviet national power in the 1930s and gave Moscow a worldwide influence which it would not otherwise have possessed. This was an immense boon to the still weak and ostracized Soviet state. Moreover, the CCP was a very important member of the Comintern. Indeed, after Hitler's destruction of the German Communist Party in 1933–1934, the CCP ranked only behind the Communist Party of the Soviet Union (CPSU) in status and importance in the international Communist movement. For Chiang Kai-shek to move against the CCP would therefore constitute a blow to Soviet interests in China.

Mao Zedong also advanced a program of national revival. While Mao, like Chiang, believed that it was imperative for China to regain its "lost territories," abolish the unequal treaties, and defeat Japan, his program differed from Chiang's in that he believed that a thoroughgoing social revolution was a necessary prerequisite to the rebirth of China.[13] Only by destroying the political power of the ruling classes, which had been willing to cooperate with foreign imperialism, could the bonds of imperialist control and exploitation be smashed. The elimination of exploitative class relations was also necessary, according to Mao, to win the enthusiastic support of the masses for efforts at national construction, upon which national wealth and power could be based. Finally, only a socialist economic system, with its state planning and centralized accumulation of capital, could effectively and rapidly transform China into a powerful industrial country. Once such a social revolution were carried through, a "new" independent and powerful China would emerge to resume its rightful place in the world.

Just as was the case with Chiang's program of national grandeur, the Soviet Union played a central role in the achievement of Mao's program of national rejuvenation via social revolution. Mao Zedong was one of the great revolutionaries of our age. He succeeded in knitting together a movement of intellectuals and peasants which was able to seize power and then begin transforming China into a unified socialist country. Yet his success as a revolutionary and, consequently, his success in implementing his program of national revival, depended on his success in breaking the bonds of Soviet control over the CCP.

While Mao was an ardent Chinese nationalist, he was also the leader of a component of the international Communist movement founded upon loyalty to the Soviet Union and commanded by Moscow. It is all too easy to forget from the perspective of the post-Tito and post-Mao era that in the 1930s there was, in fact, a coherent, disciplined international Communist movement and that Mao, like Tito, had to make a revolution within the confines of that movement. The fragmentation of the monolithic, Soviet-led Communist movement by forces of nationalism was pioneered by Mao. In this sense, too, Chinese nationalism had to come to terms with the Soviet Union during 1937–1945. Other studies have analyzed elements of Mao's revolutionary strategy and traced the course of the CCP rise to power under Mao's tutelage. Some studies have also analyzed Mao's views of the great powers, including the Soviet Union.[14] What has not been adequately analyzed, and what this study will investigate, is how Mao was able to carry out a revolution within the confines of, and even against the strictures of, the Third International.

To understand CCP-Comintern relations during this period, one must understand the nature and organization of the Comintern, of which the CCP was a "branch party." Conceived and organized as a world revolutionary party by the Bolshevik leaders in 1919, the Comintern was based on the principles of democratic centralism. The relationship between the "international leadership" in Moscow and each "branch party" was, in theory, the same as that between the Politburo and lower level organs of a particular national party. In both cases the lower levels were to be strictly and unconditionally obedient to the upper levels. Various "branch parties" were not only obligated to implement loyally the "line" promulgated by the International, but the International leadership could overrule the policies or doctrines of various branch parties if those policies or doctrines violated the International's line.

Various organizational mechanisms existed to ensure the obedience of branch parties. The Executive Committee of the Communist International (ECCI) had the right to remove any officers of a branch party. It could send various types of representatives and plenipotentiaries to the branch parties, armed with the power to attend and participate in all meetings and wielding the full powers of the ECCI in guiding the affairs of the branch party. The employment of such plenipotentiaries by the Comintern during the 1920s and 1930s was not infrequent. Usually these special representatives were of a nationality other than that of the party to which they were sent—an arrangement designed to guard against nationalist loyalties interfering with enforcement of international discipline.[15]

The effectiveness of Comintern control over the CCP was dramatically demonstrated by the manner in which the last pre-Mao leadership of the CCP came to power in 1931. In December 1929 the Comintern, in line with that body's radical "third period," had directed the CCP to simultaneously develop the guerrilla movement in the countryside and organize general strikes in the cities as part of a "revolutionary upsurge" supposedly underway in China. This directive prompted CCP leader Li Lisan to decide to throw the CCP's new peasant armies into assaults on such central China cities as Wuhan, Changsha, and Nanchang. Moscow soon began having second thoughts, however, about the consequences such radical actions might have on Soviet-Japanese relations, and was dismayed by Li's impetuousity in ordering offensives without adequate preparation. When Li failed to rein in his radicalism promptly in response to Comintern urging, Moscow decided to replace him as leader of the CCP. The Comintern then sent a representative, Pavil Mif, to China to supervise Li's ouster personally. Mif briefly put the CCP into Comintern receivership, oversaw the removal of Li and his lieutenants, and installed in power a number of young Chinese students who had preceded Mif to China from the Soviet Union by several months. Foremost among these students was Mif's star protégé, Wang Ming.[16]

Wang Ming was Moscow's main representative in the CCP throughout the war. His rise to prominence within the CCP and the international Communist movement was largely a result of his long and loyal service to Moscow. In 1925, at the age of twenty-one, he was sent to Moscow by the CCP to study at Sun Yat-sen University. He soon mastered the Russian language and Marxist-Leninist philosophy and became the protégé of Pavil Mif, a leading Soviet sinologist and rector of Sun Yat-sen University. Wang acted as interpreter and liaison for the Comintern and CCP on several occasions in the late 1920s, and in 1930 he led the group of "returned students" back to China which helped Mif oust Li Lisan. Wang returned to Moscow in the fall of 1932 to act as the CCP representative to the Comintern, leaving such fellow "returned students" as Bo Gu and Zhang Wentian in charge of the CCP center. Over the next few years Wang supported from Moscow the efforts of these men to bring Mao Zedong's rural peasant armies and soviet government under "central" control. While in Moscow between 1933 and 1937, Wang was a prolific propagandist for the Comintern line, explaining every twist and turn of that line and applying it to China. He also had responsibility for liaison with the Latin American Communist Parties. In 1933 Wang was appointed to the ECCI, and at the Seventh Congress in 1935 he became a member of the Presidium of the ECCI. In other words, Wang served as a loyal Comintern apparatchik for over a decade.[17]

Stalin's purges of the 1930s extended to the Comintern and furthered the centralization of that organization. From about 1930 on, Stalin alone had de facto control over the Comintern. Moreover, under Stalin's control the powers of such bodies as the International Control Commission—charged with eliminating any deviation from Comintern line and with rooting out anti-Comintern behavior—grew steadily. The International Control Commission worked closely with the OGPU (Unified State Political Administration) and, after 1934, with the NKVD (People's Commissariat of Internal Affairs), both names for Stalin's secret police. Stalin viewed dissident Communists and non-Communist revolutionaries as his most dangerous opponents, and such individuals were ruthlessly eliminated by these central disciplinary organs. Foreign Communists, both in the Soviet Union and abroad, were no exception. Within the Soviet Union, émigré Communists were especially vulnerable to suspicion of oppositionist activities, and the leadership of several Communist Parties (Yugoslavian, Polish, and German) in exile in the Soviet Union were virtually annihilated by Stalin's police. On occasion these purges extended to foreign lands, where dissident Communists and revolutionaries were liquidated in large numbers in order to root out opposition to Stalin's control. [18] While the Seventh World Congress of the Comintern ostensibly gave greater autonomy to "branch parties," the leadership of the International over questions of policy remained unchanged.

It is also important to keep in mind the stature of Stalin and of the Soviet Union within the international Communist movement during the 1930s. Stalin's cult of personality was then reaching its height, with almost supernatural intelligence being attributed to the "great leader" of the world revolutionary movement. The myth of the Soviet Union as the fatherland of the world revolution and the international proletariat was also still widely accepted within the Communist movement. Indeed, this seemed to be an almost self-evident truth, since the Soviet Union was the only socialist country in a capitalist world characterized by grave economic depression and virulent racist movements. The brutality and other shortcomings of Stalin's rule of the Soviet Union were exposed only later. While some people within the CCP may have seen through the Stalinist myths prevalent in that era—and Mao Zedong may well have been one of these people—most Chinese Communists must have shared them to a greater or lesser degree. All of this meant that when the Sino-Japanese War broke out, Moscow still had considerable ideological and organizational leverage within the CCP. Moscow's loyal supporters within the CCP are referred to by various appellations. The most common, and the one we shall use in this study, is "Internationalists."

Up to 1935 the Comintern effectively controlled the CCP. CCP policy loyally followed every twist and turn of Comintern line, usually with one set of CCP leaders being blamed for the "failures" of Moscow's previous line. Indeed, it makes sense to interpret CCP history prior to 1935 as an effort by one or another group of Chinese to put into practice whatever directives arrived from Moscow. One of the central characteristics which distinguished Mao's leadership of the CCP from that of his predecessors was his sensitivity to discrepancies between Soviet interests, as embodied in Comintern directives, and the revolutionary interests of the CCP. Indeed, his 1927–1935 struggle to win leadership of the CCP was characterized by affirmation of policies—such as the creation of rural peasant-based soviets and reliance and highly fluid, rural guerrilla war waged by small irregular units—which conflicted with the Comintern line at one stage or another. Several of these differences were fundamental, from a Marxist-Leninist point of view.

One such fundamental issue had to do with the class nature of the Chinese revolution. Was the urban proletariat or the rural peasantry to provide the main motive force to overthrow China's *ancien régime*? Mao believed that the social dynamite necessary to demolish the old order was to be found in the countryside. While Moscow recognized the utility of peasant movements, it saw them as a sort of second-best option which carried with them all sorts of ideological dangers. The

Comintern believed that the sooner the CCP was able to base itself in the cities and replace its peasant cadres with people from ideologically reliable working class backgrounds, the better it would be. Just as Moscow did not deny the revolutionary role of the peasantry, Mao did not deny a role for the urban classes and, more especially, a "leadership role" for the proletariat. But again there was an important difference in emphasis from which arose myriad policy differences.[19]

During the wartime debates between Mao and Wang Ming, the two men frequently founded their contrary positions in these theoretically different peasant-rural versus proletarian-urban orientations. Each man strove to show that his own theory conformed with orthodox Marxism-Leninism while that of his opponent deviated from the precepts of that body of thought. While these theoretical debates are interesting from the standpoint of Marxist-Leninist theory, it is unnecessary for our purposes to go into them in detail. The true significance of theory lay in the contrary policy prescriptions which it justified, and it is on such policy differences that this study will focus.

Mao won leadership of the CCP if not in the face of Comintern opposition, at least without Comintern support. During the last phase of the Jiangxi soviet in southern China just prior to the beginning of the Long March in late 1934, Mao was removed from his position as a top-level leader of the Party. Once the Long March was under way, the severance of radio contact between the CCP Politburo and the Comintern was critical to Mao's victory at the expanded Politburo conference at Zunyi (Guizhou province) in January 1935.[20] Once ensconced in Baoan northern Shaanxi province after the conclusion of the Long March, Mao resisted for almost a year the Comintern's new line of a united front with the "antifascist bourgeoisie" (i.e., with Chiang Kai-shek) against Japan. In mid-1936 Mao finally accepted the Comintern's new united front line but important differences of interpretation arose between Mao and Moscow over such issues as the rebellion against Chiang by the southwestern warlords in June 1936 and the kidnapping of Chiang by warlords Zhang Xueliang and Yang Hucheng in December 1936. Thus when the Sino-Japanese War broke out in 1937, the Comintern leadership (Stalin, Georgii Dimitrov, and Wang Ming) had plenty of reason to view Mao as a dissident Communist who refused to accept the "iron discipline" of the International Workers Movement.

Notes

1. Sun Yat-sen, *San Min Chu I, The Three Principles of the People*, Taibei: China Publishing Company, n.d., pp. 1, 5, 7, 37.
2. Robert Payne, *Chiang Kai-shek*, New York: Weybright and Talley, 1969, pp. 50–51.
3. Raymond F. Wylie, *The Emergence of Maoism, Mao Tse-tung, Ch'en Po-ta, and the Search for Chinese Theory*, Stanford, Calif.: Stanford University Press, 1980, pp. 2–3; 283–284.
4. Stuart R. Schram, *Mao Zedong, A Preliminary Reassessment*, New York: St. Martin's Press, 1983, pp. 3–7; 24–25.
5. *See* John Israel, *Student Nationalism in China, 1927–1937*, Stanford, Calif.: Stanford University Press, 1966.
6. *See* Chalmers Johnson, *Peasant Nationalism and Communist Power*, Stanford, Calif.: Stanford University Press, 1962.
7. For an interpretation of Wang Jingwei as a nationalist, *see* John Hunter Boyle, *China and Japan at War, 1937–1945, the Politics of Collaboration*, Stanford, Calif.: Stanford University Press, 1972.

8. A variation of this theme is in Johnson, *Peasant Nationalism*.
9. Allen S. Whiting, *Soviet Policies in China, 1917–1924*, Stanford, Calif.: Stanford University Press, 1954.
10. George A. Lensen, *The Damned Inheritance, The Soviet Union and the Manchurian Crises, 1924–1935*, Tallahassee, Fla.: Diplomatic Press, 1974.
11. *See*, for example, the pamphlet circulated by China's representatives at the Nine-Power Conference in Brussels in November 1936, *Japan's Dependence on Foreign Supplies of War Materials*, China Reference Service, vol. 1, no. 3 (15 December 1937), New York: Trans-Pacific News Service, 1937.
12. Alvin D. Coox, "The Japanese-Soviet Confrontation, 1935–1939," in *Deterrent Diplomacy, Japan, Germany and the USSR, 1935–1940*, James Morley, editor, New York: Columbia University Press, 1976, pp. 113–129.
13. Regarding the origin and intensity of Mao's determination to restore China to its rightful place in the world see Stuart R. Schram, *The Political Thought of Mao Tse-tung*, New York: Praeger Press, 1963, pp. 103–110. Regarding Mao on the recovery of Outer Mongolia, Taiwan, and other territories, *see* Edgar Snow, *Red Star over China*, New York: Grove Press, 1968, p. 96.
14. James Reardon-Anderson, *Yenan and the Great Powers: The Origins of Chinese Communist Foreign Policy, 1944–1946*, New York: Columbia University Press, 1980. Steven Goldstein, *Yenan's American Policy: 1937 to 1941*, paper presented to the Conference on Sino-American Relations in the 1940s, sponsored by the Institute of American Culture of Academia Sinica, Taibei, Taiwan, 29–30 December 1982.
15. Gunther Nollau, *International Communism and World Revolution, History and Methods*, New York: Frederick Praeger, 1961. pp. 125–133. *See also* Franz Borkenau, *World Communism*, Ann Arbor: University of Michigan Press, 1962.
16. The exact nature of the relation between Li Lisan and Moscow is a matter of some debate. A consensus exists, however, regarding the nature of Li's ouster. See Richard C. Thornton, *The Comintern and the Chinese Communists, 1928–1931*, Seattle: University of Washington Press, 1969; Stuart R. Schram, *Authority, Participation and Cultural Change in China*, Cambridge: Cambridge University Press, 1973, pp. 9–18. A.M. Grigoriev, "The Comintern and the Revolutionary Movement in China in the Late 1920s and the Early 1930s," in R.A. Ulyanovsky, ed., *The Comintern and the East, A Critique of the Critique*, Moscow: Progress Publishers, 1979, pp. 5410–451; Stuart R. Schram, Review of *The Comintern and the Chinese Communists*, in *Slavic Review*, No. 4, December 1973, pp. 821–23.
17. *See* Howard L. Boorman, editor, *Biographic Dictionary of Republican China*, Vol. 3, New York: Columbia University Press, 1967, pp. 231–234. Donald W. Klein and Anne B. Clark, *Biographic Dictionary of Chinese Communism, 1921–1965*, Cambridge, Mass.: Harvard University Press, 1971, pp. 127–134. Zheng Xuejia, *Di San Guojishi* [History of the Third International], vol. 2, Taibei: Shangwu Yinshu Guan, 1977, pp. 1450–1452.
18. Robert Conquest, *The Great Terror, Stalin's Purge of the Thirties*, New York: Macmillan, 1973, pp. 587–588.
19. John Rue, *Mao Tse-tung in Opposition, 1927–1935*, Stanford, Calif.: Stanford University Press, 1966. Benjamin Schwartz, *Chinese Communism and the Rise of Mao*, Cambridge, Mass.: Harvard University Press, 1951. Harold Isaacs, *The Tragedy of the Chinese Revolution*, Stanford, Calif.: Stanford University Press, 1961.
20. Xiang Qing, "Gongchan Guoji he Zhongguo Gongchandang Guanyu jianli kang Ri minzu tongyi zhanxian de celu" [The Comintern and the CCP regarding the strategy of forming an anti-Japanese national united front], *Dangshi Tongxun* [Bulletin of Party History], no. 11–12, 1983, pp. 16–25.

Chapter II

The Sino-Soviet Alliance
of 1937–1939

The Politics of Alliance

During the first two years of the Sino-Japanese War, Soviet Union–Republic of China relations constituted a multifaceted alliance. With the August 1937 Treaty of Nonaggression as a basis, diplomatic and military cooperation expanded rapidly and became a key element of both countries' efforts to deal with Japanese aggression. Diplomatically the Soviet Union and the Republic of China worked in tandem to increase the Western democracies' opposition to Japan. Militarily, each country bolstered the other's efforts to check Japan. While this brief alliance proved effective and extremely useful to both powers, there were major tensions within it. One of the most important of these had to do with the question of direct Soviet participation in the war. Chiang Kai-shek desperately desired such participation, while Stalin was determined to avoid war with Japan if at all possible. There were also disputes over the level of Soviet material assistance. The situation of the Republic of China was desperate and its material needs were immense. Moscow's assistance was generous, but far less than Chiang felt he needed. Finally, the alliance was also complicated by the rapid growth of CCP power and by KMT suspicions of Soviet complicity in that growth. Ultimately, however, the alliance was torn apart not by such internal tensions but by the Soviet Union's international realignment in the fall of 1939.

There was a strong parallelism between the global diplomacy of Stalin and Chiang during the first twenty-four months of the Sino-Japanese War. Both hoped that Sino-Soviet cooperation in resisting Japan would catalyze the Western democracies to join in a common front against Japan. In line with this, the Republic of China strongly supported Moscow's calls for collective security arrangements between the Soviet Union and the Western democracies, while Moscow fully supported China's efforts to persuade the Western powers to adopt sanctions against Japan. Both Stalin and Chiang wanted to see an "antiaggressor peace camp" formed including the Republic of China, the Soviet Union, the United States, and the British and French Empires. Chiang hoped that once this "peace camp" was consolidated it would guarantee the security of the European borders of the Soviet Union, thereby allowing—even condoning—the Soviet Union's entry into the Sino-Japanese War. Chiang understood very well the gravity of Moscow's concern with its two-front threat and saw the realization of a Soviet-Western antiaggressor camp as a way of stabilizing the European situation so that Moscow could adopt a more vigorous policy in the Far East.

15

A second basis for the Sino-Soviet alliance was its practicality in dealing with the Japanese military threat. As long as both the Republic of China and the Soviet Union were involved in active or potential military confrontation with Japan, Tokyo was unable to concentrate its forces to deal with either in isolation. From China's perspective, as long as large Soviet forces were maintained along the borders of Manchuria and Korea, Japan was forced to deploy large countervailing forces thereby limiting its ability to mass forces in China. Chiang also hoped for more direct cooperation; he hoped ultimately to persuade Moscow to enter the war against Japan in alliance with China. From the Soviet perspective, China was the Far Eastern counterpart of the antifascist struggle underway in Spain. China's conduct of a determined and protracted war against Japan tied down Japan's armies in China and made it less likely that Tokyo would decide to risk war with the Soviet Union. The success of Soviet deterrence of Japanese attack from 1937 to 1941 depended in large part on China's ability to sustain its war against Japan.[1] It should be noted, however, that Moscow's policy of deterrence was predicated on a desire to avoid war with Japan.

The converse of Chiang's hope for Soviet intervention was a fear that Moscow might reach an accommodation with Tokyo at China's expense. Moscow's willingness to come to terms with Japanese aggression in China had been demonstrated by the tenacity of its "peace policy" toward Japan after the Mukden Incident, including its repeated proposals for a mutual nonaggression treaty, its various de facto arrangements with the new Manchukuo regime, and its sale of the Chinese Eastern Railway to Japan in March 1935. Only after the conclusion of the German-Japanese Anti-Comintern Pact in November 1936 had Stalin decided to take China's side against Japan.[2] Chiang always had to consider the possibility that Stalin would decide that Soviet interests would be better served by making a deal with Japan than by supporting China against Japan. Such a deal might take the form of Soviet recognition of Japanese domination of Manchuria and northern China in exchange for Japanese recognition of Soviet domination of Outer Mongolia, Xinjiang, and perhaps part of China's northwest. Chiang's fear was not idle. As we shall see, after the German-Soviet Nonaggression Pact of 1939 Stalin came close to striking such a deal with Japan. During 1937–1939, Chiang was able to prevent this by fostering close cooperation between the Republic of China and the Soviet Union.

During the 1937–1939 period, three individuals served as Chiang Kai-shek's key advisors on relations with the Soviet Union. These men were Jiang Tingfu, who was China's ambassador to the Soviet Union from October 1936 to November 1937; Sun Ke, who was head of the legislative *Yuan* (the legislative organ of the Republic of China government) and son of Sun Yat-sen; and Yang Jie, who was deputy chief of the general staff of the army from 1935 to 1937 and ambassador to Moscow from May 1938 to May 1940. All three men had quite different personalities and political views, and each had a significant impact on Sino-Soviet relations during the war.

Of the three, Jiang Tingfu took the most pessimistic view about the probability of Soviet entry into a Sino-Japanese war. Jiang was an established authority on Russian-Chinese diplomatic history and chairman of the history department at Qinghua University in Beiping (as Beijing was called in the 1930s) when the Mukden Incident occurred. After that pivotal event, Jiang Tingfu emerged as one of the leaders of antiwar opinion in China. He favored closer relations with the Soviet Union in order to help moderate Japanese pressure on China, but throughout the 1930s he remained convinced that Moscow was unwilling to go to war with Japan because of China.[3] In Jiang's opinion, Chinese illusions regarding the likelihood of Soviet entry into a Sino-Japanese conflict were extremely harmful—encouraging China to undertake a war which it was highly likely to lose. Rather than undertaking a losing war which would leave China in an even more pitiful condition than before, Jiang maintained that it was better to continue backing down before superior Japanese strength while strengthening China's own military situation. It seemed elementary to Jiang that a nation should not undertake a war which it had no realistic hope of winning.[4] Chiang Kai-shek was attracted to Jiang by his prominent pro-peace activities and by his reputation as an authority on Russian-Chinese relations and by 1935 was relying on Jiang for advice regarding the Soviet Union.

Like Jiang Tingfu, Yang Jie and Sun Ke were also early advocates of closer relations with the Soviet Union. They differed from Jiang, however, regarding the likelihood of Soviet entry into a Sino-Japanese war. Yang, like Chiang Kai-shek, was a military man. Like Chiang, Yang had attended the *shimnbu gakko* (military preparatory school) in Japan, enrolling the year after Chiang left. Yang became associated with Chiang during the Northern Expedition in 1926–1927 when he served first as a division commander and then as director of Chiang's field headquarters. During 1930, Yang was Chiang's chief of staff during the bloody showdown with warlords Feng Yuxiang and Yan Xishan. After entering the Central Executive Committee of the KMT in 1931, Yang became head of the Chinese Army Staff College, a post he formally held until he became ambassador to the Soviet Union in 1938.[5]

During the mid-1930s, Yang developed strong beliefs on the issue of probable Soviet entry into a war against Japan. During 1933–1934 he undertook a military investigation tour of Europe and the Soviet Union and returned to write a book arguing that a Soviet-Chinese bloc would eventually defeat Japan. In his capacity as vice-chief of staff, Yang was close to Chiang and in a good position to make his opinion heard. Late in 1937 Chiang Kai-shek sent Yang to Moscow, ostensibly to inspect the Soviet defense industry, but in fact to persuade Stalin to extend more military assistance to China.[6]

Throughout the latter half of 1937, Jiang and Yang gave diametrically opposite advice to Chiang regarding the probability of Soviet entry into the Sino-Japanese War. In his memoir Jiang Tingfu recalls that "the winter of 1937 was the most difficult one that I had ever experienced. While General Yang sent [Chiang] messages of hope and confidence, I had to send messages of disappointment."[7] After the fall of Nanjing in December 1937, Jiang sent Chiang a very pessimistic report saying that he was absolutely certain the Soviet Union would not enter the war unless directly attacked by Japan. When Foreign Minister Wang Chonghui read Jiang's report at a secret meeting of the Supreme National Defense Council, Sun Ke denounced Jiang's "failure" in Moscow and his "misreading" of Soviet intentions. "On account of this, and perhaps for other reasons as well," Jiang later wrote, "I was recalled."

On 12 May 1938, Yang Jie formally replaced Jiang as ambassador to the Soviet Union, a position he retained until 18 April 1940.[8] Chiang Kai-shek first considered appointing veteran diplomat Wellington Koo as Jiang's replacement. Koo declined and suggested Sun Ke. The reasons why Chiang finally decided on Yang Jie remain unclear, but they probably had to do with Yang's military background and long association with Chiang, as well as his fervent belief in the probability of Soviet entry into the war. During 1937–1938, Yang continually told Chiang that Soviet entry into the Sino-Japanese War was imminent. He was also the agent of more manipulative efforts to provoke a Soviet-Japanese conflict.

Sun Ke was Chiang Kai-shek's third Soviet expert. Prominent because of his father, Sun led one of the left-leaning factions of the KMT. Sun saw a linkage between friendly Sino-Soviet ties and "progressive" government within China, and he was a firm advocate of both. Throughout the mid-1930s, Sun advocated immediate war with Japan and alliance with the Soviet Union. He tended to have a somewhat romantic notion that the Soviet Union supported countries struggling for justice, and concluded from this that if Japan attacked China, the Soviet Union would soon enter the war on China's side in support of justice.

Jiang Tingfu felt, as mentioned earlier, that such views were pernicious, and after the Xian Incident in December 1936, he urged Chiang Kai-shek to have Sun Ke undertake a special mission to the Soviet Union in the hope that Sun would learn firsthand of Soviet determination to stay out of a Sino-Japanese war. Chiang, however, turned down this recommendation, "for reasons of his own," according to Jiang.[9] It was not until November 1937 that Chiang sent Sun to Moscow as head of a special secret mission to solicit aid from the Soviets. Sun's group arrived in Moscow in January 1938.[10] Eventually Sun emerged as one of Chiang's most durable advisors on Soviet affairs. During 1938–1940, he gradually shed many of his illusions about Soviet foreign policy, but to the end of the war he retained his belief in a link between a pro-Soviet orientation and "progressivism" within China.

The Formation of the Sino-Soviet Alliance

The Sino-Soviet Nonaggression Treaty of August 1937 formed the basis for the close alignment and cooperation between those two countries during 1937–1939. Discussions about the conclusion of a treaty of mutual nonaggression and/or mutual security had begun in 1932 when the Soviet and Chinese governments were discussing the normalization of bilateral relations. At that time Chinese Foreign Minister Luo Wengan had staunchly favored such a treaty and had even submitted a draft for a nonaggression treaty to the Central Political Council of China's National Government in April 1933.[11] Chen Lifu, a member of the Central Executive Committee of the KMT and one of Chiang's close supporters, had revived the discussion of possible Soviet assistance to China in the event of a Sino-Japanese war during his talks with Soviet Ambassador Dimitri Bogomolov in 1935. Chen resurrected Lo Wengan's 1932 proposal of a mutual security treaty, but found Bogomolov unreceptive. Such a treaty was "too dangerous," Bogomolov said. Chen interpreted this to mean that while the treaty would precipitate a Japanese reaction to growing Soviet influence in China, China was too weak to give the Soviet Union much real assistance in the event of a Soviet-Japanese war. Chen continued discussions with People's Commissar for Foreign Affairs Maxim M. Litvinov during a secret mission to Moscow in February 1936. Again Moscow was extremely cautious. No agreement was reached but some progress in that direction was made.[12]

By late 1936, as Chiang was maneuvering to prepare for either an accommodation or war with Japan, he moved to consolidate potential Soviet support. When Jiang Tingfu was dispatched as ambassador to the Soviet Union in October 1936, one of his key missions was to negotiate a Soviet-Chinese treaty.[13] During his first year in Moscow, Jiang discussed both a mutual security treaty and a nonaggression treaty with Soviet officials. Commissar Litvinov rejected a mutual security treaty because he feared that Soviet involvement in a conflict in the Far East would put his country in an inferior position in Europe while simultaneously increasing Western suspicions of the Soviet Union and diminishing Western sympathy for China.[14] In Litvinov's opinion, the Soviet Union should support China only to the same extent that the Anglo-American powers did; it should not be in front of these powers in supporting China, but neither should it lag too far behind them.[15] Litvinov was willing to conclude a nonaggression treaty which would provide a political basis for loans to China for the purchase of Soviet military equipment. He specified, however, that such a treaty must be signed in Nanjing (then China's capital), not in Moscow, a provision which Jiang believed reduced the political significance of the pact. Apparently, both Jiang and Litvinov saw the literal distancing of the treaty from the Soviet Union as symbolizing a limitation of Soviet commitment, perhaps by giving the treaty a regional rather than a global significance. In any case, Jiang reported to Chiang Kai-shek that the conclusion of a mutual security treaty was impossible and that, in his opinion, the terms attached to a nonaggression treaty would make such a treaty inconsequential. He therefore advised Chiang to work instead for a multilateral alliance including not only China and the Soviet Union, but other powers as well.

Litvinov's cautious approach was overruled by Stalin. A month before the Marco Polo Bridge Incident which sparked the Sino-Japanese War on 7 July 1937, the Soviet Union did in fact propose to the Chinese government the conclusion of a treaty of mutual security. On 5 June 1937, Ambassador Bogomolov informed Chinese Foreign Minister Wang Chonghui that, since the Soviet Union and China sought a similar "environment" in the Far East, the Soviet Union wished to see China united and strong. China had no aggressive aspirations, Bogomolov said, and the Soviet Union thus viewed a strong China as a guarantee of peace in the Far East, while a weak China would be a cause of war. In line with this, the Soviet government suggested that Nanjing propose to the British, American, French, Dutch, Japanese, and Soviet governments the convocation of a convention to draw up a treaty of regional collective security for the Pacific Ocean area. The Soviet government would support this proposal and would lobby with other countries to persuade them to participate. If it proved impossible to reach a regional collective security agreement, then the Soviet Union was prepared to sign a strongly worded mutual security treaty with China—a draft of which Bogomolov handed to Wang. In Bogomolov's opinion, it would be better to convene an international security conference before a bilateral treaty was signed, since it was possible that the outcome of such a conference might make a bilateral treaty unnecessary. In response to a query by Wang as to why the Soviet Union could not itself convene such a Pacific rim conference, Bogomolov responded that Soviet sponsorship would rouse many suspicions.[16]

Surprisingly, Wang Chonghui did not promptly inform Chiang Kai-shek of Bogomolov's important proposal. Not until 8 July, the day after the Marco Polo Incident and a full month after Bogomolov made his offer, did Wang pass the proposal on to Chiang. According to Zhou Xicai, who was then the head of the Soviet desk of China's foreign ministry, Wang Chonghui was very suspicious of the Soviet proposal that China sponsor a conference of Pacific rim nations. Wang felt that such an international conference should not be convened by China alone, but jointly with Britain, France, and the United States. According to Zhou, talks between Wang and Bogomolov over this issue were still in progress when the Marco Polo Bridge Incident occurred.[17]

The outbreak of fighting on 7 July compelled Chiang to override Wang's caution. On 8 July, Chiang Kai-shek summoned Wang and Sun Ke to Lushan (a famous mountaintop resort in northern Jiangxi province where for centuries China's rulers have escaped the torrid heat of central China's summers). Chiang was uncertain whether the Marco Polo Bridge Incident of the day before could be contained, but he felt it was necessary to make preparations for the possible expansion of the incident. If the fighting expanded, he said, it would become a total war of resistance. In such a war the "most critical factor" would be reaching an agreement with the Soviet Union for the supply of military equipment and the conclusion of a Soviet-Chinese treaty of mutual security. After Wang informed Chiang of Bogomolov's 5 June proposals, Chiang ordered Wang and Sun to go to Shanghai to conclude an agreement with Ambassador Bogomolov along the lines the ambassador had proposed a month earlier.[18]

After the meeting at Lushan, mention of a mutual security treaty disappears from the diplomatic record. According to Zhou Xicai, once Wang Chonghui and Sun Ke resumed discussions with Bogomolov in Shanghai, Bogomolov insisted that it was already too late for a mutual security treaty. The purpose of such a treaty, Bogomolov reportedly said, was to prevent the outbreak of war. Now war had already begun. Had such a treaty been signed after the Mukden Incident, it might have prevented Japan from launching a war of aggression. Now it was too late. Moreover, if the Soviet Union now signed such a treaty, it would probably be attacked by Japan. The Soviet Union was not prepared for such a war and it would not be wise, Bogomolov said, to provoke a Japanese attack. Therefore, a treaty of mutual nonaggression was now the most appropriate, Bogomolov suggested.[19]

Chiang had little choice but to accept the second best option of a nonaggression treaty, and on 1 August 1937 he initialed such a treaty. On 21 August, Wang Chonghui and Bogomolov formally signed the treaty in Nanjing. The treaty was publicly announced on 29 August and approved by a meeting of the Supreme National Defense Council on 31 August.[20] Oddly enough, however, it was not until 26 April 1938 that the Supreme National Defense Council, which Chiang headed, sent the treaty to the legislative *Yuan* for approval and to the executive *Yuan* for implementation.[21] This delay may have reflected lingering doubts regarding the consequences of alignment with the Soviet Union on the actions of the Western powers. On 16 May 1938, the legislative *Yuan* ratified the treaty.

Since the August 1937 treaty is only the first of several nonaggression treaties we shall encounter in our study, it is well to consider the meaning of this now rather archaic diplomatic instrument. "Nonaggression" in the 1930s meant much more than a passive relationship which the term seemed to imply. Rather, it meant active political, economic, diplomatic, and military cooperation short of a commitment to actual belligerency. A treaty of nonaggression in the 1930s was much closer to what in the 1980s would be called a treaty of friendship and cooperation.

Essentially the 1937 pact did two things. First, it provided the political basis for large-scale Soviet military sales and assistance to the Republic of China. Second, it ensured that neither side would strike a deal with Japan while the war was still under way. According to the treaty, if either signatory were attacked by Japan, the other signatory was to provide Japan with no assistance of any kind, either direct or indirect, and would refrain from taking any action or entering into any agreement which might be used to advantage by Japan. When ratifying the treaty on 16 May, the legislative *Yuan* stated that it felt this article of the treaty was especially important.

Chiang Kai-shek also felt that the second, negative aspect of the treaty was highly important because it created some constraints against a possible Soviet double cross.[22] Chiang was skeptical, however, about how effective a treaty would ultimately be in this regard. Commenting in his diary when he approved the treaty on 1 August, Chiang said that the Soviet Union hoped to use the agreement to pressure Japan and then to sign a similar agreement with Japan ensuring Soviet neutrality.[23] Moscow would ultimately decide, in other words, to strike a deal with Japan at China's expense. The fear of a possible Soviet-Japanese partitioning of China was a central element of Chiang's thinking which would appear again and again throughout the war. A key deterrent to such a Soviet-Japanese deal was the possibility of a Chinese-Japanese or Chinese-German deal. As Shao Lizi, a KMT veteran who would succeed Yang as ambassador to Moscow in 1940, pointed out in a public analysis of the 1937 treaty, the opposite side of Moscow's promise not to strike a deal with Japan was a Chinese promise not to join Japan, Germany, or Italy in an anticommunist pact.[24] In many regards, the Sino-Soviet Treaty is best interpreted, at least from Moscow's perspective, as the Soviet response to the Anti-Comintern Pact of November 1936, as Moscow's effort to ensure that China would not join the anti-Comintern bloc.

Many Chinese hoped that the 1937 treaty, along with a supportive attitude by Britain and the United States, would provide the basis for active Soviet participation in the war. Some indication of how widespread such beliefs were is given in Jiang Tingfu's memoir. Jiang recalls that his appointment as ambassador to Moscow in October 1936 was received with the "greatest, wildest expectations." Public and private bodies gave him a series of receptions and at each gathering Jiang felt that people hoped and prayed that he might, somehow, manage to get the Soviet Union to fight with China against Japan. Some believed that he could successfully perform this "mission"; others hoped without believing. Such feelings mirrored general public sentiment, Jiang recalled.[25]

Jiang believed that Moscow manipulated Chinese hopes for Soviet involvement in order to push China into war with Japan and then to keep it fighting once the war began. Moscow's submission of the draft for a mutual security agreement in June 1937 may be interpreted in this light, that is, as a Soviet effort to bolster Chinese courage in a situation of increasingly tense Sino-Japanese relations. In his memoirs, Jiang recalls that Bogomolov continually used this ploy to encourage pro-war sentiment in China.[26] Especially when meeting with private Chinese citizens, politicians, and reporters, Bogomolov would indicate that the Soviet Union was prepared to provide all the necessary assistance if China went to war with Japan, but with Chinese officials Bogomolov was more cautious. On at least one occasion, however, Bogomolov told Jiang that the Soviet Union was willing to sign a mutual security agreement and that in the event of Sino-Japanese war the Soviet Union would give China practical military assistance.[27]

Throughout the first eighteen months of the war, Chiang Kai-shek attempted to persuade Stalin to order the Red Army into the war against Japan. Stalin was cautious in rejecting Chiang's pleas, afraid perhaps that too unequivocal a rejection might induce Chiang to make peace with Japan.

The Quest for an Anti-Aggressor Front

Moscow used both government-to-government and party-to-party channels to foster collective security in the Far East. While the primary aspect of the Republic of China–Soviet Union alliance was at the state level, Moscow also threw the considerable assets of various Communist Parties and front groups into the "International Anti-Aggressor Campaign," which was launched in late 1937. With branches in some thirty-five countries, this well-organized campaign boycotted Japanese goods, generated propaganda exposing Japanese atrocities, and collected funds for Chinese refugees and wounded soldiers. Several well-publicized international conferences were held in 1938 and 1939.[28] Such activities were a significant factor winning public opinion in the democratic countries to sympathy with China's cause.

At the state level, both Nanjing and Moscow were hopeful that a Sino-Soviet treaty would become an integral part of a Pacific rim system of collective security including the United States, Britain, and other Western powers. During the first few months after the Marco Polo Bridge Incident, Chinese officials hoped for forceful action by the Western powers against Japan.[29] On 16 July, the Chinese government sent a memorandum to Britain, France, the United States, Belgium, Holland, Italy, Germany, and the Soviet Union, charging that Japan's invasion of northern China constituted a clear violation of China's sovereignty and of the letter and spirit of the Nine-Power Treaty of 1922, the Paris Anti-War Agreement, and the Covenant of the League of Nations.[30] From 21 through 27 July, Chiang Kai-shek met with the British, American, Italian, German, and French ambassadors to solicit support for China's struggle.[31] Nanjing's early efforts to draw the Western powers into active cooperation with the Sino-Soviet coalition focused on the Nine-Power Conference convened in Brussels from 3 through 24 November 1937. Nineteen nations attended, including the United States and the Soviet Union, but not Japan or Germany. According to Tsien Tai, who was then China's ambassador to Belgium and one of the representatives of the Republic of China to the Brussels Conference, China's representatives in Europe had high hopes for the conference when it convened. Specifically, they hoped that the conference would decide to provide material aid—military equipment, munitions, credits, and loans—to China, and this would, in turn, make possible a show of force by Soviet forces on the border of Manchuria simultaneous with a naval demonstration in the Pacific by French, British, and American forces.[32] At a minimum, China's delegates hoped that the powers would agree to adopt economic sanctions against Japan.

Officials in Nanjing were less optimistic, focusing not on the conference but on the aftermath of its probable failure. About a week before the Brussels Conference opened, Wang Chonghui sent a top-secret directive to China's delegation at Brussels outlining how to handle the conference. There was no chance that the conference would succeed in mediating the Sino-Japanese dispute, Wang said. Nevertheless, China should adopt a moderate attitude toward all countries and not seek to embarrass them. It should also express the hope that the conference would solve the Sino-Japanese conflict on the basis of the Nine-Power Treaty. China's objective was to persuade the Western powers to adopt sanctions against Japan after the inevitable failure of the conference. Moreover, China's delegates at Brussels were to "actively seek ways of causing England and America to approve and encouraging *the Soviet Union* to use armed force against Japan" [emphasis added].[33]

China's program of collective Soviet-Western action against Japan dovetailed with Moscow's own strategy of collective security. The importance Moscow attached to the Brussels Conference was indicated by the fact that it was represented by none other than Foreign Affairs Commissar Litvinov. At Brussels, Litvinov strongly supported China's call for collective sanctions against Japan and for unity among the "peace-loving nations." Attempts to mediate the Sino-Japanese conflict had already been tried and failed, Litvinov told the conference. The Soviet Union felt that effective common measures to restrain Japan should be adopted and stood ready to participate in such measures.[34] Unfortunately for Chongqing, in southeastern Sichuan province, which became China's wartime capital on 20 November 1937 while the conference was still in session, the United States was more concerned with conciliating Japan than in cooperating with the Soviet Union against it. Thus, the chief delegate of the United States proposed the exclusion of the Soviet Union from a subcommittee set up to consider the plan of action to be adopted by the conference in the hope that, with Moscow excluded, Tokyo would be more likely to participate. Litvinov was outraged by this move and withdrew from the conference on the grounds that the Soviet Union was being discriminated against.

This was a major blow to Chongqing's diplomacy. According to Tsien Tai, after the Soviet Union walked out there was no more discussion of "positive steps" in support of China. Chinese diplomats such as Jiang Tingfu were puzzled by the "persistent effort" of the United States and Britain to exclude the Soviet Union from the settlement of the Far Eastern problem. It seemed to Jiang that *any* Soviet action at the League of Nations or at Brussels was deemed undesirable by Washington and London—an approach which Jiang believed was extremely shortsighted.[35] The Brussels Conference finally adopted a resolution encouraging both China and Japan to avail themselves of assistance by other countries to bring the conflict to an early end. China's delegates were very disappointed with this meager result.[36] The failure to secure support of the West pushed the Republic of China into greater dependency on the Soviet Union.

While the Nine-Power Conference was under way, Moscow continued to hint that it might enter the Sino-Japanese War. According to Chiang Kai-shek, during the conference Stalin summoned the counselor of the Chinese embassy in Moscow to praise the determined resistance of China's armies and to tell him that if China's situation became desperate, the Soviet Union might declare war on Japan.[37] Yang Jie also concluded from his discussions with Stalin and People's Commissar for Defense Kliment E. Voroshilov that Soviet intervention was imminent. On 12 November, Yang Jie sent Chiang two cables dealing with the possibility of Soviet entry into the war. In the first cable, Yang quoted Stalin to the effect that Soviet entry would only further unite the Japanese people about the Japanese government and stifle the Japanese antiwar movement. "Therefore," Yang reported Stalin as concluding, "the Soviet Union must wait for the arrival of the opportune time to go to war against Japan [*Gu Sulian dui Riben zhi kaizhan dengdai shiji zhi daolai*]."[38] Yang's second cable summarized his recent discussions with Voroshilov. According to Yang, Voroshilov agreed with Chiang that Soviet entry into the war could with one blow lay the basis for peace in the Far East. But the Soviet Union had many worries, Voroshilov said. If it went to war in the East, the West "would soon follow" and the Soviet Union had no guarantee of victory in a two-front war. Thus, at present the Soviet Union had to continue preparations. But Yang could tell Chiang, Voroshilov said, that such preparations would "be rapid."[39] Again Soviet officials were careful not to squelch entirely Chinese hopes for Soviet entry.

On 6 December, another cable from Yang conveyed to Chiang the substance of further discussions with Voroshilov about the question of Soviet "dispatch of troops [*chu bing*]" to China. Stalin was afraid, Yang reported, that such a move would incite the whole world to go to war against the Soviet Union. Therefore, the Soviet Union could only provide China with material assistance. Stalin knew, Yang continued, that China's war of resistance was extremely difficult, but he was convinced that final victory would be China's if it continued to "resist to the end." Yang concluded the report with the observation that it was "not impossible" that the Soviet Union would enter the war even though it had many worries. China should try, Yang suggested, to encourage Britain, the United States, and France to give the Soviet Union an "appropriate guarantee" to enable it to take such a move.[40]

A speech in late 1937 by the commander of the Soviet Special Far Eastern Red Army, General Vasilii K. Bluecher (who served in China in the early 1920s under the pseudonym "Galin") also encouraged hope in China that the Soviet Union was about to intervene. According to Propaganda Ministry official Hollington Tong, whose job at that time included monitoring the Soviet press, Bluecher said that when it was necessary to preserve world peace, the armed forces of the Soviet Union would not hesitate to cross her boundaries to wage war. Tong concluded that the purpose of Bluecher's speech was to slow down the Japanese drive into China in order to prevent a decisive Japanese victory.[41]

According to Jiang Tingfu, Yang Jie received the impression during his talks with Voroshilov that once Japan occupied Nanjing (China's pre-war capital in the coastal province of Jiangsu), the Soviet Union would enter the war, and he cabled this "intelligence" to Chiang Kai-shek. Yang did not clear this cable with Jiang, who was "shocked by the fertility of [Yang's] imagination," and once Jiang learned of it he sent his own cable to Chiang urging him to discount Yang's report. Nevertheless, after the fall of Nanjing in mid-December, Chiang cabled Stalin and used Yang's discussions with Voroshilov as the basis for requesting immediate Soviet entry.[42]

Stalin and Voroshilov replied with an explanation of the difficulties involved in Soviet entry into the war. If the Soviet Union sent troops to China other than in direct response to Japanese provocations, then "the world would say the Soviet Union was an aggressor and sympathy for Japan around the world would immediately increase." Such a development would not be advantageous to either China or the Soviet Union. Only if the nine powers, or at least the major ones, agreed to deal with Japan in cooperation with the Soviet Union could Moscow immediately send troops to China, "for in such a situation, the Soviet Union would be seen as just." Moreover, the Soviet tyrant said, the policy of nonintervention could be changed only by the Supreme Soviet, which would not meet for another six weeks. In the meantime, the Soviet Union would increase its aid to China in every possible way.[43] Again Stalin was saying "not now" while still keeping open the possibility of Soviet involvement. In effect he was telling Chiang that the way to achieve Soviet entry into the war was to persuade the United States and Britain to join the Soviet Union's proposed "peace camp."

Jiang Tingfu had not been informed of Chiang's direct appeal to Stalin, and when Litvinov conveyed Stalin's negative reply to Jiang, flatly denying in the process that Soviet officials had ever made a promise of the sort indicated by Yang, Jiang suggested that because Stalin had received Chiang's cable via Yang he should reply via the same channel. Litvinov refused and insisted that Jiang relay Stalin's message. The "other channel," Litvinov said, had been found to be unreliable.[44]

Soviet reservations about the reliability of Yang's reportage to Chiang raises the possibility that Yang let his own hope regarding Soviet entry into the war color his reports to Chiang. It is also possible that some Soviet statements—perhaps those by Ambassador Bogomolov and General Bluecher—may not have been fully consistent with Stalin's policy. Such factors may have led Chiang to overestimate the probability of Soviet involvement. But Stalin's policy itself was not unambiguous. Stalin was careful to leave room for possible Soviet involvement, probably because he realized that by unconditionally ruling out Soviet intervention he would encourage Chiang to make peace with Japan. Chiang also understood this linkage and tried to use it to China's advantage by threatening to make peace with Japan unless Stalin increased Soviet support.

According to Jiang Tingfu, Yang Jie was willing to use more devious methods to secure Soviet entry into the war. In mid-1937 as Jiang, along with H.H. Kung, Chiang Kai-shek's brother-in-law and key financial expert, and other Chinese officials, was about to depart for London to participate in the coronation of Britain's King George VI, Yang attempted to persuade him that while in London he should announce to Reuthers press agency that the Soviet Union would enter the war against Japan within two weeks. Although this was entirely groundless, Yang felt, according to Jiang, that once the Japanese heard it they would immediately launch a preemptive attack on the Soviet Union, thus precipitating Soviet entry into the war. Jiang rejected Yang's plan.[45]

Nanjing fell on 13 December and the barbarous savaging of that city's people began. When the Soviet Union failed to intervene after Nanjing's fall, Yang Jie sent a long letter to Chiang Kai-shek on 5 January 1938 reporting on his work. In it he laid out three reasons why the Soviet Union was unable to intervene at present. First, public opinion in Britain and the United States sympathized with China in a Sino-Japanese war, but would side with Japan in a Soviet-Japanese war. (Here again, Stalin was indirectly indicating his view of the Sino-Japanese War as a way of drawing the United States and Britain into his proposed antiaggressor camp.) Second, the Soviet Union hoped for an antifascist united front of Britain, the United States, and France, but until this front materialized it would be hard for the Soviet Union to deal with its two-front danger. Third, Stalin suspected that Britain was unwilling to see China defeat Japan, but hoped for a Soviet-Japanese war in which Britain could aid the weaker side. Yang then advanced his opinion about how Soviet involvement could be secured:

> In my opinion, the Soviet Union has all sorts of worries about war with Japan. Would it be possible to use a rather more effective method of inciting Japan or of uniting with other interested countries? In sum, if we want Soviet participation in the war, in my humble opinion, we must create an environment in which the Soviet Union cannot but participate in the war. The way to do this is to first of all find a way to have Britain and America back up the Soviet Union and perhaps to give a guarantee in the West of Europe's security. Secondly, the closer Sino-Soviet relations become, the more disadvantaged Japan will feel and the more provocatively it will act toward Russia. The Soviet Union could not tolerate such a situation and would be drawn into the vortex.[46]

In other words, closer Sino-Soviet relations might in themselves hasten a Soviet-Japanese conflict. Such thinking was one element of Chongqing's close alignment with Moscow during the first phase of war.

Of Chiang's three emissaries to the Soviet Union, Sun Ke was most successful in establishing rapport with Soviet leaders. During a long night time drinking session with Chiang's special representative Sun Ke on 4 February 1938, Stalin urged China to be patient, while still holding out the possibility of eventual intervention. The international situation was not yet right for Soviet intervention, Stalin said. It was still necessary to wait for the opportunity to ripen. If Britain, France, and the United States became willing to act together with the Soviet Union, then it would be possible for the Soviet Union to send troops to China. If the Soviet Union alone sent troops, Stalin continued, it would only encourage Germany and Italy to assist Japan, lessen international sympathy for China, and encourage the misperception that the Soviet Union wanted to communize China. All of this would be contrary to the interests of China's war of resistance. For these reasons, the Soviet government had decided to continue its current policy of no direct intervention. Nevertheless, the Soviet Union would assist China materially and would encourage Britain, France, and the United States to support China. But in order not to disillusion China's leaders entirely of their hope for future Soviet intervention, Stalin added that the Soviet Union's armies in the Far East would "continue active maneuvers and await the moment to move." Sun uncritically reported this conversation to Chiang on 7 February.[47]

Peace Talks and Soviet Support

The failure of Chiang's efforts to secure Western support and Soviet intervention opened the way for peace talks between Chiang and Tokyo, first via German mediation and then directly. This strategy of talking while fighting was linked to Sino-Soviet relations. Whereas Chiang had initially sought to precipitate Soviet intervention via Anglo-American guarantees and support, he now sought to induce Soviet intervention, or at least to increase the level of Soviet material assistance, by raising the specter of peace with Japan. This is not to say that securing increased Soviet support was Chiang's only concern as he explored the possibilities of peace in late 1937 and 1938. It was not. Chiang certainly hoped that Tokyo could be induced to grant him an honorable peace. He also hoped to increase support from the United States and Britain for China's war effort. But Chiang was, as we shall see, clearly aware of the utility of a possible Sino-Japanese peace settlement in influencing Soviet behavior.

Chiang's first move was to accept a standing German offer of mediation. Throughout the latter half of 1937, Berlin tried to resolve the contradiction between its long-standing (since 1928) friendship with China and new (since the Anti-Comintern Pact of 1936) alignment with Japan by mediating a settlement of the dispute between those two countries. Reliance on German mediation offered Chiang several tactical advantages vis-à-vis Moscow. German involvement would subtly exacerbate Soviet fears of possible Chinese alignment with the anti-Comintern bloc. If Berlin succeeded in persuading Tokyo to offer China a lenient peace, then Germany, Japan, and China might move forward with anticommunist cooperation. Moscow's fear of such a possibility would encourage it to be more generous and firm in its support for China's resistance against Japan.

On 5 November, German Ambassador Oskar Trautmann conveyed Japan's peace terms to Chiang Kai-shek along with Tokyo's warning that the longer the war continued, the harsher Japan's terms would become. Chiang rejected the Japanese terms out of hand. The Western powers were just then meeting in Brussels and Chiang did not want to do anything which would ease the pressure on that conference to find a solution to the Sino-Japanese conflict. As Chiang told Trautmann: "China cannot formally recognize Japan's demands because China is just now the object of consideration by the Nine-Power Conference at Brussels. The various powers intend to find a way to peace on the basis of the Nine-Power Treaty."[48]

On 6 December, shortly after the end of the Brussels Conference, Chiang informed Trautmann that China now welcomed German mediation. Before talks could begin, however, Nanjing fell and a new, much harsher set of Japanese terms were presented. Tokyo's new terms were conveyed by Trautmann to the Chinese government on 26 December. Tokyo now insisted that China formally recognize Manchukuo, abandon its policy of cooperating with communism, and adopt a policy of anticommunist cooperation with Japan and Manchukuo. China was to agree to the establishment of a demilitarized region in Inner Mongolia and northern China and to the creation of a "special political structure" in northern China. An agreement on economic cooperation between China, Japan, and Manchukuo was to be signed, and China was to pay an indemnity for war damages. Finally, the Japanese government was prepared for direct, bilateral negotiations with the Chinese government if the latter completely accepted these conditions.[49] China's acceptance of these terms would have been a severe blow to Soviet security. They would have allowed Japan to consolidate its southern front and turn north against the Soviet Union. They would have added China's resources to the Japanese-German anti-Soviet bloc. And they would have placed Japanese armies on the inner Asian borders of the Soviet Union.

The day after Trautmann conveyed Japan's new terms to China, the Supreme National Defense Council met to consider them. At this meeting on 27 December, Chiang firmly maintained that Tokyo's new terms could not be the basis for peace, saying "Today there can be no peace without surrender, no survival without resistance."[50] Chiang felt, however, that negotiations could be used to gain time to reorganize China's defenses. To achieve this, Chiang ordered that for the time being there would be no formal reply to Japan, while Tokyo's new terms would be conveyed to the United States, the Soviet Union, Britain, and France.[51] By forwarding Japan's terms to Stalin, Chiang was hinting that China might be forced to settle with Japan if Soviet support was not adequate.

Stalin called Chiang's bluff, no doubt confident that Chiang could not accept the humiliating terms demanded by Japan and survive politically. Regarding the terms of the Trautmann proposal, Stalin said in his December cable to Chiang, China should discuss peace with Japan only if Tokyo agreed to withdraw from northern China and restore the status quo ante bellum of 7 July. Moreover, Japan would violate any armistice agreement it signed and was merely stalling for time with German help. It was the duty of the Chinese government, Stalin urged, to speak in its capacity as the government of a great people and not submit to coercion.[52] The Soviet ambassador supplemented Stalin's message on 26 December. The Soviet Union sympathized with China, Bogomolov told H.H. Kung on that date, and would assist it materially to the extent that this was possible. It could not, however, unilaterally dispatch troops to assist China.[53]

Chiang replied to Stalin saying that he agreed with the Soviet appraisal of Trautmann's mediation effort. He also added that he hoped the Supreme Soviet would decide to give China "powerful assistance [shili yuanzhu]" in order to lay the basis for peace in the Far East.[54] Stripping away diplomatic ambiguities, Chiang was telling Stalin: We will stand by our agreement not to align with Germany and Japan and hope you will soon enter the war. The implicit threat, of course, was "or else."

H.H. Kung met with Trautmann late on 27 December and began implementing Chiang's policy of slowing Japan's advance and gaining time through protracted negotiations. Kung also tried to exacerbate German fears of expanded Soviet and Communist influence in China in the hope that this would help induce Berlin to moderate Tokyo's terms. China was determined to continue the war, Kung told Trautmann, and the longer the war went on the more closely China would have to align with the Soviet Union and the stronger bolshevism within China would become.[55]

Chiang's delaying tactics further antagonized Tokyo. In late December Tokyo declared that, unless Chiang fully accepted Japan's terms by the end of 1937, Japan would be "forced to treat the present situation from an entirely different point of view."[56] This was the basis for Prime Minister Konoe Fumimaro's declaration on 16 January 1938 that Japan would henceforth not deal with Chiang Kai-shek's government. Subsequent Japanese clarifications hardened this position and Japan began moving toward the creation of a collaborationist regime in China. Shortly afterward Chiang ordered the recall of China's ambassador to Japan and then publicly released the details of Japan's peace terms. Tokyo replied by recalling its own ambassador from China, thereby formally severing diplomatic ties between the two countries.[57] This final rupture of relations between China and Japan in early 1938 reduced Chiang's leverage with Moscow. Stalin could be even more confident that Chiang could not arrive at a politically acceptable peace with Japan. To reestablish this leverage with Moscow, it became imperative for Chiang to reestablish ties with Tokyo.

After the collapse of the German-mediated peace talks, Chiang opened direct talks with Japan. To conduct these talks, Chiang turned to an informal group of antiwar adherents close to KMT veteran Wang Jingwei. These men shared a belief that a protracted Sino-Japanese war would exhaust and devastate China, opening the way for a Communist takeover. They also believed that the hysterical anti-Japanese climate then prevailing in China was forcing the government to acquiesce to Chinese Communist efforts to expand their power.[58] Such concerns ultimately led Wang Jingwei and several others in this group to decide late in 1938 to abandon resistance and collaborate with Japan. Our concern here, however, is with an earlier period when these men were still instruments of Chiang Kai-shek's diplomacy.

Early in 1938 the Japanese representative of the South Manchurian Railway approached an old friend, head of the Asian section of the Chinese Foreign Ministry Gao Songwu, about prospects for peace. As a result of these initial contacts, in February Dong Daoning, chief of the Japan desk of the Foreign Ministry and a core member of the antiwar faction, traveled to Japan for discussions. When he returned to China two weeks later, Dong carried with him letters from the head of Japanese secret operations in China, for the latter's old friends Minister of War He Yingqin and Secretary of the Supreme National Defense Council Zhang Qun. On 5 April, Gao Songwu reported to the government on these secret contacts, thereby indicating Chiang's knowledge, if not prior approval, of these secret talks.[59]

A week later Gao met with Japanese representatives in Hong Kong. Gao told the Japanese that China understood that Japan's objectives were twofold: first, to achieve security against the Soviet Union, and second, to protect its involvement in China's economic development. Regarding the question of the Soviet Union, China was prepared to set aside discussions of Manchuria and Inner Mongolia, that is, China was prepared to acquiesce to Japan's presence there. The rest of north China would, however, have to be returned to China, and Japan would have to pledge to respect China's territorial and administrative integrity in the area south of the Great Wall. If these principles were acceptable to Japan, Gao proposed, Japan should first declare a cease-fire and peace negotiations would then begin.[60]

When there was no Japanese response to these proposed terms by mid-May, Chiang ordered Gao Songwu to discontinue his peace probes and limit his Hong Kong activities to intelligence-gathering operations.[61] Conditions in Japan seemed increasingly favorable to a compromise peace, however, and other channels, via people closer to Chiang, were soon opened. On 3 June 1938, Ugaki Kazushige replaced Hirota Koki as Konoe's foreign minister after securing major concessions from Konoe which would facilitate the quest for a settlement of the Sino-Japanese War. Ugaki strongly favored a negotiated settlement of the war, fearing that even if Japan were successful in crushing Chiang's government, it would be saddled with long and large-scale war against China's Communist guerrillas. It was better, Ugaki believed, to end the war with China by granting Chiang a generous peace such as Bismark had granted to Austria after the latter's defeat in 1866.[62]

Ugaki was an old friend of Zhang Qun and when Zhang learned of Ugaki's appointment he sent him a letter of congratulations. In this letter Zhang expressed not only his hope for Sino-Japanese friendship and for a negotiated peace, but also his own willingness to undertake peace negotiations. Ugaki replied promptly to Zhang's letter, suggesting that Zhang send a representative to Hong Kong to meet with the Japanese consul general there, Nakamura Toyokazu. On 16 June, H.H. Kung's private secretary, Jiao Fusan, met with Nakamura in Hong Kong.[63] Since Kung was Chiang's brother-in-law and a member of Chiang's inner circle, it was most likely that Kung's actions had at least Chiang's tacit approval.

On 18 July, Jiao presented an extremely conciliatory seven-point peace plan to Nakamura. Jiao's proposal provided that China would sign treaties with Japan and Manchukuo, thereby implicitly recognizing Manchukuo's independence. The autonomy of Inner Mongolia was to be recognized, and in north China the Chinese government would undertake to develop the resources of that region in cooperation with Japan on the basis of mutual equality and benefit. The Chinese government would also undertake to suppress anti-Japanese activity throughout China. Moreover, Chongqing was willing to consider Japan's demand for a "demilitarized zone" in north China in which no Chinese troops would be stationed. Finally, and for our purposes most important, China was willing to consider concluding an anti-Comintern agreement with Japan.[64] Once again, the implementation of these terms would greatly have strengthened Japan's position vis-à-vis the Soviet Union. Taken together, these terms amounted to a willingness to scrap the united front with the CCP and the Soviet Union and become a part of a broad anti-Soviet bloc. In spite of the extremely conciliatory nature of the proposed terms, they were insufficient for Ugaki who insisted that only Chiang Kai-shek's retirement from public life could pave the way for peace. The Jiao–Nakamura talks continued until early September without finding a way around this obstacle. Ugaki resigned as foreign minister on 29 September and the talks were suspended.

Clearly, the terms of these proposed peace agreements stand in stark contrast to the vision of China as a great power. How are we to reconcile this contradiction? Because of the sensitivity of this issue and the use to which it has been put by the CCP in undermining Chiang's credibility as a nationalist, little has been published by Taiwan explaining Chiang's rationale in permitting such proposals. Indeed, the KMT's usual reaction to discussions of these peace bids has been to deny either that they took place or, at least, that Chiang Kai-shek had anything to do with them. But as we have seen, the evidence indicates that Chiang was very probably privy to these peace maneuvers. How does this square with Chiang's professed desire to restore China as a great power? Chiang was clearly desperate. The United States and Britain had refused to become involved. Soviet support was far less than Chiang desired and, to preview our discussion of the next chapter, the Soviet-linked CCP was rapidly expanding its infrastructure behind Japanese lines in north China. The war had already gone on longer than Chiang had anticipated—he had originally thought in terms of a six-month war. Was Chiang desperate enough by mid-1938 to accept a harsh Brest-Litovsk-type treaty, turning over vast areas of China to a Japanese sphere of influence but giving him an opportunity to consolidate his regime? Was Chiang ready, in other words, to become a "traitor to the Han race," a *han jian*? This is an important point which, if an affirmative answer is given, would necessitate major modifications in my argument about Chiang as a determined Chinese nationalist. Unfortunately, documentary evidence is not available which permit us to probe Chiang's innermost thoughts on this issue. I personally suspect that such evidence may never turn up and that this is an issue which will be debated for many years yet. What is clear, however, is that Chiang was quite cognizant of the tactical benefits vis-à-vis Moscow and Washington of appearing ready to capitulate to Tokyo and that he cleverly capitalized on these benefits. Whatever, Chiang's innermost fears and hesitations, these tactical calculations of diplomatic leverage provide at least a partial, and perhaps a full, explanation of his peace diplomacy of 1938.

The linkage between Chiang's peace talks with Tokyo and his calls for greater Soviet assistance worked in several not entirely consistent ways. On the one hand, the peace talks pressured Moscow to increase its support to China in order to forestall China's capitulation. Increased Soviet support for Chiang might then either help persuade Tokyo to moderate its peace terms for the sake of drawing Chiang away from his Soviet alignment or, as Yang Jie had suggested in his 5 January 1938 cable to Chiang, it might provoke Japan to attack the Soviet Union. Either outcome would be helpful to Chiang. Of course this assumes that Stalin knew of the secret talks in 1938 and that Chiang knew that Stalin knew. Given the efficiency of Soviet intelligence services in China and the frequency with which Chinese and Japanese newspapers carried reports about the secret peace talks, this seems a fair assumption. If this assumption is correct, then we might paraphrase Chiang's message to Stalin in this fashion: We are willing to fight Japan for you, but we are at the extreme limits of our strength. If we surrender, the consequences will be extremely detrimental to your country's security interests. If you want us to keep fighting, you must at least give us greater assistance or, better yet, join us in the fight to check Japan. Chiang's peace negotiations with Tokyo and his entreaties for greater Soviet assistance were two sides of the same coin. While some of Chiang's emissaries were trying to hammer out peace terms with Japan, others were desperately trying to secure augmented Soviet aid to deal with an expanded Japanese offensive.

The Battle for Wuhan and the Quest for Soviet Intervention

Early 1938 saw a major expansion of the Sino-Japanese War. In March, the Japanese army launched a drive south from Shandong province toward the city of Xuzhou in northern Jiangsu province, thereby spreading the fighting across north China. Xuzhou was an important rail junction and was strongly defended by China's armies. The campaign to seize it required the redeployment southward of Japanese reserves previously held in Manchuria for use in the event of war with the Soviet Union. This sapped the Japanese forces confronting the Red Army. In this situation, Soviet intervention, or even the threat of such intervention through maneuvers on the Manchurian frontier, would assist China's efforts to hold Xuzhou.

On 10 March, Chiang cabled Yang Jie ordering him to meet with Voroshilov and press for a Soviet assault into Manchuria. Japan had deployed eight to twelve divisions to China, Chiang said, leaving northern Manchuria weakly defended. Yang should tell Voroshilov that if Soviet forces struck Manchuria or Korea they would achieve good results because of the depleted state of Japanese defenses. Picking up on Stalin's 4 February mention of Soviet manuevers to Sun Ke, Chiang also told Yang Jie that if direct Soviet military involvement were not possible, Yang should urge Voroshilov to concentrate Soviet forces on the frontiers of Manchuria and Korea, thereby preventing Japan from redeploying still more units in the south to fight China's armies. Such a move would also be "very useful," Chiang said.[65]

Xuzhou fell on 21 May.[66] There is no evidence that the Soviet Union responded to Chiang's plea for a massing of troops on the borders of Korea and Manchuria in time to support the Chinese defense of Xuzhou. After the fall of Xuzhou, the battle for Wuhan began. On 12 June, Anqing on the north bank of the Yangtze River in southwestern Anwei province fell and Japanese forces began concentrating around Hefei, the capital of Anwei, for an advance along the great river's northern bank to Wuhan.[67] Wuhan, the capital of Hubei province, was the last of China's major industrial cities not yet in Japanese hands. It was China's most important iron and steel center outside of Manchuria. It sat astride the north–south rail line and the east–west axis of the Yangtze, and in the center of the rich and densely populated upper Yangtze basin. Its fall would be, and was, a major blow to China's war effort. The battle for Wuhan marked the decisive stage of the first fifteen months of the war. Japanese logistic lines had been stretched thin and its forces spread out and worn down. Chinese patriotic fervor, and unity between the KMT and the CCP, were at unprecedented heights. If Japan's advance was to be checked, it would be at Wuhan. If Soviet entry into the war was to occur, it would be most effective during the battle for Wuhan.

As Japanese armies marched toward Wuhan in June, an intense debate within the German elite was being resolved in favor of Foreign Minister Joachim von Ribbentrop's pro-Japanese line. This shift in German policy meant the loss of an important foreign support by the ROC and led to a further strengthening of Sino-Soviet ties. A number of moves marked the shift in German policy, including German recognition of Manchukuo and the suspension of deliveries of German war matériel to China.[68] Then on 21 May the German advisors serving with China's armies were recalled. Among the German military advisors to leave was Chiang's trusted and able advisor General Alexander von Falkenhausen.[69] Berlin's abandonment of China further increased Chongqing's dependence on Moscow.

Chiang promptly requested Soviet advisors to replace the departing Germans. On 2 June, Chiang cabled Yang Jie, who had by then replaced Jiang Tingfu as ambassador, instructing him to ask Stalin and Voroshilov to dispatch an able general advisor, such as General Bluecher, to Wuhan to assist him as "general advisor."[70] As mentioned above, Bluecher was the commander of the Soviet Union's Special Far Eastern Army headquartered at Khabarovsk. His appointment as Chiang's "general advisor" to replace von Falkenhausen would have been a powerful symbolic demonstration of Soviet support for China. On 28 June, Chiang again cabled Yang asking him if the recall of the Soviet ambassador from Wuhan indicated a change in Soviet policy. Chiang noted the recent changes in German policy and argued that, in his opinion, "the Japs and Germany will inevitably take special action toward the Soviet Union before long."[71] In effect, Chiang was saying to Stalin that China had fully sided with the Soviet Union rather than its anti-Comintern enemies, that those enemies were themselves drawing closer together, and that it would be wise for Stalin to join his Chinese ally in a swift knockout blow against Japan before Germany was in a position to act.

The occurrence of heavy fighting near Changgufeng Hill immediately west of Lake Khasan on the Soviet-Korean border in July and August 1938, the first of the Soviet-Japanese border clashes in which division-size units, armor, and air power were used, greatly encouraged Chinese hopes for Soviet entry into the war.[72] The fighting at Changgufeng Hill was the topic of discussion at a dinner banquet in Wuhan in mid-July. According to Jiang Tingfu, then just returned from his post in Moscow in order to assume the position of director of the Office of Political affairs of the executive *Yuan*, many people at the banquet believed very strongly that the incident signaled the beginning of a Soviet-Japanese war.[73] Zhang Jiluan, the editor of *Da Gong Bao*, one of China's major newspapers, was among the optimists. Some of those present even went so far as to assert that Japan would collapse financially by September. Jiang, however, argued that the Soviet Union would not intervene. It was possible, he said, that the incident was not even the result of orders by the central governments of the two countries, but had been instigated by officers in command at the border. It was even possible that General Bluecher had violated discipline by seizing the hill. Jiang felt that much of the optimistic talk at the banquet was an attempt to please Chiang Kai-shek. Toward the end of the evening, however, Chiang endorsed Jiang Tingfu's view and said that China should continue as though the incident had not occurred. According to Jiang, while Chiang Kai-shek may have had illusions about Soviet entry into the war before, by mid-1938 he had shed such illusions.[74]

Chiang Kai-shek may not have been as fully disillusioned as Jiang believed. Chiang realized the debilitating effect that an overconfidence in foreign intervention could have, and even if he personally hoped for such intervention, it would be best for him to disparage such ideas—at least at such occasions as dinner banquets. As early as January 1938, for example, Chiang warned a conference of staff officers that among the errors China had committed during the early period of the war, was the false belief that, since the great powers would act against Japan, China could limit herself to defensive tactics.[75] It seems likely that regardless of how much hope Chiang had in Soviet intervention in mid-1938, he would not want unduly to encourage such hope among his subordinates. In any case, whatever Chiang's private views, he continued to work for Soviet intervention.

On 27 July, Chiang cabled Yang Jie asking him how resolute the Soviet response to the Changgufeng Incident would be. Marshaling his arguments for Yang to present to Soviet officials, Chiang raised the possibility that Japan would suggest the establishment of a border commission in order to defuse the crisis in Soviet-Japanese relations while redeploying all its troops southward to force a truce in China. Then, once China was out of the war, Japan would be free to use all its strength to deal with the Soviet Union. Japan's intent was clear, Chiang said, and the Soviet government should not be deceived. Yang was to ask the Soviet government just how resolute the Soviet position vis-à-vis Japan was. Chiang's sense of urgency, and possibly his dissatisfaction with Yang's efforts, was indicated by his queries about whether or not Yang had met with Bogomolov since the ambassador's recall, when the ambassador would return to China, and by his request for a prompt reply by Yang.[76]

The Soviet handling of the Changgufeng Incident was not what Chiang had hoped for. Not only was Moscow willing to settle the border issue peacefully with Japan, but it agreed to negotiate a boundary settlement with Tokyo, thereby tacitly accepting Japan as the de facto successor state to China in Manchuria.[77] Chiang Kai-shek recorded in his diary his bitterness about the peaceful settlement of the Changgufeng Incident. Had Japan been sincere in its proposals for an anticommunist cooperation with China, Chiang wrote, it would not have submitted so meekly after its defeat by the Red Army at Changgufeng.[78]

In late September, as the battle for Wuhan was entering the final stage with Japanese forces advancing on that city from three directions, Chiang made his last attempt in 1938 to secure Soviet entry into the war. On 30 September, Chiang Kai-shek summoned the Soviet ambassador and urged that the Soviet Union act to restrain Japan.[79] Two days later Chiang cabled Yang to inform him of his discussions with the Soviet ambassador. In line with a suggestion in a cable from Sun Ke on 7 August, Chiang now ordered Yang to propose a comprehensive treaty of alliance with the Soviet Union. Yang was to ask Stalin and Voroshilov whether the Soviet Union was prepared to adopt "military sanctions" against Japan. If so, China and the Soviet Union should then sign a mutual security agreement similar to the Soviet-French and Soviet-Czechoslovakian agreements. With the recent Four-Power Munich Agreement in mind, Chiang instructed Yang to tell Stalin that

> China believes that at this point the Soviet Union should take the most effective sanctions against the Far Eastern aggressor, and move a step closer to China. . . . At the present, one can hope for temporary stability in the European situation so that there would be no worry to your back. To use this extremely advantageous opportunity to teach the Far Eastern aggressor Japan a lesson would also prevent Germany from making trouble another day. You should tell them [Stalin and Voroshilov] that the Chinese people generally believe the Soviet Union's policy has been one of helping oppressed nations and is China's truest friend through thick and thin. Now our war of resistance has already reached its fifteenth month and the struggle against aggression has entered its most difficult and critical stage. China's own strength is stretched to the limit. The Soviet Union cannot be ready to see China fail within reach of success and thus see the arrogance of the Far Eastern aggressor further increased and the world situation become even more irretrievable.[80]

Chiang instructed Yang to explain this reasoning thoroughly and sincerely to Stalin and Voroshilov. He was also to lobby with Foreign Ministry officials and use all his strength to encourage the Soviet Union to adopt an "active policy." Chiang also ordered Yang to reply promptly to his cable.[81] On 9 October Chiang again met with the Soviet ambassador.[82]

The Soviet Union did not, of course, enter the Sino-Japanese War in 1938. Chiang ordered the withdrawal from Wuhan on 19 October and the city fell to Japanese forces on 21 October.

The Twilight of the Alliance

Both the intensification of Sino-Soviet cooperation during the first eight months of 1938 and its subsequent lessening must be viewed against the background of European events. During 1938 Europe was plunged into crisis by Germany's territorial demands. In March, Germany annexed Austria. Then Hitler escalated his agitation demanding that Czechoslovakia, which was allied to both France and the Soviet Union, cede its Sudeten territory to Nazi Germany. Czechoslovakian President Eduard Benes ordered a partial mobilization for war on 20 May, and ten days later Hitler issued an order for German mobilization against Czechoslovakia. The crisis over Czechoslovakia deepened throughout the summer and carried the very real possibility of a general European conflagration. Such an outcome was, of course, averted by Anglo-French acceptance of Germany's demands at the Munich Conference in September.

Chiang welcomed Western appeasement of Nazi Germany because the outbreak of a European war in 1938 would have been a devastating blow to Chinese efforts to secure international intervention in the Far Eastern crisis. If the Soviet Union, Britain, and the United States had to cope with a war in Europe, they would be far less willing to confront Japan in the Far East. Thus, the organizational paper of the KMT, *Zhongyang Ribao* (Central Daily News), lauded the Munich agreement.[83]

From Moscow's standpoint, however, Chongqing was working at cross-purposes to Soviet policy. As the crisis over Czechoslovakia mounted in 1938, Moscow worked with might and main to persuade London and Paris to stand firm beside Prague and Moscow, and against Hitler's outrageous claims. Chongqing, however, was lauding and encouraging the very appeasement policies which Moscow opposed. While Moscow certainly realized the China's influence on European events was nominal, Chongqing's European policy probably still increased Soviet suspicion of Chiang's aims and embittered Soviet leaders toward him. Given the level of Soviet diplomatic and military assistance to China, Soviet leaders probably expected more from their Chinese allies than sympathy for Hitler and encouragement of Western appeasement of Nazi expansion to the east.

More significantly, events in Munich signaled the collapse of Moscow's strategy of collective security with the Western democracies and the beginning of Soviet efforts to reach a *modus vivendi* with Nazi Germany. By the spring of 1939, intense Soviet-German negotiations were under way.[84] This reorientation of Soviet policy weakened China's strategic value to Moscow. As we have seen, Moscow saw its support of Nationalist China as a way of catalyzing Anglo-American-Soviet security cooperation. Once Moscow abandoned hope of such cooperation in favor of an understanding with Nazi Germany, this element no longer helped bind the Soviet Union and the Republic of China together. During January and May 1939, the representatives of the two countries at the League of Nations continued to work together to push for collective economic sanctions against Japan.[85] Such cooperation was by now a minor theme of Soviet diplomacy, however, analogous to the Anglo-Soviet talks which continued throughout the summer of 1939 while Molotov and von Ribbentrop were working out the terms of the Soviet-German partnership.

But the second foundation of the Sino-Soviet alliance, a combined military challenge to Japan, remained intact. Indeed, from the Soviet perspective, its need of China in this regard was even more acute in 1939 as the scale of combat along the Manchurian-Mongolian border escalated during the spring and summer of that year. In 1939, the situation of Moscow and Chongqing were the opposite of what they had been in mid 1938. Now it was Moscow which sought Chinese action to ease Japanese pressure in the north, and Chongqing which procrastinated to "await developments" in the international situation.

The denouement of the Soviet-Japanese border crisis of the 1930s began building early in 1939 in the Nomonhan region near the trijuncture of the borders of Manchuria, Inner Mongolia, and Outer Mongolia. Cavalry patrols from Outer Mongolia into contested areas of this region were challenged by Japanese forces beginning in March and April 1939. An armed clash on 28 May resulted in the annihilation of a Japanese cavalry regiment. Further Soviet deployments to the region in June convinced Japan's Manchurian army that Soviet and Mongolian actions were deliberately provocative and had to be met by a strong counterattack. This came in the form of a bombing raid by 130 Japanese planes on a Soviet-Mongolian air base some 100 kilometers (sixty-two miles) inside Outer Mongolia on 27 June, and an offensive on 1 July by a Japanese force of 15,000 soldiers supported by armor, artillery, and aircraft. Soviet forces once again proved superior to the Japanese both in quantity and quality, and within eleven days the Japanese invasion force was routed. A renewed Japanese offensive on 23 July also failed. By July the Soviet Union was rapidly sending reinforcements to the Nomonhan region. A powerful Soviet army of five infantry divisions and five tank brigades, under the command of General Georgii Zhukov, opened an offensive against Japanese forces on 20 August. Very heavy fighting continued for several weeks with the Soviet force finally winning an overwhelming victory. The Red Army advanced to the boundary line it claimed, halted, and began fortifying that position.[86]

While the Nomonhan conflict was escalating in June and July, Soviet military advisors in China began pushing Chiang Kai-shek to launch a major offensive in central China which would limit Japan's ability to redeploy forces from China to the Manchurian-Mongolian border. According to Aleksandr Kalyagin, a senior Soviet advisor in China, after the clash near Nomonhan on 28 May the head of the Soviet advisory mission, General A.I. Cherepanov (who had also been a military advisor to the KMT during the early 1920s) drew up plans for two major offensives by Nationalist forces that were to be launched in June and July. The objective of these offensives was nothing less than the recapture of Wuhan and the restoration of the battle situation that existed in China prior to 1 June 1938.[87] Cherepanov's plans were based on the observation that Japanese forces were deployed in the shape of a dumbbell along the Yangtze River. Large forces were deployed in the Nanchang-Yueyang-Wuhan interior region and in the Shanghai-Nanjing-Hangzhou coastal region. But only one division held the Yangtze artery linking these two concentrations. If that artery were severed, the forces in the upper Yangtze valley would be isolated and could be defeated. The first step of Cherepanov's plan called for the recapture of Jiujiang at the northern tip of Jiangxi province midway between Nanjing and Wuhan. The second step was to be an offensive to retake Wuhan itself. Nine Chinese armies were to take part in these offensives. When Cherepanov presented his plans to Chiang Kai-shek on 16 June, he noted that the mounting battle at Nomonhan had forced Japan to draw down its forces about Wuhan and that the balance of forces there now favored China.[88]

Cherepanov presented his plan to Chiang six days after the third Soviet credit agreement with China was signed. As we shall see below, this was the largest of the

Soviet Union's various wartime loans to China. Having just received Soviet largess, and still desiring to ensure actual Soviet delivery of goods, Chiang could hardly decline the Soviet request for an offensive. But perhaps with the experience of 1938 in mind, and with one eye on the rapid expansion of Chinese Communist power behind Japanese lines, Chiang was also in no mood to agree with the request. Thus, according to Kalyagin, he procrastinated. Cherepanov's plan was discussed at a session of the KMT military council on 20 June. Chiang approved the plan and set mid-July as the day for launching the offensive. On postponement and delay followed another, however, and in August the starting date was postponed until 15 September.[89]

On 9 July 1939, Stalin and Defense Commissar Voroshilov sent a letter to Chiang Kai-shek urging him to launch the offensive proposed by Cherepanov.[90] Stalin pledged continued support for China and gave an optimistic prognosis for the Soviet-British talks then underway in Moscow. If these talks bore fruit, Stalin said, this would inevitably lead to "effective measures" and to a united organization of peace-loving nations in the Far East. "Moreover," Stalin hinted cryptically, "this united organization is in the process of being formed."[91] After describing recent Japanese moves against the Soviet Union and Outer Mongolia, Stalin said that the Soviet Union was "giving Japan an answer." The United States and Britain were also awaiting an appropriate moment to move to check Japan. And China would soon deliver a blow against Japan "a hundred times more powerful."[92]

Stalin's talk of a united Sino-Soviet-American-British action against Japan was deliberate misinformation. Such a development was extremely unlikely by mid-1939; the Soviet-German rapprochement was well under way by that time. Apparently Stalin believed it expedient to pull out this old talisman to encourage Chiang to launch a new offensive in order to draw Japanese troops away from the borders between the Soviet Union and Outer Mongolia.

Soviet military advisors in China felt that Chiang was deliberately stalling to "await developments in the international situation," a euphemism for a Soviet-Japanese war.[93] It is interesting to speculate about what Chiang would have done had the Nomonhan Incident escalated into a broader Soviet-Japanese war. Would he have reproposed a Sino-Soviet mutual security arrangement to Stalin? Or would he have explored the possibility of a more moderate attitude in Tokyo? Probably he would have done both. In any case, it is clear that by late 1938 both Chiang and Stalin suspected the other of attempting to maneuver them into conflict with Japan in order to serve their own purposes. And each was determined to avoid the snares laid out by the other while seeking ways to heighten the degree of conflict between the other and Japan. There was never much trust in the Sino-Soviet alliance, and by 1939 what little there had once been was nearly depleted.

Soviet Military Assistance to China

Perhaps the most important dimension of the Sino-Soviet alliance during 1937–1939 was the large-scale and multifaceted Soviet assistance to China's war effort. Three credit agreements for $50 million, $50 million, and $150 million U.S. were signed on 1 March 1938, 1 July 1938, and 10 June 1939, respectively.[94] While these amounts were large, they were, not surprisingly, substantially less than the amounts initially requested by China. According to Sun Ke, who was the chief negotiator of the loan agreements, China initially sought $150 million U.S. for the first loan and $300 million U.S. for the second loan.[95] The Soviet loans were generally repaid with shipments of Chinese raw materials and agricultural goods over a five- to thirteen-year period and carried a three percent interest rate.[96]

The actual amounts of military equipment shipped from the Soviet Union to China during the years 1937–1941 are shown in Table 2.1. Conclusion of credit agreements and actual shipments of goods were two quite distinct matters. Goods were shipped to China before the conclusion of the first loan; the initial credit agreement retroactively covered goods shipped in late 1937 and early 1938. The conclusion of the July 1938 and June 1939 agreements were followed by long negotiations over the specific type, amounts, and prices of goods that were to be sold under the credit agreements. Even once sales agreements were reached, the specified goods might or might not be shipped to China, depending on a number of bilateral and international factors. With regard to the latter, it is especially important to understand the shift in Soviet policy toward China which occurred after the German-Soviet Nonagression Treaty of 1939 and to distinguish between the assistance before and after August 1939—a distinction Soviet sources are loath to make. Although the implications of this temporal distribution of aid are discussed in Chapter 4, the particular schedule of deliveries is noted in Table 2.1 for the sake of convenience of comparison.

Table 2.1 Soviet Aid to China, 1937–1941

Item	Total number, 1937–1941	Delivered during 1937–1939		Delivered Dec. 1940– Jan. 1941	
		Number	As percentage of total	Number	As percentage of total
Bombers	348	278	80	100	29
Fighters	542	452	83	150	28
Special aircraft	44	100[a]			
Total aircraft	904[a]				
T-26 tanks	82				
		Delivered "in significant part" before March 1938			
Motor vehicles	2,118	1,315	62	300	14
Artillery pieces	1,140	960	84	250	22
Artillery shells	2,000,000	2,000,000	100	200,000	.06
Machine guns	9,720	8,300	85	1,300	13
Rifles	50,000	100,000	50		
Ammunition (millions of rounds)	180	130	67	18	1
Aerial bombs	31,600				

Sources: Aleksandr Ya. Kalyagin, *Along Alien Roads,* New York: Columbia University East Asian Institute, 1983, pp. 8–9, Zhanshi Waijiao, pp. 509–512, 526.
[a]As in original.

Prior to Guangzhou's occupation by Japanese forces in October 1938, some 60,000 tons* of Soviet equipment, the bulk of Soviet aid, moved through that port and then by rail to China's southwest. Some material also came overland from a rail head at Saryozek, north of Alma Ata on the Turkestan-Siberian rail line in the Soviet Union, by road some 2925 kilometers (1814 miles) to Lanzhou (capital of Gansu province). According to one Soviet study, between October 1937 and February 1939, 5640 "goods wagons" were used to move freight to China's borders and 5260 trucks were used to carry it through Xinjiang.[97] Laborers kept the Saryozek-Lanzhou road open in winter by shoveling snow, while thousands of camels carried supplies to the supply depots along the route.[98] The condition of the road to Lanzhou was very poor, however, and this limited the amount of traffic it could carry. To overcome this bottleneck, during the first two years of the war, 100,000 Chinese workers labored to improve the Xinjiang road under the direction of the Soviet Union's Defense Commissariat.[99]

Soviet arms deliveries were of great value to China's armies; they substantially reduced the superiority of firepower which Japan's armies enjoyed in the initial months of the war. Soviet-supplied guns and T-26 tanks were instrumental in achieving the first clear victory of the Nationalists at Taierchuang in southern Shandong province in March 1938, at which two of Japan's best divisions were decimated.[100] According to Soviet Colonel Aleksandar Kalyagin, who served as senior advisor to the head of the Chinese Army Engineers from May 1938 to November 1939, as the battle for Wuhan intensified during the summer of 1938, the armament of the Chinese armies was actually superior to that of their Japanese enemies in terms of number of light and heavy machine guns, and was inferior to the Japanese only in terms of aircraft, armor, and artillery.[101] Again, during the successful defense of southern Guangxi province in December 1939, a detachment of fifteen T-26s played an important role.[102]

Modeled after six ton Vickers tanks purchased from Britain in 1932, the T-26 was one of the main battle tanks of the Red Army during the 1930s. Some 12,000 were produced and many saw service not only in China but in Spain, at Nomonhan, and during the Winter War against Finland. It weighed nine tons, had a top speed of twenty kilometers (twelve miles) per hour, carried a radio, and could climb an incline of forty degrees. Most of the eighty-two T-26s sent to China were single-turret models armed with a 45-millimeter cannon and two 7.62-millimeter machine guns. In the expert opinion of Soviet Marshal Gregorii Zhukov, the T-26 had poor off-road maneuverability, was too vulnerable to artillery fire, broke down often, and was inadequate in combat.[103] Yet it remained in front-line service with the Red Army until it came up against German armor in mid-1941.

The aircraft the Soviet Union sent to China varied in quality. They included superior performance fighters such as the I-16 and bombers such as the SB-2, as well as aging biplane fighters of the I-15 type. The I-16, of which at least ninety-four were delivered to China by 14 February 1938, was then one of the most advanced fighter aircraft in the world. First flown in prototype in December 1933, it was the world's first cantilever single-wing fighter and also included retractable landing gear.

---

*Unless otherwise noted all tonnages are metric. In many cases, however, sources do not specify what system of weights is being used and I have had to assume that Chinese, Soviet, or German documents give weights in metric tonnages.

It made its first operational appearance in Spain in 1937 and remained in front-line service with the Soviet army until the summer of 1943. The dual-engine SB-2 bomber was also a superior aircraft in 1938. With a crew of three, it had a range of 1200 kilometers (745 miles), a top speed of 412 kilometers (255 miles) per hour, a ceiling of 9510 meters (31,200 feet), and could carry a bomb load of 600 kilograms (1320 pounds). It was the Soviet Union's first truly advanced bomber. The Soviet army itself employed it against Japanese forces during the 1938 and 1939 clashes on the Soviet Union's Far Eastern borders, and again during the Winter War with Finland. The bi-wing I-15 biplane, on the other hand, was inferior to most of the aircraft Japan was then testing in China.[104] China, again like Spain, provided a useful testing ground for the new weapons systems being developed by the major powers.

The Soviet Union also sent about 1500 military advisors to China during this period. Included were some of the Red Army's best officers. General Georgii Zhukov, who later defeated Japanese forces at Nomonhan and went on to become the outstanding Soviet Marshal of World War II, served briefly as military attaché in late 1938. General Vasilii I. Chuikov, who later commanded the defense of Stalingrad, General P.F. Batitsky, later a Marshal of the Soviet Union, and Colonel Andrey A. Vlasov, one of the Red Army's outstanding field commanders during the opening months of World War II—until he defected to the Nazis—also served as military advisors for a period.[105] Like Spain, China served as a training ground for Soviet officers.

The first group of high level Soviet advisors arrived in China in June 1938, just after the departure of the last of the German advisory mission.[106] The Soviets were assigned to the National Government's central headquarters as well as to the regional military zones, and were specialists in artillery, armor, transportation, military engineering, communications, intelligence, antiaircraft, and aviation. According to one Soviet study, by February 1939, 3665 Soviet "military specialists" were serving in China.[107] This figure probably included volunteer Soviet pilots.[108] Whatever their precise numbers, it is clear that these advisors substantially enhanced the combat effectiveness of China's armies. Colonel Kalyagin, for example, stressed the use of camouflage and firing from concealed positions as two major improvement in China's military style to which he contributed.

The duties of the Soviet advisors were, however, confined to technical matters. With a few exceptions, such as General Cherepanov's role in planning the offensive to retake Wuhan in mid-1939, Soviet advisors were excluded from staff work, let alone from consideration of political issues. In this regard the Soviet role in the 1930s was much more limited than it had been during the period of Soviet-KMT cooperation from 1923 to 1927. This limitation reflected Chiang's interpretation of Soviet intentions and activities during that earlier united front. While Chiang was ready to cooperate with Moscow diplomatically and militarily, he remained extremely suspicious of Soviet efforts to foster revolution in China and, for this reason, limited Soviet activities to a relatively narrow role.

One prominent component of the Soviet aid program was in aviation. In 1937–1938, the armies of the world were just moving into the era of combined air-ground operations and long-range strategic bombing. Prior to the outbreak of the Sino-Japanese War, China's National Government had looked to Italy and the United

States for assistance in developing its embryonic air force. This air force was soon swept from the skies by Japanese warplanes, and the most urgent of Chiang Kai-shek's demands on his Soviet ally was for help in rapidly building a combat-worthy air force. The Soviet Union responded by supplying aircraft, aviation equipment, infrastructure, and personnel. Aviation schools were established with Soviet aid at Dihua and at Kuldja (as Urumqi and Yining were then called) in Xinjiang, and at Chengdu in Sichuan. A large Soviet air base was established at Lanzhou in Gansu province, and equipment such as radios, refueling machinery, aviation gasoline, and air weapons were supplied to China's air force.[109]

The Soviet Union also sent volunteer pilots to fly many of the aircraft it was providing. These volunteers were regular air force units commanded by their own officers and with their own ground crews and logistics support. They wore civilian clothes but retained their air force rank and received an automatic promotion upon return to the Soviet Union.[110] Soviet pilots served six-month tours in China and at any one time numbered about 200–300. All together about 2000 served in China. They were very good pilots and played an important role in the first two years of the war, shooting down 986 Japanese planes, limiting the freedom of action of the Japanese air force, effectively bombing Japanese bases and lines of communications (including at least one raid on Taiwan), and greatly boosting Chinese military and civilian morale. More than 200 Soviet pilots died in China.[111] During the 1950s, a monument to commemorate them would be built in Wuhan.

The first group of volunteer Soviet pilots began arriving in the cities of Xuzhou and Lanzhou in November 1937. Shortly afterward, the first group of twenty-three Soviet I-16 fighters and twenty SB-2 bombers landed in Nanjing in time to assist in the defense of that city.[112] By the spring of 1938, eighty-five Soviet warplanes were based at Wuhan, forty at Nanchang (Jiangxi province) with squadrons also at Changsha and Hengyang (Hunan province), and Guangzhou (Guangdong province).

On 29 April 1938, Soviet pilots and planes played an important role in what proved to be the largest pre-World War II aerial battle. Expecting a Japanese raid on Wuhan on Emperor Hirohito's birthday, Chinese and Soviet officers planned a trap. While ground crews moved out conspicuously by truck on 28 April, air defense squadrons were flown away from Hankou. After Japanese spies reported these movements, the planes and support units moved quietly back to nearby auxiliary fields during the night. When Japanese bombers arrived the next day, they lost several dozen planes to the combined Soviet-Chinese defenses.[113]

Aid Negotiations

The Sino-Soviet alliance of 1937–1939 was continually strained by the discrepancy between China's immense needs for assistance and the Soviet Union's limited ability to provide such assistance. This fundamental problem was compounded by Chinese disorganization and inefficiency. Moreover, negotiations about Soviet arms sales to China were closely linked to shifts in the broader pattern of Sino-Soviet relations.

During the first eight months of the war, the Soviet aid program was conducted on an ad hoc basis with a substantial degree of confusion. Chiang involved both

Jiang Tingfu and Yang Jie in negotiations regarding the same types of arms, thereby establishing parallel channels through men who were not on very goods terms with each other. Chiang repeatedly cabled new requests for aid to Jiang and Yang, and a sense of great urgency pervaded his directives to his emissaries in Moscow.[114]

On 2 November 1937, Yang sent Chiang a memo detailing his talks with Stalin. The Soviet Union was willing to help China set up an arsenal manufacturing field artillery of all calibers and an aircraft factory with an initial output of fifty aircraft per month, with the engines for these aircraft to be sent from the Soviet Union. (This was the origin of the Dihua aircraft factory which later figured so prominently in the Sino-Soviet relations in Xinjiang—a problem discussed in Chapter 6.) Stalin was also willing to send petroleum experts and equipment to China to help expand petroleum output in Shaanxi, Sichuan, and Xinjiang so that within a few months China's domestic production from these sources would be adequate to meet its needs. The cable also reported that Stalin felt China should accept military supplies from Britain, the United States, France, and Germany, if these countries were willing to supply them.[115]

The size of Chiang's demands for Soviet aid grew steadily. On 28 August, Chiang requested 200 fighters and 100 heavy bombers. Then on 10 December, Chiang instructed Yang to seek the purchase of "several hundred" twin-engine fighters along with the materials necessary for the manufacture of aircraft engines, 100 tanks, 60 antiaircraft guns, and 300 pieces of artillery.[116] At the end of December, Chiang ordered Yang to seek complete equipment for twenty divisions—all to be delivered within three months—along with 150 planes to be delivered within a month.[117] On 5 January, Chiang cabled further supplemental orders to Yang, saying that Yang should seek more heavy artillery, antitank guns, and machine guns for each of the twenty divisions being outfitted by the Soviet Union.[118] Later in January, Chiang ordered Yang to request 30,000–50,000 pistols from the Soviet Union.[119]

By early 1938, the ad hoc nature of Chinese demands and irregularities in the use of Soviet aid were becoming unacceptable to Moscow. In a cable of 22 January, Yang Jie cryptically informed Chiang Kai-shek that the Soviets were unhappy with the "unloading and loading" of ships delivering Soviet equipment and returning with Chinese raw materials to the Soviet Union. According to Yang, until Soviet officials had definite confirmation of Chinese receipt of the cargo of the second ship already chartered to carry goods to Canton, they were unwilling to charter additional ships.[120] The precise nature of Soviet concerns in this instance is unclear, but it could well have been that corrupt Chinese officials were siphoning off Soviet aid even before its receipt was acknowledged.

Some key Chinese representatives responsible for handling Soviet aid were apparently corrupt, a fact which did nothing to strengthen Soviet understanding of China's difficulties. Early in 1939, for example Ambassador Yang Jie was implicated in serious irregularities involving arms purchases in France. According to Jiang Tingfu, Yang had been employing questionable people and making false reports to Chongqing about purchases from the Soviet Union. He was also implicated in a scheme to sell Chinese visas to European Jewish refugees. Chongqing sent a vice-foreign minister to investigate these allegations and in June 1939 the Foreign Ministry decided to recall Yang. Difficulties arose in selecting a replacement for Yang, however, and his recall stalled; Yang remained in his post in Moscow until April 1940 when he resigned on the grounds of opposition to Chongqing's policy toward the Soviet-Finnish Winter War. Before leaving, however, Yang attempted to retain his position by mobilizing Soviet support against his own government. Upon being informed in mid-1939 of his impending recall, Yang appealed to Voroshilov for help, saying that when in China he had always obeyed Chiang Kai-shek, but when in the Soviet Union his duty was to listen to and follow Voroshilov. Yang's Chinese translator reportedly initially refused to translate these remarks and did so only at Yang's insistence.[121] This episode reportedly became something of a joke in Chongqing. Clearly, Yang's personal integrity did nothing to contribute to Sino-Soviet cooperation.

Procedural factors also contributed to the troubled course of Soviet-Chinese aid negotiations. While Sun and Yang Jie were negotiating matters relating to Soviet assistance to China, both men were simultaneously involved in negotiations in Paris over a Sino-French mutual security treaty. This quixotic effort required that Sun and Yang continually shuttle between Paris and Moscow in early 1938, and these interruptions contributed to the difficulties encountered in the Moscow negotiations. One also suspects that Paris was a rather more enjoyable place to live than austere Moscow.

Chiang Kai-shek responded to Soviet displeasure in late 1937 by sending Sun Ke to the Soviet Union to negotiate a regularization of the Sino-Soviet aid relationship. During the next year and a half, Sun functioned as Chiang's key troubleshooter in the frequently turbulent negotiations with the Soviet government over assistance to China. Sun Ke was more successful than Yang in dealing with Soviet leaders. Several times when Yang's efforts reached an impasse, Sun moved in to break the deadlock. Sun's first meeting with Stalin was on 4 February, when the two men sat drinking and talking late into the night. On 25 February, Sun sent a long cable to Chiang Kai-shek outlining Soviet grievances regarding the assistance program. Stalin felt it was not convenient to deal with continual miscellaneous demands, Sun reported. Rather, the two sides should sign a general arms sales agreement specifying amounts of credit to be extended. Moreover, "to the extent that it is possible," China should export raw materials to the Soviet Union to pay for Soviet equipment. By doing this, China would prove its sincerity and the Soviet Union would be more willing to aid China. Overlapping channels of communication should also be avoided, Sun reported. If China's military attaché to Moscow, Zhu Shiming, was ordered to negotiate a particular issue, then Yang Jie should not also be ordered to approach Soviet officials about the same issue. Moreover, military matters should be discussed with the Soviet military attaché in Wuhan, not with the Soviet ambassador.[122] In spite of these objections, Stalin agreed to an initial credit loan of $50 million U.S. Shortly after signing the agreement on 1 March, Sun departed for Paris.

After this agreement had been concluded and after Sun Ke had left Moscow, Yang, in line with Chiang's cable of 5 January, approached Voroshilov on 12 March 1938 with a long list of Chinese requests.[123] It is not clear why Yang did not coordinate his actions with Sun, but instead waited until after the latter's departure to present his requests. Possibly his personal relations with Sun were strained. Possibly he felt that he would be able to secure higher levels of assistance than Sun had negotiated and did not want to share this accomplishment with Sun.

Voroshilov responded to Yang's demands by saying that it was time to regularize the Soviet aid program to China. In a cable to Chiang Kai-shek on 15 March, Yang outlined Voroshilov's proposals for such a regularization. Three separate contracts covering different items should be signed, Voroshilov proposed. Moreover, each contract would involve different terms of repayment, with a substantial part of the Soviet credits to be repaid not with Chinese raw materials but in hard currency. This was appropriate, Voroshilov insisted, because Soviet goods had been sent to China very expeditiously and at great cost to the Soviet Union. [124] Moreover, since the Soviet Union often bought its military supplies from abroad with foreign currency, it was reasonable, Voroshilov said, that China do likewise. [125]

Regarding the general principles governing Soviet assistance, Voroshilov insisted that it was essential first to reach agreement on the method of payment and then to discuss the problem of increasing the volume of assistance to China. To make his point, Voroshilov told Yang that 120 aircraft engines bound for China would have to be paid for in cash before they would be delivered. [126] If China henceforth wanted the Soviet Union to increase the amount of any type of aid, it should present a detailed request to this effect. The Soviet Union would then do all that it could to assist China, "as long as this does not interfere with [the Soviet Union's] own preparations for war." Regarding the scope of future assistance, Voroshilov suggested that 500 million yuan over a two-year period would be an appropriate figure for discussion. [127] The day after Chiang received Yang's cable, he received another from T.V. Soong in Hong Kong informing him that the shipment of sixty-five light bombers to China was being suspended until China delivered the mineral ores which it had contracted to deliver to the Soviet Union. [128]

On 21 March 1938, six days after he received Yang's cable describing Voroshilov's proposals, Chiang Kai-shek replied to Voroshilov. Subtly raising the possibility that China might make peace with Japan, Chiang said that he hoped the Soviet Union could "first" send fifty or sixty bombers to China. "This is related to the common interest of China and Russia," Chiang said. "I cannot believe that Russia will stand by and watch us in difficulty with no way to deal with the war [*ying zhan*]." Regarding the overall level of Soviet assistance, Chiang agreed with Voroshilov's proposal of Soviet assistance of 500 million yuan, but insisted that only one-fifth of this should go for infantry weapons, while four-fifths should go for the purchase of aircraft. Moreover, the loan should be repaid entirely through shipments of Chinese goods at a rate of 50 million yuan per year (i.e., over a ten-year period). [129]

Voroshilov responded to Chiang's intrasigence, and to his hinted threat of making peace with Japan, by presenting Yang with three bills of lading for all Soviet equipment sent to China between 24 October 1937 and 14 February 1938, and by demanding that Yang inspect and sign the three lists. Yang responded by sending Voroshilov lists of Chinese officials who had already signed for the receipt of these goods, and affirming that he himself had inspected these lists to verify that there was "no discrepancy." [130] According to Zhou Xicai, Yang was unwilling himself to sign the three documents until he could return to Wuhan to verify the deliveries. [131] Whatever the reasons for Yang's reluctance, Voroshilov informed him that the Soviet reply to his extensive requests of 12 March was contingent upon China's acceptance of these three bills of lading. [132] These three bills of lading are an interesting itemization of Soviet aid to China during the first six months of the war and are summarized in Table 2.2.

In a cable to Chiang Kai-shek on 22 March, Yang explained the reasons for Voroshilov's demand for an itemized confirmation of receipt of goods. Voroshilov was concerned, Yang explained, because he was personally responsible for the goods already sent. The equipment for twenty divisions had already been shipped to China, but no agreement regarding the method of repayment had yet been reached. Until the Chinese government informed the Soviet government how and when it intended to repay the 600 million yuan for this equipment, Yang reported Voroshilov as saying, "There is no way to continue discussions of assistance." Regarding all discussions of future aid, "the problem which must first be solved is the amount of credit and the method of repayment."[134]

Chiang responded to this crisis in relations with Moscow by again ordering Sun Ke, then in Paris, to return to Moscow to assist Yang. Sun complied and was apparently able to resolve the question of confirmation of Voroshilov's three bills of lading—at least this issue is not subsequently mentioned in the diplomatic record. In a cable to Chiang Kai-shek on 29 May 1938, Sun reported to Chiang that negotiations for a second loan were scheduled to begin in Moscow and that Stalin had agreed that Yang should sign the resulting document. Agreement as to the amount of Chinese purchases under the second Soviet loan was reached by late June, but signature of the contract was postponed until Moscow received from T.V. Soong a list of Chinese goods which were to be sent to the Soviet Union.[135] Again, it was apparent that the Soviets were unhappy with the amounts of Chinese raw materials being sent to the Soviet Union in repayment for Chinese arms purchases.

Table 2.2 Soviet Aid to China, 24 October 1937–14 February 1938

Item	Number	Value (U.S. $)
I-16 Fighter (single-wing)[a]	94	3,760,000
I-15 Fighter (double-wing)[a]	62	2,170,000
SB Light bombers	62	6,820,000
TB-3 Heavy bombers[a]	6	1,440,000
N-15 Fighters (double-wing)	60	2,100,000
YT Trainer aircraft	13	417,500
Aircraft motors, parts, and ammunition		12,009,956
T-26 Tanks, with radios and parts	82	2,120,840
3NC-5 Motor vehicles	400	448,000
Guns and ammunition (76-mm and 115-mm)	240	6,492,800
76-mm antiaircraft guns and antiaircraft equipment	20	1,042,387
Guns and ammunition (37-mm and 45-mm)	130	994,936
Artillery shells		3,178,810
Machine guns and ammunition	1,880	1,017,500
Military instruments		311,800
Repair work on roads		54,547
Handling, railway, and other fees		2,987,853
TOTAL		47,262,929

[a] See note 133.
Source: Zhanshi Waijaio, pp. 483–491.

46 CHINESE-SOVIET RELATIONS, 1937–1945

On 1 July 1938 the second Soviet-Chinese credit agreement was signed. There was some delay, however, in the conclusion of a contract for delivery of specific goods. On 10 July, Chiang cabled Yang to inquire why a purchase contract for the second period had not yet been signed.[136] Chiang also had to order Yang to remain in Moscow and continue negotiations until a purchase contract was signed and a delivery schedule worked out.[137] Four days later Chiang appealed directly to Stalin and Voroshilov in an attempt to overcome the delay. The war in China was entering its critical stage, Chiang said in his cable to Stalin. China was in urgent need of fighters, bomber aircraft, and ammunition. Could the Soviet Union accelerate the delivery of these items? Delivery even one day sooner would increase China's chances for victory by one percent, Chiang said.[138] On 25 July, Chiang again asked Yang if he had conveyed this message to Stalin and requested that Yang file a detailed report as to why there was a delay in signing a purchase contract agreement. Yang replied on 2 August, citing a technicality as the apparent obstacle. According to precedent, Yang said, the agreement should be signed by a representative with plenipotentiary powers (*quanquan daibiao*), while he had only liaison powers (*tongquan daibiao*).[139]

On 17 August 1938, as the battle for Wuhan intensified, Chiang appealed to Stalin and Voroshilov. The war in China was entering a decisive stage, Chiang explained. China desperately needed all war matériel already contracted for. Such matériel should be delivered to Hong Kong by mid-September, Chiang urged, since an all-out Japanese drive for Wuhan was expected during September. "This decisive battle would be the most critical stage of China's war of resistance and of the crisis of East Asian security," Chiang told Stalin.[140] Finally, on 20 August, the Chinese embassy in Moscow was able to report to Chiang that an order for Soviet war matériel worth 120 million yuan had been accepted by Moscow. The contents of this contract are shown in Table 2.3.

Moscow apparently complied with Chiang's request for accelerated delivery of contracted purchases. On 3 October, Yang reported to Chiang that part of the goods contracted for during the second period were being sent to Hong Kong aboard a ship then being loaded in Odessa, Ukraine. Larger goods, such as aircraft, were being sent overland by truck.[141]

Talks about a third Soviet credit began in March 1939. As was the case with earlier loan negotiations, these talks did not proceed smoothly. Sun apparently worked

Table 2.3 Contents of August 1938 Purchase Agreement

Item	Quantity
Light bombers	120
Heavy bombers	10
Fighters	220
Training aircraft	100
Spare aircraft engines	200
Disassembled fighters	200
Antiaircraft guns	100
Aircraft manufacturing equipment	U.S.$ 1,000,000
Aviation instructional equipment	U.S.$ 500,000
Spare parts	U.S.$ 2,500,000

Source: Zhanshi Waijiao, p. 510.

out the general principles of the third credit loan, left the details in Yang's hands, and then departed for Paris. Once again Yang proved unable to conclude the negotiations. Again, personal factors may have played a role. According to the memoir of a man then working in Chiang Kai-shek's staff office, during Sun Ke's stay in Moscow in the spring of 1939, Sun sent Chiang Kai-shek reports which were highly critical of Yang. Sun allegedly said that Yang's attitude during negotiations with the Soviet officials was extremely arrogant and that Soviet leaders were very dissatisfied with him. Sun also reported that Yang was neglecting his duties as ambassador to pursue "pleasurable activities" and that he was careless in his actions.[142]

Once again Chiang Kai-shek turned to Sun Ke, ordering him to return to Moscow from Paris and assist Yang. Sun complied and by 14 May was able to report to Chiang that on the basis of his talks with Stalin, Voroshilov, and Molotov (who had replaced Litvinov as foreign minister on 5 May 1939), the Soviet Union absolutely would continue to assist China in resisting Japan. Rumors that the Soviet Union had changed the direction of its policy were absolutely without basis, Sun reported.[143]

Two days after Sun's optimistic report, however, the Soviet side suddenly suspended the aid negotiations. This move came as a bolt out of the blue to Sun Ke, at least so he reported to Chiang on 16 May. That very morning, Sun said, he had conducted cordial and satisfactory talks with Voroshilov. The reason given for the suspension of the talks was that "some people" in the Chinese embassy in Moscow were spreading reports that China had requested that the Soviet Union "come quickly to China's assistance." Sun was skeptical about whether this was the real reason and believed, as he reported to Chiang a few days later, that the true reason for the suspension was a Soviet fear that they would influence the delicate Soviet-British talks then underway.[144] In retrospect it seems that Sun's surmise was wrong. Assuming that the Soviet complaints were accurate, such provocative fabrication of rumors would have been adequate to rouse Soviet ire. Moscow had to tread a thin line between provocation and deterrence in its relations with Japan. Reports of possible Soviet entry into the Sino-Japanese War at a time when the battle at Nomonhan was escalating rapidly were undoubtedly viewed as provocative actions which could not be tolerated.

After learning of Moscow's suspension of talks on 16 May 1939, Chiang ordered Yang Jie, who was once again back in Paris, to return to Moscow to ascertain why the talks had been suspended.[145] Chiang also sent a cable directly to Stalin on 24 May petitioning for a resumption of the talks, pleading: "I deeply believe that Your Excellency's sense of justice is very great and absolutely will not be shaken because of any partial differences, and that you will certainly aid China's sacred revolutionary war of resistance to aggression through to the end."[146] China's battle against Japanese aggression was intensifying, Chiang said. Could Stalin please accelerate the dispatch of Soviet weapons to China?

Chiang's appeal to Stalin, along with the deteriorating situation in the Nomonhan region, had some effect. The third loan was finally signed on 10 June 1939. It was to run from 1 July 1939 to 1 July 1941, carried a three percent rate of interest, and was to be repaid over a ten-year period beginning in 1941 with deliveries of Chinese agricultural goods and raw materials.[147]

Six days after the third credit agreement was signed, a new commercial treaty was also concluded in Moscow. This further added to the nexus of bilateral Sino-Soviet cooperation. Only one aspect of the cooperation conducted under this treaty was commercial; another important aspect had to do with intelligence operations. When Sun submitted a draft commercial agreement to Soviet officials, the latter expanded it to include the establishment of Soviet trade offices in the coastal cities of Shanghai, Wuhan, Tianjin, and Guangzhou, as well as Lanzhou in the interior. Except for Lanzhou, all of these cities were under Japanese occupation. As such, they could not serve as entrepôts for strategic ROC-USSR trade. But Soviet commercial representatives enjoying diplomatic status and immunity—including the right to communicate with their home offices by secret telegraphic codes, as was provided for in the revised commercial agreement—would be well positioned to observe and report on Japanese activities in China.[148] Japan was compelled to tolerate such legal niceties because it insisted that no state of war existed between China and Japan. The conflict was an "incident" not a "war," a distinction which once led a German diplomat in occupied Nanjing to quip to his Japanese counterpart that he had fought in the First World Incident.

Once the third credit agreement was signed, Chiang continued to press for accelerated delivery of Soviet equipment. During July, he cabled further arguments to Yang to be conveyed to Voroshilov. The international situation was increasingly tense, Chiang said, and China was in extreme need of replenishment of its supply of weapons. If weapons from the Soviet Union did not arrive in China before war broke out in Europe, their delivery would become much more difficult. Were this to happen, Chiang said, China's plans for resupply and counterattack would be adversely influenced. Chiang inquired when precisely Soviet weapons would be sent to China.[149]

Although the Soviet loan of June 1939 was one-third larger than the combined total of the first two loans, it was not fulfilled as faithfully as earlier loans. By 1940, improvements in Soviet-Japanese relations and a deterioration of Japanese-American relations produced major changes in Soviet policy toward China. The shifts in Moscow's international alignments which led to a suspension of Soviet aid to China are discussed in Chapter 4.

As noted earlier, China undertook to repay Soviet loans with shipments of Chinese raw materials and agricultural goods. As of December 1938 China had delivered via Lanzhou 10,000 cattle hides, 280,000 goat skins, 2000 buffalo hides, 56 tons of pig bristles, and 2548 tons of tea.[150] Between February 1939 and November 1940, China delivered 8000 tons of antimony, 5000 tons of tin, 7000 tons of tungsten, and 50 tons of mercury.[151] The total value of mineral deliveries, including all transportation costs, between November 1938 and October 1939 was $6,942,400 U.S.[152] This represented about fourteen percent of the value of the goods on Voroshilov's three bills of lading of March 1938. These minerals were vital strategic materials and in a world furiously preparing for war they represented an important contribution to Soviet war preparations.

Nonetheless Moscow felt Chongqing could have done more. Chinese deliveries of tungsten to the Soviet Union in 1939 and 1940, for example, amounted to only fifty-three percent of Chinese tungsten shipments to Germany in 1938 and 1939. Even during 1939, long after German assistance to China had ended, 4000 tons of Chinese tungsten went to Germany.[153] Moscow undoubtedly felt that Chongqing should have been more scrupulous in fulfilling its obligations to the Soviet Union rather than repaying old debts to Germany.

The Soviet Aid Effort: Scope and Problems

The rapid and timely extension of generous Soviet aid during the first twelve months of the war was influenced by a Soviet desire to encourage Chiang to wage a determined, total, and protracted war against Japan. In this regard, it is important to keep in mind that during the aid negotiations during mid-1938, Sino-Japanese peace talks were under way and that China's representatives were offering terms tantamount to surrender and anti-Soviet cooperation with Japan. The implied message to Moscow was that unless the Soviet Union effectively supported China's war of resistance, the results could be very unfavorable for the Soviet Union. Chiang Kai-shek was aware of China's role in tying down Japanese armies for Moscow and he naturally demanded for China's services as high a price as the market would bear. Chiang's basic strategy for pressuring Moscow to supply substantial aid was to threaten to make peace with Japan. Time and again, Chiang intimated that continued aid was the *sine qua non* of continued Chinese resistance. Both Chiang and Stalin understood that if China continued to fight Japan, Japanese armies would be less able to march against Siberia.

Aside from such broad political problems, the Sino-Soviet aid relationship was plagued by several sorts of bilateral frictions. First, there was the ad hoc nature of Chinese demands and continual requests for accelerated delivery. These were inconvenient for the Soviet bureaucracy to deal with. Moreover, the satisfaction of such ad hoc demands disrupted Soviet efforts to equip systematically its own armies. Second, the Soviet side apparently feared that its aid was being misappropriated. Third, the Chinese side did not meet its obligations to repay its loans with deliveries of raw materials and agricultural products. The Chinese response to this particular Soviet complaint was that during the negotiations they had made clear that unforeseen and unavoidable circumstances might make it impossible to meet delivery deadlines. Nor could agricultural goods be delivered before they were ready for harvest. Tea, for example, could not be processed before October or it would mildew. Moreover, the Soviet side itself was frequently tardy in picking up deliveries of Chinese goods. A fourth Soviet complaint regarded the redundancy of channels and a lack of regard for correct Soviet procedures by the Chinese side. The Chinese responded that dealing with the Soviet foreign trade monopoly was also cumbersome and time-consuming.[154]

In spite of these frictions, Soviet aid to China during the first two years of the war was generous. The amount of hardware transferred to China represented a significant proportion of the annual Soviet production of such goods. The 376 fighter aircraft and eighty-two tanks sent to China during the first eighteen months of the war, for example, represented 6.8 percent and 3.6 percent respectively of Soviet production of modern aircraft and tanks during 1938.[155] At a time when the Soviet Union was rushing to prepare for war, these exports represented a significant sacrifice. Moreover, this aid came at a time when the United States, Britain, and Germany were all unwilling to sell military hardware to China.

One useful yardstick for measuring the scale of Soviet aid is subsequent American aid to China. Between mid-1941 and the end of 1943, the United States transferred to China $201 million U.S. in Lend-Lease supplies.[156] Assuming that all of the Soviet Union's $191.2 million U.S. in aid went for military assistance, then Soviet military assistance during the 1937–1941 period was ninety-five percent of that provided by the United States during the 1941–1943 period. By this yardstick, Soviet military aid to China was clearly generous. If one takes nonmilitary assistance into consideration, however, aid to China from the United States far exceeded that of the Soviet Union. Four U.S. Export–Import Bank loans between December 1938 and November 1940 provided $120 million U.S. in credits, to be repaid by shipments of Chinese tung oil, tin, tungsten, wolframite, and antimony. After Pearl Harbor, another $485 million U.S. was loaned to China for the purchase of gold, bank notes, and goods.[157] If total American and Soviet aid to China are compared, the respective figures are $686 U.S. and $191.2 U.S. Soviet aid, in other words, was about twenty-eight percent of the American total. Still, considering the differing levels of Soviet and American economic development, Soviet aid was not paltry.

Conclusion

The 1937–1939 alliance worked reasonably well for both Chiang and Stalin. For Chiang it secured Soviet support for the military defeat of Japan and, as the next chapter will examine, for China's internal unification. Both were key elements of Chiang's program of national revival. Soviet support against Japan did not, of course, go as far as Chiang hoped. It did not extend to direct Soviet entry into the war. When Chiang finally realized that his initial hopes for Soviet entry had been an illusion, he was bitter. This bitterness was offset, however, by the Soviet Union's massive and timely assistance. Soviet equipment, advisors, and pilots stood in sharp contrast to the cautious detachment of the Western powers. Whatever complaints Chiang had regarding his Soviet ally, he kept in mind that Moscow was doing more to help China's military effort than any other power.

The brief alliance with Chiang was also valuable for Stalin, because with nearly a million Japanese troops tied down in China's interior, it was considerably easier for the Red Army to muster local superiority over Japanese forces during the critical 1938–1939 border clashes. Since it was the Soviet victories in these clashes which ultimately persuaded Tokyo that war with the Soviet Union would be too risky, we can conclude that China's war of resistance made a direct and important contribution to keeping the Soviet Union out of a war with Japan.

Many of the frictions which plagued the Sino-Soviet alliance later emerged during the 1942–1945 Sino-American alliance. This suggests that they may have been endemic to the Nationalist regime. The taint of corruption on the Chinese side undoubtedly diminished Soviet respect for their allies. Chinese disorganization—the constant shuttling of Yang Jie and Sun Ke between Moscow and Paris, the overlapping lines of authority between Jiang Tingfu and Yang Jie, and the ad hoc nature of Chinese requests—did not contribute to cooperation or trust. Nor did the lack of discipline apparent among China's representatives, for example, Yang Jie's provocative actions and his later appeal to Soviet officials against his own government. The defects apparent in Yang Jie's character during his service in Moscow lead to the question of why Chiang chose such a person to be the key representative to his major ally. The answer almost certainly lies in Yang's long and loyal association with Chiang. If this was the case, however, it was an unfortunate instance in which personal loyalty was placed above competence as a diplomat.

There was another element of the Sino-Soviet alliance which also foreshadowed the later Sino-American alliance. This was Chiang's reliance on the threat of defection from the alliance to influence his ally. The German mediation of late 1937, the mid-1938 talks with Japanese representatives in Tokyo and Hong Kong, and the threats of a settlement with Japan which they implied were akin to Chiang's 1942–1943 hints to the United States that, unless certain desired measures were taken, China's "morale" and its resistance to Japan might collapse. Chiang was a shrewd Machiavellian who concluded that China's allies, whether the Soviet Union or the United States, would be more appreciative of China's resistance to Japan if they feared that that resistance might end. From Chiang's perspective, what he was doing was turning China's weakness into a bargaining asset. While such manipulation undoubtedly diminished trust and fed long-term suspicions, in the short run it worked.

The greatest failure of the Sino-Soviet alliance for both Chiang and Stalin was undoubtedly its failure to catalyze the broad anti-Japanese front they had hoped for. For Chiang, who saw great dangers in exclusive alignment with either the Soviet Union or Japan, this was a major defeat. As Chiang later explained, too close an alignment with the Soviet Union might enable Moscow to dominate China. On the other hand, a compromise peace with Japan would lead to a *modus vivendi* between the Soviet Union and Japan under which they would partition China. To avoid this dilemma, Chiang hoped to "internationalize" China's diplomacy, to raise it above the Far Eastern triangle of Japan, the Soviet Union, and China. If other powers— the United States, Britain, and Nazi Germany—could be involved in the "Far Eastern problem," China would have more room for maneuvering; that is, the influence of the other powers would help restrain Moscow and Tokyo.[158] The refusal of the United States and Britain to become involved in the Sino-Japanese conflict therefore greatly increased the dangers Chiang perceived as inherent in alliance with Moscow. Not least among these dangers was Soviet support for the CCP.

Chiang was extremely fearful that the Soviets would take advantage of their partnership with the KMT to strengthen the CCP—as they had done during the 1923–1927 period of Sino-Soviet cooperation. To guard against this, the activities of Soviet advisors in China were, as noted earlier, restricted to military affairs. Moreover, the comings and goings of Soviet personnel were closely monitored by Chiang's secret police.[159] The flow of Soviet war matériel was also closely monitored to ensure that none of it went to the CCP.

An understanding between Chiang and Stalin that the Soviet Union would not support the CCP was one element of the Sino-Soviet alliance. Chiang may also have demanded Soviet assistance in controlling the actions of the Chinese branch of the Comintern. On the face of it, it is almost inconceivable that Chiang would not demand that Stalin restrain the CCP in exchange for Chiang's aligning the Republic of China with the Soviet Union against Japan. Moreover, there is some evidence that Chiang's and Stalin's representatives discussed the political orientation of the CCP and what might be done to check its radicalism. Shortly after the Marco Polo Bridge Incident, Chiang Kai-shek dispatched Zhang Chong, a protégé of Chen Lifu who had been centrally involved in the united front negotiations between the KMT and the CCP in 1936–1937, to Moscow as a permanent liaison representative. Wang Ming met with Zhang Chong in late 1937 and proposed that Zhang obtain permission from Nanjing for his (Wang's) return to China. Zhang accepted Wang's proposal and received authorization from Nanjing.[160] Assuming that both Stalin and Chiang Kai-shek were involved in this decision, it might have been part of a larger understanding regarding Sino-Soviet alliance and the CCP. Chiang was pushing throughout this period for CCP submission to the national government and for the incorporation of the CCP army into the central government's army. As we shall see in the next chapter, Stalin was in fact doing all he could to assist Chiang's efforts to check the CCP. Even if such cooperation was not by agreement, it nonetheless constituted an important aspect of the Stalin–Chiang partnership during the first years of the war.

In Chiang's mind the possibility of Soviet support for the CCP was closely tied to a Soviet-Japanese deal to partition China. On the one hand, if Stalin decided to support the CCP, this would mean that he no longer wished to cooperate with Chiang against Japan. On the other hand, if Stalin agreed with Japan to carve out spheres of influence in China, the CCP would probably be the local agent of Soviet influence. Thus, Soviet refusal to support the CCP seemed to Chiang a good barometer of Soviet intentions toward both the Republic of China and Japan.

Notes

1. *See* the introduction by Steven I. Levine in Aleksandr Ya. Kalyagin, *Along Alien Roads*, New York: Columbia University East Asia Institute Press, 1984, pp. 2–3.
2. *See* George A. Lensen, *The Damned Inheritance, The Soviet Union and the Manchurian Crises, 1924–1935*, Tallahassee, Fla.: Diplomatic Press, 1974.
3. *See*, for example, the correspondence between Jiang and Hu Shi in *Hu Shi Laiwang Shuxin Xuan* [Collection of Hu Shi's correspondence], vol. 4, Beijing: Zhongguo Shehui Kexueyuan Jiandaishi Yanjiusuo, May 1979.
4. Jiang forcefully developed this argument in a brief interpretive history of modern China which he wrote after his return in 1938. *See* Jiang Tingfu, *Zhongguo Jindaishi Dagang* [Outline of modern chinese history], Taibei: Qiming Shuju, n.d.
5. Howard L. Boorman, editor, *Biographical Dictionary of Republican China*, vol. 4, New York: Columbia University Press, 1970, pp. 3–4.
6. *See* Wu Xiangxiang, "Yang Jie yu guofang xinlun" [Yang Jie and the new theory of national defense], *Zhuanji Wenxue* [Biographical Literature], vol. 8, no. 6 (June 1966), pp. 28–30. The other members of Yang Jie's mission to Moscow were the shadowy but pivotal Zhang Chong and Wang Shuming.
7. Tsiang Ting-fu (Jiang Tingfu) memoir, Chinese Oral History Project of the East Asia Institute of Columbia University, New York, Rare Book and Manuscript Library, p. 211.
8. *Zhongguo Zhuwai Shiling Nianbiao, 1912–1949* [Yearbook of China's foreign ambassadors and consuls, 1912–1949], Nanjing: Zhongguo Kexueyuan Jiandaishi Yanjiusuo, 1963, pp. 14–15. Jiang left Moscow in January 1938. In May 1938 he became the director of the Political Affairs Office of the executive *Yuan*. Tsiang Ting-fu memoir, p. 220.
9. Tsiang Ting-fu memoir, p. 210.
10. Sun was allowed to select three other members from his own faction to accompany him. *See* Xia Jinlin, *Wo Wudu Sanjia Waijiao Gongzuo de Huiyi* [Memoirs of my fivefold participation in diplomatic work], Taibei: Zhuanji Wenxue Chubanshe, January 1978, p. 45. Xia was one member of Sun's mission. The others were Fu Binchang, head of the international relations committee of the legislative *Yuan* and ambassador to the Soviet Union from 1943 to 1945, and Wu Shang, head of the economic committee of the legislative *Yuan*.
11. Archive on the 1937 treaty, Guo Shi Guan [Academia Historica], Taibei. File "Wai 02.1 12."
12. Charles R. Kitts, *An Inside View of the Kuomintang, Chen Li-fu, 1926–1949*, doctoral dissertation, St. Johns University, N.Y., 1978, p. 65. Kitts interviewed Chen in 1977 regarding, inter alia, his 1935–1936 discussions with Soviet officials.
13. *Milu*, vol. 12, p. 76.
14. *Jiang Tingfu Huiyilu* [Memoir of Jiang Tingfu], Taibei: Zhuanji Wenxue Chubanshe [Biographical Literature Publishing Company], congkan no. 48 (March 1979), p. 196. This is a Chinese translation of Jiang's English memoir held by the Chinese Oral History Project of Columbia University, New York.

15. Jiang perceived differences between Litvinov and Soviet ambassador to China Bogomolov on this issue. He believed that Bogomolov favored the conclusion of a mutual security treaty and even Soviet entry into the war against Japan in the hope that this would lead to Stalin's downfall.

16. *Zhanshi Waijiao*, p. 325. Other information on the 5 June meeting is in Weigesiji (translit. from Russian), editor, *Waijiaoshi* [Diplomatic history], vol. 3, Dalian: Dalian Waiyu Xueyuan, 1979, p. 896. This is a Chinese translation of a Soviet work published in Moscow in 1956.

17. Zhou Xicai, *Zhong Su Guanxi Neimu* [The hidden history of Sino-Soviet relations], Taibei: Shidai Chubanshe, p. 55, n.d.

18. Ibid., p. 56.

19. Ibid.

20. *China Handbook, 1937–1944, A Comprehensive Survey of Major Developments in China in Seven Years of War*, first published in 1944 (reprint) Taibei: Cheng Wen Publishing Company, 1971, pp. 109–110. This handbook contains an English text of the 1937 treaty.

21. Archive on the 1937 treaty, Guo Shi Guan, Taibei.

22. Huang Guowen, *Kangzhan Shiqi Woguo Dui Ri Waijiao Molüe, 1937–1945* [Our country's diplomatic strategies toward Japan during the war of resistance, 1937–1945], masters thesis, Political Warfare College, Taiwan, 1977, pp. 99–100.

23. *Zongtong Dashi*, vol. 4, p. 1142.

24. Shao Lizi, "You Zhong Su hubu qianfan tiaoyue dao Zhong Su shangyue" [From the Sino-Soviet Treaty of Mutual Nonaggression to the Sino-Soviet Treaty of Commerce], *Zhong Su Wenhua* [Sino-Soviet Culture], vol. 4, no. 1 (August 1939), p. 2.

25. Tsiang Ting-fu memoir, p. 201.

26. *Jiang Tingfu Huiyilu*, p. 191.

27. After his recall from China Bogomolov was executed in Stalin's purges. *See* Arthur Upham Pope, *Maxim Litvinoff*, New York: L.B. Fisher, 1943, p. 419. It would be interesting to know the grounds for Bogomolov's liquidation. Could he, along with General Vasilii Bluecher, the commander of the Soviet Far Eastern Army in 1937 who was also executed by Stalin, have been involved in genuine attempts to precipitate a Soviet-Japanese war in hopes that this would lead to Stalin's downfall?

28. *See* Hsu Long-hsuen and Chang Ming-kai, *History of the Sino-Japanese War (1937–1945)*, Taibei: Chung Wu Company, 1971, p. 32.

29. *See* William L. Tung, *V.K. Wellington Koo and China's Wartime Diplomacy*, New York: St. Johns University Press, 1977, Asia in the Modern World series no. 17, pp. 29–30.

30. Tsien Tai, *China and the Nine-Power Conference at Brussels in 1937*, New York: St. Johns University Press, 1964, Asia in the Modern World series no. 4, p. 1.

31. *Zongtong Dashi*, vol. 4, p. 1139. *Milu*, vol. 11, p. 68.

32. Tsien Tai, *China and the Nine Power Conference*, pp. 8–10. Wellington Koo in fact approached French, British, and American representatives at Brussels and urged a combined naval demonstration in the Pacific. *See* Tung, *Wellington Koo*, pp. 38–39.

33. Directive of 24 October 1937 from Wang Chonghui, in *Waijiaoshi Ziliao (1937–1945)*, pp. 132–133.

34. Tsien Tai, *China and the Nine Power Conference*, p. 6.

35. Tsiang Ting-fu memoir, p. 210.

36. The conference's final resolution of 24 November is in *China Handbook, 1937–1944*, p. 85.

37. *Milu*, vol. 12, p. 92.

38. *Zhanshi Waijiao*, pp. 335–336.

39. Ibid., pp. 336–337.

40. Ibid., p. 470.

41. Hollington K. Tong, *China and the World Press*, 1948, p. 47, no place of publication given. Regarding Bluecher's subsequent execution, see note 27.

42. Tsiang Ting-fu memoir, p. 211.

43. *Zhanshi Waijiao*, pp. 339–340.

44. Tsiang Ting-fu memoir, p. 211.

45. *Jiang Tingfu Huiyilu*, p. 200. Yang was not the only Chinese who took it upon himself to secure Soviet entry. A more comical incident involving KMT veteran Li Shizeng occurred in late 1937–early 1938. In December 1937 Li was in Paris in association with the Nine-Power Conference in Brussels. When CCP functionary Wu Yuzhang arrived in Paris to do propaganda work for the Communist International, Li approached him and urged Wu to accompany him to Moscow to persuade the Soviet leadership to dispatch troops to China. (*Wu Yuzhang Zizhuan* [Autobiography of Wu Yuzhang], *Lishi Yanjiu* [Historical Research], Beijing, no. 4, 1981, p. 20.) When Wu rejected Li's proposal, Li traveled on his own to Moscow. Once in Moscow, he presented himself to Ambassador Jiang Tingfu as a special representative of Chiang Kai-shek, H. H. Kung, and T.V. Soong. When Zhang cabled the Chinese Foreign Ministry, however, they said they knew nothing about Li. Li had many friends in the French Popular Front government of that time, and planned to use France as an intermediary

to bring about closer Sino-Soviet relations. Unfortunately for Li, the officials in the French embassy in Moscow disdained the Popular Front government in Paris and dismissed his proposal of a Soviet-French-Chinese alliance as unrealistic. Jiang Tingfu accompanied Li to meet with Litvinov, but Litvinov too dismissed Li's plans, telling Li and Jiang that France would not and did not want to help China. Nor did it want the Soviet Union to assist China. (*Jiang Tingfu Huiyilu*, pp. 201–202.) Li left Moscow critical of Jiang's "lack of experience" in dealing with Soviet officials and may have played a role in persuading Chiang Kai-shek to replace him as ambassador. (Tung, *Wellington Koo*, p. 21.)

46. *Zhanshi Waijiao*, pp. 473–474.
47. Ibid., p. 407.
48. From "Documents on German Foreign Policy, 1918–1945," U.S. Department of State, cited in John Hunter Boyle, *China and Japan at War, 1937–1945, The Politics of Collaboration*, Stanford, Calif.: Stanford University Press, 1972, p. 68. *See also* Thomas Leroy Lauer, *German Attempts at Mediation of the Sino-Japanese War, 1937–1938*, March 1973, doctoral dissertation, Stanford University, Stanford, Calif., pp. 35–36. Cheng Tien-fang, *A History of Sino-Russian Relations*, Washington, D.C.: Public Affairs Press, 1957, p. 212.
49. Jiang Yongjing, "Kangzhan chuqi de waijiao yu Guolian yu Deshi zhi tiaoting" [The diplomacy of the early period of the war of resistance, the League of Nations and the mediation of the German ambassador], *Zhongguo Xiandaishi Lunji* [Essays on Modern Chinese History], Zhang Yufa, ed., vol. 9, Taibei: Lian Jing Company, 1982, pp. 365–366. *See also* Boyle, *China and Japan at War*, p. 74.
50. *Zongtong Dashi*, vol. 4, p. 1204.
51. Jiang Yongjing, "Kangzhan chuqi de waijiao," p. 378.
52. *Zhanshi Waijiao*, p. 340.
53. Jiang Yongying, "Kangzhan chuqi de waijiao," p. 378.
54. *Zhanshi Waijiao*, p. 340.
55. Lauer, *German Attempts at Mediation*, pp. 78, 91, 98, 99. *Zongtong Dashi*, vol. 4, p. 1205.
56. Boyle, *China and Japan at War*, p. 74.
57. *Milu*, vol. 11, p. 107.
58. Boyle, *China and Japan at War*, pp. 170–174.
59. *Duiwai Guanxishi, 1840–1949*, p. 60. *Milu*, vol. 11, pp. 172–173.
60. Boyle, *China and Japan at War*, pp. 182–187.
61. Ibid., pp. 185–187. Gao disobeyed Chiang's order and, with the approval of Wang Jingwei's lieutenant Zhou Fohai, made a secret trip to Tokyo in July to explore peace possibilities. This was the beginning of Gao's and Wang Jingwei's *independent* search for peace, a search which would lead them to defect to Japan at the end of 1938. This story is beyond our consideration of *Chiang's* diplomacy.
62. Ibid., p. 156.
63. Zhang Bofeng, "Guanyu kang Ri zhanzheng shiqi Jiang Jieshi fandong jituan de jizi tuoxie tuoxiang huodong" [Regarding several instances of the capitulationist and appeasement activities of the reactionary Chiang Kai-shek clique during the war of resistance against Japan], *Jindaishi Yanjiu* [Research on Modern History], no. 2, 1979, p. 216. *See also Milu*, vol. 11, p. 177. Boyle also discusses the Kung-Ugaki talks in some detail (*China and Japan at War*, pp. 156–160).
64. Japanese Foreign Ministry archive no. 5487, cited in Zhang Bofeng, "Guanyu kang Ri zhanzheng," p. 217.
65. *Zhanshi Waijiao*, pp. 479–481.
66. *See* Dick Wilson, *When Tigers Fight, the Story of the Sino-Japanese War, 1937–1945*, New York: Viking Press, 1982, p. 110.
67. The battle of Wuhan is reviewed in *Renmin Ribao* [People's daily], 18 July 1983, "Wuhan huizhan" [The battle of Wuhan], p. 5.
68. William C. Kirby, *Germany and Republican China*, Stanford, Calif.: Stanford University Press, 1984, p. 235.
69. Lauer, *German Attempts at Mediation*, p. 133.
70. *Zhanshi Waijiao*, p. 341.
71. Ibid., p. 342.
72. Regarding the mid-1938 clashes, *see* O. Edmund Clubb, *China and Russia, the Great Game*, New York: Columbia University Press, 1971, p. 312.
73. *Jiang Tingfu Huiyilu*, p. 211.
74. Ibid.
75. Wilson, *When Tigers Fight*, p. 87.
76. *Zhanshi Waijiao*, pp. 341–342.

77. "Xinnian: Su De hubu qinfan tiaoyue de chenggong jiqi suo geiyu women de jiaoxun" [A new year: the success of the Soviet-German treaty of mutual non-aggression and what we have learned from it], initially printed in *Qun Zhong* [The masses], 3 September 1939, reprinted in *Xiandai Guoji Guanxishi Cankao Ziliao (1933–1939)* [Research materials on the history of modern international relations (1933–1939)], Beijing: Guoji Guanxi Xueyuan, 1958, pp. 332–339.
78. *Milu*, vol. 12, p. 9.
79. *Zongtong Dashi*, vol. 4, p. 1297.
80. *Zhanshi Waijiao*, p. 343.
81. Ibid.
82. *Zongtong Dashi*, vol. 4, p. 1297.
83. *Zhongyang Ribao* initially displayed a certain degree of criticism of the Munich agreement. A cartoon on page four of the 1 October issue, for example, showed a screaming child labeled "Czechoslovakia" being thrown to a hungry tiger by John Bull and a Frenchman. An article in the next day's paper was entitled "national territory of Czechoslovakia shrinks; the people feel a great tragedy." After the second, however, such implied criticism was absent and coverage was generally laudatory. *See Zhongyang Ribao*, 2 October 1938, p. 3; 4 October 1938, p. 3; and 8 October 1938, p. 2.
84. *See* A. Rossi, *The Russo-Germany Alliance, August 1939–June 1941*, Boston: Beacon Press, 1951, pp. 15–19.
85. *See Monthly Summary of the Proceedings of the League of Nations*, vol. 19, no. 1 (January 1939), p. 19; vol. 19, no. 5 (May 1939), p. 181.
86. Hata Ikuhiko, "The Japanese-Soviet Confrontation," in *Deterrent Diplomacy, Japan, Germany and the USSR, 1935–1940*, James Morley, editor, New York: Columbia University Press, 1976, pp. 157–170.
87. Kalyagin, *Along Alien Roads*, pp. 236–238; 258.
88. Ibid., p. 258.
89. Ibid., p. 276.
90. This letter was in response to one from Chiang Kai-shek conveyed to Stalin by Sun Ke when the latter participated in the signing of the commercial agreement on 16 June 1939. (Chiang Kai-shek, *Soviet Russia in China, A Summing-up at Seventy*, Taibei: China Publishing Company, 1969, p. 89.)
91. *Zhanshi Waijiao*, p. 425.
92. Ibid.
93. Kalyagin, *Along Alien Roads*, p. 276.
94. *China Handbook, 1937–1944*, p. 110. These figures for total credits roughly correspond to the figure of $191.2 million U.S. given in a study by Soviet historian M.I. Sladkovsky, cited by Steven I. Levine in his introduction to *Along Alien Roads*, p. 8.
95. Sun Ke, "Bashi Shulüe" [Overview at eighty], *Zhuanji Wenxue* [Biographical Literature], vol. 23, no. 5 (November 1973), p. 16.
96. Raisa Mirovitskaya and Yuri Semyonov, *The Soviet Union and China, a Brief History of Relations*, Moscow: Novosti Press Agency, 1981, p. 31.
97. Mirovitskaya and Semyonov, *Brief History*, pp. 330–331.
98. Arthur N. Young, *China and the Helping Hand, 1937–1945*, Cambridge, Mass.: Harvard University Press, 1963, p. 51.
99. Kalyagin, *Along Alien Roads*, p. 8.
100. Young, *Helping Hand*, p. 51.
101. Kalyagin, *Along Alien Roads*, p. 144.
102. Wilson, *When Tigers Fight*, pp. 163–164.
103. Georgii K, Zhukov, *The Memoirs of Marshal Zhukov*, New York: Delacorte Press, 1971, p. 139.
104. Enzo Angelucci, *The Rand McNally Encyclopedia of Military Aircraft, 1914–1980*, New York: The Military Press, 1983, pp. 217, 223, 263, 286.
105. James C. Bowden, "Soviet Military Aid to Nationalist China, 1923–1941," in *Sino-Soviet Military Relations*, Raymond Garthoff, editor, New York: Frederick Praeger, 1966, p. 55. Young, *Helping Hand*, p. 54. Otto P. Chaney Jr., *Zhukov*, Norman: University of Oklahoma Press, 1971, pp. 35–36. Sven Steenberg *Vlasov*, New York: Alfred A. Knopf, 1970, pp. 9–11.
106. Mirovitskaya and Semyonov, *Brief History*, pp. 32–33.
107. Cited by Levine in *Along Alien Roads*, p. 9.
108. Immanuel Hsu says that by the end of 1939 the Soviet Union had sent 500 military advisors to China and 2000 volunteer pilots. Immanuel C.Y. Hsu, *The Rise of Modern China*, New York: Oxford University Press, 1970, p. 696.
109. Kalyagin, *Along Alien Roads*, p. 46.
110. Young, *Helping Hand*, p. 54.

111. Ibid., p. 10. *See also* Bowden, "Soviet Military Aid," pp. 54–55. Bowden says that 100 Soviet pilots died.
112. Kalyagin, *Along Alien Roads*, p. 43.
113. Young, *Helping Hand*, pp. 54–55.
114. *See* Chiang's 28 August and 23 September cables to Jiang and his 16 and 17 September cables to Yang, in *Zhanshi Waijiao*, pp. 465, 467.
115. *Zhanshi Waijiao*, pp. 335–336. Stalin's willingness to see Germany continue as one of China's benefactors probably reflected a belief that this would create frictions between Berlin and Tokyo thereby slowing movement toward a closer Axis alignment.
116. Ibid., p. 470.
117. Ibid., p. 471.
118. Ibid.
119. Ibid., p. 476.
120. Ibid., p. 477
121. Wellington Koo, *Reminiscences of Wellington Koo*, Chinese Oral History Project of the East Asia Institute of Columbia University, New York, Rare Book and Manuscript Library, p. 895.
122. *Zhanshi Waijiao*, pp. 477–478.
123. These demands were (1) increasing the level of armaments being supplied to China's twenty divisions; (2) securing the immediate dispatch of sixty-five light bombers to China; (3) setting up seven aircraft repair shops, ammunition factories, and aviation schools; (4) purchasing several thousand trucks; (5) forming three mechanized divisions at Lanzhou; (6) purchasing Soviet gasoline; and (7) developing petroleum resources in Xinjiang. Yang reported these items in a 29 March cable to Chiang. *Zhanshi Waijiao*, p. 485.
124. *Zhanshi Waijiao*, pp. 481–482.
125. Ibid., p. 485.
126. Ibid., pp. 481–482.
127. Ibid.
128. Ibid., p. 491.
129. Ibid., p. 482.
130. Ibid., p. 483.
131. Zhou Xicai, *Zhong Su Guanxi Neimu*, p. 57.
132. *Zhanshi Waijiao*, p. 485.
133. The source lists the fighters as U-15 and U-16 type aircraft. Other sources, however, refer to "I"-designated aircraft as the major type supplied to China by the Soviet Union. Moreover, standard aircraft handbooks do not identify a "U"-designated Soviet fighter in 1937–1938. I conclude, therefore, that the Chinese documents must be in error. Perhaps the difficulty lies in the similarity of the English letters "I" and "U" or in the kinship of these letters to their Cyrillic equivalent, especially as seen by a Chinese secretary. Moreover, these Cyrillic and English letters were translated into Chinese by using a Chinese writing brush, frequently in a quite cursive style. Similarly, the heavy bombers are identified as "T6-3." Other sources identify "TB-3" bombers as the main type of Soviet heavy bombers during the 1930s while not listing a "T6" type. Again a Cyrillic "TB" apparently made it into English via cursive Chinese as "T6". It is also possible that "N-15" type fighters were actually I-15s.
134. *Zhanshi Waijiao*, p. 483. It is possible that the three bills of lading were the same as the three contracts suggested by Voroshilov and described by Yang in his 15 March cable to Chiang. However, Yang does not mention the problem of signing the lists until his cable of 22 March. Moreover, both Voroshilov's and Chiang's reference to 500 million yuan clearly referred, at least in part, to future purchases which were to be covered by the three contracts. There was a partial overlap between the two sets of three documents, for example, the equipment for twenty divisions which had already been sent by March 1938, but which were included in Voroshilov's initial three contracts.
135. *Zhanshi Waijiao*, p. 497.
136. Ibid., p. 498.
137. Ibid., pp. 498–499.
138. Ibid., p. 499.
139. Ibid., pp. 500–501.
140. Ibid., pp. 502–503.
141. Ibid., p. 506.
142. Li Tianrong, "Wo zai Jiang Jieshi shicongshi gongzuo de pianduan huiyi" [Partial memoir of my work in Chiang Kai-shek's staff office], *Guangzhou Wenshi Ziliao Xuanji* [Guangzhou Selection of Literary Materials], vol. 26, p. 113. Li also insinuates that Yang was mentally unbalanced by early 1939. He reports that Yang urged Chiang Kai-shek to allow him to sign a contract with a Dutch

inventor who claimed to have invented a death ray which would destroy Japanese ships. The man was to be paid a certain amount for each ship sunk by his device (p. 128).

143. Sun Ke, "Bashi shulüe," p. 16.
144. *Zhanshi Waijiao*, pp. 514–515, 517.
145. Ibid., p. 515.
146. Ibid., p. 516.
147. Ibid., p. 514.
148. Zhou Xicai, *Zhong Su Guanxi Neimu*, p. 58.
149. *Zhanshi Waijiao*, pp. 518–519.
150. Ibid., pp. 507–509.
151. Ibid., pp. 509–512. The values of all ores were calculated in U.S. dollars on the basis of prices prevailing on the London commodity market.
152. Ibid.
153. Kirby, *Germany and Republican China*, p. 248.
154. The Chinese version of these frictions is presented in a long memorandum by H.H. Kung to Chiang on 9 December 1938, in *Zhanshi Waijiao*, pp. 507–509.
155. Zhukov, *Memoirs*, pp. 139–140.
156. United States Department of State, *United States Relations with China*, Washington, D.C., 1949, p. 470.
157. Ibid.
158. Chiang Kai-shek, *Soviet Russia in China*, p. 56.
159. Edgar Snow, *The Battle for Asia*, New York: Random House, 1941, p. 181. Cited in Bowden, "Soviet Military Aid," p. 55.
160. Wang Jiaxiang, "Huiyi Mao Zedong tongzhi yu Wang Ming jihui zhuyi luxian de duozheng" [Recollection of comrade Mao Zedong's struggle with Wang Ming's opportunist line], *Renmin Ribao* (People's Daily), 27 December 1979, p. 2.

Chapter III

Revolution in China and Soviet National Security

Revolutionary Chinese Nationalism and Soviet National Interests

Mao Zedong, like Chiang Kai-shek, believed that out of war a great China would emerge. But revolution, Mao believed, was a necessary precondition for the creation of a powerful China, and the Sino-Japanese War presented an unparalleled opportunity to engineer just such a revolution. Like the early Bolsheviks, Mao understood the profound links between war and revolution. The war with Japan presented the opportunity, Mao believed, for the Chinese people led by the "proletariat," that is by the CCP, to prepare to seize power. During the initial months of the war, Mao envisioned an actual revolutionary seizure of power during the war, as in 1917, as the *ancien régime* disintegrated under the war's impact. He soon realized, however, that the essence of the problem lay in the expansion of revolutionary power, in the expansion of the political and military forces led by the CCP, and that compromises could be made in other areas as long as this one essential was upheld. If the revolutionary forces were powerful, they would be able to utilize whatever opportunities developed either during or after the war to smash the counterrevolutionary forces.

Such revolutionary ideas conflicted with Stalin's desire to bolster Chiang's resolve and the Republic of China's war effort. Revolutionary upheaval in China would at best divert Nationalist energies from fighting Japan. At worst it might push Chiang into peace with Japan. A Communist drive for power in China would also make Britain and the United States less willing to cooperate with the Soviet Union against Japan. Thus, for the sake of his diplomatic objectives, for the defense of the "fatherland of socialism," Stalin had to rein in Mao's revolutionism.

The fact that relations between the CCP and the Soviet Union functioned within the framework of the Comintern meant that the conflict between Stalin and Mao was closely tied to factional conflict within the CCP. When the war began, Mao's authority over the CCP was still weak. He had been the preeminent leader of the party only since January 1935 and had yet to prove his ideas and leadership capable of winning broad domestic, let alone international, support. Moreover, he still faced major rivals within the party. Aside from Wang Ming, such senior leaders as Zhang Guotao, Zhou Enlai, Zhu De, Bo Gu, Peng Dehuai, and Yang Shangkun were all critical of aspects of Mao's leadership. Had these men united against Mao in support of Wang Ming's internationalism, they almost certainly could have ousted Mao. In a sense, the conflict between Stalin and Mao was a contest for control of the CCP fought by winning the loyalties of key CCP cadres.

The conflict between Mao and Stalin boiled down to an attempt by Mao to emancipate the CCP from Comintern control without alienating Stalin. Aside from the weakness of Mao's control over the CCP, Mao believed that the ultimate realization of his ideas of a revolutionary transformation of China would require substantial Soviet support. This meant that Mao could not break with Stalin even had he been confident that he could carry the CCP with him in the event of such a rupture.

When the Sino-Japanese War began, the Comintern's political line centered on the "antifascist united front." After belatedly realizing the threat posed to the Soviet Union by Hitler's rule of Germany, by 1934 Stalin began abandoning his previous policies of hostility toward the Western capitalist democracies—chiefly Britain, France, and the United States—and attempting to cooperate with those "bourgeois democracies" against Germany and Japan. The Seventh Comintern Congress in July–August 1935 authoritatively promulgated this new line, scrapping the ultraradical line of the Comintern's "third period" and calling for the establishment of united fronts of all groups and classes willing to resist Germany or Japan. The key objective of these antifascist united fronts was to make the bourgeois democracies of Britain, France, and the United States willing to undertake "collective security" cooperation with the Soviet Union against the "fascist" powers. Moscow realized that these capitalist democracies were unlikely to cooperate with the Soviet Union as long as the Comintern was actively fomenting revolution. In other words, Moscow recognized a contradiction between a drive to establish Communist power by the Comintern's branch parties and anti-German and anti-Japanese cooperation between the Soviet Union and the capitalist democracies. It resolved this contradiction by temporarily shelving the drive for revolution.

Spain and China

China and Spain were the two countries where Moscow had to deal with this contradiction between revolution and collective security in the late 1930s. Strong revolutionary movements and Comintern-linked Communist Parties existed in both countries, and Moscow had to guide those movements along lines which would strengthen the security of the Soviet Union. Moscow's efforts in achieving such an accommodation were similar to both China and Spain, and it is useful to begin with a look at Soviet efforts in dealing with the problem on the Iberian Peninsula.

In July 1936, General Francisco Franco's coup against the Spanish Republican government touched off the explosive political situation which had developed over the previous several months and plunged the country into a thirty-two month civil war. Italy and Germany soon began supporting Franco, while the Soviet Union began supporting the Republican government.[1] Stalin aided the Spanish Republic because he hoped that protracted and determined resistance to German-Italian expansionism in Spain would be a catalyst for an effective international collective security arrangement, and because he wanted to tie down Hitler's forces in areas far away from Soviet borders. Stalin believed that France would not tolerate the establishment of a German client state south of the Pyrenees and that Britain would reach a similar conclusion about one north of Gibraltar and astride its "lifeline to India." Soviet support would sustain the Republic until the slow-moving democracies realized the danger and roused themselves to action.[2]

A major problem arose, however, from the fact that the Republican camp included anarchist workers and peasants, Trotskyists, and radical socialists who wanted to carry out a social revolution. Stalin feared that these radical forces would bring about an uncontrollable revolution in Spain which would rouse Western fears and alienate the bourgeois democracies from the notion of cooperation with the Soviet Union against the fascist powers. From Stalin's perspective, the interests of the Soviet Union, the "fatherland of the world proletariat," necessitated that revolution be prevented in Spain. Spain's Communists were therefore ordered to prevent the implementation of revolutionary measures. By the spring of 1937, the Communist-supported moderate Socialist government of Largo Caballero was everywhere trying to slow down the process of revolution.[3] When Caballero's government proved insufficiently conservative in May 1937, the Communists withdrew their support and helped bring to power a cabinet dominated by bourgeois liberal Republicans.[4]

The Spanish Communist Party's efforts to control dissident revolutionary elements was aided by a powerful political police apparatus controlled by Stalin's murderous secret police, the NKVD. At the end of 1936, an "Administration of Special Tasks" was set up within the NKVD and charged with the assassination of noncompliant leftists outside the Soviet Union, especially in Spain.[5] The NKVD unleashed a terror against the Spanish Trotskyists and anarchists in late 1936.[6] Throughout 1937 and 1938, mobile NKVD teams roamed Republican Spain arresting and killing deviationists.[7]

From the standpoint of Soviet diplomacy during 1936–1938, China and Spain played similar roles.[8] Just as Moscow hoped that Spanish resistance to German-Italian aggression would mobilize the Western democracies, so it hoped that Chinese resistance would mobilize the West against Japan. As Japan expanded in China, especially in the Yangtze River valley where Anglo-American interests were centered, Britain and the United States would come to realize that it was in their interest to support Chinese resistance to Japan—together with the Soviet Union. But in China as in Spain, Stalin's strategy came into conflict with the indigenous forces of social revolution.

Mao Zedong: Resistance and Revolution

The first attempt of the CCP to formulate its wartime strategy was at a Politburo conference at the village of Luochuan in Shaanxi province, in late August 1937. At Luochuan, Mao and CCP Secretary General Zhang Wentian maintained that because of the reactionary nature of the KMT it would be unable to mobilize China's people to wage a victorious war against Japan. The defeat of the KMT was therefore certain and would result, Mao said, in a split in that party, with the right wing surrendering to Japan and the left wing continuing resistance together with the CCP. The CCP should therefore maintain full independence from the KMT while exposing its reactionary nature, and should put maximum energies into expanding its organization and forces in the areas deep behind Japanese lines. Rather than massing to wage big battles with

Japan's armies in the early phase of the war, Communist military forces should be broken into small groups and dispersed behind Japanese lines to expand the "anti-Japanese forces" as quickly as possible. Communist forces should neither take orders from Nationalist authorities nor allow Nationalist staff officers to be attached to them. The CCP had to maintain a high level of vigilance toward the KMT and constantly expose its reactionary nature. In this fashion, when the KMT was defeated and the CCP-led anti-Japanese base areas and guerrilla armies had grown powerful, the CCP would emerge as the full leader of China's national liberation struggle and lead the Chinese people to victory.[9] In sum, Mao's program combined resistance to Japan and the rapid expansion of Communist strength in preparation for the final revolutionary struggle.

Mao and Zhang Wentian's proposals encountered strong opposition at Luochuan. Zhang Guotao and Zhou Enlai were two senior leaders who spoke against them. Zhang Guotao had been a founding member of the CCP and in the mid-1930s had commanded an army which rivaled Mao's and Zhu De's in size and fame. By early 1937 Zhang had already lost most of his real power, but he retained substantial prestige. At Luochuan, Zhang forthrightly contradicted the arguments of Mao and Zhang Wentian. It was wrong to look with equanimity on Chiang Kai-shek's defeat by Japan, Zhang argued. If Chiang was defeated by Japan, China would become Japan's colony and this would be a great disaster for all of China including the CCP. Moreover, rather than being weakened by the war, the rule of the KMT had been strengthened by enhancing its standing in the eyes of the people. And even if there were a right wing of the KMT willing to surrender to Japan, Zhang said, its mainstream group would not capitulate. In such a situation, for the CCP vigorously to assert its independence would only undermine the united front and invite the catastrophe of national defeat.[10]

Zhou Enlai also doubted whether Chiang would surrender. Chiang's character and domestic political constraints would, Zhou argued, probably prevent it. Moreover, since nationalist passions were rising, the CCP should seek to increase its national status by waging big battles against Japanese forces if conditions were advantageous. To minimize friction with the KMT, Zhou proposed that the CCP maintain the form of the ROC governmental structure when setting up base areas behind Japanese lines.[11] Regarding the military forces of the CCP, Zhou was willing to accept supplies and pay from the National Government and to abolish the system of political commissars and political departments, as Chiang was demanding.[12]

Mao's concept of a dispersed and initially low-intensity, protracted guerrilla war also met with substantial opposition from his generals, including the commander and deputy commander of the Eighth Route Army, Zhu De and Peng Dehuai. Zhu and Peng did not dispute the principle of operating behind Japanese lines or of attacking the enemy's weak points and flanks at times and places of their own choosing— all essential elements of Mao's military strategy. They maintained, however, that CCP forces should mass and engage the Japanese in direct support of friendly armies engaged in ongoing battles.[13]

The term "mobile war" was used to distinguish the strategy initially preferred by the CCP generals, and by Moscow, as opposed to Mao's strategy of protracted guerrilla war. Since this was to become a major issue of dispute between Mao and Moscow, it is well to be clear about the precise meaning of mobile war. Tetsuya

Kataoka concisely summarized mobile war as consisting of four main points. First, the National Government's armies were seen as constituting China's major armed strength. Second, while relying chiefly on guerrilla warfare, under certain conditions Communist forces could join friendly forces in positional warfare against Japan. Third, Communist forces should coordinate their mobile operations behind Japanese lines with the operations of friendly forces, but without giving up their independence. Fourth, the Communist forces should strive to develop rapidly toward regular force status by securing equipment from the National Government.[14]

The political consequences of guerrilla war and mobile war were very different. Under Mao's strategy, Communist cadres would concentrate on building mass organizations and systems of government in the vast rural areas through which Japanese armies had swept but did not effectively rule. The great bulk of CCP military personnel and resources would go toward establishing effective control of these areas: organizing militia, peasant associations, systems of revenue collection and social control; collecting the weapons abandoned by the retreating Chinese armies; and politically educating the populace to support the CCP. Under the doctrine of mobile war, on the other hand, CCP military forces would concentrate on fighting Japanese armies. Military forces and civilian cadres would be concentrated in areas where they could conduct operations in support of the Nationalist armies. Cadres would be channeled primarily into military tasks, not into the maximal expansion of the territorial and popular base of the CCP. More generally, the relations between the National Government and CCP would remain more harmonious because the KMT would not fear a CCP effort to use the war to prepare for a future seizure of power.

Mao's strategy was admirably designed to carry out an eventual social revolution in China. The relatively moderate character of the specific policies implemented in the vast new CCP base areas was less important than the fact of CCP control over those areas; that control could provide the base for a future national seizure of power. In terms of inflicting maximum casualties on Japan and tying down the maximum number of Japanese troops, however, mobile warfare made greater sense. Moreover, from the standpoint of promoting anti-Japanese cooperation between the Soviet Union and the Republic of China, and between both of those countries and the United States and Britain, CCP concentration on military operations against Japan was much more useful than expanding CCP power behind Japanese lines.

The result of the debate at the Luochuan Conference was a compromise between Mao and his critics. All references to revolutionary struggle or the inevitability of Chiang Kai-shek's defeat were deleted from the outline for propaganda and agitation endorsed by the conference. Nevertheless, that outline remained highly critical of the "reactionary" policies of the KMT, that is, its failure to mobilize the masses fully and to carry out sweeping political reforms. These mistaken policies, the propaganda outline said, would "bring disaster to the war of resistance." Responsibility for this would fall on those who tried to postpone political reforms until after victory. A ten-point program was also endorsed which basically called for the democratization of China's political system.[15] A compromise was also worked out regarding military strategy. Communist armies were to cooperate with friendly armies and obey the orders of the National Government's Military Council during the initial stage of the war. But once Japan's armies broke through Chinese lines and penetrated deep into China's interior, Communist forces were to break into small units and infiltrate into the northern provinces of Hebei, Rehe, and Shandong, where they would operate independently.[16]

After the Luochuan Conference, most of the top leaders of the CCP dispersed to northern and central China to participate in the war effort, leaving Mao and Zhang Wentian in charge of Yan'an and in a position to radicalize CCP policy.[17] One month after the Luochuan Conference, Mao Zedong sent a "directive" to Zhou Enlai, Liu Shaoqi, and Yang Shangkun in north China ordering that guerrilla war "should be the sole direction of all work in north China." "All work, such as popular movements, the united front, and so on," Mao's directive said, "should revolve about guerrilla war. If conventional warfare in north China fails, we will not be held responsible, but if guerrilla war fails, we will necessarily bear heavy responsibility.[18]

Mao's orders apparently went unheeded; his directive was in sharp contrast to the actual direction of the work then being carried out by the North China Bureau. Later CCP accounts say that at this juncture a number of CCP leaders felt that the Eighth Route Army should concentrate on the defense of important centers in Shanxi province, especially the capital of Taiyuan, in cooperation with "friendly" armies. These leaders felt that the chance of halting the Japanese advance into Shanxi was good and that the Eighth Route Army's energies would be directed toward this end, not toward organizing for a long-term protracted guerrilla war.[19]

The mobile warfare perspective then dominating the North China Bureau was embodied in a directive of 8 October, almost two weeks after Mao's directive, from the north China military council of the CCP, then headed by Yang Shangkun. This directive was a flat affirmation of positional warfare. "Shanxi has currently become the most important objective in the final battle for north China," the directive said. If Taiyuan and the mountain ranges of central Shanxi could be held, they might become a fortress from which to launch a strategic counteroffensive to retake the Beiping–Wuhan railway. Such a counteroffensive might transform the whole strategic situation in north China, and with "favorable domestic and international changes," might secure final victory in the war of resistance. The directive concluded: "The possibility exists to hold Shanxi and to launch a counter-attack to transform the situation in the battle for north China. Struggling for this prospect has become our central political and strategic duty at present."[20] It was the North China Bureau's 8 October directive rather than that of Mao on 25 September which was implemented.[21]

The opposition which Mao's revolutionary line encountered at Luochuan and during the following months indicated the political constraints he would face in his upcoming struggle with Wang Ming. The opposition of such people as Zhou Enlai, Zhu De, Peng Dehuai, Yang Shangkun, and Zhang Guotao did not automatically translate into support for Wang Ming, but it did mean that many top leaders were predisposed to accept Wang's arguments. It meant that Mao had to tread carefully and consolidate his support before moving against Stalin's emissary. To lead, Mao had to persuade and cajole; he could not merely command.

The fall of Taiyuan on 9 November was a victory for Mao. As the 8 October directive had indicated, the defense of Taiyuan was the pivot of the defense of Shanxi province. Its fall demonstrated the inability of the Nationalist armies to hold the

Shanxi plateau and meant that all of north China would soon be under Japanese occupation. In line with the compromise reached at Luochuan, this meant that the phase of mobile warfare in north China was over and that guerrilla warfare was now the main thrust of CCP work there.[22]

On 12 November Mao issued a major report on the situation after the fall of Taiyuan, outlining the new direction of policy. Mao's report stridently attacked the reactionary policies of the KMT which, Mao charged, had produced the recent defeats in Shanghai and Taiyuan. (Shanghai fell on 9 November after a determined three-month resistance.) The Kuomintang as it was then constituted, Mao said, was capable only of waging a partial war which was doomed to defeat. In fact "the Kuomintang's partial resistance cannot last long." The right wing of the united front would soon split away from the united front and surrender to Japan. The center elements of the united front were tending toward the CCP. In this situation, the key political question facing China was: "Will the proletariat lead the bourgeoisie in the united front, or the bourgeoisie the proletariat? Will the Kuomintang draw over the Communist Party, or the Communist Party the Kuomintang?"[23]

After the fall of Taiyuan, most Communist military commanders accepted Mao's line on guerrilla warfare.[24] Mao also took a number of organizational measures to ensure central control over CCP military forces. Zhou Enlai also apparently began supporting Mao at this juncture, at least concerning north China.[25] These were all important victories for Mao. Mao also revived an earlier campaign to criticize Zhang Guotao's "errors" during the Long March.[26] This further reduced Zhang's influence. There remained, however, strong opposition to Mao's revolutionary line. According to the annotation in Mao's *Selected Works*, his report on the post-Taiyuan situation "met with immediate opposition from the Right opportunists in the Party, and not until the Sixth Plenary Session of the Sixth Central Committee in October 1938 was the Right deviation basically overcome."[27]

Wang Ming's Injection into China

Late in 1937, Wang Ming ended his ten-year residency in the Soviet Union and returned to China. As we saw in the last chapter, in late November, Wang Ming arrived at Yan'an, the capital of the CCP's Shaan-Gan-Ning (Shaanxi, Gansu, Ningxia) special border district, aboard a Soviet aircraft along with Kang Sheng, Chen Yun, Yang Song, and a group of Soviet military advisors. Kang Sheng and Yang Song had been Wang's loyal lieutenants in Moscow. After the Zunyi Conference in January 1935, Kang had helped prevent the Comintern from conferring its blessing on Mao Zedong and had lobbied instead for Comintern endorsement of Wang Ming as head of the CCP. Yang Song and Kang Sheng had both helped Wang Ming assert direct Comintern control over the CCP organization in Manchuria in 1935–1936—a matter of some significance which will be discussed in Chapter 8.[28] The plane that brought Wang and his group to Yan'an was the first Soviet aircraft ever to land there and carried a large radio in order to improve communications between Yan'an and Moscow.[29] This, along with Wang's high-ranking status in the Comintern and the discussions between Wang and Zhang Chong in Moscow regarding Wang's return (discussed in the last chapter), indicates that Wang's return had Stalin's approval.

Unfortunately, we still do not know precisely what Comintern powers Wang Ming held when he flew into Yan'an. Numerous People's Republic of China sources agree that Wang spoke as a "representative" of the Comintern at a Politburo conference convened soon after his return.[30] One Chinese historian, for example, states that "the Comintern went through Wang Ming's waving of the banner of internationalism to force the CCP to appease the KMT and Chiang Kai-shek, to surrender and unite the armed strength of the people into the KMT military. Moreover, Wang Ming always followed the orders of the Comintern and unreservedly implemented Comintern policy.[31] Wang may well have carried powers as a representative of the Comintern's International Control Commission which was responsible for investigating deviations from Comintern line by branch parties. During this period, the International Control Commission frequently sent special representatives abroad to review the work of various parties. It is also possible that Wang was a Plenipotentiary Representative of the Executive Committee of the Communist International (ECCI)—a representative who carried extraordinary powers, including the power to overrule decisions and reshuffle the personnel of the Central Committee of a branch party.[32] At a minimum, Wang was a member of the Presidium of the ECCI—a position not held by Mao.[33] This meant that Wang outranked Mao in the international Communist hierarchy. Wang also enjoyed the prestige of close personal association with Stalin and Comintern head Georgii Dimitrov.

While Wang's precise status at this juncture remains uncertain, it is clear that he was treated with extraordinary deference by Mao and other top CCP leaders, and that he was able to bring about abrupt changes in the Politburo's political line and leadership. As Zhang Guotao says, Wang Ming was an "angel" armed with a "precious sword" from Moscow.[34]

Shortly after Wang's arrival, a Politburo conference convened in Yan'an on 9 December to hear the Comintern's "instructions" carried to Yan'an by Wang and to summarize the recent work of the CCP.[35] Wang began the conference by conveying a three-point "Comintern instruction." Moscow's "instruction" charged that Mao did not understand Marxism–Leninism, lacked an internationalist perspective, and decided matters on the basis of narrow empiricism. But, since Mao was already the top leader of the CCP, the Comintern was willing to help him overcome his ideological weaknesses by sending Russian-educated cadre. The instruction also charged that Zhang Wentian was unsuitable for the post of Secretary General. The party cell at Sun Yat-sen University which Zhang had headed in the 1920s was later discovered to be filled with Trotskyites, and although there was no direct proof that Zhang was himself a Trotskyite, he still came under "heavy suspicion." Finally, the Comintern directive said, the campaign against Zhang Guotao had gone too far. So prestigious a leader should not be publicly criticized.[36] All three points raised by the Comintern instruction directly challenged Mao's power. As we have seen, Zhang Wentian was one of Mao's closest allies, while Zhang Guotao was a key rival. And if Mao was a defective Marxist-Leninist, then his recent line was open to question.

After delivering the Comintern directive, Wang proceeded to challenge Mao's radical approach toward the KMT. The KMT, Wang explained, was actively resisting Japan, and the CCP should cooperate fully with it in this resistance. This was essential, Wang explained, since it would lessen the danger of Japanese attack on the Soviet Union. If China was able to resist Japan powerfully for a long period of time, this would make it impossible for Japan to attack the Soviet Union. This would be very advantageous for the world proletariat revolution.[37] Increased CCP pressure on the KMT, on the other hand, escalated the danger of surrender by the KMT, a danger which was great now that Nanjing's fall was imminent and Germany was mediating peace. In such circumstances, the CCP should do everything possible to stiffen KMT resolve to continue the war.[38] Wang also explained how cordial CCP–KMT relations would help bring the United States and Britain into the international anti-fascist front.[39]

Wang then made what amounted to a point-by-point refutation of Mao's line as laid down at Luochuan and in the post-Taiyuan speech. Wang said that victory in the war against Japan was not to be won by struggling against the KMT's reactionary policies, as Mao had argued, but by strengthening the unity between the CCP and the KMT. The defeats of the early stage of the war were not due, as Mao had argued, to the reactionary character of the KMT, but to Japan's overwhelming power and had therefore been unavoidable. Resistance to Japan was the sole criterion of unity. The KMT was not made up of a right wing, center, and left wing, but was willing as a group to resist Japan and should therefore be united with completely and thoroughly. It followed that cooperation between the KMT and the CCP in all areas had to be expanded. Instead of seeking to weaken and undermine the Nationalist regime, Wang said, the CCP should strengthen it in every way possible. The CCP should not look forward to the demise of the KMT but should join with it in creating a united government and a united army of national defense. Rather than claiming leadership over the united front, the CCP should stress the common leadership of both the KMT and the CCP. Both parties should enjoy equal positions within the united front and together exercise joint, cooperative leadership over it. To argue for an "independent" Communist position within—let alone Communist leadership over—the united front would give a pretext to pro-Japanese groups and Trotskyites seeking to disrupt the united front.[40]

Wang also laid out "concrete methods" for establishing a united national army. The sixth method listed by Wang was probably the most important. It called for establishing a "truly unified" system of command, discipline, armament, supply, and war planning. Wang agreed that the Eighth Route Army should "guarantee its independence" by being built around a core of Communist cadre and by conducting political work within the ranks.[41] But in spite of this caveat, it was clear that with command, discipline, planning, and supply unified under the National Government, Communist forces would end up concentrating on fighting Japan rather than on expanding their base areas and guerrilla armies.[42]

Wang Ming's report was unanimously endorsed by the December Politburo conference. Even Mao abandoned his earlier line and endorsed Wang's line.[43] Mao was able, however, to prevent Wang's report from becoming a formal "resolution."[44] This was an important tactical victory for Mao. Wang Ming later complained that this oversight caused political damage to the party.[45] Nevertheless, Wang's ability to force Mao into accepting a drastic reorientation of the Party's line confirms both Mao's weakness and Wang's special Comintern powers.

Wang Ming also moved to weaken Mao's organizational control of the CCP by bringing Chen Yun and Kang Sheng into the Politburo and making them secretaries of the Central Committee, ousting Zhang Wentian as Secretary General and reducing him to seventh rank in the Politburo, and by halting the criticism campaign against Zhang Guotao. Kang's relation to Wang has already been discussed. Chen, it will be recalled, had also arrived in Yan'an aboard the same aircraft as Wang. Prior to that he had spent two and a half years in the Soviet Union. This may have led Wang to believe that Chen Yun would support him, especially as he (Wang) was now advancing Chen's career. As for Zhang Guotao, he had defended himself against Mao's criticisms of his actions in the mid-1930s by maintaining that he had merely been following Comintern orders. This, together with Zhang's opposition to Mao at Luochuan, probably led Wang to hope that Zhang would support his challenge to Mao. Wang Ming also attempted to have himself made General Secretary. Mao was able to block this, however, by having that position abolished.[46]

Finally, Wang proposed, and the December conference accepted, the convocation of the Seventh Congress of the CCP in the near future. Wang hoped to use this congress to downgrade Mao's position further. Several times over the next year he called for its prompt convocation, and each time he was blocked by Mao. The Seventh Congress did not meet until April 1945, after Mao had fully consolidated his control over the Party.

The Question of "Trotskyite Influence"

Charges of "Trotskyite influence" were one of Wang Ming's major weapons in his attack on Mao. Within the world Communist movement in 1937–1939, the charge of being a "Trotskyite" was not a frivolous one. At a minimum, being labeled a "Trotskyite" meant excommunication from the Communist movement. Frequently the consequences were more serious. In the Soviet Union, tens of thousands of people were then being executed or imprisoned for purported involvement in fantastic "Trotskyite" conspiracies. In Spain, Trotskyists were also being "liquidated" in large numbers by the NKVD.

During December 1937, Wang frequently raised the issue of Trotskyism. In a report of 27 December, Wang set forward a very long critique of "Trotskyite" ideas held by "a small number" of people within the KMT and the CCP. He began the report with the assertion that the most dangerous aspect of the present situation was not Japan's greater strength or China's weakness, but Japan's attempts to "use Chinese to control Chinese, in the plots of traitors to the Han race . . . and Trotskyite bandits" to disrupt the national united front. Wang then proceeded through a list of mistaken Trotskyite ideas. These included overlooking the extreme importance of cooperation between the KMT and the CCP, neglecting "the simple truth" that "resistance to Japan is above all else and that everything should be subordinated to resistance to Japan," instigating unnecessary friction between the KMT and the CCP, trying to undermine the position of the KMT, saying that the KMT contained a fascist faction or that it would turn against the Communists, and spreading the idea that the Communists would win control over China through the war against Japan.[47] These "Trotskyite" ideas clearly referred to Mao's views. If Wang was not saying that Mao himself was a Trotskyite, at least he was saying that many of his ideas were.

There was, in fact, a high degree of agreement between Mao and Trotsky at this juncture. In late July 1937, Trotsky gave an interview in which he argued that

China's revolutionaries should give nominal support to Chiang as leader of China's anti-Japanese struggle while criticizing his failure to mobilize fully the nation in waging that struggle. In this fashion, Trotsky argued, China's revolutionaries could expand their influence, discredit Chiang, and prepare eventually to seize power themselves and lead the Chinese people to victory over Japan. Trotsky differed from Mao primarily in his belief that the urban proletariat was the key social base for revolution in China, and in his belief that the CCP was a pliant vassal of the Comintern.[48] Ironically, however, Mao and Trotsky were agreed that Soviet control of the CCP would prevent the CCP from exploiting the war to lay the basis for a revolutionary seizure of power.

Two specific instances of "Trotskyite" infiltration of the CCP were raised at the December Politburo conference. The first involved Zhang Wentian's tenure as Secretary General of the Party which was discussed above. The second involved the readmission of Chen Duxiu to the CCP. To understand this latter issue, it is necessary to digress momentarily.

Chen was the leader of the CCP prior to 1927, who founded and led a genuine Trotskyist group after his expulsion from the CCP in 1929. He was imprisoned by the KMT in October 1932 and released from prison in August 1937 under the united front agreement that all political prisoners would be released. When he emerged from prison in 1937, Chen was still renowned as one of China's foremost intellectuals and revolutionary leaders, and was a man whose name and words attracted a good deal of attention and respect. Shortly after Chen's release, Chiang Kai-shek tried to persuade him to organize "a new communist party" to compete with the CCP.[49] Chen Duxiu rejected this proposal. Instead he contacted the CCP and asked for readmission, indicating that he "warmly embraced" the line of a united front against Japan and wished to "return to work under the leadership of the Party."[50] The Politburo and Mao Zedong considered Chen's request and, "for the sake of uniting all possible anti-Japanese strength," decided to welcome Chen into the Party under certain conditions. These conditions were stated in a cable sent to Chen by none other than Mao and Zhang Wentian.[51] After receiving and analyzing Mao's three conditions, Chen drafted a reply containing a seven-point program. The CCP Politburo in turn considered this program and concluded that Chen's position was basically the same as the line of the CCP. Zhou Enlai and Dong Biwu then began talks with Chen in Wuhan. These talks were under way when Wang Ming returned from Moscow.

It is now possible to return to our discussion of the December Politburo conference. At that conference Wang adamantly opposed Mao's proposed readmission of Chen Duxiu to the CCP. Moreover, he "prohibited [di hui]" continued talks between Chen and the CCP. Chen was a paid Japanese agent, Wang charged, a "traitor to the Han race," and under no circumstances could the Party cooperate with him or other Trotskyites. While it could unite with the most reactionary and anticommunist of Chiang Kai-shek's "special agents," the CCP could never unite or cooperate with Trotskyites.[52]

Wang then used the incident of Chen Duxiu's attempt to "infiltrate" the CCP to educate his listeners about the purges then underway in the Soviet Union. The Communist Party of the Soviet Union (CPSU) had already purged many famous people who had previously made great contributions to the Party, Wang warned the December conference. Past contributions were no guard against present treason. Stalin's use of the purge was one of his "creative developments of Leninism" and a reflection of his genius. The struggle against Trotskyites by the CCP had to be intensified, Wang said. If so many Trotskyites had infiltrated the CPSU, was it possible that the CCP had remained free of them? Of course it was not. There were still many Trotskyites and antiparty elements hiding within the CCP. The struggle against them was not yet sharp and thorough enough, Wang said.[53]

As one Chinese historian has concluded, the motive underlying Wang's outlandishly inaccurate attack on Chen Duxiu was to use Chen as a pretext for opposing Mao Zedong.[54] After Wang Ming's attack on Trotskyism, the CCP broke off negotiations with Chen Duxiu. Mao also moved to minimize further his vulnerability by ordering the recall of the Chinese translation of Edgar Snow's *Red Star over China*, a book in which Mao had acknowledged Chen Duxiu's early political and personal influence.[55]

Wang's campaign against Trotskyite conspiracies to infiltrate the CCP and disrupt the united front intensified in early 1938 when Kang Sheng, who had become head of the Politburo's political protection bureau, the equivalent of its political police, published a series of articles in *Jiefang Zhoukan* (Liberation Weekly) and *Xinhua Ribao* (New China Daily) charging that Chen Duxiu was the linchpin of a pervasive Trotskyite–fascist conspiracy. Chen was plotting, Kang's articles charged, to "murder the top leader of the Eighth Route Army" and infiltrate the organization of the CCP. While cunningly holding up the banner of resistance to Japan, Chen was taking Japanese money and working in close cooperation with Japanese intelligence organizations to disrupt KMT–CCP cooperation in every way possible. Because the Trotskyites were using frictions between the KMT and CCP to provoke division, Kang warned in an article in *Jiefang Zhoukan* on 28 January 1938, "everyone must stand on the line that resistance to Japan is above all else and not be misled by any Trotskyite divisive provocations."[56]

Wang Ming and Kang Sheng were charging, in short, that Trotskyite ideas were rampant within the CCP. Even the basic line of the Luochuan Conference had been flawed by Trotskyite ideas. Furthermore, there was a ramified Trotskyite conspiracy to infiltrate the CCP and to murder its leaders, the latter charge being eerily reminiscent of the charges of plots to murder Kirov and Stalin which preceded the first of Stalin's great purges. Even Chen Duxiu himself was trying to infiltrate the Party, while the Party's top officers were under heavy suspicion of being Trotskyites. Under the Stalinist practices then current in the Soviet Union, suspicion of Trotskyism was more than enough to send people to their death, and Wang strongly implied that this was just what the CCP needed. Vigilance against Trotskyites had to be increased. Trotskyites should be weeded out and Trotskyite ideas thoroughly extirpated.

It may well be that the episode involving Chen Duxiu helped Mao discredit Wang Ming. Chen was a respected and capable figure whom the top leadership of the CCP had carefully considered and judged able to make a useful contribution to the Party's work. Yet this was prevented because Wang Ming insisted that whatever developments took place in the Soviet Union should automatically be copied in China. This was an immediate and clear example of the shortcomings and costs of Wang's dependency on Moscow, and Mao, being an astute tactician, turned it to his advantage. The fact that Wang Ming, having himself launched the campaign against Chen Duxiu, found himself branded a few months later as a proponent of Chen Duxiu's brand of "rightist surrenderism," is testament to Mao's skill at political maneuvering.[57]

There was another more personal factor prompting some CCP leaders to support Mao: fear that Wang Ming and Kang Sheng would introduce Stalin's murderous style of "intra-Party struggle" into the CCP. At least some CCP leaders were aware of the nature and scope of the purges underway in the Soviet Union. Zhang Guotao, for one, believed that Wang Ming wanted to apply Stalin's "cruel methods" to purge the CCP of the many "Trotskyites" he thought were lurking in it. Even though Zhang basically agreed with Wang Ming's political position, he was fearful that he would be killed in Wang's purges and decided to defect to the KMT rather than help Wang.[58] Zhang was probably not the only CCP leader who reached similar conclusions about Wang's aims. There may have been a strong element of self-preservation encouraging the CCP leadership to rally about Mao and reject Wang's bid for influence over the next year or two.

Wang Versus Mao

The December Politburo conference also set up a Yangtze River Bureau of the CCP in Wuhan headed by Wang Ming with Zhou Enlai and Bo Gu as his assistants. This post put Wang in a good position to implement his policy of broader CCP–KMT cooperation. On the other hand, being in Wuhan while the Party center remained in Yan'an handicapped Wang's efforts to rectify the Party leadership. In retrospect, the latter aspect appears to have been the most important. Wang's Wuhan assignment may have represented an early victory by Mao, perhaps one accomplished without Wang's understanding his own defeat.[59]

In Yan'an, Mao continued to implement his revolutionary line. From Wuhan, Wang continued to oppose it. Shortly after his arrival in Wuhan, Wang directly challenged Mao's policy of expanding revolutionary power behind Japanese lines. In January, representatives from Communist base areas across north China assembled to establish a border district government, the first Communist-controlled "new democratic" regime to be established behind Japanese lines. The "provisional executive committee" of the new government broadcast an announcement of its formation and then sent cables to Chiang Kai-shek and Yan Xishan calling on them to recognize it.[60]

Wang Ming deemed this action rash and provocative, and on 28 January he sent a cable to the Politburo strongly condemning the manner in which the new border district government had been established. The cable asserted that the Politburo had already agreed to respect the form of existing governmental structures. Therefore, to establish new administrative bodies unilaterally in this fashion, and simply to present Chiang Kai-shek with a *fait accompli*, would undermine the united front. Henceforth only if Republic of China authorities gave prior approval should new governmental organs be set up.[61]

Wang also used *Xinhua Ribao* (New China Daily), the first CCP newspaper to be published openly in KMT-controlled areas, to attack Mao's radical line. Wang served as *Xinhua Ribao's* chairman, and after beginning publication on 11 January 1938 the paper reflected Wang's line on several key issues. Perhaps the most important of these had to do with the efficacy of guerrilla warfare versus regular warfare. In repeated articles and editorials, the paper denigrated guerrilla war and extolled Wang's idea of building a new army with united command, supply, armaments, pay, discipline, and planning.[62]

Another Politburo conference convened at Yan'an from 27 February through 1 March 1938, probably at Wang Ming's demand, to discuss the war situation and to prepare for the convocation of the Seventh Party Congress. Of the eight people who attended this conference, only Zhang Wentian and Ren Bishi actively supported Mao and opposed Wang.[63] The thrust of Wang's criticism of Mao was embodied in his report "on the current situation and how to continue the war of resistance and win victory."[64] Regarding military strategy, Wang argued that "principle reliance had to be on mobile war coordinated with positional war and supplemented by guerrilla war." Key cities such as Wuhan had to be defended "by taking mobile war as the key supplemented by guerrilla war and coordinated with positional warfare." At the present stage, Wang's report asserted, the defense of Wuhan was critical and all possible strength should be used to achieve this objective. To contribute to this, the army of the CCP should become part of a truly united national army under Chiang Kai-shek's command. Regarding the question of the governmental forms appropriate to the united front, Wang reiterated his opposition to unilateral CCP establishment of new administrative organs without the authorization of the central authorities. Moreover, all personnel appointed to executive organs in areas recovered from Japanese occupation should be approved by the appropriate ROC officials.

Regarding the mobilization of the masses, Wang urged that they be organized "on the basis of their occupation and areas of residence." That is, urbanites should not be siphoned off to rural areas as Mao urged. Existing mass organizations should be utilized, rather than creating new ones. Moreover, mass organizations should be led by the government and should register with the government. In areas under KMT control, the CCP should operate only via legal methods. Moreover, a major object of the efforts of mass organizations should be "to help the government's armies." Finally, Wang linked the "mistakes" in CCP line to its peasant-dominated nature and inadequate theoretical level. To counter these defects, Wang called for a deliberate proletarianization of the CCP and intensified study of Marxism–Leninism.

Wang's February report constituted a major challenge to Mao's strategy of an independent guerrilla war and all-out expansion of Communist power in the vast rural areas behind Japanese lines. It urged a shift of the Party's energies from the countryside back to the cities and a concentration on mobile war in coordination with the armies of the KMT. Moreover, while not directly challenging Mao's leadership, the clear implication was that he lacked an understanding of Marxism–Leninism and was unfit to be leader of the party.

Wang's views prevailed at the February conference. But once again Mao was able to win a tactical victory. Because of the opposition of Mao, Zhang, and Ren, Wang's report was not voted on or formally adopted, and no "conclusion" or "summary" was reached by the March conference.[65]

After the February Politburo conference, the split between the Yan'an center and the Yangtze Bureau in Wuhan became more pronounced. Mao accelerated the expansion of the anti-Japanese base areas, which had apparently been slowed since Wang's return at the end of November. In February and March, the fourth column of the New Fourth Army was dispatched to the Hubei–Anwei provincial border area, and in March–April the New Fourth Army's first, second, and third columns were deployed south of the Yangtze River to southern Anwei. In May, the Politburo ordered the New Fourth Army to expand base areas in Japanese-occupied zones to its east and north and in June and July the New Fourth Army expanded into Jiangsu and Anwei provinces north of the Yangtze.[66] These areas were well beyond those designated by the National Government as the areas of operation for the armed forces of the CCP. Moreover, these moves implied a substantial expansion of those armed forces beyond the 20,000-man strength authorized by the KMT.

In Wuhan, Wang Ming proceeded to implement his own line. In March he proposed to the provisional national congress convened in Wuhan, a plan for CCP participation in a reorganized government. He did this without prior Politburo clearance. Indeed, he sent a copy of his proposal to the Politburo at the same time he submitted it to the provisional congress. Upon receipt of Wang's plan, the Politburo rejected it and cabled an alternative to Wang with orders that it be passed on to the congress. Wang replied that Yan'an's plan had arrived too late and that his own plan had already been submitted to the congress. He thus declined to withdraw his plan and urged the Party center not to propagandize their plan, since to do so would have an adverse impact both within the CCP and between it and the KMT.[67] Then, on 23 April, the magazine Qun Zhong (The Masses), which was controlled by Wang's Yangtze Bureau, published Wang's report to the February Politburo conference and falsely asserted that it was a "summary" unanimously approved by the Politburo. Again, this was done without the permission of the Party center.[68]

While Wang was isolated in Wuhan and becoming increasingly reckless in his defiance of CCP discipline, several developments further strengthened Mao's hand. Zhang Guotao's defection on 4 April—while participating in a KMT-sponsored Qing Ming ceremony at the tomb of the Yellow Emperor—removed one of Mao's key opponents from the Politburo. It also strengthened Mao's arguments about the danger of rightist capitulation within the CCP and discredited Wang by association with Zhang. More important, by this time the generals of the CCP were becoming aware of the opportunities offered by Mao's military line and the defects of Wang's line.[69] More generally, the dedicated revolutionaries constituting the CCP Politburo probably began to realize that Mao's strategy held the opportunity for eventual Communist rule of China, while Wang's strategy could well sacrifice that opportunity for the defense of the Soviet Union.

In May 1938, Mao published two lengthy essays on guerrilla war rebutting Wang Ming: "Problems of Strategy in Guerrilla War against Japan," and "On Protracted War." As the annotation to "Problems of Strategy" in Mao's Selected Works pointed out, this essay was necessary because "many people inside and outside the Party belittled the important strategic role of guerrilla warfare and pinned their hopes on regular warfare alone, and particularly on the operations of the Kuomintang forces."[70] When Mao finished his magnum opus, "On Protracted War," the Politburo ordered Wang Ming to publish the work in *Xinhua Ribao*. Wang replied that it was too long. The Politburo then ordered Wang to publish the work serially.[71]

Mao's strategy of guerrilla war is well known and can be summarized here in a few sentences. It entailed a long first period of low-intensity conflict with Japanese forces, during which emphasis would be placed on establishing, consolidating, and expanding the organizational infrastructure and territorial base of the CCP. Eventually, once these base areas had been built up, the war would move into its second stage in which more powerful attacks could be launched on enemy forces. Finally, after the revolutionary forces had grown more powerful, they would attack and overwhelm the isolated enemy-occupied cities.

This much is straightforward and well known. One other aspect of Mao's tract on protracted war is less well understood: Mao fully expected the Soviet Union to intervene in the war with Japan at some stage, and expected that this intervention would be critical to winning final victory. In "On Protracted War" Mao explained the international and domestic factors which would make possible China's victory over Japan. Among the most important international factors was anticipated Soviet support:

> The existence of the Soviet Union is a particularly vital factor in present-day international politics and the Soviet Union will certainly support China with the greatest enthusiasm. . . . All these factors have created and are creating important conditions indispensable to China's final victory. *Large-scale direct assistance is as yet lacking and will come only in the future*, but China is progressive and is a big country and these are the factors enabling her to protract the war and to *promote as well as await international help*. . . . As for international support, *though direct and large-scale assistance is not yet in sight it is in the making*, the international situation being fundamentally different than before [emphasis added].[72]

Soviet assistance to China was, as we saw in Chapter 2, quite large by May 1938; loans and arms sales to the KMT were not "lacking." This sort of aid was apparently not the type of Soviet assistance Mao had in mind. In the context of mid-1938, "direct and large-scale" assistance from the Soviet Union meant the dispatch of Soviet armies to fight Japan. Mao reassured his readers that such assistance "is in the making" and "will come in the future." With this vision of the future defeat of Japan, Mao could hardly afford to break with Moscow.

From the standpoint of expanding Communist power in China, Mao's strategy was shrewd. It was, in fact, a brilliant way of combining revolution and resistance. From Moscow's standpoint, however, it meant that fewer Japanese troops would be killed and tied down during the long first phase of Mao's protracted war. It is also important to remember that the first, low-intensity stage of Mao's protracted war came at a time when the Soviet commitment to Nationalist China's war effort was at its maximum and concentrated on halting the Japanese advance on Wuhan. The contrast between Moscow's efforts in support of the defense of Wuhan and Mao's military strategy in mid-1938 brought into clear focus the contradiction between revolution in China and Soviet national security concerns.

The People's Defense of Wuhan

As we saw in the last chapter, the defense of Wuhan was the focus of Republic of China–Soviet Union military cooperation during mid-1938. The defense of Wuhan meant big battles in areas far away from Soviet borders and in the heartland of Anglo-American influence in China. This served Moscow's dual objectives of tying down Japan's armies and drawing Britain and the United States into the Sino-Japanese War. The defense of Wuhan also provided a rallying point for Chinese resistance to Japan, just as the defense of Madrid was then doing in Spain. The defense of Madrid from mid-1936 onward was one of the critical military successes of the Spanish Republic which provided time to organize Republican forces for a protracted struggle. (Madrid fell in June 1939.) Moscow hoped that Wuhan would play a comparable role in China. It is also relevant that during the initial epic defense of Madrid, a newly formed workers' militia played a critical role.

Parallels between Madrid and Wuhan were common in Soviet and leftist Chinese media in 1938. The Madrid-Wuhan analogy also played a prominent role in Wang Ming's program. In his report to the February 1938 Politburo conference, Wang Ming proposed that the CCP use "all possible strength" to defend Wuhan, which, Wang said, was to be China's Madrid. Wang stressed that even though China could continue to resist if Wuhan fell, its loss would greatly weaken that resistance.[73] Again, this was not an esoteric point, but had to do with such basic issues as where cadres should be assigned and what activities Communist armed forces should undertake.

Mao made his position on this issue clear in a directive from the Central Committee Secretariat to Wang Ming's Yangtze Bureau on 22 May 1938—just as the Japanese drive for Wuhan was beginning—ordering the Yangtze Bureau to place the emphasis of *all* of its work on preparations for guerrilla war in Hubei, Hunan, and Anwei provinces. Students, unemployed workers, and revolutionary activists were to be sent back to their homes in the countryside, where they were to organize and lead guerrilla war. A large part of the cadres of the CCP in Wuhan were also to be assigned to rural areas to build up the Party's leadership organs and expand the Party's work. This was to be done even if it injured the Party's work in Wuhan.[74] This directive flatly contradicted Wang's emphasis on the defense of Wuhan, and he ignored it.[75]

Instead, on 15 June, Wang issued without Politburo authorization his own program on the war of resistance and defense of Wuhan. This program termed the defense of Wuhan "the strategic center of the present stage of the war" and said that its loss would have extremely adverse consequences both domestically and internationally. According to Wang, the defense of Wuhan was "extremely important" to waging a protracted war of resistance and in winning final victory. Wuhan was the only major economic center of China not in Japanese hands and provided the base of defense industries which would make possible a strategic counteroffensive. Wuhan had a large proletariat and a long history of revolutionary struggle. The 1911 revolution had begun there, Wang noted, and it had been the stormy petrel of the 1925–1927 revolution. Now Wuhan was to become China's "Madrid." The roused workers and people of Wuhan would stop the Japanese advance, just as Madrid's residents had held Franco's armies before the walls of their city. The defense of Madrid demonstrated, Wang said, that the Chinese people and army could defend Wuhan. To achieve this vital objective, "all possible military forces" should be rushed to Wuhan's defense. Workers and other groups within the city should be organized into armed militias, just as had been done in Madrid. Moreover, "several tens" of new regiments should be formed by amalgamating the best units of all existing armies (presumably including Communist armies) and arming them with the newest weapons. These new units would then undertake mobile warfare in Henan and Anwei provinces to delay and wear down the Japanese forces advancing on Wuhan.[76] Again Wang insisted on copying the experiences of foreign, European revolutionary movements.

In line with this perspective, Wang refused to obey the Politburo's orders to reassign CCP cadres and activists to the rural areas far from the front lines. In April he refused to accept the dispatch to Wuhan of a Yan'an representative to reorganize the Party's work. He also refused to organize special classes to train cadres in the organization of guerrilla war, preferring instead to permit their attendance in classes organized by the KMT.[77]

The credibility of Wang's line suffered a severe setback in August when Nationalist authorities disbanded the Communist-led workers' militias in Wuhan. The organization of these militias had been a main focus of the Yangtze Bureau's work and, in line with his concern for Nationalist laws, Wang had ordered them to register their membership with Republic of China authorities as required by government regulations. Having gone a long way to placate Nationalist concerns about Communist activities, however, Wang found these concessions inadequate to protect the organizational base of the CCP. This gave Mao further proof both of the reactionary nature of the KMT and of the imbecility of mechanically copying foreign experiences—in this case respect for the laws of the "progressive" bourgeois government leading the united front.[78]

Chiang Kai-shek ordered withdrawal from Wuhan on 19 October, as Japanese forces were encircling the city and after they had seized Guangzhou, the strategic coastal terminus of the Hubei–Guangdong railway. The fall of Wuhan signaled a shift of Japanese efforts from military advance to consolidation of areas already conquered. Wang Ming's failure to expand vigorously base areas in central China in early 1938 meant that the CCP infrastructure there was weak as Japanese forces and their Chinese collaborators now turned their attention to these areas. Because of Wang Ming's influence, the CCP had concentrated its forces on defending Wuhan and failed to utilize fully the great opportunity created in 1938 by the disintegration of governmental power and authority in the Yangtze valley and to fill that vacuum before either the KMT or Japan could.[79] By the fall of 1938, the powerful bases of the CCP in north China, built up by following Mao's line, contrasted sharply with the weaknesses of the infrastructure of the CCP in central China. This was perhaps the most important factor in persuading the revolutionaries on the CCP Politburo that Mao's leadership was superior to that of Moscow's minions.

The Comintern's Endorsement of Mao Zedong

In the fall of 1938, the Comintern finally endorsed Mao's leadership of the CCP, three and a half years after the Zunyi conference which had established Mao's paramountcy. Several factors underlay this important shift in Soviet policy. Perhaps the most important was Mao's defeat of the Comintern's Internationalist agents. By the fall of 1938 it was increasingly apparent that Mao had outmaneuvered Wang Ming; Wang was simply not Mao's equal. Mao had won the support of a majority of the Politburo and the loyalty of most of the generals of the CCP, and was able to implement his plans to expand revolutionary power in northern China in spite of Wang's opposition. Mao had thwarted Wang's efforts to launch a rectification and purge within the CCP and to convene the Seventh Party Congress. Wang had been relegated to a role of ineffectual and increasingly public opposition at Wuhan. Thus, if Stalin wanted to retain some leverage over the CCP, he had to make a deal with Mao.

But Stalin still wished to uphold the Republic of China–Soviet Union alliance as a way of coping with Japan. This meant that he could not afford to alienate Chiang by unleashing Mao. Stalin saw the possible uses of the large guerrilla armies being created by Mao in northern China. But those forces were far from being adequate compensation for loss of the ROC as an ally against Japan. Mao, for his part, wished to avoid a break with Stalin. The lingering influence of Soviet Union-style "internationalism" among the backbone cadre of the CCP made an attempted break with Stalin a very risky proposition. Stalin could still publicly denounce Mao as a Trotskyite possibly producing a revolt against Mao's leadership within the Party or at least the defection of many veteran cadres. Moreover, Mao still hoped to receive Soviet arms and to cooperate actively with the Red Army at some stage in the struggle against Japan. Out of these considerations arose the first wartime compromise between Mao and Stalin. Mao won Comintern endorsement and approval of his drive to build peasant armies. Stalin secured CCP pledges of loyalty and submission to Chiang and the Republic of China which would, Stalin hoped, reassure Chiang.

Early in 1937, Politburo member Wang Jiaxiang (later to become the first ambassador of the People's Republic of China to the Soviet Union) went to Moscow for medical treatment of wounds. When Wang Ming returned to China in November 1937, Wang Jiaxiang replaced him as CCP representative to the Comintern. Throughout his stay in Moscow in 1937 and 1938, Wang Jiaxiang actively supported and propagandized Mao's principle of "independence within the united front," opposed Wang Ming's "capitulationist" line, and was instrumental in winning Comintern endorsement of Mao.[80]

In April 1938, Ren Bishi arrived in Moscow to replace Wang Jiaxiang as head of the CCP Comintern delegation. Ren carried with him a special report of the situation in China which he hoped would win Comintern approval.[81] Ren was also charged with actively lobbying Comintern officials in order to win their support for Mao. Fortunately one of Ren's associates has left an account of his activities in Moscow. Ren initially faced substantial opposition. In the words of his associate:

> A few people in the Comintern believed in the stuff Wang Ming was saying and did not understand the actual situation of our Party's leadership of the Chinese revolution, even to the extent that they believed that the Chinese revolution had failed after the Long March. They absolutely did not understand the line advanced by our Party in the War of Resistance, but thought Wang Ming's line was Marxism and that Wang Ming was the leader of the Chinese revolution.[82]

Ren set about to educate these "few people." Shortly after his arrival he presented to the ECCI his report "on the victories won by the CCP under Mao's leadership." In his report to the ECCI, Ren demonstrated how Mao had succeeded in building up large rural bases and Communist armies in the 1920s and early 1930s and how these successes demonstrated the correctness of Mao's line. The establishment of Mao as supreme leader at the Zunyi Conference had been due, Ren explained, to a recognition of the correctness of Mao's line. Ren's central point was simple: "Only comrade Mao Zedong is the leader of our Party."[83]

Ren Bishi also organized his comrades in Moscow to translate Mao's writings for perusal by Comintern officials and to write articles explaining various aspects of Mao's thinking about the Chinese revolution. When Ren found that the representatives of many "fraternal parties" were "very concerned" about the state of the Chinese revolution, he recruited his comrades to call on them and explain Mao's strategy of building rural base areas and surrounding the cities from the countryside. The representatives from the fraternal parties had not read of such things in Marx and Lenin, but they were willing to listen to Ren's explanation of these strategies. Ren also set about rectifying the delegation of the CCP in Moscow. Pictures of Wang Ming were torn down and replaced with those of Mao and Zhu De. The membership of the CCP Moscow mission was organized to study Mao's writings. Ren stressed this ideological remolding, and when comrades had "ideological problems" he would work with them individually and at length. Some cadres were sent back to Yan'an to study. Ren also investigated the cases of CCP cadres who had crossed Wang in one way or another and had been sent to Soviet labor camps as a result. The release of a number of such cadres was secured.

By August 1938, Wang Jiaxiang had fully recovered from his wounds and was ready to return to China. Shortly before Wang Jiaxiang's departure from Moscow, he and Ren discussed China's situation with Dimitrov. Wang and Ren explained how the present KMT–CCP united front differed from that of 1923–1927. After some discussion, Dimitrov accepted a CCP Politburo report and then endorsed Mao's leadership of the CCP, saying:

> You should tell the entire Party that they should support Comrade Mao Zedong as the leader of the CCP. He is a leader tempered by the actual experience of struggle. Other people such as Wang Ming, should not again hold leadership positions. [84]

Dimitrov's words elated Wang Jiaxiang, for they indicated that Mao's prestige and authority had at last been accepted by the Comintern and its "highest authorities." Wang then returned to China with Dimitrov's endorsement and some important documents from the Comintern for the CCP Politburo and Mao Zedong.[85]

The terms of the agreement between Mao and Stalin were laid out in a "Declaration by the CCP Center" in September 1938. This declaration began with an affirmation of Moscow's interpretation of the Xian Incident of December 1936, thereby indicating Mao's acceptance of the Soviet position on an old dispute between them.[86] The declaration then went on to accept Moscow's analysis of the utility of China's war of resistance to Soviet national defense. China's war of resistance was a great success, the declaration said straightforwardly, because it was tying down large numbers of Japanese troops.

> This resistance [by China] has inflicted huge losses on Japan and caused its attack on China to become a very complex protracted war. In this war Japan is daily being forced to use ever greater military strength. The longer the war continues, the greater become Japan's difficulties and the closer comes the day of complete defeat for Japanese aggression.[87]

The declaration then went on to affirm Chiang Kai-shek's leadership, calling for political and military unification under Chiang. But the declaration also upheld Mao's line on independent guerrilla warfare behind Japanese lines and the organization of peasants into base areas supporting this political expediency. Here logical consistency suffered for the sake of political expediency. The CCP was to submit to the National Government while moving forward at high speed to expand its own strength.

After Dimitrov and Stalin considered and approved a document submitted by Ren Bishi (probably a version of the same report that Ren carried to Moscow in April), the ECCI issued two declarations of its own. The first said that the ECCI "completely agreed" with the political line of the CCP and approved the expulsion of Zhang Guotao.[88] The second promised to increase support from the Comintern for China's national liberation war against Japanese aggression.[89]

These statements, and the compromises and understandings between Stalin and Mao which they embodied, laid the basis for the convocation of the Sixth Plenum of the Sixth CCP Central Committee.[90] On 29 September 1938, the first full plenary session of the Central Committee to be held since Mao took over as leader of the Party opened in Yan'an. It was the longest meeting of the CCP center since the Sixth Congress in Moscow in 1928. It met for almost two months, over twice as long as the Sixth Congress which had been the longest CCP central meeting up to that point, and represented a major step forward in the consolidation of Mao's leadership of the CCP.[91] It was also a classic example of a trade-off of policy for power. Mao accepted Stalin's line on the national united front, including Chiang's leadership role, while Stalin accepted Mao's leadership of the CCP and his drive to establish CCP power throughout the Japanese-occupied hinterland.[92]

Wang Ming was extremely reluctant to attend the Sixth Plenum. According to Wang Jiaxiang, Wang Ming rejected an order by Mao to attend the plenum and instead proposed that the plenum be convened in Wuhan or Xian, that is, in an area under KMT control. When the Politburo rejected Wang's proposal, Wang Ming reportedly urged Wang Jiaxiang to travel to Wuhan to tell him personally the contents of the Comintern's directives. Only after repeated urging and direct orders from Mao and Wang Jiaxiang, did Wang Ming report to Yan'an for the plenum.[93]

The Sixth Plenum formally began with a recitation by Wang Jiaxiang of the Comintern's directives and of Dimitrov's comments to him regarding Mao's leadership position.[94] Mao then took the floor to deliver the first of several long reports.[95] In none of these speeches (nor in the final resolution based on these speeches) did Mao claim proletarian or Communist leadership of the united front.[96] The closest he came to this was in his talk on the role of the CCP, when he maintained that Communists should play "an exemplary vanguard role" through hard work, honesty, and selflessness.[97] In one instance, Mao went so far as to recognize that "the Kuomintang is the party in power," and the final resolution of the plenum referred to "the leadership of Chairman Chiang" over the "Chinese people." Mao's general emphasis, however, was on mutual support, cooperation, and independence between the CCP and the KMT. He made frequent reference to such mutual support. He began his talk on independence and initiative within the united front, for example, with the words: "All political parties and groups in the united front must help each other and make mutual concessions for the sake of long-term cooperation."[98] Mao, in other words, adopted the line which the Comintern had pressed on him, via Wang Ming, for the previous year. In one other critical respect Mao also accepted the Comintern's line. In spite of the dire straits in which the KMT then found itself, Mao did not raise the possibility of Nationalist surrender, or of a split between the right and left wings of the KMT. Rather, he implied that the united front between the CCP and the KMT could and would last as long as China's war against Japan. This, too was a striking departure from Mao's position in late 1937.

Stalin also conceded several important points to Mao. One was Stalin's approval of Mao's rural strategy of protracted guerrilla war. The Sixth Plenum fully endorsed the expansion of base areas and guerrilla armies, even if doing this created friction with the KMT. Such friction was to be minimized, however, by conducting tension-provoking activities clandestinely whenever possible.[99] Stalin's second concession to Mao was his endorsement of Mao's leadership of the CCP.

Comintern endorsement was not the only factor enabling Mao to push aside Wang Ming, but it was an important one. As Mao told the Seventh CCP Congress in April 1945, if it had not been for Comintern "instructions" it would have been very difficult to solve the problem of right-wing capitulationism during the Sixth Plenum.[100] Wang's major ideological weapon against Mao had been that Mao was not a good internationalist. But once Dimitrov and Stalin personally endorsed Mao, such charges no longer rang true. Thus Mao could tell the Sixth Plenum: "Only those who are politically muddle-headed or have ulterior motives talk nonsense about our having made a mistake and abandoned internationalism."[101]

One other critical theme introduced by Mao at the Sixth Plenum probably had not been approved by Moscow but followed logically from Soviet approval of Mao's theoretical innovations. This was the "sinification of Marxism." During the latter half of 1937, Mao began developing a philosophical basis for the transformation of Marxism in the process of adapting it to China. By the fall of 1938, his ideas in this regard had progressed from modifying Marxist doctrine to take into account China's practical social and political environment, to the assimilation of China's entire cultural and historical heritage. This "sinification of Marxism" had far-reaching implications. In the first instance, it enhanced the appeal of Marxism in China by increasing the congruence between that doctrine and China's own heritage. In terms of CCP–Comintern relations, it provided a theoretical justification for doctrines qualitatively different from those propounded by Moscow. Moreover, the process of "sinification" could perforce be led only by Chinese, not by Moscow. It was, in other words, a justification of the independence of the CCP from Moscow. Mao first raised the idea of "sinification" of Marxism in his report to the Sixth Plenum, but it was not incorporated into the final resolution in order not to antagonize Moscow.[102]

Adjustments in the United Front

The CCP had rapidly expanded its infrastructure across northern China during the first months of the war. Then after several months of restraint due, as we have seen, to opposition within the CCP and pressure from Moscow, in early 1938 Mao threw the full weight of his forces into a renewed effort to establish base areas deep behind Japanese lines in northern China. After the repudiation of Wang Ming's line at the Sixth Plenum and the elimination of his independent center at Wuhan, CCP expansion in central China also began to accelerate.

By the end of 1938, many KMT leaders were thoroughly alarmed by the speed and scope of CCP expansion. One group led by Wang Jingwei believed that the choice facing them was between collaboration with Japan and Communist rule of China. They chose the former, and on 18 December 1938 Wang Jingwei fled from Chongqing to Hanoi where he began working out a deal with Japan.[103] Chiang Kai-shek believed that the path taken by Wang Jingwei would lead to several centuries of Japanese colonial rule over China and was unwilling to accept such a consequence. Nevertheless, he too thought the CCP was using the war to prepare for a future seizure of power and felt that more forceful measures had to be taken to check its growth.

Mao's defeat of Wang Ming at the Sixth Plenum of the CCP was also a defeat for Chiang's initial wartime strategy for controlling the CCP. When Chiang began the war with Japan, he had hoped to use Comintern pressure to force Mao and the CCP into subservience within the united front. This was to be part of the price that Stalin was to pay for alliance with the ROC against Japan. Stalin had tried to fulfill his part of the bargain but had been outmaneuvered by Mao. The Sixth Plenum of the Central Committee meant, in effect, that Chiang's first wartime strategy for dealing with the CCP was in a shambles. During the last months of 1938, Chiang was forced to rethink the nature of the relationship between Stalin and Mao, and to devise a new strategy for dealing with the CCP.

Chiang had a general understanding of the outcome of the Sixth Plenum. Indeed, when Wang Ming, Bo Gu, and Wu Yuzhang left the plenum early to return to Chongqing, Chiang received them, talked with them for five or six hours, and urged them to join the KMT as top-level officials.[104] Chiang understood very clearly Wang Ming's relation to Moscow and must have concluded that Wang's defeat by Mao at the Sixth Plenum meant that Stalin's ability to restrain Mao was, in fact, rather limited. Chiang also knew that very little Soviet material was going to the CCP. This too indicated a rather loose relationship between the CCP and the Soviet Union. Chiang had several liasion officers in Yan'an who reported to him on relations between the CCP and the Soviet Union. When reports of Soviet arms going to the CCP did occasionally reach Chiang, he protested to the Soviet government with apparently satisfactory results.[105]

Yet while Chiang was aware of the differences between Mao and Stalin, and of

Stalin's limited control over Mao, he could not be entirely certain that Moscow would stand aside and allow him to suppress the CCP. Nor could he be sure that Moscow would not at some point alter its policy of "noninterference" in China's domestic affairs and begin supporting the CCP on a substantial scale. The CCP remained, after all, an important branch party of the Comintern and provided considerable assets which Moscow could use to achieve its ends in China. Moreover, the Republic of China remained in desperate need of continued Soviet military assistance. All of this meant that Chiang had to watch constantly for Moscow's reaction as he moved cautiously against the CCP.

Chiang's second wartime strategy for coping with the CCP was revealed at the Fifth Plenum of the Fifth Central Executive Committee (CEC) of the KMT in January 1939. This new strategy was based on an assumption about relations between Moscow and the CCP which in one respect was the exact opposite of the assumption which had underlain Chiang's first plan. Whereas Chiang's initial strategy had assumed that Stalin would be able to restrain Mao because of the intimacy of CCP–CPSU cooperation, Chiang now assumed that relations between the CCP and the Soviet Union were much looser and that, consequently, Stalin would sacrifice the CCP as a pawn in the great-power chess game. If Stalin could not control Mao, Chiang concluded, then he should be willing to stand aside while the KMT armies moved against the CCP. If Mao was not Stalin's proxy, then Stalin should be willing to sacrifice him for the sake of maintaining good relations with China's National Government in order to offset Japanese pressure.

The January KMT plenum formulated a new policy of limiting the growth of CCP power while maintaining good relations with the Soviet Union. The plenum rejected a CCP proposal that Communists join the KMT while retaining their CCP membership and instead adopted a number of measures designed to contain communism. Among these were the restoration of the fourteenth-century *baojia* system of collective family responsibility for individual actions, intensified anticommunist propaganda, and a set of tough regulations designed to restrict Communist activities. Most important for our purposes, however, was the plenum's decision to contest Communist control of Japanese-held areas. To this end, two zones of KMT guerrilla operations were established.[106] Over the next several months as the KMT moved to implement these measures, tension and conflict between the KMT and the CCP mounted.

The impact this new anti-CCP orientation would have on Chongqing's relations with Moscow was a critical question. In a secret speech to the Fifth Plenum on 26 January 1939, Chiang Kai-shek analyzed the relationship between this hard-line approach to the CCP and the Republic of China ties with the Soviet Union. Good relations with the Soviet Union were still essential, Chiang said, and must continue even while the power of the CCP was being reduced.[107]

During the spring and summer of 1939, KMT military pressure on the CCP steadily mounted. According to CCP calculations, during 1938 KMT forces had advanced into the Shaan-Gan-Ning special border district only twelve times, with 60 people being killed in the ensuing clashes. During 1939, however, there were 50 KMT incursions with 11,404 people killed.[108] Between December 1938 and October 1939 the CCP also counted 150 incidents of "friction" with government forces in its base areas. Among these incidents were 28 military attacks on CCP cadres or forces.[109] A number of these clashes were serious. On 12 June 1939 at Ping Jiang in Hunan province, for example, government troops surrounded and attacked, according to the Communist version, a liaison office of the New Fourth Army. Two high-level New Fourth Army cadres were killed and a number arrested in the ensuing clash. Throughout the spring and summer of 1939 such attacks on Eighth Route Army forces continued. Again according to CCP calculations, between June and December 1939 there were 90 clashes between government forces and those of the CCP, resulting in 1350 soldiers of the Eighth Route Army killed and 812 people arrested.[110]

Publicly the CCP responded quite moderately to this escalating government pressure throughout the summer of 1939. It initially protested the KMT encroachments in a letter from Zhou Enlai to Chiang Kai-shek.[111] When it issued a public protest of anticommunist moves as preparation for surrender to Japan, it did not even mention, let alone condemn, the increasingly frequent armed clashes, including the one at Ping Jiang two weeks earlier which later became a focus of Communist condemnation.[112] Nor did the statement issued by the CCP on the 7 July 1939 second anniversary of the Marco Polo Bridge Incident mention the increasingly frequent incidents. Instead, that statement expressed the CCP Politburo's "great respect" for "Chairman Chiang." The statement did go to great lengths to condemn the efforts of "traitors to the Han race" of the Wang Jingwei type who were trying to create disunity, and harm and malign the CCP. But the manifesto did not link these "capitulationist" activities to the anticommunist decisions of the KMT's Fifth Plenum. Nor, for that matter, did it demand the recension of the various anticommunist ordinances promulgated after the Fifth Plenum.[113]

A memorial meeting for the "martyrs" killed in the 12 June Ping Jiang clash was not held until 1 August. On that date, Mao finally demanded the cancellation of the various Fifth Plenum anticommunist ordinances. But even then Mao did not condemn the National Government, but called only for the punishment of those responsible for the Ping Jiang clash. Nor did Mao raise the possibility of using armed force to resist KMT encroachments and attacks.[114]

It was not until after the conclusion of the Soviet-German nonaggression pact on 23 August that the CCP began *publicly* taking a firm line against KMT encroachments. In an interview on 16 September, Mao sharply condemned the recent armed attacks, insinuated that the central government was behind them, and publicly announced a new policy of armed retaliation to future attacks: "Our attitude is, we will not attack unless we are attacked; if we are attacked, we will certainly counterattack."[115] In fact, CCP units had been following such a hard line since early spring. In February 1939, the CCP center had issued a directive instructing various units that attacks by the KMT were to be dealt with by counterattacks and not be met with "easy compromises."[116] Mao was unwilling to let anything stand in the way of the expansion of revolutionary power. He was willing, however, to conceal the implementation of this policy when expedient.

The moderate response of the CCP to mounting Nationalist pressure during mid-1939 was probably linked to the escalating conflict between Japanese and Soviet forces then underway on the border of Manchuria and Outer Mongolia. As we saw in

Chapter 2, during June and July, both Stalin and General Cherepanov in Chongqing were urging Chiang Kai-shek to launch a major offensive against Wuhan to relieve Japanese pressure in Manchuria. Chiang would be less willing to undertake such an offensive if the CCP were militantly resisting Chiang's efforts to check its expansion. To the contrary, the more docile the CCP seemed, the more likely it was that Chiang would risk depletion of his strength fighting Japan. Mao had won Stalin's endorsement in the fall of 1938 by convincing Stalin that he, Mao, was a good internationalist. Less than a year later, Mao had to demonstrate his "internationalism" to Stalin's satisfaction.

There is some evidence of Comintern intervention in the decision-making process of the CCP at this point. As part of his effort to persuade Chiang to launch an offensive to retake Wuhan in mid-1939, Stalin sought to reassure him that the CCP would pose no threat to him. Stalin made this pledge at a banquet held in Moscow in June 1939 to celebrate the conclusion of the Sino-Soviet Commercial treaty. After reporting on the heavy fighting on the Mongolian-Manchurian border, Stalin commented about China's domestic situation:

> Prior to the war of resistance, China's leftists, including the CCP, did not understand the national policies of China and the Soviet Union. After these mistakes and through the sincere advice and guidance of the Soviet Union, these forces now honestly uphold and protect Your Excellency's leadership of the war of national resistance and of national construction. Henceforth China's unity will grow steadily stronger. There absolutely will be no problem between the KMT and the CCP. [117]

The possibility of a peace settlement between Chongqing and Tokyo was also closely related to the escalating confrontation on the Mongolian-Manchurian border, and also helped moderate CCP policy in mid-1939. Here the concerns of Stalin and Mao coincided: both men did not want Chiang's armies disengaged from fighting Japan. The possibility of Nationalist capitulation to Japan was the central concern of a speech by Mao on 30 June 1939. International conditions, especially the efforts of Britain and the United States, to arrange a compromise peace between China and Japan were creating a great danger of capitulation by the KMT, Mao said. The "peace group" within the KMT hoped that Japan's exhausted state and "international pressure" would induce Japan to make concessions, thus opening the way to peace. This "peace camp" hoped to arrange an international conference to negotiate peace terms. Thus, Mao concluded, "With some people in our anti-Japanese front wavering more than ever . . . capitulationism has become the main danger in the present political situation." [118]

An increased "danger of peace" is not, however, in and of itself an adequate explanation of the moderation of CCP policy in mid-1939. At other times—for example in late 1937 and again in 1940—increased danger of KMT surrender led not to greater Communist restraint, but to an accelerated CCP drive to expand the "anti-Japanese forces" at the expense of the KMT. Other factors must have been operating in mid-1939. Among these factors were the "international" ones (e.g., Comintern pressure) and concern for Soviet security in the midst of the escalating Soviet-Japanese border crisis.

Notes

1. David T. Cattell, *Soviet Diplomacy and the Spanish Civil War*, Berkeley: University of California Press, 1957, pp. 32–37. Hugh Thomas, *The Spanish Civil War*, New York: Harper and Row, 1961, pp. 295–298.
2. Cattell, *Soviet Diplomacy and the Spanish Civil War*, pp. 35, 37.
3. Thomas, *Spanish Civil War*, p. 366.
4. David T. Cattell, *Communism and the Spanish Civil War*, Berkeley: University of California Press, 1956, pp. 155–161.
5. See Cattell, *Communism and the Spanish Civil War*, pp. 118, 136-137. *See also* Thomas, *Spanish Civil War*, pp. 363–365. Robert Conquest, *The Great Terror, Stalin's Purge of the Thirties*, New York: Macmillan, 1973, pp. 587–588.
6. Cattell, *Communism and the Spanish Civil War*, pp. 9, 117, 136.
7. Conquest, *Great Terror*, p. 588.
8. Spain and China were the first and second most frequent topics in the Comintern's *International Press Correspondence* during the years 1936–1938. Charles B. McLane, *Soviet Policy and the Chinese Communists, 1931–1945*, Berkeley: University of California Press, 1958, pp. 104–105.
9. There are three firsthand accounts of the Luochuan Conference. Tu Cheng-neng, then secretarial chief of the Central Committee of the CCP, later defected to the Nationalists and provided much of the inside information for Warren Kuo's study. Warren Kuo, "The Conference at Luochuan," *Issues and Studies*, vol. 5, no. 1 (October 1968), pp. 36–56. Zhang Guotao was also there and discusses it in *Wo de Huiyi* [My memoir], vol. 3, Hong Kong: Ming Bao Chubanshe, 1974, pp. 1294–1295. *See also* Otto Braun (then a Comintern military advisor to Yan'an), in *Comintern Agent in China, 1932–1939*, London: Hurst and Co., 1982, pp. 211–213. These accounts are corroborated by post-1949 CCP accounts of the Luochuan Conference. Zhonggong Zhongyang Dangxiao Dangshi Jiaoyanshi Ziliaoju [The party history instructional materials office of the CCP Central Committee], *Zhongguo Gongchandang Lizi Zhongyao Huiyiji* [Historically important meetings of the Chinese Communist Party], Shanghai: Renmin Chubanshe, 1982.
10. Zhang Guotao, *Wo de Huiyi*, p. 1297. Braun, *Comintern Agent*, p. 212.
11. Zhang Guotao, *Wo de Huiyi*, pp. 1298–1299.
12. Kuo, "Conference at Luochuan," p. 43.
13. Peng Dehuai, *Peng Dehuai Zishu* [Peng Dehuai remembers], Beijing: Renmin Chubanshe, 1981, p. 221. On this point the memoir of Peng Dehuai is confirmed by several other recent Chinese accounts. *See* Shi Feng, *Fandui Wang Ming Tuoxiang Zhuyi Luxian de Duozheng* [The struggle against Wang Ming's capitulationist line], Shanghai: Renmin Chubanshe, 1976; He Shifen, "Mao Zedong tongzhi zai kangzhan chuqi junshi zhanlüe zhuanbian zhong de jiechu gongxian" [The outstanding contributions of comrade Mao Zedong to the changes in military strategy during the early period of the war of resistance], *Dangshi Yanjiu* [Research on Party History], no. 1, 1984, p. 35. The Red Guard journal *Zhan Bao* (24 February 1967), cited in Warren Kuo, "The 6th Plenum of the CCP 6th Central Committee," part 2, *Issues and Studies*, vol. 5, no. 7 (April 1969, p. 37. Zhang Guotao, *Wo de Huiyi*, p. 1244.
14. Tetsuya Kataoka, *Resistance and Revolution in China, the Communists and the Second United Front*, Stanford, Calif.: Stanford University Press, 1974, p. 71.
15. Mao Zedong, "For the Mobilization of all the Nation's Forces for Victory in the War of Resistance," 25 August 1937, *Selected Works of Mao Tse-tung*, vol. 2, Beijing: Foreign Languages Press, 1967, pp. 23–29 (hereafter cited as Mao, *Selected Works*). Otto Braun says that the Ten-Point Program was drafted by Wang Ming in Moscow, approved by the secretariat of the ECCI, and recommended to the Central Committee of the CCP by the ECCI (Braun, *Comintern Agent*, p. 211). This is flatly contradicted by the annotation of Mao's *Selected Works*, which says that the outline of the program was "written by Comrade Mao Tse-tung in August 1937."
16. Zhang Guotao, *Wo de Huiyi*, pp. 44–45.
17. Ibid., p. 1317.
18. *Cankao Ziliao*, vol. 8, p. 78. Liu and Yang then headed the North China Bureau of the CCP. Zhou was in northern China on an "investigation," which Zhang Guotao says was a maneuver designed to express his opposition to Mao's line.
19. Ma Qilin, "Kangzhan chuqi de Wang Ming tuoxiang zhuyi luxian zuowu" [The incorrect capitulationist line of Wang Ming during the early period of the war of resistance], *Dangshi Ziliao Congkan* [Compendium of Materials on Party History], no. 1, 1981, pp. 130–131. *See also Zhongguo Gongchandang Lizi Zhongyao Huiyi Ji*, p. 207.

20. *Cankao Ziliao*, vol. 8, p. 79. According to Zhang Guotao, the divergence between Mao's views and those of his generals was also reflected in his response to the famous ambush of a Japanese column at Pingxing Pass in northern Shanxi on 25 September 1937. Zhang says that after that battle, which was a classic example of successful mobile war but in which 1000 Eighth Route Army soldiers were killed, Mao issued orders that henceforth battles of this type were to be avoided (Zhang Guotao, *Wo de Huiyi*, p. 1318).
21. Peng Dehuai, *Peng Dehuai Zishu*, pp. 222–223.
22. Kataoka, *Resistance and Revolution*, p. 66.
23. "The Situation and Tasks in the Anti-Japanese War after the Fall of Shanghai and Taiyuan," Mao, *Selected Works*, vol. 2, pp. 61–74.
24. He Shifen, "Mao Zedong tongzhi kangzhan chuqi," p. 37.
25. See Zhou's 13 November cable to Mao in Zhou Enlai, "Fandui touxie qiuhe, jinchi Huabei kangzhan" [Oppose capitulationism and seeking peace and resolutely uphold the war or resistance in northern China], *Zhou Enlai Xuanji* [Selected works of Zhou Enlai], vol. 1, Beijing: Renmin Chubanshe, 1980, pp. 79–80.
26. Ning Jinan, *Zhang Guotao he "Wo de Huiyi"* [Zhang Guotao and his "Memoir"], Chengdu: Sichuan Renmin Chubanshe, 1982, p. 278.
27. Mao, *Selected Works*, vol. 2, p. 61.
28. Zhong Pei, *Kang Sheng Ping Zhuan* (Critical biography of Kang Sheng), Beijing: Hong Qi Chubanshe, 1982, p. 52. Chong-Sik Lee, *Revolutionary Struggle in Manchuria, Chinese Communism and Soviet Interests, 1922–1945*, Berkeley: University of California Press, 1983, pp. 230–237.
29. Yan Jingwen, *Zhou Enlai Ping Zhuan* [Critical biography of Zhou Enlai], Hong Kong: Powen Shuju, 1974, p. 232. Kuo, "Conference at Luochuan," p. 36. Kuo's informant regarding the circumstances of Wang's return was Tu Cheng-neng.
30. Liu Yixun says that the December conference affirmed the leadership of the Comintern with Dimitrov's help (Liu Yixun, "Gongchan Guoji he Sidalin dui Zhongguo kang Ri zhanzheng de taidu he fangzhen" [The attitude and policy of the Comintern and Stalin toward China's war of resistance with Japan], *Dangshi Ziliao Congkan* [Compendium of Materials on Party History], no. 2, 1983, p. 139). *See also* Liao Gailong, "Guanyu Gongchang Guoji, Sulian he Zhongguo geming" [On the Communist International, the Soviet Union and China's revolution], *Dangshi Tongxun* [Party History Bulletin], no. 11–12, 1983. Tang Manzhen, "Wang Ming wei 'yiqie jingguo tongyi zhanxian' de zuowu fanan shi tulao de" [It is futile to try to reverse the judgment regarding Wang Ming's incorrect line of "everything through the united front"], *Dangshi Yanjiu* [Research on Party History], no. 3, 1983, pp. 53–58. Peng Dehuai, *Peng Dehuai Zishu*, p. 227. Zhang Rixin, "Wang Ming youqin touxiang zhuyi shi heshi xingcheng de" [When did the rightist capitulationist line of Wang Ming materialize], *Jiangxi Daxue Xuebao* [Jiangxi University Journal], no. 4, 1983, p. 206.
31. Ma Qilin, "Kangzhan chuqi de Wang Ming," pp. 126–155.
32. Gunther Nollau, *International Communism and World Revolution*, New York: Frederick Praeger, 1961, pp. 132–133, 158–159. Warren Kuo concludes that Wang's return was "comparable to a Comintern envoy's inspection of its Chinese branch." (Warren Kuo, "The Conflict between Chen Shao-yu and Mao Tse-tung," part 1, *Issues and Studies*, vol. 5, no. 2 [November 1968], p. 35). Wang Fan-hsi, who was active in the Chinese Trotskyist movement in the 1930s, says that Wang Ming was the Comintern's "inspector general" and quoted H.H. Kung to the effect that Wang was the "direct representative of the Third International" in China (Wang Fan-hsi, *Chinese Revolutionary, Memoirs, 1919–1949*, New York: Oxford University Press, 1980, pp. 220).
33. Zheng Xuejia, *Di San Guojishi* [History of the Third International], vol. 2, Taibei: Shangwu Yingshuguan, 1977, p. 1452.
34. Zhang Guotao, *Wo de Huiyi*, p. 1333.
35. *Zhongguo Gongchandang Lizi Zhongyao Huiyi Ji*, p. 208.
36. Kuo, "Conflict between Chen Shao-yu and Mao Tse-tung," part 1, p. 36. Tu Cheng-nung's account is corroborated by Otto Braun, who says that at the end of 1937 Stalin and Dimitrov directed the "Marxists" within the CCP to prevail on Mao to form a solid united front with the KMT, but not to contest Mao's personal leadership of the CCP (Braun, *Comintern Agent*, p. 221).
37. Zhang Guotao, *Wo de Huiyi*, p. 1327.
38. Kuo, "Conflict between Chen Shao-yu and Mao Tse-tung," p. 40.
39. Wang Ming, "Ruhe jixu quanguo kangzhan zhengchu kangzhan shengli ne?" [How can we continue a nationwide war of resistance and win victory in that war?], *Cankao Ziliao*, vol. 8, pp. 102–107.
40. Ibid., vol. 7, pp. 102–107.
41. Ibid.
42. This is confirmed by Peng Dehuai in *Peng Dehuai Zishu*, p. 229.

43. Kuo, "Conflict between Chen Shao-yu and Mao Tse-tung," part 1, pp. 39–40. Zhang Guotao, *Wo de Huiyi*, p. 1329.
44. *Zhongguo Gongchandang Lizi Zhongyao Huiyi Ji*, p. 210. A "declaration" issued in the name of the Central Committee on 25 December, two weeks after the conference closed, did closely reflect Wang's line. A resolution involves a collective decision of the Politburo and is therefore more authoritative than a declaration by the center in the name of the Central Committee.
45. Ibid., p. 211.
46. Zhang Guotao, *Wo de Huiyi*, p. 1333. Kuo, "Conflict between Chen Shao-yu and Mao Tse-tung," part 1, pp, 36, 43. Ning Jinan, *Zhang Guotao he "Wo de Huiyi"*, p. 278.
47. Wang Ming, "Wanjiu shiju de guanjian" [The crux of rescuing the current situation], *Cankao Ziliao*, vol. 7, pp. 110–114.
48. Steven I. Levine, "Trotsky on China: The Exile Period," *Papers on China*, vol. 18, Cambridge, Mass.: Harvard University East Asian Research Center, December 1964, pp. 90–128.
49. Tang Baolin, "Jiu an xin kao" (Reexamining old cases), in *Chen Duxiu Pinglun Xuanbian* [Selection of essays on Chen Duxiu], Wang Shudi, editor, Zhengzhou (?): Henan Renmin Chubanshe, August 1982, p. 213. Chiang also made other offers to Chen. Hu Shi tried to persuade Chen to go to the United States, or to serve as an advisor to the National Defense Consultative Council. *See also* Sun Qiming, "Chen Duxiu shifo hanjian wenti de tantao" [An investigation of the question of whether Chen Duxiu was a traitor to the Han race], also in the Wang Shutang volume, p. 202.
50. Tang Baolin, "Jiu an xin kao," p. 201.
51. These conditions were that Chen publicly renounce all Trotskyist theories and openly break with the Trotskyist organization, that he recognize his mistake in entering the Trotskyist faction, and that he publicly embrace the anti-Japanese national united front and demonstrate his sincerity through practical actions. Tang Baolin, "Jiu an xin kao," p. 202.
52. Tang Baolin, "Jiu an xin kao," p. 203.
53. Zhang Guotao, *Wo de Huiyi*, p. 1332.
54. Sun Qiming, "Chen Duxiu shifo hanjian," p. 203.
55. Wang Fan-hsi, *Chinese Revolutionary*, pp. 240–241.
56. Kang Sheng, "Chanchu Rikou zhentan minzu gongdi de tuoluo sidi feitu" [Root out, expose, and snare Jap spies, public enemies, and diehard national traitors], in Wang Shutang, *Chen Duxiu Pinglun Xuanbian*, p. 216–233.
57. Wang Fan-shi, *Chinese Revolutionary*, pp. 222–223.
58. Zhang Guotao, *Wo de Huiyi*, p. 1336.
59. If this author's conclusion about Zhou's defection to Mao's camp in November 1937 is correct, one of the reasons for Zhou's assignment as Wang's assistant may also have been to keep an eye on Wang.
60. Shi Feng, *Fandui Wang Ming Touxiang Zhuyi*, p. 37.
61. *Cankao Ziliao*, vol. 7, p. 135.
62. Yang Fangzhi, "Cong Nanjing dao Wuhan" [From Nanjing to Wuhan], *Xinhua Ribao de Huiyi* [Memoir of the New China Daily], Chengdu: Sichuan Renmin Chubanshe, 1983, pp. 154, 476.
63. *Zhongguo Gongchandang Lizi Zhongyao Huiyi Ji*, pp. 211–213. Ma Qilin, "Kangzhan chuqi de Wang Ming," pp. 126–155. The other participants were Mao, Wang Ming, Zhang Guotao, Kang Sheng, Zhou Enlai, and Gai Feng.
64. *Cankao Ziliao*, vol. 7, pp. 120–133. Wang's report was also printed in *Qun Zhong* (The Masses), no. 19 (23 April 1938), pp. 322–332.
65. Xia Honggen, "Wang Ming meiyou zai sanyue zhengzhi huishang zuoguo zongjie" [Wang Ming did not make a summary at the March Politburo conference], *Dangshi Yanjiu* [Research on Party History], no. 3, 1983, p. 81.
66. *Zhonggong Dangshi Dashi Nianbiao* [Chronology of CCP history], Nanjing: Jiangsu Renmin Chubanshe, 1981, pp. 55–56.
67. Ma Qilin, "Kangzhan chuqi de Wang Ming," pp. 138–139.
68. Xia Honggen, "Wang Ming meiyou zai sanyue zhengzhi huishang zuoguo zongjie," p. 81.
69. Peng Dehuai, *Peng Dehuai Zishu*, p. 229.
70. Mao, *Selected Works*, vol. 2, p. 79.
71. Ma Qilin, "Kangzhan chuqi de Wang Ming," p. 143. Wen Dahong, "Wuhan shiqi de 'Xinhua Ribao'" ["New China Daily" during the Wuhan period], in *Xinhua Ribao Huiyi*, p. 476.
72. Mao Zedong, "On Protracted War," in *Selected Works*, vol. 2, pp. 126, 128.
73. "Sanyue zhengzhiju huiyi de zongjie" [Summary of the March Politburo conference], *Qun Zhong*, no. 19 (23 April 1938), pp. 322–332.
74. *Cankao Ziliao*, vol. 8, p. 152.
75. Ma Qilin, "Kangzhan chuqi de Wang Ming," p. 140. Wen Dahong, "Wuhan shiqi de 'Xinhua Ribao,'" p. 475.

76. Tang Manzhen, "Wang Ming wei 'yiqie jingguo tongyi zhanxian' de zuowu fanan shi tulao de," 1983, p. 56. Ma Qilin, "Kangzhan chuqi de Wang Ming," p. 140. Wen Dahong, "Wuhan shiqi de 'Xinhua Ribao,'" p. 476.

77. Ibid.

78. Tang Manzhen, "Wang Ming wei 'yiqie jingguo tongyi zhanxian,'" p. 56.

79. Ma Qilin, "Kanzhan chuqi de Wang Ming," pp. 149–150.

80. Wang Jiaxiang, "Huiyi Mao Zedong tongzhi yu Wang Ming jihui zhuyi luxian de duozheng" [Recollection of comrade Mao Zedong's struggle with Wang Ming's opportunist line], *Renmin Ribao* [People's Daily], 27 December 1979, p. 2. Xu Zehao, "Wang Jiaxiang dui Mao Zedong sixiang de renshi ji qi gongxian" [Wang Jiaxiang's understanding of and contribution to the thoughts of Mao Zedong], *Dangshi Yanjiu* [Research on Party History], no. 1, 1984, p. 41.

81. Wang Jiaxiang, "Huiyi Mao Zedong Tongzhi yu Wang Ming." Shi Zhe, "Chen Tanqiu tongzhi zai Mozeke" [Comrade Chen Tanqiu in Moscow], in *Huiyi Chen Tanqiu* [Remembering Chen Tanqiu], Wuhan: Hubei Shehui Kexueyuan, Huazhong Gongxueyuan, July 1981, p. 125.

82. Gao Jun, *Weida de Zhanshi Ren Bishi* [Great warrior Ren Bishi], Beijing: Qingnian Chubanshe, 1980, p. 100.

83. Ibid.

84. Wang Jiaxiang, "Huiyi Mao Zedong tongzhi yu Wang Ming."

85. Wang Jiaxiang, "Huiyi Mao zhuxi geming luxian yu Wang Ming jihui zhuyi luxian de duozheng" [Recalling the struggle between Chairman Mao's revolutionary line and Wang Ming's opportunist line], *Hongqi Piaopiao* [The Red Flag Waves], no. 18, pp. 47–63.

86. Specifically, the declaration said that the incident had resulted from a Japanese plot to trigger civil war in China. Mao had argued that it resulted from the basically patriotic motives of Zhang Xueliang and Yang Hucheng. Zhang Xuejia, *Di San Guojishi*, pp. 1468–1469. Gao Jun, *Weidi de Zhanshi*, p. 100.

87. *Cankao Ziliao*, vol. 7, pp. 30–31.

88. *See* Gongchan Guoji zhixing weiyuanhui zhuxituan de jueyi" [The resolution of the Presidium of the Executive Committee of the Communist International], in *Cankao Ziliao*, vol. 7, pp. 32–33.

89. "Gongchan Guoji zhixing weiyuanhui zhuxituan zhi shengming" [The declaration of the Presidium of the Executive Committee of the Communist International], in *Cankao Ziliao*, vol. 7, p. 33.

90. All of these three documents are merely dated "September 1938," so it is impossible to determine their exact relationship to each other. Since Wang Jiaxiang addressed the Sixth Plenum shortly after it opened on 29 September, the negotiations in Moscow surrounding these declarations must have taken place in August and early September 1938. Travel between Moscow and Yan'an was not speedy in those days, and Mao certainly would have waited to learn where Moscow stood before convening the Sixth Plenum. Again, this fits with Ren Bishi's arrival in Moscow in April carrying a report on the situation in China for Comintern approval.

91. *Zhonggong Gongchandang Lizi Zhongyao Huiyi Ji*, p. 1.

92. This interpretation of the Sixth Plenum differs sharply from that advanced by Tetsu Kataoka (Kataoka, *Resistance and Revolution*). Kataoka argues that the Sixth Plenum was a "stand-off" between Mao and Wang Ming and that many of the key documents issued by the plenum, including the resolution and Mao's report "On the New Stage," were products of compromises between Wang and Mao. To support this hypothesis, Kataoka argues that, since prior to the plenum one set of arguments represented Wang's line while another set of arguments represented Mao's line, the appearance of both sets of arguments in the same document must, perforce, have been a compromise between Wang and Mao. While this was a plausible explanation, it is contradicted by Wang Jiaxiang's and Gao Jun's memoirs—both of which were published after Kataoka's excellent and pathbreaking work.

93. Wang Jiaxiang. "Huiyi Mao Zedong tongzhi yu Wang Ming."

94. *Zhongguo Gongchandang Lizi Zhongyao Huiyi Ji*, p. 214. Ma Qilin, "Kangzhan chuqi de Wang Ming," p. 144.

95. "The Role of the Chinese Communist Party in the National War," October in *Selected Works*, vol. 2, pp. 195–212; "The Question of Independence and Initiative within the United Front," 5 November, ibid., pp. 213–217; "Problems of War and Strategy," 6 November, ibid., pp. 219–235. *See also* "Lun Xin Jieduan" [On the new stage], in *Cankao Ziliao*, vol. 7, pp. 200–209. The resolution of the plenum is in *Cankao Ziliao*, vol. 7, pp. 172–177.

96. This conclusion is contrary to the orthodox CCP interpretation of this plenum. The discussion of the Sixth Plenum in *Zhongguo Gongchandang Lizi Zhongyao Huiyi Ji*, for instance, says that Mao "especially explained the position and responsibility of the CCP in the national revolutionary war, stressing the Party's leadership position in the war of resistance to Japan" (p. 215). The annotation of Mao's 6 November 1938 speech to the plenum on "Problems of War and Strategy" in his *Selected Works*, to cite one more example, asserts that "in his 'Problems of Strategy in the Guerrilla War

against Japan' and 'On Protracted War' [both of May 1938] Comrade Mao Tse-tung had already settled the question of the Party's leading role in the War of Resistance against Japan" (*Selected Works*, vol. 2, p. 219). This author's reading of the available documents, including the original versions of those annotated in *Selected Works*, does not support such a conclusion. Indeed, one of the striking aspects of Mao's speeches and reports of 1938, including both those of May and those to the Sixth Plenum, was the absence of explicit discussions of leadership of the national united front. What little comment there was of such leadership in Mao's original speeches seemed to indicate formal approval of the dominant position of the KMT within the united front. It is possible to argue that the *practical consequences* of Mao's line of expansion of base areas and guerrilla armies laid the basis for eventual CCP leadership of the united front. This author would not dispute such an assertion, but a statement of this sort is very different from one saying that at the Sixth Plenum Mao advanced the idea of CCP leadership of the united front. The original versions of Mao's writings, along with subsequent alterations, are in *Mao Zedong Ji* [Collected Works of Mao Zedong], Tokyo: Sososha Company, 1971.

97. Mao, *Selected Works*, vol. 2, pp. 197–198.
98. Ibid., p. 213.
99. Mao Zedong, "Question of Independence and Initiative Within the United Front," ibid., p. 216.
100. Cited in Xu Zehao, "Wang Jiaxiang dui Mao Zedong sixiang de renshi," p. 41.
101. "Role of the Chinese Communist Party," in Mao, *Selected Works*, vol. 2, p. 197.
102. Raymond F. Wylie, *The Emergence of Maoism, Mao Tse-tung, Ch'en Po-ta, and the Search for Chinese Theory*, Stanford, Calif.: Stanford University Press, 1980, pp. 49, 57, 91–92, 97.
103. John Boyle, *China and Japan at War, the Politics of Collaboration*, Stanford, Calif.: Stanford University Press, 1972.
104. Wu Yuzhang, "Wu Yuzhang Zizhuan" [Autobiography of Wu Yuzhang], *Lishi Yanjiu* [Historical Research], no. 4, 1981, pp. 22.
105. For example, a December 1937 protest by Yang Jie regarding reported diversions of Soviet arms to CCP forces in northern China (*Zhanshi Waijiao*, p. 505–506).
106. Regarding the anticommunist measures of the Fifth Plenum, *see* Tang Manzhen, "Zhongguo Gongchandang shi ruhe datui di yi ci fangong gaochao de" [How it was that the CCP beat back the first anticommunist high tide], *Jiaoxue yu Yanjiu* [Teaching and Research], no. 3, 1981, p. 220. *See also* Pan Guohua and Lin Dazhao, "Kang Ri zhanzheng shiqi Zhongguo Gongchandang zai sixiang lilun zhanxian shang dui Guomindang wangupai de duozheng" [The ideological struggle of the CCP against the Kuomintang die hards during the war of resistance), *Lishi Jiaoxue* [Teaching History], 1982, pp. 3, 10. Kataoka, *Resistance and Revolution*, p. 153. Annotation in Mao, *Selected Works*, vol. 2, p. 255. Robert C. North, *Kuomintang and Chinese Communist Elites*, Hoover Institute series B, Elite Studies no. 8, Stanford, Calif.: Hoover Institute Press, July 1952, p. 17.
107. Aleksandr Ya. Kalyagin, *Along Alien Roads*, New York: Columbia University East Asia Institute Press, 1984, p. 206. It would be totally inappropriate to cite a source such as this to document this point were it not for the mystery surrounding Chiang's 26 January 1939 speech. Other sources also mention a speech by Chiang on 26 January. Liu Shaotang, for example, says that Chiang's 26 January speech dealt with the relationship between foreign and domestic policy (Liu Shao-tang, *Minguo Dashi Rizi* [Chronicle of major events of the republic], vol. 1, Taibei: Zhuanji Wenxue Chubanshe, 1978, p. 598). Such a speech was not included, however, in the half-dozen or so compendium of Chiang's speeches and writings printed either prior to or after 1949. Indeed, none of Chiang's speeches to the Fifth Plenum published in those volumes even mention China's relations with the Soviet Union. This in itself is suspicious. It is virtually inconceivable that Chiang would not have addressed the question of the impact of this new domestic orientation on relations with the Soviet Union, China's major foreign supporter at that point. Moreover, a report on foreign policy by Chiang was a standard event for such important meetings. Yet no such speech to the Fifth Plenum is included in the published compendium of Chiang's speeches and writings. Moreover, in a speech several months later on 18 November 1939, Chiang Kai-shek stated that at the Fifth Plenum he had said that China's war aim was the restoration of the pre-7 July 1937 status quo. (*Jiang Zongtong Sixiang Yanlun Ji (Yanjiang)* [Collected speeches and essays of President Chiang (Speeches)], vol. 15, Taibei, p. 218). Again, this issue was not mentioned in any of the published speeches of Chiang to the Fifth Plenum. This again suggests that at least one of Chiang's critical speeches to the Fifth Plenum remains unpublished. To complicate the matter further, the speech dated 26 January 1939 in two English-language translations of Chiang's speeches are, in fact, the same speech which is dated 21 January in the Chinese-language editions of Chiang's speeches. *See* "China Cannot Be Conquered," in *Resistance and Reconstruction; Messages during China's Six Years of War, 1937–1943*, New York: Harper and Row, 1943, pp. 70–83. The same speech in *The Collected Wartime Messages of Generalissimo Chiang Kai-shek, 1937–1945*, compiled by the Chinese Ministry of

Information, (New York: John Day Company, 1943, pp. 158–173), is also dated 26 January 1939. While this could have been an accident, it could also have been, and in this author's opinion was, a deliberate attempt to cover up Chiang's original 26 January speech, which was later deemed too sensitive. Chiang's published speeches to the Fifth Plenum include: "Kai mu zi" [Opening words], in *Dongfang Zazhi* [Oriental Miscellany], 16 February 1939, pp. 53–61; "Yi shishi zhengming diguo bi bai ji woguo bi sheng" [Using facts to prove that the enemy will inevitably be defeated and our country will triumph], January 1939, in *Jiang Zongtong Sixiang Yanlun Ji (Yan Jiang)*, vol. 15, Taibei, pp. 17–32.

108. Ding Yongnian, "Guanyu di yi ci fangong gaochao de yi xie shishi" [Several facts regarding the first anticommunist high tide], *Dangshi Yanjiu Ziliao* [Research Materials on Party History], no. 12 (20 June 1980), p. 22.

109. Tang Manzhen, "Zhongguo Gongchandang shi ruhe datui di yi ci fangong gaochao de," pp. 220–221.

110. Ibid. *See also Zhonggong Dangshi Dashi Nianbiao* [Chronology of major events in CCP history], Beijing: Renmin Chubanshe, 1981, p. 60.

111. *See* Sai Guoyu, "Kangzhan shiqi Guo Gong jian de junshi shangtan" [Military talks between the KMT and CCP during the war of resistance], *Gongdang Wenti Yanjiu* [Research on the CCP Problem], vol. 9, no. 7 [15 July 1983], Taibei, pp. 48–64. In his letter of 7 June, a "statement of opinion," Zhou called for the National Government to respect the originally designated eighteen-county Shaan-Gan-Ning border district, to recognize an additional five-county defense zone in eastern Shaanxi, to grant the Eighth Route Army the right to establish liaison offices, hospitals, and depots throughout Ningxia, Gansu, and Shaanxi provinces, and to accept the expansion of the Eighth Route Army to three corps. In his talk with reporters on 16 September 1939, Mao said that Zhou wrote to Chiang "as early as July" (*Selected Works*, vol. 2, p. 271). Presumably the letter Mao was referring to was the same as the one discussed here. I have chosen the more precise date which accompanies the full text of the letter released in the Taiwan source.

112. "Oppose Capitulationist Activity," 30 June 1939, in Mao, *Selected Works*, vol. 2, pp. 251–255.

113. The 7 July 1939 CCP manifesto is reprinted in *Zhongguo Waijiao Ziliao (1937–1945)* [Selection of materials on China's diplomatic history, vol. 3 (1937–1945)], Beijing: Waijiao Xueyuan, 1958, p. 34. The evil actions of domestic splitters and capitulationists were said to be in league with the activities of those international reactionaries who were trying to carry out a "Far Eastern Munich" to sacrifice China and appease Japan through a Sino-Japanese peace settlement.

114. *See* "The Reactionaries Must Be Punished," Mao, *Selected Works*, vol. 2, pp. 257–261.

115. *See Selected Works*, vol. 2, p. 272.

116. *Zhonggong Dangshi Dashi Nianbiao*, p. 59.

117. *Zhanshi Waijiao*, p. 423.

118. "Oppose Capitulationist Activity," in Mao, *Selected Works*, vol. 2, p. 253.

Chapter IV

China and Soviet-Axis Alignment

The Divergence of Global Alignments

The Soviet alignment with Nazi Germany initiated by the Nonaggression Pact of 23 August 1939 destroyed the parallelism between Soviet and Chinese policies which had characterized the first two years of the war. As long as the Soviet Union hoped for collective security cooperation with the Western democracies, Chinese and Soviet policies were generally parallel. But once the Soviet Union aligned with Nazi Germany, Soviet and Chinese ways parted. Moscow now sought cooperation with the incipient Axis bloc while Chongqing increasingly aligned with the Anglo-American camp. By mid-1940, Chiang and Stalin found themselves on opposite sides of the global camps rushing toward world war.

It was the Soviet position more than the Chinese which changed during 1939–1941, and an evaluation of Sino-Soviet relations during this period must begin with an understanding of the extent of Soviet-German cooperation. Moscow's adverse reaction to China's growing security relations with the West during this period can be understood only against the background of close Soviet cooperation first with Germany and then with Berlin's partner, Japan. Soviet-Nazi cooperation during this period was quite close, at least until the end of 1940.

Soviet-Nazi cooperation was manifested in numerous ways. Soviet diplomacy and propaganda assisted Hitler's peace initiatives during this period of "phony war" in the West. Soviet exports of strategic ores, petroleum, and cotton to Germany expanded rapidly. Not only were Soviet goods supplied, but Soviet railways carried goods from the entire Pacific littoral through Siberia to Germany. Such Soviet assistance substantially diminished the significance of British denial of the Atlantic Ocean and Mediterranean Sea to German commerce.[1] There was also repeated and important military cooperation between Moscow and Berlin. Such military cooperation occurred during Germany's invasion of Poland and again during the Soviet Union's attack on Finland, but by far the most important instance was during Germany's offensive in France during May–June 1940.[2] Because of the Soviet Union's friendly, nonthreatening attitude toward Germany, Hitler was able to concentrate his forces in the West for that offensive, leaving only five to eight divisions in the East. As Molotov reminded Hitler during their discussions in Berlin on 13 November 1940, this was an important factor underlying the German success in France.[3] While Soviet-German relations grew quite cordial, Soviet-British and Soviet-American relations deteriorated right up to 22 June 1941.[4]

Moscow's realignment was a devastating blow to Chiang's diplomacy, which had sought to catalyze a Soviet-Western-Chinese front. Chiang would still continue these efforts, but they became increasingly forlorn. To a significant degree, between September 1939 and June 1941 Chiang had to decide whether to improve relations with and seek the support of *either* the United States *or* the Soviet Union. Chiang attempted to finesse the contradiction between his retention of Soviet support and his efforts to secure greater American support. He desired desperately to maintain good relations with both Moscow and Washington and to persuade Moscow to support the growing sanctions by the United States against Japan. He also attempted to reassure Moscow that China's expanding ties to the United States, and China's political alignment with the Western Camp, did not constitute a threat to the Soviet Union. These efforts had only limited success, however, and Sino-Soviet relations steadily deteriorated.

A second component of the international upheaval of September 1939 was the beginning of the war between Britain, France, and Germany on the first of that month. This too was a harsh blow to Chiang's diplomacy, which, as we have seen, had sought peace in Europe in order to encourage the powers to adopt a more active policy in the Far East. Chiang tried to recoup these losses by aligning China with the Anglo-French camp. Coming at a time when the Soviet Union was moving closer to Germany, however, this created major tensions in Republic of China–Soviet Union relations.

A few days after the beginning of the European war, China's ambassador to France, Wellington Koo, proposed to Chongqing that China formally declare its alignment with France and Britain and offer Chinese manpower and raw materials to the Allied war effort. Koo believed that such a declaration would help prevent France and Britain from aligning with Japan. The Soviet-German treaty had been a major blow to Japanese-German cooperation. Japan might now attempt to improve its ties with Britain and France to offset Germany's defection. There was a danger, Koo felt, that London and Paris might respond to such a Japanese bid in order to drive a wedge between Tokyo and Berlin. But if China formally affiliated with the Allies it would be more difficult for Japanese efforts to cut off British and French support for China to succeed. Koo realized that a Chinese declaration of affiliation with the Allies would have to be worded carefully so as not to offend the Soviet Union, but he believed that this difficulty could be overcome.[5]

Chongqing replied favorably to Koo's plan, and directed him and Ambassador Guo Taiqi in London to inquire into the attitudes of the French and British governments toward such a plan. As it turned out, Paris was not enthusiastic about the plan, fearing that Chinese affiliation with the Allies might push Japan back into alignment with Germany. London was not opposed to Chinese affiliation but doubted if China would be able to provide much real help. Ultimately it was Soviet opposition, however, which killed projected Chinese affiliation with the Allies. As Koo pointed out in his memoir, his plan was conceived and initiated prior to the Soviet invasion of eastern Poland on 17 September. Chinese affiliation with the Allies was based, in other words, on an assumption of continuing Soviet nonparticipation in the war. But once it became clear that the Soviet Union would be an active partner of Germany, and not merely neutral, Chongqing had to be much more circumspect about aligning with Paris and London.[6]

Immediately after the outbreak of the European conflict, Chiang Kai-shek tried to gauge the direction of Soviet policy in Europe. On 4 September he cabled Sun Ke, directing him to inquire as to the Soviet attitude toward the European conflict. A week later he again cabled Sun instructing him to solicit Soviet views regarding *China's* attitude toward the war. China was considering its orientation toward the European conflict, Chiang told Sun. The general tendency in China was to sympathize with Poland as a victim of aggression and to uphold the League of Nations. But before reaching a final decision, Chiang would like to know Stalin's views on the matter of China's response to the war.[7]

Sun replied to Chiang on 13 September. Neutrality in the European conflict would be the best policy for China, Sun told Chiang.[8] On 18 September (the day after the Red Army invaded eastern Poland) Sun provided further elaboration. In spite of Moscow's professed policy of neutrality in the European war, Sun told Chiang, its invasion of Poland amounted to helping Germany.[9] In other words, Moscow and the Anglo-French powers were aligned on opposite sides of the European conflict.

Stalin's objections effectively killed the plan to align China with the Anglo-French camp in September 1939. The Chinese Foreign Ministry explained the reasons for dropping the scheme in a cable to Koo on 27 October. Chinese affiliation with the Allied power was "unnecessary" for several reasons, the cable explained. The first three reasons cited had to do with the Soviet intention to remain neutral and not to ally with either side in the European conflict. The fourth factor cited was Moscow's assurances that Soviet aid and support to China would continue "as heretofore." Moscow had given assurances that talk of the Soviet Union joining with other powers to present some sort of set of demands on China was "vicious propaganda without any basis in fact." The last three points made by the Foreign Ministry had to do with Chongqing's ties with Britain and France, the central idea being that China would pledge to remain neutral in the event of Soviet entry into the war on Germany's side in exchange for continuing British and French support of China against Japan. This was a sly ploy: having decided to stay out of the European war because of Soviet objections, Chiang was attempting to get what he could from Paris and London for remaining noninvolved. But at bottom, as Koo attested in his memoir, "the suggested declaration was vetoed for fear of causing unpleasantness in Russia."[10]

While trying to secure Soviet endorsement of China's participation in the Anglo-French camp, Chiang also tried to persuade Moscow to continue to cooperate with the Western democracies in the Far East. Even though the Western democracies and the Soviet Union took different positions vis-à-vis Nazi Germany, it still might be possible for them to cooperate against Japan. If so, this would eliminate the potential conflict between China's links to Moscow and its links to the Western democracies. It would also counter the tendency of Paris and London to appease Japan. What Chiang sought was effective, even if strained, Soviet-Allied (Allied referring here to the incipient Anglo-French-American bloc) neutrality in Europe, but active Soviet-Allied-Chinese cooperation in the Far East. Such a strategy made sense from Chongqing's point of view; it would allow Moscow to concentrate its energies on the solution of the Far Eastern question while limiting British and French tendencies to appease Japan. It would also lay the basis for Soviet-American cooperation against Japan.

In cables to Chiang on 25 and 26 August, Koo laid out the aspects of the new international system which might facilitate such a plan. The fact that the Soviet Union was not involved in the European conflict which was engaging the energies of the other European powers, might itself encourage Moscow to adopt a more forceful policy toward Japan. The conclusion of the German-Soviet pact had also eased Moscow's two-front concerns by destroying the strategic basis of the German-Japanese partnership. This too might embolden the Soviet Union to confront Japan. China should take advantage of Japan's isolation, Koo told Chiang, by approaching Moscow about the possibility of undertaking "positive military cooperation" against Japan in conjunction with the United States. If Moscow could be persuaded to increase its forces along the Manchurian border, and if the United States could be persuaded to send its fleet to the western Pacific, then Tokyo would understand that it faced the combined strength of the Soviet Union, the United States, and China.[11]

Chiang endorsed Koo's proposal in two cables on 29 August, that is, after the conclusion of the Soviet-German pact but before the outbreak of the European conflict. Chiang ordered Koo to urge the French and British governments to cooperate with the Soviet Union in the Far East. The key to the situation, however, was in American hands. If Roosevelt could be persuaded to urge Soviet, British, and French cooperation in the Pacific, Chiang said, Moscow would respond positively.[12] A short while afterward Chiang directed Sun Ke to urge the Soviet Union to cooperate with the United States, Britain, and France in the Far East.[13]

Early in September, Koo put this plan for Allied-Soviet cooperation in the Far East into action during meetings with the American and Soviet ambassadors in Paris. Soviet Ambassador Souritz was not encouraging: the Soviet Union had not concluded the Nonaggression Pact with Germany in order to concentrate on Far Eastern affairs, but because of a lack of sincerity from Paris and London. Nor did the Soviet Union think that developments in Europe made possible a more active posture in Asia. Moreover, the Soviet Union did not trust the motives of London and Paris.[14] In Moscow, meanwhile, Soviet officials were telling Sun Ke that no "practical basis" existed for cooperation between the Soviet Union and the United States, Britain, or France in the Far East. American attitudes were insincere, and Washington secretly harbored a desire to see a Soviet-Japanese war. China would do best "not to listen too much" to Washington, London, and Paris.[15]

On 17 September 1939, Sun Ke cabled Chiang from Moscow saying that since Moscow suspected that the British and Americans wanted to incite a Soviet-Japanese war in order to ease pressure on themselves, it would be extremely difficult to bring about cooperation between the Soviet Union and the Anglo-American powers. Before Moscow would be willing to cooperate with London and Washington, Sun reported, it would be necessary for the Anglo-American powers to move actively to check Japan. Otherwise the Soviet Union would be suspicious of closer relations between China and the United States and Britain, and would suspect China of doing the bidding of the United States.[16] The next day Chiang received a message from Stalin (via Sun and foreign trade commissar A. Mikoyan). He was happy to hear that the United States was giving China real assistance, Stalin said. But in spite of Washington's July 1939 cancellation of its 1911 Commercial Treaty with Japan, the United States was still supplying Japan with essential military matériel. "Under such circumstances," Stalin said, "there is no need for Soviet unity with the United States in the Far East."[17] In short, Soviet cooperation with the Western democracies was out of the question.

While rejecting Chongqing's plea for Soviet-Western cooperation against Japan,

Moscow did not oppose Anglo-American support of China's war effort. Shortly after the conclusion of the Nazi-Soviet Nonaggression Treaty, Yang Jie reported to Chiang Kai-shek on recent talks with the Soviet vice-commissar for foreign affairs. The Soviet Union still viewed Japan's New East Asian Order as equivalent to the annexation of China and as a threat to the Soviet Union. Consequently, Moscow still hoped that China would achieve liberation and that China would maintain "necessary relations" with Great Britain in order to secure support from it. "The Soviet Union has never urged China to abandon a policy of uniting with England," Yang reported the Soviet vice-commissar as saying.[18] Of course, expanded Anglo-American aid for China at a time when Soviet aid to China was declining would facilitate Soviet-Japanese rapprochement and Japanese-American confrontation.

Chiang was skeptical—and became increasingly so during 1940—of Moscow's pledges of continued support for China and of its endorsement of China's deepening links to the United States. Chiang felt that such Soviet assurances were subterfuges designed to minimize China's adverse reaction to Moscow's alignment with Japan. When Chiang met with Soviet Ambassador Aleksandr S. Paniushkin on 8 November 1939, he countered Paniushkin's condemnation of Britain and France for protracting the war in Europe (this was in line with Hitler's campaign for "immediate peace" at that time) with a plea for joint Soviet-American efforts to settle the Far Eastern problem. China and the Soviet Union should continue the policy they had previously agreed on—that is, encouraging the United States to step forward and solve the Far Eastern question together with the Soviet Union. The United States was now becoming increasingly active in the Far East, Chiang said, pointing to Washington's cancellation of the 1911 treaty. This was precisely what China and the Soviet Union had long predicted and sought, Chiang said. Now was the time for the Soviet Union to step forward and cooperate with the United States. If, however, the Soviet Union showed itself willing to appease Japan, the United States would change its policy and retreat before Japan.[19] When Paniushkin assured Chiang that Soviet policy toward China absolutely would not change, Chiang pushed him to clarify reports that the Soviet Union, Japan, and Germany were preparing to partition China. Paniushkin dismissed these reports as rumors. When Chiang asked about the possibility of harmonious relations between Japan and the Soviet Union, the Soviet ambassador replied that there were no obstacles blocking expanded commercial relations.[20]

Chiang then advanced what was to become his major argument to the Soviet Union against Soviet-Japanese rapprochement. Efforts at such rapprochement would backfire, Chiang warned, and lead to a Japanese-American alignment against the Soviet Union. If the Soviet Union opened commercial relations with Japan, Chiang argued, this would be a "major blow" against the United States, rendering ineffective American economic sanctions against Japan. If Japan could simply turn to the Soviet Union to purchase raw materials and other goods, the United States would not adopt economic sanctions against Japan since to do so would merely force Japan and the Soviet Union together. The effectiveness of an American economic blockade of Japan, the "only weapon that the U.S. could currently use to solve the Far Eastern problem," thus "completely depends," Chiang said, on the attitude of the Soviet Union.[21]

Chiang elaborated on these arguments in a letter to Stalin on 1 December. (The delivery of this letter would be delayed until April by the Soviet-Finnish Winter War.)

After expressing gratitude for the fact that Soviet aid to China had not decreased since the outbreak of the European war, Chiang noted that the United States was becoming increasingly active in the Far East. Thus, opportunities were beginning to ripen for the success of the "traditional" Soviet policy of uniting with other Pacific rim powers to check Japan. Unity of the Soviet Union, the United States, and Britain was the most important condition for the solution of the Far Eastern problem, Chiang told Stalin. While differences might exist among the Soviet Union, Britain, and the United States in Europe, the interests of these countries in the Far East were identical. Britain and the United States deeply hoped to unite with the Soviet Union in dealing with Japan, Chiang assured Stalin.[22]

There were two probable paths of development for the Far East, Chiang told Stalin. One was for the Soviet Union, the United States, and Britain to unite, "beginning with the Soviet Union." This bloc would then coordinate its activities with China's war of resistance and form a powerful anti-Japanese front. The second possible path of development was toward the formation of an Anglo-American-Japanese anti-communist camp. The creation of such a camp was the objective underlying Japan's move to improve relations with the Soviet Union, Chiang argued. Tokyo would use its rapprochement with Moscow to pressure London and Washington into accepting Japan's New East Asian Order. Then after solving the China problem with Anglo-American help, Tokyo would turn all its strength against the Soviet Union. Japan's rapprochement with the Soviet Union was devoid of sincerity, Chiang warned. Both of the two main factions in Japan were anti-Soviet. "That Japan and the Soviet Union are enemies, this sort of ideology is deeply embedded in the psychology of all levels of Japanese society," Chiang continued. Moscow should also not expect to cause a deterioration of Japanese-American relations by executing a rapprochement with Japan. For each step Moscow took in improving relations with Japan, Washington and London would take two steps. Japan could appease Britain and the United States by guaranteeing their interests within its New Order, whereas Tokyo could never accommodate such "revolutionary countries" as China and the Soviet Union. In short, the ultimate result of Soviet effort at rapprochement with Japan would be a Japanese-American alignment against the Soviet Union.[23]

Chiang's efforts failed, of course. It is ironic that what in fact materialized was almost the exact opposite of what Chiang sought. Instead of Soviet neutrality in the European war and joint Soviet-Western efforts in the Far East, what developed was Soviet noninvolvement in the Far Eastern war and joint efforts in Europe.

Soviet-Japanese Rapprochement

The parallelism in Chinese and Soviet policies toward Japan which had underlain Sino-Soviet cooperation from July 1937 to August 1939 also began to disappear in September 1939. A gradual improvement in Soviet-Japanese relations began in September 1939 and continued through the spring of 1941. This process of Soviet-Japanese rapprochement further sharpened the contradictions between Soviet and Chinese international orientations.

Changes in Japanese attitudes due to the Soviet-German Nonaggression Treaty and to the catastrophic defeat of Japanese forces at Nomonhan were largely responsible for this Soviet-Japanese rapprochement. But the Soviet Union welcomed and responded to Japan's overtures. The Soviet view was expressed by Stalin when replying to a question by von Ribbentrop in August 1939 about the future of Soviet-Japanese relations. If Japan wanted peace the Soviet Union was willing, Stalin said. If Japan wanted war, the Soviet Union was also willing.[24] Since 1936, Japan's strategy in dealing with the Soviet Union had centered on constraining Moscow by presenting it with a two-front threat through Tokyo's link to Berlin. As late as 3 August 1939, the Japanese General Staff had decided to conclude promptly a military alliance with Germany and Italy, largely for the sake of making the Soviet Union more amenable.[25] Stalin had deftly demolished this strategy by his Nonaggression Pact with Hitler while dealing a shattering military defeat to Japan's best army. Tokyo now began searching for an accommodation with Moscow.[26]

The Soviet government welcomed Japan's new orientation. Shortly after a cease-fire on 15 September 1939 defused the Nomonhan conflict, bilateral conferences were set up to discuss other outstanding issues such as Japanese mining concessions on northern Sakhalin Island, trade, and Japanese fishing rights off Siberia.[27] Both Moscow and Tokyo hoped to formalize their new cordiality with a treaty. From September 1939 to April 1941, Moscow and Tokyo maneuvered and debated the pros and cons of a nonaggression agreement as opposed to a mere neutrality agreement. As the Sino-Soviet treaty of 1937 and the German-Soviet treaty of 1939 had demonstrated, a nonaggression treaty in those days implied fairly intimate cooperation on a wide range of political, economic, and military issues. A neutrality agreement, on the other hand, meant a much looser tie. In effect, a neutrality agreement bound each side *not* to join the enemies of the other, whereas a nonaggression treaty meant active cooperation in the defeat of common enemies.

Between the fall of 1939 and the summer of 1940, the Soviet government favored a nonaggression treaty with Japan. Moscow pushed for a closer "nonaggression" relationship, arguing that a mere neutrality agreement would complicate Soviet relations with China and with the United States while not guaranteeing the borders of Soviet Siberia against Japanese attack. Tokyo, however, placed priority on preventing a further deterioration of relations with the United States and Britain, and was skeptical of too close ties with Moscow. Tokyo therefore preferred a looser neutrality agreement. In mid-1940, however, Moscow and Tokyo switched positions. With the dramatic collapse of France in June and Japan's accelerating preparations to move into the power vacuum newly created in Southeast Asia, Moscow became ready to accept a "mere" neutrality agreement, but only if Tokyo was willing to pay for it by liquidating its concessions on northern Sakhalin. Japan's ambassador to Moscow favored acceptance of Moscow's demands, but wanted in turn, to link the northern Sakhalin issue to the termination of Soviet aid to Chiang Kai-shek. Throughout the Japanese-Soviet talks of 1939–1941, Soviet aid to China was a major topic of discussion.[28]

Chiang Kai-shek was extremely concerned that Soviet alignment with Germany would lead to improved Soviet-Japanese relations and to a consequent reduction of Soviet assistance to China. During September, both Yang Jie and Sun Ke reported to Chiang that Moscow hoped for better relations with Japan.[29] If Japan abandoned its provocative policy toward the Soviet Union, Sun reported on 17 September, the Soviet

Union would be willing merely to "defend its own borders" and cease fighting with Japan. Moscow did not want war with Japan and was afraid that its aid to China might touch off just such a war. Future Soviet aid to China would therefore be limited to equipment and technology, and it would be hopeless for China to seek Soviet entry into the war against Japan.[30]

But Chiang's fears of Soviet intentions were not limited to decreased probabilities of a Soviet-Japanese war and cuts in Soviet aid to China. Rather, old fears of a possible Russian-Japanese division of China were revived. In September 1939, Chiang received intelligence reports of a plan reportedly given to Wang Jingwei's pro-Japanese group by Japanese military headquarters and proposing a partition of China into Soviet and Japanese spheres of influence. Xinjiang, Outer Mongolia, Tibet, and China's northwest were to be a part of the Soviet sphere.[31] Chiang also received reports from China's embassies in Washington and London of newspaper accounts that Soviet-Japanese discussions of a nonaggression treaty were already under way. Such reports sometimes asserted that mutual Japanese-Soviet recognition of spheres of influence in China was to be one component of this treaty.[32]

Chongqing naturally attempted to thwart the budding Soviet-Japanese rapprochement. On 5 September, Zhang Chong proposed to Chiang that he cable Yang Jie and Sun Ke directing them to urge Moscow not to sign a nonaggression treaty with Japan on the grounds that to do so would create an unfavorable response among the Chinese people, and would violate both the Sino-Soviet Treaty of 1937 and the spirit of the various League of Nations resolutions regarding China.[33] These arguments were certainly valid, but when juxtaposed to the realpolitik mood of Moscow, as reported by Yang Jie's and Sun Ke's cables, the futility of advancing such legal arguments was clear.

Chiang's representatives in Moscow inquired repeatedly about reports that Moscow and Tokyo might strike a deal. Moscow's response to these queries was less than entirely truthful. On 2 September, Yang Jie reported that Molotov had told him that he had no reports of Germany encouraging Japan to sign a nonaggression treaty with Moscow.[34] Later in September Yang reported that the Soviet vice-foreign minister had told him that Japan had still not mentioned a nonaggression treaty to Soviet officials, and dismissed press reports to the contrary as false and as provocations.[35] Then on 18 September Sun reported that Stalin had said (via Foreign Trade Commissar Mikoyan) that Japan had not proposed a nonaggression treaty to the Soviet Union, and that reports to the contrary were inaccurate. Moreover, there were no political conditions attached to the Nomonhan cease-fire agreement. Soviet support for China would continue to be demonstrated by facts, and China should not doubt or be mistaken about this.[36] Soviet remarks about Japan not proposing a nonaggression treaty were technically correct. It was not Japan, but the Soviet Union itself which was then proposing such a treaty!

Chiang attempted to check Moscow's drift toward Tokyo by reviving his earlier offer of a Sino-Soviet alliance against Japan. Unlike his 1937–1938 proposals, however, his 1939–1940 offers were sweetened with hints of postwar bases and special privileges for the Soviet Union in China. On 19 December 1939, Chiang approved a very significant change in the wording of a letter he had sent to his personal emissary He Yaozu on 1 December for delivery to Stalin. At He Yaozu's suggestion, Chiang changed a general call for close diplomatic cooperation between the Soviet Union and the Republic of China to a call for Soviet entry into the war against Japan in exchange for Soviet bases in postwar China.[37] We shall return to this question later.

Chiang hoped that the greater security of the Soviet Union's European borders after the conclusion of the Soviet-German Nonaggression Pact and the outbreak of the European war would make Moscow willing to strike at Japan. There was, however, another utilitarian aspect to Chiang's proposal of Sino-Soviet alliance, one which did not hinge on an expectation of Soviet willingness to go to war with Japan—which both Yang and Sun had indicated was unlikely. If Chiang's proposal of 19 December became known to Japan's intelligence service, it would increase Japanese suspicion of Moscow. It would also make Tokyo more willing to compromise with Chiang in secret negotiations then underway between Chiang and Japanese intermediaries in Hong Kong.

In Soviet eyes, such proposals of Sino-Soviet alliance against Japan were tantamount to Chinese provocations. In his memoir, General Vasilii Chuikov, who became the Soviet military attaché to China in late 1940, recounts such Chinese efforts at "provocation." Madame Chiang repeatedly told him that Soviet entry into the war against Japan would be the greatest Soviet assistance to China, and frequently passed on to him false information designed to damage Soviet-Japanese relations. Such attempts to provoke a Soviet-Japanese war were, in Chuikov's view, one of Chiang Kai-shek's "main duties."[38]

Chinese spokesmen also attempted to limit Soviet-Japanese rapprochement by waxing effusive about Japan's military threat to the Soviet Union and by stressing the historic Soviet-Chinese unity against Japan. At a ceremony held at the Soviet embassy in Chongqing on 23 February 1940 commemorating the 1918 founding of the Red Army, for instance, Zhang Chong praised the strength, discipline, and ideals of the Red Army. The Red Army and China's National Revolutionary Army were brother armies formed in the same mold and joint fighters against aggression.[39] In November of 1940, Foreign Minister Wang Chonghui marked the twenty-third anniversary of the Bolshevik insurrection with a contribution to the magazine Zhong Su Wenhua (Sino-Soviet Culture). At a time when Soviet-German relations were most intimate and just as Moscow's rapprochement with Japan was shifting into high gear, Wang argued that Japan was the common enemy of China and the Soviet Union. Since the 1917 revolution, Wang said, the Soviet Union had cooperated with and supported the Chinese revolution, while Japan had opposed and threatened both the Chinese revolution and the Soviet Union. Japan planned to conquer China and then use its manpower and resources to conquer the world, beginning with the Soviet Union. The Soviet Union was the primary hypothetical enemy of the "big war" being prepared by Japanese imperialism, Wang asserted. In light of this, the only way to check Japan was to strengthen relations between the Soviet Union and China. Wang also reminded his readers that Japan had repeatedly demanded that China sign an anti-Soviet agreement and that China continually refused.[40]

Chongqing's efforts to thwart Soviet-Japanese rapprochement were to no avail. China was simply too weak to offset the advantages Moscow saw in making a deal with Tokyo. In spite of Chongqing's pleas, arguments, inducements, pledges, and threats, Moscow continued step by step to improve its relations with Japan. It was ironic that just as Moscow was becoming less hostile toward Japan, Washington was at last beginning to increase its military preparations in the Pacific region and to consider actions to check Japanese aggression, terminating its 1911 Commercial Treaty with Japan and then instituting a system of embargo cum licensing in July 1940.[41] Chongqing welcomed the new American course and, as we have seen, urged Moscow to return to its previous policy of "antiaggressor" cooperation in the Far East with the United States and Britain. It also tried to reassure Moscow that the deepening American involvement in China would not threaten the Soviet Union or be deleterious to Soviet interests in China. Unfortunately for Chongqing, developments showed that growing alignment of the Republic of China with the West conflicted in very immediate ways with its link to the Soviet Union.

China and the Russo-Finnish Winter War

While Chongqing had been able to avoid a conflict with Moscow in September 1939 by shelving the plan to associate with the Anglo-French Allies, and the emergence of Soviet-Japanese rapprochement created new strains in Sino-Soviet relations, it was the Russo-Finnish Winter War which brought into focus the new contradiction between Chongqing's and Moscow's global orientations and forced Chongqing to choose between the Soviet Union and the Western democracies. China in effect chose the latter, and by the spring of 1940 it was apparent that China and the Soviet Union were aligned on opposite sides of the global polarization then taking shape.

The Winter War began with a Soviet attack on Finland on 29 November 1939 and ended with a peace agreement signed on 12 March 1940. As noted earlier, Berlin supported Soviet efforts during the Winter War, and a German warning to Norway was instrumental in persuading Oslo not to permit Western aid for Finland to transit Norwegian territory. Western public opinion, on the other hand, was strongly pro-Finnish. Moreover, in the view of the British and French governments, the Soviet attack on Finland was tantamount to Soviet entry into the European conflict on Germany's side. The British and French governments therefore sent substantial amounts of munitions and even considered sending troops to assist Finland.

From Chongqing's perspective it would have been best if it could have ignored the Winter War which was, after all, far away and of little direct consequence to China. When the issue of the Winter War was brought before the League of Nations in Geneva, however, Chongqing found itself in a quandary. On the one hand, China was trying to rally popular support for China's own cause in the United States and Britain by appeals to international law and morality. China was trying to portray itself as a weak victim of aggression by a rapacious imperialist power, and trying to cultivate a sense of moral outrage in the West at the spectacle of "lawless" aggression by great powers against weak countries. The pursuit of these objectives would not be facilitated if China's representatives in Geneva defended Soviet actions against Finland. On the other hand, Chongqing was trying to retain Soviet support and friendship and to convince Moscow that China was a valuable and reliable ally. Moreover, Chongqing wanted to retard or abort Soviet-Japanese rapprochement. Alignment with the West against the Soviet Union over the issue of faraway Finland would run counter to these objectives. Guo Taiqi, the ambassador to Britain, explained the conflicting pressures operating in China in a cable to the ambassador to the United States, Hu Shi, on 8 December 1939. Regarding the debate in Geneva over the Soviet-Finnish dispute, Guo said, from the standpoint of legality and morality, there was no room for silence or neutrality: Finland should be supported. China's own interests, however, demanded that it not offend the Soviet Union. Yet China had to be careful not to lose world sympathy, especially in the United States.[42] China's status as one of nine nonpermanent members of the League's Council, the executive organ of the League of Nations, and the provision of the League Covenant that the expulsion of any member state from the organization required a unanimous vote of the Council, further complicated China's position. This meant that China had the power to veto the expulsion of the Soviet Union. If it exercised that power it would alienate Western opinion. If it did not, it would alienate Moscow. China's position was further complicated by its desire to retain its Council seat—a position which was quite useful in its efforts to focus world attention on the Sino-Japanese War. Non-permanent Council members normally served three-year terms, but China had already twice been declared eligible for reelection. It was seeking, and obtained, a third extension of eligibility during the League's December 1939 session.

On 9 December the Finnish government appealed to the world body to intervene in the conflict with the Soviet Union. On 13 December, Argentina introduced a resolution in the Assembly calling for the expulsion of the Soviet Union from the League. The Latin American countries, which had an interest of their own in minimizing bigpower bullying of smaller neighbors, took the lead in the Assembly in pushing for action against the Soviet Union. The next day a special committee set up to consider the question issued a report condemning Soviet actions plus a resolution which inter alia expelled the Soviet Union from the League. This report and the resolution were then approved unanimously by the Assembly, with Bulgaria and China abstaining. The matter was then considered by the Council and on 14 December the Council also passed a resolution condemning the Soviet Union and expelling it from the organization, and calling for member states to take action in support of Finland. China did not vote against this resolution but abstained along with Greece and Yugoslavia.[43] In other words, the Republic of China did not veto the expulsion of the Soviet Union as it had the power to do.

Wellington Koo sought instructions from Chongqing when he learned that a move was afoot to expel the Soviet Union.[44] Chongqing ordered Koo to abstain from measures condemning Soviet actions and to resign from the Council if this was necessary to avoid embarrassment and "complications." Koo was either reluctant to give up China's Council seat or he was unclear about Chongqing's intentions, for he cabled Chongqing for further instructions. Events moved more quickly than cables between Geneva and Chongqing, and when the issue of expelling the Soviet Union came before the Council on 14 December, Koo had received no further clarifications from Chongqing. In such a situation, he abstained from voting.

Koo spoke briefly during both the Assembly and Council debates. In the Assembly he stated that in circumstances known to the Assembly, China would abstain from voting on any part of the special committee's report. In his statement to the Council, Koo declared that in conformity with his declaration to the Assembly, and in the absence of final instructions from his government, he would abstain from voting. There was, however, a distinct anti-Soviet tone to Koo's brief statements on the fourteenth. His reference to "circumstances known to the assembly" was a veiled plea to be excused for sacrificing principles for expediency; in other words, it implied that the Soviet Union was in the wrong. Moreover, in abstaining, Koo, unlike the Yugoslavian and Greek representatives, did not note his opposition to the expulsion provision of the Assembly resolution.[45]

Moscow was extremely unhappy with China's refusal to veto its expulsion from the League. On 19 December, Chiang's special representative in Moscow He Yaozu informed Chiang of Soviet displeasure. Because of Moscow's displeasure, and because of a concomitant deterioration in Soviet relations with Britain and France, it "was not convenient" for He to convey to Stalin Chiang's letter of 1 December.[46] Three weeks later on 6 January 1940, Wang Shijie, the minister of information and a member of Chiang's inner circle, cabled Hu Shi regarding the Soviet-Finnish question. Relations with the Soviet Union had become the most difficult and urgent diplomatic problem facing Chongqing, Wang said. The Soviet Union was insisting that China cast its vote in the League Executive Council blocking sanctions against the Soviet Union on account of the Winter War.[47] Chinese abstention was not enough for Moscow; it demanded active support.

During talks with Yang Jie in early January, Molotov linked the question of continuing Soviet assistance to China with China's policy toward the Russo-Finnish War. The Soviet Union was willing to find ways of continuing its aid to China, Molotov said, but this would depend in part on China's attitude toward the Soviet Union. If China had opposed the move to expel the Soviet Union from the League, Britain and France could not have succeeded. As it was, China's actions had assisted Paris and London in attacking the Soviet Union. Moreover, Molotov said, China had still not explained to the Soviet government the intentions behind its recent actions in Geneva. Chinese public opinion should understand, Molotov said, that Soviet demands and offers to Finland were reasonable and that Finland was being manipulated by foreign powers.[48]

Disagreement with Chiang's diplomatic handling of the war between Finland and the Soviet Union was part of the reason for Yang Jie's resignation as ambassador to the Soviet Union in January 1940. According to the memoir of an associate of Yang's at that time, Yang disagreed with Chiang's "anti-Soviet, pro-American" policy and advocated instead "improvements in Sino-Soviet relations." Because of these views, Chiang was "unwilling to let Yang continue" as ambassador.[49] Yang himself left no memoir (he was assassinated, probably by KMT special agents, in Hong Kong in 1949), but it seems probable that he was unhappy with the reorientation of Chiang's policy toward the West which was then under way.

On 10 and 12 January He Yaozu, who had taken over Yang's responsibility for conduct of military aid talks with the Soviet Union, cabled Chiang requesting instructions about how to respond to Molotov's demands for an explanation of why China's representative had not defended the Soviet Union at Geneva.[50] He also sent Chiang a cable analyzing Moscow's broader intentions. The Soviet Union's expulsion from the League of Nations would further isolate it, He Yaozu said, and in its quest for security, Moscow would turn to the Axis. Moscow's increasingly cold attitude toward

China was designed to facilitate its talks with Japan. Moreover, Moscow wanted to see how far China would go in aligning with Britain and the United States against the Soviet Union.[51]

Chiang replied to He Yaozu's queries on 13 January. The move to expel the Soviet Union from the League had taken China's representatives by surprise, Chiang explained. It was unfortunate that when Wellington Koo had met with the Soviet representative at Geneva three or four times before the "incident," the Soviet representative had not raised the issue of possible moves to expel the Soviet Union. "Henceforth," Chiang said, "so long as Soviet Russia is able to sincerely discuss issues with China in advance, China will be happy to do everything possible to see that its diplomatic direction is in accord with that of Soviet Russia." Chiang then proceeded to up the ante by directly raising the issue of tardy Soviet assistance to China. If the Soviet Union had not changed its policy and was not now trying to appease Japan, it should fulfill its agreements with China and send the fighters, bombers, and other munitions already contracted for and which China urgently needed. China was willing to ship to the Soviet Union all the materials demanded by Moscow, but China's transportation system was poor and the Soviet Union would have to assist China in transporting these materials. In any case, Sino-Soviet relations could not be compared to purely commercial relations, but were based on broader political interests. "In fact, matters touching on the common interests of the two countries and whether or not agreements will be implemented and aid continue as it has in the past, depends on Soviet sincerity and on whether or not Soviet policy toward China has changed. This depends on the Soviet Union, rather than on China, and cannot, therefore, be achieved by pleas by China."[52]

Chiang's message to Stalin indicates that, like He Yaozu, he believed that Soviet displeasure over China's behavior at Geneva was contrived. Moscow was attempting to distance itself from China for the sake of better relations with Japan, and China's actions at Geneva were merely a pretext to facilitate this. Moscow had pledged repeatedly that its policy toward China had not changed since the fall of 1939, and Chiang was now demanding that Moscow deliver the goods, literally, to prove this. The imbroglio at Geneva was minor compared to parallel interests vis-à-vis Japan previously agreed upon between Moscow and Chongqing. If Moscow changed its policy toward China, it would not be because of China's votes at Geneva, but because it no longer perceived common interests regarding Japan.

Chiang's instructions to He Yaozu did not assuage Soviet bitterness. On 19 January, He Yaozu informed Chiang that Defense Commissar Voroshilov (who was still responsible for conducting the military aid talks with China) was demanding an explanation of China's actions at Geneva before he was willing to meet with He.[53] These objections were apparently overcome as He and Voroshilov met the next day. The meeting—the first between He Yaozu and Voroshilov—did not go well, however. He Yaozu expressed Chongqing's concern that the beginning of the European war might enable Japan to close China's sea lines of communication via Haiphong and Rangoon and that transportation via the Soviet Union was therefore even more vital. Voroshilov replied that He's attitude revealed that he was not concerned with the Soviet side of things and did not have a "friendly attitude." Voroshilov then raised the issue of China's failure to meet its deliveries of raw materials to the Soviet Union. He

Yaozu attempted to respond to Voroshilov's charges, but the latter found his replies unsatisfactory.[54] Chiang later rebuked He Yaozu for not being firmer with Voroshilov on this occasion. If the Soviet attitude remained cold, Chiang subsequently directed He Yaozu that he could go to visit some old friends of his (He's) in Turkey.[55]

Chiang himself presented a detailed defense of China's voting at Geneva when he met with the chief Soviet advisor to China in Chongqing on 22 January. China's failure to block the expulsion of the Soviet Union from the League of Nations was a result of confusion rather than of deliberation, Chiang said. The Chinese government had instructed its representatives at Geneva to abstain from any vote condemning the Soviet Union for its war with Finland. However, no one had expected Britain and France to move to expel the Soviet Union from the League. Had China known this was their intention, Chiang said, it certainly would have opposed such a move and not merely abstained. It was unfortunate that the Soviet representative at Geneva did not raise this question when he met with Wellington Koo several times prior to the Anglo-French move. Chiang also rebutted Molotov's charge that China had not condemned the Soviet expulsion once it had occurred. This was not true, Chiang said. In fact, the day before the League session closed, Chiang himself had met with Soviet ambassador to China A.S. Paniushkin and told him that the League's action was "unthinkable." Moreover, Foreign Minister Wang Chonghui had already informed Paniushkin that as a member of the executive Council of the League, China would block any move to adopt sanctions against the Soviet Union.[56] Chiang did not need to explain that nonpublic assurances such as he and Wang offered the Soviet ambassador did not injure China's image with public opinion in the United States and Britain.

While minimizing the significance of the Geneva imbroglio during his talks with the Soviet advisor, Chiang indirectly raised the question of whether Soviet policy toward China had changed, and challenged Moscow to demonstrate that it had not. Regarding Molotov's query to Yang Jie in January about whether Britain, France, and the United States were able to assist China's war of resistance, Chiang said that Molotov's "tone of voice" was very strange. China had never begged for help, Chiang said. It was good if other nations assisted China, but even if they did not, China would continue to resist. Chiang then questioned Moscow's general orientation:

> For the past several months the authorities of my humble country, both in Moscow and in Geneva, and I myself, have repeatedly discussed with Soviet representatives the policy of unison of Soviet and Chinese diplomatic actions. We have advanced various opinions about this and asked for replies from the Soviet Union. However, we have received no answer. Does this sort of reaction reflect a belief that China does not have the status to jointly discuss policy, or is not fit to be a friend? There is no way of knowing. But China, for its part, has discussed all matters with the Soviet Union and carried out all the duties and responsibilities of friendship.[57]

By the end of February, the Finnish crisis in Sino-Soviet relations had passed and talks about Soviet military assistance to China resumed.[58] They did not progress, however. The mutuality of interests which had characterized the first two years of the war no longer existed. Moscow's basic global orientation had changed: it was aligned with Germany and against the Western democracies and wished to conciliate rather than antagonize Japan. Moscow and Chongqing had parted ways.

The Suspension of Soviet Aid in 1940

Perhaps the single most critical question regarding Soviet-Chinese relations during the period of Soviet-German alliance is whether or not Soviet assistance to China declined and if so, by how much. The evidence is ambiguous, but it seems that there *was* a substantial decline during 1940. Such a decline was not, of course, reflected by the formal conclusion of loan agreements. As indicated in Chapter 2, the third and largest ($150 million U.S.) agreement was concluded in July 1939 and was to run throughout 1940. But as we have seen, the conclusion of loans, and even of purchase agreements, and the actual delivery of goods were two very different things.

A letter dated 11 November 1939 from Economics Minister Weng Wenhao to Ambassador Hu Shi indicated that as of that time Soviet aid was "substantial and generous."[59] Zhou Xicai also says that after the conclusion of the June 1939 agreement and the formal ratification of that agreement by the Chinese government in December 1939, "the Soviet Union uninterruptedly supplied China with weapons."[60] There is substantial contrary evidence, however, indicating that Soviet aid was in fact suspended during the imbroglio over the Winter War in early 1940. Shao Lizi, who formally replaced Yang Jie as ambassador to Moscow on 18 April 1940, states, for example, that while Moscow provided substantial assistance to China in 1939, "Not long afterwards, assistance suddenly ceased."[61] The flow of aid apparently resumed only late in 1940. Shao says that on 7 July 1940 (the anniversary of the Marco Polo Bridge Incident) the Soviet general advisor in Chongqing informed the Chinese government that *nonaviation* aid was being prepared and would be shipped to China via Xinjiang *that winter*.

There was much discussion and conflict, but little concrete action regarding Soviet assistance to China during the first ten months of 1940. On 20 January 1940, He Yaozu presented to Voroshilov an order for $30 million U.S. worth of Soviet equipment.[62] Moscow was still studying this request in mid-March when He Yaozu requested an additional 800,000 rifles and ninety-six howitzers to replace items included in the January request but which the Soviet Union had indicated it was unable to supply. The Soviet Union then protested this ad hoc revision of China's earlier request. On 28 April, He Yaozu finally deemed it appropriate to present Chiang Kai-shek's December letter for Stalin to Molotov. Accompanying Chiang's letter was a long list of equipment which Chiang hoped to purchase, including 200 aircraft, 10,000 machine guns, and 560 antiaircraft guns.[63] There is no indication that the Soviets accepted this request at that time. Not until September did Shao Lizi present a purchase order combining both He Yaozu's 20 January and mid-March requests.[64] Again this seems to indicate that from January through September 1940 the Soviet side refused to consider Chinese requests for the purchase of goods under the July 1939 credit agreement.

As Table 2.1 showed, only thirteen percent of the rifles, fourteen percent of motor vehicles, one percent of ammunition, and twenty-eight percent of fighter aircraft supplied by the Soviet Union during the war were provided during 1940 and 1941. Most of this amount was probably included in the late-1940 shipments discussed later. Again this leads to the conclusion that throughout most of 1940 little or no Soviet aid was going to China.

The suspension of Soviet aid facilitated the process of Soviet-Japanese rapprochement. On 2 July 1940, Japan's ambassador in Moscow Togo Shigenori broached with Molotov the question of Soviet aid to China in the context of discussing the possibility of a Soviet-Japanese neutrality agreement. Molotov reassured Togo that Soviet aid to Chiang was insignificant because of Soviet preoccupation with its own national defense.[65]

A dispute over the quality of Soviet aircraft being supplied to China also contributed to the disruption of Soviet aid to China during 1940. On 9 January 1940, Yang Jie informed Chiang Kai-shek that the Soviet Union had decided to implement the agreement concluded by Sun Ke in the summer of 1939 under which the Soviet Union was to establish a jointly owned aircraft factory in Dihua (today's Urumqi) to produce 300 fighters per year.[66] According to Shao Lizi, War Minister He Yingqin and Commandant of the Central Air Force Academy Zhou Zhirou felt that the I-16 and SB aircraft to be built in the Dihua factory, while perhaps adequate in 1938, were obsolete by the standards of 1940.[67] In line with this view, Chiang cabled Shao on 13 April instructing him that the factory should be built only if it would produce the newest-model aircraft. The I-16 fighter was too slow and the SB bomber had too short a range, Chiang said.[68] Chinese officials may have been aware that a new generation of Soviet fighters (the MiG-1) and bombers (the Il-4) which were, in fact, greatly superior to the I-16 and SB were just coming into production in the Soviet Union.[69] If Stalin was going to buy Chinese soldiers to fight against Japan, Chiang wanted him to pay in good coinage.

Securing the resumption of Soviet assistance was the major task of Shao Lizi when he arrived in Moscow in April 1940. In his memoir, Shao cites an editorial from *Da Gong Bao* of 16 May 1940 which reflected the arguments he used to urge Soviet officials to resume Soviet aid to China. The article read:

> China's war of resistance against Japan is a direct defense of itself, but an indirect shield for others. Regarding the Soviet Union, Soviet aid to China increases our war making power and helps us to resist the enemy, thus making Japan unable to attack the Soviet Union and causing the Japan-German pact to abort and Japan-German relations to develop as they otherwise did [i.e., toward Japan-German estrangement]. This proves that Sino-Soviet friendship has been mutually beneficial to both. Thus far this situation has not changed.[70]

In line with this analysis, in June Shao requested that the Soviet Union supply China with 300 aircraft of the latest types. Soviet officials refused, saying that if China needed aircraft it should not block the completion of the Dihua factory.[71] If China's need for aircraft was so urgent, the Soviet vice-foreign minister asked, why did China procrastinate about setting up the proposed factory? The responsibility for the nonoperation of that factory lay with the Chinese side, not with the Soviet side, the Soviet vice-foreign minister said.[72]

Chiang also revived the idea of a Soviet-Chinese alliance as part of his attempt to revive Stalin's flagging interest in cooperation with China. This time, however, the proposal was sweetened by offers of bases and other special rights in postwar Manchuria. As noted earlier, on 28 April 1940 He Yaozu was finally able to deliver Chiang's December 1939 letter to Molotov. He Yaozu began his interview with Molotov with a carte blanche endorsement of Moscow's recent territorial annexations "in the Baltic region," that is, in Finland. He Yaozu then moved on to solicit, once again, Soviet entry into the Sino-Japanese War, in exchange for which the Soviet Union would be granted certain privileges in China after Japan's defeat. Chinese "public opinion" hoped, He Yaozu said, that the Soviet Union would be able "within an appropriate time to adopt an active policy in the Far East and restrain the aggressor." Then followed He's cryptic but critical proposition:

> At this time the Chinese government is prepared to immediately conclude an agreement with the Soviet government regarding all problems related to the road to eternal peace in the Far East, to economic and provisional measures as well as permanent constructions, and to assume responsibility for a portion of the honor.[73]

The phrase "provisional measures" implied transit rights for Soviet forces across Chinese territory during wartime, rights such as the Soviet Union had sought from Czechoslovakia during the European crisis of 1938 and which China would agree to in August 1945. The reference to "the road to eternal peace in the Far East" implied Soviet military bases in China after the defeat of Japan. From the Soviet perspective, and perhaps from the Chinese as well, "eternal peace" could only be guaranteed by a strengthening of the Soviet position vis-à-vis Japan. The phrase "permanent constructions" also hinted at railway rights across Manchuria, such as those which Moscow had sold to Tokyo in 1935 and which it was to regain in 1945, and to naval bases such as those at Luxun (Port Arthur) and Dairen, relinquished by imperial Russia in 1905 and reacquired by Moscow in 1945. There is no record, as far as this author knows, of whether He Yaozu or other Chinese diplomats elaborated orally in 1940 on the precise meaning of these phrases. But even if they did not, Stalin and Molotov would have understood what was meant. These diplomatic seeds would bear fruit in 1945.

He Yaozu also held out prospects for an expanded Soviet economic position in China. The problems related to Japan and Sino-Soviet relations were complex, He Yaozu said, but once agreement between China and the Soviet Union was reached, there would be no limit to the development of Sino-Soviet economic relations. The Soviet Union should recommend an economic expert to be hired by the Chinese government to investigate ways of expanding Sino-Soviet economic cooperation. Again, stripped of its diplomatic ambiguity, this was an offer of special economic privileges for the Soviet Union in China.[74]

He Yaozu then went on to explain to Molotov that the close Sino-Soviet bloc he was proposing would align with the Anglo-American bloc. He recalled that Chiang had warned Paniushkin in December 1939 that Japan's objective was to win London and Washington over to an anti-Soviet alliance. The recent changes in Europe and the Pacific region now made this danger even greater, He Yaozu explained. Japan's plot could, however, be thwarted by a Soviet-American-British-Chinese understanding. The Soviet Union and the United States should adopt a vigilant attitude toward Japan. They should reach an understanding and act in coordination with China's war of resistance. American anti-Japanese sentiments were increasing, and Washington would not object to Soviet actions against Japan. If the Soviet Union used its armed might to deal with the Japanese "barbarians," "no one would think anything of it."[75]

Moscow did not respond to Chongqing's sweeping April 1940 proposal for a Sino-Soviet-American-British alliance against Japan. Three months later Chiang tried again. On 18 July, Shao Lizi received a cable from Chiang instructing him to urge Moscow to oppose the closure of the Burma–Yunnan road by Britain under Japanese pressure. Coming just after U.S. Secretary of State Cordell Hull's statement of opposition to London's move, Tokyo would take note of such parallel Soviet and American measures.[76] Again Moscow rejected Chiang's plan. In his reply to Chiang the next day, Shao said that the Soviet Union "was not willing to listen to talk" of Soviet-American cooperation. In the Soviet view, Shao reported, American sympathy for China was long on words and short on action. The United States was afraid to implement even an economic embargo, much less to use military force against Japan. Regarding the specific issue of a Soviet protest over the closing of the Burma Road, Shao reported that the Soviet press had already expressed "appropriate opposition." Further Soviet response was "under study."[77]

Later in September, Chiang accepted a proposal by Shao Lizi that China use the opportunity of new tensions emerging in Soviet-German relations to push for increased Soviet cooperation with the West and China. Shao was to tell Soviet officials that "the Soviet Union must encourage the United States in order for it to become active quickly. . . . We must not lose this opportunity; this point is extremely important, and we deeply hope the Soviet Union will pay attention to it."[78]

Meanwhile, Chiang's representatives in Washington were broaching the same arguments to American officials. U.S. leaders were more receptive to China's proposals and in fact attempted to persuade Moscow to coordinate its China aid efforts with the United States. On 4 October, T.V. Soong reported to Chiang that the United States was willing to aid China in cooperation with the Soviet Union, but that Moscow still rejected American proposals to this effect.[79] At the end of December, after the third American loan to China, T.V. Soong again reported that U.S. Treasury Secretary Henry Morgenthau had proposed to Soviet Ambassador Litvinov a long-term Soviet-American trade agreement exchanging Soviet molybdenum for American industrial goods. The political condition for such an agreement, T.V. Soong reported, was that the Soviet Union increase its aid to China. The Soviet reply had been that until overall Soviet-American relations improved, it was premature to discuss American-Soviet cooperation in aiding China.[80]

Not until late November were Shao's efforts to reopen the Soviet aid pipeline successful. On 25 November, Chiang cabled Shao informing him that the Soviet ambassador had told him that the Soviet Union was prepared to continue aiding China with aircraft, artillery, machine guns, and gasoline. When Chiang asked the Soviet ambassador whether the amounts of the goods to be delivered corresponded to the requests presented in April by He Yaozu, the Soviet official gave an evasive reply. Therefore, Chiang directed, Shao was to negotiate specific amounts and dates of deliveries—and to thank Soviet officials for their generosity. Chiang also directed Shao to seek delivery of all goods by February 1941 at the latest.[81]

The flow of Soviet aid to China resumed in December 1940. Moreover, Stalin acceded to Chiang's request for urgent shipment of equipment. By mid-December 1940 some 300 truckloads of equipment had been delivered by the Soviet Union to Hami in Xinjiang—and had returned to the Soviet Union with loads of tin, tungsten, wool, and hides.[82] On 16 January 1941, Soviet military attaché General Vasilii Chuikov enumerated the quantity of Soviet equipment delivered to China in December 1940–January 1941.[83] Chuikov's list is shown in Table 2.1 on page 38. Chinese sources do not give a figure for the total amount of the late-1940 aid transfer. A report by American military intelligence, however, gave $50 million U.S. as the amount.[84]

While some Soviet material continued to reach China as late as August 1941, the late-1940 deal was the last large-scale Soviet assistance to China until 1945.[85] Finally, on 24 October 1941, Moscow informed Chongqing that because of the pressing demands of its own war it would no longer be able to provide assistance to China.[86]

Moscow's resumption of aid to China at the end of 1940 was linked to the deterioration of Soviet-German relations which began after the failure of the Molotov and von Ribbentrop talks in November 1940.[87] Mounting Soviet-German tensions meant that Chongqing was increasingly important to Moscow. Keeping China at war with Japan was Stalin's insurance policy against a two-front war, and arms shipments to Chongqing were the premiums on that policy. While Germany's power was directed to the West and while tensions between Moscow and Berlin were still low (in early and mid-1940), Stalin felt that his costly Chinese insurance policy was less necessary. Moreover, the payment of the premium on that policy obstructed the improvement of Soviet-Japanese ties. With the expansion of German power into the Balkans at the end of 1940, Stalin apparently reconsidered the utility of his costly Chinese insurance.

Soviet thinking about China at the end of 1940 was indicated by the instructions given by Semen K. Timoshenko and Stalin to General Chuikov just before the latter departed for China at the end of the year. (Timoshenko succeeded Voroshilov as Commissar of Defense in May 1940, a post he held until July 1941.) In their talks with Chuikov, both Timoshenko and Stalin stressed the growing danger of German attack on the Soviet Union and China's role in preventing Japan from joining that attack. Timoshenko stressed his concern about a possible simultaneous attack by both Japan and Germany and the great difficulties such an attack would pose. Japanese troops numbering 1,120,000 were bogged down in China, Timoshennko said. This was up from only 132,000 in 1937. Timoshenko expected Japan either to concentrate all its forces to defeat Chiang Kai-shek during 1941, or to use peace negotiations to contract the area of military operations in China. Tokyo's objective was to free its forces in order to join together with Hitler in attacking the Soviet Union. Chuikov's mission, Timoshenko informed him, was to use his influence as Chiang's general military advisor to cause the Chinese military to actively wage war against Japan. The Soviet Union would continue aiding Chiang's military forces, but this aid should be actively used against Japan. Stalin's directions to Chuikov were equally forthright. Chuikov's duty, and the duty of all Soviet personnel in China, was, Stalin said, to "tie the hands and feet of the Japanese aggressors. Only when they are bound and tied in this way will we be able to avoid a two-front war if the German aggressors attack our country."[88] This Soviet fear of Sino-Japanese peace was not unrelated to Chiang's "peace diplomacy" of 1940.

The Quest for Peace and a "Far Eastern Munich"

Chiang outlined his views on the international situation in the fall of 1940 in a long disquisition in his diary on the occasion of his fifty-fourth birthday on 31 October. There were three possible courses China could follow, Chiang wrote. The worst path would be to make peace with Japan. Since no treaty could force Japan to withdraw its troops from China, this would mean continued Japanese occupation of Chinese territory. A moderately acceptable policy would be for China to join the Anglo-American camp. Such a policy would, however, meet with Soviet suspicion, perhaps even causing Moscow to sever relations with China or ordering the CCP to reach an accommodation with Japan against the KMT. On the other hand, if China awaited the outbreak of a Japanese-American war, it could enter that war at an opportune moment when Britain and the United States needed China's armies. By that time the Soviet Union might once again be aligned with Britain and the United States, or at least Moscow would "not make it difficult" for China to cooperate militarily with them. This was the best policy for China to follow: to take Japan as the sole enemy, continue a neutral policy toward both the Anglo-American and the German-Italian blocs, and wait until the Soviet Union clarified its attitude. In this fashion, China would retain room for maneuver with regard to the United States, Germany, and the Soviet Union. Such an autonomous policy was, Chiang concluded, the only viable policy at present.[89]

This policy of keeping options open and waiting watchfully would be enhanced by testing the climate in Tokyo. Of course, talks with Japan would have to be clandestine, that is, deniable. But if conducted in an appropriate fashion, peace talks with Japan would help pressure Moscow and warn it that its rapprochement with Japan threatened to trigger the Sino-Japanese-American anti-Soviet bloc of which Chiang had warned Stalin. If offers of special rights in China and visions of Soviet-Chinese-American-British cooperation were the positive aspect of Chiang's efforts to align the Soviet Union against Japan during 1939–1940, the negative aspect was a threat that China might align with Japan. This negative aspect had been laid out by Chiang in his 1 December letter to Stalin: a United States-facilitated settlement of the Sino-Japanese War might lead to the formation of a broad anti-Soviet front. This threat was given substance by movement toward what China's leftist press was pleased to call a "Far Eastern Munich."

The term "Far Eastern Munich" was used frequently during 1939–1940 and it is useful to consider just what this phrase meant. A Munich-type settlement implied, of course, the avoidance or termination of great-power conflict through the cession of territory or special rights by a weak country to a powerful aggressor country under the aegis of third powers seeking themselves to avoid conflict with the aggressor. This much is straightforward. There was, however, another very important meaning to a Munich-type settlement, a meaning which was rooted in the Soviet perception of the 1938 Munich Conference. From this perspective, a Munich-type settlement represented an attempt by the Western imperialist powers to direct German or Japanese aggression away from themselves and toward the Soviet Union. It was, in short, an attempt by the Western powers to avoid an inter-imperialist war by precipitating a

Soviet-German or a Soviet-Japanese war.[90] A Far Eastern Munich implied, in other words, a settlement of the Sino-Japanese conflict on terms which would lead to a Japanese attack on the Soviet Union rather than to a Japanese advance into Southeast Asia and war with Britain and the United States.

Chiang used the threat of a "Far Eastern Munich" to influence Soviet policy. In other words, Chiang's counter to Soviet tendencies to cut a deal with Japan at China's expense, was to threaten to cut a deal with Japan at Soviet expense. One component of such a deal would be settlement of the Sino-Japanese conflict, possibly via American mediation, on terms which would better position Japanese forces for a strike against Siberia. One of the premises of such an arrangement would be Japanese renunciation of a southern advance in favor of security cooperation against the Soviet Union. Such a settlement would have been, in the parlance of that era, a "Far Eastern Munich."

To give substance to this threat, Chiang reopened peace talks with Japan. This is not to say that increased leverage with Moscow was the only objective behind Chongqing's 1939–1940 peace talks. It was not. Chiang also wanted to explore the possibility that the breakdown (until mid-1940) of the Tokyo–Berlin axis, the now-apparent futility of Japan's earlier hope of military victory over China, and Tokyo's desire to extricate itself from the China quagmire in order to be better able to take advantage of the European preoccupations of the colonial powers in Asia, might have persuaded Tokyo to grant Chiang peace terms which he could accept. Chiang was also aware of the efficacious impact that possible Sino-Japanese peace might have on U.S. aid to China. But of prime concern to us here was Chiang's hope that the possibility of a "Far Eastern Munich" might staunch the erosion of Soviet support for China.

Foreign Minister Wang Chonghui made the opening move in Chongqing's new peace gambit when he met with an American reporter on 28 September 1939. China had always been ready to discuss peace with Japan, Wang said. As long as the terms of peace were honorable, China would be happy to accept. China especially hoped, Wang said, that a peace-loving country such as the United States would mediate the Sino-Japanese conflict.[91] Head of the executive *yuan* H.H. Kung elaborated on this proposition on 16 October. Regarding the question of peace talks, Kung told another American reporter, the key issue was not whether China was willing to discuss peace, but whether Japan was willing to abandon its policy of aggression against China. If Japan abandoned its dream of conquering China, peace could be restored. Kung also proposed a United States-sponsored international conference to settle the Sino-Japanese conflict.[92]

Chongqing also sought German involvement in its peace efforts. If Washington was not able to arrange acceptable terms, then perhaps Berlin would be. Early in October 1939, the counselor of the Chinese embassy in Berlin, Ding Wenyuan, presented a plan for a German-mediated settlement of the Sino-Japanese War to the German Foreign Ministry.[93] Once steps had been taken to involve both the United States and Nazi Germany in mediation efforts, Chiang began to lay out his peace terms. In a major speech on 18 November 1939 Chiang publicly restated the peace terms he had outlined in a secret speech at the Fifth Plenum in January. China's war aim, Chiang said, was restoration of the 7 July 1937 status quo ante bellum. Chiang also again raised the idea of an international conference to settle both the European and the Far Eastern problems.[94]

After these preliminary moves, and just as He Yaozu in Moscow was preparing to present to Stalin Chiang's proposal for a comprehensive Soviet-Chinese military alliance, Chiang moved to open secret peace talks with Japan. In November 1939, Chiang ordered the head of his secret service Dai Li to send an agent to Hong Kong to establish contacts with Japanese operatives there. Dai made the necessary arrangements, and talks began in Hong Kong on 7 March 1940. They continued intermittently until 8 October 1940.[95] By early June the two sides were close to agreement. Chiang's peace terms in mid-1940, simply stated, included the following points. First, Japan could station troops in Inner Mongolia and at certain points in north China. Second, China would sign an anticommunist agreement with Japan directed against "external communism," that is, against the Soviet Union. Third, China would not contest the loss of Manchuria to Japan. Finally, Japan would have extensive economic and political privileges in China. The implementation of these terms would have been a serious threat to the Soviet Union. Moreover, if a Sino-Japanese settlement were linked to improvements in Japanese-American relations, as the idea of a U.S.-sponsored international conference suggested would be the case, such an arrangement would diminish prospects for a Japanese drive south into Southeast Asia. Again, in the lexicon of that era, it would have been a "Far Eastern Munich."

These secret peace talks of 1940 amounted to a threat by Chiang to become a partner to an anti-Soviet settlement of the Sino-Japanese War. This was in part a response to Moscow's increasingly cool attitude toward China—the crisis over China's role during the Winter War and the suspension of Soviet aid—and to Moscow's increasingly cordial relations with Japan. Chiang was trying to abort Soviet-Japanese rapprochement by persuading Stalin that efforts at such rapprochement would backfire and lead instead to a Far Eastern Munich. It did not matter to Chiang Kai-shek whether it was Anglo-American or German-Soviet pressure which forced Japan to compromise. Chiang was, in effect, pitting these great global blocs against one another, asking both to pressure Japan to be reasonable, hinting that China would tilt toward that bloc which was most successful in this effort, and watching to see which bloc would, in fact, prove of most use to China.

The formation of the second Konoe cabinet in Tokyo on 16 July 1940 (just after the collapse of France) undermined the Sino-Japanese peace talks. Rejecting the idea of working out a *modus vivendi* with the United States and Britain, the new Konoe government decided instead to strike a deal with the Soviet Union and march against the European colonies in Southeast Asia. Part of the 16 July reorganization in Tokyo was the appointment of Hideki Tojo as minister of war. Tojo was strongly opposed to the talks then underway with Chiang Kai-shek, preferring instead to settle the China Incident by militarily cutting off Chiang's international supply lines in Southeast Asia and through agreement with the Soviet Union.[96] Consequently, after mid-July little progress was made at the Hong Kong talks and on 1 October Tojo ordered their termination.

Chiang's peace ploy was partially successful. While it did not thwart Moscow's rapprochement with Tokyo, it may well have been a factor inducing Stalin to resume aid to China at the end of 1940. Regarding the United States, Chiang's stratagem of threatened settlement with Japan enjoyed quite substantial success. But that is another story.

China and the Axis Treaty

While the formation of the second Konoe government doomed Chiang's efforts to maneuver the Soviet Union into confrontation with Japan, it greatly increased the prospects for an American-Japanese clash. One element of Konoe's diplomatic preparation for the planned drive into Southeast Asia was the conclusion of a military alliance with Germany to deter American intervention. A second component of Konoe's diplomatic strategy was the conclusion of a neutrality agreement with the Soviet Union. The Tri-Partite Treaty of September 1940, the Soviet-Japanese Neutrality Treaty of April 1941, and Japan's drive into Southeast Asia were inextricably linked.

Chiang was aware of and pleased with the implications of the shift of power in Tokyo in mid-July. Commenting in his diary on 17 July, Chiang said that with Konoe's reassumption of power, Japan's expansion into Southeast Asia would accelerate. Such developments "would not be unbeneficial" to China, Chiang concluded.[97] When the Tri-Partite Treaty was finally signed on 27 September 1940 Chiang was quite satisfied, commenting in his diary the next day:

> The alliance of Germany, Italy, and the Japs has finally materialized. As far as the war of resistance and the international situation is concerned, this is something we have long sought but have not obtained. The situation for inevitable victory in the war of resistance has been achieved.[98]

Chiang welcomed the Tri-Partite Treaty because he believed it would hasten a Japanese-American clash over Southeast Asia. But he also believed that the Treaty was directed against the Soviet Union, or at least that it would rouse Soviet fears regardless of German and Japanese intentions. Chiang gave his appraisal of the threat to the Soviet Union presented by the Tri-Partite Treaty in a speech to the Standing Committee of the KMT Central Executive Committee shortly after the treaty's conclusion. The treaty would lead, Chiang said, to the polarization of the world into two camps. In the antiaggressor camp would stand China, the United States, Britain, *and the Soviet Union*.[99] Clearly, Chiang felt that the Tri-Partite Treaty threatened the Soviet Union. Perhaps he believed that it contained secret anti-Soviet protocols, such as the 1936 anti-Comintern agreement had in fact contained. In any case, it was this assumption of a threat to the Soviet Union which underlay Chiang's final pre-world war bid for an alliance with Moscow.

In Moscow, Ambassador Shao Lizi also concluded that the Tri-Partite Treaty was directed against the Soviet Union and deduced from this that the time was ripe for China to propose, once again, expanded cooperation with the Soviet Union. Shao cabled specific proposals to this effect to Chiang who accepted his advice and incorporated it into a cable to Stalin on 29 September.[100] Chiang's cable of that date asserted that the Tri-Partite Treaty marked the beginning of even more adventurous actions by Japanese imperialism. This had important implications for Sino-Soviet relations and China hoped for unanimity with the Soviet Union in the present situation. Thus, Chiang requested that Stalin inform him of what approach China and the Soviet Union should take to the new world situation.[101] The fact that German Foreign Minister von Ribbentrop was then pressuring Chiang to join the new Axis bloc as part of a German-mediated peace settlement with Japan gave added weight to Chiang's query to Stalin as to where Moscow preferred China to stand.[102]

The Soviet response was not what Chiang had hoped for. When Shao Lizi delivered Chiang's message to the Soviet vice-foreign minister, the latter told Shao that the Soviet Union still intended to remain neutral in the ongoing wars in Europe and the Far East. China need not be overly concerned about the Tri-Partite Treaty, the Soviet official told Shao, since it would intensify the Japanese-American confrontation to the advantage of China.[103] On 16 October 1940, Stalin himself replied to Chiang's message. The Soviet leader's reply is a masterpiece of diplomatic innuendo and reveals much about the Soviet view of the world in the fall of 1940. It is thus worth quoting at length:

> It is difficult for me to make proposals to Your Excellency because I am not sufficiently informed regarding the situation of China and Japan. But regarding the problem under consideration [e.g., the Tri-Partite Treaty] I perhaps have a relatively accurate opinion which I may convey to Your Excellency. It seems to me that the conclusion of the three power alliance may slightly injure China's situation, just as it will that of the Soviet Union in some regards. . . . But the three power treaty has a contradictory nature and under certain international conditions it may be disadvantageous to Japan, namely by demolishing the basis for Anglo-American neutrality toward Japan. . . . This will create several advantages for China. The American embargo of scrap metal and other goods to Japan and the reopening of the Burma road are indirect proofs of this. Under such a complex and contradictory situation, my own opinion is that China's chief duty is to preserve and strengthen its national army. The national army of China holds the destiny of China and carries the responsibility for its freedom and independence. If Your Excellency's armed forces are resolute and powerful, then China cannot be destroyed. Regarding the possibility of making peace with Japan, there is much talk and I cannot know which of these rumors are in accord with the facts. But no matter what, I believe without doubt that as long as China's national army is resolute and strong, China will be able to conquer all difficulties.[104]

There were several salient aspects of Stalin's reply. First, he refused to be drawn into the Sino-Japanese conflict: he was "uninformed" about Sino-Japanese relations; it was the responsibility of *China's* army to achieve China's independence and freedom. Second, the Tri-Partite Treaty opened the road to a Japanese-American war, not to a Japanese-Soviet conflict. Stalin was, in fact, well informed on this point by Richard Sorge's spy ring then active in Tokyo. The third striking characteristic of Stalin's reply was Soviet disinterest in closer cooperation with China: it "was difficult for [Stalin] to make proposals" to Chiang. Stalin saw the capitalist world racing headlong toward another inter-imperialist world war and he intended to do everything possible to keep the Soviet Union out of that war. In line with this, Stalin was more interested in a neutrality agreement with Japan than in an alliance with China.[105]

Six days after Stalin cabled his message to Chiang, Chiang replied with a message of thanks for the Soviet leader's "kind words and encouragement." "No matter what," Chiang said, Japan was the common enemy of China and the Soviet Union. Regarding Stalin's observations about future developments in the international situation (i.e., the likelihood of an American-Japanese war), Chiang implied that in this regard China and the Soviet Union shared common interests and should adopt parallel policies. In this regard, Chiang said, he deeply hoped to receive Stalin's "instructions" frequently.[106]

The Soviet-Japanese Neutrality Agreement

In the fall of 1940, Soviet-Japanese rapprochement moved into high gear. Tokyo was preparing for its drive south and needed to guarantee Soviet noninvolvement in any conflict which might result from that drive. Moscow faced mounting tensions with a Germany which now controlled most of Europe. In October German troops entered Romania, and the next month that country, along with Hungary and Slovakia (the rump state left after Bohemia became a protectorate of Germany), entered the Axis bloc. In March 1941 Bulgaria allied itself with Germany and in April Greece and Yugoslavia were overrun by German forces. As Hitler turned his attentions to the Balkans, Soviet-German tensions mounted, and as they did, Moscow became increasingly desirous of a neutrality agreement with Japan. By the spring of 1941 Moscow was receiving intelligence from numerous sources that Germany was preparing to invade the Soviet Union. Stalin, of course, discounted much of this information as British trickery designed to further disrupt Soviet-German ties. Still, he made preparations. If it came to a Soviet-German war, a neutrality agreement with Japan would lessen the danger of a two-front war. Much hard bargaining over peripheral issues such as mineral rights on Sakhalin Island and offshore fishing rights remained, but both Moscow and Tokyo now clearly desired an agreement.[107]

Chiang Kai-shek wondered whether Moscow's accelerating rapprochement with Japan was not designed to touch off a Japanese-American war. Commenting on Soviet relations with the Axis bloc shortly after the conclusion of the Tri-Partite Treaty, for instance, Chiang wrote in his diary:

> Although Russia has not entered the [Axis] alliance, Russia's Stalin was its principal instigator. Henceforth, if Japan does not promptly move south, Stalin will use a Russian-Jap non-aggression treaty to encourage a southern advance by Japan. This is precisely Stalin's intention, since in this fashion he can realize his plot of global inter-imperialist war.[108]

Chiang was not unhappy with Moscow's effort to engineer a Japanese-American war. In his disquisition on foreign affairs in his diary on 31 October 1940, Chiang recognized that Soviet machinations to trigger such a war would benefit China. Once the Soviet Union "permitted" Tokyo a nonaggression treaty, Chiang wrote, Japan would be able to carry out its policy of southern advance. Given Soviet support for Tokyo, American efforts to prevent a southern advance by Japan would be futile. "The factors making it necessary for Japan to move South and go to war with the

U.S. already exist," Chiang said. "Therefore America's hopes of moderating the Japs will absolutely come to nothing. The major factors lie entirely with Russia and the Japs." The anticipated results of Soviet policy "would not be extremely harmful to us," Chiang concluded.[109]

While Chiang was not unhappy with what he believed to be Soviet efforts to precipitate a Japanese-American clash, he was appalled by the Soviet desire to remain neutral in such a war. Chiang thus tried to persuade Stalin that it was worthwhile to continue cooperating with China. One way Chiang did this may have been by signaling Chongqing's willingness to recognize Soviet special rights in Xinjiang — a development discussed in Chapter 6. Chiang also found opportunities to underline his friendship for the Soviet Union and his hope for continued Soviet support. On 23 April 1941, for example, he visited the Soviet embassy in Chongqing for the first time (according to Chuikov's memoir), to participate in the celebration of the twenty-third anniversary of the Soviet Union's Red Army.[110]

Such efforts were unsuccessful, and on 5 April 1941 a five-year neutrality agreement between Japan and the Soviet Union capped the process of rapprochement which had begun in September 1939. This neutrality agreement represented an understanding between Moscow and Tokyo which was to endure, though not without challenge, until 5 April 1945 when Moscow announced its intention to terminate the agreement. The April 1941 agreement had a great impact on Sino-Soviet relations.

During negotiation of the neutrality agreement, Tokyo originally hoped to reach agreement with Moscow on their respective spheres of influence in China. Japan would recognize the Soviet position in Outer Mongolia and Xinjiang, while Moscow would recognize Japan's position in north China and Inner Mongolia. Relations between the Soviet Union and areas within its sphere of influence would be determined solely by the Soviet Union and China. The same would be the case with Tokyo and regions within its sphere. Moreover, the Soviet Union was to agree to stop helping China's war against Japan.[111] As finally signed, the neutrality agreement applied the idea of spheres of influence only to "Manchukuo" and the "Mongolian People's Republic" [Outer Mongolia]. Tokyo and Moscow each pledged to respect the territorial integrity and inviolability of the boundaries of the other's client state. The status of north China, Inner Mongolia, or Xinjiang was not specified by the agreement. Nor was there explicit mention of Soviet aid to China or of its termination. Yet as Japanese Foreign Minister Yosuke Matsuoka explained to the German ambassador to Moscow, the agreement would exert great pressure on the Chinese government, which would perhaps make it possible to force China to submit.[112]

The conclusion of the April 1941 agreement did not take Chiang by surprise. When Matsuoka left on 12 March 1941 for Moscow and Berlin, Chiang accurately surmised Tokyo's objective. Commenting in his diary on the day Matsuoka began his mission, Chiang concluded that Matsuoka's purpose was to increase cooperation between Germany and Japan and to conclude a Japanese-Soviet nonaggression agreement. China should attempt to counter this plot, according to Chiang, by the "active use" of diplomacy toward Germany.[113]

The day after the conclusion of the April agreement, Foreign Minister Wang Chonghui made a public protest against it. His first objection was that Moscow's action violated the provision of the 1937 Sino-Soviet Nonaggression Treaty that neither party would render assistance of any kind, direct or indirect, at any time during the duration of the conflict, to a third party who was carrying out aggression against either China or the Soviet Union. Moreover, the 1937 agreement had specified that both powers would refrain from taking any action or entering into any agreement which in any way could be used by the aggressor to its advantage, and to the disadvantage of the party subjected to aggression. Wang also protested the pledge by Moscow to respect the integrity of Manchukuo and of Japan to respect the Mongolian People's Republic. "It is an indisputable fact that the four Northeastern Provinces and Outer Mongolia are an integral part of the Republic of China and [will] always remain Chinese territory," Wang protested. China would not recognize any engagement entered into by third parties which were detrimental to China's territorial and administrative integrity. Finally, the Soviet and Japanese declarations would have no binding force whatsoever on China. Wang's protest was designed primarily to put on record China's claim to Manchuria and Outer Mongolia. To let such an agreement pass without protest would have implied tacit Chinese acceptance of the independence of those areas. In a sense, Chongqing's April 1941 protest laid the diplomatic basis for Chiang's recovery of Manchuria at Cairo two years later when Chiang was able to use American influence to undo the Japanese-Soviet understanding of April 1941.

Moscow's reply to Chongqing's protest agreed that the Soviet-Japanese agreement had no binding power on China; China was still free to recover Manchuria and to make war to this end. (Moscow did not, of course, grant such "freedom" to China regarding Outer Mongolia.) Furthermore, the agreement would not be an obstacle to continued Soviet assistance to China.[114]

Chiang also feared that there might be secret protocols relating to China attached to the April 1941 agreement. When Ambassador Shao queried Molotov in detail about the possibility of such secret protocols, however, Molotov insisted that the agreement was designed exclusively to maintain peace between Japan and the Soviet Union. It was in no way related to the China problem. Indeed, Molotov said, the two sides had not discussed relations with China during the negotiations.[115] Ambassador Paniushkin made the same points when he discussed the treaty with Chiang Kai-shek on 19 April. The agreement contained nothing touching on the China problem and Soviet policy toward China would not change, Paniushkin assured Chiang.[116]

Even without such secret codicils, the Soviet-Japanese neutrality agreement symbolized the final collapse of Chiang's Soviet diplomacy. It was now clear that the hope which had buoyed Chinese resistance since 1937, that the Soviet Union would enter the war against Japan, was futile. Moreover, the agreement punctured Chiang's hope for parallel Soviet-American actions in the Pacific. Most important, it represented the realization of the long-dreaded Russo-Japanese partition of China. More important than the limitation of the geographic scope of that partition to China's outlying areas was the direction of Soviet policy indicated by the treaty: Moscow had switched from supporting China against Japan, to carving up a weak China in cooperation with Japan.[117]

To prevent demoralization Chiang put the best face on the immense diplomatic setback of April 1941. He chose, therefore, not to admit defeat but to reinterpret his recent Soviet policy in a way which would turn diplomatic defeat into success. He did this by stressing the probable consequences of the treaty for Japanese-American relations. Chiang presented a detailed analysis of the treaty and its consequences in a report to governmental and military leaders on 24 April. Ignoring the fact that Chinese diplomacy had consistently tried to thwart Soviet-Japanese rapprochement, Chiang concluded that the April agreement would benefit China by hastening a Japanese-American war. The treaty was entirely a result of Soviet initiative and represented the success of Soviet policy toward Japan, Chiang asserted. Through the agreement Moscow hoped to accomplish two things. Its most important objective was to uncouple Japan from Germany, thereby eliminating Soviet concerns for the security of Siberia and permitting the concentration of Soviet forces in the West. In this fashion, Moscow hoped to prevent Germany from attacking the Soviet Union. Moscow's second objective, according to Chiang, was to precipitate a Japanese-American war. By guaranteeing the tranquility of Japan's northern flank, Moscow hoped to encourage Japan to advance into Southeast Asia. This would lead to a clash between Japan and the Anglo-American powers, a clash which would "destroy" Japan's navy and leave that island nation in a "hopeless situation."[118]

Regarding China, Chiang said, the treaty had several implications. The agreement would allow Japan to withdraw six divisions from Manchuria and redeploy them to China or to Southeast Asia. It was unlikely that these forces would be sent to China, however, because renewed Japanese offensives in China would require much time and matériel and would bring only limited results. Several times the forces used to attack Wuhan in 1938 would be necessary for an assault on Chongqing, Chiang said, and even then Chongqing was an "impregnable fortress." Moreover, if Japan used all its strength to attack Sichuan province, "other countries" (e.g., the United States and Britain) would take advantage of the opportunity to attack Japan from behind. The utilization of the newly available divisions in Southeast Asia would thus make much more sense for Japan, Chiang concluded. Henceforth, the defense position of the United States in the Far East was the "most critical factor" for China. The United States and Britain were accelerating their war preparations, Chiang said, and a "warlike" situation now existed in the Pacific. This was a "great loss" to Japan, Chiang said, and "greatly strengthened" China's position. The most aggravating element of the April 1941 agreement, Chiang told his audience of top Chinese officials, was Tokyo's and Moscow's cross-recognition of Outer Mongolia and Manchukuo. This, however, was only a "temporary problem." Once China achieved victory it would recover its lost territory.

Conclusion

The period between September 1939 and June 1941 was the nadir of Chiang's effort to secure Soviet support for and overcome Soviet opposition to, his plans to reestablish China's greatness. During this period, Soviet support for China's war effort diminished and by the spring of 1941, not only was Soviet entry into the war extremely unlikely, but it was clear that future Soviet aid would be marginal. Moscow also came down squarely against the recovery of key lost territories by the Republic of China; Moscow's response to Chongqing's protest of the April 1941 neutrality agreement made it clear that China could not expect Soviet support for the recovery of

Manchuria. Moreover, Tokyo's and Moscow's counterpledges to respect the territorial integrity and border inviolability of the Mongolian People's Republic and Manchukuo implied mutual support for the status quo and common opposition to Chinese efforts to change that status quo.

From Chiang's perspective, the shift in Soviet policy during 1940 amounted to a shift from Soviet support for China against Japan, to cooperation with Japan to weaken and partition China. Chiang tried mightily to thwart this shift but without success. His chief handicap was China's own weakness: China was strong enough to be useful to the Soviet Union if Moscow was determined to confront Japan, but not strong enough to offset the advantages Moscow could derive from neutralizing the Japanese threat through agreement with Tokyo. China's international assets were also at a minimum during these midwar years. The Soviet Union was moving toward partnership with the Axis while support from the United States for China was still uncertain. American aid to China increased substantially during 1940, but it was not until the conclusion of the Tri-Partite Treaty in September 1940 that Washington decided that China's continued resistance to Japan was vital to U.S. security. Until that point, the United States still seriously explored the possibility of a compromise settlement with Tokyo which might detach Japan from Germany at China's expense. This meant that from September 1939 to September 1940 China was without a firm and powerful international partner. It was on its own to confront both Japanese and Soviet demands. Earlier the Sino-Soviet alliance had given Chiang substantial leverage. Later, the conjunction of the Sino-American and Soviet-American alliances would give Chongqing an extremely effective lever with Moscow. For a year or so, however, China stood alone.

In several other ways Moscow cooperated actively with Japan against China during these midwar years. As we shall see in the next chapter, Soviet policy toward the CCP and especially toward Xinjiang became less solicitous of Chiang's objective of national unity. The reorientation of the international alignment of the Soviet Union in late 1939 and 1940 induced Moscow to give a somewhat freer reign to Mao's revolutionism, while in Xinjiang Moscow moved to detach that territory from China. Chiang tried desperately but without success to reverse these Soviet policies. It was not until the creation of the Chongqing–Washington and Washington–Moscow links and the immersion of the Soviet Union in a life-and-death struggle against Nazi Germany that Chiang regained Soviet support for his program of establishing China as a great power.

Notes

1. See A. Rossi, *The Russo-German Alliance, August 1939–June 1941*, Boston: Beacon Press, 1951. pp. 109–113. David J. Dallin, *Soviet Russia and the Far East*, New Haven, Conn.: Yale University Press, 1948, p. 151.
2. Regarding German assistance to Moscow during the Winter War *see* Arthur Upham Pope, *Maxim Litvinoff*, New York: L.B. Fisher, 1943, p. 455–456.
3. Rossi, *Russo-German Alliance*, pp. 92–93, 119.
4. Harriet L. Moore, *Soviet Far Eastern Policy, 1931–1945*, Princeton, N.J.: Princeton University Press, 1945, p. 126.
5. Wellington Koo, *Reminiscences of Wellington Koo*, part 2, reel 2, Chinese Oral History Project of the East Asia Institute of Columbia University, New York, Rare Book and Manuscript Library, pp. 864–866; 775–800.

6. Koo, *Reminiscences*, pp. 864–866.
7. *Zhanshi Waijiao*, pp. 428–429.
8. Ibid., p. 430.
9. Ibid., pp. 432–433.
10. Koo, *Reminiscences*, pp. 865; 893.
11. Ibid., pp. 713–714. Koo also speculated that Germany, under Soviet influence and as part of Berlin's strategy of cooperation with Moscow, might once again adopt pro-Chinese policies.
12. Ibid., p. 717.
13. *Zhanshi Waijiao*, pp. 428–429.
14. Koo, *Reminiscences*, pp. 769–771; 721–722.
15. Ibid., p. 870.
16. *Zhanshi Waijiao*, pp. 431–432.
17. Ibid., pp. 432–433.
18. Ibid., pp. 348–349.
19. Ibid., pp. 351–352.
20. Ibid.
21. Ibid., pp. 350–355.
22. Ibid., pp. 356–357.
23. Ibid.
24. Li Zhongyuan, *Zhong Su Buqinfan Tiaoyue yu Ri Su Zhongli Xieding zhi Yanjiu* [Research on the Sino-Soviet Nonaggression Treaty and the Russian-Japanese Neutrality Agreement], masters thesis, Taiwan National University, 1980, p. 44.
25. Li Zhongyuan, *Zhong Su Buqinfan Taioyue*, p. 39.
26. George A. Lensen, *The Strange Neutrality, Soviet-Japanese Relations during the Second World War, 1941–1945*, Tallahassee, Fla.: Diplomatic Press, 1972, p. 2. Regarding the Nomonhan battle, *see* Hato Ikuhiko, "The Japanese-Soviet Confrontation," in *Deterrent Diplomacy, Japan, Germany, and the USSR, 1935–1940*, James W. Morley, editor, New York: Columbia University Press, 1976, pp. 157–178.
27. Lensen, *Strange Neutrality*, pp. 2–3.
28. Ibid., pp. 3–6.
29. *Zhanshi Waijiao*, pp. 345–346.
30. Ibid., pp. 431–432.
31. Li Zhongyuan, *Zhong Su Buqinfan Tiaoyue*, p. 56.
32. *Hu Shi Ren Zhu Mei Dashi Qijian Wanglai Diangao* [Hu Shi's cable correspondence during the period as ambassador to the United States], Zhonghua Minguoshi Ziliao Zonggao, Zhuanti Ziliao Xuanji, Di San Ji [Compendium of materials on the Republic of China's history, selection on specialized topics, vol. 3], Beijing: Zhongguo Shehui Kexueyuan Jindaishi Yanjiusuo, Zhonghua Minguoshizhu, 1978, p. 23.
33. *Zhanshi Waijiao*, p. 346.
34. Ibid., p. 345.
35. Ibid., pp. 348–349. Sun Ke to Chiang Kai-shek, 23 September 1939.
36. Ibid., pp. 432–433.
37. Ibid., p. 361–362.
38. Wa. Zui Ke Fu [Vasilii Chuikov], *Zai Hua Shiming* [Mission to China], Beijing: Xinhua Chubanshe, 1983. Originally published in Russian in the Soviet journal, *New World*, nos. 11, 12, in 1979.
39. "Zhu Sulian hongjun jie" [In celebration of Soviet Red Army Day] *Zhong Su Wenhua* [Sino-Soviet Culture], vol. 5, no. 2 (1 February 1940), pp. 10–11.
40. Wang Chonghui, "Sulian guoqing jinian chengyan" [Sincere words commemorating Soviet national day], *Zhong Su Wenhua* [Sino-Soviet Culture], special issue commemorating the twenty-third anniversary of the Bolshevik insurrection, November 1940, pp. 5–6.
41. Herbert Feis, *The Road to Pearl Harbor*, New York: Atheneum, 1965, pp. 21–22; 72–74.
42. *Hu Shi Laiwang Shuxin Xuan* [Selected correspondence of Hu Shi], vol. 2, Beijing: Zhongguo Shehui Kexueyuan Jindaishi Yanjiusuo, May 1979, p. 449. Guo also wondered if the American government and people adequately understood China's difficulties and its positions in this case.
43. *The Appeal of the Finnish Government to the League of Nations, a Summary Based on the Official Documentation*, special supplement to the Monthly Summary of the League of Nations, December 1939, pp. 42–69.
44. Koo, *Reminiscences*, pp. 938, 959.
45. Ibid., pp. 62–65, 69.
46. *Zhanshi Waijiao*, p. 358.
47. *Hu Shi Laiwang Shuxin Xuan*, p. 449.

120 CHINESE-SOVIET RELATIONS, 1937–1945

48. *Zhanshi Waijiao*, pp. 362-363.
49. Yang Chunzhou, "Yang Jie beihai qian de fan Jiang huodong" [The anti-Chiang activities of Yang Jie prior to his assassination], *Yunnan Wenshi Ziliao Xuanji* [Yunnan Selection of Literary Materials], no. 2, pp. 172–173. According to the memoir of another of Yang's associates, Yang was "forced" to resign as ambassador and return to China. Wang Kaiting, "Wosuo zhidao de Yang Jie jiangjun" [The General Yang Jie I knew], *Kunming Wenshi Ziliao Xuanji* [Kunming Selection of Literary Materials], no. 1, p. 120. Kunming: Renmin Zhengzhi Xieshang Huiyi, n.d. After Yang's return to China he gave frequent public speeches lauding the Soviet Union's military strength and its certain victory over Germany. During World War II he helped organize the anti-Chiang group Three Principles of the People Comrades Alliance, one of the "third force" groups which stood between the CCP and the KMT after the defeat of Japan. He was assassinated in Hong Kong in 1949 while preparing to return to the newly founded People's Republic of China to assume a position in the People's Political Consultative Conference.
50. *Zhanshi Waijiao*, pp. 363–365.
51. Ibid., p. 367.
52. Ibid., p. 365.
53. Ibid., p. 367.
54. Ibid., p. 368.
55. Ibid., p. 371.
56. Ibid., p. 370. Memorandum of Chiang's meeting with the general Soviet advisor, 22 January 1940.
57. Ibid.
58. Ibid., pp. 372–375.
59. *Hu Shi Laiwang Shuxin Xuan*, pp. 439–441. Weng went on to raise the possibility that Moscow's desire to "adjust" its relations with Japan would lead to a reduction of aid to China.
60. Zhou Xicai, *Zhong Su Guannxi Neimu* [The secret history of Sino-Soviet relations], Taibei: Shidai Chubanshe, n.d., p. 58.
61. Shao Lizi, "Chushi Sulian de huiyi" [Memoir of ambassadorship to the Soviet Union], *Wenshi Ziliao Xuanji* [Selection of Literary Materials], vol. 60, Beijing: Zhongguo Renmin Zhengzhi Xieshanghui, pp. 181; 185–186. Chiang Kai-shek himself provides other evidence. In his diary Chiang recorded the monthly tonnage of war supplies reaching China over various routes in the spring of 1940. Some 31,000 tons ran the Japanese blockade to come through various Chinese ports. 15,000 tons came over the rail line through northern Vietnam. 10,000 tons came through Rangoon and over the Burma Road. Only 500 tons came via the Xinjiang route (*Milu*, vol. 12, p. 42). Assuming that no Soviet aid came by sea, these figures indicate that Soviet aid had fallen to a bare minimum.
62. *Zhanshi Waijiao*, pp. 530–531.
63. Ibid., pp. 374–375.
64. Ibid., pp. 530–531.
65. Lensen, *Strange Neutrality*, p. 32.
66. *Zhanshi Waijiao*, pp. 520–521.
67. Shao Lizi, "Chushi Sulian," p. 182.
68. *Zhanshi Waijiao*, p. 522. The published KMT document indicates the aircraft were "E-16" types. For reasons discussed in note 33 of Chapter 2, I have concluded that this is probably an error.
69. Enzo Angelucei, *The Rand McNally Encyclopedia of Military Aircraft, 1914–1980*, New York: The Military Press, 1983, pp. 223, 286.
70. Shao Lizi, "Chushi Sulian," pp. 181–182.
71. Ibid., pp. 185–186.
72. *Zhanshi Waijiao*, p. 523.
73. Ibid., pp. 373–374. This wording was somewhat different and more ambiguous than that originally proposed by He Yaozu on 19 December and approved by Chiang. His original proposal provided: "If an appropriate situation is reached and the Soviet Union adopts an active policy in the Far East, China and Russia will mutually cooperate in waging war against Japan. After the war, the arrangement of political and economic measures related to the eternal peace of the Far East, and military measures, will be satisfactorily discussed and agreement reached."
74. Ibid.
75. Ibid.
76. Ibid., p. 378.
77. Ibid.
78. Ibid., p. 379.
79. Ibid., p. 380. Also, Hu Shi's cable of 9 June 1940 to Chen Bulai and of 19 August 1940 to Chiang Kai-shek, in *Hu Shi Ren Zhu Mei Dashi Qijian Wanglai Diangao*, pp. 43, 61.

80. *Zhanshi Waijiao*, pp. 384–385.
81. Ibid., pp. 523–524.
82. Shao Lizi, "Chushi Sulian," p. 188.
83. *Zhanshi Waijiao*, p. 526.
84. Cited in Charles B. McLane, *Soviet Policy and the Chinese Communists, 1931–1946*, New York: Columbia University Press, 1958, p. 129.
85. Cheng Tianfang, then China's ambassador to Berlin, says that Soviet arms deliveries declined to a minimum after January 1941 (Cheng Tien-fong, *A History of Sino-Soviet Relations*, Washington, D.C.: Public Affairs Press, 1957, p. 220). Cheng implies that the termination of Soviet aid was due to the clash between CCP and KMT armies in Anwei in January. Vasilii Chuikov says in his memoir that in April 1941, 150 seventy-five millimeter Soviet cannons were sent to China via Lanzhou (Wa. Zui Ke Fu, *Zai Hua Shiming*, p. 87). Charles McLane cites American sources to the effect that Soviet supplies continued to reach China as late as August 1941, but that no contracts for further shipments were made after the onset of the German invasion of the Soviet Union (*FRUS*, 1941, vol. 4, pp. 10–15; cited in McLane, *Soviet Policy*, p. 136).
86. *Milu*, vol. 12, p. 184.
87. Rossi, *Russo-German Alliance*, pp. 173–176.
88. Wa. Zui Ke Fu, *Zai Hua Shiming*, pp. 31–32, 36.
89. *Milu*, vol. 12, pp. 60–62.
90. This interpretation of the Munich Conference had been conveyed to Sun Ke at the conclusion of his August–October 1939 mission to Moscow. *See* Sun Ke, "Guoji xianshi yu Zhongguo" [The present international situation and China], *Zhong Su Wenhua* [Sino-Soviet Culture], vol. 5, no. 2 (1 February 1940), pp. 1–8.
91. *Cankao Ziliao*, vol. 8, p. 309.
92. *Da Gong Bao*, 17 October 1939; *Cankao Ziliao*, vol. 8, p. 311.
93. Reprinted in *Waijiaoshi Ziliao (1937–1945)*, pp. 169–171.
94. Chiang Kai-shek, 18 November 1939, "Zhongguo kangzhan yu guoji xingshi" [China's war of resistance and the international situation], in *Jiang Zongtong Sixiang Yanlun Ji*, [Collected speeches and writings of President Chiang], vol. 15, p. 218. According to a note in Mao Zedong's *Selected Works*, Chiang had declared this to be his objective at the Fifth Plenary Session of the Fifth Central Executive Committee of the KMT in January 1939 (*Selected Works of Mao Tse-tung*, vol. 2, Beijing: Foreign Languages Press, 1967, p. 255).
95. John Hunter Boyle, *China and Japan at War, 1937–1945, the Politics of Collaboration*, Stanford, Calif.: Stanford University Press, 1972, pp. 289–292. *Duiwai Guanxishi, 1840–1949*, pp. 65–66.
96. *Duiwai Guanxishi, 1840–1949*, p. 79. *See also* Hosoya Chihiro, "The Tripartite Pact," in *Deterrent Diplomacy*, James Morley, editor, pp. 214–226.
97. *Milu*, vol. 12, p. 46.
98. Ibid., p. 52.
99. Zuo Lu, *Huiyilu* (Memoir), vol. 2, Taibei: Duli Chubanshe, 1956, p. 549.
100. Shao Lizi, "Chushi Sulian," p. 181.
101. *Zhanshi Waijiao*, p. 379.
102. William C. Kirby, *Germany and Republican China*, Stanford, Calif.: Stanford University Press, 1984, p. 251.
103. *Zhanshi Waijiao*, p. 379.
104. Ibid.
105. Chiang apparently took to heart Stalin's advice that the main duty was to preserve and strengthen China's army. According to Yan Yuqing, who then worked in Chiang's staff office, at the end of October Chiang sent orders to the commanders of the various war districts instructing them to conserve their strength. (Yan Yuqing, "Wo suo zhidao de Chen Bulai" [The Chen Bulai that I knew], *Wenshi Ziliao Xuanji*, vol. 81, p. 165.)
106. Shao Lizi, "Chushi Sulian," p. 188.
107. Lensen, *Strange Neutrality*, p. 186.
108. 24 October 1940, in *Milu*, vol. 12, p. 54.
109. *Milu*, vol. 12, p. 62.
110. Wa. Zui Ke Fu, *Zai Hua Shiming*, p. 83.
111. Lensen, *Strange Neutrality*, pp. 12–13. *See also* Li Zhongyuan, *Zhong Su Buqinfan Tiaoyue*, pp. 49–50.
112. Li Zhongyuan, *Zhong Su Buqinfan Tiaoyue*, p. 54.
113. *Milu*, vol. 12, p. 127.
114. Li Zhongyuan, *Zhong Su Buqinfan Tiaoyue*, p. 57.

115. Shao Lizi, "Chushi Sulian," p. 190. Shortly before the treaty had been signed, Shao asked Soviet leaders about reports carried by Japanese newspapers that the two sides had discussed a possible division of China. Soviet officials dismissed these reports as untrue. When Shao insisted that Soviet officials should not discuss the China problem with Japan, Molotov replied that, of course, this was correct (*Zhanshi Waijiao*, p. 388).
116. *Milu*, vol. 12, p. 132.
117. Ibid., p. 127.
118. Ibid., pp. 132–134.

Chapter V

The CCP and Soviet-Axis Alignment

The Comintern and the "Second Imperialist War"

The diplomatic upheaval of August–September 1939, specifically the Soviet-German Nonaggression Treaty and the beginning of the European war, had important consequences for the KMT–CCP contest and the Soviet role in that duel. The Comintern's analysis of the European war reflected, of course, the alignment of the Soviet Union with Nazi Germany. Throughout the twenty-one months of Soviet-Nazi cooperation, the Comintern publication *Communist International* scarcely mentioned Germany and fascism, while bitterly condemning the aims and motives of the British and French "monopoly capitalist ruling classes." The war was an unjust, imperialist war and its continuation was primarily a result of the greed and evil ambitions of the British and French governments. The Communist Parties of France and Britain sought to undermine their countries' war efforts while the Communist Party of the United States sought to prevent American involvement in the war, that is, to thwart American aid to Britain and France.[1]

Regarding the united front, the Comintern now concluded that a united front "from above," with the bourgeois ruling circles of various capitalist countries, was no longer possible because the bourgeoisie had betrayed the proletariat through its policy of appeasing fascism. A "united front from below," between the working classes and various middle groups, was now the order of the day. As Georgii Dimitrov explained in November 1939, "In the present situation, working class unity can only be achieved from below, on the basis of the development of the movement of the working masses themselves and in a resolute struggle against the treacherous . . . leaders of the Social Democratic parties." The goal of these "united fronts from below" was the creation of "democracies of a new type" which would carry out programs of social reform.[2]

While these formulations applied chiefly to the industrialized capitalist countries, they also had important implications for such "semicolonial" countries as China. In colonial and semicolonial countries a united front with the ruling bourgeoisie was still possible if that bourgeoisie was willing to struggle against imperialism. In some colonial countries this caveat was ignored, and the local Communist Parties promptly reasserted a much more radical line, only to be reined in again by the Comintern. In India, for example, the application of the new line by the Indian Communist Party promptly brought that party into opposition to Mohandas Gandhi's National Congress Party on the grounds that it was not sufficiently opposed to Indian involvement in the war. The Indian Party's radical interpretation of the new line was overruled by the ECCI, however, and it soon began pursuing a policy of "both unity and struggle" with the Congress Party.[3] As we shall see, developments in China followed a similar pattern.

There was another very important but less publicized element of Comintern policy during the period of Soviet-Nazi cooperation. This had to do with the revolutionization of the masses of the various belligerent countries which the war was to bring about, and the role of the Red Army as an agent of revolution. Comintern leaders imagined that "the second imperialist war" would end as the first one had, with revolutionary uprisings by the peoples forced to bear the sacrifices of the war. The international situation at the end of the second imperialist war would, however, be quite different from that of 1918–1919. Now a powerful working-class state existed to assist and support the revolutionary movements of other countries. Moreover, Stalin's deft strategy of aligning with the Axis meant that the relative strength of that socialist state would be greatly increased by the time the current war among the imperialists ended. While the imperialists were exhausting one another with their war, the industrial and military might of the Soviet Union would grow powerful in peace. Then, when the time was right, the Red Army would act to assist the revolutionary masses struggling to overthrow the ruling classes in other countries. The "revolutionary role" of the Red Army in fact became a central characteristic of Soviet foreign policy during the first year of the "second imperialist war."

There were numerous examples of the use of the Red Army to "expand the frontiers of socialism" during 1939–1940. The "liberation" of eastern Poland in September 1939, of Finland's Karelian Isthmus and a strip of territory along the northern Soviet-Finnish border in April 1940, of Romania's province of Bessarabia and northern Bukovina in June 1940, and of Lithuania, Latvia, and Estonia in July–September 1940, were all cases in point. Soviet aspirations in Finland may have gone well beyond the Karelian Isthumus. On 1 December 1939, when the Winter War was just beginning, a Provisional People's Government of Finland headed by the Finnish Comintern apparatchik Otto Kunsinen was established at Terijoki on Finnish territory but behind Soviet lines. A program issued by this provisional government called on the Red Army to help "liberate" the Finnish people.[4] It is quite possible that the realization of this aim was thwarted by the military setbacks suffered by the Red Army in Finland and by the strong Western reaction to the Soviet attack, which threatened to drag the Soviet Union into the European conflict alongside Germany.

Nor was the use of the Red Army in such a fashion to be limited to small countries on the immediate periphery of the Soviet Union. After a detailed study of the strategy of the French Communist Party during these years, A. Rossi concluded that that Party sought to take power in Vichy France largely via cooperating with the German authorities and by engineering a type of Brest-Litovsk peace settlement with Berlin, and then waiting until a powerful Soviet Union could dictate the terms of peace to the war-weary belligerents. Then the frontiers of socialism could be expanded to France.[5] As we shall see in the next chapter, the Xinjiang region of China was the area of the Far East most likely to be "liberated" by the Red Army during 1940–1941.

Mao Zedong responded promptly to the shift in Comintern line in September 1939. During that month Mao found four occasions to endorse all aspects of the momentous shifts in Soviet policy.[6] In these talks, Mao unequivocally endorsed the Hitler–Stalin pact as a brilliant victory for Soviet peace diplomacy which had thwarted Anglo-French efforts to instigate a Soviet-German war and Japanese efforts to encircle the Soviet Union. Regarding the European war, Mao explained that it was an internecine war of imperialists for the redivision of spheres of influence, colonies, and semicolonies just as the 1914–1918 war had been. All the belligerents were motivated entirely by lust for conquest. There was nothing noble or just about the war from the standpoint of either side. It followed that the war efforts of neither side should be supported.

In line with Comintern orientation during this period, the anti-British and French theme of Mao's line was much stronger than the anti-German. Moral responsibility for the war, Mao strongly implied, lay with Britain and France, who had refused to cooperate with the Soviet Union in support of Spain, China, and Czechoslovakia. London and Paris had not wanted peace but a big war which they hoped to use to their advantage. In his 28 September speech, for example, Mao said:

> Many people around the world have been blinded by the honeyed words of Chamberlain and partners, and do not know the harm that lurks in the laughter of these men. They do not know that when Chamberlain and Dalider decided to reject the Soviet Union, they had decided to carry out imperialist war. Only then was the Soviet-German treaty of non-aggression concluded. . . . Everyone knows that in today's world, to reject the Soviet Union is to reject peace.[7]

Britain had become, according to Mao, the most reactionary country in the world. Chamberlain was the ringleader of hostility to socialism, to the people, and to democracy. His plan was first to defeat Germany and then to attack the Soviet Union. This implied that Germany's struggle against Anglo-French imperialism was the first line of defense of the Soviet Union. Mao explicitly recognized the possibility of Germany's war acquiring a "progressive" character. If Britain attacked the Soviet Union, Mao said in his 28 September speech, Germany's war would change its character and become beneficial to socialism. Under such circumstances, the Soviet Union might form an alliance with Germany.

Mao also believed that the new imperialist war would create the conditions for world revolution. The war would be protracted and would bring unparalleled death and suffering, Mao said. This would create a revolutionary consciousness among the masses and turn the people against the war policies of their governments. When this had happened during the first imperialist war, Mao said, only one socialist state had been produced. Now, however, there were many countries which had powerful Communist movements and there was a powerful socialist country, the Soviet Union, willing to assist the liberation movements of oppressed peoples. Mao pointed to the "liberation" of the "White Russians and Ukrainians" of eastern Poland as an example of such assistance. The Red Army's occupation of eastern Poland had been "completely just," Mao said, because it was taking back what had been stolen from the young Soviet Republic by German imperialism, and because it involved the "liberation" of weak peoples.

The world was on the eve of a new era of revolution, Mao said. The Soviet Union, the national liberation movements of the colonial and semicolonial countries, and the people's movements within the imperialist countries made up a powerful revolutionary camp. Their objective was nothing less than the overthrow of the entire reactionary camp, the warmongers and the bourgeoisie. Its method was to use revolutionary war to defeat imperialist war. In countries such as China and India, the duty of revolutionaries was to strengthen the united front and resistance to aggression, Mao said. In short, Mao saw the new war as creating favorable conditions for a new upsurge in the world revolution. China, of course, was to be a key arena of the world revolutionary struggle.

The alacrity of Mao's endorsement of Moscow's new line is striking. The speed and comprehensiveness with which Mao embraced Moscow's new line stood in sharp contrast, for example, to his foot-dragging response in 1935–1936 to the promulgation of the united front line, or his 1937–1938 response to Moscow's moderate interpretation of that line. This leads one to suspect that Mao's enthusiasm for Moscow's new orientation was genuine. Mao probably welcomed the leftward swing in Comintern line because he realized it would make possible a reassertion of his claim to Communist leadership of China's national liberation struggle. He may also have hoped that it would open the door to Soviet assistance of the CCP.

New Democracy and World Revolution

The upheaval of fall 1939 prompted both the CCP and the KMT to adopt sterner policies toward the other. Each was apparently convinced that the new international situation would make Moscow more willing to envision a loosening of the bonds of the shotgun marriage of the second united front. This appraisal was only partially accurate.

The policy of the CCP moved leftward with the Comintern's line. Armed proletarian revolution against the bourgeoisie was once again placed on the theoretical, if not the immediate, agenda of the Chinese revolution. In his October 1939 introduction to the new CCP journal *The Communist*, Mao termed China's "big bourgeoisie" "comprador in character" and "a target of the revolution." However, because of the contradictions between the various imperialist powers to which different segments of the "big bourgeoisie" were linked, some parts of the bourgeoisie could be won over to the proletariat during certain stages of the revolution. Even then, however, the proletariat would have to wage a peaceful and bloodless struggle against such "progressive" bourgeoisie in order to avoid and prepare for the day when the proletariat would wage a "stern and resolute armed struggle against the bourgeoisie."[8] This line was a sharp contrast to Mao's earlier talk of mutual help and concessions and long-term cooperation which had characterized Mao's speeches and writings since the end of 1937.

Mao also used the new international circumstances to reestablish his claim to CCP leadership of China's united front and national liberation struggle. Mao's most famous and comprehensive explication of the revived Communist claim to leadership of China's national liberation struggle was his tract "On New Democracy," published in January 1940. "On New Democracy' firmly rooted China's revolution in an international context. In brief, it argued that the existence and power of the Soviet Union made possible a proletarian-led (i.e., CCP led) revolution in China. The syllogism

Mao laid out in "On New Democracy" began with the orthodox notion of the historical inevitability of "democratic revolutions" whose "historic tasks" were securing national independence and unity, and eliminating "feudalism." Prior to the Bolshevik Revolution, the bourgeoisie had led the democratic revolutions of various countries, making them "bourgeois democratic revolutions." After the October Revolution and the establishment of a Soviet state, however, history entered a new era. It now became possible for the proletariat to lead the "democratic revolution," making them a "new type of democratic revolution." This was the case in China. Under circumstances after 1917, China's bourgeoisie, especially its big capitalists, was unwilling and unable to break completely with imperialism. Rather, they would try to appease imperialism and would refuse to overthrow feudalism in China. The inconsistent reaction of China's bourgeoisie to the May Fourth movement of 1919 had proved, Mao asserted, that "at most [the bourgeoisie] could serve to a certain extent as an ally during revolutionary periods, while inevitably the responsibility for leading the [revolutionary] alliance rested on proletarian culture and ideology. This is an undeniable fact."[9] It followed, therefore, that only the proletariat could lead China's struggle against imperialism and feudalism. Because of these new international circumstances, China's "democratic revolution" was a "new type of democratic revolution led by the proletariat."

Mao's new line also revived socialism as the explicit (albeit future) goal of China's revolution. This was something the CCP had not done since early 1936. China's revolution was divided into two stages, Mao now wrote. During the first stage, there would be a "revolutionary democratic dictatorship" of several classes to carry out the antiimperialist and antifeudal tasks of the revolution. Then, once these objectives had been accomplished, new international circumstances and the proletariat leadership of China's revolution would make it possible for the revolution to move into the second, socialist stage.[10] Although Mao's "two-stage" formulation provided a basis for maintaining the CCP–KMT united front as long as the war with Japan continued, it also made explicit the ultimate rejection of long-term cooperation between those two parties. It said, in effect, that KMT–CCP cooperation was temporary, a "stage," and that as the revolution moved into its second, socialist stage, the "big bourgeoisie" and the KMT which represented it, would become counterrevolutionary.

A final theme of Mao's "On New Democracy" was the critical role the Soviet Union was to play in the victory of the Chinese revolution. China's New Democratic revolution had to proceed in close alliance with the Soviet Union, Mao explained. There were now three camps in the world: the imperialist camp made up of the capitalist countries, the socialist Soviet Union, and countries such as China where there was a united front of several revolutionary classes led by the proletariat. It was inevitable that countries such as China would align with the socialist countries against imperialism. China's revolution could not act as an "allied army" of the "counterrevolutionary, world bourgeois camp" but had to serve as an "allied army" of the "world socialist revolution." Mao was unequivocal about the Soviet Union's role: "In today's world, all imperialism is our enemy. China wants independence, and absolutely cannot do without the assistance of the socialist nations and the international proletariat." The victory of the Chinese revolution depended on international support. "The assistance of the Soviet Union, is the indispensable condition for the final victory of the war of resistance," Mao said. "Refuse the assistance of the Soviet Union and revolution will fail."[11] A corollary of China's close alignment with the Soviet Union was that it should distance itself from the Anglo-American camp then confronting the Soviet Union.

> The conflict between the socialist Soviet Union and imperialist England and America has already intensified. If China does not stand to one side, it must stand on the other. This is an inevitable tendency. How could it be possible not to lean to one side? This is a day dream. The whole world will be drawn into these two camps. Henceforth "neutrality" is merely a word used to deceive people. Moreover, China is struggling against an imperialist that has penetrated deeply into the national territory and *without Soviet assistance, it can forget about final victory* [emphasis added].[12]

Mao recognized the possibility that China might obtain some assistance from Britain and the United States, but he believed that this should not be done at the expense of offending Moscow. In a passage of "On New Democracy" which was deleted from later versions of that work, Mao said:

> During the first two years of the war of resistance, because the great imperialist war had not yet broken out, it was still possible to use the contradictions between England and America and Japan. But with the outbreak of the [European] war, although this sort of contradiction has not been eliminated, it has been lessened, and if not used gingerly [*bu de dang*] England and America will demand that China join them in opposing the Soviet Union. If China relies on them, it will immediately stand in the reactionary camp of imperialism and any national independence will be finished.[13]

Stripped of its theoretical ambiguities, Mao's new line was this: (1) The CCP not the KMT would lead China's war against Japan; (2) China should distance itself from the Anglo-American camp and align more closely with the Soviet Union; (3) at some point the CCP would break with the KMT and carry out a socialist revolution; (4) China's socialist revolution would be carried out with the assistance of the Soviet Union; and (5) this would occur when the war-weary proletariat of the imperialist countries rose in revolt against their governments. In many ways Mao's late-1939 line represented a return to the radical position he had staked out in the opening months of the war. Comintern pressure had forced Mao to moderate his policy during 1938 and most of 1939. Now Mao welcomed the opportunity to revive his earlier claim to Communist leadership of the Chinese revolution. In effect, Mao's reinterpretation of the duties and tasks of the revolution in late 1939 was a brilliant manipulation of the shift in Comintern line. Mao was utilizing the August 1939 revolution in Soviet foreign policy and Comintern line to recover much of the ideological ground he had conceded to Stalin in mid-1938.

The First Anticommunist High Tide

The renewed radicalism of the CCP of late 1939 reflected not only changes in Comintern line, but also escalating KMT pressure against the CCP. As we saw in Chapter 3, Mao had responded moderately to this mounting pressure during the first nine months of 1939. Now, Mao seized the opportunity to adopt publicly a harder, less conciliatory attitude toward KMT encroachments on the newly established revolutionary base areas.

The Nationalist effort to hem in the CCP moved into high gear in the fall of 1939. In October, the National Government suspended the disbursement of 600,000 yuan and allotments of ammunition which had previously gone to the CCP. Then in December, the combined forces of Shanxi warlord Yan Xishan and those of the central government commanded by Hu Songnan began moving against the Shaan-Gan-Ning special district.

Yan Xishan was a member of the KMT Central Executive Committee (CEC), and in December 1937 he was appointed commander of the Second War District, which included Shanxi and Suiyuan provinces. Shanxi was a major target of CCP expansion and throughout 1938 Yan's control over that province was undermined by the growth of the CCP. As a result, in March 1939 Yan concluded that the CCP represented a more serious threat to his power than the Japanese and decided to focus his efforts on checking the CCP. This led to a de facto cease-fire with Japan. Then, in the spring of 1939, in conformity with the decisions of the recent Fifth Plenum of the KMT, Yan began setting up special committees to contest CCP control of areas behind Japanese lines. Tension with the CCP naturally escalated. As it did, Yan began coordinating anticommunist actions with local Japanese forces. Early in December, Yan's forces launched an operation against a column of the Eighth Route Army operating in northwestern Shanxi province. The Communist column broke out of the encirclement and joined other Communist forces to counterattack Yan's armies.[14] Hu Songnan's forces joined in the battle on 11 December, moving first to occupy the northeastern corner of Gansu province and then to expand their control to all of eastern Gansu.[15] In this position Hu's forces sat astride the road from Shaanxi to Outer Mongolia via the provinces of Ningxia and Suiyuan, thereby shutting off one of the possible lines of communication between the CCP and the Soviet Union.

Fighting between Communist and Nationalist forces, dubbed the "First Anti-Communist High Tide" by the CCP, escalated throughout December 1939 and continued into March 1940. The CCP strongly and repeatedly protested what it termed the attempted suppression by the KMT of the people's anti-Japanese forces.[16] Yet both the CCP and the KMT publicly treated the incidents as "local" in character and refrained from blaming them on the central authorities of the other party.[17] Neither Chongqing nor the CCP desired a formal rupture in the united front.

Nor did the Soviet Union. Moscow used its leverage with Chongqing to help force the suspension of Chongqing's first concerted wartime military move against the CCP. The eruption of major fighting between CCP and KMT forces in early 1940 coincided with the suspension of Soviet military assistance to the Republic of China, a development discussed in Chapter 4. Both Chinese and Soviet sources agree that this linkage was not coincidental. Aleksandr Kalyagin claims, for example, that Soviet aid to China was closely linked to the continuation of the united front, thereby implying that as the united front deteriorated Soviet aid declined.[18] A Soviet polemic of 1981 was even more explicit, asserting that the suspension of Soviet aid to Chongqing in late 1939 and early 1940 was a response to the KMT suspension of deliveries of supplies to the CCP and the beginning of military operations against the base areas of the CCP.[19] Other Nationalist sources say that on 1 March 1940 the Soviet Union "indirectly" indicated to Chongqing that "unless the problem of the CCP is resolved, it will be impossible to continue economic assistance" to China.[20]

A reading of the record of diplomatic interactions between Moscow and Chongqing in late 1939 and early 1940 does *not*, however, indicate that the clashes between the CCP and the KMT were a major issue in Sino-Soviet relations at this point. Indeed, the published Nationalist archives for this period indicate no discussion whatsoever of the mounting clashes between CCP and government forces. There *was* continual discussion about China's alignment at the League of Nations during the Soviet-Finnish Winter War, but apparently none about KMT–CCP "friction."[21] This leads to the conclusion that China's voting at the League of Nations and, more generally, the international alignment of the Republic of China, was a much more important problem in Sino-Soviet relations at that time. Nonetheless, there is no reason to discount entirely the Nationalist and Soviet assertions that Soviet aid was used to force Chiang Kai-shek to ease pressure on the CCP. Moscow may well have abstained from diplomatic protests because it preferred not to hand to Chongqing or other interested parties ready evidence of Soviet interference in China's internal affairs. More subtle methods, perhaps an off-the-record comment by Kalyagin or some other ranking Soviet representative, could have been used. There were probably multiple objectives behind the Soviet suspension of aid in early 1940: to retaliate for China's alignment at Geneva, to facilitate better relations with Japan, and to prevent civil war in China. Like the United States four years later, the Soviet Union was pressuring both the KMT and the CCP to moderate their policies toward one another, and used its assistance to the National Government as one instrument in its effort to achieve this. Chiang in any case concluded that there was a linkage between his anti-CCP moves and Moscow's suspension of aid. Writing in his diary on 1 March 1940 he asserted that he was ready to call Stalin's hand over this issue:

> If the CCP does not calmly accept discipline, our government absolutely cannot let them betray the nation. Regarding the matter of whether or not Russia will give us economic assistance, this is not on my mind. We absolutely cannot hope for favors from foreign countries, nor can we accept internal calamities bequeathed on us by foreign countries.[22]

In spite of these bold words, Soviet pressure was one factor persuading Chiang to halt Hu Songnan's offensive against the Shaan-Gan-Ning base area. The Republic of China was then extremely isolated and could not afford to alienate the Soviet Union further. The early-1940 suspension of the anti-CCP campaign under Soviet pressure represented a setback for Chiang's strategy of winning Soviet acquiescence to the restriction of the CCP which he had outlined at the Fifth Plenum in January 1939. It also represented the utility of Mao's deal with Stalin. Soviet influence had helped protect the CCP.

The Comintern and Mao's New Democracy

Just as Moscow was not enthusiastic about Chiang's anticommunist campaign, it was also unenthusiastic about Mao's radical new line. Early in 1940, Moscow moved again to reign in Mao's drive for revolutionary power. This time, however, Moscow's efforts were less successful than in December 1937 and September 1938.

Soviet media attention to the CCP between August 1939 and June 1941 dropped to the lowest level since the early 1920s. The Soviet press did not report important CCP gatherings and events during this period, although it did report on KMT meetings. In spite of the fact that this period was one of Mao's most prolific periods of writing, the Soviet press carried only two statements by Mao, both of which were within six months of the signing of the Hitler–Stalin pact. Mao's most important essay during this period, "On New Democracy," was not mentioned in the Soviet press. Indeed, it was not mentioned until after the war. Soviet media coverage of guerrilla activities in China also declined during 1940 and ceased altogether by the end of that year. Previous coverage of such activities had been comparable to that given to China's regular forces. Soviet media also praised continued KMT–CCP cooperation and reported no basic problems in that united front. It did, however, publish CCP accounts and interviews which referred to KMT–CCP tensions and conflicts. Perhaps most important, the Soviet media continued to laud china's war of national liberation and *the KMT for leading that war* and for leading China toward democracy.[23] This was in stark contrast to the theory of "proletarian" leadership which Mao advanced during this period.

Low media attention probably signaled greater Soviet skepticism about Mao's radical line and a desire to minimize its association with that line.[24] Yet lower public attention did not mean that Moscow washed its hands of the CCP. To the contrary, there is substantial evidence that Moscow continued to pressure Yan'an to moderate its expansionist drive for the sake of keeping Chiang in the war against Japan.

Regular communication between Moscow and Yan'an continued throughout the 1940–1941 period.[25] Soviet journalists were stationed in Yan'an, and the information they collected allowed the chief Soviet advisor to Chiang Kai-shek, General Vasilii Chuikov, and presumably Moscow, to keep informed of developments there.[26] Moreover, Chiang routinely, albeit grudgingly, approved Soviet requests for the dispatch of Comintern representatives to Yan'an and of CCP military cadres to the Soviet Union for training. As late as January 1941, Chiang Kai-shek approved the rotation of three Soviet reporters stationed in Yan'an and the dispatch of two Soviet doctors to that city.[27] Presumably this flow of Soviet personnel brought whatever equipment was necessary to maintain in good repair the large radio apparatus brought to Yan'an by Wang Ming in November 1937. When the new Comintern representative Peter Vladimirov arrived at Communist headquarters in 1942, he found the radio decrepit but still operating.[28] There was also radio contact between Yan'an and the Soviet Union via Xinjiang warlord Sheng Shicai's transmitting station in Dihua. When Zhou Enlai passed through Dihua in February 1940 on his way back from Moscow, he instructed the personnel operating that equipment to change regularly the codes used to communicate with CCP headquarters.[29]

The CCP also still found it necessary to report to the Comintern during the interregnum of Soviet-Axis cooperation. In September 1939, senior Politburo member Zhou Enlai went to Moscow for treatment of a broken arm he had sustained in a fall from horseback earlier that year. Zhou stayed in Moscow for six months, returning to Yan'an in March 1940.[30] Zhou's mission to Moscow also had a political objective:

to respond to Comintern doubts about Mao's interpretation of "new democracy" and, if possible, to secure Comintern approval of that new, radical line. Zhou may well have carried with him a draft of Mao's tract on new democracy.

Zhou's Moscow mission took place against the background of the first open revolt by a national Communist Party against Moscow. Immediately prior to the Winter War the secretary general of the Finnish Communist Party rejected a direct order from Stalin to report to the Soviet Union to assume the premiership of the Terijoki government. Then, once the Soviet attack began, the Finnish Communist leader called on the proletariat, and mobilized the Finnish Communist Party, to defend the Finnish homeland against Soviet imperialist attack.[31] While there was no direct connection between the nationalist revolt by the Finnish Communists and Zhou's visit, events in Finland certainly roused Comintern sensitivities to the dangers of "nationalist deviations" and colored its reception of Zhou.

Zhou's trip to Moscow may also have been related to Moscow's recall of Comintern military advisor Otto Braun in September 1939. Braun had long been critical of Mao Zedong's leadership, and the fact that Braun was now to have an opportunity to report fully and personally to the Comintern leadership may have figured in the CCP decision to send Zhou to the Soviet Union at this juncture. Perhaps Zhou hoped to minimize the damage to Comintern–CCP relations which Braun might inflict. In any case, Zhou's and Braun's trips to Moscow were related in an immediate sense: they both travelled there aboard the same Soviet aircraft. Once in Moscow Braun wrote a long report summarizing his seven years' experience in China. Braun says little about this report, but one can safely assume that it contained many of the same conclusions which he expressed in his memoir, that is, that Mao Zedong was a petty bourgeois national deviationist who had little understanding of the primary duty of a true Communist to defend the Soviet Union. Shortly after completing this report, Braun joined Zhou, Mao Zedong's brother Mao Zemin, and "several leading members of the ECCI" for a series of day-long discussions of the CCP's political-military strategy.[32]

Several years later, during the campaign to extirpate Comintern influence in the CCP during World War II, Zhou described briefly his 1940 discussions in Moscow. Comintern leaders had feared, Zhou reported, that the ideology of the CCP would deviate from Marxism–Leninism because it was not rooted in the workers' movement. Zhou reassured the Comintern that this would not happen. Indeed, the long struggle of the CCP in the villages had proved, Zhou argued, that under Mao's leadership the Party could thoroughly "bolshevize" itself and maintain proletarian ideology. Such a development was, however, both historically unprecedented and contrary to all Comintern writings on the subject, Zhou said, and when "some comrades in the Comintern" heard such a proposition, they laughed skeptically.[33]

According to Gao Jun, the associate of Ren Bishi who was still in Moscow in 1940 and who worked with Zhou during the latter's 1939–1940 visit, Zhou worked assiduously to overcome Comintern "misunderstandings" of Mao Zedong's line and leadership. In his capacity as CCP representative to the Comintern, Ren Bishi asked Zhou to make a detailed report to the ECCI on the war situation in China and on the political and military line of the CCP. When Zhou finished his report, Georgii Dimitrov asked him to explain "some other matters," and Ren Bishi then suggested that Zhou explain the entire situation which had occurred after Wang Ming's return to China at the end of 1937. These discussions continued into a second day, with Zhou explaining to the ECCI how Wang Ming had put himself in opposition to the Party line represented by Mao Zedong and how he had implemented his rightist capitulationist line, thereby causing serious injuries to the revolution.[34] Apparently these discussions involved charges that Mao had violated the international line during his conflict with Wang Ming, with Zhou countering by elucidating Wang Ming's own violations of CCP discipline. Interestingly, Dimitrov disowned Wang Ming's earlier opposition to Mao. When Dimitrov heard Zhou's account of Wang's opposition to Mao, an account which apparently included reference of Wang's use of his affiliation with the Comintern to intimidate other CCP members, Dimitrov reportedly became very angry and denied that Wang had acted with Comintern support in 1937–1938. Dimitrov reportedly told Zhou:

> When Wang Ming returned to China I told him, "You are one of the secretaries of the Comintern, but you cannot exhibit [*chuxian*] your Comintern secretary status. You should respect the comrade leaders within China, especially Comrade Mao Zedong." At that time Wang Ming had reservations about what I said, but I never imagined that when he returned to China he would act in such a fashion.[35]

There is no reason to take Dimitrov's words, as reported, at face value. Indeed, the prima facie assumption would be to discount them, since time and again the Comintern had responded to the failure of its line in China by disowning various CCP leaders who had faithfully implemented that line. Perhaps more creditable was Dimitrov's explanation of how the purge of Wang Ming's mentor, Pavil Mif, had undermined Wang's political credibility in Moscow. Mif had fallen victim to the NKVD and was executed at the age of thirty-eight on 10 September 1939.[36] Dimitrov explained to Zhou and Ren that Wang Ming had been introduced to Stalin by Mif. But as early as 1937, Dimitrov said, Mif had been "struggled against" as a Trotskyite due to his earlier connections with the first president of Sun Yat-sen University, A.I. Rykov, who had himself been "exposed" as a Trotskyite. At the same time, the Comintern had also considered the "problem" of Wang Ming because of his affiliation with Mif and, by extension, Rykov. At this point in his talk with Zhou and Ren, Dimitrov reportedly laughed and said, "Wang Ming is a clever fellow, he changed very quickly thereby saving his political life." Dimitrov concluded by saying, "The leader of the Chinese Communist Party is none other than Mao Zedong."[37]

Given the fantastic nature of the conspiracy stories then being concocted by Moscow to justify the purges, accounts which frequently fabricated stories of traitorous activities stretching back for years, there is again no reason to credit Dimitrov's story about Mif being under suspicion of Trotskyism in 1937, two years before his execution. What was significant, however, was that once Mif had been sucked into the maelstrom of Stalin's purges, Wang lost an influential backer in Moscow and all Mif's associates, including Wang Ming, came under suspicion. It would be interesting to know the "evidence" which led to Mif's execution. Did it have to do with developments in China? Could Ren Bishi have been involved in supplying that evidence?

The account of Gao Jun says that Zhou's report caused a few "responsible people" in the Comintern to "change their views" about the CCP.[38] Zhou's 1944 report, however, gives the impression that Comintern leaders were not very receptive to Mao's heretical ideas. The hallmark of international Communism in 1940 was not a creative search for effective revolutionary strategies, but rigid loyalty to Stalinist dogma. This leads one to suspect that the draft of Mao's New Democracy presented by Zhou (if such a draft was in fact submitted) was toned down somewhat before he left Moscow.

Another important matter discussed by Zhou Enlai and Soviet leaders during Zhou's visit had to do with the transfer of several hundred Soviet-trained military personnel from Xinjiang to Yan'an. As we shall see in the next chapter, a Soviet-sponsored military academy was set up in Xinjiang in 1937 to train CCP cadre in such elements of modern warfare as mechanized operations, aviation, signal communications, and artillery. While in Xinjiang en route to Moscow in September 1939, Zhou addressed the several hundred men of this academy and urged them to concentrate on their technical studies because "very soon we will establish our own special units."[39] Shortly after Zhou left Dihua for Moscow, preparations began for the transfer of the cadre to Yan'an.[40] Then in January 1940, the order came for most of these cadres to move to Yan'an. When the group arrived in Yan'an they carried Soviet "supplies."[41]

The implication of this decision to transfer several hundred highly trained military personnel to Yan'an is not entirely clear. The maneuvering between Moscow and Yan'an for influence in Xinjiang was extremely complicated (again a subject which is dealt with in the next chapter), and Moscow's approval of this transfer may have been linked to a desire to eliminate an inconvenient CCP military presence in that region. On the other hand, the transfer seems to imply a qualitative change in the military effort of the CCP. The intriguing and still unanswerable question is whether Yan'an hoped, and whether Moscow gave it reason to hope, that its new modern service arm would be equipped with Soviet weapons. It is quite possible that having rejected Yan'an's request for weapons, perhaps conveyed by Zhou, Moscow allowed the return of these expert military cadres as a sort of compensation. It is also significant that Moscow was willing to risk antagonizing Chongqing at this juncture by sending top-quality, Soviet Union-trained military personnel to Yan'an.

In March, Zhou Enlai, Ren Bishi, and Shi Zhe (another of the CCP's "Soviet hands" who would play a prominent role in post-1949 Sino-Soviet relations) returned to Yan'an by way of Xinjiang.[42] It seems probable that Zhou carried with him some sort of Comintern directive. Momentous changes in the international situation had led to similar changes in Comintern line. The ECCI remained unhappy with certain aspects of the CCP policy and had called Zhou Enlai to account for those shortcomings. Just as had been the case with Wang Jiaxiang in mid-1938, it is likely that Zhou carried some sort of document representing approved direction for CCP policy back to Yan'an. But even lacking such a document, it is certain that Zhou conveyed Moscow's views and criticisms when he returned to Yan'an.

In March 1940, the same month that Zhou returned from Moscow, Wang Ming renewed his struggle against Mao and his policy by republishing a 1931 polemic entitled *Two Lines: The Struggle for a More Thorough Bolshevization of the CCP*. This 100-page booklet had originally been published as part of the Comintern's efforts to blame Li Lisan for the setbacks suffered by the CCP when it had implemented the radical line Moscow had imposed on it in 1929. It was also an effort to explain and justify the dramatic Comintern intervention in CCP affairs which had led to Li's ouster in early 1931. As such, it was a scathing attack on those Chinese Communist leaders who violated and ignored the Communist International's line. Its key theme was the vital importance of Comintern assistance in overcoming basic errors in Party line. The final words with which Wang ended his original polemic reflected this:

> All members of the Chinese Communist Party certainly will resolutely resist this opposition to the program of the Communist International. All China's Bolsheviks certainly will unite as though one man to carry out the line of the Communist International. The indefatigable work of the proletariat and the Bolshevik struggle to resolutely and bravely implement the line of the Executive Committee of the Communist International, certainly will lead the Chinese Communist Party to new and great victories of the Chinese Revolution.[43]

In the preface to the 1940 edition of *Two Lines*, Wang Ming explained his motive for republishing the work. Many comrades needed to understand, he said, the history of the CCP during this critical earlier stage. By studying the events of 1931, Communists could gain insight into the problems of 1940:

> Any sincere dialectical materialist and historical materialist realizes that although one cannot deal with problems apart from actual conditions of time and place, neither can one look upon the events of yesterday as irrelevant to today's events, or say that the events of some other time and place are entirely different from the events one faces today, or assert that different sets of events cannot be compared.[44]

In plain speech, Wang was saying that the CCP under Mao's leadership had gone far astray and should be put into receivership by the Comintern just as it had been in 1931.

The republication of *Two Lines* was a bold attempt by Wang Ming to recoup through direct Comintern intervention his recent losses at Mao's hands. There is some evidence that Wang's action was not entirely reckless and that Moscow may indeed have intervened at this juncture to restrain Mao's radicalism. According to KMT sources, the month after Wang's polemic was republished, a Comintern representative in Yan'an spoke at a CCP meeting and demanded that the CCP abandon its policy of armed struggle with the KMT. The CCP was not considering the time and circumstances under which it was carrying out its policy of armed struggle and was touching off a war with the KMT, the Comintern representative reportedly said. By doing this, the CCP was inadvertently creating a situation in which it would be defeated and which would, moreover, lead to unfortunate anti-Soviet changes in the Far East. Mao reportedly rejected the Comintern proposal and went so far as to call for an end to Soviet military assistance to the KMT.[45]

Another source also refers to conflict between Yan'an and Moscow at this juncture. According to a pamphlet probably published in Chongqing in 1943, in 1940 the CCP Politburo debated mistakes in the "international line" during the 1928–1935 period. Ultraleft policies such as elimination of the bourgeoisie and killing landlords, and mistaken military policies such as attacking big cities and denying the importance of guerrilla war, were all linked to Comintern "mistakes."[46] If this report is correct, Mao must have been defending himself against Comintern criticisms by pointing out that the Comintern had been wrong many times in the past. These fragments of evidence all point in the same direction. It seems that what was under way was a full-blown, but highly secret debate within the top levels of the CCP regarding the relationship between the Chinese revolution and the Soviet Union. The central element of the Comintern's criticisms of Mao was that his drive to expand revolutionary power was increasing the danger of KMT surrender to Japan.

Mao did not necessarily desire defeat of the KMT by Japan. As Tetsuya Kataoka pointed out, Mao realized that such a development would allow the KMT to turn against the CCP. Mao probably saw a protracted war of attrition between the KMT and Japan as creating the best conditions for the expansion of revolutionary power in China. Yet, as a revolutionary, Mao also appreciated the beneficial conditions which would result from a Japanese defeat of the KMT and KMT acceptance of a Carthaginian peace.

Mao's relative equanimity about a possible KMT surrender and his determination that such a possibility would not tie the hands of the CCP was made clear in a central directive of 19 January 1940 which ordered the New Fourth Army to expand as rapidly as possible "as long as the National Government has not yet surrendered."[47] But the clearest expression of Mao's sanguine "revolutionary defeatism" was in a CCP central directive of 10 September 1940. There were three possibilities regarding China's war of resistance, the directive said. The first possibility was American intervention in China after a British defeat of Germany. American aid to the KMT and active Anglo-American intervention in the Far East was the path of development hoped for by the "die-hard reactionaries" in China and the path most advantageous to the one-party dictatorship of the KMT. The second possibility was that the "diehards" would be forced to make some compromises with the "national bourgeoisie." This would mean adopting a pro-Soviet orientation internationally and abandoning anticommunism domestically. Such a positive policy had been pursued by the National Government prior to the fall of 1938 but had later been interrupted by the pro-Anglo-American, anti-Soviet, anticommunist policy. The third possibility was a Japanese capture of Chongqing and the surrender of part of the KMT to Japan. Such a development, the directive said, would result in chaos within China's ruling class and the emergence of powerful, popular anti-Japanese, antitraitor movements.[48] This last option was clearly less desirable than the second—concessions by the "national bourgeoisie" to the "proletariat" and continuing Chinese national unity in the war against Japan together with the Soviet Union. But the option of KMT surrender was better than that of active Anglo-American intervention in China against Japan and in support of the KMT—the path of development most advantageous to the "die-hard reactionaries" and "one-party dictatorship of the KMT." In short, Mao preferred to see Japan defeat the KMT rather than see the KMT defeat Japan together with the United States and Britain. This was quite different from Moscow's set of preferences.

Mao was aware that in the event of a Republic of China–Japan peace, Japan might use its newly available forces against the CCP. Moreover, systematic Japanese suppression of guerrilla forces had been relatively effective in Manchuria and Mao was certainly aware of this fact. While it is possible that Mao minimized this possibility simply to put the best interpretation on an otherwise grim situation, it seems more probable that he, like Chiang Kai-shek, thought Japan wanted to disengage from

China in order to strike into Southeast Asia. By September 1940, Japan's strike south was well under way, with relations between Japan and the United States deteriorating rapidly as a consequence. Mao probably concluded that, since the bulk of Japan's newly available forces would be used against the Americans and British, the cost of increased Japanese pressure against the CCP would be more than offset by the establishment of the CCP as the sole sincere representative of Chinese nationalism. There was another, perhaps even more important, consideration. A KMT surrender in the face of deteriorating American–Japanese relations would abort the rapidly crystallizing special relationship between Chongqing and Washington. This would have been an immense boon for the CCP. In such an eventuality Chiang would either face the CCP without a foreign sponsor or, more likely, would move closer to Japan, thereby further undermining his nationalist credentials. Again, the conclusion was that a KMT settlement with Japan was preferable to United States-backed continued KMT resistance to Japan.

To understand Mao's orientation on this issue, it is essential to consider the probable political consequences of the surrender of the National Government to Japan.[49] Such a surrender would have demolished the nationalist credentials of the KMT. The astonishingly little support which Wang Jingwei's collaborationist regime received from Chinese during this period was testament to this.[50] If the CCP then continued to fight on against Japan, it stood a good chance of winning the loyalty of a broad spectrum of patriotic Chinese. The peace terms imposed on Chongqing by a victorious Japan were certain to be harsh enough to fire Chinese resentment and bitterness. Patriotic military units and leaders of the KMT might defect to the Communists rather than accept surrender to Japan. The KMT would certainly attempt to mount campaigns against the Communists, but it would do so as "puppets of the Japanese." These conditions would allow the CCP to emerge as the representative of Chinese nationalism. Chiang Kai-shek probably understood these possibilities fully as well as did Mao Zedong, and it was precisely considerations of this sort which were instrumental in preventing Chiang from accepting a harsh, compromise peace with Japan.

Mao was first and foremost a revolutionary. He realized that the continuing war between the KMT and Japan was useful, and this was his preferred scenario. But like his mentor Lenin, he also realized that lost wars tend to delegitimize regimes and that defeat of the KMT by Japan would fuel revolution in China. Whichever set of conditions developed, Mao could and would utilize. The one *sine qua non* was the expansion of revolutionary power. Nothing must stand in the way of that goal—not possible surrender by the KMT, not even the national defense concerns of the Soviet Union.

From Moscow's perspective the costs and benefits of a harsh KMT–Japan peace were quite different. Unlike the CCP, Moscow would derive few benefits from the destabilization and delegitimization of Chiang's regime which would follow such a peace. The costs were still there—Japan's armies would be freed for possible use against the Soviet Union—but without the offsetting benefits which would accrue to the CCP. Stalin's calculations were easier than Mao's: continuing Sino-Japanese war was Stalin's insurance policy against a joint German-Japanese attack against the Soviet Union. It followed that the Kuomintang had to be kept in the war against Japan.

Stalin indicated his views on this question during a discussion with General Vasilii

Chuikov in December 1940, just as the latter was about to depart for Chongqing to serve as military attaché. (Chuikov had commanded an army during the invasion of eastern Poland and again during the Winter War. He remained in China until February 1942.) Stalin was skeptical of the CCP at the end of 1940. The social base of the CCP was the peasantry, he told Chuikov, and such a nonproletarian base inevitably led to serious ideological defects. Among these defects were a tendency toward nationalism and an inadequately developed sense of internationalism. Stalin also indicated his apprehensions about the consequences of the radical policies of the CCP. The Chinese "red army," like Chiang Kai-shek's army, was willing to launch a civil war regardless of the crisis into which this would plunge China. Chuikov should therefore, Stalin said, seek to mediate the conflict between the CCP and KMT armies. A CCP assault on Chiang's position would drive him toward Japan. Once Chiang felt he was about to lose power, he would imitate Wang Jingwei. Chiang could "easily" unite with Japan to oppose the CCP, Stalin warned Chuikov. Only Chiang Kai-shek could lead a continuing war of resistance against Japan, Stalin continued. The CCP and the Chinese proletariat were still too weak to lead China's antiaggression struggle and would need more time to win over the Chinese masses. Just how much time would be needed was uncertain. Nor would the imperialist powers ever allow the CCP to overthrow Chiang Kai-shek. The Soviet Union also had treaties and diplomatic relations with Chiang's government, Stalin said, and the Soviet Union could not "export revolution" to nations with which it had such ties. It followed from this that the Soviet Union could not aid the CCP, and Stalin told Chuikov that he was to carry out his work in strict accordance with existing Soviet-Chinese treaties which specified that all Soviet assistance would go exclusively to the National Government. Stalin also warned Chuikov to beware of those in the CCP who thought that a Japanese defeat of the KMT would benefit China's revolution.[51]

Moscow's demand for CCP moderation put Mao in a quandary. On the one hand, he did not want to slow his drive for revolutionary power. On the other hand, he could not say openly that he was willing to accept KMT surrender to Japan if this was the price that had to be paid for revolution in China. Mao resolved this dilemma by cleverly turning Moscow's argument on its head: expansion of CCP power would not push the KMT toward surrender to Japan, Mao argued, but would prevent it from surrendering. Mao rebutted Comintern charges by agreeing with the premise that the danger of KMT surrender had increased and that such a surrender should be averted, but by disagreeing about how this was to be done. Mao replied to Moscow's criticism by replying that the expansion of China's anti-Japanese forces, that is of the power and influence of the CCP, diminished rather than increased the danger of KMT surrender.

Mao elaborated his theory of defeating capitulationism by expanding CCP power in a long directive of 4 May 1940. This directive was aimed, according to the annotation in Mao's Selected Works, at Xiang Ying, secretary of the Southeast Bureau of the CCP, who "held strong rightist views."[52] The CCP should understand, Mao explained in the directive, that while the danger of capitulationism had greatly increased, it was still possible to avert it by freely expanding the progressive forces, winning over the middle forces, and isolating the "diehards." The stronger the CCP and its armies grew throughout the country, Mao said, "the greater will be the possibility of averting the danger of capitulation. . . . It is wrong to make the op-posite appraisal . . . that the more our forces expand, the more the diehards will tend toward capitulation, that the more concessions we make, the more they will resist Japan."[53]

The outcome of the dispute within the CCP and between Moscow and Yan'an in 1940 seems to have been a power-for-policy trade-off similar to that of mid-1938. On the one hand, Mao further reduced the organizational position of the Internationalist faction. After 1940, Wang Ming no longer attended the Political Consultative Assembly in Chongqing, and, after temporarily serving as the Party's united front representative during Zhou Enlai's mission to Moscow, he stepped down as CCP representative in Chongqing. Instead, he served as president of the Yan'an Chinese Women's University, not a prestigious post in male-dominated China.[54] The criticism of earlier mistakes in the Comintern line also probably signaled a reduction in Wang's rank standing within the Politburo.[55]

On the other hand, Mao modified CCP policy in response to Moscow's criticisms by incorporating some of Moscow's demands into CCP policy and by making a number of moderate, conciliatory moves toward Chongqing. In June the CCP issued a fairly conciliatory set of proposals to the KMT regarding the avoidance of future conflict and renewing the CCP's 1937 pledges of subordination to Chiang Kai-shek. At the same time, however, it called for KMT recognition of the expansion of the Shaan-Gan-Ning border district to twenty-three counties and expansion of Communist military forces to a total of eight divisions.[56]

Mao also modified his earlier rejection of the possibility of cooperating with the United States against Japan. On 7 July 1940, the CCP Politburo issued a resolution warning of an "unprecedented danger of surrender and unprecedented difficulties." Japan's Axis partners wanted it to end the war in China in order to facilitate its southern advance. The Anglo-American powers, on the other hand, "want to sacrifice China in order to protect Southeast Asia." Thus, "We can make use of the conflict between the Anglo-American-French and the German-Italian-Japanese imperialist camps, especially the heightening contradictions between Japan and America in the Pacific."[57] This should not violate close Soviet-Chinese ties, however. The fall of France indicated that an anti-Soviet, anticommunist policy would lead to national collapse. To avoid a similiar collapse, China should avoid such anti-Soviet policies.

The key reason why Mao was willing to placate Moscow at this juncture had to do with his view of the probable Soviet role in future international developments. This estimate was embodied in the 7 July 1940 resolution. According to this resolution, the world was on the eve of a new era of world revolution, a process in which the Soviet Union would play a critical role. The world was moving rapidly toward an all-out imperialist war which would lead to "unprecedented disruption of the whole world order" and to the "rapid revolutionization" of the peoples of the capitalist and the oppressed countries. There would be growing revolutionary movements, especially in Europe and India. The faith of the masses in the Communist Party and in the Soviet Union was already increasing rapidly. This situation was most advantageous for China's war of resistance and for the world revolution. The CCP should "especially emphasize the great might of the Soviet Union" as "the reliable friend" of China's war of resistance:

> The Soviet Union, which has remained outside the imperialist war, is moving a step further toward resolving the question of defense of the Baltic coast, and is consolidating

its security in the Balkans and the Near East. It is preparing the great revolutionary strength to respond to the huge changes in the world and to struggle to win eternal world peace.[58]

Of course, from a Marxist-Leninist viewpoint, "eternal world peace" could be achieved only after monopoly capitalism was replaced by socialism around the world. The scenario envisioned by Mao in mid-1940 was, in other words, one in which the Soviet Union grew powerful in peace while the imperialists bled one another white and radicalized the masses by imposing upon them the senseless sufferings of imperialist war. Then at some point the masses would rise up and the Soviet Union would use its strength to assist the world revolution, toppling forever capitalism and imperialism. Operating on the basis of this scenario, Mao and the CCP needed to retain the good graces of Moscow. One of Yan'an's most important conciliatory moves toward Moscow was the Hundred Regiments Campaign of 1940.

The Hundred Regiments Campaign

In the summer of 1940, the CCP launched its biggest military offensive of the entire war—at least until the general offensive in the weeks immediately preceding Japan's surrender in September 1945. The offensive lasted from the end of July until the end of December 1940 and involved 400,000 Communist-held troops in 115 regiments, thus giving the offensive its name, the Hundred Regiments Campaign. The chief targets of the offensive were transportation and communications lines, coal mines, and other economic installations in north China that served Japan's war effort. According to CCP sources, the offensive inflicted 46,000 casualties (killed, wounded, and captured) on Japanese and puppet forces. Of these, 20,900 were Japanese. But while the offensive was successful in inflicting heavy losses on Japan, it also cost the CCP 22,000 casualties. Just as important, the offensive caused the Japanese to intensify their "mop-up" operations against CCP base areas. After the offensive and under increased Japanese pressure, the population in areas under CCP control fell from 44 to 25 million, while the Eighth Route Army decreased from 400,000 to 300,000 troops.[59]

The Hundred Regiments Campaign was a dramatic departure from Mao's strategy of protracted guerrilla war. In speeches in September 1939 and again in March 1940, Mao had clearly indicated that the war was still in its second stage of strategic stalemate (*xiangchi jieduan*).[60] In his 1938 essay "On Protracted War," Mao had outlined the military strategy which was appropriate to the stage of strategic stalemate. During this stage, Mao wrote, guerrilla warfare would be developed extensively in the unguarded areas of the enemy's rear. Base areas would be rapidly established in order to make possible extensive guerrilla warfare, supplemented by mobile war. Except for the troops engaged in frontal defense against the enemy, CCP forces would be deployed to the enemy's rear "in comparatively dispersed dispositions" to conduct "extensive, fierce guerrilla warfare."[61] While these strictures do not entirely preclude an offensive on the scale of the Hundred Regiments Campaign, they do point toward a strategy emphasizing building up the organizational and territorial infrastructure of the CCP plus small-unit military operations. Certainly they would not include launching massive assaults on strategic enemy-held positions. From the standpoint of expanding the organizational and territorial base of the CCP, the Hundred Regiments Campaign did not make sense. Indeed, it was a colossal failure. It meant that CCP cadres concentrated on fighting Japan rather than on organizing base areas and mass organizations. Moreover, it forced the CCP to turn and face Japan just as the KMT was maneuvering its forces into position to attack the CCP.

According to vice-commander of the Eighth Route Army Peng Dehuai, Mao was unenthusiastic about the Hundred Regiment's Campaign. Indeed, the offensive was launched without prior authorization by either Mao or the Military Affairs Commission (MAC) of the Central Committee which Mao headed. The Eighth Route Army headquarters began preliminary planning for such an offensive in December 1939. Actual preparations for the offensive began in July 1940, and on 22 July army headquarters "informed" the MAC of their plans. Authorization from the MAC had still not been received by army headquarters when the offensive was launched in late July.[62]

Peng's memoir also explains that the campaign was launched to offset the factors then working to pressure the KMT into making peace with Japan. Britain's closure of the Rangoon–Kunming road in response to Japanese pressure after the fall of France, and Japan's declared intention of seizing Xian by August to cut off the last of the major international supply lines of the KMT, were seen as shaking KMT determination to continue the war. Moreover, the "international movement" for a "Far Eastern Munich" was influencing people in the Japanese-occupied areas. All of these developments were creating a serious danger of KMT surrender to Japan. The KMT was also spreading rumors that the Eighth Route Army was only interested in fighting friendly armies, not the Japanese, and it was necessary to refute these "rumors."[63] As we have seen previously, in mid-1940 Mao believed that the way to counter KMT capitulationism was to expand the anti-Japanese forces of the CCP as quickly as possible. He had continually rejected the argument that the way to prevent KMT surrender was by having CCP forces attack Japan's armies rather than by establishing and expanding revolutionary power. In short, the Hundred Regiments Campaign was anathema to Mao.

There is some evidence linking the Hundred Regiments Campaign to Moscow. In December 1939, Chongqing's forces launched a powerful winter offensive against the entire Japanese front. This offensive continued into March 1940 and came very close, according to reports of the Japanese army, to defeating the Japanese army defending Wuhan. Japanese intelligence also reported a meeting of the Far Eastern Bureau of the Comintern in Chita, Soviet Union, on 22 February 1940, which ordered the CCP to intensify its military activities in coordination with the Nationalist offensive then under way.[64] It was just at this juncture that Zhou was called to account for deviations from Comintern line, Wang Ming issued his veiled polemical attack on Mao's violation of international policy, and the CCP Politburo debated earlier mistakes in the international line. It could well be that Moscow was pushing the CCP in early 1940 to take military action on the scope of the Hundred Regiments Campaign.[65] There is, of course, a danger of seeing the Comintern behind every difference of opinion within the CCP. Nonetheless, there is a general pattern of events and evidence which points toward a Comintern role in the launching of the offensive. Stalin clearly wanted the CCP to fight Japan more and the KMT less. Mao generally favored the reverse emphasis. Stalin was very apprehensive of possible surrender by Chiang Kai-shek to Japan. Mao, however, viewed this possibility with greater equanimity.

The Second "Anti-Communist High Tide"

After Hu Songnan's forces compressed the Shaan-Gan-Ning special district in late 1939 and early 1940, Chiang Kai-shek began maneuvering to implement an even more drastic rollback of the area under CCP control. The central element of this plan was to force all Communist armies to withdraw north of the Yellow River. In March 1940, during negotiations ending clashes between Nationalist and Communist forces in eastern Anwei, the Nationalists had raised this demand. The Seventh Plenum of the Fifth Central Executive Committee of the KMT in July 1940 discussed the prospects for continuing the war against Japan and for dealing with the CCP, and decided to enforce the demand for Communist withdrawal north of the Yellow River. This demand was then embodied in a "draft central directive" presented by Chief of Staff He Yingqin to Zhou Enlai on 16 July 1940. This "draft central directive" provided that the Shaan-Gan-Ning special district was to be limited to eighteen counties (as opposed to the twenty-three the CCP had demanded in June), that the total size of Communist armies was to be reduced from about 500,000 to 100,000 men, that operations of the Eighth Route and New Fourth Armies be confined to Hebei, Chahar, and Shandong north of the Yellow River, and that all Communist military forces move to these areas within one month.[66]

Implementation of this plan would have been a severe blow to the CCP. It would have necessitated relinquishment of the base areas painstakingly built up not only in the provinces of Jiangsu, Hubei, and Anwei, but also in those portions of Henan and Shandong which were south of the Yellow River—areas which, according to a CCP directive of 19 January 1940, "offered the best opportunities in the whole country for expansion." Moreover, as a 1 February 1940 cable from Mao to the New Fourth Army (NFA) pointed out, if the CCP's armies withdrew north of the Yellow River, they would be wedged between Japanese and KMT armies, and with a frontier along the Yellow River which could be easily blockaded.[67]

Base areas south of the Yangtze River were another matter. The NFA had originally been assigned, in May 1938, to develop base areas in Jiangsu province south of the Yangtze. By early 1939, however, the CCP center had decided that the lower Yangtze valley offered fewer opportunities than central China north of the Yangtze, and began ordering the NFA to redirect its efforts northward toward central China. Zhou Enlai had personally conveyed such instructions to the NFA headquarters during February–March 1939. But NFA commander Ye Ting and secretary of the CCP Southeast Bureau and vice-commander of the NFA Xiang Ying were extremely reluctant to redirect the activities of the NFA and to relocate its bases. On 19 January 1940, 1 February 1940, 4 May 1940, and 12 May 1940, the CCP center sent directives to the NFA ordering it to cross to the north bank *of the Yangtze* and begin expanding base areas in eastern Anwei. Having decided that southern Jiangsu and Anwei did not offer the most profitable area for investment of CCP energies, the CCP center decided to use withdrawal from that area as a "concession" to placate Chiang and demonstrate its reasonableness. As the CCP center explained to Xiang Ying and Ye Ting in a cable of 21 November 1940, the CCP had decided to withdraw from southern Anwei in order to win over the "middle elements.'"[68]

Xiang Ying and Ye Ting were reluctant to abandon their bases south of the Yangtze. They may also have been supportive of Wang Ming's criticisms of Mao's leadership. According to a high-level CCP defector, Xiang felt that Stalin's endorsement of Mao at the Sixth Plenum had been wrong and that Mao's personal degeneracy had been proven when he divorced his Long March comrade He Zuchen and remarried in 1940 a young movie actress from Shanghai.[69] Xiang also objected to Mao's policies of forcing landlords to reduce rent and rapidly expanding liberated areas and guerrilla forces. Such radicalism would, Xiang feared, frighten Chiang Kai-shek and the Kuomintang away from the united front.[70]

It was a tactical blunder for Chiang to assist Mao's consolidation of power by attacking Xiang Ying's "independent kingdom" in southern Anwei. Perhaps Chiang's intelligence services did not inform him about the conflict between Xiang and Mao. Or perhaps Chiang felt that Xiang was more dangerous precisely because he was politically closer to Wang Ming, and to Chiang's old *dipan* (political base) in the lower Yangtze. In any case, when Chiang renewed his pressure against the CCP, Xiang's NFA was his primary target.

While the CCP's Hundred Regiments Campaign was under way in the fall of 1940, Chiang intensified his effort to force the CCP out of Central China. On 19 October, He Yingqin sent a cable to Zhu De charging that the Eighth Route and New Fourth Armies were moving around arbitrarily in disregard of designated military zones and central orders, taking over friendly armies, and arbitrarily expanding the size of their forces. He also ordered that all Communist military forces were to be withdrawn north of the Yellow River within one month. On 9 November, the commanders of the Communist armies replied to He Yingqin rejecting withdrawal north of the Yellow River as "unreasonable." This did not satisfy Chongqing and on 2 January 1941 KMT units began deploying around NFA units still situated south of the Yangtze.[71]

Mao Zedong was probably almost as unhappy as Chiang Kai-shek that Xiang Ying's NFA forces were still in southern Anwei in January 1941. As late as 23–26 December 1940, the CCP center had ordered Xiang Ying to move all his forces across the Yangtze by the end of the month. On 4 January 1941, Xiang's forces finally began moving southward out of their base areas and clashes began occurring between them and government units surrounding them. Then on 9 January government forces launched a general assault on the NFA units remaining in southern Anwei.[72] Fighting continued throughout January, with the NFA suffering very heavy casualties. Of the 9000 NFA soldiers still south of the Yangtze when the fighting began, over 7000 were killed, deserted, or were taken prisoner.[73] This fighting was dubbed the "Second Anti-Communist High Tide" or the "Southern Anwei Incident" by the CCP.

Chiang Kai-shek believed that Moscow's increasing alignment with Japan necessitated this drastic move against the CCP. While Chiang had initially thought that the Tri-Partite Treaty was directed against the Soviet Union as well as against the United States, after Stalin's 16 October 1940 cable (discussed in Chapter 4) indicating Moscow's determination to continue improving relations with Japan, Chiang became increasingly apprehensive of a Soviet-Japanese condominium. If the CCP were allowed to grow too powerful, Chiang indicated in his diary on 31 October 1940 a few days after He Yingqin's ultimatum to Zhou Enlai, Moscow would be tempted to switch its support from the National Government to a Chinese soviet government. It was now clear, Chiang wrote, that the Tri-Partite Treaty had accelerated the tendency toward both a Japanese-American war *and* Soviet-Japanese cooperation. One of the manifestations of such Soviet-Japanese cooperation might be Soviet recognition of Wang Jingwei's regime in exchange for Japanese recognition of a Chinese soviet regime in China's northwest. Chiang feared, in other words, that in the event of a U.S.–Japan war in which the Soviet Union was friendly toward Japan while the ROC was allied to the United States, Moscow might be tempted to support the CCP and divide China in cooperation with Japan. This possibility could be averted, Chiang believed, by limiting the power of the CCP. As he wrote in his diary on 31 October,

> If our strength is further weakened, Russia will help the Chinese Communists organize a Chinese soviet people's government, order them to appease the Japs, and cause them to plot to extinguish the Kuomintang and the National Government. But if we are able to maintain our strength, then Russia cannot actively harm us.[74]

Given the extent of Soviet cooperation with Nazi Germany at that time, the accelerating development of Soviet-Japanese rapprochement, and the negotiations then under way between Moscow and Berlin regarding possible Soviet entry into the Axis bloc, Chiang's apprehensions were quite plausible. Throughout October 1940 German leaders were sounding out their allies in Vichy and Madrid about possible Soviet entry into the Axis alliance, and word of this activity probably reached Chongqing. Moscow was, in fact, moving closer and closer to the German-Japanese camp. Moreover, Soviet cooperation in Europe with Nazi Germany had led to the establishment of a Soviet sphere of influence in Eastern Europe. Might not a Soviet-Japanese "understanding" lead to similar efforts in China? If Stalin reached an understanding with Tokyo comparable to the one he had reached with Berlin, might he not demand territorial cessions in China similar to those he had demanded and obtained in Europe? This was Chiang Kai-shek's fear. In the international situation existing in 1940 it was quite plausible. Indeed, it is quite possible that such an outcome was averted chiefly by the insanity of Adolf Hitler and his invasion of the Soviet Union.

Chiang was in a quandary. Moscow's deepening relations with the Axis added impetus to the need to move against the CCP. Yet such a move was now more dangerous precisely because Soviet-Japanese cordiality eased the Soviet security concerns which had previously induced Moscow to be understanding of Chiang's efforts to discipline the CCP. Thus, the precise circumstances of the move against the CCP, and its impact on the Soviet Union, had to be considered carefully.

The calculations regarding the specific timing of the move against the CCP and its expected impact on the Soviet Union were laid out in a memorandum of February 1941 prepared for Chiang Kai-shek by Wang Shijie, then with the staff office of the National Government's Military Commission. Steeper inflation and grain shortages leading to major famine were possible later in 1941, Wang said in the memo. If the weather was good, this could be avoided, but if not, the situation in the summer and fall of 1941 would be quite difficult. Japanese action to close Rangoon harbor was also likely later in 1941. This would further increase economic difficulties. By cutting off the flow of Chinese silk, tea, and minerals to Western markets, and of foreign goods into China, Japanese closure of the Rangoon-Kunming road would exacerbate inflation in China. "Therefore," Wang concluded, "now is perhaps the best time to thoroughly check the Communists."[75]

Wang Shijie also addressed the question of how a move against the CCP would affect relations with the Soviet Union. It was necessary, Wang's memo explained, to maintain a "minimum level of cordiality" with the Soviet Union. China "could not but accommodate" the Soviet Union. To this end the government should order the army to use the minimum force necessary against the CCP and to use political methods to seek a solution so as to "avoid a break" with the Soviet Union. Elsewhere in the memo Wang said that London and Washington could only cautiously support Chongqing's repression of the CCP because they too feared offending the Soviet Union. This clearly implied a linkage between the Soviet Union and the CCP on the one hand and the restrained nature of the 1941 anti-CCP campaign on the other. In other words, Chongqing's campaign against the CCP was still being shaped by apprehensions about Moscow's reaction to a more far-reaching move.

The Soviet Response to the "Second Anti-Communist High Tide"

The Southern Anwei Incident occurred just as Soviet aid to Nationalist China had resumed after a hiatus of almost a year. As we saw in the last chapter, in November 1940 Ambassador Shao Lizi finally secured the resumption of Soviet aid and throughout December 1940 and January 1941 hundreds of Soviet trucks delivered munitions to Nationalist China. Moreover, as we saw earlier in this chapter, there had been a link between the termination of Soviet aid and the KMT move against the Shaan-Gan-Ning special district in early 1940. A key question for Soviet-Chinese relations in the midst of the Southern Anwei Incident thus becomes whether Moscow once again suspended, or threatened to suspend, the flow of aid to Chongqing in an effort to pressure Chiang into suspending his renewed anticommunist operations.

If, as Chiang feared, the Soviet Union were tending toward a spheres-of-influence deal with Japan, then Moscow might be expected to use its aid to Chongqing as leverage to protect its putative proxy, the CCP. If, on the other hand, Moscow still viewed the KMT's war against Japan as the more important factor, then it would continue to aid Chongqing in spite of its move against the CCP. Thus, Chiang wrote in his diary on 17 January 1941: "We can use [the Southern Anwei Incident] to gauge the sincerity of Russia's assistance to our war of resistance."[76]

Unlike the situation in early 1940, Moscow did not suspend its aid to Chongqing in response to the moves by the KMT against the CCP in early 1941. It did, however, gently pressure Chiang to suspend his drive against the CCP. Moscow urged Chongqing to suspend its anti-CCP drive but did this in a very low-key fashion and did not use its aid as leverage to enforce this demand. When General Vasilii Chuikov was preparing to leave for China in late 1940, Stalin and Defense Commissar Semën

Timoshenko instructed him to foil Chiang's plots to use Soviet weapons against the CCP rather than against Japan.

In line with these directions, when the NFA incident erupted in January 1941, Chuikov worked to prevent expansion of the conflict. Shortly after his arrival in Chongqing, Chuikov called on He Yingqin and asked if Soviet-supplied weapons were being used against the NFA. He Yingqin replied that none were and went on to explain that what was involved in the Southern Anwei Incident was simple insubordination: the NFA had refused to obey the orders of the supreme commander, and disciplinary measures were thus necessary. Chuikov countered that in that case the removal and court-martial of the commander would have been more appropriate than armed assault on his units. One should not, Chuikov admonished He Yingqin, fire on one's own army. Chuikov then called on vice-chief of staff Bai Zhongxi and told him that the Soviet Union could not accept such incidents. He would have to report to Soviet Defense Commissar Timoshenko, Chuikov said, that the Chinese government had carried out a premeditated attack against the NFA. When meeting with other Chinese officials, Chuikov also intimated that the outbreak of civil war in China would cause the Soviet Union to cease all assistance to China. It was hard for the Soviets to understand, Chuikov told them, why China did not concentrate on fighting Japan.[77]

On 16 January 1941, Chuikov met with Chiang Kai-shek and again pressed him about the incident at Anwei. Although the main purpose of Chuikov's visit was to discuss the recent deliveries of Soviet military equipment to China and to warn of renewed Japanese offensives in central or northern China, he took the occasion to press Chiang for information about the development, scope, and significance of the Anwei incident. Chiang refused to discuss the incident saying only that it was a matter of maintaining military discipline and thus such incidents could be avoided if orders were obeyed. The Soviet attaché thereupon dropped the subject, praised Chiang's leadership of China, and forcefully asserted that all military units should obey his orders.[78]

Chiang carefully weighed his move against the CCP against Moscow's response. The day after the Soviet attaché's moderate response, Chiang ordered the formal dissolution of the NFA and the court-martial of its commander, Ye Ting.[79] Yet, even this, Chiang felt, was a gamble. The same day he ordered the disbandment of the NFA, Chiang commented in his diary on the possibility that the Soviet Union would cease aiding Nationalist China in retaliation. Regarding his disbandment and court-martial orders, Chiang wrote:

> This affair is extremely important for relations with Russia. If we are to act to further the independence of the nation, to let outsiders interfere with strict military discipline would be to lead to national calamities more evil than even defeat at the hands of the Japs. Therefore I have given orders to deal with this in a strict fashion. Even if the weapons and planes which Russia has already sent to China's borders do not arrive because of this, this does not matter greatly [*yi suo bu xi*].[80]

A week after Chiang's disbandment of the NFA (two weeks after the initial clash in southern Anwei), Ambassador A.S. Paniushkin called on Chiang Kai-shek to inquire about the Southern Anwei Incident and to express his government's "extreme concern" about it. The Soviet government feared the incident would touch off a civil war which would injure China's war of resistance, Paniushkin explained. Chiang insisted that the incident was purely a problem of maintaining military discipline and that strengthening such discipline could only have a beneficial effect on China's war effort. Being solely a matter of military discipline, the Anwei incident did not touch on the question of relations between the CCP and the KMT. Thus, it was not an issue of civil war. When Paniushkin asked about future policy, Chiang said that he was determined to continue resisting Japan until final victory was achieved.[81]

Although Soviet officials clearly used their leverage to prevent expanded civil conflict in China, Moscow did not suspend the flow of aid to China in early 1941, as it had done in early 1940. This was probably due to the increasingly tense relations between the Soviet Union and Nazi Germany. As the possibility of war with Germany loomed larger, Stalin's Chinese insurance policy against the eventuality of Japanese entry into a Soviet-German war became more valuable.

Soviet representatives also attempted to pressure the CCP into moderating its policies for the sake of greater KMT–CCP unity against Japan. General Chuikov's memoirs recount an early-1941 meeting with Zhou Enlai and Ye Jianying, the Eighth Route Army representative in Chongqing. Chuikov was shocked when Zhou and Ye told him that the CCP and its armed strength, rather than Japan, was Chiang Kai-shek's major enemy. Zhou and Ye refused to give clear answers to Chuikov's questions about how the united front should be maintained and refused to elaborate on the state of CCP guerrilla operations behind Japanese lines.[82] Like the United States five years earlier, the Soviet Union was finding out that its ability to guide the course of developments within China was very limited.

Mao Versus Stalin

The gap in 1940 between Mao's view of the future Soviet role in achieving the final victory of the Chinese revolution and Stalin's view of the future role of the CCP in China was great. Mao believed (perhaps hoped is a better word) that at some point in the future—when the imperialist powers had exhausted each other through internecine war, and when the peoples of those countries had been revolutionized by that war, and when the Soviet Union had grown even more powerful in peace—the Soviet Union would start arming the CCP and that the Red Army would enter the war against Japan, thereby laying the basis for socialist revolution in China. Stalin, on the other hand, believed that the CCP and the Chinese proletariat were too weak to overthrow Chiang Kai-shek, and that an attempt to do so would precipitate Chiang's surrender to Japan. Moreover, the Soviet Union enjoyed friendly treaty and diplomatic relations with the Republic of China. In short, Stalin saw the Republic of China, not a revolutionary China, as the most appropriate buffer between the Soviet Union and the imperialist powers.

There is a pattern to the fragmentary evidence we have about Comintern policy toward the CCP during 1939–1940. Otto Braun's negative report on the CCP in late 1939, the Chita Comintern conference of February 1940, Zhou Enlai's early-

1940 debates in Moscow, Wang Ming's reissuance of his 1931 polemic in March 1940, the report of the Comintern criticism of the CCP in April 1940, and Stalin's comments to Chuikov at the end of 1940—all indicate continuing Soviet apprehensions about the drive of the CCP for revolutionary power. The question then becomes: how was it possible for Mao to defy Stalin? What were the sources of Mao's strength?

One element of Mao's strength was organization: the support he enjoyed in the Politburo. By early 1940 Wang Ming was virtually isolated within the top leadership of the CCP. His slavish imitation of the Comintern line and of Soviet experience was both too glaringly out of line with the revolutionary objectives of the CCP and too irritating to Chinese nationalist sensibilities. Indeed, Mao's appeal to Chinese nationalist sentiments was probably a key weapon in his isolation of Wang Ming. Conversely, Mao's strong nationalist resistance to Soviet intervention in the CCP via Wang Ming was probably one important reason why other CCP leaders rallied around him after the Sixth Plenum.

Mao could probably have defeated a direct Comintern intervention against him in 1940. Moscow, however, was loath to undertake such intervention since it would have complicated Soviet relations with both Japan and the United States. It could well have been viewed as provocative by Japan's anticommunist extremists and bolstered their arguments for a strike north against the Soviet Union rather than a strike south into Southeast Asia. While Stalin hoped that the CCP and the KMT would continue to cooperate against Japan, he did not want to play too prominent a role in facilitating this because he did not want to disrupt the Soviet rapprochement with Japan or the Japanese collision with the United States, both of which were well under way by then.

Faced with this balance of interests and assets, Stalin and Mao were forced to strike their second compromise of the war in early 1940. Very probably this deal was worked out by Mao's "foreign minister" Zhou Enlai during Zhou's six-month stay in Moscow. While the mechanics of the negotiation of that deal remain unclear, its general contours are not. Mao utilized the Comintern's shift in line in the fall of 1939 to set forth a policy akin to the one he had been forced to drop at the end of 1937. He then had to retreat several steps under Soviet pressure and grudgingly conceded several major points to Moscow. Perhaps the most important of these concessions was the Hundred Regiments Campaign.

Notes

1. See Kermit E. McKenzie, *Comintern and World Revolution, 1928–1943, the Shaping of Doctrine*, New York: Columbia University Press, 1964.
2. McKenzie, *Comintern and World Revolution*, pp. 174–175. For example, the program of "new democracy" advanced by a People's Congress sponsored by the British Communist Party in January 1941 called for increases in wages and social security, better air-raid defenses, a "restoration of trade union rights," the nationalization of banks, land, transport, and big industries, and independence to India and other colonies.
3. Ibid., p. 175.
4. *See* Arvo Tuominen, *The Bells of the Kremlin, an Experience in Communism*, Hanover, N.H.: University Press of New England, 1983, pp. 315–332.
5. A. Rossi, *A Communist Party in Action, an Account of the Organization and Operations in France*, New Haven, Conn.: Yale University Press, 1949, pp. 52–54.

6. "Interview with a New China Daily Correspondent on the New International Situation," 1 September 1939, in *Mao Tse-tung Selected Works*, vol. 2, Beijing: Foreign Languages Press 1967, pp. 263–268. (hereafter cited as Mao, *Selected Works*). "Di er ci diguo zhuyi zhanzheng jiangyan tigang" [Outline of a lecture on the second imperialist war], September 1939, in *Lun Muqian Guoji Xingshi yu Zhongguo Kangzhan* [On the present international situation and China's war of resistance], Chongqing: Xinhua Ribao, December 1939. "Interview with Three Correspondents from the Central News Agency, the Sao Tang Pao and the Hsin Min Pao," in Mao, *Selected Works*, vol. 2, pp. 269–274. "Sulian liyi yu renlai liyi de yizhi" [The interests of the Soviet Union and of mankind are one], 28 September 1939, in *Lun Muqian Guoji Xingshi yu Zhongguo Kangzhan*.

7. Mao, *Selected Works*, vol. 2, p. 51.

8. "Introducing the Communist," in Mao, *Selected Works*, vol. 2, pp. 285–296.

9. *Lun Xin Minzhu Zhuyi* [On new democracy], 15 January 1940, pp. 11–17, no place of publication given.

10. Ibid., p. 12.

11. Ibid., pp. 22–23.

12. Ibid., pp. 64–65.

13. *Mao Zedong Ji* [Collected works of Mao Zedong], vol. 7, Tokyo: Sososha Company, 1971, p. 181. This multivolume collection of Mao's work juxtaposes the original versions of all Mao's writings with post-1949 versions, indicating portions that were subsequently deleted or altered.

14. Zhao Rui, "Yan Xishan tongdi panguo zuixing jiyao" [The essence of Yan Xishan's traitorous crime of contact with the enemy], *Wenshi Ziliao Xuanji* [Selection of Literary Materials], vol. 29, Beijing: Zhongguo Renmin Zhengzhi Xieshanghui, p. 158.

15. Ding Yongnian, "Guanyu di yi ci fangong gaochao de yi xie shishi" [Several historical facts regarding the first anticommunist high tide], *Dangshi Yanjiu Ziliao* [Research Materials on Party History], no. 12, 20 June 1980, p. 23. Tang Manzhen, "Zhongguo Gongchandang shi ruhe datui di yi ci fangong gaochao" [How the CCP beat back the first anticommunist high tide], *Jiaoxue yu Yanjiu* [Teaching and Research], no. 3, 1981, p. 14. According to Ding Yongnian, Hu's offensive was part of a plan developed by Zhu Shaoliang and approved by Chiang Kai-shek in March 1939.

16. Zhu De and Peng Dehuai issued a "letter to the whole nation" on 25 December protesting recent anticommunist moves, and on 29 December Zhu sent a cable to the National Government demanding punishment of the individuals responsible for the incidents and cancellation of various anticommunist ordinances. Further CCP protests followed on 23 January and 13 February 1940. Charles B. McLane, *Soviet Policy and the Chinese Communists, 1931–1946*, New York: Columbia University Press, 1958, p. 140.

17. Tetsuya Kataoka, *Resistance and Revolution: The Communists and the Second United Front*, Berkeley: University of California Press, 1974, p. 175.

18. Aleksandar Ya. Kalyagin, *Along Alien Roads*, New York: Columbia University East Asia Institute, 1984, *passim*.

19. Raisa Mirovitskaya and Yuri Semyonov, *The Soviet Union and China, a Brief History*, Moscow: Novosti Press Agency, 1981, pp. 28–29.

20. *Milu*, vol. 12, p. 93.

21. *Zhanshi Waijiao*, pp. 359–375.

22. *Milu*, vol. 12, p. 93.

23. McLane, *Soviet Policy*, pp. 138, 144–146.

24. McLane suggested that the decline in Soviet media attention was due to decreasing Soviet concern for the Far Eastern situation as Soviet-Japanese relations improved, and to new restrictions on foreign reporters contacts with Yan'an and reporting from Chongqing.

25. Again this conclusion is contrary to that of Charles McLane, who asserted, on the basis of Soviet press coverage of Chinese affairs, that contacts between the CCP and Moscow were minimal between the fall of 1939 and the spring of 1941. See McLane, *Soviet Policy*, p. 154.

26. Wa. Zui Ke Fu [Vasilii Chuikov], *Zai Hua Shiming* [Mission to China], Beijing: Xinhua Chubanshe, 1983, p. 64.

27. *Zhanshi Waijiao*, p. 529.

28. Peter Vladimirov, *The Vladimirov Diaries, Yenan China: 1942–1945*, New York: Doubleday, 1975, pp. 6–7.

29. Wang Yunxue, "Huiyi Tanqiu tongzhi zhanduo zai Xinjiang" [Recalling comrade Tanqiu's struggle in Xinjiang], in *Huiyi Chen Tanqiu* [Recollections of Chen Tanqiu], Wuhan: Huazhong Gongxueyuan Chubanshe, 1981, p. 136.

30. Li Tien-min, *Chou En-lai*, Taibei: Institute of International Relations, p. 220. Howard Boorman, *Biographical Dictionary of Republican China*, vol. 1, New York: Columbia University Press, p. 396. During his stay in Moscow, Zhou made a speech to a session of the Fifth Supreme Soviet of the Soviet Union.

31. Tuominen, *Bells of the Kremlin*, pp. 315–321. When the tenacity and unity with which the Finns fought is compared with the disintegration of French resistance before German military might several months later, one gains some insight into the value of Communist loyalty to Comintern orders as an instrument of Soviet national policy. Regarding the French Communist role in the collapse of France in 1940, see William L. Shirer, *The Collapse of the Third Republic*, New York: Pocket Books, 1976, pp. 509–858.

32. Otto Braun, Comintern Agent in China, 1932–1939, New York: C. Hurst and Co., 1982, p. 263.

33. Zhou Enlai, "Guanyu dang de 'liu da' de yanjiu" [Research on the Party's Sixth Congress], 3 March 1944, in *Zhou Enlai Xuanji* [Selected works of Zhou Enlai], vol. I. Beijing: Renmin Chubanshe, 1983, pp. 178–179.

34. Gao Jun, *Weida de Zhanshi Ren Bishi* [The great warrior Ren Bishi], Beijing: Zhongguo Qingnian Chubanshe, 1980, p. 101.

35. Ibid.

36. *The Great Soviet Encyclopedia*, New York: Macmillan, 1981, vol. 16, p. 281.

37. Gao Jun, *Weida de Zhanshi*, pp. 101–102.

38. Ibid., p. 101.

39. Wen Feiran, "Xinjiang kang Ri minzu tongyi zhanxian de xingcheng yu polie" [The formation and collapse of the anti-Japanese national united front in Xinjiang], *Xinjiang Wenshi Ziliao Xuanji* [Xinjiang Selection of Literary Materials], no. 8, p. 7. Wen mistakenly places Zhou's visit to Moscow in June 1939.

40. Wang Yunxue, "Huiyi Tanqiu tongzhi," p. 135.

41. Hu Hua, editor, "Chen Tanqiu" [Chen Tanqiu], *Zhonggong Dangshi Renwu Zhuan* [Biographies of historic CCP personalities], Xian (?): Shaanxi Renmin Chubanshe, 1983, pp. 35. Ji He, "Chen Tanqiu tongzhi zai Xinjiang" [Comrade Chen Tanqiu in Xinjiang], *Xinjiang Wenshi Ziliao*, no. 8, p. 29. Another People's Republic of China chronology says that the transfer took place at the end of 1939; *see* "Zhongguo Gongchandangren zai Xinjiang huodong jishi" [Record of activities of Chinese Communist personnel in Xinjiang], in *Xinjiang Wenshi Ziliao Xuanji*, no. 1, p. 34. Wen Feiran also says that the transfer took place "at the end of 1939" and that upon their arrival in Yan'an the men formed a mechanized unit of the Eighth Route Army.

42. Zhang Qi, "Liang shi yi you" [Good teacher and excellent friend], in *Huiyi Chen Tanqiu*, p. 127.

43. *See* Wang Ming, "Liang Tiao Luxian: Wei Zhonggong Gengjia Buersaiweike Hua Er Duozheng" [Two lines: The struggle for a more thorough Bolshevization of the CCP], *Wang Ming Xuanji* [Selected works of Wang Ming], vol. 3, Tokyo: Ji Gu Shuyuan, 1973, p. 174.

44. Wang Ming, "Liang Tiao Luxian," p. 111.

45. *Milu*, vol. 12, pp. 93–94. The identity of the Comintern representative in Yan'an between Otto Braun's recall in September 1939 and Peter Vladimirov's arrival in early 1942 is, as far as I know, unknown.

46. *Gongchang Guoji Jiesan yu Zhonggong* [The dissolution of the Communist International and the CCP], Fenduo Congshu di 33 Zhong, Tongyi Chubanshe. There is no date or place of publication listed on this booklet, but it seems to have been published in Chongqing in 1943 shortly after the disbandment of the Comintern.

47. Huang Kaiyuan, et al., "Wannan shibian dashiji" [Chronology of the Southern Anwei Incident], *Dangshi Ziliao Congkan* [Compendium of Materials on Party History], no. 2, 1981, p. 138.

48. *Cankao Ziliao*, vol. 8, p. 356.

49. Tetsuya Kataoka's outstanding work was marred by a failure to take this factor into consideration. Kataoka assumed that had Chiang signed a Carthaginian peace with Japan he would have retained control over his armies and could have thrown them against the CCP much as he did after the defeat of Japan. In fact, this is a very problematic assumption. Many historical examples indicate that lost wars profoundly delegitimize regimes, and if this experience is any guide, Chiang would have faced the rapid disintegration of much of his army if he had settled with Japan. He would have forfeited the mantle of Chinese nationalism, and that mantle could well have passed to the CCP several years earlier than it did. Kataoka's assumption that the military assets Chiang controlled would have remained essentially constant after he accepted a harsh peace with Japan was, moreover, shared by neither Chiang Kai-shek nor Mao Zedong. It follows from this that Mao was much less fearful of Chiang's possible surrender than Kataoka argues.

50. *See* John Hunter Boyle, *China and Japan at War 1937–1945, The Politics of Collaboration*, Stanford, Calif.: Stanford University Press, 1972.

51. Wa. Zui Ke Fu, *Zai Hua Shiming*, pp. 35–36. Stalin also told Chuikov that the United States and Britain were likely to increase their aid to Chiang because of the situation in Europe. This was a good development, since such aid, along with Soviet assistance, would enable Chiang to continue the

war against Japan. This aspect of Stalin's December comments probably differed from his views on this subject in late 1939 and early 1940. By late 1940 the Soviet-German honeymoon was over and tensions were mounting rapidly.

52. *See* "Freely Expand the Anti-Japanese Forces and Resist the Onslaughts of the Anti-Communist Die-hards," in Mao, *Selected Works*, vol. 2, p. 431.

53. Ibid., p. 434. According to later CCP accounts, there were also "leftist tendencies" within the CCP in 1940. These leftists reportedly felt that the "First Anti-Communist High Tide" was equivalent to the 1927 suppression by the KMT of the CCP. Thus, they believed that the time had arrived for a revival of land revolution and were ready for a fight to the finish with the KMT. They felt that "friction" with the KMT could continue and did not understand that the "antifriction" battle was for the purpose of maintaining unity with the KMT. *See* Xu Haining, "Lun kang Ri minzu tongyi zhanxian zai xiangchi jieduan zhong de 'zuo' qin weixian" [On the "leftist" danger in the anti-Japanese national united front during the period of strategic stalemate in the war of resistance], *Xueshu Yanjiu Congkan* [Compendium of Academic Research], no. 2, 1983, pp. 59-64.

54. Donald W. Klein and Anne B. Clark, *Biographic Dictionary of Chinese Communism, 1921–1965*, Cambridge, Mass.: Harvard University Press, 1971, vol. 1, p. 132.

55. There is another interesting incident which may have figured in this second compromise between Stalin and Mao. In 1940, Mao sent his two sons by his second wife Yang Kaihui (executed by the KMT in 1930) to Moscow for middle-school study. These two boys, Mao Anying and Mao Qinying, had been given to peasant families to raise at the beginning of the Long March in 1934. They were later tracked down and sent to Yan'an by Zhou Enlai in 1938. After completing middle school in Moscow, the two boys then entered university there. Mao Anying returned to China briefly in 1944 and then again returned to Moscow. Both sons returned to China permanently in 1949. *See* Huang Yuchuan, editor, *Mao Zedong Shengping Ziliao Jianbian, 1893–1969* [Materials on the life of Mao Zedong, 1893–1969], Hong Kong: Youlian Shubao Gongsi, 1970, p. 185. Given the role of Chiang Kai-shek's son Jiang Jingguo as Stalin's hostage during the years 1927–1936, it is possible that Mao Anying and Mao Qinying performed a similar role in the 1940s. Stalin may have tried to keep Mao in line by keeping his hands on Mao's sons. But other explanations are also plausible. The most simple and plausible explanation, of course, was that Mao was concerned with the education and safety of his sons.

56. Kataoka, *Resistance and Revolution*, p. 209.

57. "Zhongyang guanyu muqian xingshi yu dang de zhengce de jueding" [Central resolution on the present situation and the party's policy], in *Cankao Ziliao*, vol. 8, pp. 351–354.

58. In *Cankao Ziliao*, vol. 8, p. 351.

59. *See* Suo Shihui, "Bai tuan dazhan ying zhongfen kending" [The Hundred Regiments Offensive should be substantially upheld], in *Zhonggong Dangshi Yanjiu Lunwen Xuan* [Selection of research essays on CCP history], Zhu Chengya, editor, Changsha: Hunan Renmin Chubanshe, 1984, pp. 147–148. Dick Wilson, *When Tigers Fight, the Story of the Sino-Japanese War, 1937–1945*, New York: Viking Press, 1982, p. 177. James Reardon-Anderson, *Yenan and the Great Powers: the Origins of Chinese Communist Foreign Policy, 1944–1946*, New York: Columbia University Press, 1980, p. 15.

60. "Xiangchi jieduan zhong de xingshi yu renwu" [The situation and our duties during the stage of strategic stalement], in *Mao Zedong Ji*, vol. 7, pp. 213–226. Huang Yuchuan, *Mao Zedong Shengping Ziliao Jianbian*, pp. 189–190.

61. "On Protracted War," in Mao, *Selected Works*, Vol. 2, p. 138. Further evidence of a discrepancy between Mao's military strategy in 1940 and the Hundred Regiments Campaign is provided by the secretary of a CCP branch in a cavalry unit of the Eighth Route Army who defected to the KMT. This man had undergone a year's training in Yan'an, and after defection he reported a speech by Mao to his training class early in 1940. In this speech Mao reputedly said that the CCP should use seven-tenths of its effort to expand its strength, two-tenths to deal with the KMT, and one-tenth to fight Japan. Li Faqing, *Zhongguo Gongchandang Zai Kangzhan Qijian zhi Zhengge Yinmo* [The complete plot of the CCP during the period of the war of resistance], 10 May 1940, p. 2, no publisher or place of publication given. This purported statement by Mao figured prominently in later KMT propaganda against the CCP. While its source and subsequent importance to the KMT make its veracity questionable, it does provide another fragment of evidence confirming the hypothesis that the Hundred Regiments Campaign contradicted Mao's preferences.

62. Peng Dehuai, *Peng Dehuai Zishu* [Peng Dehuai remembers], Beijing: Remin Chubanshe, 1981, pp. 235–236. Other evidence substantiates Peng's account. The evaluation of the Hundred Regiments Campaign has been a troublesome issue for the CCP. Prior to the Cultural Revolution, the campaign was lauded as a great and heroic victory. During the Cultural Revolution, however, both Red Guard publications and more establishment media such as *Peking Review* charged that the campaign was launched by Peng Dehuai and Zhu De in violation of Mao's line and without his consent. (e.g.,

Lin Hsin-kung, "Settle Accounts with Peng Teh-huai for his Heinous Crimes of Usurping Army Leadership and Opposing the Party," *Peking Review*, 1 September 1967, no. 36, pp. 12–15; 34.) In 1984 Chinese historians still openly disagreed about the campaign. Some argued that "militarily the Hundred Regiments offensive violated the strategic direction set by the Party center for the period of strategic stalemate, exceeded the limits of strategic defense, and because of errors of command, caused heavy losses which could have been avoided." Other Chinese writers, while not denying these points, extol the objectives and results of the campaign. The evidence presented in this debate agrees that Mao Zedong was not enthusiastic about the campaign. *See* Suo Shihui, "Bai tuan dazhan," pp. 147–148, 155–156.

63. Peng Dehuai, *Peng Dehuai Zishu*, pp. 234–236.
64. *See* Kataoka, *Resistance and Revolution*, pp. 171, 199.
65. Other fragmentary evidence supports this hypothesis. During the Cultural Revolution, Chinese sources asserted that Peng Dehuai and Zhu De were supporters of Wang Ming's line and linked their initiation of the Hundred Regiments Campaign to their support for Wang. See Lin Hsin-kung, "Settle Accounts with Peng Teh-huai"; *see also* Shi Feng, *Fandui Wang Ming Tuoxiang Zhuyi Luxian de Duozheng* [The struggle against Wang Ming's capitulationist line], Shanghai: Renmin Chubanshe, 1976, pp. 68–69. In a radio broadcast from Moscow in 1969, Wang Ming himself said that as late as 1942, Zhu De and Peng Dehuai were supporters of his "international line." Cited in Huai Yuan, "Wang Ming, Mao Zedong yu Sulian" [Wang Ming, Mao Zedong and the Soviet Union], in *Feidang Neibu Duozheng Wenti Lunji* [Collection of essays on the internal struggle of the bandit party], Yao Menggan, editor, Taibei: Guoji Guanxi Yanjiusuo, 1975, p. 200.
66. Huang Kaiyuan, "Wannan shibian dashiji," pp. 147–148. *Milu*, vol. 12, pp. 97–98. These two sources agree on the contents of He's plan, but disagree on Zhou's immediate response to it. *Milu* says that Zhou "immediately agreed" and only raised objections after visiting Yan'an. The CCP source does not mention Zhou's meeting with He and Bai.
67. Huang Kaiyuan et al., "Wannan shibian dashiji," p. 139.
68. Ibid., pp. 136, 139–142, 146.
69. Warren Kuo, "The CCP after the Government Evacuation of Wuhan," part 1, *Issues and Studies*, vol. 5, no. 8 (may 1969), pp. 34–42.
70. Hu Chiao-mu, *Thirty Years of the Communist Party of China*, Beijing: Foreign Languages Press, 1959, p. 61. Shi Feng, *Fandui Wang Ming Tuoxiang Zhuyi Luxian*, p. 69. Kataoka, *War and Resistance*, pp. 159–160.
71. Huang Kaiyuan et al., "Wannan shibian dashiji," pp. 144, 145.
72. Ibid., p. 15.
73. Shi Feng, *Fandui Wang Ming Tuoxiang Zhuyi Luxian*, p. 69.
74. *Milu*, vol. 12, p. 26.
75. Memorandum from the archives of the staff office of the military commission of the National Government, no. 031, first catalog, vol. 94. In *Waijiaoshi Ziliao (1937–1945)*, pp. 186–187.
76. *Milu*, vol. 12, p. 115.
77. Wa. Zui Ke Fu, *Zai Hua Shiming*, pp. 58–59.
78. *Zhanshi Waijiao*, pp. 527–529.
79. Huang Kaiyuan et al., "Wannan shibian dashiji," p. 154.
80. *Milu*, vol. 12, p. 115.
81. *Zhanshi Waijiao*, pp. 387–388.
82. Wa. Zui Ke Fu, *Zai Hua Shiming*, p. 46.

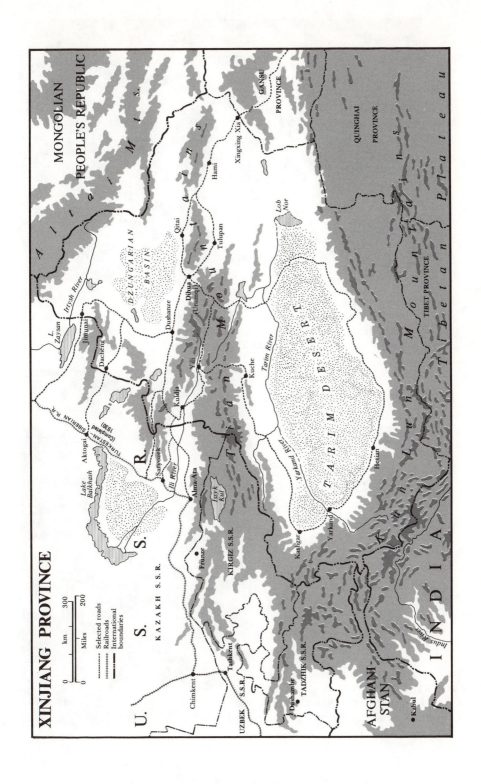

XINJIANG PROVINCE

MONGOLIAN
PEOPLE'S REPUBLIC

A l t a i   M t s.

GANSU
PROVINCE

QUINGHAI
PROVINCE

Xingxing Xia

Hami

T i a n   M o u n t a i n s

Qitai

Tulupan

Lob
Nor

DZUNGARIAN
BASIN

Dushanze

Dihua
(Urumqi)

Vili

Kuche

Tarim River

T A R I M   D E S E R T

Jimunai

Dacheng

L.
Zaisan

Irtysh River

Kuldja

Yarkand River

K u n   L u n   M o u n t a i n s

T i b e t a n   P l a t e a u

TIBET PROVINCE

Hetian

Lake
Balkhash

Aktogai

Saryozek

TURKESTAN-
SIBERIAN R.R.
(completed
1930)

Ili River

Alma-Ata

Issyk
Kul

T i a n

Kashgar

Yarkand

U.   S.   S.   R.

KAZAKH S.S.R.

Frunze

KIRGIZ S.S.R.

I N D I A

Chimkent

Tashkent

UZBEK   S.S.R.

Dushanbe

TADZHIK S.S.R.

AFGHANI-
STAN

Kabul

Indus River

km   300

Miles   200

Selected roads
Railroads
International
boundaries

President of the Legislative Yuan and Chiang's special representative Sun Ke (firing rifle) on the firing range of the officers club outside Moscow, 1938. Rear, right to left: Xia Junlun, Ambassador Yang Jie (center rear), Yu Ming, and future ambassador Fu Bingchang (on outside). Courtesy of KMT Committee on Party History, Taibei.

President of the Legislative *Yuan* Sun Ke making a speech at the opening of the Fifth National Sports Meeting in 1933. Courtesy of The Commercial Press, Taibei.

Soviet supplied I-15 fighter in service in China, circa 1938. Courtesy of Dr. Wen Liang-yen and Ministry of Defense, Taibei.

Soviet supplied SB-2 bomber in service in China, circa 1938. Courtesy of Dr. Wen Liang-yen and Ministry of Defense, Taibei.

I-16 fighter in service in China, circa 1938. This advanced fighter was the mainstay of China's Soviet-supplied air force. Courtesy of Dr. Wen Liang-yen and Ministry of Defense, Taibei.

Wang Chonghui. Foreign Minister 1937–1941. Courtesy of KMT Committee on Party History, Taibei.

Chiang Kai-shek inspecting a squadron of Soviet supplied T-26 tanks, circa 1938. Courtesy of KMT Committee on Party History, Taibei.

Wang Ming and other leading members of the Executive Committee of the Communist International at that organization's seventh World Congress. Left to right (front): Georgii Dimitrov, Palmiro Togliatti, Wilhelm Florin, Wang Ming; (rear) Otto Kuusinen, Dmitri Mannilski, Klement Gottwald, Wilhelm Pieck. Courtesy of Dietz Verlag, Berlin.

Mao Zedong and Ren Bishi shortly before Ren's dispatch to Moscow in 1938 to negotiate Stalin's endorsement of Mao's leadership. Courtesy of China Youth Publishing Company, Beijing.

Ren Bishi and Zhou Enlai. Probably taken during Zhou's early 1940 mission to Moscow. Courtesy of China Youth Publishing Company, Beijing.

Xinjiang ruler Sheng Shicai, circa 1940. Courtesy of KMT Committee on Party History, Taibei.

China joins the Big Four. Ambassador Fu Bingchang signs the Four Power Declaration for China at October 1943 Foreign Minister's Conference in Moscow while U.S. Secretary of State Cordell Hull, Soviet Foreign Minister Vyacheslav Molotov, and U.S. Ambassador Averell Harriman look on. Courtesy of KMT Committee on Party History, Taibei.

Chiang Kai-shek signing the United Nations treaty, 1945. Courtesy of KMT Committee on Party History, Taibei.

Foreign Minister Wang Shijie. Courtesy
of Dr. Wang Chi-wu, Taibei.

Chinese delegation arrives in Moscow, 30 June 1945 to negotiate treaty of alliance and
friendship. Front row from right: Ambassador Fu Bingchang, Foreign Minister T.V. Soong, Foreign Minister Vyacheslav Molotov, President Mikhail I. Kalinin. Second row far left: Ambassador Appolon Petrov. Courtesy of KMT Committee on Party History, Taibei.

Chapter VI

The Xinjiang Cockpit

Pawn and Pivot

Throughout the wartime period, Xinjiang province in China's west was a major arena of both Chinese-Soviet rivalry and cooperation. While Sino-Soviet relations in Xinjiang were largely a function of the broader policies of Chongqing, Moscow, and Yan'an, they merit a separate discussion both because of the prominence of the Xinjiang issue in Republic of China–Soviet Union relations and because of the importance of the vast and mineral-rich region of Xinjiang in the establishment of China as a great power. Xinjiang was the territory in which Soviet special interests in China were focused in the 1930s and the region where Chinese nationalism and Soviet national interests came into most direct conflict throughout the war. If, in other words, Xinjiang had become an independent nation similar to Outer Mongolia, China's future as a major power would have been significantly less bright.

Stalin, Chiang Kai-shek, and Mao Zedong all wanted to direct the development of Xinjiang along lines compatible with their own particular vision of China. To Chiang Kai-shek, Xinjiang was a part of the once-great Chinese nation that had been seized by Russian imperialism during China's period of weakness. From Chiang's perspective, Xinjiang was the Soviet equivalent of Japan's Manchukuo and the territorial concessions along China's coast and waterways made to Western imperialists. Just as the Western powers in their extraterritorial concessions, so the Soviet Union in Xinjiang exercised extensive special powers while still professing to uphold China's sovereignty and territorial integrity. For Chiang Kai-shek, China's return to national greatness demanded the reestablishment of the full authority of China's central government over Xinjiang and the expulsion of the Soviet imperialist presence there.

This flatly contradicted Stalin's objective, which was to draw Xinjiang into the orbit of the Soviet Union. While recognizing the formal sovereignty of China over Xinjiang in order not to undermine the Soviet Union–Republic of China united front against Japan, Stalin sought, with a considerable degree of success, to establish Soviet political and military hegemony over the region, while integrating it into the economy of the Soviet Union. During periods when China's anti-Japanese cooperation was less critical to Moscow, such as during the period of Soviet-Axis cooperation in 1940, Soviet respect for China's formal sovereignty in Xinjiang was less solicitous.

The rivalries of Moscow, Chongqing, and Yan'an for control of Xinjiang unfolded under the rule of the shrewd and ruthless warlord Sheng Shicai. Ruling Xinjiang from 1933 to 1944, Sheng sought to manipulate and balance Stalin and Chiang to enhance his own power. Ruling a province where rebellion was endemic and the level of economic and cultural development was quite low, Sheng realized that he needed outside help. Like other rulers of Xinjiang before him, Sheng frequently had to turn to outside support to put down rebellions against his rule and to counter threats from Japan, India, or China itself. Sheng was a ruthless opportunist who accepted or rejected overtures from Moscow and Chongqing as his own interests demanded.[1]

To understand the wartime contest for control of Xinjiang, it is necessary to understand the extent of Soviet control of that province when the war began. In the mid-1930s, the Soviet Union began expanding its penetration into Xinjiang well beyond the areas immediately adjacent to the Soviet Union's borders where Russia had more traditionally exercised its influence. According to Allen S. Whiting, there were four key mechanisms of Soviet penetration in Xinjiang in the 1930s. The first was military intervention to suppress revolts which Dihua (as Urumqi, the capital of Xinjiang, was then called) was incapable of suppressing. In 1933–1934 and again in early 1937, Soviet forces intervened in Xinjiang in support of Sheng's regime.[2]

Economic influence, including loans which indebted Dihua to Moscow and trade which oriented Xinjiang's economy toward the Soviet Union, was a second mechanism of Soviet penetration.[3] In 1934, Moscow granted Sheng a five-year loan of 5 million gold rubles for the purchase of Soviet military and industrial equipment.[4] The next year a Soviet mission headed by Stalin's brother-in-law A. S. Svanidze arrived in Dihua to help draw up a plan to Xinjiang's economic development. Then in 1937, a further Soviet loan of 15 million gold rubles was extended to help finance a three-year development plan. With Soviet financial and technical assistance, roads and bridges were built, telegraph and telephone lines were strung, and new industrial facilities, schools, and hospitals were built. Trade between Xinjiang and the Soviet Union burgeoned.[5] Xinjiang's rich mineral resources were also developed with Soviet assistance. Xinjiang was discovered to have rich petroleum deposits and in 1935 Soviet engineers began drilling for oil in the Dushanze area on the southern edge of the Dzungarian basin. A refinery with an annual capacity of 50,000 tons was soon built at that site. Soviet operations at Dushanze were carried on under an "oral agreement" between Sheng and Soviet officials, and would play a prominent role in subsequent Soviet-Xinjiang relations.[6] So extensive did economic cooperation between the two become by the late 1930s that Allen Whiting suggests the integration of Xinjiang into the economies of the Soviet central Asian republics through the newly completed Turkestan-Siberian Railway was Moscow's objective.[7]

A third mode of Soviet penetration was ideological. Especially important was the appeal of a tolerant nationalities policy modeled after that of the Soviet Union, a policy which was popular among the Turkic peoples of Xinjiang long used to chauvinistic policies imposed by the ruling Han Chinese authorities.[8] Sheng combined such a tolerant nationalities policy with ruthless "class struggle" and Marxism–Leninism. According to the memoir of one man who was a cadre in Sheng's administration, in 1936 the Soviet Union began pressing Sheng to arrest Xinjiang's wealthy and confiscate their property in order to help repay recent Soviet loans. Sheng agreed and invited the Soviet Union to send personnel to assist in this "class struggle." Over 100,000 people were then arrested and sent to prisons and concentration camps by the end of 1937.[9]

A fourth mechanism of Soviet influence took the form of direct penetration by Soviet advisory personnel. Soviet military, financial, and economic advisors and instructors assisted Sheng's administration.[10] Soviet advisors helped Sheng establish a political police system modeled after the Soviet Union's NKVD. The efficiency and cruelty of this organization was reflected by the numerous executions it carried out, estimates of which range from several hundred to 100,000.[11] According to the memoir of Wen Feiran, one of Sheng Shicai's intelligence officers in the 1930s, the Soviet Union also expanded the Comintern's secret intelligence apparatus in Xinjiang.[12]

By 1937, Xinjiang was clearly in the Soviet sphere of influence. The effective authority of China's National Government was minimal while that of Moscow was overwhelming. Yet Xinjiang remained formally a part of the Republic of China. Xinjiang's status was summarized by Jiang Tingfu in a letter of 8 June 1934 to his friend Hu Shi. (As we saw in Chapter 2, Jiang served as China's first wartime ambassador to the Soviet Union; Hu was later ambassador to the United States.) Jiang explained that the Soviet Union recognized Chinese sovereignty over Xinjiang and still requested approval of the Chinese Foreign Ministry before sending its consuls there. Moreover, Moscow denied that it had any "ambitions" in Xinjiang, even though it enjoyed "special relations" with it. Sheng Shicai was also superficially subordinate to the National Government, with provincial officials nominally appointed and removed by Nanjing. Yet Nanjing exercised no real power in Xinjiang.[13]

The Republic of China was not powerful enough in the 1930s to permit Chiang to consider ousting the Soviet Union from Xinjiang. To have even attempted this would have driven Sheng closer to Moscow and tempted Stalin to sponsor a declaration of independence by Xinjiang. Again, the Chinese perspective on Xinjiang was elucidated by Jiang Tingfu's 1934 letter. Jiang drew an interesting analogy between China's relation to Xinjiang and Britain's relation to Canada. Both Xinjiang and Canada were next to powerful neighbors and far away from the mother country which had sovereignty over it. In such a situation, Jiang said, it would be foolish for the mother country to oppose close and friendly relations between her faraway province and its powerful neighbor. To do so would create greater danger of driving the province even more into the orbit of its neighbor. Rather than opposing increased contacts between Xinjiang and the Soviet Union, Jiang said, China's National Government should merely insist that the Soviet Union not stand in the way of improved relations between the central and provincial governments. Moreover, it should try to find ways of reducing Xinjiang's dependency on the Soviet Union.[14] Given the preponderance of Soviet power in Xinjiang, Chiang Kai-shek had to move cautiously in his efforts to limit Soviet influence, wean Sheng Shicai from the Soviet Union, and maintain his own claim to de jure sovereignty there.

Xinjiang and the Sino-Japanese War

The onset of the Sino-Japanese War greatly increased the importance of both Xinjiang and of Soviet goodwill to Chiang. Soviet protection of China's northwestern supply route against Japanese raids now became vital to China's war effort. Moreover, Chongqing could no longer risk Soviet displeasure and a possible reduction or suspension of Soviet aid by pressuring Moscow over the Xinjiang issue. This meant that

Chinese efforts to limit or reduce the Soviet presence in Xinjiang were shelved while the Soviet position there expanded to a previously unparalleled degree.

The main overland route for Soviet aid to China ran through Xinjiang. From railheads in Soviet Kazakhstan, hundreds of Soviet trucks carried cargoes to Dihua. From there the route continued through Hami to Lanzhou, the eastern terminus of the supply line. As we saw in Chapter 2, Soviet trucks often carried cargoes of Chinese antimony, tungsten, hides, and foodstuffs on their way back to the Soviet Union. Xinjiang's airspace also provided the major corridor for the rapid movement of diplomatic and advisory personnel between China and the Soviet Union. After the conclusion of the Sino-Soviet Nonaggression Treaty, an organizational infrastructure was quickly built up to facilitate the flow of men and material through Xinjiang. Sheng Shicai established a liaison office in Chongqing and a Xinjiang mineral products office in Lanzhou. He also agreed to the establishment of a Nationalist air base at Kuldja (Yining) to facilitate the movement of government personnel to and from the Soviet Union. The National Government organized a special diplomatic group at Lanzhou to negotiate with Soviet officials and to receive incoming and departing Soviet advisors. Refueling and repair depots for the truck convoys were set up along the route and tens of thousands of camels were organized into caravans to carry fuel to these supply dumps. Soviet radio and air stations were established at Dihua, Qitai, and Yili, while a Soviet military base developed at Lanzhou with a large contingent of Soviet aircraft and personnel.[15] Behind Lanzhou at Hami stood a self-contained Soviet mechanized infantry force known as the "Eighth Regiment." Stationed in Xinjiang in January 1938 at the request of Sheng Shicai, this force strengthened the guard against either Japanese raids or KMT penetration into Xinjiang via Suiyuan, and protected from pillaging by local warlords and bandits the large volume of Soviet military goods then flowing across Xinjiang. The Eighth Regiment remained at Hami until 1943.[16]

A joint Sino-Soviet air transport company was also organized to ferry personnel between China and the Soviet Union. Discussions regarding the creation of this company began in 1938 and actual operations began in April 1939. A formal agreement between the Soviet and Chinese governments establishing the company was not concluded until September 1939, however. As finally formalized in 1939, the company carefully respected mutual equality and reciprocity, and in this regard stood in sharp contrast to the mining agreement which would be imposed on Xinjiang a year later. Chinese aircraft flew Chongqing–Hami portion of the route, while Soviet aircraft flew the Hami-Dihua-Alma Ata-Moscow portion. The agreement also provided for training opportunities for Chinese pilots and technical personnel.[17]

Chongqing's war effort against Japan was served in 1937–1939 by the Soviet presence in Xinjiang. Yet even during this period of most intimate Sino-Soviet alliance, Chiang sought to limit Soviet penetration. The growing Soviet presence in Xinjiang was a realization of Chiang's fear that Moscow would take advantage of its alliance with the ROC to expand its influence in China. Chiang realized that the Soviet presence in Xinjiang benefited China's war effort, but he struggled to ensure that China's de jure sovereignty over that region would not be eroded by that presence.

During his discussions with Stalin in February 1938, Sun Ke raised the issue of the expanding Soviet position in Xinjiang. Stalin reassured Sun that the Soviet Union had no territorial interest in either Outer Mongolia or Xinjiang and urged China to begin construction of a rail line through Xinjiang to the Soviet Union, promising Soviet technological assistance for this endeavor.[18] By placing Outer Mongolia and Xinjiang in the same category, Stalin inadvertently raised the specter which haunted Chinese minds: that Xinjiang would eventually go the way of Outer Mongolia, achieving de factor independence and claiming de jure independence under the protection and tutelage of the Soviet Union. During his discussions with Stalin in 1939, Sun again raised the question of Xinjiang and was once again assured by Stalin that the Soviet Union had no interests there which clashed with those of Chongqing. The Soviet role in Xinjiang was "indirectly helping the Chinese government," Stalin insisted.[19]

Such discussions of Xinjiang were, however, exceptions. Xinjiang did not figure prominently in Sun's or other Chinese officials' talks with Soviet leaders during the period of Sino-Soviet alliance. The lack of prominence given to the Xinjiang issue was based, in part, on the circumspection of Soviet policy there. To a substantial degree, Moscow was careful to respect two of Chongqing's vital interests in Xinjiang during 1937–1939: it did not challenge Chinese de jure sovereignty there and it did not allow CCP influence in Xinjiang to grow strong.

The CCP, Xinjiang, and the Chinese Revolution

Like Chiang Kai-shek, Mao Zedong hoped to use Soviet influence in Xinjiang to further his own rule of China. From Mao's perspective, Xinjiang could play an important role in the Chinese revolution. Under Soviet patronage and through a united front with Sheng Shicai, Xinjiang could be developed into a base area which could complement and support the Shaan-Gan-Ning special district. Perhaps even more important, Xinjiang provided access to the Soviet Union. Soviet weapons, advisors, and supplies might one day roll through Xinjiang to the CCP's forces. The achievement of all these objectives would be facilitated, or so Mao hoped, by a Soviet protectorate over Xinjiang. But Mao was also a Chinese patriot. As such he believed that Xinjiang should one day return to the embrace of the motherland. No less than Chiang Kai-shek, Mao wanted to maintain Chinese sovereignty over Xinjiang and looked forward to the day when the effective control of China's central government—a Communist-led one—could be imposed through the length and breadth of that rich province.

Stalin, as we have seen, was well aware of Mao's tendencies toward "nationalist deviation" and this undoubtedly helped persuade him that CCP influence in Xinjiang should be kept to a minimum, along with that of the KMT. If Soviet interests in Xinjiang were to be protected, neither Yan'an or Chongqing could be allowed to establish a hold there. According to Wen Feiran, Stalin personally instructed Soviet personnel about to depart for service in Xinjiang in the late 1930s that they were to turn Xinjiang, under the support of the Third International, into a third political force in China. This third force would not belong to the KMT and would also be different from the CCP.[20]

Until the late 1930s, CCP influence in Xinjiang was minimal. A few CCP cadres had infiltrated into Xinjiang in the early and mid-1930s, but their modest activities paled in significance beside the powerful peasant armies and rural soviets then being built up by the CCP in southern China.[21] It was not until 1937, as Moscow, Nanjing, and Yan'an were maneuvering toward the creation of an anti-Japanese united front, that the CCP was able to establish a significant presence in Xinjiang under the auspices of a united front with Sheng Shicai.[22] A number of CCP sources clearly indicate that the main purpose in forming this united front with Sheng was to "open lines of international communication."[23] Moreover, once this united front was formed, Yan'an did in fact have easy access to the Soviet Union. From 1937 through 1941, the main line of CCP transportation to the Soviet Union ran from Yan'an to the Eighth Route Army liaison office in Xian, to a similar liaison office in Lanzhou, to the CCP's New Camp (discussed below) in Dihua, to Alma Alta where the train for Moscow could be caught. The flow of CCP personnel to and from Moscow via Dihua became so heavy that a hotel (*jiaodaisuo*) was set up there for personnel in transit.[24]

Easy access to the Soviet Union via Xinjiang conferred a number of benefits on the CCP. Some supplies, weapons, and ammunition were in fact sent to Yan'an from Xinjiang, although it is not clear whether these were sent by the Comintern or by the CCP apparatus in Xinjiang without Soviet approval.[25] One way or another, however, it is likely that they came from Soviet arsenals. Sums of money also reached Yan'an from Moscow via Xinjiang. Moscow was rumored to have sent $300,000 U.S. to Yan'an via Sheng Shicai in late 1937.[26] While this amount was paltry compared to the lavish Soviet aid then flowing to Chiang Kai-shek, still, it whetted CCP hopes for future Soviet generosity once Soviet policy toward Chiang Kai-shek changed—as it did in 1940.

Chiang Kai-shek took precautions to ensure that none of the Soviet material flowing across Xinjiang was diverted to the CCP. On 12 December 1937 he sent an order to Gansu governor Zhu Shaoliang, instructing him that all trucks, planes, or goods arriving at Lanzhou most be turned over directly to the Nationalist commander of the military district. Moreover, any plane or truck wishing to go to northern Shaanxi would have to be personally approved by Chiang Kai-shek and obtain a passport issued by the National Government. Similar orders were also sent to the governor of Shaanxi, Jiang Dingwen.[27] A year and a half later, in the summer of 1939 following the anticommunist decisions of the KMT's Fifth Plenum, the 34th Group Army under Hu Songnan was assigned to the Ningxia–Gansu region to reinforce the provincial forces of various Moslem warlords. Once Hu's forces were in place, all commerce between Xinjiang and the Shaan-Gan-Ning border area was severed as part of the general blockade of the CCP instituted in the fall of 1939.[28]

Chiang's safeguards and, perhaps more important, Soviet discretion, were effective in preventing much Soviet material from reaching the CCP during this period. Other forms of Soviet assistance to the CCP were more significant. One of these was ready access to Soviet medical facilities by top-level CCP cadres. A fairly substantial number of CCP cadres went to Moscow for medical treatment during these years.[29] When Ren Bishi arrived in Moscow in April 1938 to take over as head of the CCP delegation to the Comintern, for example, he found eighteen top-level CCP cadres undergoing medical treatment there.[30]

Aside from "lines of communication," the CCP also established a direct presence in Xinjiang under Soviet auspices during the 1937–1941 period. This presence took two main forms. The first was the New Camp. Consisting of the approximately

400-man remnant of Zhang Guotao's once-powerful Fourth Front Army which had fled into Xinjiang in 1935, the New Camp was in effect a small military academy. From September 1937 until January 1940, these men studied artillery, motor vehicle operation and repair, logistics, aviation, armor, medicine, radio, infantry operations, and foreign languages.[31] In the winter of 1939, some forty men from the New Camp were sent to the Soviet Union to study intelligence work.[32] Given the extent of Soviet control over Xinjiang and over Sheng Shicai, the New Camp military school could not have functioned without Soviet consent. Moreover, at least some of the instructors at the school, especially those in aviation and in Marxist-Leninist ideology, were Soviets.[33]

The New Camp in Dihua represented an important form of covert Soviet support for the military effort of the CCP. (By way of comparison, the first class at the Whampoa Military Academy in 1925 had numbered 500 men.) From Moscow's perspective the New Camp was a way to satisfy the demands of the CCP for military assistance in a covert fashion which would not be detrimental to Republic of China–Soviet Union relations. Great efforts were taken to camouflage the activities of the New Camp. Its cadets wore Nationalist uniforms, previous unit designations were dropped, and the innocuous-sounding name "New Camp" was adopted. In Xinjiang the academy was far away from the eyes of both KMT agents and foreigners. The camp also operated under very strict discipline. Deng Fa, the camp's commander, had been in charge of the CCP's counterespionage work and the protection of top Communist leaders from 1931 to 1935.[34] Working in cooperation with Sheng Shicai's efficient political police, Deng kept tight security about the New Camp.

While Yan'an undoubtedly hoped for more Soviet military assistance than that represented by the New Camp. it was grateful for even this support. Such men as those being trained under Deng Fa would clearly be an important asset in the effort to turn a collection of poor peasants and urban intellectuals into a fighting force which could challenge the modern divisions of the National Government or Japan. In fact, these men became core officers in building up a new Communist army after their return to Yan'an.[35]

The second major form of CCP presence in Xinjiang was through the assignment of its cadre to positions with Sheng Shicai's administration. Agreement between Sheng and Yan'an over the terms of such cooperation was reached in late 1937 and by the end of 1938 some 120 CCP cadre had assumed positions in Xinjiang under Sheng.[36] Sheng welcomed the CCP personnel and assigned them prominent positions within his administration, something he had been unwilling to do with KMT personnel.[37] These positions provided important bases for the expansion of CCP influence.[38] CCP cadres used their new positions to "raise the political consciousness" of the people of Xinjiang, efforts which coincided with the strong Marxist bent of Sheng himself. So extensive did CCP influence in Xinjiang become that by 1938–1939 people were calling Dihua "the second Yan'an."[39]

By early 1938, Sheng's policies were becoming steadily more "progressive" and Soviet and CCP influence was expanding steadily. It must have seemed to Yan'an that under Soviet protection there could well be a confluence of the revolutionary bases in Xinjiang and north and northwest China. Such a notion did not accord with

Stalin's own ideas about China's future, however, and it was vetoed by him. This divergence of interests between Moscow and Yan'an was manifested in the question of whether Sheng Shicai should join the Chinese or the Soviet Communist Party.

When Wang Ming had passed through Dihua on his way to Yan'an in November 1937, Sheng requested membership in the CCP.[40] The CCP Politburo welcomed Sheng's petition for Party membership and Ren Bishi, who traveled to Moscow to report on CCP work in early 1938 (see Chapter 3), discussed Sheng's request with him on his way through Dihua. Ren told Sheng that the Politburo had unanimously approved his application but that "because of the many years of close relations between Xinjiang and the Soviet Union" and "because of the importance of [Sheng's] position," the matter would have to be reported to the Comintern and to Stalin.[41]

As Allen Whiting pointed out, the significance of Sheng's application for CCP membership "cannot be over stressed."[42] It meant that Sheng was willing to pledge ultimate loyalty to Yan'an rather than to Chongqing. The CCP Politburo's approval of Sheng's request is equally significant; it implies that Mao hoped for an ultimate merging of the revolutionary forces of Xinjiang and northwest China. Both regions would contribute toward the construction of a revolutionary China. This was not to be. Later in 1938 Ren Bishi reported to Sheng that, while the Comintern and Stalin realized that Sheng was well qualified for CCP membership, "They believe you should refrain temporarily from joining the CCP. . . . The delicate role [Xinjiang] now occupies in the international scene," Ren said, "and the importance of your own position in China combine to make your present membership undesirable."[43]

There are two not mutually exclusive explanations of Stalin's actions. On the one hand, Stalin wanted to minimize Chinese influence, whether Nationalist or Communist, in Xinjiang. He was apprehensive of Mao's "nationalist tendencies" and may have realized that closer ties between Dihua and Yan'an would mean a lessening of Soviet influence in Xinjiang over the long run. Stalin hinted at this line of reasoning in his subsequent explanation of his decision to Sheng. Xinjiang was the innermost base of resistance to Japan, Stalin said. Its key mission was to guard the international lines of communication for the war against Japanese, German, and Trotskyite penetration. If China could get help from Allied countries (e.g., from the United States and Britain), Japan could be defeated after which there would be a period of "peaceful coexistence" between the CCP and the KMT. During this postwar period, Xinjiang should maintain close contact with both Chiang Kai-shek and Mao Zedong. Ultimately, however, the CCP would defeat the KMT.[44] Stalin's prognosis for Xinjiang, in other words, seems to have been this: Xinjiang should maintain its autonomy by balancing the CCP against the KMT. It should maintain good relations with both, while keeping both at arm's length. In this way Chinese influence in Xinjiang would be minimized and Soviet predominance protected. This also meant that Xinjiang would not become a base for the revolutionary efforts of the CCP against the KMT.

A second reason for Stalin's veto of Sheng's membership in the CCP may have been that such membership, had it become known to Chiang Kai-shek, would have antagonized Chongqing. Had Chiang Kai-shek witnessed Dihua and Yan'an growing closer, he certainly would have questioned whether or not Moscow was honoring its pledge not to aid the CCP. If Chiang concluded that Stalin was willing to harness

Xinjiang's resources to Yan'an's efforts, he might well reappraise his whole alignment vis-à-vis Japan and the Soviet Union. Sheng's membership in the CCP might, in other words, have undermined the Sino-Soviet united front against Japan.

Following Stalin's veto of Sheng's application to join the CCP, Sheng decided to go to Moscow to discuss the situation directly with the Soviet leader. According to Sheng, he felt that his role and that of Xinjiang were very important to both Stalin and Mao, and that if there were any disputes as to his future relationship with these two men, "it seemed only natural that I should iron out the problem with Stalin himself."[45] Thus, in August 1938, Sheng made a secret trip to Moscow to discuss the role of Xinjiang in the war against Japan and in the Chinese revolution, and the role of the Soviet Union in Xinjiang. During the long train ride to Moscow, Sheng was apprehensive of the fate awaiting him, fearful that he might be detained indefinitely in the Soviet Union. Upon arrival, however, Sheng was warmly and grandly received and conducted extensive discussions with Stalin, Molotov, and Voroshilov.[46]

During these talks, Stalin responded generously to Sheng's requests for greater Soviet support. After Sheng outlined his plans for developing Xinjiang into a "model socialist state," Stalin directed Molotov to speed the delivery to Xinjiang of industrial equipment needed for a three-year development plan. When Sheng requested that military equipment ordered five to six years earlier by his predecessor be delivered within two months, Voroshilov readily agreed. Regarding the status of Xinjiang, Sheng claims that he advocated continued "autonomous status" for the province. Neither he nor Stalin raised the possibility of Xinjiang becoming an independent republic or of it joining the Soviet Union.[47] Regarding the question of Sheng joining the CCP, Stalin decided that Sheng, on Stalin's personnel recommendation, was to be admitted to the CPSU, rather than to the CCP. Sheng says that he had qualms about joining the CPSU, but felt that he had no choice but to agree.[48] Sheng's entry into the CPSU was obviously a major gain for Soviet influence in Xinjiang.

Xinjiang and the Soviet-Axis Alignment

The Xinjiang relationships between Moscow, Chongqing, Dihua, and Yan'an began to shift in late 1939 as Moscow moved toward alignment with Germany and Japan. Moscow's preeminence in Xinjiang grew even greater: Xinjiang's media became more extravagant in praising the Soviet Union and Stalin; Soviet–Xinjiang trade grew, and Soviet advisors in Xinjiang become omnipresent. In 1940, a long-discussed Soviet-built aircraft factory also came into operation. Chongqing had tried to persuade Moscow to establish the plant in Lanzhou, but Moscow insisted on a site outside of Dihua. When production began in 1940, the plant was heavily fortified and included a garrison of 1500 Soviet soldiers plus some twenty tanks. This gave Moscow two garrisons in Xinjiang and added substantially to its ability to orchestrate events there.[49]

Chongqing vainly attempted to stem this growing Soviet hegemony. In October 1940, Soviet Ambassador Paniushkin passed on to his government Chongqing's protest about the stationing of "uninvited" Soviet troops in Xinjiang, apparently a reference to the new garrison at the Dihua aircraft plant.[50] Out of concern for the growing

Soviet presence in Xinjiang, Chongqing rejected a Soviet request to open a consulate at Lanzhou.[51] Such protests and denials were, however, inadequate to stem the rapid growth of Soviet influence in Xinjiang.

In November 1940 Moscow took a dramatic step toward full control over Xinjiang. This came in the form of a "mining agreement" concluded with Sheng Shi-cai on 26 November 1940. This agreement established an exclusively Soviet-owned and -managed company, named "Xin Tin," with rights to develop Xinjiang's deposits of tin and its "ancillary minerals" for thirty years. Xin Tin was given extensive economic rights and immunity from supervision or control by Chinese authorities.[52] The far-reaching and one-sided terms of this agreement were reminiscent of the Chinese Eastern and the South Manchurian railways in Manchuria and would have completed the integration of Xinjiang into the Soviet economy.

In his memoir Sheng claims that he initially resisted the demand of the Soviet Consul General I.V. Bakulin that he sign the "mining agreement." He first raised several technical objections, only to be told by Bakulin that Stalin had said that not a single word of the agreement could be changed and that no one but Sheng was to see the contents of the agreement. When Sheng compared the treaty to the Twenty-One Demands presented to China by Japan in 1915 and with the ninety-nine year concessions held by the Western powers in China, Bakulin insisted that he would not discuss "ideology." Sheng could write Stalin about any questions he might have regarding the agreement—after he had signed it. Bakulin assured Sheng that Stalin was fully aware of the terms of the agreement and that Stalin himself decided important affairs of state, especially foreign affairs. Bakulin then gave Sheng one day to decide whether or not to sign the agreement, ominously warning him in leaving: "We hope you will make a wise and cautious decision on a matter which affects not only the future of Xinjiang, but also of yourself."[53]

As a member of the CPSU, Sheng was bound by Party discipline to obey the orders of Stalin—a fact of which Bakulin reminded him. What persuaded Sheng to sign the agreement, however, was a fear that if he did not, he would be overthrown by the Soviet forces at Hami and Dihua. Thus when Bakulin returned the next day Sheng addressed him "with honeyed words" and signed the treaty.[54] He refused, however, to affix the official seals of the Xinjiang provincial government and of the Border Defense Commission on the grounds that this could be done only with specific authorization from Chongqing. He would later use this as a pretext to declare that the agreement was null and void. After signing the tin mines agreement, Sheng kept it secret from Chongqing.

Chiang Kai-shek may, however, have received word of the treaty. In any case, he was clearly apprehensive about the growing Soviet role in Xinjiang. Late in 1940, Chiang ordered the ROC transportation ministry to suspend work on a road through Xinjiang to the Soviet Union on the grounds that if the road were completed, "It would become their world"—apparently referring to Soviet and CCP control over Xinjiang.[55]

Stalin was apparently preparing to move still further toward turning Xinjiang into a Soviet satellite after the conclusion of the Soviet-Japanese neutrality agreement in April 1941. The Japanese consul in Shanghai reported to his government that on 23 April Sun Ke had been appointed head of a "Committee for the Adjustment of Sino-

Soviet Relations." Sun Ke then reportedly approached the Soviet ambassador about expanded cooperation with the Soviet Union in mining and highway construction. The Soviet Union was expected to request the establishment of a Soviet sphere of influence in Xinjiang, the Japanese consul reported. The next month the consul reported that Sheng Shicai was sending representatives to Chongqing to discuss a Soviet proposal regarding Sino-Soviet "cooperation" in mining operations in Xinjiang.[56] This evidence seems to indicate that negotiations were under way between Chongqing and Moscow in April–June 1941 regarding Chinese recognition of Soviet gains in Xinjiang acquired via the November 1940 tin mines agreement.[57] Chongqing may well have been trying to limit Soviet rapprochement with Japan and ensure continuing aid to China by compromising with Moscow on the Xinjiang issue. If so, and if Chiang condoned these negotiations, this was certainly the nadir of Chiang's nationalist efforts.[58]

If the Japanese reports of early 1941 are accurate, and this author is inclined to believe that they are, then perhaps the best way to explain them is that Chiang simply believed the Soviet role was so critical in prying loose Japan's hold over China, that some way, any way, had to be found to prevent Moscow from giving Japan carte blanche in China. Chiang was trying desperately to outbid Tokyo for Soviet affections.

While Moscow was moving to take over Xinjiang, the CCP and Sheng Shicai were maneuvering to see who would rule the new soviet Xinjiang which seemed to be in the making. In January 1940 and again in January 1941, Sheng proposed to Moscow the creation of a soviet government in Xinjiang.[59] Sheng believed that Moscow did not think him reliable enough to act as its man in Xinjiang and feared a plot by the Soviet Union and the CCP to oust him. The CCP had, in fact, begun to expand its organization in Xinjiang in late 1939 in violation of its 1937 understanding with Sheng.[60] By April 1941 the organizational paper of the CCP in Xinjiang, *Xinjiang Ribao*, was allegorically attacking Sheng and his regime.[61]

Beneath the complex and murky maneuvering between Moscow, Sheng, and the CCP in Xinjiang in 1939–1941 lay the question of that province's future. Stated simply, the question was whether Xinjiang would be integrated into the Chinese or the Soviet revolutionary process. Stalin had apparently decided that it should draw nearer to the Soviet. Mao hoped to add the expanse of Xinjiang to China's revolutionary forces. Moreover, he probably hoped to do this with Soviet support.

The CCP's view of Xinjiang and the Soviet role in Xinjiang in 1940 and early 1941 was reflected in Yan'an's propaganda. As we saw in Chapter 5, the CCP was then lauding the "revolutionary role" of the Red Army in "liberating" eastern Poland, Bessarabia, Bukovina, Lithuania, Latvia, Estonia, and parts of Finland. In many ways Xinjiang was comparable to those areas. Like them it had a tradition of being within the Russian sphere of influence. When Yan'an talked of the Red Army's role in assisting the Chinese revolution, they probably had in mind, among other things, a Soviet intervention in Xinjiang which would install them in power and allow them to harness Xinjiang's resources to their struggle against Chongqing. According to Wen Feiran, "Wang Ming's line was responsible for not adequately developing the CCP organization in Xinjiang." "Wang Ming" is often an euphemism for the Soviet Union in CCP writings. Wen goes on to note that in Xinjiang the combined strength of the Red Army (at Hami and at the Dihua aircraft factor) and of the CCP New Camp were about equal to Sheng's forces in terms of numbers and superior in terms of combat ability. In such a situation, Wen explained in his memoir, not to have developed the CCP organization was a mistake for it allowed the reactionaries to "break unity" and kill and arrest many Communists.[62] Stated plainly, Wen Feiran thinks that the Soviet forces and the CCP should have taken over from Sheng and established a CCP regime. Wen's views may well have been those of the CCP leaders in 1939–1940. Of course, in the event of a Soviet move to oust Sheng, there was no guarantee that Stalin would choose Mao to lead a soviet Xinjiang. Mao, like Sheng, had to try to win Stalin's support and prove his loyalty to Moscow. He had to try to outbid Sheng as a loyal supporter of the Soviet Union.

The Chinese Recovery of Xinjiang

The German invasion of the Soviet Union changed everything. Previously the military assets that Moscow could potentially bring to bear in Xinjiang far exceeded those that Chongqing could muster. Likewise, as long as the Soviet Union remained an island of peace while China fought desperately for its national survival, Moscow could assume far greater risks in Xinjiang than could Chongqing. But as Hitler's armies penetrated deeper and deeper into Soviet territory and as the Soviet government came face to face with the prospect of military defeat, the tables were turned in Xinjiang. Now Moscow could divert precious few forces to Xinjiang and needed at all costs to avoid a confrontation with China. The beginning of war between Japan and the United States in December 1941 also allowed Chiang to act more boldly in Xinjiang. Chiang could now be fairly confident that a diversion of Chinese strength to Xinjiang and away from the Japanese front would not be fatal for China. Thus, from 1942 through 1943, Chongqing used the shift in power relations in Xinjiang to eradicate the Soviet position there. Just as Moscow had utilized Chongqing's darkest hour in 1940 to expand its position in Xinjiang, so Chongqing used the Soviet crisis of 1942–1943 to uproot that position. Moscow attempted to stall and to divert Chongqing's efforts, but without success. By the time Moscow was able to look eastward once again after the summer of 1943, the status quo in Xinjiang was altogether different from that existing there two years earlier.

As German troops advanced on Moscow late in 1941, Sheng Shicai sensed the shifts under way and began improving his relations with Chongqing. Guo Dequan, the newly appointed Chinese military attaché to the Soviet Union, was one of the first to detect the shift in Sheng's position. When Guo traveled through Dihua on his way to Moscow in December 1941, Sheng received him cordially and made repeated gestures of his respect for Chiang. Guo responded by stressing the importance of Chiang's newly acquired American and British support. Upon arriving in the Soviet Union, Guo sent a cable to Chiang indicating that Sheng was reevaluating his position and that he might be ready to improve relations with the National Government.[63]

Chiang moved rapidly by dispatching Eighth War District commander Zhu Shao-liang to Dihua in March 1942 for talks with Sheng. Progress was made and in May Economics Minister Weng Wenhao accompanied Zhu to Dihua for further talks with Sheng. Meanwhile the journal of the pro-Soviet, leftist Anti-Imperialist Society ceased publication in Dihua.[64] Sheng and Zhu soon agreed on a strategy for pushing the Soviets out of Xinjiang. Sheng was to present demands on the Soviet Union and create problems in Soviet–Xinjiang relations. Chongqing would then intercede in these disputes, disclaiming responsibility for the unpleasant circumstances while insisting that such problems could be avoided in the future if Moscow dealt directly with Chongqing. Chongqing could thus maintain an attitude of reasonableness and friendship, while Sheng did the dirty work of applying the pressure. Relations between Chongqing and Moscow would be insulated, to some extent, from adverse consequences arising from Dihua's anti-Soviet drive.

Spring and summer of 1942 marked the high tide of the German offensive against the Soviet Union and the nadir of Soviet fortunes of war. The situation on the Soviet-German front was watched closely by all the participants in the Xinjiang game and had a great impact on the outcome of that rivalry. The Red Army's "Stalin Offensive" opened on 9 April 1942 with an assault against German forces on the Kerch Peninsula of the Crimea. It stalled within three days, and within a month German forces occupied the entire Kerch Peninsula and were driving on Sevastopol. German forces captured 100,000 Soviet prisoners and 200 tanks in the operation. The second stage of the Soviet offensive opened in early May with an attack on the Volkhov River front—an offensive commanded by General A. Vlasov who had served in China in 1938. The Red Army broke through the German lines, then stalled and was encircled. The main Soviet attack opened on 12 May with assaults by Marshal S. Timoshenko's forces north and south of the city of Kharkov. The northern pincer of Timoshenko's forces stalled while the southern one drove 113 kilometers (seventy miles) westward through weak Romanian divisions. On 18 May, German forces counterattacked the southern flank of the Soviet salient and by 23 May had sealed off the Soviet spearhead. The Germans claimed the capture of 240,000 prisoners and 1200 tanks. The German spring offensive then opened on 28 June with a drive by three armies across the Ukrainian steppes toward the Don and the Volga rivers. One of the four defending Soviet armies collapsed within forty-eight hours. Two others were soon rapidly retreating eastward in disorderly fashion, their command structure degenerating to divisional, then brigade, and finally the regimental level. The firepower of the German armies was vastly superior. By July the Red Army was evacuating the coal and industrial center of the Donetz basin as rapidly as possible.[65]

It was in this dark situation that Moscow was forced to deal with Sheng Shicai's pressure and demands. On 29 March 1942 Sheng Shicai's younger brother Sheng Shiqi was murdered, and Sheng seized on this incident as a pretext to arrest some 300 Soviet and CCP personnel. On 10 May Sheng sent a letter to Molotov charging that Consul General Bakulin and chief military advisor Latoff had perpetrated his brother's assassination as part of a conspiracy to overthrow the existing government of Xinjiang. Sheng also raised questions regarding the extralegal status of some Soviet activities in Xinjiang, such as the Dushanze oil wells, which, as we have seen, were operating under an "oral understanding" of 1935.

On 27 June, Soviet Vice-Commissar of Foreign Affairs Vladimir G. Dekanozov, who also happened to be an operative of the NKVD,[66] arrived in Dihua to bring Sheng back into line with a combination of blackmail and a generous offer regarding the Dushanze oil field. One of Dekanozov's objectives was to increase production at the Dushanze field and to regularize the Soviet presence there by concluding a formal agreement. In line with this, Dekanozov carried with him a letter from Molotov proposing the joint operation of the Dushanze oil field. Molotov's letter embodied an extremely conciliatory proposal for a genuine joint operation of the field, including joint management and a substantial increase in Xinjiang's share of production. Both the conciliatory tone and the substance of Molotov's proposal indicate that it was a serious effort to halt the rapprochement under way between Dihua and Chongqing.[67] It was also a desperate attempt to keep the oil from that field flowing to the Red Army–a matter discussed below.

On 3 July Sheng received a second letter from Molotov dealing with the history of relations between Sheng and the Soviet Union. Replying to Sheng's charges of Soviet involvement in his brother's death and of a plot to overthrow Sheng, Molotov denied such charges as "baseless and malicious slander." Molotov also warned Sheng that his "repressive policies" were endangering Xinjiang's stability and opined that this was the work of imperialist agents who had infiltrated Sheng's police. Molotov then proceeded to attempt to blackmail Sheng by enumerating a number of Sheng's past "mistakes" which had involved conspicuous disloyalty to Chiang Kai-shek: Sheng's 1934 petition to the Soviet Union for the establishment of a soviet government, his 1941 proposal that Xinjiang become an independent soviet country allied with the Soviet Union, and his support for the rebellious warlord Zhang Xueliang during the Xian Incident of 1936 when Chiang Kai-shek had been kidnapped. Molotov concluded: "The Soviet government deeply hopes that Your Excellency will draw the necessary conclusions from these matters and find a way for the normal solution of problems and prevent relations from deteriorating."[68] Implicit in Molotov's accusations was the message that Sheng's past actions would make him unacceptable to Chiang Kai-shek.

Dekanozov met with Sheng several times during July. According to Sheng's memoir, at their first meeting Dekanozov urged Sheng to remember past Soviet aid to Xinjiang and to Sheng personally. Dekanozov also reminded Sheng that he, Sheng, was a member of the Soviet Communist Party and that he should continue to have unwavering faith in Marxism. Sheng responded that while he would never forget the positive things Stalin had done for him and for Xinjiang, neither could he forget the bad things he had done—such as the imposition of the unequal tin mines agreement and the recent plot to kill him. Sheng then proceeded to disavow belief in Marxism and in Stalin as the leader of the world revolution, and to charge that Stalin had turned Lenin's policy of aiding the people of Asia into a policy of aggression. Dekanozov retorted that the tin mines agreement had been necessary for the struggle against fascism and left Sheng with the warning: "My present visit. . .has much to do with your future and that of your province. It is the final chance for restoring friendly relations between [Xinjiang] and Soviet Russia on the one hand, and Stalin and your honorable self on the other."[69]

By their third meeting, Dekanozov was using open threats and blackmail to influence Sheng. Sheng must remember that he was a member of the CPSU, Dekanozov warned, and that the CPSU would never allow one of its members, especially an important one, to forsake the Party and attack Marxism with impunity. Sheng should also recall that he had previously done a number of things fundamentally antagonistic to China's National Government and to Chiang Kai-shek. Dekanozov then recounted the embarrassing actions enumerated in Molotov's 3 July letter. "All these actions will prove to be serious predicaments for your political future if you change sides," Dekanozov warned. Sheng attempted to rebut some of the Soviet charges, but ultimately he challenged Dekanozov to give this extortionary information to Chongqing. Chiang Kai-shek knew that he was formerly a communist, Sheng said, and the actions cited by Dekanozov were entirely logical and consistent from a communist point of view. But now he had rejected Marxism and had embraced Sun Yat-sen's Three Principles of the People. Chiang Kai-shek knew this and had told him that what was important was Sheng's future loyalty to KMT principles and orders. Dekanozov then despaired of changing Sheng's mind, but upon leaving, told Sheng, "Whenever you need me, I can come to Xinjiang at any time."[70]

Moscow then proceeded to hand over to Chiang Kai-shek its incriminating information on Sheng Shicai. Moscow seems to have calculated that once Chiang learned the extent of Sheng's previous pro-Soviet orientation, he would conclude that Sheng could not be trusted and had to be removed from office. Sheng would then realize that it was too late in the game to change sides and would call Dekanozov back to Dihua and beg Soviet forgiveness and support. Such a sequence of events did not occur, in part because of Chiang's leniency toward Sheng's past indiscretions.

On 9 July Ambassador Paniushkin met with Chiang. He had been ordered by Stalin to meet with Chiang, the ambassador explained, because of the recent "unreasonable actions" against Soviet personnel in Xinjiang. Paniushkin then passed on to Chiang a copy of Molotov's 3 July letter to Sheng. He was revealing this letter, Paniushkin said, so that the Chinese government could be clear about the situation in Xinjiang and about Sheng's actions toward the Soviet Union and toward China's own government. It was clear, Paniushkin said, that the people behind such actions as these were "enemy spies." Chiang was unmoved by Paniushkin's demand that a "conclusion must be reached" on this affair. In closing his talk with Paniushkin Chiang made his most important point: "Any matters regarding Xinjiang should be negotiated between your honorable country's government and my humble country's central government, and cannot be discussed with the Commissioner's [Sheng Shicai's] Office."[71]

On 11 July Chiang received a long letter of self-criticism from Sheng Shicai. After his discussions with Dekanozov. Sheng anticipated Moscow's next move and decided to present his own version of events to Chiang. In this letter Sheng explained the mitigating circumstances surrounding the actions described in Molotov's epistle. Sheng confessed his past pro-Soviet, procommunist inclinations but assured Chiang that such beliefs were now a thing of the past. Moscow had not responded appropriately to his friendship, but had provoked repeated incidents. Most recently, it had organized a plot to kill Sheng and all his loyal officers, and to establish a soviet regime under the CCP. The CCP hoped, Sheng told Chiang, to seize Xinjiang and use it as a base from which to expand its power in China. Sheng also revealed to Chiang his membership in the CPSU and his signature of the 1940 tin mines agreement under direct Soviet orders. All of these things had led Sheng to realize, he now told Chiang, that the Soviet Union was really an imperialist country using Marxism as a mask to cover its aggression. Finally, Sheng embraced the Three Principles of the People, swore loyalty to the KMT, to Chiang Kai-shek, and to the National Government, and renounced any future cooperation with the Soviet Union.[72]

On 13 July—four days after Paniushkin gave the copy of Molotov's letter to

Chiang, two days after Chiang received Sheng's confession, and just as the German drive toward the Volga River was gaining steam—a top-level meeting convened in Chongqing to decide on policy toward Xinjiang. Minister of War He Yingqin presented a long memorandum embodying a comprehensive strategy for recovering Chinese sovereignty over Xinjiang.[73] Since Chongqing's policy in Xinjiang over the next two years generally corresponded to He's plan, it is worth considering in some detail.

According to He's plan, China should take advantage of the current period of "Sino-Soviet alliance" to recover Xinjiang. But since the strength of the central government was still inadequate, it would have to act indirectly through Sheng Shicai. Chongqing should support Sheng and gradually bring him under central government control while simultaneously "mollifying" [fuyan] the Soviet Union. This would slow down the implementation of Moscow's Xinjiang strategy and give China time to strengthen its military positions in Gansu, Qinghai, and Tibet.

Xinjiang would be recovered in two stages, according to He's plan. During the first stage, China should continue its "good neighbor policy" toward the Soviet Union and use "stratagem" to "prevent it from adopting decisive action in Xinjiang"—in other words, to prevent the Soviets from militarily occupying Xinjiang. Moscow's objective, according to He's memorandum, was to annex Xinjiang. The Soviets had adequate strength to do this, but open use of military force would reveal Moscow's aggressive attitude toward China. This "would be disadvantageous [to Moscow] in terms of both stratagem and strategy." Moscow was therefore forced to resort to more devious methods, such as its attempt to blackmail Sheng. Moscow hoped to estrange Sheng from Chongqing, and then once Sheng was isolated, eliminate him and establish another puppet to protect Soviet interests in Xinjiang. By using the appropriate stratagem, however, Chongqing could turn Soviet pressure on Sheng to its own advantage. Sheng was very afraid of the Soviet Union and would have to rely on the central government for support against it, He Yingqin explained. Chongqing should thus uphold Sheng's position and encourage him to rely on the central government for support. It should send top officials to Dihua to confer with Sheng and, once Sheng agreed, should send cadres and "secret agents" to Xinjiang.

Closer ties between Sheng and the central government would increase Soviet suspicions, He Yingqin continued, but Moscow "would not dare to take violent actions" as long as Chongqing acted cautiously. He proposed a number of immediate measures to "mollify" Moscow. Chongqing should thank Moscow for passing on Molotov's letter to Sheng, while explaining that the matters mentioned in the letter had already been reported by Sheng to the central government. Chongqing should avoid mentioning its future attitude toward Sheng and if the Soviet side raised this issue, Chinese officials should say that the matter was under study. Chongqing should assure Moscow of its desire for continued friendly relations and explain that the "unpleasant situation" existing between the Soviet Union and the Xinjiang authorities arose from direct negotiations between Moscow and Dihua. To avoid this in the future, and since China and the Soviet Union were allies, all diplomatic matters regarding Xinjiang should henceforth be dealt with through "proper channels," that is, by discussions with Chongqing. A special diplomatic mission should be dispatched to Dihua to conduct these negotiations and to "reduce direct Soviet pressure on Sheng." Meanwhile, China should find a way to have British and American missionaries enter Xinjiang in order to "add a few worries and constraints" to Soviet actions. Chongqing should also station a division at Yumen in western Gansu on the pretext of defending the mining district near there. "Less than a division" should be stationed in southern Xinjiang on the pretext of defending Xinjiang's airfields.

The second stage of He Yingqin's plan, during which time sovereignty over Xinjiang would actually be recovered, would begin when the Soviet Union was on the brink of military defeat by Germany and Japan. "Once the Jap pirates attack the Soviets, or the Soviets are defeated by Germany, or other situations even more advantageous to our international situation develop," He's memorandum read, "then China could propose to the Soviet Union the resolution of outstanding diplomatic problems." Among the unresolved problems which China should raise at that time were the "cancellation of recognition of the puppet regimes of Manchukuo and Outer Mongolia," Soviet support for the CCP, and Soviet evacuation of Xinjiang. Main force units of the Nationalist army would then enter Xinjiang, purge all "unstable elements," and recovery sovereignty. He Yingqin warned against revealing Chinese objectives before the Soviet Union was in dire straits. Although the Soviet Union had not yet used military force to annex Xinjiang, it still had adequate strength to "deal with incidents." Therefore, the central government should not at present directly aid Sheng or demand that the Soviet Union withdraw from Xinjiang. The Soviet Union could "ignore" such demands until it was on the brink of military defeat.

Chongqing promptly began to implement He's plan. On the same day that He presented his memorandum, Chiang Kai-shek decided to keep Sheng Shicai in place and "to leave room for compromise" with the Soviet Union over Xinjiang.[74] Writing in his diary, Chiang commented that he must guard against Soviet attempts to incite insurrection against Sheng, even though the Soviet probably would not attempt this during the war. As long as the Soviet Union and Japan remained at peace, Chiang wrote, he would bolster Sheng's rule of Xinjiang while negotiating with the Soviet Union for a thorough resolution of the Xinjiang problem.[75]

On 16 July, Chiang met again with Ambassador Paniushkin to implement steps outlined in He Yingqin's plan. After thanking Paniushkin for the copy of Molotov's letter and telling him that Sheng had already reported to Chongqing the events mentioned in it, Chiang made his main point. In order to avoid a repeat of the "misunderstandings" of the past, all matters relating to Xinjiang should henceforth be negotiated by the Chinese and Soviet governments, not by the Xinjiang and Soviet governments. These negotiations would be conducted on the basis of equality and sincerity, and since China and the Soviet Union were allies in the struggle against aggression, all problems could be settled fairly and peacefully. In preparation for such negotiations, Chiang informed Paniushkin, Economics Minister Weng Wenhao had already been sent to Dihua to negotiate economic matters. Chiang also rejected Molotov's charge that Sheng was an "enemy agent" who should be removed from office.[76]

The Sino-Soviet Negotiations over Xinjiang

Negotiations over the status of Soviet interests in Xinjiang began in mid-1942 and continued into 1943. There was a division of labor between Chongqing and Dihua in the talks with Moscow over Xinjiang. While Chongqing handled questions of "economic cooperation," especially the Dushanze oil fields and the Dihua aircraft factory, Sheng Shicai handled talks over the withdrawal of Soviet advisors, technical personnel, and military units from Xinjiang. According to Sheng, his assumption of responsibility for negotiations regarding the withdrawal of Soviet personnel was intended to insulate broader ROC-USSR relations from possible adverse consequences.[77] The Soviet holdings at Dushanze and at Dihua were especially vulnerable to Chinese pressure. Since no agreements had been signed regarding these operations, the Soviet presence at these localities was, in a strict sense, extralegal. Moscow used a combination of conciliation and pressure to try to reach agreements which would legitimize and continue its Xinjiang interests. Chongqing preferred to leave the issues unresolved while steadily upping the ante.

Sino-Soviet negotiations over the Dushanze oil field must especially be viewed against the background of the Soviet-German war. One of the strategic objectives of the German drive on Stalingrad was to use that city to anchor the left flank of a drive to the southeast to seize the Soviet Union's main oil fields at Baku on the western shore of the Caspian Sea. The loss of the Baku fields would be a devastating, possibly fatal, blow to the Soviet Union's war effort. During the Third Five-Year Plan (launched in 1938), a prime objective had been the development of industry in the Ural Mountains and western Siberia. In most industrial sectors this relocation had been fairly successful, but not in petroleum. By June 1941, only twelve percent of the Soviet Union's petroleum output came from the regions east of the Urals.[78] Most of the remaining domestic oil came from the Baku fields.

The seizure of those supplies was a major objective of the Nazi armies. On 23 July 1942, a German army group received orders to swing south and occupy the Caucasus "with its oil resources," while a second army group drove eastward toward Stalingrad. On 9 August, the first of the Caucasus oil fields at Maikop fell. On 25 August, the oil fields at Mozdok, midway between the Black and Caspian seas, fell to German forces. Just ahead lay the Grozny fields, and only 300 kilometers (186 miles) further to the southeast were the vital Baku fields.[79] Had the German drive succeeded, the Dushanze field would have become extremely critical to the Soviet war effort.

In August 1942 negotiations over the Dushanze field were begun between Moscow's and Chongqing's representatives in Dihua. No progress was made, however, and the talks collapsed a year later. Moscow demanded formal "equality," which had previously meant Soviet control in practice, while Chongqing insisted on clear Chinese preeminence in terms of both ownership and managerial authority. Meanwhile, the oil from those fields continued to flow to the Soviet Union.[80]

While these talks were under way, the Chinese side made a number of military preparations. During the summer of 1942, Sheng ordered the organization of a 100,000-man paramilitary force and the construction of air-raid shelters in Dihua and fortifications along the border between Xinjiang and the Soviet Union. Sheng did not expect the Soviet Union to resort to military force because of its war with Germany, but he wanted to convince Moscow that he would not back down.[81] If Moscow were persuaded that intervention would not be an easy affair, it might be deterred. Similar considerations underlay Chongqing's military deployments. In a talk at Lanzhou on 20 August 1942, Chiang Kai-shek announced that the Forty-second Army was being ordered from Lanzhou to Yumen in western Gansu in order to be in a better position to check the Soviet Eighth Regiment at Hami.[82] The day before Chiang's announcement the first serious German effort to storm Stalingrad began.[83] It is ironic to think that in those dark days Moscow was probably quite apprehensive about a possible military clash with its Chinese "ally."

During October 1942 Chongqing's efforts to recover Xinjiang entered the second stage outlined in He Yingqin's 13 July plan. Chiang Kai-shek was following closely the intensifying battle at Stalingrad and believed that Japan might well be about to join in the Axis attack on the Soviet Union.[84] Thus, when Sheng and the new Soviet Consul General G.M. Pushkin began their talks in Dihua on 5 October about the status of Soviet personnel, Sheng demanded nothing less than the complete withdrawal of all Soviet technical and military personnel from Xinjiang within three months. Only authorized diplomatic personnel would be allowed to remain. When Pushkin protested that many Soviet personnel were in Xinjiang under the terms of the 1940 tin mines agreement, Sheng retorted that that agreement had been forced upon him and, in any case, had not been approved by the central government, as indicated by the absence of the appropriate official seals on the document. The 1940 agreement must be abrogated and all Soviet personnel of Xin Tin promptly leave Xinjiang, Sheng demanded.[85]

By the third meeting between Sheng and Pushkin, a reply to Sheng's initial note had arrived from Moscow. Soviet military units and the personnel of Xin Tin were in Xinjiang in accordance with the terms of previous agreements and would not therefore be withdrawn. Soviet advisory and technical personnel would be withdrawn when they completed their regular two years of service. This reply was unacceptable to Sheng, and he reiterated his arguments about the invalidity of the 1940 agreement and his demand for the complete Soviet evacuation of Xinjiang within three months. When Pushkin told Sheng, "But it is the decision of our government not to withdraw these people" and asked "What can you do if we refuse to leave?" Sheng replied:

> If you are deaf to reason, we will take all steps necessary to protect the sovereignty and territorial integrity of Sinkiang. Tell Stalin that the four million [sic] people of my province, particularly the Commissioner and the armed forces under his command, will not hesitate to fight to the bitter end against any foreign aggression.[86]

While Sheng and Pushkin were meeting in Dihua on 16 October, Chiang Kai-shek and Ambassador Paniushkin met in Chongqing. Chiang first turned aside a query from Paniushkin as to whether or not China's "understanding" of the Soviet Union had changed. "As long as our two countries are frank and honest with one another," Chiang assured the Soviet ambassador, "there are no problems that cannot be solved by discussions, no point on which we cannot reach mutually harmonious understanding." Chiang then proceeded to raise the issues of the Dushanze oil fields and the Dihua aircraft factory. These two "unresolved problems" had to be settled rapidly and agreements regarding them signed if Sino-Soviet relations were to "become more intimate," Chiang said. Regarding the Dihua plant, China had proposed negotiations three or four years ago, but a contract had still not been signed even though the facility was already producing aircraft. Soviet operation of this factory without a contract was injurious to China's sovereignty, Chiang said, and this problem must be "solved" soon.[87]

At the end of their discussion, Chiang passed on some interesting intelligence regarding Germany and Japan. During the next month Japan would attack the Soviet Union in order to help the German army at Stalingrad.[88] Regardless of the origin of this information, passing it on to Stalin at that moment would have helped make Moscow more amenable to Chinese demands in Xinjiang. Soviet positions at Stalingrad had been reduced to a few pockets of rubble seldom more than three hundred yards deep bordering the west bank of the Volga, and Soviet victory at Stalingrad was by no means certain.[89] Much of the Red Army's vital petroleum then came from American fields via Vladivostok, carried on neutral Soviet tankers. If Japan entered the war, this would have promptly shut off the flow of American crude through Vladivostok. Without the Caucasus fields and Vladivostok, Soviet concern with guaranteeing supplies from the Dushanze fields by ensuring Chongqing's goodwill would have been very great.

On 21 October Sheng and Pushkin met again. Further Soviet concessions were forthcoming. All Soviet technical advisors and experts would be withdrawn, Pushkin said, but he did not have adequate information to express a view about the personnel of Xin Tin. Moreover, the Commissariat of Foreign Affairs was in no position to make a decision regarding the withdrawal of military personnel including military advisors and the Eighth Regiment at Hami. Sheng dismissed these explanations as mere stalling. *All* Soviet personnel must leave within three months, he said. If they did not, Xin Tin personnel would be struck from personnel rosters and not paid, while the people of Hami would be ordered not to sell food or fodder to the Eighth Regiment. In such circumstances, Sheng continued, he could assume no responsibility for any incidents involving Soviet personnel. Rather, the Soviet Union would be held entirely responsible for all consequences arising from Soviet refusal to withdraw. Finally, Sheng threatened to publicize "to the world" such a Soviet refusal.[90] Officials in Moscow understood that such publicity could create problems in Soviet-American relations.

At their next meeting on 26 October, Pushkin made a few more concessions and Sheng again upped the ante. The withdrawal of all Xin Tin personnel would begin immediately, Pushkin said, and troops were to be withdrawn within six months. Sheng reiterated his three-month deadline and then added the demand that after the tin mine personnel were withdrawn, "the secret agreement concerning the lease shall be abrogated in full." When Pushkin insisted that he had no instructions regarding the abrogation of the 1940 agreement and that "further procedures must be explored," Sheng replied that such explorations were not necessary. The Xinjiang government would gladly buy any buildings, equipment, and materials owned by Xin Tin which it did not wish to ship back to the Soviet Union.[91]

According to Sheng's account, while these negotiations were under way, on 26 October twenty Soviet tanks crossed into the Yili region of Xinjiang in defiance of Chinese border guards and advanced toward Dihua. Sheng interpreted this as an attempt at intimidation and demanded that Pushkin halt the Soviet tanks. Sheng told Pushkin that he had put the Yili garrison on alert and ordered it to stop the Soviet tanks, even if that meant destroying the bridges in their path. "The Xinjiang provincial government will bear no responsibility for any incident which may arise," Sheng said. According to Sheng's account, Pushkin was able to stop the Soviet column by the next morning.[92]

Pushkin did not call on Sheng again for several weeks. When he did, on 14

November, it was to inform Sheng that all Soviet advisors and Xin Tin personnel, as well as the Eighth Regiment at Hami, would be withdrawn. The armor "reinforcements" which had entered Xinjiang on 26 October would also leave Xinjiang immediately.[93]

In addition to taking advantage of German and Japanese pressure on Moscow to achieve the objectives of the second stage of its recovery plan, Chongqing mobilized American influence to pressure the Soviets. In October 1942 the director of the American desk of the Chinese foreign ministry suggested to U.S. Ambassador Clarence Gauss that the United States open a consular office in Dihua. Gauss accurately accessed this offer as an attempt to offset Soviet influence in Xinjiang. Washington accepted Chongqing's proposal and in April 1943 the new U.S. Consul, O. Edmund Clubb, assumed his post in Dihua.[94] That September, when Chiang Kai-shek reflected on the mounting victories of Soviet arms over Germany, he concluded that the American-British "attitude" was a major factor in preventing a Soviet reoccupation of Xinjiang.[95]

Meanwhile, Chinese pressure continued to mount. In March 1943 Sheng, acting on orders from Chongqing, notified the commander of the Eighth Regiment at Hami that unless that unit withdrew immediately, it would be transferred to the front to fight Japan.[96] Although there was no possibility that such a threat could be carried out, the fact that Chongqing might attempt this must have figured in Moscow's calculations about how to keep Japan from joining Germany's war against the Soviet Union.

Mounting Chinese pressure had the desired effect. In March 1943 Moscow decided to withdraw from Xinjiang. Apparently a decision had been made in Moscow that the Soviet Union's critical military situation did not allow it to risk conflict with China over Xinjiang. On 17 March, Ambassador Paniushkin notified the Chinese government that the Soviet Union was prepared to withdraw all Soviet personnel and equipment from both the Dihua plant and the Dushanze field. Chongqing was content, however, to leave the issue unresolved, perhaps out of a desire to present an image of reasonableness. On 6 May, Vice-Foreign Minister in charge of Xinjiang Wu Guozhen informed Paniushkin that the Chinese side was still "researching a draft proposal for cooperative operation of the [Dihua] plant."[97] On 10 April 1943, Pushkin had informed Sheng that all Xin Tin geological exploration teams and equipment would be withdrawn from Xinjiang. Five days later, Pushkin informed Sheng that the Soviet government had decided to withdraw the Eighth Regiment from Hami and to abolish the aircraft factory at Dihua, withdrawing all Soviet personnel, equipment, and materials at that site.[98] A short while later Pushkin informed Sheng that all Soviet personnel and equipment at the Dushanze field, and all Soviet military and technical advisory personnel throughout Xinjiang, would be withdrawn to the Soviet Union. Moreover, the operations at the Soviet trading company would be substantially contracted.[99]

Chiang Kai-shek feared that these drastic Soviet moves would destabilize Sheng's regime and Xinjiang's economy. The suspension of trade with the Soviet Union would especially have an adverse effect on Xinjiang's economy. Moscow was trying, Chiang believed, to pressure Sheng into signing agreements recognizing the Soviet position at Dushanze and Dihua.[100] In order to divert Soviet pressure from Sheng, Chiang ordered the Foreign Ministry to take up the issues with Paniushkin. On 6 May,

Wu Guozhen protested the "unilateral" Soviet decision to withdraw. The Chinese government was just then researching a plan for joint operation of the Dushanze field "in accord with Chinese law and on the basis of the spirit of Sino-Soviet cooperation." Regarding Moscow's decision on the Dihua factory and Xin Tin personnel, these actions were "extremely surprising," Wu told Paniushkin. "Just in the middle of Sino-Soviet negotiations" over these issues, the Soviet government suddenly announced that it was preparing to withdraw completely all equipment and technical personnel, Wu disingenuously protested.[101]

Once Moscow agreed to abandon the Dushanze and Dihua facilities, Chongqing moved to ensure that the Soviet would leave intact the industrial equipment at those sites when they withdrew. Chiang hoped that Moscow would turn over to China the valuable machinery at Dihua and Dushanze in order to avoid further complications. But even if Moscow was unwilling to do this, Chongqing should still push to get the Soviets out of Xinjiang as rapidly as possible without rupturing Sino-Soviet friendship.[102]

Chiang's efforts to protect the production facilities at Dihua and Dushanze were unsuccessful. The Dushanze equipment was rapidly shipped back to the Soviet Union, and Economics Minister Weng Wenhao was reduced to sending a letter to Paniushkin asking him to ensure that cement was used to seal the oil wells to prevent damage to the field. If cement were lacking, Weng explained, the Chinese side would provide it.[103] Regarding the Dihua factory, Director of China's Aviation Commission Zhou Zhirou inspected the factory in August 1943 and found that eighty percent of the equipment had already been evacuated. The machinery remaining in the plant was largely axillary equipment such as sawmills, and motor vehicle repair and oxygen-producing equipment. Even most of the electrical transmission cable at the plant had already been taken down and shipped out.[104] Zhou also found 400 Soviet soldiers and seventeen tanks of the Eighth Regiment encamped in the gutted factory. Informed by the Soviet consul that if China purchased the facility these troops would be withdrawn, Zhou recommended to Chongqing the rapid purchase of the plant so that the remaining Soviet troops could be removed from Xinjiang before there was a change in the Soviet Union's war situation.[105] When Wu Guozhen protested the delays in Soviet withdrawal, Ambassador Paniushkin explained that until China purchased the structures remaining at Dushanze and Dihua, it would be "difficult for the Soviet Union to determine a date for withdrawal."[106] Finally, in February 1944, Chiang authorized the purchase of the remaining equipment at Dushanze for $1,700,000 U.S.[107]

The withdrawal of Soviet personnel and equipment did not go smoothly. Calculated Soviet use of delaying tactics to pressure the Chinese combined with the mutual animosity and tension under which local commanders operated to create considerable danger of incidents as the Soviet withdrawal proceeded during mid-1943.[108]

Chongqing seized on the withdrawal of the Soviet air squadron from Hami to demand the closing of the Soviet air and radio stations at Yili, Dihua, Qitai, and Hami and to abolish the special procedures which Soviet aircraft had previously enjoyed when entering Xinjiang's airspace. By the spring of 1944, the Soviet withdrawal from Xinjiang was complete.

The Collapse of the CCP in Xinjiang

The CCP position in Xinjiang collapsed along with that of the Soviet Union. As the ability of the Soviet Union to protect its interests in Xinjiang declined, the position of the CCP became more precarious. A purge of the CCP was in fact one component of the agreement reached between Sheng and Chiang Kai-shek in mid-1942.[109] The CCP quickly sensed the shift under way in Xinjiang in 1942 and adopted a twofold policy to protect its position. On the one hand, it tried to prevent an erosion of the Soviet position in Xinjiang. On the other hand, it explored the possibility of striking a deal with Sheng independently of the Soviet Union. Both policies ultimately failed with catastrophic consequences for the CCP.

Representatives of the CCP monitored early anti-Soviet moves by Sheng—for example, Sheng's accusation of complicity by the Soviet consulate in the murder of several Soviet advisors in February 1942—and tried to smoke him out regarding possible shifts in his political orientation.[110] Representatives Mao Zemin and Chen Tanqiu cautiously explored various possibilities with Sheng. Mao and Chen called on Sheng early in 1942 to request permission to travel either to Yan'an or to the Soviet Union for "medical treatment," an obvious pretext to flee an impending anticommunist coup. While talking with Sheng, Mao and Chen hinted that the CCP might be willing to continue working with Sheng even if he broke with the Soviet Union.[111] Chen Tanqiu was not optimistic about such efforts; his reports to the CCP Politburo at this point continually linked Sheng's anti-Soviet and his anti-CCP policies.[112] Still, Chen and Mao Zemin probed to see if it might not be possible to work out a *modus vivendi* which would allow the CCP to continue work in Xinjiang without Soviet support.

This was not to be. Sheng rejected the CCP bid in order to fulfill his pledge to Chiang to crush the CCP in Xinjiang. As mentioned earlier, the assassination of Sheng Shicai's younger brother on 29 March 1942 triggered the arrest of approximately 300 Soviet and CCP personnel. Sheng Shicai subsequently charged that a plot had been under way, organized out of the Soviet consulate and in close liaison with Mao Zemin in Dihua and Zhou Enlai in Chongqing, to kill Sheng and his family and overthrow his regime, replacing it with a CCP-led government. This conspiracy was a concoction of Sheng's troubled imagination; he himself had ordered his brother's death.[113]

Immediately after the murder of Sheng's brother, Mao Zemin asked Sheng to cable Yan'an for permission to transfer all 400 CCP cadres in Xinjiang to the Soviet Union for political study. Sheng agreed and cabled Mao's petition to Yan'an.[114] The Politburo did not respond promptly. Apparently Yan'an was loath to abandon its foothold in Xinjiang; perhaps it was under pressure from Moscow not to pull out of Xinjiang. Zhou Enlai in Chongqing and Chen Tainqiu in Dihua were closely monitoring the negotiations under way between Sheng Shicai and Chiang Kai-shek during April and May, and trying to determine whether Chiang and Sheng would be able to reach an understanding.[115] If no agreement were reached, then there might still be a role for the CCP in Xinjiang.

On 8 May, Yan'an finally approved a phased withdrawal of CCP personnel from Xinjiang to the Soviet Union.[116] A month later, Chen Tanqiu again urged immediate "preparations" for withdrawal in order to avoid an anticommunist coup.[117] Again in early July, Yan'an approved the withdrawal of all CCP cadres to the Soviet Union. Soviet consent was necessary, however, and it was not until mid-August that Moscow approved the plan.[118] Before word of Soviet approval could arrive, however, Sheng's police cut the CCP's lines of communication with the Soviet Union and rounded up 160 CCP personnel, including Mao Zemin and Chen Tanqiu.[119]

The reliance by the CCP on Soviet protection in Xinjiang was indicated by the final orders given by Chen Tanqiu to his comrades when Sheng's police came to arrest him. Chen's first order regarded who was to take command. The second was that the Comintern was to be informed of developments in Xinjiang.[120] Several days later the Soviet consul general did in fact intervene on behalf of the arrested Communists. On 2 October, Pushkin inquired about the status of the arrested men and requested that they be allowed to return to Yan'an via the Soviet Union. The Soviet government and Stalin personally were especially concerned that Mao Zemin and Chen Tanqiu be released, the consul said. Sheng replied that those arrested were Chinese citizens subject to Chinese law and that the Soviet Union ought not involve itself in a domestic Chinese affair.[121] Soviet efforts to assist the arrested Communists were to no avail. The following February they were transferred to prison and in September 1943 most of the leaders of the group, including Chen Tanqiu and Mao Zemin, were executed after enduring prolonged torture to extract "confessions."[122] These events ended the efforts by the CCP to build a revolutionary base in Xinjiang. Not until 1949 would the CCP again build up a significant presence there under the auspices of the victorious People's Liberation Army.

Conclusion

The elimination of the direct and massive Soviet presence in Xinjiang was a brilliant diplomatic success by Chiang. It was a major step toward the achievement of Chiang's program of national revival. By acting when the time was right—while the Soviet Union was on the verge of military collapse before the might of Nazi Germany—Chiang was able to force Moscow to relinquish its substantial and important position in Xinjiang. China's government had not been able to do that earlier, and it might not have been able to do it in 1945. Indeed, it is just possible that Chiang saved Xinjiang for the Chinese nation. Had he not acted to eradicate Soviet influence when he did, it is quite possible that in 1945 Moscow would have demanded that China recognize the "status quo" in Xinjiang as well as in Outer Mongolia. Xinjiang, in other words, might have gone the way of Outer Mongolia.

In 1944–1945, Moscow tried to reassert its influence in Xinjiang by supporting the rebellion of Turkic peoples which culminated in the establishment of the Eastern Turkistan Republic in November 1944. This episode is best understood in the context of the maneuvering between Stalin and Chiang over the terms of a postwar settlement and is therefore discussed in the next chapter. It is important to note here, however, that by that time it was Stalin, and no longer Chiang, who was attempting to alter the status quo. Had Soviet forces remained scattered throughout Xinjiang, had Soviet advisory personnel and economic interests remained deeply entrenched, and had KMT authority remained nominal in Xinjiang in 1944–1945, then the establishment of the

Eastern Turkistan Republic would not have been a rebellion challenging the established authority of China's central government, but merely a legalistic change consolidating the preexisting de facto situation.

From one perspective, the overriding nationalism embodied in Chiang's Xinjiang policies is breathtaking. It almost seems that Chiang had no great preference as to whether Hitler or Stalin won the titanic battle in which they were engaged. It is important to remember, however, that other prominent third-world nationalists reached conclusions similar to those of Chiang. Mohandas Gandhi, whom Chiang visited in 1942, also concluded that the liberation of his country required that the powerful movement that he led not support the British war effort even though Japan's armies were advancing across Burma. To Chiang, the reestablishment of China's national grandeur entailed the recovery of lost territories, or at least the major ones. There might be subtle shades of difference between the intentions of the imperialist powers, but in the final analysis they were all alike in oppressing China and opposing the revival of its national power. It mattered little to Chiang whether the Stalinist Soviet Union helped China recover north China from Japan, whether Nazi Germany helped China recover Xinjiang from the Soviet Union, or whether democratic America helped China recover Manchuria and Taiwan. They were all imperialist powers to be manipulated as the need arose.

Conflict over Xinjiang contributed substantially to the deterioration of ROC–USSR relations during 1942–1944. This tension created major difficulties for Chongqing's efforts to secure Soviet support on other critical issues during the last two years of World War II. While relations between the Republic of China and the Soviet Union were at a nadir because of the expulsion of the Soviet Union from Xinjiang, Chiang had to secure Soviet support for China's claim to great-power status and the return of Manchuria to China, and Soviet non-support for the Chinese Communists. Securing such Soviet support was not an easy feat, and it is to a discussion of this that we now turn.

Notes

1. Allen S. Whiting and Sheng Shih-ts'ai (Sheng Shicai), *Sinkiang: Pawn or Pivot?*, East Lansing: Michigan State University Press, 1958. Pages 151 through 273 of this work are Sheng Shicai's memoir and are cited as such.
2. Ibid. See also Wang Boyu, "Su jun liang ci ru Xin huanzhu Sheng Shicai shimo" [The full story of the Soviet army's twofold entry into Xinjiang to assist Sheng Shicai], *Zhong Ya Yanjiu Ziliao* [Research Materials on Central Asia], no. 2, 1983, p. 33. Hu Jian, "Mizi qi de jianglou" [The Union Jack's fall], *Xinjiang Wenshi Ziliao Xuanji* [Xinjiang Selection of Literary Materials], no. 1, p. 19. *See also* Sheng Shicai memoir, p. 164.
3. Whiting, idem. See also Owen Lattimore, *Pivot of Asia*, Boston: Little, Brown, 1950, p. 76. Liang Daoheng, "Wo suo renshi de 'Xinjiang wang' Sheng Shicai," [The 'Xinjiang king' Sheng Shicai that I knew], *Xinjiang Wenshi Ziliao Xuanji*, no. 2, p. 1.
4. Whiting, *Pawn or Pivot?*, p. 27.
5. Lattimore, *Pivot of Asia*, pp. 76–77.
6. Whiting, *Pawn or Pivot?*, p. 66. One KMT source estimated the annual production of the Dushanze field at 1000 tons. Whiting, however, suggests that the actual output was substantially higher.
7. Whiting, *Pawn or Pivot?*, pp. 126–127.
8. Ibid., pp. 126–127.
9. Liang Daoheng, "Wo suo renshi de 'Xinjiang wang' Sheng Shicai," pp. 4–5, 10.

10. Ibid., pp. 8–9.
11. Shi Yuanpu, "Xinjiang mimi shenpan weiyuanhui jiepo," [Expose of the secret investigation committee of Xinjiang], *Xinjiang Wenshi Ziliao Xuanji*, no. 1, pp. 77–78. *See also* Whiting, *Pawn or Pivot?*, p. xiv.
12. Wen Feiran, "Xinjiang kang Ri minzu tongyi zhanxian de xingcheng yu polie" [The formation and collapse of the anti-Japanese national united front in Xinjiang], *Xinjiang Wenshi Ziliao Xuanji* [Xinjiang Selection of Literary Materials], no. 8, pp. 13–14. According to Wen, under the rule of Sheng's predecessor Jin Shuren, a Comintern intelligence organization had been set up in the Soviet consulate in Dihua. After Sheng took power, this apparatus was given better cover by making it part of Sheng's office. Still later it was made part of Sheng's Border Affairs Office of the Border Defense Commission. Seven Soviet personnel, fifteen or so Chinese Communists, and a few nonparty people with "relatively progressive thinking" ran the operation "under the leadership of the Comintern." Operating under the strictest discipline, the organization undertook intelligence and counterintelligence operations, including operations into India and into China's northwest to determine the disposition of military forces there. Sheng reportedly had two informants in this organization but did not control it.
13. *Hu Shi Laiwang Shuxin Xuan* [Selected correspondence of Hu Shi], vol. 2, Beijing: Zhongguo Shehui Kexueyuan Jindaishi Yanjiusuo, 1979, pp. 245–246. Moscow's respect for Nanjing's de jure jurisdiction over Xinjiang was stated forthrightly by Molotov the year after Jiang's letter to Hu Shi. Speaking to the Seventh All-Union Congress of Soviets, Molotov affirmed, "The Soviet Union considers as incompatible with its policy the seizure of foreign territories, and is an absolute adherent of the independence, integrity, and sovereignty of China over all her parts, including Sinkiang." Cited in Whiting, *Pawn or Pivot?*, p. 39.
14. *Hu Shi Laiwang Shuxin Xuan*, pp. 245–246.
15. Jin Shaoxian, "Guomindang fandong shili jinru he tongzhi Xinjiang" [The entry and control of reactionary Kuomintang power in Xinjiang], *Xinjiang Wenshi Ziliao Xuanji*, no. 2, p. 21. Whiting, *Pawn or Pivot?*, p. 62.
16. *Zhanshi Waijiao*, p. 448. Whiting, *Pawn or Pivot*, p. 51. According to Wen Feiran, the proposal to station a Soviet unit at Hami had been made by Sheng Shicai to Chen Yun when the latter arrived in Dihua from Moscow in April 1937. Wen Feiran, "Xinjiang kang Ri minzu tongyi zhanxian," pp. 35–36.
17. Whiting, *Pawn or Pivot*, p. 65.
18. *Zhanshi Waijiao*, p. 408.
19. Sun Ke interview with Allen Whiting, 19 December 1957, cited in Whiting, *Pawn or Pivot?*, p. 63.
20. Wen Feiran, "Xinjiang kang Ri minzu tongyi zhanxian," pp. 21–22.
21. "Kang Ri zhanzheng shiqi Zhongguo Gongchandang zai Xinjiang geming duozhengshi" [History of the revolutionary struggle of the Chinese Communist Party in Xinjiang during the war of resistance against Japan], *Xinjiang Daxue Xuebao* [Xinjiang University Journal], no. 1, 1981, pp. 44–63 (hereafter cited as "Zhongguo Gongchandang zai Xinjiang").
22. Regarding the interactions leading to the establishment of a CCP presence in Xinjiang in 1935–1937, *see* Hu Hua, editor, "Chen Tanqiu," in *Zhonggong Dangshi Renwu Zhuan* [Biographies of Chinese communist historical personalities], vol. 9, Xian(?): Shaanxi Renmin Chubanshe, 1983, p. 30. "Zhongguo Gongchandang zai Xinjiang," p. 57. Wen Feiran, "Xinjiang kang Ri minzu tongyi zhanxian," p. 30. Hu Hua, editor, "Mao Zemin," in *Zhonggong Dangshi Renwu Zhuan*, vol. 9, p. 63. "Zhongguo Gongchandang ren zai Xinjiang huodong jishi" [Record of the activities of Chinese communist personnel in Xinjiang], *Xinjiang Wenshi Ziliao Xuanji*, no. 1, p. 30 (hereafter cited "Zai Xinjiang huodong jishi").
23. Wang Yunxue, "Huiyi Tanqiu tongzhi zhanduo zai Xinjiang" [Recalling comrade Tanqiu's struggle in Xinjiang], in *Huiyi Chen Tanqiu* [Recollections of Chen Tanqiu], Wuhan: Huazhong Gongxue Yuan, 1981, p. 131. Hu Hua, "Mao Zemin," p. 63. Hu also implies that the CCP expected Soviet assistance to begin flowing to the CCP over these newly opened "lines of international communism." Wen Feiran also says that in addition to keeping "lines of international transportation" open, the CCP sought to "win international assistance" by establishing itself in Xinjiang (Wen Feiran, "Xinjiang kang Ri minzu tongyi zhanxian," p. 8).
24. "Zhongguo Gongchandang zai Xinjiang," pp. 58–59. The establishment of the Eighth Route Army liaison offices in Lanzhou and Xian had been part of the united front agreement worked out with the KMT. Other liaison offices were in Hankou, Changsha, Guilin, and Chongqing.
25. Hu Hua, "Chen Tanqiu," p. 33.
26. Whiting, *Pawn or Pivot?*, p. 55. Mao reportedly thanked Sheng profusely and sent him a gift of a fur coat for forwarding the Soviet money on to Yan'an.

27. Tang Manzhen, "Zhongguo Gongchandang shi ruhe datui di yi ci fangong gaochao de" [How it was that the CCP was able to beat back the first anticommunist high tide], in *Jiaoxue yu Yanjiu* [Teaching and Research], no. 4, 1981, p. 25.

28. Lyman P. Van Slyke, *The Chinese Communist Movement, A Report of the United States War Department, July 1945* (reprint), Stanford, Calif.: Stanford University Press, 1968, p. 71.

29. "Zhongguo Gongchandang zai Xinjiang," p. 61. Donald W. Klein and Anne B. Clark, *Biographic Dictionary of Chinese Communism, 1921–1965*, Cambridge, Mass.: Harvard University Press, 1971, p. 502. Xu Linqiu, Zhong Zhibing, He Zhizhen, Sai Shupan, Liu Ying, and "other comrades" in December 1937, Mao Zedong's brother Mao Zemin, Lin Biao, Ren Bishi, and Ma Mingfang in 1938, and Zhou Enlai and his wife Deng Yingqiao in 1939, are among the CCP leaders listed by Klein and Clark as receiving medical treatment in the Soviet Union during these years. I suspect that the provision of such medical treatment was important in cultivating friendly feelings toward the Soviet Union among these ambitious men.

30. Gao Jun, *Weida de Zhanshi Ren Bishi* [The great warrior Ren Bishi], Beijing: Zhongguo Qingnian Chubanshe, 1980, p. 103.

31. "Zai Xinjiang huodong jishi," p. 31. "Zhongguo Gongchandang zai Xinjiang," p. 57. Wen Feiran, "Xinjiang kang Ri minzu tongyi zhanxian," p. 6.

32. Hu Hua, "Chen Tanqiu," p. 38.

33. Wang Yunxue, "Huiyi Tanqiu tongzhi," p. 132.

34. Yang Shilan, "Deng Fa," in *Zhonggong Dangshi Renwu Zhuan* [Biographies of Chinese communist historical personalities], vol. 1, Beijing: Zhongguo Shehui Kexueyuan, p. 359.

35. Wen Feiran, "Xinjiang kang Ri minzu tongyi zhanxian," pp. 6–7. Sheng Shicai's motives for accepting the New Camp were more complex. On occasion he seemed to use the New Camp cadets as a sort of palace guard. He may also have wanted to curry favor with Yan'an. Moreover, he was in no position to refuse a request by Moscow.

36. Among Sheng's conditions were that the Communists not publicly reveal their party affiliation, not set up party organizations in Xinjiang, and not propagandize Marxism–Leninism. "Zhongguo Gongchandang zai Xinjiang," p. 63. "Zai Xinjiang huodong jishi," pp. 31–32.

37. Whiting, *Pawn or Pivot?*, p. 55.

38. "Zhongguo Gongchandang zai Xinjiang," pp. 61, 63. Hu Hua, "Chen Tanqiu," p. 33. Hu Jian, "Mizi qi de jianglou," pp. 2–9. Wang Boyu, "Su jun liang ci ru Xin," p. 34. Hu Hua, "Mao Zemin," p. 65.

39. Hu Hua, "Chen Tanqiu," p. 33. "Zhonggong Gongchandang zai Xinjiang," p. 62.

40. "Zai Xinjiang huodong jishi," p. 31. "Zhongguo Gongchandang zai Xinjiang," p. 61. Sheng Shicai memoir, p. 187. Sheng later repeated his request to Deng Fa, who reportedly told Sheng that he was not qualified for membership in the CCP and refused to approve his request (Yang Shilan, "Deng Fa," p. 362). Deng could not, of course, have himself approved or rejected Sheng's request for party membership.

41. Sheng Shicai memoir, p. 187.

42. Whiting, *Pawn or Pivot?*, pp. 5–6.

43. Sheng Shicai memoir, p. 188.

44. Ibid., pp. 198–199, 203.

45. Ibid., p. 189.

46. Ibid., p. 192.

47. Ibid., pp. 200, 204. Wen Feiran says that Sheng Shicai's secretary told him that Sheng went to Moscow to test Stalin's attitude toward the possibility of "turning Xinjiang into an allied republic and joining the Soviet Union" so that Sheng "could become the leader of a socialist country." (Wen Feiran, "Xinjiang kang Ri minzu tongyi zhanxian," pp. 9, 21). The accounts of Sheng and Wen are not necessarily mutually exclusive. Sheng would not necessarily have had to raise directly the issue of Xinjiang becoming independent to "test" Stalin's attitude toward this possibility. There are, however, very important differences of nuance. Sheng implies that he was, fundamentally, a Chinese patriot. Wen implies that Sheng was basically a "traitor to the Han race." Both Sheng's and Wen's accounts were written with political purposes in mind, but at least Sheng's has the benefit of being firsthand.

48. Sheng Shicai memoir, pp. 201, 206. Here again Wen Feiran's account differs from Sheng's. According to Wen, Sheng personally asked Stalin to admit him to the CPSU. Stalin, however, did not "formally reply" to his request. Indeed, he never approved or rejected Sheng's request. Again Wen claims to have learned this from Sheng's secretary (Wen Feiran, "Xinjiang kang Ri minzu tongyi zhanxian," p. 21). Given Sheng's later admission of joining the CPSU in his 1942 letter of confession to Chiang Kai-shek, Wen's account of this seems questionable.

49. *Zhanshi Waijiao*, pp. 448, 451. Whiting, *Pawn or Pivot?*, p. 62.

50. Whiting, *Pawn or Pivot?*, p. 51. This protest is not mentioned in the KMT archives published in Taibei in 1981.
51. Ibid., *Pawn or Pivot?*, p. 64.
52. This agreement is reproduced in Sheng Shicai's memoir, pp. 280–286.
53. Sheng Shicai memoir, pp. 223–224.
54. Ibid., pp. 225–227; 258–259.
55. Du Yuming, "Zhongguo Yuanzhengjun ru Mian dui Ri zuozhan shulie" [General description of the entry into Burma and war against Japan of China's Expeditionary army and its war with Japan], in *Wenshi Ziliao Xuanji*, national edition, vol. 8, pp. 4–5.
56. Whiting, *Pawn or Pivot?*, p. 81.
57. Ibid.
58. The KMT's published archives contain no information about these negotiations; indeed, records dealing with Xinjiang begin only in July 1942 when Chongqing began trying to recover that region from the Soviet Union. This silence is itself suspicious, and it suggests that the Japanese reports of early 1941 were accurate.
59. The January 1940 date is from an 11 July 1942 letter of confession from Sheng to Chiang Kai-shek, reproduced in *Zongtong Dashi*, vol. 4, p. 1985. The January 1941 date is mentioned in Molotov's 3 July 1942 letter to Chiang, in *Zhanshi Waijiao*, p. 437. It is possible that both sources refer to the same letter.
60. Shi Yuanpu, "Xinjiang mimi shenpan weiyuanhui jiepo," p. 78. Hu Hua, "Chen Tanqiu," p. 35. Shi Zhe, "Chen Tanqiu tongzhi zai Mozike" [Comrade Chen Tanqiu in Moscow], in *Huiyi Chen Tanqiu*, p. 125. "Zai Xinjiang huodong jishi," p. 33. Ji He, "Chen Tanqiu tongzhi zai Xinjiang" [Comrade Chen Tanqiu in Xinjiang], *Xinjiang Wenshi Ziliao Xuanji*, no. 8, p. 29. Regarding the conditions Sheng imposed on CCP activities in Xinjiang, see note 36.
61. "Zai Xinjiang huodong jishi," p. 34.
62. Wen Feiran, "Xinjiang kang Ri minzu tongyi zhanxian," pp. 22–23.
63. Guo Dequan, *Kangzhan Shiqu Zhu E Wuguan Huiyi Shilu* [True record of service as military attaché to Russia during the war of resistance], Taibei: Guofangbu Shizheng Bianyiju, 1982, p. 89. Guo went so far as to suggest that Sheng might be willing to resign from his position in Xinjiang.
64. Whiting, *Pawn or Pivot?*, pp. 83–84.
65. Alan Clark, *Barbarossa, The Russian-German Conflict, 1941–1945*, New York: William Morrow, 1965, pp. 198–210.
66. Robert Conquest, *The Great Terror, Stalin's Purges of the Thirties*, New York: Macmillan, 1973, p. 610. Dekanozov had played an important role in the purges of the 1930s and was a Candidate Member of the CPSU Central Committee at the time of his mission to XinJiang. He was executed in December 1953, along with secret police head Lavrenti Beria. *The Modern Encyclopedia of Russian and Soviet History*, Joseph L. Wieczyuski, editor, vol. 9, Gulf Breeze, Fl. : Academic International Press, 1978, p. 33.
67. Whiting, *Pawn or Pivot?*, p. 84. *See also Zongtong Dashi*, vol. 4, p. 1967.
68. *See* Sheng Shicai memoir, pp. 243–254. *Zhanshi Waijiao*, p. 436–437. For some reason, Sheng does not mention either of Molotov's letters in his memoirs. The substance of Dekanozov's talks with Sheng, as recorded in Sheng's memoirs, parallels Molotov's 3 July letter, however. The collection of documents published by the KMT and which contains the 3 July letter, states that the letter was presented to Chiang Kai-shek on 9 July, and that it was a copy of one addressed to and presented to Sheng Shicai.
69. Sheng Shicai memoir, pp. 244–247.
70. Ibid., pp. 248–253.
71. *Zhanshi Waijiao*, p. 436.
72. *Zongtong Dashi*, vol. 5, p. 1980–1985. The wording of the 11 July letter indicated that it was written after Sheng received Molotov's accusative epistle of 3 July. Given the amount of time which was probably necessary to compose such a letter and the difficulties of communication between Dihua and Chongqing, it is probable that this letter was written after Sheng's talks with Dekanovoz and sent by Sheng to Chongqing before Paniushkin called on Chiang on 9 July.
73. *Zhanshi Waijiao*, pp. 439–440.
74. *Zongtong Dashi*, vol. 4, p. 1987.
75. Ibid.
76. *Zhanshi Waijiao*, pp. 441–443.
77. Sheng Shicai memoir, p. 255.
78. Gordon Wright, *The Ordeal of Total War, 1939–1945*, New York: Harper and Row, 1968, p. 57.
79. Clark, *Barbarossa*, pp. 190–191; 211–212.
80. *Zongtong Dashi*, vol. 4, p. 1992. Whiting, *Pawn or Pivot?*, pp. 84–88.

81. Sheng Shicai memoir, p. 260.
82. *Zongtong Dashi*, vol. 5, p. 2021.
83. Clark, *Barbarossa*, p. 216.
84. *Zongtong Dashi*, vol. 5, p. 2062. On 27 October Chiang noted Japanese antiaircraft exercises in the vicinity of Zhangjiakou and took this as possible indication of an imminent Japanese attack against the Soviet Union.
85. Sheng Shicai memoir, pp. 256–259.
86. Ibid., p. 262.
87. *Zhanshi Waijiao*, p. 536.
88. Ibid., p. 537.
89. Clark, *Barbarossa*, p. 270.
90. Sheng Shicai memoir, pp. 262–263.
91. Ibid., p. 263.
92. Ibid., pp. 264–265.
93. Ibid., p. 266.
94. Whiting, *Pawn or Pivot?*, p. 101.
95. Chiang Kai-shek diary, 30 September 1943, in *Zongtong Dashi*, vol. 5, p. 2245.
96. Whiting, *Pawn or Pivot?*, p. 89.
97. *Zhanshi Waijiao*, p. 440.
98. Ibid., pp. 447–448. Sheng informed Chiang Kai-shek of these developments by cable on 17 April.
99. *Zongtong Dashi*, vol. 5, pp. 2151–2152. Sheng informed Chiang of these developments in a cable of 5 May.
100. Ibid.
101. *Zhanshi Waijiao*, p. 450.
102. Ibid.
103. Lattimore, *Pivot of Asia*, p. 80. *Zhanshi Waijiao*, p. 455.
104. *Zhanshi Waijiao*, pp. 451–452.
105. Ibid., p. 452. *See also*, Whiting, *Pawn or Pivot?*, p. 90.
106. *Zhanshi Waijiao*, p. 452.
107. *Zongtong Dashi*, vol. 5, p. 2320. Whiting, *Pawn or Pivot?*, p. 86. *Zhanshi Waijiao*, pp. 456–457.
108. Whiting, *Pawn or Pivot?*, p. 91.
109. *Zongtong Dashi*, vol. 5, p. 2021.
110. Wen Feiran, "Xinjiang kang Ri minzu tongyi zhanxian," pp. 25–26.
111. Sheng Shicai memoir, pp. 232–237, 241.
112. Hu Hua, "Chen Tanqiu," p. 40.
113. Wen Feiran, "Sheng Shicai tewu tongzhi xia de Xinjiang" [Xinjiang under the rule of Sheng Shicai's special agents], *Xinjiang Wenshi Ziliao Xuanji*, no. 7, pp. 12–15.
114. Sheng Shicai memoir, pp. 238–239.
115. Hu Hua, "Chen Tanqiu," p. 40.
116. Ji He, "Chen Tanqiu tongzhi zai Xinjiang," p. 31. Top-level cadre and aviation personnel were to be withdrawn first. Medical personnel and patients would then follow. Then the remaining Communist personnel would be evacuated.
117. Hu Hua, "Chen Tanqiu," p. 38.
118. Wang Yunxue, "Huiyi Tanqiu tongzhi zhanduo zai Xinjiang," p. 140.
119. Ji He, "Chen Tanqiu tongzhi zai Xinjiang," p. 31. Sheng Shicai memoir, pp. 238–239. Hu Hua, "Mao Zemin," p. 71. Idem., "Chen Tanqiu," p. 42.
120. Ji He, "Chen Tanqiu tongzhi zai Xinjiang," p. 32.
121. *Zongtong Dashi*, vol. 5, p. 2055. Sheng Shicai memoir, pp. 243–244.
122. Hu Hua, "Chen Tanqiu," p. 42. Zhang Dalun, "Chen Tanqiu, Mao Zemin lieshi bei Jiang Jieshi, Sheng Shicai guojie mosha de neimu" [The secret story of the collaboration between Chiang Kai-shek and Sheng Shicai to murder the martyrs Chen Tanqiu and Mao Zemin], *Wuhan Wenshi Ziliao Xuanji* [Wuhan Selection of Literary Materials], vol. 3 (June 1981), pp. 68–70.

Chapter VII

China and World War II

China and Soviet-Japanese Neutrality

The German attack on the Soviet Union on 22 June and the Japanese attack on the United States on 7 December 1941 merged the Sino-Japanese conflict into a truly global war. Chiang Kai-shek's policies toward the Soviet Union during this world conflagration were premised on the peculiar pattern of alignments associated with it. In Europe, the Soviet Union and the United States were active allies. In the Far East, however, the Soviet Union and Japan maintained an effective if strained neutrality until literally the last days of the war. Chiang initially concluded that the continuation of such an arrangement posed grave dangers for China. Chief among these was that confinement of the Soviet-American alliance to Europe increased the danger that Japan would be appeased at China's expense. If the experience of World War I was any indication, the war against Germany would prove long and costly, and the Soviet Union might become even more willing to accept Japan's domination of China than it had been in April 1941. The United States, too, might be forced to reach some sort of compromise peace with Japan, permitting the U.S. to concentrate its forces in Europe in exchange for American recognition of some part of Japan's position in China. Even if the war in the Far East were not settled prior to the European war, Soviet neutrality in the Far East could well mean that when Germany was finally defeated, Japan's position would still be quite powerful. This danger increased as it became apparent in 1942 that Washington and Moscow had agreed to place first priority on the defeat of Germany. If the Soviet Union and the United States concentrated on Europe and became exhausted in the process, by the time Germany was defeated the Allies might be so war-weary that they would grant Japan a compromise peace. China would have sacrificed for many years, only to find Moscow and Washington accept some part of Japan's position in China.

This fear was reinforced by China's experience at the Versailles Conference of 1919. Then, too, the interests of an allied China had been betrayed to Japan in order to reward Tokyo for not siding with Germany. One of Chiang's primary concerns throughout World War II was to ensure that the experience of 1919 was not repeated. One way of doing this was to see to it that the Soviet Union and the United States did not leave China to deal with Japan alone while exhausting themselves in the European war. Again, this pointed toward Soviet entry into the war against Japan. The danger of Soviet appeasement of Japan and an American compromise peace with Japan would both be diminished if the Soviet Union became an active ally of the United States and China against Japan.

182

Of course, the more enemies Japan had the smaller share of the fighting China would have to carry, and the more grateful those other cobelligerents would be to China for taking on a large part of Japan's forces. That is, China would have more leverage with Moscow if the Soviet Union's military situation were directly dependent on the continuation of China's military operations against Japan. Had the Soviet Union entered the Pacific war, in other words, China would have been in a position to use exactly the same ploy it used so effectively against the United States: the threat of peace with Japan if China's demands were not met.

Of all the Allied powers in World War II, only the United States was forced to conduct large wars simultaneously against Germany and Japan. The necessity of coping with a war on two fronts while rushing desperately to mobilize its economy and manpower, meant that the continuation of China's war against Japan was critical to the United States. This, in turn, meant that the United States was very important to China's Soviet policy. Throughout World War II Chiang's Soviet policy relied heavily on the United States. While Chiang had little leverage with Moscow, he had substantial leverage with Washington; and Washington, in turn, had significant leverage with Moscow. Exactly what Chiang sought from Moscow via Washington varied from period to period, but time and again his road to Moscow led through Washington.

Staggering under German blows in Europe, the Soviet Union wanted at all costs to avoid provoking or tempting Tokyo to join its Axis partners in a crusade against communism.[1] One element of this policy was an effort to disengage from China and the Far East. Once again Soviet and Chinese interests diverged. While Stalin acted with increasing caution to avoid provoking Japan, Chiang Kai-shek sought through a combination of direct and indirect methods to bring the Soviet Union into the Far Eastern war. These efforts overlapped with conflicts over Xinjiang to produce a downward spiral in Sino-Soviet relations.

China's intelligence services, like those of several countries, picked up information indicating an imminent German attack on the Soviet Union well in advance of the actual beginning of that invasion. According to the memoir of Shao Lizi, then China's ambassador in Moscow, China's military attaché in Berlin cabled a warning of the imminent German attack to Chongqing in early May.[2] On 10 May Chiang Kai-shek passed this intelligence on to the American ambassador in Chongqing, along with the admonition that the United States should carefully refrain from actions which might irritate Berlin and cause it to shelve its planned eastern advance. Chiang was quite frank with the American ambassador about his desire for a German-Soviet conflict. Three days later, Chiang amplified his warning by explaining to the ambassador that if the United States entered the war against Germany at that point (e.g., prior to a German attack on the Soviet Union), it would push Berlin and Moscow closer together, a situation which would be most dangerous.[3] Chiang hoped, in other words, that the United States would do nothing to prevent or delay the onset of a German-Soviet war.

Chongqing was quite pleased once the German attack began. Nationalist officials commonly believed that Japan would eventually be obligated to honor its commitments under the Tri-Partite Treaty by attacking Siberia or Outer Mongolia.[4] Four days after the German onslaught began, Ambassador Shao Lizi met with the American ambassador in Moscow and expressed his satisfaction with recent developments. The Soviet-German war meant that Japan was "surrounded," Shao said. He had feared that the Soviet Union might join the Axis, but now a Soviet-Japanese conflict could not be far off.[5]

Chongqing moved quickly to align with the Soviet Union. On 2 July 1941, Chongqing severed diplomatic relations with Germany and Italy ostensibly in retaliation for their recognition of the Wang Jingwei regime the previous day.[6] While this move did derive in part from Chongqing's determination to isolate Wang's Nanjing government, it also helped merge Far Eastern and European events. On the same day that Chongqing broke relations with Berlin and Rome, Chiang sent a message to Franklin Roosevelt's special representative in China, Lauchlin Currie, informing him of intelligence indicating that a *Japanese* attack on the Soviet Union was imminent. Japan was about to abrogate the April 1941 agreement, Chiang said, and declare war on the Soviet Union. Tokyo's hope was that the United States would remain neutral and allow Japan and Germany to defeat the Soviet Union.[7] Regardless of the source of this information, Chiang's decision to pass it on to Washington was a reflection of its utility to his larger plan. By clarifying Japan's sinister intentions, Chiang hoped to make Washington more willing to support the Soviet Union. This, in turn, would strengthen Soviet resolve to confront Japan.

Chiang also revived the idea of a Soviet-Chinese military alliance against Japan. A treaty of alliance was drafted and submitted to chief Soviet advisor and military attaché General Vasilii Chuikov. The latter promptly rejected the proposal, believing that it was an American-inspired attempt to precipitate a Soviet-Japanese war in order to prevent a Japanese advance into Southeast Asia.[8] Chiang also lobbied for a U.S. initiative launching a Sino-Soviet-British-American alliance. On 8 July, Chiang informed Roosevelt that according to "most reliable sources" in Tokyo, Germany and Japan had reached a secret agreement providing for a Japanese strike against Siberia and into the South Seas. To counter this Axis advance Chiang proposed a four-power military alliance. Since the outbreak of the Soviet-German war, Chiang ingeniously told Roosevelt, the Soviet Union had "repeatedly announced their desire to conclude definite military arrangements with us against Japan." Would President Roosevelt favor such an arrangement, Chiang queried, and did he believe that the situation was "ripening" for a military pact between China, the Soviet Union, and Britain with the friendly support of the United States?[9] Roosevelt's response on 11 July said that because the United States was not a party to Sino-Soviet military arrangements, it could assume no responsibility for them. But in his own opinion, Roosevelt ventured, such arrangements would definitely be to China's benefit.[10]

Roosevelt's cautious response did not discourage Chiang. In early August he met with his American political advisor Owen Lattimore and reformulated his argument for a four-power anti-Japanese alliance. China had already fought for four years and was still isolated and without allies, Chiang told Lattimore. Japanese propaganda was using this fact to persuade Chinese that China was being used as an anti-Axis tool by the Western democracies—propaganda which was having "unfortunate effects," according to Chiang. This was a veiled threat that, isolated and demoralized,

China might leave the war. To counter Japanese propaganda, Chiang suggested, Roosevelt should propose to Moscow and London a military alliance with China. If this were not possible, Chiang urged, then China should at least be invited to participate in the existing defense conferences of the United States, Britain, and Holland. In explaining Chiang's reasoning to Roosevelt, Lattimore noted that the Japanese warning to Moscow following the recent conclusion of the Anglo-Soviet mutual security agreement had led Chiang to believe that the time was ripe for an antiaggressor alliance.[11] In other words, the proposed four-power alliance would well presage a Soviet-Japanese war.

While pushing for American action to initiate a four-power alliance as a means for securing Soviet entry into the war with Japan, Chiang launched a press campaign to reinforce his diplomatic efforts. On 8 July the Sino-Soviet Cultural Association, the China Branch of the International Anti-Aggressor Association, and the China National Diplomatic Association sent a joint cable to the Soviet people. The cable lauded the struggle of the Soviet Union and linked that struggle to China's struggle against the Far Eastern aggressor. In order to eliminate the evil of aggression from the world, the cable said, "We deeply hope that China, the Soviet Union, Britain, and the United States can establish a solid anti-aggressor camp, increase and strengthen their mutual trust, and share sorrows and joys together in order to exterminate their common enemy."[12]

General Chuikov also began noticing many articles in Chinese newspapers written by Madame Chiang Kai-shek and people close to her lauding Soviet military aid to China. The articles complained that Britain and the United States had not given China as much aid as the Soviet Union had, and pointed out that, unlike London and Washington, Moscow was willing to sell munitions to China. In Chuikov's opinion, the purpose of these articles was to anger Japan and persuade it that the Soviet Union was more threatening to it than were Britain or the United States. Chuikov believed that these articles along with Chongqing's severance of relations with Germany and Italy, and its push for a Soviet-Chinese military alliance were all part of a Chinese effort to precipitate a Japanese attack on the Soviet Union.[13]

Immediately after Japan's attack on Pearl Harbor, Chiang tried still once again to coalesce a Soviet-Chinese-American alliance against Japan. This time Chiang tried to persuade Washington to link American support for the Soviet Union against Germany to Soviet involvement in the war against Japan. On 8 December, Chiang met with the Soviet and American ambassadors and proposed a simultaneous American declaration of war against Germany, a Soviet declaration of war against Japan, and a Chinese declaration of war against both Axis powers. The Allies were also to pledge not to conclude a separate peace with Japan. This was to be followed by the conclusion of a treaty of military alliance and the creation of a unified command to direct the forces of all allied powers.[14] Chiang also cabled this proposal directly to Stalin. In Washington, Chinese Ambassador Hu Shi also urged Roosevelt to press the Soviet Union to declare war on Japan, thereby making possible a coordinated Sino-Soviet offensive against Japan. China was afraid, Hu said, that if it declared war on Japan ahead of the Soviet Union, Moscow would wait even longer to enter the war against Japan. Simultaneous declarations of war by Moscow, Washington, and Chongqing were best, Hu argued.[15]

What Chongqing was in effect proposing was that Washington should tell Moscow that American support for the Soviet Union in Europe was contingent on Soviet support for the war against Japan.

American leaders agreed with Chongqing regarding the desirability of Soviet entry into the Far Eastern war.[16] They were not prepared, however, to make support in Europe contingent on Soviet entry into this war. On 9 December, Under-Secretary of State Sumner Welles advised T.V. Soong that China should go ahead and declare war on the Axis powers.[17] Chongqing did so the same day.[18]

Stalin and Molotov wanted nothing to do with Chinese, or for that matter American, proposals that the Soviet Union willingly undertake a two-front war. Stalin replied to Chiang's cable the same day it was sent, 8 December. While Stalin agreed with Chiang's proposition that the Pacific war and China's war of resistance were both parts of the anti-Axis struggle, he felt that the struggle against Germany was the most decisive and most important component of that struggle. Moreover, since the Soviet Union was currently carrying the main burden of the war against Germany, Soviet strength could not be dispersed to the Far East. To do so would be to ease the difficulties facing the German armies. Thus, Stalin "sincerely urged" Chiang not to demand that the Soviet Union immediately declare war on Japan. Stalin ended his message with the cryptic words:

> Naturally the Soviet Union must go to war against Japan, because Japan will uncondi-
> tionally violate the neutrality agreement. We should prepare to deal with this sort of
> situation, but preparations take time. For this reason, I once again sincerely urge Your
> Excellency not to demand that the Soviet Union immediately declare war on Japan. [19]

The day after Stalin's cable arrived, the head of Chongqing's foreign advisors office met with Chuikov seeking clarification of the last phrase of Stalin's message. Stalin had not meant to imply, Chuikov explained, that the Soviet Union would enter the war against Japan once Germany were defeated. Soviet action in the Far East was contingent on many factors, such as concentration of troops, movements of supplies, and so on.[20] Four days after Stalin's cable arrived in Chongqing, T.V. Soong forwarded a copy of it to the U.S. State Department.[21] In Chongqing there was still hope, however. The following June when Winston Churchill visited Washington, Chinese newspapers openly urged the Anglo-American powers to bring the Soviet Union into the war against Japan.[22]

As Chongqing was trying to precipitate a Soviet-Japanese war, Moscow was distancing itself from Chongqing in order to minimize just such a possibility. During the second half of 1941, Moscow was extremely worried about future Japanese policy and sought repeated assurances from Tokyo. Japan's initial responses to Soviet entreaties were evasive while the Japanese elite debated whether or not to join in the attack on the Soviet Union. Finally, on 5 August 1941, Japan's Foreign Minister Toyoda Teijiro gave a definite pledge to Soviet Ambassador Konstatin Smetanin that Japan would respect the April 1941 agreement. In exchange, Toyoda demanded that the Soviet Union promise inter alia to cease all direct and indirect aid to Chiang Kai-shek. Twice during August Toyoda protested the increased deliveries of American goods arriving in Vladivostok. Japan was concerned, Toyoda explained, that these goods were destined for Chiang Kai-shek's forces. The Soviets reassured Tokyo that the American supplies were for Soviet use only—and that any attempt to stop their flow would be an unfriendly act.[23]

To protect Japanese-Soviet neutrality and the flow of vital American equipment through Vladivostok, Stalin terminated Soviet aid to China. On 13 August, Ambassador Smetanin responded to Toyoda's demands of 5 August. Regarding Soviet aid to China, Smetanin said, Japan had no more right to object to Soviet dealings with China than the Soviet Union had to object to Japanese dealings with Germany and Italy. The April 1941 agreement did not affect either country's relations with third parties, Smetanin said. Nonetheless, the ambassador reaffirmed the 2 July 1940 statement by Molotov that Soviet aid to Chiang Kai-shek was insignificant because the Soviet Union was preoccupied with its own national defense. Since 22 June 1941, Smetanin said, this was even more the case. Smetanin also assured Toyoda that the Soviet Union would not grant military bases or territorial concessions to any third power (i.e., the United States or China) in the Soviet Far East.[24] That October, Ambassador Litvinov in Washington told the American government that because of its own needs, the Soviet Union would no longer be able to continue aiding China.[25]

The issue of Soviet aid to China continued to rankle Sino-Soviet relations for the remainder of the war. Shortly after China's new ambassador to the Soviet Union, Fu Bingchang, arrived in Kuybyshev [the wartime capital of the Soviet Union about 965 kilometers (600 miles) east of Moscow] in early 1943, he discussed the matter with Soviet Foreign Trade Commissar Anastas Mikoyan. During their meeting on 24 February 1943, Mikoyan reassured Fu that the termination of Soviet aid to China had been entirely due to the inability of the Soviet Union to provide such aid. Moreover, Mikoyan said, such aid would resume in the future. Fu cabled Mikoyan's comments to Chongqing along with his own impression that Moscow desired to improve relations with China but was afraid to act openly because it still feared Japan and because Soviet strength was still inadequate to assist China.[26] Soviet explanations did not assuage Chiang Kai-shek's bitterness toward Moscow. From Chiang's perspective, Moscow's suspension of aid represented Soviet appeasement of Japan. Not only did Moscow refuse to join into an alliance with China, it even bowed to Japanese pressure and stopped aiding China. How, Chiang must have asked himself, could Stalin expect him to be understanding of Soviet concerns in Xinjiang when the Soviets were so unresponsive to Chinese concerns regarding Japan?

The Question of Transit Rights via Soviet Central Asia

China's situation in early 1942 was ironic. It now had two powerful allies, Britain and the United States, but it was more isolated than it had ever been since embarking on its war against Japan. The termination of Soviet aid in the fall of 1941 and the Japanese occupation of Rangoon in March 1942 cut off China's two remaining international supply lines. The Haiphong–Kunming railway had been severed since mid-1940. China's only source of foreign aid was now the small amount which could be ferried by aircraft over the mountains between India and southwestern China. There were, however, alternative ground routes over which U.S. Lend-Lease aid might move to China: via Soviet Siberia or Soviet Central Asia. After Japan's occupation of Burma, Chongqing sought to open one of these routes. Even though Moscow had terminated its own assistance, Chongqing hoped that it would allow U.S. Lend-Lease supplies to move from Iran, through Soviet Turkestan and Kazakhstan, to Xinjiang. After all, the Soviet Union was claiming that it had suspended its aid to China only because its own needs were so great—and not because it wanted to placate Japan.

Chiang's desire to open an aid pipeline was compelling, because his armies desperately needed the equipment. But there were other considerations as well. The question of transit rights via the Soviet Union was closely tied to the question of Soviet-Japanese neutrality. China and the United States were allies against Japan, just as the Soviet Union and the United States were allies against Germany. If the Soviet Union helped the United States help China make war, this might persuade Japan to respond to Germany's increasingly desperate calls for a Japanese attack on Siberia. As we shall see, Stalin was apprehensive about just such a possibility. Chiang welcomed it for many of the same reasons that Stalin rejected it.

On 23 May 1942, Chiang Kai-shek ordered Shao Lizi to request the Soviet government to grant transit rights via Soviet territory. At a meeting of the Pacific War Council in Washington, Chiang told Shao, Roosevelt had indicated that he also hoped that a route through Soviet territory could be found for American aid to China. But it would be best, Roosevelt had suggested, for China's ambassador in Moscow to raise this issue directly with the Soviet government. The United States and Britain would then support China's initiative.[27]

Chiang's directive to Shao was a repetition of an earlier directive by China's foreign ministry. According to the memoir of Guo Dequan, China's military attaché to Moscow during the war, Shao Lizi was initially unwilling to ask the Soviet government to provide such transit rights. Shao felt that China should seek ways in which to assist the Soviet Union during its time of trouble, rather than making demands on the Soviet Union. According to Guo, after Chongqing repeated its order to request transit rights, Guo himself approached the American and British ambassadors and asked them to intercede on China's behalf.[28]

The day after Chiang's directive, Shao presented a request to the Soviet Foreign Ministry that 4000 tons of supplies per month be allowed to transit Soviet territory en route to China. The Soviets expressed sympathy for China but insisted that the technical aspects of the request would have to be studied.[29] On 25 May Shao reported the Soviet response to Chiang. If Roosevelt could earnestly mention this matter to Stalin, this would certainly be effective, Shao suggested.[30]

Guo Dequan believed that Shao's efforts to secure Soviet consent were perfunctory and that Moscow was in fact prepared to grant Chongqing's request. The British and American ambassadors told him, Guo recounts in his memoir, that Shao himself tried to sabotage the request for transit rights and, had he not done so, China's petition might well have been granted.[31] While Guo's account of Shao's behavior may well be accurate (Shao's own memoir recounts his disagreements with Chongqing's Soviet policy at this juncture), it is unlikely that China's petition failed because of Shao's lack of enthusiasm. American officials, including Roosevelt, discussed the possibility of supplying China via Soviet territory with Molotov during the latter's May–June 1942 visit to Washington.[32] For the next eighteen months, Moscow "studied" China's request for transit rights for American war matériel.[33] When Fu Bingchang raised the issue with Mikoyan on 11 March 1943, the Soviet trade commissar was sympathetic but again cited technical difficulties such as the limited railway capacity. If such transportation problems could be solved, he said, it would not be difficult to reach agreement on transit rights.[34] Chiang Kai-shek believed that such "technical problems" were mere pretexts. Moscow's real concern, he felt, was to avoid offending Japan.[35]

As had happened with both Jiang Tingfu in 1937 and Yang Jie in 1940, the new orientation in Chiang Kai-shek's Soviet policy met opposition from his ambassador in Moscow. According to his memoir, Shao's resignation in October 1942 was due to his opposition to the "anti-Soviet" orientation of Chiang's policy. Shortly after the German invasion of the Soviet Union, Shao urged Chiang to order China's armies to launch a general offensive against Japan to divert Japan's armies and prevent them from joining in the attack on the Soviet Union. Chiang was not enthusiastic about Shao's suggestion and replied to it, according to Shao, with a one-sentence cable: "You may indicate to the Soviet Government that you have received instructions to express active sympathy." During the summer and fall of 1941, Shao also urged Chiang to send a top-level official to Moscow for discussions. Just as Roosevelt had sent Harry Hopkins and Churchill had sent Anthony Eden to Moscow for confidential talks with Stalin, so Chiang should send a top-level official to discuss the international situation with the Soviet leader. Perhaps Guo Taiqi could stop in Moscow on his way from London to Chongqing (where he was to replace Wang Chonghui as foreign minister upon his arrival in July). The absence of such top-level exchanges, Shao thought, led Stalin to underemphasize China. Shao believed that Chiang Kai-shek ignored these suggestions because he was under the influence of hard-line anticommunists in Chongqing who wanted to weaken, rather than strengthen, the Soviet Union.[36] Apparently Shao concluded that such weakening was to be brought about by enmeshing Moscow in war with Japan. On 8 December 1942, Fu Bingchang, a professional diplomat with links to Sun Ke, was appointed to succeed Shao Lizi as ambassador to Moscow.[37]

Shortly before his departure from the Soviet Union, Shao submitted to Mikoyan a draft of a transit agreement providing for Soviet shipment of 2000 tons of goods and 1200 tons of petroleum per month from Aschabad on the Soviet-Iranian border to Hami. In exchange, 2000 tons of Chinese wool, tin, wolframite, raw silk, hides, and tung oil would be delivered to the Soviets each month. Several counterproposals were exchanged, with the final Soviet offer providing for a monthly exchange of 2000 tons including 300 tons of oil, and Xingxing Xia on the Xinjiang–Gansu border, rather than Hami in Xinjiang's interior, as the point of exchange.[38]

But still Moscow stalled. The Soviets now insisted that the Turkestan-Siberian Railway was already fully occupied and that shipment of these goods would have to be by road. For this, large numbers of trucks would be necessary. The Soviet Union could not provide these trucks, and China should ask the United States and Great Britain to provide a thousand or so trucks.[39] The lack of American and British trucks then became the major "technical problem" stalling a transit agreement from

October 1942 through May 1943. Whenever the Chinese side urged the Soviet Union to accelerate negotiations, the Soviets replied that the lack of any agreement for the American supply of trucks made any urgency unnecessary.[40]

Moscow's decisions on aid transit involved careful calculations. On the one hand, Moscow wished to honor American requests for such transit rights and was glad to see American aid strengthen China's fighting capability. On the other hand, it did not want to provoke Japan while the Soviet Union was still weak. Thus, Moscow procrastinated until early 1943. By that time Paulus's armies had surrendered at Stalingrad and Moscow probably felt confident enough of the situation on the European front to run a somewhat greater risk of provoking Japan. But even then it insisted on secrecy.

Late in March 1943 a transit agreement was finally reached. Monthly deliveries of 2000 tons of American and British war matériel plus 500 tons of Soviet petroleum were to be made to China by the Soviet Union in exchange for 1000 tons of Chinese raw materials. The discrepancy in the tonnage exchange was due to China's inability to make larger deliveries because of its dilapidated domestic transportation system and was to be compensated by a cash payment covering seventy-five percent of the cost of sending the empty trucks back to their loading point in Iran. The exchanges were to begin as soon as China secured several thousand trucks from the United States.[41] Two months later, in May, the United States and Britain agreed, "for the political effect," to provide the necessary trucks.[42]

Because of the extreme delicacy of this matter, Moscow was unwilling to put the March 1943 agreement in writing.[43] Such a document might fall into Japanese hands, while without such a document Moscow could more easily deny any reports Tokyo might receive. Such precautions were futile. While preparations were under way to implement the secret transit rights agreement, the Ministry of Information in Chongqing made a public announcement about China's new international supply route. A reporter from the London *Evening News* picked up the announcement and wired it to his home office. The paper's London bureau got confirmation of the story from the Chinese embassy in London and then, on 6 July 1943, printed the story.[44]

Once the transit arrangement became known to Tokyo, Moscow could not permit it to continue. Thus, in early September, when the first two convoys under the transit exchange agreement arrived at the designated entry point on the Soviet-Iranian border, they were refused entry into the Soviet Union. Moscow then cancelled indefinitely all arrangements to ship goods to China over this route on the grounds that Soviet transportation facilities were inadequate.[45]

It is uncertain whether Chiang himself initiated or approved this clumsy ploy. The Chinese government was then considerably more disorganized, undisciplined, and faction-ridden than most governments normally are, and the critical leak from the Information Ministry may well have been the work of some enterprising bureaucratic underling. Still, it must be noted that this move was consistent with Chiang's approach to Soviet-Japanese relations; over the previous several years he *had* made clear his desire for a Soviet-Japanese war. Moscow must have wondered just how much Chiang had to do with the July 1943 episode. It added still another increment to Sino-Soviet hostility and suspicion.

Considering Chiang's policies toward the Soviet Union in 1942–1943, the question must be asked: did Chiang Kai-shek desire the defeat of the Soviet Union? Was this why he tried so persistently to undermine Soviet-Japanese neutrality and threatened the Soviet Union with war in Xinjiang? There is some evidence that several members of Chiang's entourage did, in fact, harbor such hopes. As we saw in the last chapter, He Yingqin's 13 July 1942 plan for the recovery of Xinjiang clearly looked with favor on Soviet defeat. This author knows of no documentary evidence permitting a similar conclusion regarding the views of Chiang Kai-shek. Moreover, Chiang consistently sought, at least after July 1937, the military defeat of Japan. It follows that Chiang must have understood that the extension of Japanese rule to, say, Lake Baikal or the partition of the Soviet Union by Germany and Japan would have virtually ensured continued Japanese domination of China. But it is also clear that if Chiang did not desire Soviet defeat, at least he wanted to see a much weakened Soviet Union. Had the Soviet Union been forced to deal with a combined German-Japanese attack in 1941–1942, it would have suffered greater destruction and would have emerged as a much weaker power after the war, even if it still emerged victorious. This would have greatly strengthened China's hand vis-à-vis the Soviet Union, especially if China could conserve and built its own strength during the war.

Many of Chiang's officials, if not Chiang himself, held such views. In June 1942, the vice-chairman of China's National Resources Board explained to the second secretary of the American embassy that a Soviet-Japanese war was highly desirable because it would enhance China's bargaining position with the Soviet Union.[46] The vice-chairman mentioned only the securing of Soviet aid as one possible Chinese demand once it was in such an improved bargaining position, but other possibilities come readily to mind: elimination of the Soviet position in Xinjiang, return of Outer Mongolia to China, and complete severance of all Soviet ties to the CCP. Regarding the CCP, Economics Minister Weng Wenhao agreed with a suggestion by the counselor of the American embassy in September 1942 that once Japan attacked the Soviet Union it might be possible for Chongqing to solve the CCP problem by reaching an "understanding" with Moscow.[47] In other words, a Soviet-Japanese war would put China in a position to demand that Moscow concede to Chinese demands.

Chiang's Demarche toward Soviet Entry into the Far East War

Chiang Kai-shek's attitude toward Soviet-Japanese relations changed in mid-1943. From that point onwards, Chiang no longer thought that Soviet entry into the war with Japan would be favorable to China. He believed, however, that such Soviet entry was increasingly likely. Commenting on Soviet-Japanese relations in his diary on 31 July 1943, Chiang said, "If the Soviet Union does not join in the war against Japan, China's sacrifices will be greater, but we are nevertheless willing to do this. Unfortunately this is not likely."[48] Another comment at the end of August made the same point and also suggested a possible way of preventing Soviet entry. It would be best if the Soviet Union did not enter the war against Japan, Chiang wrote, but it was inevitable that Moscow would want to take advantage of the opportunity the war presented. This was not, however, a situation which could not be influenced by China's diplomacy. Henceforth one of the "major duties" of China's diplomacy should be to "make it impossible" for the Soviet Union to join in the Far Eastern war. To this end, China should seek the organization of a Sino-American-British United Pacific War Council. Then if the Soviet Union at some point wished to enter the war against Japan, its request would have to be approved by this council.[49] Consistent with this strategy, on the second day of the Cairo Conference on 24 November 1943, Wang Chonghui presented to Harry Hopkins a memo proposing the creation of a far eastern commission consisting of the United States, Britain, and China. Future Soviet participation in the commission would be welcomed at any time.[50]

Deterring Soviet entry into the war in the Far East also seems to have been a major reason why Chongqing rejected Roosevelt's June 1943 proposal for a four-power conference and suggested, instead, two tripartite conferences—a development which is discussed more fully in the next section. By separating the Pacific Allies from the European Allies, it might be possible to establish some arrangements exclusive to the situation in the Pacific, which could then serve to constrain, perhaps even prevent, future Soviet entry into the Pacific war. If Chiang had still wanted to undermine Soviet-Japanese neutrality in mid-1943, he would have leaped at Roosevelt's offer for a four-power conference for precisely the same reasons that Stalin rejected it: its adverse impact on Soviet-Japanese neutrality.

The reason for the shift in Chiang's orientation was probably a growing confidence that the United States would push the war against Japan through to the end and then accept China's basic demands at the peace conference. Early in the war in the Pacific, Chiang feared that the priority given to the war in Europe might lead Britain and the United States to make a compromise peace with Japan, leaving it with some portion of its position in China. This was one reason why Chiang was so sensitive to perceived breaches of faith and slights of China's formal status as a great power by the Allies. Developments in early 1943, however, somewhat assuaged these fears. The inclusion of Chinese representatives in Anglo-American joint staff meetings and the scheduling of the Cairo Conference, both indicated that China would be treated as an equal at the future peace conference. Moreover, the scheduling of an offensive in Burma and Roosevelt's announcement of the goal of "unconditional surrender" of both Germany and Japan at the January 1943 Casablanca Conference, and the mounting success of the American-Australian-New Zealand naval-amphibious campaign in the Solomon Islands and New Guinea during the spring, must have reassured Chiang that the United States intended to pursue vigorously the war against Japan. This, in turn, probably reassured Chiang that Japan could be thoroughly defeated without Soviet intervention.

Soviet Support for China's Rise to Great-Power Status

By 1943 Chiang was turning his attention to ensuring the establishment of China as a great power in the postwar era. Early in the year, Chiang presented his view of China's future power and greatness in his book, *Zhongguo zhi Mingyun*, or *China's Destiny*.[51] From the standpoint of Sino-Soviet relations, Chiang's basic diplomatic dilemma was this: to achieve the restoration of China's national greatness, Chiang needed Soviet cooperation. Yet the very achievement of these objectives conflicted with the Soviet Union's own interests. Several of the "lost territories" which Chiang sought to reintegrate into the Republic of China—Xinjiang, Outer Mongolia, and Manchuria—were historic spheres of Russian influence.[52] Could Moscow be expected not to resist Chinese efforts to recover these territories? And then there was the overriding question of the Chinese Communist Party. How could Moscow be persuaded to accept the elimination or subordination of that party, a move which Chiang viewed as essential to the creation of a united nation?

Chiang's diplomatic management of this Soviet dilemma centered on manipulation of the United States. He first secured American support for his program of national grandeur and then used American influence to secure Soviet support. The most important of Chiang's diplomatic levers was the utilization of American fears of a separate peace between China and Japan. Confronted with a two-front war and forced to fight a holding action in the Pacific, American leaders valued China's role in tying down well over a million Japanese troops. Chiang's basic diplomatic tactic was to convince Washington via this leverage to pressure Moscow into acceding to Chinese demands.

While our purpose is not to analyze Sino-American relations, it is important to note that in establishing China's formal rank as a great power, Chongqing was not a mere passive beneficiary of American generosity. It is, of course, quite true that the United States had a historic policy of support for China's national independence and territorial integrity, a policy which culminated in Roosevelt's and U.S. Secretary of State Cordell Hull's wartime vision of China as the major power in postwar Asia. There is also no question that without American support China could not have entered the ranks of the great powers during 1942–1943. But the fact that American support was forthcoming was, to a considerable extent, a result of Chongqing's manipulation of American fears and hopes. In other words, Chongqing's repeated hints about a tacit Chinese separate peace with Japan struck a responsive chord in Washington. American leaders were willing to grant China at least symbolic status as an equal allied great power, to make China one of the Big Four to compensate for the low levels of material support going to China and the low priority assigned to the war against Japan. They were reluctant, however, to give substance to China's great-power status in ways which might interfere in the efficient functioning of the war effort, such as inclusion of China in the joint Anglo-American staff conferences or inclusion of Chinese representatives in the various summit conferences at which basic allied decisions were made during the war. Because we are concerned with the Sino-American relations only in so far as they relate to Sino-Soviet ties, it will suffice to say that throughout 1942 and early 1943 Chiang Kai-shek's representatives worked continually to pressure the United States into giving substance to China's great-power status. By mid-1943, these efforts had borne fruit: during the Washington Conference of May and the Quebec Conference of August 1943, China was represented as one of the major Allied powers. Moreover, a summit meeting between Chiang and Roosevelt was under discussion. Chongqing then used American pressure to secure Soviet acceptance of China's entry into the ranks of the great powers.

The issue of formal Soviet acceptance of China's formal admission to the Big

Four was decided at the foreign ministers' conference in Moscow in October 1943. At a 5 October White House planning meeting for that conference, American leaders decided to push for British and Soviet acceptance of Chinese participation in various Allied commissions. Both Allies were expected to present "difficulties," but American leaders believed that, with regard to the Soviet Union, a way could be found to absolve Moscow of involvement in the Pacific question until after the defeat of Germany. China, it was felt, was too important a factor to be alienated.[53]

Once the foreign ministers' conference began, Molotov strongly objected to consideration of a four-power declaration on security and cooperation, as was proposed by the United States. It had been agreed, Molotov said, that the conference would be a three-power conference. The declaration of that conference should therefore be a tripartite declaration. Moreover, because China was not a party to the conference, how could a declaration be issued in its name? Secretary of State Hull tried to persuade Molotov by hinting that failure to allow China to sign the declaration might cause China to make a separate peace with Japan. The exclusion of China, Hull said, would "create, in all probability, the most terrific repercussions, both political and military, in the Pacific area."[54] Molotov countered by saying that if the *three* powers could not reach an agreement, that indeed would create serious problems. It was not necessary to consider a four-power declaration, Molotov said. Eventually, however, Molotov accepted Anthony Eden's suggestion that if the three powers could reach an agreement on a joint declaration, and if the Chinese government could give its consent to this declaration before the end of the conference, then the three-power declaration might be transformed into a four-power one. This was on 21 October.[55]

The question of China's signature of the declaration was not discussed again until 26 October when Hull raised the issue with Molotov. Molotov then said that the Soviet government had no objection to the inclusion of China as an original signatory but doubted whether it would be possible for Fu Bingchang, China's ambassador in Moscow, to receive authorization in time. At Hull's suggestion, Fu then formally demanded full Chinese participation in the issuance of the joint declaration, citing China's long resistance to aggression and its sacrifices. How could China hope for an equal position after the war if it was not treated equally during the war, Fu asked.[56] The final text of the declaration was wired to Chongqing at midnight on 26 October. By this time, however, only four days remained before the conference was scheduled to adjourn, whereas an exchange of cables between Moscow and Chongqing normally took seven to eight days.[57] American assistance enabled Fu to overcome this difficulty. Secretary Hull authorized the use of the U.S. Navy transmitter in Moscow to radio a message to Chongqing via Washington requesting delegation of plenipotentiary powers to Fu and authorization of his signature of the joint declaration. Chiang had known the general substance of the proposed declaration for some time, because Hull had given a copy of the American draft to T.V. Soong on 20 September,[58] and was therefore able to radio authorization, again via American transmitters, back through Washington to Moscow. After the declaration was signed on 30 October, Roosevelt cabled Chiang: "I am delighted that such excellent progress is being made for our proposal. We have cracked the ice and I think that you and I have successfully established the principle."[59] Fu Bingchang thanked Hull for his assistance in hushing up the "difficulties" involved in China's signature.[60]

Given the exceedingly cool state of Sino-Soviet relations in mid-1943, securing Soviet acceptance of China's entry into the Big Four was no easy accomplishment. Chongqing's efforts to undermine Soviet-Japanese neutrality had antagonized Moscow, just as Moscow's efforts to distance itself from China for the sake of that neutrality had antagonized Chongqing. These tensions overlapped and intensified the conflict arising from Chongqing's drive to oust the Soviet Union from Xinjiang. Moreover, as both Moscow and Chongqing began to look beyond the war, old suspicions began to grow. Stalin feared that postwar China might become an anti-Soviet base for a revived Japan or the United States. Chiang was concerned about a possible revival of recent Soviet claims in Manchuria and Xinjiang, and about the extent of Soviet demands regarding Outer Mongolia. And above all, Chiang feared Soviet support for the CCP insurgency.

After the pivotal Soviet victories at Stalingrad in early 1943 and at Kursh that summer, the Soviet Union began showing renewed interest in Far Eastern affairs. This, combined with the strained state of Sino-Soviet relations, produced increased Soviet pressure on Chongqing. In August 1943, the Soviet media began to criticize the Chongqing government for the first time since June 1941. After the onset of the German-Soviet war, Soviet media had largely confined its coverage of China to reports on fighting or to articles commemorating Chinese historical events. Without exception, these articles praised Chinese resistance to Japan and expressed great friendship for the Chinese people. Mention of the CCP or unfavorable comments about the KMT were avoided.[61] Then suddenly, on 6 August 1943, the Soviet journal *War and the Working Class* carried an article condemning "defeatists" and "capitulationists" high within the KMT who wanted peace with Japan in order to wipe out the CCP.[62] Other similar articles followed in the Soviet press. Chiang believed that this Soviet media campaign was an attempt to undermine American support for him.[63] He responded by directing China's media to charge Moscow with leadership of the CCP and with responsibility for revolts in Xinjiang.[64]

In Xinjiang, too, Moscow increased its pressure on Chongqing. In November 1943 the Soviet consul general in Dihua rejected a Chinese bid to reopen trade between Xinjiang and the Soviet Union. The embargo on trade between the Soviet Union and Xinjiang thus continued and greatly contributed to the economic collapse underway in Xinjiang.[65] This, in turn, destabilized political conditions and prepared conditions for the insurrections which Moscow began supporting the next spring.

Throughout 1943 and into 1944, Chiang showed little interest in responding to mounting Soviet pressure by trying to improve relations with Moscow. Instead, he tried to mobilize American pressure against the Soviet Union. From Chiang's perspective, American involvement in Sino-Soviet relations held great dangers as well as great opportunities. American pressure on Moscow might help compel Soviet acceptance of China's recovery of lost territories, internal unification, and admission to the Big Four. But if the United States sided with Moscow on any of those issues, China's case would be nearly hopeless. This was the overriding danger which Chiang sought to avoid throughout the last three years of the war: the imposition of a Soviet-American diktat to China at the war's end. One especially dangerous possibility was that Washington might recognize Manchuria as a Soviet sphere of influence, perhaps in exchange for Soviet recognition of Japan as an American sphere of influence. A related danger was that Washington might acquiesce in a postwar Communist rebellion in China. For the sake of continued Soviet-American amity, Washington might refuse to support the Nationalists in a postwar showdown with the CCP, or refuse to force Moscow to abandon the CCP. To minimize these dangers, Chiang sought to ensure that Washington approached its mediation of Sino-Soviet relations with an attitude of bolstering China against a hostile Soviet Union, rather than one of an impartial mediator trying to bring two friends together.

In considering the linkage between Chongqing's Soviet and American diplomacy in 1943 and early 1944, it is also essential to keep in mind the strained state of Soviet-American relations at that point. During mid-1943, relations between Moscow and Washington–London were at a low ebb. Soviet leaders were bitter about the Anglo-American failure to open a second front in France and suspected that this failure was an attempt to let the Nazis and the Communists bleed one another white.[66] Chiang Kai-shek was well informed about the dispute over the second front in Europe and reflections in his diary in mid-1943 indicate not only that he credited such Soviet interpretations of Anglo-American motives, but that he lauded those motives.[67] Anglo-American demands on the Soviets regarding the postwar period absolutely must be settled during the war, Chiang wrote in his diary on 25 August 1943. Moreover,

> If the Soviets will not accept Anglo-American demands, then they will not open a second front. . . . In sum, unless the Soviet Union thoroughly abandons its schemes for world revolution, its contradictions with America and Britain will increase day by day. The Anglo-Americans hold the dominant position, have more than enough strength to deal with both the Soviet Union and the Axis countries, and absolutely will not be pushed around by Russian bullying.[68]

Chiang believed, in other words, that Washington was in a position to demand Soviet acceptance of China's great-power position because Moscow dared not break with the Anglo-American camp. Moreover, he believed that Washington would do this because the United States wanted to keep China in the war with Japan and because they saw China as a postwar ally in balancing and containing the Soviet Union. These perceptions guided Chiang's approach toward his famous summit conference with Roosevelt and Churchill at Cairo in November 1943.

The Conferences at Cairo and Teheran

The fact that there were two tripartite conferences at the end of 1943 rather than one four-power conference reflected, in part, Chiang's desire to secure American support against the Soviet Union. Both Stalin and Chiang, each for their own reasons, rejected the idea of a single four-power conference. On 7 June 1943, Roosevelt told T.V. Soong that he hoped for a *four-power* summit in the near future and that several days before that summit he hoped to meet privately with Chiang Kai-shek. Three days later Chiang directed Soong to tell Roosevelt that, because the Soviet Union and

Japan were not at war, it would be "inconvenient" for China and the Soviet Union to participate in a four-power conference.[69]

Chinese sources are remarkably quiet about the reasons for Chiang's decision not to meet with Stalin in 1943—a decision which may well have been one of the most important of Chiang's wartime decisions about relations with the Soviet Union. Some sources explain Chiang's decision as arising from his embitterment from the 1941 Soviet-Japanese neutrality agreement and by Soviet support for the CCP.[70] Patrick Hurley, who went to Chongqing as Roosevelt's special representative in late 1943 to arrange the Cairo summit, felt that Chiang hesitated to meet with Stalin because he suspected him of wanting to communize China and to annex a portion of China to the Soviet Union.[71]

Neither of these explanations is entirely satisfactory. Chiang was certainly apprehensive about Soviet intentions, but why didn't he want to sit down with Roosevelt and Stalin and try to get the appropriate guarantees underwritten by the United States? If we assume that Chiang thought this issue through, which seems to be a fair assumption for a decision of this magnitude, the answer seems to be that Chiang preferred to sit down with Roosevelt and warn him about the sinister motives of Stalin, something he could not very well do with the Soviet leader present. This fits with Chiang's views of the antagonistic nature of the Soviet-American relations in mid-1943. Chiang may also have feared that he would be presented with a set of demands previously agreed upon by the Soviet Union, the United States, and Britain. Were he confronted by such three-power unanimity, refusal to accept these demands would be tantamount to Chinese self-expulsion from the ranks of the Big Four. Chiang may also have feared that Stalin would call him to account before Roosevelt for China's recent policy in Xinjiang.

One of Chiang's key objectives at the late-1943 conferences was to secure American, Soviet, and British acceptance of China's basic territorial claims, in other words, its claims to Manchuria, Outer Mongolia, and Taiwan. Madame Chiang had conveyed these demands to Roosevelt during their talks in February 1943, and on 1 March she reported to Chiang that Roosevelt had agreed that after the war, Manchuria, Taiwan, the Pescadores Islands and the Ryukyu Islands (!) would be returned to China.[72] Chongqing's claims to Taiwan and the Pescadores were easily satisfied without prejudice to the Soviet Union. Its claims to Outer Mongolia and Manchuria, however, touched directly on Soviet interests.[73] Yet through the dual tripartite conferences at Cairo and Teheran in November–December 1943, Chiang won Soviet endorsement of his claim to Manchuria. He raised the issue of Outer Mongolia, but won no commitment from either Roosevelt or Stalin in this regard.

During their discussion over dinner at Cairo on the evening of 23 November, Chiang and Roosevelt agreed that Manchuria, including the Liaodong Peninsula ports of Luxun (Port Arthur) and Dairen, along with Taiwan and the Pescadores, should be returned to China. Roosevelt also inquired about Chiang's opinion of the status of Tannu Tuva. Tannu Tuva was an area 170,400 square kilometers (65,800 square miles) in the upper reaches of the Yenisei River valley on the northwestern border of Outer Mongolia inhabited by the Turkic-speaking Tuvans. It had been a province of Outer Mongolia until 1911 and in 1914 had become a Russian protectorate. Reoccupied briefly by Chinese forces during the Russian Civil War, in 1921 it was established as an independent country, the Tuvinian People's Republic, under the aegis of the Red Army. In reply to Roosevelt's query at Cairo, Chiang replied that Tannu Tuva had been an integral part of China's Outer Mongolia until it was forcibly taken and annexed by Russia. Together with Outer Mongolia its status would have to be settled in the future through negotiations with the Soviet Union.[74] As we shall see, China's claim to Outer Mongolia, including Tannu Tuva, was one of the basic problems in Soviet-Chinese relations.

These territorial questions, and especially the postwar disposition of Manchuria, were linked to the broader issue of postwar Sino-Soviet relations and to China's rise to great-power status. If China were to be the primary power in postwar East Asia, it would have to recover resource-rich and industrially developed Manchuria. Conversely, Soviet control of Manchuria would vastly strengthen the Soviet position in the Far East and the Pacific. Soviet seizure of Manchuria would also probably doom hopes for postwar amity and cooperation between the Soviet Union and China, an amity which Roosevelt saw as one basis of future world peace. If, as the United States hoped, the Soviet Union entered the war against Japan after the defeat of Germany, Soviet armies would very probably control Manchuria at the war's end. In such a situation, China's recovery of Manchuria would depend on Soviet intentions — and perhaps on American pressure on Moscow. On the other hand, the Soviet Union could be expected to be a responsible postwar power only if its "legitimate security concerns" were fulfilled. This meant first and foremost Soviet access to warm-water ports on the Liaodong Peninsula and rail rights across Manchuria to those ports. This was to be the price that China was to pay for Soviet support for Chiang's program of national grandeur.

The question of Soviet access to warm-water ports on the Liaodong Peninsula was discussed by Roosevelt and Madame Chiang during the latter's stay in Washington in February thru May 1943. No record was kept of these discussions, but in a cable to his wife on 18 June, Chiang instructed her to tell Roosevelt that China was prepared to use Dairen and Luxun jointly only with the United States. In her reply at the end of the month, Madame Chiang informed her husband that Roosevelt had approved of joint use of Dairen, Luxun, and Taiwan by the American and Chinese navies.[75] Chiang repeated the offer of a joint Sino-American base at Luxun during his dinner with Roosevelt at Cairo on 23 November.[76] It is important to realize that Chiang's offer implied the existence of American military bases on the Soviet Union's territorial periphery and Chinese military cooperation with the United States. It implied, in other words, Chinese support for an American effort to contain the Soviet Union. American acceptance of such an offer would have roused Soviet suspicions about the postwar orientation of American foreign policy.

Roosevelt was more concerned with securing Soviet rather than American access to Manchurian ports and countered Chiang's Cairo proposal for Sino-American bases by inquiring about the possibility of converting Dairen into a free port after the war. Chiang replied that he was willing to consider such a possibility when the time came, providing that such an arrangement did not include terms which infringed on China's sovereignty.[77] This was the signal Roosevelt needed to proceed with his mediation of a Soviet-Chinese accommodation.

From Cairo, Roosevelt and Churchill went to Teheran. Stalin was generally disparaging about the possibility of China playing a great-power role in the postwar era, but he endorsed the agreement just concluded at Cairo that Manchuria be returned to China after the war. Stalin also confirmed that the Soviet Union was prepared to enter the war against Japan once Germany was defeated. He expected, however, to be adequately compensated for this effort, noting in this regard that the Soviet Union had no ice-free ports in the Far East. Roosevelt then suggested, and Stalin accepted, the idea of a free port at Dairen under international (i.e., American) guarantee. There was no mention of Luxun or of the status of Outer Mongolia at Teheran.[78]

Chiang learned of Soviet approval of the return of Manchuria to China when he received a cable from Roosevelt just after the Teheran Conference indicating Soviet acceptance of the Cairo communiqué.[79] He learned the cost of this concession from Roosevelt in mid-January 1944: a Soviet presence at Dairen and rail access across Manchuria.[80]

Regarding the issue of Outer Mongolia, Chiang had grounds for cautious optimism. When Chiang raised this issue with Roosevelt at Cairo and explained China's claim to historical suzerainty there, Roosevelt did not reject these claims.[81] In fact, Chiang could well have taken Roosevelt's broaching of the Tannu Tuva issue as implying that he thought Outer Mongolia should be returned to China. Otherwise, why raise the issue of Tannu Tuva at all? The fact that Stalin had not raised the issue of Outer Mongolia at Teheran must also have encouraged Chiang. At worst, Chiang probably concluded, even if he did not formally recover Outer Mongolia, at least he would not be required formally to cede it.

Chiang's Efforts to Rouse American Suspicions

Early in 1944, Chiang moved to strengthen American support for China against the Soviet Union by attempting to exacerbate American fears of the Soviets. American mediation of Sino-Soviet relations would most benefit China if the United States was willing to use its leverage to compel Moscow to moderate its demands, especially regarding Manchuria and the CCP. At Teheran, Stalin had agreed to the return of Manchuria to China, but as the case of Xinjiang had shown, there was a great difference between formal ownership and actual control. It was still possible that China's sovereignty over Manchuria might turn out to be a hollow formality, with real power and control remaining in Moscow's hands. From Chiang's perspective, this danger could be minimized by making Washington more suspicious of Moscow. Increased American anti-Soviet sentiment would also serve another purpose: securing American support in repressing the CCP. If Washington viewed Moscow with suspicion and hostility, and if it viewed the CCP as Moscow's proxy, it was more likely to cooperate with Chongqing in the forcible disarmament of the CCP. Greater U.S. suspicions regarding Moscow would also facilitate Chiang's efforts to use American influence to counter mounting Soviet-Outer Mongolian pressure on Xinjiang.

In the correspondence between Chiang and Roosevelt during 1942 and 1943 there is virtually no mention of Sino-Soviet relations. The one or two references to Sino-Soviet relations have to do with arrangements for the conferences at Cairo and

Teheran. Then, in the early spring of 1944, there was a flurry of exchanges about clashes between China and Outer Mongolia in the Altai region of the border between Outer Mongolia and Xinjiang. Regardless of the exact origin of those incidents, Chiang's response to them was tough. On 19 March, about a week after the original incident, Chiang ordered Eighth War District commander Zhu Shaoliang to deploy two infantry regiments plus antiaircraft and antitank units to Qitai.[82] The forces in the Eighth War District had been among the main recipients of U.S. Lend-Lease equipment, and the use of this equipment to oppose Outer Mongolian forces would not go unnoted in Moscow.

Chiang also used the Altai clashes to educate the American leaders about the sinister nature of Soviet intentions. On 17 March Chiang sent Roosevelt a cable advising that "For your personal information, I should like to advise you of recent significant developments which are matters of grave concern to the prosecution of the war in the Far East." After presenting China's version of the Altai clashes, Chiang told Roosevelt, "This cannot be construed as a local incident, but as a very significant indication of Soviet Far Eastern policy both now and in the future." Chiang also informed Roosevelt that the CCP was preparing to revolt and seize Xian in Shaanxi province on the basis of an understanding reached between the Soviet Union and Japan.[83]

After a noncommittal response from Roosevelt on 20 March, Chiang repeated his warnings in another cable on 29 March. The situation in Xinjiang was quite tense because of the recent attack by Soviet planes and invasion by troops of Outer Mongolia, Chiang said. China's belief in concerted action by the Allies had been "somewhat shaken" by these activities. Moreover, the revolt in western Xinjiang and CCP activities in Shaanxi would assume an even more ominous aspect if Japan invaded Yunnan province, as it was then preparing to do, in advancement of its plan of forcing China out of the war by "bolshevizing this country."[84]

Chiang's argument about Japanese support for the "bolshevization" of China dovetailed with charges of broader Soviet-Japanese collaboration. It is important to note that a charge of Japanese support for communist revolution in China had historical precedents and would have tapped powerful "historic lessons" in the minds of people of Roosevelt's generation. Such a strategy had, in fact, been employed by the German imperial general staff in 1917 and had been effective in eliminating Russia from the war a year later. What Chiang was trying to convince Washington of, was that Tokyo, Moscow, and the CCP were all conspiring to foment revolution in China, push China out of the war, and allow Japan's armies to turn and face the American forces, while the Soviet Union carved out a sphere of influence in Xinjiang and China's northwest. Tokyo, Moscow, and Yan'an would all benefit from such a deal while Washington and, of course, Chongqing, would lose. The recent border incidents and insurrections in Xinjiang, Chiang wanted Roosevelt to believe, were merely the tip of this conspiratorial iceberg.

Roosevelt's lukewarm response to Chiang's dire warnings were instrumental in inducing Chongqing to adopt a more moderate approach to handling the Altai incident. On 1 and 2 April governmental conferences convened in Chongqing to discuss the clashes in Xinjiang and Soviet Ambassador Paniushkin's 31 March reply to

China's several protests regarding these clashes. Chiang Kai-shek was very angry about the incidents and about Moscow's response to China's protests, but Wang Shijie, secretary general of the National Defense Council and counsel to the Military Affairs Commission, advocated a cautious handling of Sino-Soviet relations. In responding to Moscow's note giving the Soviet version of a major clash on 11 March, Wang urged that China merely reiterate the facts and its legal position regarding Outer Mongolia while avoiding words which might cause the incident to expand. A press debate on the merits of the Xinjiang clashes should be avoided at all costs in order not to embarrass the Soviet Union or to complicate a settlement of the issue. Chiang Kai-shek accepted Wang Shijie's cautious approach.[85] Wang Shijie was the key architect and advocate of a conciliatory policy toward the Soviet Union and served as one of Chiang's key advisors on the Soviet Union from early 1944 well into 1948.

Chiang Kai-shek, Wang Shijie, Foreign Minister T.V. Soong, and Chiang's private secretary Chen Bulai met again on 3 April to draft a response to a Soviet TASS news agency statement of the previous day which had covered the same ground as Paniushkin's earlier statement to the Chinese foreign ministry. The meeting decided that Soong would make an oral statement saying: "The Central Government has long ago strictly ordered the anti-bandit military forces in Xinjiang not to cross the Outer Mongolian border. This order is still in effect and has been reiterated." The statement thus left open the possibility that troops from Xinjiang might in fact have crossed the border, albeit in violation of Chongqing's orders. However, Ambassador Paniushkin was also to be told that the 1936 Soviet-Mongolian treaty, which both Paniushkin and the TASS statement had mentioned, was invalid because it violated the 1924 Sino-Soviet agreement.[86]

Chongqing also seized on a Soviet-Japanese agreement of 30 March 1944 as further evidence of secret Soviet-Japanese collaboration. As publicly announced, the 30 March agreement liquidated Japanese mineral concessions on northern Sakhalin Island and extended for five years Japan's fishing rights off Siberia. Chongqing tried to persuade Washington, however, that there were secret protocols providing for broader political-military cooperation attached to the agreement. Chiang raised this issue in a cable to Roosevelt on 4 April. In replying to two earlier cables from Roosevelt urging China to minimize the recent clashes in Xinjiang, Chiang told Roosevelt that four times already he had asked the Soviet ambassador for an explanation of the clashes. No reply was forthcoming until the day after the 30 March Soviet-Japanese agreement was signed, Chiang noted.[87] Chiang did not make explicit the connection between the two events. On 8 April, the chargé d'affaires of the Chinese embassy in Washington further prodded the Americans toward enlightenment when he called at the State Department. He had been directed by his government, the Chinese chargé d'affaires explained, to inquire about American views of the recent Soviet-Japanese agreement. When the State Department official minimized the significance of the agreement, the chargé questioned the accuracy of the American assessment. Why had the agreement been signed just then, he queried?[88] At the end of April, Ambassador Wei Daoming called on Secretary of State Hull to explain in a straightforward manner to the uncomplicated Americans that the 30 March agreement indicated that the Soviet Union was expanding its political moves to the Far East.[89] Finally, early in June,

Chiang Kai-shek sent a letter to U.S. Chief of Staff George Marshall, flatly warning that there was a secret understanding between Tokyo and Moscow which had allowed Japan to withdraw fourteen divisions from Manchuria.[90]

It is unclear just where the stories of a secret Soviet-Japanese agreement originated. Such an agreement apparently did not exist.[91] From one perspective, however, the question of who first concocted the story is moot. What is clear is that Chongqing found it useful for its efforts to influence American policy toward China and the Soviet Union, and that it tried mightily to persuade Washington of the credibility of this bit of disinformation.

Chongqing's charges of secret Soviet-Japanese collusion further strained Sino-Soviet relations. It seemed to Moscow that Chongqing had switched from trying to provoke Soviet-Japanese relations to trying to exacerbate Soviet-American tensions. In talks with American ambassador to Moscow Averell Harriman on 10 June 1944, Stalin complained that Chiang Kai-shek and his entourage were spreading false propaganda about the Soviet Union having signed a secret alliance with Japan and against China. Such "nonsense" was "unfriendly to the Soviet Union," Stalin told Harriman.[92] A month later a report by the director of the Office of Far Eastern Affairs of the U.S. State Department placed Chinese propaganda about a secret Soviet-Japanese deal as the first of three principle causes of "difficulties" in Sino-Soviet relations.[93]

Washington's response to the Altai fighting and to the charges of secret Soviet-Japanese collusion was not as supportive of China as Chiang had hoped. In responding to a 10 April cable from Roosevelt urging patience and Allied unity, Chiang told Roosevelt on 13 April that he "greatly feared" that "it is not in the exercise of self-restraint on the part of China alone that the real answer [to Sino-Soviet problems] could be found." Chiang also raised the possibility of "even more serious developments" which "would not permit the problem to be postponed" and which would have unfortunate consequences "on the world as a whole."[94] American officials discounted Chongqing's charges of Soviet-Japanese collusion and even rebuked Chongqing for spreading them.[95]

On 11 April, a meeting of top-level government officials convened in Chongqing to discuss policy toward the Soviet Union in light of the American attitude. The conference considered several indications of Washington's determination to take a conciliatory approach to Moscow: Roosevelt's 8 April cable to Chiang urging that the Xinjiang incidents be "placed on ice" until after the war; Cordell Hull's 9 April radio speech stressing the necessity of close collaboration among the Four Powers; and Hull's statement to T.V. Soong that he had had Sino-Soviet relations in mind when he made the 9 April speech.[96] Wang Shijie argued that since the United States was committed to a conciliatory approach toward the Soviets, Chongqing should actively seek ways to reestablish good relations with the Soviet Union. If Sino-Soviet relations did not improve, Wang argued, they would deteriorate further. Chiang again accepted Wang's advice.[97]

Six days later, on 17 April, Chiang and Wang Shijie met again to discuss a plan to ease Sino-Soviet tension in Xinjiang as a prelude to winning Soviet support for a key role for China in the new international organization then moving toward formation. Wang's plan included three points. First, the Xinjiang authorities should be

ordered strictly to avoid all border conflicts. Second, Sheng Shicai should be removed
as governor of Xinjiang at the KMT Central Executive Committee plenary session
scheduled for May. Third, once amicable feelings had been reestablished with the
Soviet Union, Chongqing should urge Roosevelt to propose a plan for the organization
of the postwar United Nations organization. Two days later Chiang approved Wang's
plan.[98]

On 25 April, Wang began putting his plan into effect when he met with Ambassador Paniushkin. The ambassador expressed his concern about the anti-Soviet tendency emerging in China and pointed to Sheng Shicai's actions in Xinjiang in this
regard. Wang replied that there was no anti-Soviet trend in China, but only a trend
toward better Sino-Soviet relations. The coldness which then characterized bilateral
relations was merely superficial, resulting from Soviet-Japanese neutrality, Wang
said. Because of that neutrality, the Soviet Union could not speak frankly regarding
the Japanese problem, and this created certain misperceptions in China. By tying
Chinese "misperceptions" to Soviet-Japanese neutrality in this fashion, Wang cleverly exonerated Chongqing of responsibility for the sour state of Sino-Soviet relations
while implying that those relations would grow cordial once Moscow abandoned its
neutral position in the Far East war. Regarding Xinjiang, Wang told Paniushkin that
the situation there was special and could not be dealt with hastily. Sheng Shicai still
had an army of 20,000 men, Wang asserted. This implied both that Sheng would
ultimately be removed and that Chongqing recognized Sheng's responsibility for the
tense state of relations between Xinjiang and Outer Mongolia.[99]

In mid-May 1944 Paniushkin was recalled to the Soviet Union. When he called
on Chiang Kai-shek to take leave, he conveyed the Soviet Union's desire for better
Sino-Soviet relations. The Soviet Union's inability to said China was entirely due
to the demands of the European war, Paniushkin said, but apparently many Chinese
did not understand this. The Soviet Union was very concerned about the anti-Soviet
attitude of many high-ranking Chinese officials. Nonetheless, the Soviet government
felt that China and the Soviet Union needed each other and should have friendly
relations. Perhaps the ambassador's most important point was his assurance that the
Soviet Union no longer aided foreign Communist Parties and that Chiang could be
assured that the Soviet Union was not giving and would not give aid to the CCP.
Chiang responded by giving a virtual assurance of a "change in personnel" in Xinjiang,
to which Paniushkin replied that this would be good because the Soviet Union found
it impossible to work with Sheng Shicai.[100]

Once Paniushkin reached Moscow, Ambassador Fu Bingchang called on him
and reiterated Chongqing's hopes for improved relations and closer contacts. China
hoped, Fu said, for negotiations in order to exchange opinions and solve problems
with the Soviet Union, just as was the case with Soviet-American and Soviet-British
relations. To this end, Fu inquired whether Moscow would be prepared to receive
a delegation led by Foreign Minister T.V. Soong.[101] Moscow did not reply to Fu
Bingchang's suggestion of a high-level Chinese mission to Moscow. In relating this
Soviet nonresponse to the counselor at the American embassy in Chongqing, the
Soviet military attaché linked it to Chiang Kai-shek's failure to fulfill his May promise
to Paniushkin to remove Sheng Shicai.[102] (Sheng was not relieved of his Xinjiang

post until late August 1944.) While Sheng's continued tenure in office may have been one factor leading Moscow to stall on T.V. Soong's mission, a Soviet desire to further increase pressure on Chongqing before settling down to negotiations was probably more important.

Throughout the summer and fall 1944, Soviet pressure on Chongqing mounted. During June and July, the last sixty or so Soviet military advisors were withdrawn from Chengdu, Xian, and Lanzhou.[103] Negative commentary in the Soviet press about the Nationalists increased. In July an editorial in *War and the Working Class* sharply criticized the military helplessness of Chongqing's armies, comparing them unfavorably to Tito's forces in Yugoslavia.[104] In the context of 1944, such a reference to the Yugoslavian Partisans raised an obvious analogy with the forces of the CCP. During July, Moscow also indicated to Washington that it was unwilling to meet with China at the Dumbarton Oaks Conference to discuss the future United Nations organization. Two separate tripartite conferences would have to be held, Moscow said.[105] Then, in August 1944, the Tuvinian People's Republic requested admission to the USSR and in October it became the Tuvan Autonomous Oblast (Region) of the Russian Federated Soviet Socialist Republic.[106] The Soviet Union thus formally annexed a large tract of territory claimed by China—a claim about which Chiang had explicitly informed Roosevelt at Cairo. And all the while a replacement was not sent to fill the post left vacant by Paniushkin's departure in mid-May. Not until June 1945 would a new Soviet ambassador arrive. Finally, throughout the summer and fall of 1944, the Soviet-supported rebellion in western and northern Xinjiang grew. By November, the well-organized and well-armed rebels controlled the strategic and rich Yili region and proceeded formally to proclaim an independent republic.[107]

While systematically stepping up pressure on Chongqing, Stalin began increasing his demands regarding the terms of a postwar settlement, revising the Cairo–Teheran terms in the process. During discussions with American representatives in mid-1944, Stalin ignored the earlier formula for the "internationalization" of Dairen and demanded instead the straightforward "leasing" of not only Dairen but also Luxun and the Manchurian railways. Stalin also added the demand that China recognize the status quo of Outer Mongolia by recognizing its independence. Moscow's new demands regarding the lease of Luxun and Dairen (but not its demand regarding Outer Mongolia) were passed on to Chongqing by American officials in the fall of 1944.[108]

As Soviet pressure mounted, Chiang's relations with the United States were also becoming increasingly strained. On 4 July Chiang received Roosevelt's request that General Joseph Stilwell be appointed commander of all Chinese armies, Communist as well as Nationalist. In the ensuing months General Stilwell developed plans to arm Communist forces and redeploy Nationalist forces away from the borders of the Shaan-Gan-Ning special district to the front line against Japan. Then on 19 September Chiang received Roosevelt's ultimatum demanding Stilwell's appointment. As is well known, Chiang rejected Roosevelt's demand. Several considerations underlay Chiang's rejection. One relevant to our study was a fear that acceptance of Roosevelt's demand and Stilwell's plans would lead to a U.S.-Soviet partition of China. Now that the Soviet Union was committed to enter the Far East war, Chiang wrote in his diary in mid-July, Roosevelt's prime concern had become avoidance of conflict with

Moscow over China. Roosevelt was probably trying to force Chongqing to appease the CCP in order to forestall Soviet suspicions. If this were done, however, Chongqing would have to accept Communist domination of north China. The division of China into Communist and Nationalist areas would continue after the war.[109] Chiang suspected, in other words, that Roosevelt realized that Stilwell's plans would lead to the firmer entrenchment of CCP power in northwest and north China, and that Roosevelt was willing to accept this in order to ensure Soviet-American cooperation. Thus by rejecting Roosevelt's demands, Chiang believed that he was guarding against a possible great power partition of China. To further reduce this possibility, however, it was imperative that Chongqing improve its ties with Moscow.

American Good Offices

Confronted with mounting Soviet pressure and the looming reemergence of the Soviet Union as a major power in the Far East, Chiang Kai-shek desperately needed to improve relations with Moscow. If he did not, the consequences might be catastrophic: the loss of Manchuria and Xinjiang, Soviet support for the CCP, and noninclusion in the Security Council of the incipient United Nations organization. To achieve rapprochement with the Soviet Union, Chiang accepted an American offer of good offices.

American leaders were willing to facilitate Sino-Soviet rapprochement for the sake of both the war effort against Japan and postwar stability. Improved ROC–USSR relations would, they believed, help avert a KMT–CCP civil war thereby helping to keep China in the war against Japan. Poor relations between Chongqing and Moscow, on the other hand, heightened Chongqing's fear of the CCP and made it more inclined to fight the CCP rather than Japan. Poor Sino-Soviet relations also made it less likely that Moscow would restrain, and more likely at some point to arm, the CCP. If cordial Sino-Soviet relations could be reestablished, however, lack of Soviet support for the CCP and perhaps even Soviet pressure on the CCP, might help encourage the CCP to abandon its aim of overthrowing the KMT regime.[110]

America's postwar objectives also made Washington ready to facilitate Sino-Soviet rapprochement. As Roosevelt began turning his attention to creating a stable postwar order, he was confronted with the task of encouraging better Soviet-Chinese relations. Roosevelt believed that after the war a strong, united Nationalist China should fill the power vacuum created by the collapse of Japanese imperialism and the decline of British, French, and Dutch colonial empires. This united China would be encouraged to develop along liberal, pro-American lines, and Roosevelt undoubtedly hoped that China would be prepared to align with the United States against the Soviet Union if the need for that arose. But he also hoped that such a need would not arise and that Sino-Soviet amity could continue along with Soviet-American friendship. His vision of postwar peace and security was based on cooperation among all four of the big powers. Conflict between China and the Soviet Union contradicted this vision; it threatened the postwar peace.

The American effort to promote Sino-Soviet rapprochement began with the mission of Vice-President Henry Wallace to the Soviet Union and the Republic of

China in June 1944. The fact that Wallace took the Moscow–Xinjiang route to China, rather than the more common route through India was itself deemed a significant gesture by Chongqing. Wang Shijie flew to Dihua to welcome Wallace, and to warn Sheng Shicai not to criticize the Soviet Union before Wallace.[111]

Chiang Kai-shek viewed Wallace's mission as very important and put a good amount of energy into preparing for his talks with Wallace.[112] On 10 June, Wang Shijie presented to Chiang a memo outlining the best way the handle Wallace. Roosevelt was extremely concerned with the deterioration of Sino-Soviet relations, Wang's memo pointed out. Chiang should therefore tell Wallace that China desired "good neighbor" relations with the Soviet Union and was willing to listen to any proposals Roosevelt might have in this regard. Chiang should be careful to present a conciliatory attitude toward the Soviet Union. Different Sino-Soviet views on Outer Mongolia should be acknowledged, but Chiang should assure Wallace that China would not press for a settlement of that issue before the end of the war. Regarding the recent conflict in the Altai region, Chiang should deny responsibility for the incident and insist that he was dealing with it in a restrained fashion. Regarding the CCP, Chiang should indicate a willingness to seek a political solution, but stress the growing rebellion of the CCP. Wang also proposed that Chiang push for an Allied agreement that all territories liberated by Allied armies were to be returned to the administration of the original sovereign power. If such an agreement were not reached before the Red Army entered Manchuria and Korea, great problems would result.[113] During his discussions with Wallace, Chiang adhered to the suggestions of Wang's 10 June memo.[114]

Shortly after Wallace departed, Chiang sent a cable to Roosevelt saying how "touched" he had been by Wallace's repeated statements that Roosevelt was eager to see improved Sino-Soviet relations. His own views were in full accord with those of Roosevelt, Chiang said, and he would do everything in his power to help bring about a Sino-Soviet rapprochement.[115] When he left Chongqing, Wallace also carried a letter from Madame Chiang to Roosevelt emphasizing the question of improving Sino-Soviet relations. If Roosevelt had any suggestions about how this was to be done, the letter said, China was ready to accept them and act accordingly.[116]

In mid-July, Roosevelt responded to these messages. He welcomed Chiang's willingness to improve Sino-Soviet relations and was giving serious consideration to the suggestion that the United States use its good offices to arrange a Sino-Soviet conference.[117]

Meanwhile, Chiang's own policy of "active friendship" toward the Soviet Union continued. In a 7 July 1944 memorial address, Chiang praised the bravery of the Soviet Union and its contribution to the war over the past year.[118] Chiang also ordered the initiation of a pro-Soviet press campaign in preparation for more substantial subsequent steps.[119] Among the measures Chiang considered were the proposal of either a treaty of alliance modeled after the Anglo-Soviet alliance or a treaty providing for the nonfortification of the Sino-Soviet border. Eventually, however, both ideas were dropped as impractical.[120] More practical was the removal of Sheng Shicai. On 28 August, Sheng was finally removed as governor of Xinjiang and on 11 September left Dihua for Chongqing.[121] The next month, Wu Zhexiang was replaced as Chongqing's special foreign affairs representative in Dihua as part of an effort to staff Xinjiang with "persona grata" to the Soviet Union.[122] Sheng Shicai's removal was especially significant. Stalin had raised the issue of Sheng's replacement during his discussion with Ambassador Harriman on 10 June and Wallace had conveyed Stalin's wishes in this regard to Chiang. Stalin blamed Sheng for the recent clashes on the border between Xinjiang and Outer Mongolia—thereby implicitly exonerating Chiang Kai-shek—and told the Americans that his replacement would greatly facilitate the improvement of Sino-Soviet relations.[123]

But Chiang's policy of "active friendship" was inadequate to prevent further escalation of Soviet pressure in late 1944. One important element of such pressure was the Soviet attitude toward China at the Dumbarton Oaks Conference.

The Dumbarton Oaks Conference

The Allied powers met at Dumbarton Oaks from 21 August to 7 October 1944 to decide on the structure of the future United Nations organization. In the opinion of Wellington Koo, China's chief delegate at Dumbarton Oaks, the conference represented a "step backward" for China's effort to join the Big Four. Whereas American pressure had forced Soviet acceptance of China's great-power status at the October 1943 foreign ministers' conference, at Dumbarton Oaks the United States acceded to Soviet demands that China be excluded from the main part of the conference at which the key features of the future world organization were discussed.[124]

In mid-July Cordell Hull informed Ambassador Wei Daoming that the Soviet Union was unwilling to meet with China regarding the structure of the future international organization since to do so would damage Soviet relations with Japan. To accommodate Soviet concerns, the United States and Britain agreed to two separate tripartite sessions. Chiang Kai-shek agreed to this split-conference arrangement in part because his showdown with General Stilwell was looming and he did not want to complicate further his relations with Washington. The same day that Chiang accepted a bifurcated conference at Dumbarton Oaks, he received Roosevelt's cable demanding Stilwell's appointment as commander-in-chief of all forces in the China theater.[125] China's leaders were convinced, however, that Moscow's expressed concern for Soviet-Japanese neutrality was a pretext for not meeting with China at Dumbarton Oaks. The real reason, they suspected, was a Soviet reluctance to see China recognized as an equal of the other powers.[126] This interpretation was given substance by Moscow's refusal to allow a Big Four communiqué to be issued at the close of the conference. (The final communiqué referred to neither the Big Three nor the Big Four).[127] This was a year after the four-power declaration at Moscow and at a time when Moscow's military situation was much improved by the opening of the second front in Europe after the Normandy invasion. Chongqing was probably correct in interpreting the Soviet policy at Dumbarton Oaks as a way of increasing the pressure on China; Moscow's refusal to meet with Chinese representatives at Dumbarton Oaks fit with other demonstrations of Soviet displeasure with China in 1944.

The bifurcation of the Dumbarton Oaks Conference meant that China's participation was pro forma. The initial Soviet-American-British conference lasted from 21 August to 28 September, and the second Sino-American-British conference lasted from 29 September to 7 October.[128] Once the second session began, the Anglo-American representatives had already reached agreement with the Soviets on the basic issues after long and difficult negotiations. Not only did they feel that there was no way to reopen discussion of these issues with the Soviets, but the individual representatives were thoroughly exhausted and ready to go home. The strain on Sino-American relations arising from the Stilwell incident also militated against Chinese demands that their participation be more than symbolic. Thus, there was little that the Chinese delegates could do but raise minor issues.[129]

This outcome foiled Chongqing's plans to use the new United Nations organization to place limitations on future Soviet actions in the Far East. In June Chiang had proposed to Vice-President Wallace that a regional organization be set up in the Far East under the auspices of the United Nations and that, before the Soviet Union entered the war there (and by implication before it joined the U.N. Far Eastern council), the United States, China, and Britain should reach agreement on the disposition of territories liberated from Japan's rule.[130] This was consistent with the plan Wang Chonghui had presented to Harry Hopkins at Cairo. If implemented, it would have constrained, and perhaps prevented, Soviet military involvement in the Far East. At least, so Chiang hoped.

The most divisive issue at Dumbarton Oaks regarded whether or not a permanent member of the Security Council who was a party to a dispute brought before that council could be allowed to participate in the council vote, and therefore block action. The United States and Britain argued that it should not. The Soviet Union argued that it should. China had initially favored giving each permanent member a veto because it feared that the powers might unite against it.[131] By the time the Dumbarton Oaks Conference convened, however, Chongqing had shifted and supported the Anglo-American position. But by the time the second phase of the conference opened, the American and British delegations had already accepted the Soviet position and China was in no position to challenge this *fait accompli*. Wellington Koo was very unhappy with this American appeasement of Moscow's "uncompromising" attitude, but there was little he could do about it.[132] Again Chongqing's hope for a Chinese-American-British coalition which might check the Soviets came to naught.

The final collapse at Dumbarton Oaks of Chongqing's plan to establish an international structure to exclude or regulate Soviet entry into the war in the Far East made imperative for Chongqing a United States mediated settlement with the Soviet Union. In other words, it opened the door to the Yalta Conference.

By late 1944 Chongqing's repeated friendly gestures along with American urging may have helped persuade Stalin to make a bid to Chiang. In October Moscow approached Chongqing via Ambassador Harriman and Roosevelt's special representative Patrick Hurley (then in Moscow on his way to China to smooth out Sino-American relations after the Stilwell incident) about a possible summit meeting between Stalin and Chiang. Then, on 7 November, the Soviet embassy in Chongqing informed Jiang Jingguo (Chiang Kai-shek's son) that Stalin was ready to meet with Chiang Kai-shek.[133]

Chiang declined Stalin's invitation. According to KMT sources, this remarkable decision was based on Chiang's fear that Stalin's invitation was part of a plot to estrange Sino-American relations. Ties between Chongqing and Washington were then very strained because of the Stilwell affair, and Chiang believed that Stalin hoped a meeting between the two of them would lead to a further deterioration of Sino-American relations. The American government should not be led to believe, Chiang reportedly concluded, that Moscow and Chongqing were conducting secret negotiations behind Washington's back.[134] There was also speculation in China in late 1944 that Roosevelt would visit China within a year of his election to a fourth term. Chiang may have thought it would be best to wait to balance his meeting with Stalin with a second summit with Roosevelt.[135]

Chiang's rejection of a summit with Stalin also seems to have been influenced by events in Xinjiang. On 12 November the Eastern Turkestan Republic was formally proclaimed. It seemed to Chiang that Stalin was trying to recover the ground he had lost only recently in Xinjiang while professing friendship toward China and reassuring Washington that Sino-Soviet relations were getting better. The way to deal with this Soviet strategy was not by facilitating Moscow's efforts at camouflage but by exposing the true state of Sino-Soviet relations.

In mid-November Chiang approved a plan under which a 40,000-man force of the supposedly crack Second Army would attack the Xinjiang rebels. A key purpose of this offensive was to capture evidence of Soviet involvement which could be presented to the United States. The United States was also to be informed of the extent of the Xinjiang rebellion.[136] Developments in Xinjiang seemed to Chiang to be a clear demonstration of Soviet expansionism, and he hoped that once the United States was presented with evidence to this effect it would agree to help China thwart the Soviet advance. In such circumstances, it would not be useful for Chiang and Stalin to meet because such a summit would defuse Sino-Soviet tension rather than prompting American intervention against the Soviets on China's behalf. But whatever his reasons, Chiang's refusal to meet with Stalin meant that the terms of future Sino-Soviet relations would be negotiated not between Chiang and Stalin, but between Roosevelt and Stalin at Yalta.

Yalta: American Mediation

At Yalta, American and Soviet negotiators worked out the terms of future Sino-Soviet relations which were then presented to Chongqing. Domestic political considerations required that Chiang later plead surprise and outrage at this Soviet-American diktat, but as our narrative has shown, Chiang had long sought American mediation and had indicated to Roosevelt general approval of several of the key elements which were embodied in the Yalta agreement.[137] Moreover, the roots of specific terms of the Yalta agreement traced back to Chiang's 1940 offer of alliance with the Soviet Union.

Chiang did not receive a copy of the Yalta agreement regarding China until 15 June when it was formally handed to him by Ambassador Hurley.[138] But during the four months after Yalta, Chiang learned bit by bit most of what the Big Three had agreed to.[139] From Moscow, military attaché Guo Dequan and Ambassador Fu Bingchang cabled fairly specific and accurate information about the agreement to Chiang in February.[140] On 13 March, Roosevelt briefed Ambassador Wei Daoming on the agreement.[141] Then, on 22 May, Hurley "informally" told Chiang the contents of the agreement.[142]

China's treatment at the Versailles Conference haunted Chiang while he waited to learn the full content of the Soviet-American agreement. Until Chiang learned the precise contents of that agreement, he did not know whether it represented a realization of his hope for U.S. supported Soviet-Chinese rapprochement, or of his nightmare of great-power partition of China. Thus, for the first several months after Yalta, Chiang worried that there might be secret protocols to the agreement under which the Big Three agreed to recognize one another's spheres of influence or other special interests and privileges in China.[143]

Until Chiang learned the precise terms of the Yalta agreement, and until he could plumb American intentions, he needed to keep his options open. This meant delaying the opening of negotiations with Moscow. At Yalta, Stalin had told Roosevelt that T.V. Soong should come to Moscow in late April. Later in February, Soviet officials in Dihua and Chongqing told Jiang Jingguo that the Soviet Union would welcome Chinese proposals for expanded Sino-Soviet cooperation, including a mutual security treaty and intimate cooperation in the economic development of Xinjiang.[144] A further Soviet invitation to China to send a representative to Moscow for talks was extended by Molotov during a speech at the United Nations conference in San Francisco in April.[145]

As the terms of the Yalta deal gradually became clear, Chiang mulled his diplomatic response to it. There were two broad strategies Chiang could pursue. On the one hand, Chiang could seek to uncouple the Soviet Union and the United States and draw the United States into Manchuria in order to check the Soviets. In the Chinese idiom, this was *hu jia hu wei*: to borrow the fearsomeness of the tiger through clever maneuver. If this roused Soviet suspicions of the United States and vice versa, so much the better. While greater Soviet-American tensions increased the risk that Moscow would decide to support the CCP or refuse to withdraw from Manchuria, it also increased the probability that if either of these occurred, the United States would squarely back Chongqing and force Soviet compliance with American-Chinese wishes. Chiang's second diplomatic option was to make generous concessions to Moscow in order to win Soviet support. One of the most important concessions China could make concerned its general international orientation. Moscow clearly desired friendly states on the postwar borders of the Soviet Union, and as Soviet-American tension rose, China's nonparticipation in any future American anti-Soviet bloc would be increasingly valuable to Moscow. Just as Chiang had responded to growing Soviet-Japanese tension in the late 1930s by guaranteeing Moscow in the 1937 Nonaggression Treaty that China would not join the anti-Comintern pact, so in 1945 he hoped to win Moscow's gratitude by opting out of any United States-sponsored anti-Soviet arrangement.

In logical terms, these two strategies of mobilizing American pressure and making concessions to Moscow contradicted one another. Drawing the U.S. into Sino-Soviet relations, involving it in Manchuria, and lining it up beside Chongqing and against Moscow prima facie contradicted an approach in which China stood aloof from Soviet-American conflict. Yet the evidence indicates that Chiang vacillated back and forth between and two and, at times, simultaneously implemented both policies.

In May Chiang began mobilizing American involvement. Harry Hopkins was then preparing to go to Moscow as President Truman's special representative in an effort to stem the erosion of Soviet-American cooperation which had already begun. Chiang hoped that Washington would use Hopkins's trip to get assurances from Stalin regarding future Soviet actions in China. Specifically, Chiang wanted Hopkins to tell Stalin that the United States opposed the establishment of any Soviet "special installations" within China's national territory.[146] Shortly after conveying Chiang's message to Hopkins, T.V. Soong cabled Chiang a favorable prognosis of future U.S. support.[147]

In order to test American willingness to establish a direct presence in Manchuria, on 8 June Chiang ordered T.V. Soong to propose to Truman the establishment of an international air and naval base at Luxun under the auspices of the new United Nations, and to be used jointly by China, the United States, and the Soviet Union. This was a variant of the idea broached by Chiang to Roosevelt at Cairo. If such an arrangement proved unacceptable to the Soviet Union, Soong was to tell Truman, then China would agree to joint Sino-Soviet use, but sovereignty and administrative authority were to remain with China.[148] Later the same day, Chiang directed Soong that under no circumstances could China accept exclusive Soviet control of Luxun.[149] A week after ordering Soong to propose an American presence at Luxun, Chiang commented in his diary that if the United States indicated a willingness to participate in the joint use of Luxun but Moscow rejected this proposal and negotiations collapsed, this would not be unfortunate.[150]

A critical unknown for Chiang was whether or not the United States contemplated landings in north China or Manchuria. A direct American military presence there would greatly limit Moscow's freedom of action and, conversely, strengthen Chiang's hand. Thus, Chiang's 8 June cable also instructed T.V. Soong to inquire about the plans for U.S. military operations in Manchuria. Were American military landings in southern Manchuria or in Korea planned? If it was "inconvenient" for Truman to respond to this, then Soong should inquire of General Marshall. This information would have a very great influence on China's negotiations with the Soviet Union, Chiang informed Soong.[151]

It seems that at this point Chiang had still not decided to strike a deal with Moscow. If the Soviet price were too high and if the United States under its new president could be split away from its Soviet ally and lined up behind China, it might still be possible to use American pressure to moderate Soviet terms. When Chiang made these moves, he had not yet received the full text of the Yalta agreement. Had he known that that text provided for "the lease of Port Arthur as a naval base of the USSR," he probably would have designed a more skillful ploy than proposing an American naval presence at Luxun; perhaps he would have proposed U.S. participation in operating the commercial port at Dairen. As it was, unless the United States was willing to break openly with the Yalta agreement, Chiang's proposal of a multinational naval base at Luxun was doomed. Thus when T.V. Soong raised Chiang's proposal with Truman on 9 June, during the same meeting at which Truman let him read a copy of the Yalta Far Eastern agreement, Truman responded by saying that he would uphold the agreement reached by Roosevelt at Yalta.[152]

Truman's rebuff of this bid for an American presence at Luxun was highly significant to Chiang. It demonstrated the futility, at least for now, of this particular ploy, and the danger that continuing to propose an American presence in Manchuria would antagonize both the United States and the Soviet Union. Thus, on 11 June

Chiang told Soong that he absolutely must not again mention to anyone the plan regarding American participation in air and naval bases at Luxun. This was very important, Chiang warned.[153] Chiang also told him that the use of the term "lease" regarding the Soviet position at Luxun was absolutely unacceptable, and that while he could tell this to the United States, he must *not* ask the United States to raise it with the Soviet Union. It would be best, Chiang said, for China itself to negotiate directly with the Soviet Union.[154] In dropping the effort to draw the United States into Luxun and in deciding not to involve it in persuading Stalin to drop his demand for a "lease," Chiang demonstrated his intention to reassure Moscow by distancing China from the United States. Chiang's 11 June instructions to Soong seem to indicate that at this point he had concluded that as long as the United States was bound to its Soviet ally, it was best to uncouple Sino-Soviet and Sino-American relations. By doing this, he would lessen the chances for a Soviet-American diktat and perhaps win Soviet goodwill. Moreover, if the U.S. was still unwilling to challenge Moscow, it would be counterproductive to antagonize Moscow by trying to use the United States to pressure it.

On 1 June a new Soviet ambassador, Appolon A. Petrov, arrived in Chongqing to the welcome of many editorials in Chinese newspapers calling for better Sino-Soviet relations.[155] Only two days after Petrov's arrival, Chiang received him and formally proposed Sino-Soviet talks. Chiang began his 3 June talk with Petrov by welcoming Soviet participation in the war against Japan and urging Moscow to adopt a generous and farsighted attitude toward China in order to lay the basis for genuine Sino-Soviet friendship and cooperation. After the 1917 Revolution, Chiang said, the Soviet Union helped China recover its territorial sovereignty and abolish the unequal treaties. The Soviet Union should now help China recover Manchuria. Such Soviet assistance would lay the basis for "eternal cooperation" between the Soviet and Chinese peoples and would inspire China to oppose any anti-Soviet movement around the world. If the Soviet Union helped China recover Manchuria, Chiang told Petrov, China was willing to grant railway rights, commercial ports, and "joint use" of air and naval bases there.[156]

Chiang met with Petrov again on 12 June—three days before Chiang received the full text of the Yalta agreement from Hurley. Petrov advanced five preconditions for the conclusion of a treaty of Soviet-Chinese friendship, preconditions which followed the Yalta agreement's treatment regarding Luxun, Dairen, the Manchurian railways, the Mongolian People's Republic, and southern Sakhalin Island and the Kurile Islands. If Chiang agreed to these five conditions, Petrov said, the Soviet Union was prepared to begin negotiating a treaty of friendship.

Chiang's objections to the Soviet preconditions centered on the "lease" (*zujie*) of Luxun. The term *zujie* could not be used, Chiang said, because it implied national humiliation and disgrace and would undermine the very friendship which was the purpose of the treaty. Chiang left unstated the fact that use of this term would rouse charges that he had betrayed the nation, but such an implication was clear. Petrov tried to make a distinction between the term *zujiedi* (lease holding) and *zujie*, asserting that the former implied jurisdiction over an area while the latter did not. Chiang replied that neither term was acceptable. If the lease were for a specified, limited period, Petrov countered, it would not harm China's sovereignty and territorial integrity. Chiang replied that the existence of any "leased territory" would mean that China's territorial sovereignty was not complete. This term simply could not be used. Nor would its use be beneficial to the Soviet Union, Chiang said. Russia's lease of Luxun in 1898 had touched off a whole series of similar demands by other powers: Germany for Qingdao, France for Guangzhouwan, Britain for Weihaiwei. Now too, a Soviet demand on Luxun would lead other nations to make similar demands.

Petrov replied to Chiang's statement of Chinese nationalist sentiments by presenting similar Russian sentiments. In dealing with this problem, Petrov said, China should keep in mind that the Soviet Union was a Pacific Ocean nation which needed warm-water ports. Even more to the point, Petrov informed Chiang that Churchill and Roosevelt had discussed and approved of all five Soviet preconditions. When Chiang tried once again to draw an analogy between 1898 and 1945 and stress his fear of the Soviet Union setting a bad precedent which might be mimicked by other nations, Petrov insisted that the two periods were not comparable: the old Russia was imperialist while the new Russia desired only friendly cooperation with China. Chiang observed that the previous environment had not yet been completely eliminated and that, because of this, such terms as *zujie* could not be used.[157]

In his diary, Chiang explained why he pushed Petrov so hard on the *zujie* issue during their 12 June meeting. Had he not raised this issue before the beginning of formal negotiations and before he received formal notification of the Yalta terms by the United States (Hurley had told Chiang on 11 June that he had been ordered to deliver the Yalta agreement formally to Chiang on 15 June), and before T.V. Soong arrived back from the United States, then Moscow might have concluded that the United States had instigated China to raise this objection, or at least that China had raised this objection only after discussing it with the U.S. This might have caused Moscow to think that China was trying to use the United States to restrain the Soviet Union, Chiang wrote.[158]

On 15 June, Chiang finally learned the exact contents of the Yalta Far Eastern agreement from Hurley. Chiang also received a copy of a memorandum from Truman specifying additional guarantees given by Stalin to Hopkins on 28 May. According to this memo, Stalin agreed to do everything he could to promote China's unification under Chiang's leadership and stipulated that Chiang's leadership would continue after the war. Stalin also renounced any territorial claims in Xinjiang and Manchuria, and agreed to facilitate the reestablishment of Chinese administration in Manchuria.[159]

After receiving the text of the Yalta agreement and the terms of the Hopkins–Stalin note, Chiang made three counterproposals to Hurley on 15 June. One was that the United States and Britain join in any Sino-Soviet agreement. A second stipulated that all four big powers use Luxun. Finally, all four big powers, not merely China and the Soviet Union, should discuss the transfer of southern Sakhalin and the Kurile islands to the Soviet Union.[160] Shortly after Hurley left, Chiang informed Petrov that the *United States conditions* had been received and that the United States was acting as an intermediary and participating in the negotiations.[161] Thus, several days after attempting to moderate Soviet demands by distancing the Republic of China from the United States, Chiang now attempted to moderate Soviet demands by stressing the American role in the negotiations. Only four days after ordering Soong not to raise the idea of an American presence at Luxun, Chiang himself raised this notion.[162] Chiang had switched from unlinking Sino-Soviet-American relations to playing the American card.

Once again, Washington rebuffed Chiang's effort to involve the United States in the Sino-Soviet talks. On 22 June Hurley delivered Washington's reply rejecting unequivocally the possibility of U.S. participation in the use of the Luxun naval base. The United States completely approved Soviet demands, the cable said, and since the Soviet Union was unwilling for any third country to participate in the Luxun base, the United States would not seek to do so.[163] This indication of American unwillingness to pressure Moscow prompted Chiang to move back toward the strategy of uncoupling Sino-Soviet and Soviet-American relations. Thus, when Chiang met again with Petrov on 26 June and outlined the position that Soong would present when talks began four days later in Moscow, he told the Soviet ambassador:

> The Americans say that the various problems mentioned in this memorandum were discussed at the Black Sea [Yalta] conference, that the late President Roosevelt agreed to them, and that President Truman also approves. I myself feel that matters relating to Sino-Soviet relations should be discussed directly by China and the Soviet Union and that it is irrelevant whether or not the United States agrees.[164]

This statement served a dual purpose. On the one hand, it warned Stalin that Chiang would not automatically accept a Soviet-American diktat. Although such resolve would have been virtually insupportable in the face of actual Soviet-American agreement, still it was useful to stake out such a position prior to the beginning of talks. Of equal importance, Chiang was hinting to Stalin that China was ready to remain neutral in any future Soviet-American confrontation. He was careful, however, to keep testing his American option. Shortly before Soong departed for Moscow, he asked Hurley to tell Truman that he would keep the United States informed at all times of the progress of the Sino-Soviet negotiations.[165]

The Moscow Talks: Round One

The Moscow negotiations of the Chinese-Soviet treaty were divided into two rounds separated by the Soviet-American-British summit conference at Potsdam. The first round extended from 30 June until 13 July, the second from 7 to 14 August. The chief Chinese negotiators were Foreign Minister T.V. Soong and, joining the Chinese team during the second round, Wang Shijie. Jiang Jingguo and Ambassador Fu Bingchang were also top-level members of the Chinese team.[166] Stalin headed the Soviet team and himself conducted most of the negotiations assisted by Molotov and Ambassador Petrov.[167] Throughout the negotiations U.S. Ambassador Averell Harriman maintained close contact with T.V. Soong, advising him on tactics and occasionally on the substance of negotiations.[168]

The Chinese negotiating team arrived in Moscow on 30 June 1945 aboard an American aircraft. It was received cordially at the airport by Molotov, President Mikhail Kalinin, important cabinet heads, and the entire diplomatic corps. The same afternoon T.V. Soong was received by Stalin, Molotov, and Petrov.[169] During his initial discussion with Stalin, Soong expressed China's desire to restore the sort of intimate Chinese-Soviet cooperation which had existed in the early 1920s. The complete understanding and sympathy of the Soviet Union was necessary to China, he said; otherwise it would not be possible to "build the nation." Stalin also struck a cordial note in outlining the principles which underlay his China policy. Russia's present rulers were not like those of the past who had wanted to ally with Japan and divide China. Russia's new rulers wanted to ally with China to check Japan. There was also some oblique verbal sparring over China's relations with the United States. In response to an opening query by Stalin about whether his trip had been a pleasant one, Soong commented that lately he had frequently traveled to and from the United States. Stalin picked up on this insinuation and a few minutes later asked him "Has the United States helped China a lot?" Soong replied evasively.[170]

Stalin and the Chinese foreign minister began formal talks at eight o'clock the next evening, setting the pattern of nocturnal talks which was followed throughout the remainder of the negotiations. Stalin opened by throwing a copy of the Yalta Far Eastern agreement before Soong and rudely asking him if he had previously seen the agreement signed by Roosevelt, Churchill, and himself.[171] Soong answered affirmatively and handed Stalin a copy of the memo of the 28 May Hopkins–Stalin talk, stressing that this memo had been given to the Chinese government by Truman himself. Stalin confirmed that the document was accurate and that "this is our position." The two sides then proceeded to review and compare positions on a number of points.

Agreement was readily reached on Japan's cession of the Kuriles and southern Sakhalin to the Soviet Union, the return of Manchuria to Chinese sovereignty, and the problem of the CCP. Major differences existed regarding the questions of the Manchurian railways, Dairen, and Luxun. Stalin initially demanded nothing less than restoration of the full territorial limit of the 1898 concession on the Liaodong peninsula and Soviet operational control over the Manchurian railways plus associated coal mines and enterprises. Regarding Luxun, however, Stalin made a minor concession at the very outset. When Soong raised the issue of Luxun, Stalin replied that "In order to accommodate Chairman Chiang's hopes and views" he was ready to use the term "joint use" rather than "lease." He did not wish to establish a "harmful precedent" for China, Stalin said. The Soviets had long known that Chiang would object strenuously to a "lease" arrangement at Luxun and Stalin's insistence on this provision at Yalta and his subsequent abandonment of it during the first negotiating session suggest that Moscow had all along intended this as a valuable "throwaway" item. Stalin subsequently used this "major concession" to demand a Chinese *quid pro quo* on the Mongolian issue.

The issue of Outer Mongolia proved to be the most divisive issue of the Moscow talks. Indeed, it came close to torpedoing the talks entirely. This is a point which Westerners with their utilitarian orientation frequently have difficulty understanding. To grasp the importance of the Mongolian issue to Chiang it is necessary to understand how that issue was linked to Chiang's nationalist credentials. One of the precepts deeply ingrained in the consciousness of most Chinese is the notion that China is, or ought to be, a single political entity. China might be fragmented for greater or lesser periods of time, but over the long run it will, and ought to, reunite into a single, great "China." Even in ancient China, which had more of a cultural than a national or racial consciousness, leaders who relinquished parts of "Chinese territory" to "barbarian" control were condemned as vile traitors by subsequent generations. To most Chinese, both Inner and Outer Mongolia had been a part of China since the founding of the Yuan dynasty in the thirteenth century. Though largely populated by the non-Han Mongols, it was, in Chinese minds, a part of the territorial expanse of "China." To relinquish such as massive tract of "Chinese" territory as Outer Mongolia would have weakened Chiang's claim to the right to represent Chinese nationalism.

But more was involved in the issue about Outer Mongolia than mere nationalist symbols. Rather, it touched in a very real way on the future, long-term balance of power between the Soviet Union and China. Outer Mongolia had very real geopolitical importance. In the hands of a power hostile to the Soviet Union (e.g., Japan, the United States, or a future, powerful China), it could pose a great threat to the trans-Siberian rail line. In Soviet hands, it would put the Red Army within easy striking distance of Beiping and the neck of southern Manchuria. Both Chiang and Stalin recognized this. Chiang's objective was probably to maintain China's shadow suzerainty over Outer Mongolia in the long-range hope that in the future China would be powerful enough to give substance to that nominal claim. Stalin sought to prevent exactly such an eventuality.[172]

Chiang had outlined his stance on Outer Mongolia to Petrov during their 26 June meeting in Chongqing. The "status quo" in Outer Mongolia, according to Chiang, was that China still retained suzerainty (*zongzuquan*) there—as recognized by the Soviet Union in the Sino-Soviet agreement of 1924. But Outer Mongolia also enjoyed a high degree of autonomy which China was willing to continue allowing, including autonomy in the military and diplomatic spheres. Moreover, Chiang said, the question of Outer Mongolia was linked to the question of Tibet, implying that Chinese concessions to Moscow regarding Outer Mongolia would lead to demands from London for similar concessions regarding Tibet. Because of this complex situation, it would be best to avoid mention of the problem of Outer Mongolia altogether. If this was impossible, Chiang said, China was willing formally to grant Outer Mongolia a high degree of autonomy, but with a provision for retention of suzerainty by China. Such a solution meant that Chiang's government would not have to "recognize" the independence of Outer Mongolia.

Stalin made clear during the second and third sessions on 2 and 7 July that Chiang's position on Outer Mongolia was totally unacceptable. The people of Outer Mongolia did not want to be ruled by China but wished to be independent, Stalin told Soong. Moreover, Outer Mongolia was already an independent nation which had formally declared itself to be and acted as such. China must recognize this fact, Stalin said; it must recognize the status quo. Stalin rejected China's interpretation of the term "status quo" on the grounds that the Yalta agreement had been drafted by Molotov and that the phrase pertaining to Outer Mongolia had not been revised by the American or British negotiators. The authors of an agreement should know what the intent of that agreement was, Stalin insisted. Moreover, the inclusion of the phrase "Mongolian People's Republic" in parentheses in the Yalta agreement, indicated that the "status quo" involved the existence of an independent nation.

Stalin also adduced reasons of Soviet national security to require Chinese recognition of the independence of Outer Mongolia. Pulling out a map of the Far East, Stalin explained that if an enemy attacked Siberia from Outer Mongolia, as Japan had once hoped to do, the Soviet Far East would be virtually indefensible. Japan's recovery was certain, Stalin said, and although alliance with China and a naval base at Luxun might be adequate for the defense of Siberia over the next twenty or thirty years, the more distant future was uncertain and an independent and Soviet-allied Outer Mongolia was vital to the long-term security of the Soviet Union.

Soong attempted to counter these arguments by assuring Stalin that China had no objection to Soviet troops being stationed in Outer Mongolia and that China was willing to grant Outer Mongolia a high degree of autonomy. Stalin found such arrangements unacceptable. Nothing less than Chinese recognition of the independence of Outer Mongolia would do. Stalin also made clear that Chinese recognition of this independence was linked to Soviet acceptance of China's demands regarding Manchuria and the CCP.[173] After the second session deadlocked over the independence issue on 2 July, Soong sought instructions from Chiang. He also conveyed Harriman's views on this issue to Chiang. Roosevelt had never considered this problem in depth, Harriman had told Soong, but he realized that domestic political considerations would prevent China from recognizing Outer Mongolia's independence. The next day Soong asked Chiang whether negotiations should be broken off if Stalin continued to demand the recognition of Outer Mongolian independence.[174]

At this point, Chiang decided to employ a more personal diplomacy and ordered Jiang Jingguo to meet privately with Stalin and explain why Chiang could not recognize Outer Mongolia's independence. Jiang had lived, studied, and worked in the Soviet Union from 1925 until 1937, spoke fluent Russian, and had taken a Russian wife. When he met with the Soviet leader at his father's direction, Jiang outlined the domestic constraints confronting his father. China had struggled for eight years to recover lost territory, Jiang said. If the National Government now ceded Outer Mongolia, the people would not forgive it but would charge it with "selling national territory" (*chumai guotu*). In this way, the government would lose the popular support on which the war effort depended. Stalin was unmoved by Jiang's arguments. Perhaps what Jiang said was true, he replied, but China was now seeking Soviet help, not vice versa. If China was itself strong enough to defeat Japan, the Soviet Union naturally would not make demands on it. This, however, was not the case. Stalin went a bit further in revealing the future uncertainties he feared. Not only was Japan's revival as a major power certain and renewed Japanese aggression possible, Stalin said, but China itself would grow strong once it was united. There was also a possibility that the United States would someday attempt to use Outer Mongolia as a base from which to attack the Soviet Union. Treaties of alliance and friendship were unreliable, Stalin said, and only full Outer Mongolian independence would guarantee the Soviet Union against future attack from that quarter.[175]

On 5 July Chiang convened a conference of ranking officials in Chongqing to discuss the Moscow talks. Some officials favored outright rejection of Stalin's demand on Outer Mongolia. Others argued that Soviet guarantees regarding Manchuria and Xinjiang should not be discarded lightly. Moreover, without an agreement limiting Soviet actions, the Red Army might seize not only Manchuria, Xinjiang, and Inner

Mongolia, but part of northern China as well. After a long debate, the conference decided to accept conditionally Stalin's demands regarding Outer Mongolia.[176] That evening Chiang indicated in his diary that he shared the concerns voiced earlier in the day. If Stalin's demands regarding Outer Mongolia were rejected, Chiang wrote, it would be impossible to reach agreements securing the territorial and administrative integrity of Manchuria and Xinjiang or clarifying the CCP problem. In any case, Outer Mongolia had long been occupied by the Soviet Union and China's claim to it was an "empty name." It would not be wise, Chiang wrote, to risk "national calamities" for the sake of "mere formality."[177]

The next day Chiang summoned Hurley and asked that he immediately convey to Truman the news of the "maximum concessions" he was prepared to make to Stalin on Outer Mongolia, Luxun, Dairen, and the Manchurian railways.[178] T.V. Soong also sought American intervention at this point, asking Harriman to cable Washington to ascertain the U.S. interpretation of the term "status quo" and explaining to him that, in China's opinion, Stalin's demands on Outer Mongolia exceeded the terms of the Yalta agreement.[179]

Truman rejected the Chinese call for American intervention, though not in an unequivocal fashion. On 4 July he directed Harriman that the United States would not act as an interpreter on any part of the Yalta agreements in connection with the Moscow talks. But Truman bent this principle by informing Harriman that he might "informally" confirm to Soong his understanding that, as far as the United States was concerned, the absence of discussion of the term "status quo" at Yalta implied maintenance of the present factual and *juridical* status of Outer Mongolia. "For your information only," Truman told Harriman, the United States felt the Yalta agreement meant that de jure sovereignty over Outer Mongolia remained with China.[180] On 8 July Harriman conveyed this "private" "unofficial" opinion to Soong.[181]

On 7 July, Chiang had cabled a new proposal to Soong which, in effect, traded Outer Mongolia for a major reduction in Soviet demands in Manchuria. In exchange for Soviet guarantees regarding Manchuria, Xinjiang, and the CCP, Chiang's cable read, China was willing to "consider" the independence of Outer Mongolia. Regarding Manchuria, Stalin would have to agree to respect unconditionally China's sovereignty there. This would entail acceptance of Chinese jurisdiction over Dairen and civil jurisdiction over Luxun, and "joint operation" (*gongtong jingying*) rather than "joint management" (*gongtong guanli*) of the Manchurian railways. Regarding Xinjiang, all "lost areas" (e.g., areas under the sway of the Eastern Turkestan Republic) would have to be returned to the control of the central government. Regarding the CCP, Yan'an would have to submit completely to the military and civil orders of the central government. When the National Assembly convened and the government reorganized, some Communists could be taken into the cabinet, but there absolutely would not be a "coalition government." "If China could be unified to this degree," Chiang said, then he was willing to "voluntarily settle" the problem of Outer Mongolia. After the war, Chiang proposed, a plebiscite could be conducted there and if the vote favored independence, China's National Assembly could then be petitioned to recognize it. If the Assembly approved this petition, then the government would ratify it.[182]

Although Chiang's cables apparently arrived before the third session opened at eleven o'clock on the evening of 7 July, Soong chose to make one more attempt to persuade Stalin before agreeing to cede Outer Mongolia. While it is possible that he did not read Chiang's new directive before going to the 7 July session, it seems more likely that he disagreed with Chongqing's decision to yield on the issue of Outer Mongolia. As we shall see, he would step down as foreign minister rather than sign a document relinquishing China's claim to Outer Mongolia. In any case, on the evening of 7 July, Soong explained to Stalin that although China's initial position had been that the question of Outer Mongolia should not be mentioned in the Soviet-Chinese agreement, because the Soviets attached such importance to this issue, China was willing to concede this point and deal with this issue in the treaty. Consistent with the Yalta agreement, he said, China would agree to "uphold" and "agree with" the status quo; Soong carefully avoided using the pernicious word "recognize." This "status quo" included the stationing of Soviet troops in Outer Mongolia and Moscow enjoying the right to send troops there whenever the Soviet Union was threatened. China was also prepared to give Outer Mongolia a high degree of autonomy, including the power to enter into military agreements with the Soviet Union. When Stalin cut through the Chinese foreign minister's vagueness with the question "Will it be a part of China?" he did not give a direct reply. Instead, the foreign minister asked Stalin to "face reality" and understand that China's government simply could not "recognize" Outer Mongolia:

> The reason why we cannot recognize Outer Mongolia's independence is very simple. Survival is the first law of nature. Any Chinese government which signs an agreement ceding Outer Mongolia cannot continue to survive. . . . Our government does not believe that it can continue to survive it if recognizes Outer Mongolian independence. Even China's most extreme liberals adamantly oppose giving independence to Outer Mongolia. [183]

Stalin was unmoved: "We cannot compromise on this issue." China did not now object to Soviet troops being stationed in Outer Mongolia, Stalin pointed out, but what about twenty or thirty years hence? Stationing troops in Chinese territory was not like stationing them in some small country, which was "relatively natural," Stalin said. The session ended in complete disagreement on the issue of Outer Mongolia:

Soong: Marshall Stalin has frankly explained his own plan, and I am impressed by its farsightedness. But at the same time we ourselves have present and future problems, both of which involve the most urgent matter of survival. Because of this we advanced our realistic proposal about Outer Mongolia.
Stalin: But this proposal is not realistic.
Soong: In the view of my government, it is realistic.
Stalin: But we do not agree.
Soong: This is in accordance with the directions I have received.
Stalin: Let us conclude here.
Soong: It is very regretful that Your Excellency cannot understand our position. From the Chinese point of view, it is an extremely realistic position.
Stalin: It is very regretful that Your Excellency also cannot understand our position. Let us conclude here. [184]

Although he had already ordered Soong to give way on Outer Mongolia, Chiang still thought American pressure on Moscow might be useful. Thus, on 8 July, the day after he ordered Soong to accept Moscow's Mongolian demands, Chiang replied to Truman's cable of 15 June. If the president had any opinions regarding the ongoing Sino-Soviet negotiations, he would be glad to hear them, Chiang said.[185] Here again was the combination of a willingness to conciliate Moscow and the mobilization of U.S. pressure. It is possible that Chiang hoped to rouse American suspicions by making "maximum concessions" to the Soviet Union on the Outer Mongolian issue and then solicit American intervention. Chiang knew from Roosevelt's 13 March comments to Wei Daoming and Harriman's 2 July comments to Soong that the United States thought China should retain at least nominal suzerainty over Outer Mongolia. Chiang's apparent willingness to back down on precisely the issue on which the United States had repeatedly and specifically indicated its support, and his subsequent attempt to rally U.S. support on that issue, may have been a way of combining Chinese conciliatory attitudes and American pressure on Moscow in a way which would give Chongqing the advantages of both. Washington would bear the responsibility for blocking Chinese "recognition" of Outer Mongolia while Chiang would reap the benefits of a conciliatory attitude toward Moscow. More probably, Chiang was simply desperate.

The fourth negotiating session opened on 9 July at nine in the evening. Soong apparently had learned from discussions with Molotov that the Soviet position on Outer Mongolia had not changed, because he opened the session with a statement stressing the magnitude of the concession China was now prepared to make. Since 1931, he said, Japan had repeatedly tried to force China to recognize the independence of Manchuria. All such efforts had failed. China had also repeatedly refused Soviet demands that it recognize the independence of Outer Mongolia because doing so would go against the "basic nature of the Chinese people" and would undermine the stability of China's government. Now, however, China was prepared to make the "greatest sacrifice" for the sake of "eternal peace" between China and the Soviet Union. In exchange for Soviet guarantees regarding China's territorial unity and administrative integrity, China was prepared to "permit" (*yunxu*) independence for Outer Mongolia after Japan's surrender. The modalities of this "permission" would include a plebiscite in Outer Mongolia and a unilateral declaration by the Chinese government. The boundary between Outer Mongolia and China was also to be delineated on the basis of old *Chinese* maps which showed the Altai region as part of Xinjiang.[186]

Once the Chinese side had yielded on the critical issue of Outer Mongolia, Stalin proceeded to indicate the specific guarantees he was prepared to give on other critical issues. When Soong brought up Xinjiang by asking how the Soviet Union could help suppress the rebellion there, Stalin suggested, probably in jest, that the Red Army be sent to Xinjiang. The Chinese foreign minister declined the offer and suggested that action to suppress "smuggling" of arms from the Soviet Union into Xinjiang might be more appropriate. Stalin agreed. Regarding Manchuria, Stalin told the foreign minister: "I have already said that I am willing to make any declaration your side desires. We recognize China's complete sovereignty in Manchuria." On the question of the CCP, Stalin was just as unequivocal:

> Regarding the Chinese Communist Party, we do not support them and have no intention of supporting them. We believe that China has only one government. If there is more than one government in China, or something that calls itself a government, this naturally

is a problem that China itself should solve. Regarding the matter of assistance, Chairman Chiang says that it should go to the central government and this is what we have done in the past. If Your Excellency needs our assistance and we are able to help, naturally it will go to Chairman Chiang's government.[187]

Soong later returned to the matter of the CCP and asked Stalin's nonofficial, private opinion about it. Again Stalin washed his hands of the CCP:

Stalin: What does Your Excellency wish? Your Excellency has said that he wishes us not to give weapons to the Communists and to assist China, to assist the government of Chairman Chiang, did you not?

Soong: Yes.

Stalin: Very good. But what else does Your Excellency wish? Do you wish for us to send an army to help you eradicate the Communist armed forces? (*Stalin smiles*)

Soong: This is not what I had in mind. I wish for Your Excellency to be clear about our position. We are willing to use political methods to seek a solution.

Stalin: This is a good policy. They are outstanding patriots. It you are able to find a political situation, it would not be bad.

Soong: We hope that the Communist armies will be incorporated into the government's armed forces.

Stalin: This is a legitimate request. China must have only one government and one armed force.

Soong: We are prepared for them to enter the sort of wartime cabinet we have proposed and the military committee. We cannot permit them to stand against us.

Stalin: The situation at present truly does not give one a good impression.[188]

What Soong was implying was that Stalin should order, or at least pressure, the CCP to relinquish their armed forces and accept a subordinate role in China's KMT-dominated political structure. As we shall see in the next chapter, Moscow was, in fact, still cabling various instructions to Yan'an in mid-1945, although Mao accepted or ignored them as suited his purposes. Stalin no doubt concealed from Soong just how little influence he had with the CCP. Indeed, Chongqing's belief in Soviet leverage with the CCP was a useful bargaining ploy for Stalin.

The last several sessions of the first round of talks concentrated on the nuts and bolts of the Dairen, Luxun, and the Manchurian railways issues. When the talks had begun, Stalin demanded exclusive Soviet military authority over virtually the entire Liaodong Peninsula and a special maritime zone extending 100 kilometers from the Luxun harbor. Civil authority would be in Chinese hands, but the Soviet Union would exercise a veto over the appointment of civil officers. Moreover, the use of Luxun would be restricted to the Soviet and Chinese navies. Dairen harbor was to be owned jointly by China and the Soviet Union, managed by a joint Sino-Soviet commission with a Chinese chairman and a Soviet chief executive. Dairen would also be used solely by Soviet and Chinese ships. The Manchurian railways were to be jointly owned, but guarded by Soviet troops and controlled by Soviet managers. The Soviet Union would have the right to move troops over these lines in wartime. By the end of the first round of talks on 13 July, Soong had been able to whittle down these Soviet demands. Considerable differences still remained, however, regarding the administrative structures to be set up at Dairen and Luxun, the geographic limit of the

Luxun defense zone, the peacetime transit rights of Soviet troops across Manchuria, and the management structures of the two Manchurian railways.

These seemingly narrow differences reflected a clash between Chiang's determination to safeguard China's effective control over Manchuria and Stalin's determination to secure Manchuria as a security buffer for the Soviet Union. They also reflected Chiang's fears about possible Soviet sponsorship of a "people's republic" in Manchuria. Unless the Soviet presence in Manchuria was carefully contained, Moscow might be tempted to help the CCP seize control over that region. Although Moscow claimed to recognize China's sovereignty over Manchuria, if Soviet troops and personnel were free to move across the territory, and if the major transportation grid of the region were under Soviet control, then Moscow could easily find ways of rendering China's sovereignty there nominal. Chiang feared that the specific, relatively narrow gains conceded to the Soviet Union in Manchuria might be a beachhead for the establishment of Soviet hegemony there while nominally respecting Chinese sovereignty. After all, such had been the case in Manchuria prior to 1904 and in Xinjiang prior to 1942. In those instances also, relatively narrow legal rights had been used to establish effective political, economic, and even military domination. Now, Chiang feared, Moscow intended to do this once again, perhaps with Mao Zedong playing the role played by Sheng Shicai in Xinjiang during the 1930s. He bargained away Outer Mongolia to win a substantial reduction of Soviet demands in Manchuria, but even the remaining Soviet position there might serve as a basis for Soviet hegemony. Chiang needed American intervention in Manchuria not so much to alter the specific terms under negotiation, but to ensure that the terms of the treaty, whatever they were, would not be transformed into a broad Soviet hegemony.

After Potsdam: The Shift in American Policy

The Moscow talks adjourned on 13 July so that Stalin and Molotov could attend the Soviet-American-British conference at Potsdam. Chongqing then began pressing for American intercession at Potsdam. Chiang and T.V. Soong wanted the United States to raise with the Soviets the various issues remaining in dispute and to press Moscow to accept China's demands on those issues. Just before the 12 July meeting in Moscow, Soong met with Harriman and outlined the status of the talks and the "maximum Chinese concessions" he would advance at the final session the next day. "If no agreement is reached," the Chinese foreign minister hoped that Harriman would report to Truman on the points remaining in dispute. Soong also asked Harriman to tell Truman that "in order to meet Stalin's demands [Soong] had gone beyond the Yalta agreements in agreeing to recognize the independence of Outer Mongolia."[189] Soong told Harriman that he was hopeful Truman would be able either to persuade Stalin to accept the Chinese position or to work out an acceptable compromise at the forthcoming Potsdam Conference.

After Soong's preparatory work with Harriman, Chiang himself acted. On 19 July, he met with Petrov and gave him a long message for Stalin reviewing China's position on the issues of Outer Mongolia and Manchuria, and telling Stalin, "I have frankly put forward all I could to meet Soviet needs." The message closed: "Since the Yalta proposals were put forward through the American government, and since Mr. Harriman on behalf of the President has asked that the American government be kept fully informed, I shall inform President Truman of this message to you."[190] The next day Chiang sent Truman the full text of his cable to Stalin. Chiang's message to Truman ended:

> Although China was not represented at the Yalta conference, You, Mr. President, will realize that we have gone to the limit to fulfill the Yalta formula. We have even gone beyond it in the case of Outer Mongolia. We may even have already gone beyond the limit that the Chinese people will support. I trust that in your conversations with Generalissimo Stalin you would impress [on him] the eminently reasonable stand we have taken, so that he will not insist on the impossible. Hoping for your prompt action and support and awaiting your reply.[191]

Of all the issues still unresolved by the time the first round ended, the issue of Outer Mongolia, that is the territorial issue, was clearly the most critical to maintaining Chiang' nationalist legitimacy. Repeated signals from Washington indicated that the United States agreed with Chongqing's interpretation of "status quo" of Outer Mongolia. These seeming American signals probably persuaded Chiang to focus on this issue and make it the touchstone of Soviet sincerity. This was a miscalculation. The Americans proved to be much more concerned with free access for their goods through Dairen, than with who owned Outer Mongolia.

Chiang probably hoped that Soong would be called to Potsdam and that the United States would arbitrate a Sino-Soviet understanding along the lines desired by Chongqing. A number of American civilian officials in fact wanted Truman to raise with Stalin the narrower U.S. interpretation of the Yalta Far Eastern agreement and the ways in which Soviet demands on China exceeded that interpretation.[192] Indeed, a proposed Soviet-American protocol which would have narrowly limited Soviet interests in Manchuria and reaffirmed the "open door" was among the materials included in Truman's briefing book for Potsdam.[193] Under the urging of his military advisors, however, Truman rejected this advice for the sake of securing early Soviet entry into the war against Japan.[194] During his discussions with Harry Hopkins in May, Stalin had said that the date on which the Red Army began operations in the Far East was dependent on Chinese acceptance of the Yalta terms.[195] Therefore, when Truman went to Potsdam, he believed that early Soviet entry into the war in the Far East depended "a great deal" on the successful conclusion of the Sino-Soviet negotiations.[196] During the Potsdam Conference, Stalin and Molotov repeatedly reiterated this linkage.[197] In this regard, Stalin's strategy mirrored Chiang's: use the American desire to reduce its casualties in the war as a lever to compel Washington to pressure China into acceding to Soviet demands—or at least not to pressure the Soviet Union on China's behalf. During the first round of the Moscow talks, Stalin's strategy worked.

Several days after Stalin made clear at Potsdam the linkage between China's acceptance of the Yalta terms as interpreted by Moscow and Soviet entry into the war against Japan, Truman rejected Chiang's request that the United States mediate Sino-

Soviet relations. In replying on 23 July to Chiang's 20 July cable seeking American intercession, Truman said bluntly:

> I asked that you carry out the Yalta agreement but I had not expected that you make any concessions in excess of that agreement. If you and Generalissimo Stalin differ as to the correct interpretation of the Yalta agreement, I hope you will arrange for Soong to return to Moscow and continue your efforts to reach complete understanding. [198]

Chiang has asked Truman to discuss outstanding issues in the Sino-Soviet talks at Potsdam, and asked specifically for support on the issue of Outer Mongolia. The acerbic reply of 23 July did not mention either of these. Moreover, its tone was one of rebuke. Its message seemed clear: the United States would not intervene in the Moscow talks. Chiang had gambled on American support on the issue of Outer Mongolia and lost.

The failure to secure American intercession at Potsdam led to T.V. Soong's resignation as foreign minister. The day after Truman's blunt telegram arrived, Soong told Wang Shijie that he intended to resign as foreign minister and that he hoped Wang would assume that position and conclude the negotiations in Moscow. [199] Soong now faced responsibility for signing an agreement relinquishing China's legal claim to Outer Mongolia and feared that this would doom his future political ambitions. It was better to resign and let someone else bear the onus of ceding part of China's national territory. On 30 July, he resigned as foreign minister and was replaced by Wang Shijie. [200]

Wang Shijie was less concerned about Outer Mongolia than about promptly concluding an agreement which might help constrain Soviet actions in Manchuria and toward the CCP. Without such an agreement, he wrote in his diary on 4 August, the problems associated with the Soviet invasion of Manchuria would be much greater. It was even possible that the Soviet Union might recognize a CCP regime in that region. [201]

Round Two of the Moscow Talks

When the second round of Sino-Soviet negotiations began in Moscow on 7 August— the day after the atomic bomb fell on Hiroshima and the day before Moscow declared war on Japan— the calculations of Washington and Moscow had changed. The successful testing of the atomic bomb in New Mexico on 16 July 1945 led to an American reappraisal of the costs and benefits associated with a Soviet entry into the war against Japan. As it became clear to U.S. leaders that Soviet help might not be essential to achieving the early surrender to Japan, the costs of a Soviet presence in Manchuria began to weigh more heavily. This led, in turn, to a reversal of the U.S. policy of noninvolvement in the Sino-Soviet talks which had prevailed throughout the first round of those talks. Stalin, for his part, was now anxious to reach an agreement with China in order to provide a legal basis for the Soviet presence in Manchuria and thus made several important concessions during the first session of the resumed talks. [202]

On 8 August, the United States formally intervened in the Moscow talks on China's behalf. Three days earlier Truman, while still in mid-Atlantic on his way home from Potsdam, had ordered Harriman to inform Stalin that while the United States had not withdrawn its support for the Yalta agreement, it believed that Soong had already met the requirements of that agreement and hoped that the Soviet Union would not press for further Chinese concessions which might adversely affect U.S. interests without prior consultations. The United States was especially concerned about the possible inclusion of Dairen in the Soviet military zone.[203]

Harriman conveyed Truman's message to Stalin and insisted on a narrow interpretation of Soviet rights under the Yalta agreement. What Roosevelt had meant to do by recognizing Soviet "preeminence" at Dairen and on the Manchuria railways, Harriman said, was merely to protect Soviet commercial transit traffic across Manchuria and to the high seas. Stalin rejected this narrow interpretation of the Yalta agreement, insisting that "preeminence" entitled Russia to such institutional guarantees as a role in the administration of Dairen and its harbor and the inclusion of Dairen in a military zone. Unless Dairen were thus included, he said, it could not be defended against Japanese agents and saboteurs. Stalin also insisted that his demands violated neither the American "open door" policy nor the Yalta agreement and were, in fact, quite generous. Under the Yalta agreement's provisions for the reestablishment of Russia's pre-1904 rights, Stalin said, he could have demanded much more from China. The Chinese were repaying his generosity, Stalin told the American representatives, by treating the Soviets as unwelcome and undesirable guests, and wanted to put the Soviet Union in a position where it could not operate.[204]

The next day Harriman informed Wang Shijie of his talk with Stalin and urged Wang not to accept any arrangement at Dairen which violated the "open door" policy. Stalin had agreed, Harriman told Wang, to a joint Soviet-American statement about maintaining the "open door" at Dairen.[205] Later the same day, Harriman told Soong that Chinese acceptance of any demands exceeding the U.S. interpretation of the Yalta agreement (e.g., an overly large military zone at Luxun or the lease of port facilities at Dairen) would be interpreted by the United States as being made with an understanding that the United States did not support these concessions and that they were made with an eye to "obtaining Soviet support in other directions."[206]

Events moved very fast during the second round of talks and placed mounting pressure on both sides to reach an agreement. On 8 July Molotov informed Wang Shijie of the Soviet declaration of war against Japan and expressed his hopes for a joint Soviet-Chinese victory over Japan. Wang replied with an expression of gratitude for Soviet friendship toward China as demonstrated by Moscow's abolition of the unequal treaties in the 1920s and its assistance to China's war of resistance in the 1930s.[207] The next day Wang cabled Chiang that, because of the Soviet entry into the Pacific war, it was even more urgent to reach an agreement with Moscow.[208] The next day, 9 August, the second atomic bomb devastated Nagasaki.

On 10 August Wang Shijie heard a British Broadcasting Corporation broadcast announcing Japan's acceptance of the Allied Potsdam declaration calling for unconditional surrender. The Chinese delegation conferred immediately to consider the implications of Japanese surrender on Sino-Soviet relations. There was general agreement that if a treaty were not rapidly concluded, Soviet terms would harden once the Red Army occupied Manchuria. Moreover, without a treaty China would be powerless to limit Soviet support for the CCP or to ensure eventual Soviet withdrawal from Manchuria. But in spite of these pressing considerations, the Chinese delegation decided to make one final push for further Soviet concessions.[209]

Wang and Stalin opened the next plenary session that same evening at nine o'clock. During the course of the evening, Stalin made a major concession by dropping his demand for Soviet participation in the civil administration of Dairen through a joint committee (Harriman had taken objection to such an arrangement during his 8 August meeting with Stalin) and by dropping his demand for a veto over Chinese civil officials at Luxun. The Chinese side made a minor concession on the Dairen issue by agreeing to hire a Soviet as harbor pilot. Stalin also agreed that the Soviet withdrawal from Manchuria would begin within three months of Japan's defeat but refused to set a firm deadline for completion of the withdrawal. At the end of the 10 August session the two sides remained deadlocked on three issues. Moscow continued to demand exclusive military authority at Luxun as well as a Soviet chief for both the Chinese Eastern and Southern Manchurian Railways. Moscow also refused to allow Chinese recognition of the independence of Outer Mongolia to be contingent on border delimitation.[210]

The issue of independence for Outer Mongolia once again proved to be the most nettlesome. The crux of this issue now centered on the disposition of the Altai region and the delineation of the border between Xinjiang and Outer Mongolia prior to a Chinese recognition of its independence. Prior to 1911 the Altai region, an area comparable in size to the province of Zhejiang, had been a part of Outer Mongolia. When the Mongolian People's Republic was established, however, the Altai region became a part of Xinjiang—a fact that Soviet maps of the 1920s reflected. Then, in 1940, a Soviet map was published showing some 215,000 square kilometers (83,000 square miles) of the Altai region as part of the Mongolian People's Republic. In 1944, a Soviet-supported rebellion developed in the western Altai region and spread to other regions of Xinjiang. All of these facts made Chongqing fearful that unless specific agreement that the Altai region was a part of China was reached, recognition of Mongolian independence would mean implicit cession of the western Altai.[211] The fact that Stalin refused to provide a map specifying Outer Mongolia's borders further roused Chinese suspicions.

Stalin, on the other hand, suspected that Chiang Kai-shek intended to use the delimitation of Outer Mongolia's boundaries as a pretext to avoid recognition of its independence. By making such recognition contingent on final delimitation of the border, Chiang could prevent the conclusion of a boundary agreement and be technically within his rights in refusing to recognize the results of the plebiscite on independence. When the second round of talks opened, Stalin was willing to inspect and consider the Chinese maps presented by Wang Shijie. By the second session on 10 August, however, he adamantly refused to consider boundary delimitation, insisting that there was no need because the boundary was already well known and for the previous twenty years there had been no boundary dispute along the border between Outer Mongolia and Xinjiang.[212] Stalin also ensured that the pressure of the Soviet advance into Manchuria would not go unfelt on the Chinese delegation by telling T.V. Soong that unless a treaty was signed soon there was a danger of

Manchuria's falling to the CCP. Stalin also upped the ante by telling Soong that if China did not soon drop its demand for the delimitation of the border between Xinjiang and Outer Mongolia, thereby permitting the conclusion of an agreement, the people of Inner Mongolia might demand to join Outer Mongolia.[213]

On 12 August, a cable arrived from Chiang reiterating that Outer Mongolia's borders would have to be clarified before its independence could be recognized.[214] Chiang's cable touched off a debate among the members of the Chinese negotiating team. All were agreed that Chiang's proposal was unrealistic and that further delay would be extremely dangerous. T.V. Soong, Fu Bingchang, and Jiang Jingguo felt so strongly about the urgency of the situation that they were ready to ignore Chiang's most recent cable and settle with Stalin. Wang Shijie opposed this proposal on the grounds that it would divide public opinion and make it difficult for the Legislative *Yuan* to ratify the treaty. At least with regard to the question of Outer Mongolia, Chiang's instructions would have to be sought before an agreement could be reached. In line with this, further negotiations were postponed until Chiang could be apprised of the situation.[215] Later during the evening of 12 August, Wang and Soong cabled Chiang advising him that it was imperative to compromise on the remaining unresolved issues and especially regarding Outer Mongolia:

> It is impossible to fulfill Your Excellency's directive regarding Outer Mongolia. . . . We and the other members of the delegation unanimously believe that we must conclude a Sino-Soviet agreement. If we delay further, it will be extremely easy to cause unexpected changes. Therefore, we very earnestly ask Your Excellency to authorize us to deal expediently with Outer Mongolia and other still unresolved issues.[216]

The next day the following one-sentence reply arrived from Chiang: Regarding Outer Mongolia and other unresolved issues, "you are authorized to deal with them in an appropriate fashion" (*jun shouquan xiong deng quanyi chuzhi keye*). This was an ambiguous reply. What was an "appropriate fashion?" Only the day before Chiang had directed his representatives to continue insisting on clarification of Outer Mongolia's borders. Was the message of 13 August to be taken as a reversal of this position? This was unclear. The ambiguity of Chiang's message had the advantage of allowing him to avoid the onus of assuming responsibility for giving final authorization to accept Moscow's demands for an ironclad guarantee of Chinese recognition of the independence of Outer Mongolia. Again the Chinese team in Moscow was in a quandary. Wang, Soong, and Jiang Jingguo all felt it was imperative to sign an agreement immediately, but recognized that they lacked final authorization from Chiang for the acceptance of Stalin's terms. Finally, Jiang Jingguo agreed to take personal responsibility for the acceptance of Stalin's terms. It is probable that Jiang Jingguo recognized his father's dilemma and sought to give him a way out. This may have been by prearrangement.[217]

On 14 August negotiations resumed. The Chinese side dropped their demand for a delimitation of Outer Mongolian boundaries and Stalin agreed on an exchange of notes specifying that existing boundaries would be maintained. Stalin also modified his longstanding demand for exclusive military control of Luxun by agreeing to the establishment of a joint Sino-Soviet military committee there—as Chiang had demanded in his cable the day before. China gave in on the Southern Manchurian Railway issue: it, along with the Eastern Manchurian Railway, would be headed by Soviet appointees. The Chinese chairman (a position distinct from the director who actually administered the line) of the Southern Manchurian Railway board of directors was, however, given two votes. Stalin also asked for a Chinese guarantee that facilities at Luxun would not be leased to any third power. The Chinese side was willing to give verbal assurances to this effect, but refused to include it in the text of this agreement or in the ancillary documents. Stalin accepted this and expressed his deep hopes that China would not violate this promise. The issue of "war trophies," that is, of ownership of Japanese investments in Manchuria, was left unresolved.[218] This loophole later provided the basis for the Soviets to strip Manchuria of much of its industrial plant. There were also ancillary agreements establishing jointly owned companies to exploit Xinjiang's mineral deposits.

On 14 August Stalin presided over the signature of the Treaty of Friendship and Alliance by Foreign Ministers Wang Shijie and Molotov. As its name implied, the treaty provided for a full military alliance against Japan. It also provided that neither power would conclude an alliance or enter into a coalition directed against the other. After the signing, Stalin made a brief speech stressing once again the differences between imperial Russia and the Soviet Russia: the former had desired to partition China together with Japan; the latter wanted a strong China to help check Japan. China did not completely trust Soviet words, Stalin noted, but if it watched developments it would see that the words were not false.[219] At a banquet later that evening, Stalin reiterated the pledge that the Soviet Union would exert all its strength to achieve China's unification under Chiang Kai-shek's leadership.[220]

Conclusion

Overall, Chiang's Soviet policy during the 1942–1945 period met with considerable success. Up until mid-1944, Chiang's hard-line approach forced Stalin to retreat from Xinjiang. Moreover, playing the American card secured Soviet acceptance of China's entry into first the Big Four, and then the United Nations Security Council. Efforts to undermine Soviet-Japanese neutrality and the Soviet-American alliance were unproductive, but they do not ultimately seem to have been counterproductive. While these efforts contributed to the downward spiral of ROC-USSR relations up until late 1944, the resulting tensions did not prevent Chiang from securing firm guarantees from Stalin regarding Xinjiang, Manchuria, and the CCP. Of course all three of these situations were ambiguous. Soviet supported rebellions still controlled wide areas of Xinjiang. ROC authority in Manchuria remained nominal with real power in the hands of the Soviet Union's Red Army and, in the countryside, the CCP. And, of course, Stalin's pledges about not helping the CCP did not prevent the Red Army from giving the CCP large amounts of captured Japanese weapons. Still, Chiang had firm legal guarantees of China's sovereignty over Manchuria which could, and in fact ultimately did, provide a basis for full recovery of those areas once postwar China grew strong. By then, China was Communist rather than Nationalist-led. That, however, is another matter.

Chiang's cards were limited. The Republic of China had immense internal problems and its strength was far below that of the emerging Soviet superpower. From this perspective, what is remarkable is not that Chiang did not achieve more, but that, given the weakness of the Republic of China, he achieved so much. He played his limited cards shrewdly and by the war's end had secured most of what he had hoped to secure when he led China to war eight years earlier. Only the return of Outer Mongolia and Soviet assistance in bringing the CCP in line escaped his grasp. And of these, only Outer Mongolia was within Soviet power to deliver.

In Manchuria, the Soviet Union was in an excellent position to demand a full-blown sphere of influence. Indeed, this may have been what Stalin intended.[221] If it had not been for the dogged Chinese resistance during the Moscow talks, and for Chiang's skill in playing the American card, Stalin might have achieved just that. As it was, the 1945 treaty formalized an unequal relationship between the Soviet Union and China. Given the gross disparities in power between the two countries, however, it is remarkable that China did not have to give up more. That is, it is remarkable that Manchuria is today a part of China.

The pivotal role of Outer Mongolia in the 1945 negotiations was a powerful demonstration of Chiang's sensitivity to popular nationalist passions. Some of the most powerful invectives in the Chinese language refer to Chinese leaders who relinquish Chinese territory to the barbarian foreigners. *Chumai guotu* (to sell out national territory) is, as Jiang Jingguo pointed out to Stalin during the Moscow talks, one such emotive epithet. Others, such as *mai guo zai*, a criminal who betrays the nation; or, worst of all, *han jian*, a traitor to the Han race, would also cover such behavior. While the Han population of Outer Mongolia was minimal, in Chinese minds it was a part of "China." Chiang was aware that these traditional ideas had been tremendously strengthened and focused by China's experience in the twentieth century. He feared that if he gave up Outer Mongolia he would undermine his claim to be a genuine, sincere, and effective nationalist. These fears may have been well founded.

In spite of the efforts of government censors to suppress criticism of the August treaty, such influential newspapers as *Da Gong Bao* and *Dongfang Zazhi* nonetheless obliquely criticized the treaty for such issues as the relinquishment of Outer Mongolia. But it was the public disclosure of the Yalta agreement in January 1946, shortly after the government formally recognized the independence of the Mongolian People's Republic, which unleashed a torrent of condemnation. For several months, student demonstrations and newspaper editorials angrily condemned the government's seeming capitulation to great-power pressure. In the words of a study by Emily Yaung, the disclosure of the Yalta agreement and of its links to the August treaty "threw the entire nation in[to] a state of high agitation."

> The Yalta Agreement aroused apparent patriotic sentiments among the Chinese public and strong indignation against secret diplomacy and the language used in the accord. In addition, the feeling that the independence of Outer Mongolia was too high a price to pay was shared by the majority despite justifications reiterated by Chiang and other KMT leaders.[222]

The KMT right wing seized on this patriotic indignation to attack the KMT moderates such as Wang Shijie who had negotiated the treaty, and to charge that the conciliatory policies of Chiang and Wang toward the Soviet Union, plus their attempt to solve the CCP problem by political means, were ineffective. They thus demanded that Chiang adopt a military solution to the problem of internal unity.[223] The public outcry against the Yalta agreement also helped convince Chiang that the people were not ready for democracy, thus making him less willing to satisfy the widespread demand for rapid implementation of democratic reforms. But, in Emily Yaung's words:

> Above all, the most damaging effect [was] that Yalta discredited the KMT government in the eyes of the Chinese public. Although we cannot exaggerate the impact of Yalta on China's overall domestic politics . . . one cannot deny that the rather quick shift in the political tide from compromise to confrontation [between the KMT and the CCP] was closely related to the disclosure of the Yalta Agreement.[224]

The CCP was not in a position to exploit directly these sentiments; it could not itself condemn the treaty and by implication the Soviet Union. Yet it benefited indirectly, because many people concluded that events surrounding the 1945 treaty confirmed the incompetence of the government regarding the conduct of domestic and foreign affairs.[225]

Notes

1. George Lensen, *Strange Neutrality: Soviet-Japanese Relations during the Second World War, 1941–1945*, Tallahassee, Fla.: Diplomatic Press, 1972.
2. Shao Lizi, "Chushi Sulian de Huiyi" [Memoir of ambassadorship to the Soviet Union], *Wenshi Ziliao Xuanji* [Selection of Literary Materials], national edition, vol. 60, Beijing: Zhongguo Renmin Zhengzhi Xieshanghui, p. 191.
3. *FRUS*, 1941, vol. 4, p. 971. Chongqing also passed its warning of imminent German attack on to Moscow. Zhang Chong, then the head of the Overseas Department of the KMT, a central component of Chiang's foreign intelligence apparatus, told General Vasilii Chuikov that Germany was planning to attack the Soviet Union in June or July and was encouraging Japan to undertake a simultaneous move south against the British colonies in Southeast Asia. Wa. Zui Ke Fu (Vasilii Chuikov), *Zai Hua Shiming* [Mission to China], Beijing: Xinhua Chubanshe, 1983, p. 115.
4. Lyman P. Van Slyke, *The Chinese Communist Movement, a Report of the United States War Department, July 1945*, Military Intelligence Division of the War Department, (reprint), Stanford, Calif.: Stanford University Press, 1968, p.215 (hereafter cited "War Department Report").
5. *FRUS*, 1941, vol. 4, pp. 281–282.
6. *China Handbook, 1937–1944: A Comprehensive Survey of Major Developments in China in Seven Years of War*, first published in 1944, republished, Taibei: Ch'eng Wen Co., 1971, p. 89 (hereafter cited as *China Handbook, 1937–1944*).
7. *FRUS*, 1941, vol. 4, p. 289.
8. Wa. Zui Ke Fu, *Zai Hua Shiming*, p. 121.
9. *FRUS*, 1941, vol. 4, p. 1004.
10. Ibid., p. 1006.
11. Ibid., pp. 362–363.
12. *Zhong Su Wenhua* [Sino-Soviet Culture], vol. 9, no. 2–3 (n.d.), Chongqing.
13. Wa. Zui Ke Fu, *Zai Hua Shiming*, p. 121.
14. *FRUS*, 1941, vol. 4, p. 736.
15. Ibid., pp. 738–739.
16. Lensen, *Strange Neutrality*, p. 258.
17. *FRUS*, 1941, vol. 4, p. 740.
18. *China Handbook, 1937–1944*, p. 89.
19. *Zhanshi Waijiao*, pp. 391–392.
20. Ibid., p. 392.
21. *FRUS*, 1941, vol. 4, p. 747.

22. *FRUS*, 1942, China, p. 85.
23. Lensen, *Strange Neutrality*, pp. 30–34.
24. Ibid., p. 32.
25. Harriet L. Moore, *Soviet Far Eastern Policy, 1931–1945*, Princeton, N.J.: Princeton University Press, 1945, p. 130.
26. *Zhanshi Waijiao*, p. 402. Moscow also recalled Chuikov from China as part of its effort to insulate Soviet-Japanese neutrality from the world war. According to Chuikov, he was recalled to the Soviet Union in February 1942 because Moscow was not willing to take responsibility for helping the United States, China, and Britain fight Japan. Chuikov also feared that his continued presence in Chongqing might cause friction in Soviet-American relations once General Joseph Stilwell arrived there. Wa. Zui Ke Fu, *Zai Hua Shiming*, pp. 164–165. After his return to the Soviet Union, Chuikov became one of the outstanding Soviet generals of the war, commanding the defense of Stalingrad.
27. *Zhanshi Waijiao*, p. 395. *Zongtong Dashi*, vol. 4, p. 1929.
28. Guo Dequan, *Kangzhan Shiqi Zhu E Wuguan Huiyi Shilu* [True record of service as military attaché to Russia during the war of resistance], Taibei: Guofangbu Shizheng Bianyiju, June 1982, pp. 18–19.
29. *Zhanshi Waijiao*, p. 396.
30. Ibid. *Zongtong Dashi*, vol. 4, p. 1931.
31. Guo Dequan, *Kangzhan Shiqi*, pp. 18–19.
32. Robert Sherwood, *Roosevelt and Hopkins, an Intimate Portrait*, vol. 2, New York: Bantam, 1950, p. 148. The American ambassador in Moscow also lobbied with Molotov and Stalin during June and July to accept this proposal referring the Soviet leaders to the Chinese for further details. *FRUS*, 1942, China, pp. 599, 618.
33. Shao Lizi reported that shortly before his return to China in October 1942 he and Soviet officials signed an agreement for the transport of British aid through Soviet central Asia (Shao Lizi, "Chushi Sulian," p. 193). There is no mention of such an agreement in *FRUS*, although American diplomats were keeping close tabs on the transit talks and had good contacts with all sides involved. There were, however, many reports of agreements being reached, reports which ultimately proved to be false. Perhaps Shao's recollection was of some sort of preliminary agreement or for the transit of a small amount of material on a one-time basis.
34. *Zhanshi Waijiao*, pp. 402–403.
35. *FRUS*, 1942, China, pp. 591–599.
36. Shao Lizi, "Chushi Sulian," p. 191.
37. *See* Lo Hsiang-lin, *Fu Ping-ch'ang and Modern China* [in Chinese with an English title], Hong Kong: Institute of Chinese Culture, 1973.
38. *FRUS*, 1942, China, pp. 618–622.
39. Ibid., p. 621.
40. Ibid., pp. 598–599.
41. *FRUS*, 1943, China, pp. 600–602.
42. Ibid., pp. 603, 605.
43. Ibid., pp. 600–602.
44. Ibid., pp. 606–607.
45. Ibid., pp. 606–607, 612.
46. *FRUS*, 1942, China, pp. 82–84.
47. Ibid., p. 238.
48. *Zongtong Dashi*, vol. 5, p. 2181.
49. Ibid., p. 2201. At their first meeting in Cairo on 21 November, Churchill told Chiang that he hoped for Soviet entry into the war against Japan and asked Chiang what he thought of the matter. Chiang replied that he too hoped for Soviet entry (ibid., pp. 2275–2276). In this author's opinion, Chiang's response to Churchill was very probably influenced by a number of diplomatic exigencies and not representative of Chiang's true sentiments.
50. U.S. Department of State, *Conferences at Cairo and Teheran*, Washington, D.C.: Government Printing Office, 1961, pp. 387–388.
51. Jiang Jieshi, *Zhongguo Zhi Mingyun* [China's destiny], Chongqing: Zheng Zhong Shuju, March 1943. Intended as Chiang's major wartime political statement, *Zhongguo Zhi Mingyun* excoriated the foreign presence in China, blaming foreigners for virtually all of China's ills from prostitution, opium, and poverty, to liberalism and communism. The book's xenophobia was one reason for the overwhelmingly negative reaction which it encountered both in China and abroad, and a major reason why it was withdrawn from circulation shortly after publication. Regarding the reaction to *Zhongguo Zhi Mingyun, see FRUS*, 1943, China, pp. 244–248. It was later reprinted in a much toned-down version, but was not reprinted in original form until the early 1950s when the new Communist government reissued it as a good example of Chiang's "reactionary" thinking.

52. On 29 January 1943, Chiang commented in his diary that at the end of the war he hoped China could recover Manchuria, Outer Mongolia, and Taiwan. *Zongtong Dashi*, vol. 5, p. 2110.
53. *FRUS*, 1943, vol. 1, pp. 542, 640.
54. Ibid.
55. Ibid., pp. 830–831.
56. Ibid.
57. Guo Dequan, *Kangzhan Shiqi*, pp. 59–60.
58. U.S. Department of State, *The Conferences at Washington and Quebec, 1943*, Washington, D.C.: Government Printing Office, 1970, p. 1240.
59. Franklin D. Roosevelt, *Map Room Messages of President Roosevelt (1939–1945)*, Reel 8, communication between President Roosevelt and Generalissimo Chiang Kai-shek, December 29, 1941–January 26, 1945. Frederick, Md.: University Publications of America, 1981. The documents in this series are unnumbered. Hereafter cited as *Map Room Messages*.
60. *FRUS*, 1943, vol. 1, pp. 692–693.
61. Moore, *Soviet Far Eastern Policy*, p. 133. "War Department Report," p. 229.
62. Hollington K. Tong, *China and the World Press*, 1948, p. 220 (no place of publication or publisher given). *See also* "War Department Report," pp. 228–229.
63. *Zongtong Dashi*, vol. 5, p. 2194.
64. Moore, *Soviet Far Eastern Policy*, p. 135.
65. "War Department Report," p. 229.
66. Sherwood, *Roosevelt and Hopkins*, vol. 2, pp. 345–346.
67. When Chiang met with Soviet Ambassador Paniushkin on 17 January 1943, for example, Paniushkin explained Moscow's desire for a second front, regretted that it had not yet been opened, and noted that this failure made one feel "impatient." *Zhanshi Waijiao*, pp. 399–400.
68. Chiang diary, 25 August 1943. *See also* his diary for 30 August, in *Zongtong Dashi*, vol. 5, pp. 2204, 2207.
69. *Zongtong Dashi*, vol. 5, p. 2167.
70. Immanuel Hsu, *The Rise of Modern China*, New York: Oxford University Press, 1970, pp. 698–699.
71. *Conferences at Cairo and Teheran*, pp. 102–103. Hurley had reassured Chiang that Stalin had no such intentions.
72. *Zongtong Dashi*, vol. 5, p. 2127. Madame Chiang also reported that Roosevelt said that Hong Kong would be returned to Chinese sovereignty, but that China should promptly designate it as a free harbor.
73. Chiang had alluded to this in *Zhongguo Zhi Mingyun*. Because of certain problems in the 1920s, he wrote, "Sino-Soviet border issues" had not been satisfactorily resolved when diplomatic relations were established in 1924. Such problems would be solved in the future on the basis of "traditional friendship" between China and the Soviet Union (*Zhongguo Zhi Mingyun*, pp. 121–122).
74. *Conferences at Cairo and Teheran*, pp. 324–325, 367. During the same discussion Chiang rejected a claim to the Ryukyu Islands. Several days later Chiang again raised the matter of Outer Mongolia's return to China during a discussion with Harry Hopkins.
75. *Zongtong Dashi*, vol. 5, pp. 2170–2171.
76. *Conferences at Cairo and Teheran*, pp. 324–325.
77. Ibid., p. 891.
78. Ibid., pp. 566–567.
79. *Map Room Messages*.
80. On 12 January 1944 Wei Daoming, China's ambassador to the United States, attended a conference of the Pacific War Council in Washington at which Roosevelt described the recent conferences at Cairo and Teheran. The Soviet Union had no ice-free port in Siberia, Roosevelt explained, and therefore looked with favor on making Dairen a free port for all the world to use. The Soviet Union was also interested in rail access across Manchuria to Dairen, but the railway itself would be owned by the Chinese government (*Conferences at Cairo and Teheran*, pp. 868–869).
81. Ibid., pp. 257, 325, 367.
82. *Zhanshi Waijiao*, p. 460–461.
83. *Map Room Messages*.
84. Ibid.
85. Wang Shijie riji, (Wang Shijie diary), 1, 2 April 1944 [unpublished manuscript].
86. *Zongtong Dashi*, vol. 5, p. 2343.
87. *Map Room Messages*.
88. *FRUS*, 1944, vol. 6, p. 771.
89. Ibid., p. 785.
90. Ibid., p. 798.

91. George Lensen does not mention any such agreement in his detailed study of the 30 March agreement, a study based on extensive use of Soviet documents (Lensen, *Strange Neutrality*). Nor does the diplomatic records office of the Japanese Foreign Ministry have any record of the existence of secret protocols attached to the 30 March agreement (Communication with the author, Consulate General of Japan, 3 April 1986).
92. *FRUS*, 1944, vol. 6, p. 800.
93. Ibid., pp. 802–803. The second and third sources of "difficulty" were the clashes on the border between Xinjiang and Outer Mongolia, and the restrictions which Chongqing was then imposing on the activities of Soviet diplomatic and consular representatives in China.
94. *Map Room Messages*.
95. *FRUS*, 1944, vol. 6, pp. 800–801.
96. Ibid., p. 773.
97. Wang Shijie riji, 11 April 1944.
98. Ibid., 17, 19 April 1944.
99. Ibid., 25 April 1944.
100. *FRUS*, 1944, vol. 6, pp. 793, 504–505.
101. *Zhanshi Waijiao*, pp. 404–405.
102. *FRUS*, 1944, vol. 6, p. 804.
103. Ibid., pp. 794, 798, 803.
104. "War Department Report," p. 234.
105. *Zongtong Dashi*, vol. 5, p. 2398.
106. *Great Soviet Encyclopedia*, vol. 26, New York: Macmillan, 1981, pp. 522–523.
107. Wang Shijie riji, 1, 17 August 1944. *Zongtong Dashi*, vol. 5, p. 2486; Whiting, *Pawn or Pivot?*, p. 105.
108. *The Conferences at Malta and Yalta*, p. 378. *See also* William Tung, *V.K. Wellington Koo and China's Wartime Diplomacy*, New York: St. Johns University Press, p. 64.
109. *Zongtong Dashi*, vol. 5, pp. 2203, 2205.
110. Regarding American policy at this juncture *see* Tang Tsou, *America's Failure in China, 1941–1950*, 2 vol. Chicago: University of Chicago Press, 1963. Michael Schaller, *The U.S. Crusade in China, 1938–1945*, New York: Columbia University Press, 1979. Barbara W. Tuchman, *Stilwell and the American Experience in China*, New York: Bantam, 1972. Herbert Feis, *The China Tangle: The American Effort in China from Pearl Harbor to the Marshall Mission*, Princeton, N.J.: Princeton University Press, 1953.
111. Wang Shijie riji, 17 June 1944. *Zongtong Dashi*, vol. 5, p. 2384.
112. Roosevelt had his own reasons for choosing Wallace, his main purpose being to get Wallace out of the United States during the Democratic party's 1944 National Presidential Nominating Convention. As the visibly aging Roosevelt was to be nominated for his unprecedented fourth term, the question of the vice-presidency was especially important. For a number of partisan and diplomatic reasons (the latter having to do with winning Senate approval of the treaty ending the war and setting up the new United Nations organization), Roosevelt decided to ask Wallace to undertake an important mission to the Soviet Union and China, thereby clearing the decks for Senator Harry Truman's nomination as vice-presidential candidate. The Chinese side was unaware of such considerations, and knew only that Wallace had been dispatched as Roosevelt's personal representative on what the American president took to be an extremely important mission (Tuchman, *Stilwell*, pp. 593–594). Such domestic considerations should not, however, obscure the fact that Wallace's mission did have substantial diplomatic significance.
113. *Waijiaoshi Ziliao (1937–1945)*, pp. 211–212.
114. *FRUS*, 1944, vol. 6, p. 854. *Waijiaoshi Ziliao (1937–1945)*, pp. 211–212.
115. *FRUS*, 1944, vol. 6, p. 234.
116. Wang Shijie riji, 24 June 1944.
117. *FRUS*, 1944, vol. 6, p. 245. Japan was apprehensive about Wallace's visits to Moscow and Chongqing, suspecting that his talks dealt with the delivery of American aid to China via the Soviet Union. The Japanese ambassador in Moscow requested clarification on this issue, and Molotov denied that the issue had been discussed. *See* Lensen, *Strange Neutrality*, p. 57.
118. Wang Shijie riji, 7 July 1944.
119. Ibid., 11 July 1944.
120. Ibid.
121. Wang Shijie riji, 28 August 1944. *See also* Owen Lattimore, *The Sinkiang Pivot*, Boston: Little, Brown, 1950, p. 81.
122. Guo Dequan, *Zhanzhan Shiqi*, pp. 65–66. *FRUS*, 1944, vol. 6, p. 815.
123. *Zongtong Dashi*, vol. 5, p. 2417. *FRUS*, 1944, vol. 6, p. 800.

124. Wellington Koo, *Reminiscences of Wellington Koo*, Chinese Oral History Project of East Asia Institute of Columbia University, New York, pp. 636–639.
125. Wang Shijie riji, 15 July 1944.
126. Koo, *Reminiscences*, p. 626. Wang Shijie riji, 15 July 1944.
127. Koo, *Reminiscences*, p. 661–662.
128. Forest C. Pogue, "The Big Three and the United Nations," in *The Meaning of Yalta*, John L. Snell, editor, Baton Rouge: Louisiana State University Press, 1956, p. 19.
129. Koo, *Reminiscences*, pp. 656–659.
130. *Waijiaoshi Ziliao (1937–1945)*, pp. 210–211.
131. Koo, *Reminiscences*, p. 663. Koo's exact words were that China feared that it might be "shunted aside."
132. Ibid., pp. 656–657. *See also* Wang Shijie riji, 7 October 1944. Moscow took its time replying to the American proposal and the American delegation reportedly tried to prod Moscow along by pleading that the Chinese representatives at Dumbarton Oaks could not be kept waiting much longer. The Soviets were not impressed by this argument.
133. *Zongtong Dashi*, vol. 5, p. 2469.
134. Ibid.
135. Chiang's decisions not to meet with Stalin may also have been influenced by an expectation that the war against Germany would end soon. During the fall of 1944, before the German offensive in the Ardennes in December, people in China commonly believed that Germany would surrender by the end of that year. If Chiang shared these beliefs, he may have expected that tensions between Moscow and Washington would increase once they sat down to arrange affairs in postwar Europe. Comments in Wang Shijie's diary in January 1945 indicate his close attention to Soviet-American conflicts over postwar Poland, and Chiang may well have thought that if a resolution of Soviet-Chinese questions could be postponed until after the defeat of Germany, American support for China would be greater. Wang Shijie riji, 9 November 1944, 2 January 1945.
136. *Zongtong Dashi*, vol. 5, p. 2483. *FRUS*, 1944, vol. 6, p. 816.
137. Regarding the development and utility of this myth to Chiang, *see* Peter M. Kuhfus, *Die Risiken der Freundschaft: China und der Jalta-Mythos*, Bochumer Jahrbuch zur Ostasienforschung, no. 7, 1984.
138. *FRUS*, 1945, vol. 7, p. 896.
139. *Zongtong Dashi*, vol. 5, pp. 2519–2520; 2526–2527. *Zhanshi Waijiao*, pp. 542–543. Guo Dequan, *Kangzhan Shiqi*, p. 67.
140. Guo Dequan, *Kangzhan Shiqi*, p. 67. *Zongtong Dashi*, vol. 5, pp. 2519–2520.
141. *Zhanshi Waijiao*, pp. 542–543. *Zongtong Dashi*, vol. 5, pp. 2526–2527.
142. *Zhanshi Waijiao*, pp. 546–547. *Zongtong Dashi*, vol. 5, pp. 2539–2540, 2552. *Milu*, vol. 1, p. 345. Wang Shijie riji, 24, 30 April 1945. *FRUS*, 1945, vol. 7, p. 868.
143. *Milu*, vol. 1, p. 34.
144. *Zongtong Dashi*, vol. 5, pp. 2522, 2542.
145. *FRUS*, 1945, vol. 6, p. 8171.
146. *Zhanshi Waijiao*, p. 547.
147. Ibid., p. 548.
148. Ibid., pp. 554–555. *Zongtong Dashi*, vol. 5, p. 2558.
149. *Zhanshi Waijiao*, p. 555.
150. Chiang Kai-shek diary 14 June 1945, in *Zongtong Dashi*, vol. 5, p. 2566.
151. *Zhanshi Waijiao*, p. 555.
152. Ibid., p. 556.
153. Ibid., pp. 557–558.
154. Ibid.
155. *FRUS*, 1945, vol. 7, p. 861.
156. *Zhanshi Waijiao*, pp. 449–450.
157. *Zongtong Dashi*, vol. 5, pp. 2561–2564.
158. Ibid., p. 2564.
159. Harry S. Truman, *Memoirs, Volume One, Year of Decisions*, Garden City, N.J.: Doubleday, 1955, p. 269 (hereafter cited as *Year of Decisions*). According to General Albert Wedemeyer (Stilwell's replacement), who was present when Hurley gave Chiang the text of the Yalta agreement, Chiang was visibly shaken when he read its contents. Testimony before the U.S. Senate, 1951, in "The Military Situation in the Far East," part 3, pp. 2416–2417. (Cited in Richard C. Thornton, *China, The Struggle for Power, 1917–1972*, Bloomington, Ind.: Indiana University Press, 1973, p. 173.) It was this observation by Wedemeyer which long persuaded Western analysts to accept at face value

Chiang's subsequent claims that he had been presented with a surprise Soviet-American dictate on 16 June.

160. Thornton, *Struggle for Power*, p. 173.

161. *Zongtong Dashi*, vol. 5, p. 2567.

162. Even after receiving the text of the Yalta agreement from Hurley, Chiang still feared that there might be other, even harsher, terms contained in secret codicils. Such secret provisions might, he feared, link the fate Manchuria to some "third country" (*Zongtong Dashi*, vol. 5, p. 2567. *Milu*, vol. 1, p. 36). This elliptical reference seems to imply that Chiang feared that the United States might have recognized Manchuria as a Soviet sphere of influence in exchange for Soviet recognition of American preeminence over Japan.

163. *Zongtong Dashi*, vol. 5, p. 2571.

164. *Zhanshi Waijiao*, pp. 569–571.

165. *Zongtong Dashi*, vol. 5, p. 2573.

166. Other members of the Chinese team included Ka Daoming, Hu Shize, Sheng Minglie, Liu Zerong, Qiang Changzhao, and Zhang Guangmu. General accounts of the 1945 negotiations include: Wang Shijie, "Zhong Su youhao tongmeng tiaoyue zhi dijie yu feizhi" [The conclusion and abrogation of the Sino-Soviet treaty of friendship and alliance], in *Wang Shijie Xiansheng Lunzhu Xuanji* [Selected writings of Mr. Wang Shijie], Xiandian: Yutai Gongsi, 1980, pp. 347–388. Jiang Junjiang, "Song Ziwen Mozike tanpan zuiji" [Record of Song Ziwen's Moscow negotiations], *Zhongguo Yi Zhou* [China Weekly], no. 100 (24 March 1952), pp. 14–16.

167. *Zhanshi Waijiao*, pp. 573–574. *Zongtong Dashi*, vol. 5, p. 2583.

168. *FRUS*, 1945, vol. 7, pp. 910–912. *Zhanshi Waijiao*, pp. 608–609.

169. *Zhanshi Waijiao*, p. 572–574. *Zongtong Dashi*, vol. 5, p. 2583.

170. *Zhanshi Waijiao*, p. 573.

171. Jiang Jingguo, *Fuzhong zhi Yuan* [Carrying heavy burdens a great distance], Taibei, 1960, p. 63. Cited in Liang Chin-tung, "The Sino-Soviet Treaty of Friendship and Alliance of 1945: The Inside Story," in *Nationalist China during the Sino-Japanese War, 1937–1945*, Paul K.T. Sih, editor, Hicksville, N.Y.: Exposition Press, 1977, p. 373.

172. Steven I. Levine, "Comments," in Sih, *Nationalist China during the Sino-Japanese War*, p. 399.

173. *Zhanshi Waijiao*, pp. 586–587.

174. Ibid., pp. 591–593.

175. Jiang Jingguo, in *Fengyu Zhong de Ningjing* [Peace in the midst of storms], cited in *Milu*, vol. 1, pp. 46–49.

176. Liang Chin-tung, "Sino-Soviet Treaty," p. 406.

177. *Zongtong Dashi*, vol. 5, p. 2586.

178. Truman, *Year of Decisions*, p. 318.

179. *FRUS*, 1945, vol. 6, pp. 911–912.

180. Truman, *Year of Decisions*, p. 317. *FRUS*, 1945, vol. 6, pp. 912–914.

181. *Zhanshi Waijiao*, pp. 508–509.

182. Ibid., pp. 593–594.

183. Ibid., pp. 599, 602.

184. Ibid., pp. 603–604.

185. Ibid., p. 606. Hurley forwarded this cable to Truman on 10 July.

186. Ibid., pp. 611–612.

187. Ibid., p. 612.

188. Ibid., pp. 619–620.

189. U.S. Department of State, *The Conference at Berlin (the Potsdam Conference), 1945*, Washington, D.C.: Government Printing Office, 1960, vol. 2, pp. 862, 864.

190. Ibid., pp. 1226–1227.

191. Ibid.

192. These officials included Secretary of War Henry Stimson, Secretary of State James Byrnes, Chief of China Division of the State Department John Carter Vincent, and Ambassadors Patrick Hurley and Averell Harriman. *See* ibid., pp. 1224, 1225, 1228–1229, 1243, 1247.

193. Ibid., pp. 1241–1243.

194. In mid-June the invasion of Japan's southern island of Kyūshū had been scheduled for 1 November. This operation was based on the assumption of a Soviet offensive on the Asian continent which would tie down large numbers of Japanese troops. Raymond Garthoff, "The Soviet Intervention in Manchuria, 1945–1946," in *Sino-Soviet Military Relations*, Raymond Garthoff, ed., New York: Frederick Praeger, 1966, p. 61. Regarding Truman's estimate of this military imperative, *see* Truman, *Year of Decisions*, p. 411.

195. *FRUS*, 1945, vol 7, p. 885.
196. Truman, *Year of Decisions*, p. 315.
197. For example, Stalin's comments during the 17 July discussion and Molotov's comments on the modalities of the Soviet declaration of war against Japan during the 28 July discussion (*Conference at Berlin*, vol. 2, p. 476).
198. Ibid., p. 1241.
199. Wang Shijie riji, 24 July 1945.
200. Ibid., 25 July 1945. *Conference at Berlin*, vol. 2, p. 1246. *Zongtong Dashi*, vol. 5, p. 2615.
201. Wang Shijie riji, 4 August 1945.
202. *Zhanshi Waijiao*, p. 643. *Milu*, vol. 1, p. 62.
203. Truman, *Year of Decisions*, pp. 423–424. *FRUS*, 1945, vol. 7, p. 956.
204. *FRUS*, 1945, vol. 7, pp. 960–965. On 12 August, Harriman, on instructions from James Byrnes, delivered a letter to Molotov again expressing American concern with several issues remaining in dispute and asking the Soviet Union not to press for further concessions from China.
205. Wang Shijie riji, 9 August 1945.
206. W. Averell Harriman, "Statement of W. Averell Harriman, Special Assistant to the President, Regarding Our Wartime Relations with the Soviet Union, Particularly as They Concern the Agreements Reached at Yalta," *The Military Situation in the Far East*, Hearings before the Committee on Armed Services and the Committee of Foreign Relations, United States Senate, 82nd Congress, 1st Session, Part 5, Washington, D.C.: Government Printing Office, 1951, p. 3331.
207. Wang Shijie riji, 8 August 1945.
208. *Zhanshi Waijiao*, p. 644.
209. Wang Shijie riji, 10 August 1945. *Milu*, vol. 1, p. 62.
210. *Zhanshi Waijiao*, pp. 645, 648.
211. Wang Shijie riji, August 1945. *FRUS*, 1944, vol. 6, pp. 806, 808.
212. *Zhanshi Waijiao*, p. 643.
213. Hsu, *The Rise of Modern China*, p. 707. *FRUS*, 1945, vol. 7, pp. 967–969.
214. *Zhanshi Waijiao*, p. 647.
215. Wang Shijie riji, 12, 13 August 1945.
216. *Zhanshi Waijiao*, p. 649.
217. Interview with Dr. Wang Chi-wu (Wang Shijie's son), Taibei, 4 August 1983.
218. Wang Shijie riji, 14 August 1945. *Zhanshi Waiajiao*, pp. 642, 651.
219. Wang Shijie riji, 15 August 1945. Jiang Junjiang, "Song Ziwen Mozike tanpan zuiji," p. 16.
220. On 24 August a joint meeting of the Supreme National Defense Council and the Standing Committee of the legislative *Yuan* met in Chongqing. After hearing a report on the treaty's negotiation and the Yalta agreement by Chiang Kai-shek, the session unanimously approved the Sino-Soviet Treaty. The treaty was then submitted to the legislative *Yuan* the same day for discussion. Opinion was divided, but only a few people voted against the treaty when the final vote was taken on 24 August. Two days later the National Government ratified the treaty.
221. Diane Clements and Michael Schaller argue that at Yalta Stalin and Roosevelt in fact agreed that Manchuria was to be a Soviet sphere of influence. See Diane S. Clements, *Yalta*, New York: Oxford University Press, 1970, and Schaller, *U.S. Crusade*, p. 212. There is no hard evidence regarding this question one way or the other, but the Clements-Schaller hypothesis seems untenable to me for several reasons. First, it overlooks the idealistic sentiments expressed by Hopkins, Leahy, and other U.S. leaders after Yalta; they *thought* they were laying the basis for postwar peace and cooperation among the Big Four, not securing Soviet-U.S. cooperation at China's expense. Second, Yalta was the direct culmination of a U.S. effort to engineer Sino-Soviet amity which began with Wallace's mission to China. Third, the fact that Roosevelt was exhausted and on the verge of death at Yalta argues in favor of the continuing inertia of previous policy rather than bold initiatives in new directions. Fourth, contrary to Chiang's later protestations, except for Outer Mongolia, the Yalta agreement, and most especially the granting of Soviet special rights in Manchuria, *did not* represent a Soviet-American diktat but was rooted in Chiang's own 1940 proposals to Stalin.
222. Emily Yaung, *The Impact of the Yalta Agreement on China's Domestic Politics, 1945–1946*, doctoral dissertation, Kent State University, Kent, Ohio, 1979, pp. 92–93, 212, 218.
223. Ibid., pp. 197, 209–213.
224. Ibid., p. 218.
225. Ibid., p. 213.

Chapter VIII

The CCP and World War II

Proletarian Internationalism and the Great Patriotic War

Since the earliest days of the Soviet state, Communists had predicted and prepared for the time when the imperialist states would join together to invade the "land of the Soviets." Indeed, it became a key tenant of Marxism–Leninism that the defense of the socialist fatherland was the cardinal duty of all proletarian revolutionaries. With the German invasion of the Soviet Union in June 1941, this prediction seemed to have been fulfilled. Moscow mobilized all its resources to deal with the fascist onslaught. Among these resources was the international Communist movement. Moscow promptly ordered the "branch parties" of the Comintern to throw their strength into the defense of the USSR. In most countries the results were impressive. Literally overnight, Communists in France switched from collaborating with the German authorities to armed resistance to those same authorities. In the United States, the Communist party of the United States of America switched just as promptly from strident opposition to ardent support for Roosevelt's efforts to step up American support for embattled Britain. The Indian Communist Party took longer. On the subcontinent, some six months were required to change the Party line, but once this was done the Indian Communists effectively opposed the Congress Party's Quit India Movement.[1] As well shall see, the Chinese Communists also received orders to carry out their "proletarian internationalist" duty.

The Soviet-German war presented Mao Zedong with both exceptional dangers and opportunities. In the first instance, Moscow was certain to become more solicitous of Japanese concerns and more desirous of upholding its April 1941 neutrality agreement with Tokyo. This meant that Mao could now be virtually certain that the Soviet Union would not arm the CCP. Hopes that Mao entertained in this regard during the period of Soviet Union–Axis cooperation now vanished.[2] The virtual disappearance of the Soviet Union as a major Far Eastern power during the first thirty months of World War II also eliminated an important check against KMT military action against the CCP. As we saw in earlier chapters, during previous periods of increased Nationalist military pressure, Chongqing's fear of Soviet displeasure had helped check Nationalist advances. With Moscow out of the picture, Yan'an faced the specter of confronting both KMT and Japanese armies on its own.

But the Soviet Union's preoccupation with its European front also offered Mao a critical opportunity. With Moscow deliberately, if temporarily, washing its hands of Far Eastern affairs, and with its material resources strained to the limit by the German onslaught, Mao could move to eliminate the remaining elements of Soviet influence within the CCP. This was Mao's opportunity to push to a successful conclusion his struggle against the Internationalists of the CCP. Of course, this had to be done in a politically expedient fashion. The possibility of Allied victory over Germany and of Soviet reentry into Far Eastern affairs meant that Mao could not afford to break irreparably with the Soviet Union. Moreover, Mao was probably not indifferent to the fate of the Soviet Union. As a Marxist–Leninist, he probably saw the Soviet struggle against fascism as the vanguard of human progress at that point and was determined to demonstrate his loyalty to the Soviet Union. This would be done, however, on Mao's terms. This meant that Mao's assault on the Internationalists would be camouflaged; he would pour new nationalist wine into old Internationalist bottles.

The CCP responded promptly to the German attack on the Soviet Union. On 23 June, the day after the German attack began, *Jiefang Ribao* (Liberation Daily) condemned the German attack in the strongest terms and endorsed the Soviet struggle.[3] Other activities were quickly organized to demonstrate Yan'an's support for the Soviet war effort. In October, for example, an "Anti-Fascist Assembly of the Far East" convened in Yan'an and 130 "representatives" from various Asian countries resolved to struggle against Japan in order to help the Soviet Union.[4]

CCP support for the Soviet Union did not, however, extend to military action to disrupt Japanese deployments concentrating for a possible attack against the USSR. Although the German invasion of the Soviet Union took Japan by surprise, a strong faction of the Japanese military argued that Japan should join Germany in destroying bolshevism. While the debate between the "strike north" and the "strike south" factions raged in Tokyo, Japanese forces opposite the borders of the Soviet Union and Outer Mongolia grew rapidly in preparation for war.[5] Richard Sorge's spy ring in Tokyo kept Moscow informed of the debate over an invasion of the Soviet Union, while Soviet military intelligence certainly monitored the Japanese buildup. Facing such a real and immediate two-front threat, Moscow turned to the CCP for assistance.

In July 1941, Soviet authorities informed Yan'an that Japan was transferring large numbers of fully organized units from Japan to the borders of the Soviet Union and demanded that the Eighth Route Army attack Japanese concentrations in the Beiping, Kalgan, and Baotou areas and destroy the rail lines leading to those assembly areas.[6] These operations were apparently not intended to be mere guerrilla raids, but sustained operations design to tie down Japanese troops and prevent them from moving against the Soviet Union. What Moscow probably had in mind was an operation along the lines of the Hundred Regiments offensive of the year before. Otto Braun implies that Yan'an had previously agreed to such a plan.[7]

Mao procrastinated rather than flatly reject Moscow's demand. According to a postwar Soviet source, when Mao was approached about the matter of CCP military operations against Japan on 3 September 1941, he refused to give a definite answer while giving general assurances of support for the Soviet Union.[8] While asserting that Mao did not comply with Moscow's wishes, Soviet accounts do not say that he flatly rejected Moscow's request.[9] Still, Mao's de facto disobedience was a serious violation of Comintern discipline and line.

More important to Moscow than the subtleness of Mao's refusal was the practical direction of the military strategy of the CCP, which was the precise opposite of what

Moscow desired. While German armies were driving toward Moscow and while Japan was considering and preparing to join in the Axis attack, the CCP in fact reoriented its military strategy toward a more low-intensity warfare. In July 1941, General Okamura Neiji assumed command of Japan's antiguerrilla operations in north China and began implementing the savage "Three All" extermination policy, which was to devastate CCP strength over the next several years.[10] About the same time, the KMT began strengthening its forces around and tightening its blockade of the Shaan-Gan-Ning border region. The CCP responded to this stepped up Japanese and KMT pressure by redeploying units from Japanese-contested areas to areas threatened by the KMT, and by breaking up units remaining behind Japanese lines and assigning cadres and troops to villages. Orders were given to avoid large battles with Japanese forces and to conduct only small-scale guerrilla operations.[11] From the standpoint of preservation of the CCP's armed strength and territorial base, this shift of strategic direction made excellent sense. Had the CCP complied with Moscow's wishes and concentrated its forces, Okamura's task of "mopping up" Communist forces would have been greatly facilitated. But from Moscow's point of view, Yan'an's move constituted a betrayal of proletarian internationalism—a doctrine which first and foremost meant the defense of the socialist fatherland. Not only had Mao refused to implement Comintern orders designed to strengthen Soviet defense, he had acted in precisely contrary fashion.

Confronted with such blatant CCP disobedience in the hour of need, Moscow moved to strengthen its ties to Yan'an. In May 1942, a "Comintern liaison officer," Peter P. Vladimirov, arrived in Yan'an by special Soviet plane. Vladimirov was an old China hand, having served as China correspondent for TASS from early 1938 through mid-1940 and again in 1941. His Chinese was good.[12] It would be most interesting to know Vladimirov's precise Comintern status when he arrived in Yan'an, but unfortunately, this is unclear. Might he have carried extraordinary powers such as those carried by Pavil Mif ten years earlier? If so, Stalin could not have had much hope for the success of such an intervention against Mao, but perhaps the Soviet situation was so dire that such a long shot was worth a try. After all, what did Stalin have to lose? In any case, Vladimirov's duties included advising the Comintern on the situation within the CCP and in the Shaan-Gan-Ning border region. Vladimirov also brought with him some spare parts for the Yan'an radio, a new electrical generator along with gasoline to fuel it, and an additional radio operator to assist the two Soviet radiomen already stationed in Yan'an. Clearly the Comintern felt that closer contact between the Comintern and the CCP at this juncture was desirable. If Moscow could not bring Mao into line, at least it wanted to be informed of the full extent of his "deviation." Vladimirov kept an extensive diary of his activities in Yan'an, and while this account must be viewed critically, it is extremely valuable because it is one of the few firsthand sources we have regarding Soviet Union–CCP relations during this period.[13]

According to Vladimirov, shortly after his arrival in Yan'an two members of the Soviet liaison group undertook an extensive tour of the Eighth Route Army's front lines. When they returned to Yan'an, they reported to Vladimirov that the Eighth Route Army was virtually inactive and was not attempting to hamper Japan's preparations to attack the Soviet Union but withdrawing its forces to avoid clashes with

Japanese columns. Instead of tying down Japanese forces, the Eighth Route Army was deploying its forces to seize more territory from the Chongqing government. Vladimirov duly reported these observations to Moscow.[14]

This fundamental clash of interests continued into the spring and summer of 1942 as Soviet armies crumbled before the renewed Nazi offensive. As we saw in Chapter 6, the Soviet position in the spring of 1942 was dire. Moreover, the success of Japan's Pacific campaign had exceeded Tokyo's own hopes. The fortress of Singapore had fallen easily in February 1942 and the conquest of Australia seemed only temporarily delayed by the setback suffered by the Imperial Japanese Navy in the Coral Sea during the first week of May. The U.S. Navy was clearly on the defensive; in early June, a mighty fleet of 145 Japanese warships steamed confidently toward the Midway Islands, a stepping stone for the invasion of Hawaii.[15] While Stalin did not know of the planned Japanese invasion of Hawaii (the Sorge ring was broken up in October 1941), he could see clearly that Japan's ambitions had yet to be checked.

Heartened by Axis military successes in the spring of 1942, Japan renewed its buildup of mechanized forces in Manchuria. Vladimirov reported that fifty Japanese divisions were being held in reserve in Manchuria, Korea, and Japan, and had no doubt that these forces were intended for an invasion of the Soviet Union.[16] If the German offensives of mid-1942 were successful, Japan might decide to join in the war against the USSR, thereby vastly complicating the Soviet dilemma. Again it made good sense, from the Soviet perspective, for the CCP to launch maximum operations against Japanese forces. The more thinly Japanese forces could be spread, the less likely Tokyo would be to decide to tackle the Red Army.

Throughout the summer of 1942, the Soviet liaison group in Yan'an demanded that the CCP disrupt Japan's preparations to attack the Soviet Union. Again Mao turned aside Vladimirov's demands, replying that once Japan actually attacked the Soviet Union the Eighth Route Army would, of course, launch an offensive against Japanese forces.[17] Even in September 1942 when Vladimirov informed Mao that Japan was forming its first armored army with three tank divisions in Manchuria with the mission of seizing Khabarovsk in Soviet Siberia, Mao "did not heed" Soviet "requests" to take effective measures to engage Japanese forces. To the contrary, Vladimirov found that the Eighth Route Army continued to reduce the scope of its operations.[18]

From Mao's perspective, a large-scale offensive against Japanese forces in 1942 would have been suicidal. Chongqing was just then cutting off Yan'an's Xinjiang supply line and further strengthening its forces blockading the Shaan-Gan-Ning border region. Japan's "Three All" campaign was continuing and was inflicting heavy costs on the north China base areas of the CCP. (Japanese pressure would not ease until the fall of 1942 when the sharpening contest over Guadalcanal in the Solomon Islands forced Japan to begin redeploying units from north China to the South Pacific.[19]) In such a situation, to have concentrated Communist forces for major operations against Japanese units would have left the Shaan-Gan-Ning base area exposed to the KMT.

The political corollary of the Comintern's military line was that the CCP should do whatever necessary to minimize conflict with the KMT, to unify all Chinese forces to wage war against Japan, and to conduct joint military actions with the KMT. All actions of the CCP ought to be subordinated to this overriding task of unity in effective action against Japan. Vladimirov believed that Mao's policy of seizing new areas from the KMT whenever the opportunity arose contradicted this "correct" political orientation.[20]

Mao's "nationalist deviation" from Comintern line encountered resistance within the CCP, but the full extent of the opposition to Mao at this juncture is still unclear. If subsequent Soviet sources are to be believed, a large part of the top CCP leadership supported to some degree the Internationalist position of Wang Ming and Bo Gu at this juncture. Zhang Wentian, Zhou Enlai, Zhu De, Peng Dehuai, Yang Shangkun, He Long, and Xiang Ying are all named by various Soviet sources as supporting the Internationalist position in 1941–1942.[21] Chinese sources identify only Wang Ming and Bo Gu as opponents of Mao in 1941–1942. There are hints, however, that opposition may have been much more widespread. A 1982 internal CCP handbook on party rectification, for example, indicated that "Wang Ming's" influence with "a part of the CCP membership" was still "relatively big" in 1942.[22] The reticence of the CCP to divulge information regarding divisions within its top leadership at this juncture may itself be an indication that individuals who were prominent and respected in post-1949 China questioned Mao's stance in 1941–1942.[23] On the face of it, it should not be too surprising for CCP leaders to have been dismayed by Mao's nationalism. These men had, after all, risen within the CCP independently of Mao Zedong. And as Marxist–Leninists they had long looked upon the USSR as the bastion of socialism and had long anticipated an imperialist onslaught against that bastion. Now when the predicted onslaught had finally materialized, Mao pursued policies exactly the opposite of those prescribed by "proletarian internationalism." It was one thing to view with equanimity the plight of the reactionary Chinese government before Japan's invasion; it was quite something else to adopt such an attitude toward the socialist Soviet Union. It thus seems likely that one immediate cause for the beginning of the *Zheng Feng* (party rectification) campaign, which began in 1942, was internal CCP resistance to Mao's disregard for Moscow's orders. On the one hand, the Zheng Feng campaign was possible because of Moscow's preoccupation in the West. On the other hand, it was made necessary, in part, by the internal CCP repercussions of that "preoccupation."

According to Vladimirov, Mao responded to Comintern challenges to his passive military policies by trying to isolate the Soviet liaison group. By late 1941, top CCP leaders no longer met with members of the Soviet liaison group, and Kang Sheng's intelligence operatives had begun shadowing Soviet personnel. Mao terminated the practice of passing on to the liaison group information about internal CCP issues and made the internal affairs of the CCP off limits to the Soviet group.[24] Depending on Vladimirov's precise status, these moves may have in themselves constituted violations of the organizational rules of the Comintern.

Mao's resistance to Moscow's wishes, and perhaps the strong opposition to Mao among the top CCP leadership, may have emboldened Wang Ming to make what would be his final challenge to Mao. According to Vladimirov, by the end of 1941 the dispute between Mao and Wang was increasingly sharp. Mao responded by launching a campaign designed to break once and for all the influence of Wang and Moscow within the CCP.

Moscow and the Zheng Feng Campaign

The Zheng Feng or party rectification campaign which unfolded throughout the base areas of the CCP in 1942–1944 represented the final emancipation of the CCP from Moscow's control. Zheng Feng was not, of course, merely a consequence of the conflict between Mao and Wang Ming's Internationalists. It had several important aspects. It was an effort to respond to the economic and military hardships imposed by Japan's brutal "Three All" campaign and by the tightening KMT blockade. It was also designed to indoctrinate the many recently recruited Party members in the elements of Marxist–Leninist ideology. It can also be viewed as an attempt to make a complex foreign ideology, Marxism–Leninism, intelligible to the broad masses of Chinese people. It was an effort to feret out KMT and Japanese spies and to compel ideological uniformity. For our purposes, however, the most important aspect of the Zheng Feng campaign was the extirpation of the influence of the CCP Internationalists. As a 1984 CCP handbook on party rectification explained, although "opportunism" had been basically overcome at the Zunyi Conference of January 1935, because of the war with Japan and other "changes in the situation" the ideological roots of such "mistaken thought" had not been thoroughly eliminated. Wang Ming's "dogmatism" still had influence within the Party and manifested itself in such forms as "understanding only Greece [i.e., the Soviet Union], and not understanding China," and "treating Comintern directives and the experiences of the Soviet Union as sacrosanct."[25] As Boyd Compton put it, Wang Ming was the "specific target" of the Zheng Feng movement."[26]

"Subjectivism," "sectarianism," and "formalism" were all condemned during the Zheng Feng campaign, with "dogmatism" being singled out as the most dangerous and important form of subjectivism.[27] Mao later explained just what "dogmatism" was. Dogmatists, Mao explained, were people who refused to integrate the "universal truths of Marxism–Leninism" with the "concrete realities" of the Chinese revolution. The essence of dogmatism was dependency on foreign theories and formulations and a refusal to develop a sinified form of Marxism premised on the needs of making revolution in China. Indeed, Mao explained, "dogmatists" did not even understand China and the Chinese revolution, but only understood the history of foreign countries and revolutions.[28] The sinification of Marxism was Mao's solution to dogmatism. As we saw earlier, Mao had raised this theme at the Sixth Plenum in September 1938. During 1939 and 1940 Mao occasionally alluded to this idea, but it was during Zheng Feng that he formulated a specifically Chinese theory of Marxism.[29]

Mao's opening moves in the Zheng Feng campaign came on 5 May 1941 when he delivered a speech to a senior cadres conference maintaining that a correct revolutionary ideology had to begin with a study of Chinese society and then extend to the study of classical Marxist–Leninist theory. To proceed the other way around, Mao implied, would lead to acceptance of a rigid foreign doctrine without questioning its applicability to Chinese problems.[30] Mao's 5 May speech was not published until 1 July, however, a week after the German attack on the Soviet Union. Would Mao have moved against the Internationalists even without the Nazi invasion of the Soviet Union? Unfortunately, we can only speculate about Mao's calculations prior to 22 June 1941. In any case, it is clear that Mao did not move against the Internationalists until the development of the titanic Soviet-German war absorbed Soviet strength and attention in Europe. This is not to say that Mao welcomed the German invasion of the Soviet Union, although Comintern representatives in Yan'an thought that he did. Rather, as the Chinese proverb says, *zai weng shi ma, yan zhi fei fu.* (Even in calamity good fortune can be found.)

After the onset of the Soviet-German war, the Zheng Feng campaign began gaining steam. On the occasion of the twentieth founding of the CCP on 1 July 1941, the CCP center issued a resolution calling for the entire Party to submit to central discipline. In September, an expanded meeting of the Politburo formally launched the movement, calling for an "ideological revolution" within the Party.[31] The conference also debated the history of the CCP during the 1927–1937 period. According to Vladimirov, Wang Ming's violations of Party discipline at Wuhan in 1938 were criticized, and heated debate resulted.[32] The crux of Wang's 1938 lack of discipline was, as we saw in Chapter 3, his obedience to Comintern line rather than to Mao Zedong. Vladimirov's account of substantial elite disunity at this conference is indirectly confirmed by subsequent CCP sources which say that the Politburo meeting decided that it was necessary to unify the Party's thinking and to resolve the general question of theory and practice in the Chinese revolution.[33] To this end, a "study group" was set up to organize "study" among high-level cadres.[34]

Early in 1942 the campaign became full blown. The Central Party School was reorganized and a thousand top-level cadres were assembled there in February 1942. A speech by Mao on 1 February substantially intensified the campaign by calling for a thorough effort to rectify errors in party work style and thought. Further speeches by Mao and Propaganda Bureau Chief Kai Feng and authoritative articles in *Jiefang Ribao* followed. Discussions, investigations, and criticism, self-criticism activities then unfolded rapidly, stimulated by an atmosphere of terror in which each individual feared he might be made his unit's designated target for ideological remolding.[35] Rectification began with the top levels of the CCP and gradually extended downward and outward from Yan'an. By summer 1942, the campaign had extended to the party organizations of the entire Shaan-Gan-Ning border region.

As the Internationalist position was "liquidated," Mao's control over the CCP was consolidated. On 19 October 1942, a conference of the Northwest Bureau of the CCP including 266 top cadres convened to inspect and summarize, under Mao's personal leadership, the work of the border region. The conference, which continued until 14 January 1943, opened with a lecture by Mao on the need to bolshevize the CCP. Mao sharply criticized lack of discipline within the Party and called for strengthened central control.[36] A month after this conference adjourned, the Politburo itself met and institutionalized Mao's control. On 20 March 1943, the Politburo elected Mao its Chairman and General Secretary of the Central Committee Secretariat. Mao had become "Chairman Mao." The other two members of the Secretariat were Mao's close allies Liu Shaoqi and Ren Bishi.[37]

The Northwest Bureau conference also made a major stride toward the formula-tion of a Maoist Party history. The creation of an orthodox history of the CCP was a major component of Zheng Feng and of the extirpation of Soviet influence within the CCP. Again, multiple considerations were at work. Historiography has always played a central role in the exercise of power in China. Laid on top of this is the

Marxist tradition of deriving "laws" from the study of history. More specifically, the "correctness" of "Mao Zedong Thought"—which emerged from Zheng Feng—could be demonstrated by showing it to be manifest in the "concrete historical processes" of the CCP. It followed from this that the various "errors" of the Internationalists would be exposed and Mao's claim to leadership of the Party upheld. [38]

Chen Boda had written a classified preliminary Maoist version of Party history in 1938. Shortly afterward, the CCP launched a drive to collect materials dealing with the Party's history. Mao edited a history of the CCP since the Sixth Congress in 1928 early in 1941, and the senior cadres conference at the end of 1942 further elaborated and debated this history. [39] A crucial element of this revision of history was fixing the blame for the failures of the early 1930s squarely on Wang Ming. Since the Zunyi Conference, it had been held that between 1931 and 1935 only the military line, and not the political line, of the Party had been mistaken. In January 1943, however, Ren Bishi delivered a report revising this judgment. It was precisely the political errors during this period, Ren maintained, which were responsible for the catastrophes that befell the CCP during the Jiangxi soviet period. So erroneous had the 1931–1935 line been, Ren maintained, that it produced evils exceeding those of Chen Duxiu's and Li Lisan's opportunist lines. But while everyone knew that Moscow was responsible for the 1931–1935 line, Mao was careful not to point directly at the Comintern. Wang Ming and Pavil Mif were technically exonerated from responsibility for this incorrect line by dating its beginning from September 1931, when Bo Gu became Secretary General, not January 1931 when Mif had installed Wang in that office. [40]

By late 1943, the Zheng Feng campaign entered the stage of "summing up Party history." Top-level cadres met repeatedly to discuss Ren's January report and to debate the period of Wang Ming's leadership from 1931 to 1935. [41] An anthology on Party history entitled "The Two Lines" was published. This was a clear reference to Wang Ming's 1931 and 1940 polemic, and the collection indeed demonstrated Wang's repeated errors and the evolution of correct Mao Zedong Thought in struggle against those errors. [42] By April 1944 the thinking of top-level cadres on these critical historical issues had been "unified" and a "resolution on several historical problems" was drafted by Ren Bishi with the assistance of Liu Shaoqi, Zhou Enlai, Bo Gu, and Zhang Wentian. The final revision of the resolution was made by Mao himself. The production of this orthodox history, according to later Chinese sources, was a major "ideological preparation" for the "victorious convocation" of the Seventh Plenum of the Sixth Central Committee immediately prior to the Seventh Congress in the spring of 1945. [43] After a Maoist interpretation of party history had been agreed upon, preparations for the actual convocation of the Seventh Congress were begun. [44]

Once it had been agreed that the 1931–1934 line was incorrect, it followed that Wang Ming and his supporters should criticize their earlier behavior. According to Wang Ming, former supporters of the Comintern line such as Zhang Wentian, Wang Jiaxiang, Yang Shangkun, and Zhou Enlai were compelled to criticize their previous errors. Party members who had studied in the Soviet Union were especially called upon to examine their political past for "error." [45] Wang Ming himself refused to confess past errors and engage in self-criticism. [46] According to Vladimirov, Wang sought and received Soviet protection. Late in October 1943, Wang asked his Soviet doctor to cable Moscow requesting former Comintern head Dimitrov to inform Mao that

Wang's earlier actions had been in accord with Comintern guidelines and directives, and that Wang had merely been doing his duty in carrying them out. (Wang also criticized Mao's line as contradicting the interests of the antifascist united front.) Vladimirov duly radioed Wang's message to Moscow and the following January a response from Dimitrov arrived in Yan'an.[47] Mao replied by reassuring Dimitrov that Wang was being dealt with in accordance with principles of Party unity. It appears that Dimitrov's intervention protected Wang from being forced to undergo self-criticism.[48] By December 1943, however, Wang was ready for reconciliation with Mao and repented for his October appeal to Dimitrov.[49]

As in so many of his battles, during the Zheng Feng campaign Mao Zedong demonstrated a mastery of political stratagem. While Zheng Feng was a devastating attack on Moscow's loyal followers, it did not take the form of an attack on Moscow, Stalin, or Soviet-style Marxism–Leninism. Rather, as in mid-1938, Mao stressed his loyalty to Moscow while moving against Moscow's Chinese proxies. Taken at face value the polemics associated with Zheng Feng indicated acceptance of the tenants of orthodox Soviet Marxism–Leninism including dialectical materialism, materialist epistemology, the central role of the productive forces, the role and nature of the Party, the unity of theory and practice, and the class nature of all literature and art.[50] Moreover, the Communist Party of the Soviet Union (CPSU) was held up as a model in the application of these principles. As Mao himself said of the official Stalinist history of the CPSU in his 1 February 1942 speech,

The *History of the Communist Party of the Soviet Union* is the highest synthesis and summary of the world Communist movement in the last hundred years, a model for the union of theory and practice; in the whole world, this is still the one perfect model. By observing the way in which Lenin and Stalin took the universal truths of Marxism and related them to the concrete reality of the Soviet revolution and thereby developed Marxism, we can understand the manner in which we should carry out our work in China.[51]

During Zheng Feng, the CCP continually reiterated its loyalty to the Comintern. One of the campaign's study documents, "How to Be a Communist Party Member," stipulated, for example, that "Anyone who subscribes to the Constitution and regulations of the Communist International and the Chinese Communist Party [and also] obeys all the resolutions of the Communist International . . . may become a Party member."[52] In his various Zheng Feng speeches, Mao went to some lengths to appear an orthodox Stalinist. He frequently cited Stalin and extolled him as an ideal of brevity of expression, as a model in the creation of new and useful concepts and words, and as providing an example of how intra-Party struggle should be conducted.[53] Several speeches and articles by Stalin as well as articles by Dimitrov and Lenin, and the introduction to the Stalinist *History of the CPSU* were among the required study documents of the campaign.

In one sense Mao turned Stalinism against Stalin. As Boyd Compton pointed out, organization was perhaps the greatest Russian gift to revolutionary movements in Asia and it was during Zheng Feng that the CCP was "thoroughly bolshevized" under Mao Zedong's control.[54] During Zheng Feng, the first systematic and intensive survey of Soviet organizational methods was carried out by the CCP, the Soviet method of Party discipline was adopted in full, factionalism was repressed, and Mao's supremacy within the Party was consolidated. A cult of Mao, complete with icons, hero worship, and a hagiography of Mao, was created and inculcated into Party members.[55] This consolidation of Mao's control would have a significant influence on Soviet-Chinese relations in 1944–1945. Once Nazi Germany began to collapse and Stalin began considering the options he faced in the Far East, he had to consider that he no longer had much influence within CCP. He could, of course, still pressure Mao. But no longer could he do this by encouraging and supporting opposition to Mao within the CCP. The CCP was now a Stalinist Party with Mao as its leader.

There is also some evidence that we should take Mao at his word regarding his emulation of Stalin's method of conducting intra-Party struggle. During the 1940s there were reports of numerous executions associated with Zheng Feng. Recent Chinese accounts confirm that Zheng Feng was, indeed, very violent, while charging that Kang Sheng, rather than Mao, was responsible for this. As noted earlier, Kang was head of the Politburo's political protection office, the equivalent of the secret police, and played a key role in the first several years of Zheng Feng. According to one account, Kang viewed Zheng Feng as a "purge of counter-revolutionaries [*sufan*]" and used coercion and "cruel struggle" to extort confessions from cadre. "Many cadres" were subjected to repeated "mass struggle" and then "turned over to public security for treatment as counter-revolutionaries [*zui hou jiao gei shuhuibu an sufan duixiang chuli*]."[56] Arrests were made arbitrarily, people were forced to commit suicide, and a climate of fear was created. It was not until December 1943 that this "incorrect" style of rectification was brought to an end.[57] According to the subsequent leader of the Indonesian Communist Party who was in Yan'an during Zheng Feng, many people were executed during the campaign.[58] While we must be skeptical about the high figures tossed about by such sources, it does seem clear that the first two years of Zheng Feng did involve substantial violence. Moreover, as Peter Seybolt has pointed out, this violence was instrumental in persuading cadres to renounce heretical beliefs and embrace the new Maoist orthodoxy. In this regard also, Mao turned Stalin's own methods against Moscow.[59]

The Zheng Feng campaign unfolded under the eyes of the Soviet mission in Yan'an. Two of the radio operators and a TASS reporter were withdrawn in October 1943, but liaison officer Vladimirov and the four other Soviet personnel remained in Yan'an until the end of the war. (Vladimirov himself remained until November 1945.) Several days after his arrival in May 1942, Vladimirov confided in his diary that "The Comintern is worried [about] what is going on in the leadership of the Chinese Communist Party." As Zheng Feng gained steam in the spring of 1942, Vladimirov found the situation "so serious that it wholly absorbs my attention." The CCP, he believed, was trying to conceal the anti-Soviet essence of the campaign. Although Mao attempted to explain the internal CCP struggle to Vladimirov, the latter found those explanations unsatisfactory and concluded that Mao believed that Comintern policy toward China was wrong and was using "dogmatism" as a foil with which to attack the supporters of the Comintern within the CCP.[60] In Vladimirov's view, during the critical spring and summer of 1942, the CCP should have been mobilizing its forces to fight Japan, not dissipating its energies through intense intra-party struggle. The Zheng Feng campaign was possible because of the lower-intensity military strategy adopted by Mao in 1942, and from the Soviet perspective both were equally damnable.

Vladimirov believed that the conflict between Mao and Wang Ming's Internationalists—who posed the "main opposition" to Mao—had been intensifying since the end of 1941. Vladimirov does not specify the causes of this conflict, but he implies that it was over Mao's militant policy toward the KMT and the lessening of military pressure on Japan which resulted from this policy. Mao had to move carefully, since Wang was still a member of the Executive Committee of the Communist International (ECCI) and CCP representative to the Comintern.[61] Nonetheless, by early 1943 Vladimirov had concluded that Zheng Feng was a general assault on all Internationalist influence within the CCP. The Comintern officer perceived increasing pressure on all Party members who had worked for the Comintern or who had studied in the Soviet Union. Party members were being called on to confess all previous connections with the Soviet Union and with Wang Ming. Surveillance of the activities of the Soviet mission was also stepped up, and further restrictions were placed on its contacts with Chinese.[62] Vladimirov is vague about whether or not he cabled these observations and conclusions to Moscow. Presumably he did. This was, after all, his job, and he reports that the mission's three radio operators frequently worked throughout the night (when atmospheric conditions were better) communicating with Moscow. It was in this context of growing Soviet suspicions of Mao that the Comintern was dissolved in May 1943.

The Dissolution of the Comintern and the "Third Anti-Communist High Tide"

On 7 May 1943 Yan'an received a cable from the ECCI proposing the dissolution of the Communist International in order to strengthen unity in the antifascist war and allow various national Communist Parties to deal independently with the complex situations they faced in their own countries.[63] Chinese observers understood Moscow's reasoning and cryptic language.[64] Soviet policy now revolved around the imperative of a second front in Europe and Moscow did not want seeming Soviet support for foreign Communist movements to complicate its relations with the United States and Great Britain.

According to Vladimirov (who claimed that Bo Gu informed him about this matter), when the CCP Politburo met to discuss the ECCI message Mao opened the meeting by reading the recent ECCI cable. He then said that in his opinion the ECCI proposal was entirely justified and correct. The Comintern had long since outlived its usefulness as a leading body of the international working-class movement, Mao said.[65] The Politburo endorsed Mao's position and moved to "agree completely" with the ECCI proposal. "In the course of the revolutionary struggle," the statement issue by the Politburo concluded, "the Chinese Communist Party has received much assistance from the Communist International. Nonetheless, China's Communists have long since been capable of independently determining their own political direction, policy and activities on the basis of their concrete circumstances and special conditions of their own people's liberation."[66] These themes were expanded upon in the CCP newspaper, *Xinhua Ribao.* The paper was careful to point out, however, that the dissolution of the Comintern would not mean the dissolution of the Chinese Communist Party.[67] Such a demand had been raised by various groups in the provincial capital of Xian.[68] There is fragmentary evidence that Wang Ming or others within the CCP in fact proposed a "Browderist"-style dissolution of the CCP.[69]

The dissolution of the Comintern was a windfall for Mao Zedong. It confirmed ipso facto his contention that the CCP had to define its own political line rather than being guided by Moscow. It also indicated to the Internationalists that they could not expect Comintern intervention. It made clear that the internal Party struggle would be decided solely on the basis of the forces that each side could rally within China; the Internationalists were on their own. Thus, there is reason to credit Vladimirov's recollection that shortly after the dissolution of the Comintern, Mao announced that the time had finally arrived to convene the long-delayed Seventh Congress. By early September, again according to Vladimirov, all of Wang Ming's previous supporters except for Bo Gu had broken with Wang and criticized him for his earlier errors.[70]

But even though the Comintern no longer existed, Moscow could still influence the CCP. According to Vladimirov, throughout 1943 Mao sent misleading cables to Moscow "camouflaging the actual situation" in the Shaan-Gan-Ning border area and especially the nature of the differences between Mao himself and Wang Ming.[71] Apparently Vladimirov did his best to disabuse Moscow of Mao's disinformation, for on 3 January 1944 a cable from Georgii Dimitrov arrived in Yan'an expressing apprehension about the repression of the "Moscow Group" within the CCP, and about Kang Sheng's violent methods. Mao promptly cabled his own views about CCP policy and objectives to Dimitrov and assured him that Wang Ming was being treated according to the principles of strengthening Party unity. Mao also became more cordial toward the Soviet mission in Yan'an. Two days after Dimitrov's cable arrived Mao invited Vladimirov to attend an opera and in the course of the evening lauded Stalin, the CPSU, and the Soviet Union, and expressed his gratitude for Dimitrov's sincere desire to help the CCP. Several days later Mao invited several members of the Soviet mission to dine with him and other top CCP leaders.[72]

Vladimirov is of the opinion that the arrival of Dimitrov's cable persuaded Mao of the need to win over Wang Ming in order to defuse charges of anti-Sovietism. While keeping Wang ignorant of Dimitrov's cable, Mao had a long talk with him on 6 January 1944 and held out the possibility of reconciliation if Wang confessed his past errors. Mao reportedly succeeded in persuading Wang to accept this arrangement.[73] While we have only Vladimirov's account of this episode, there is a certain logic to it. Wang, along with Bo Gu, was in fact reelected to the Central Committee at the Seventh Congress in April 1945 while going along with the Maoist version of CCP history promulgated on that occasion. It therefore makes sense to presume that a deal such as the one described by Vladimirov must have been made.

Mao had good reason to avoid alienating Moscow from mid-1943 onward. After the catastrophic German defeats at Stalingrad in January and at Kursk (in southern Russia some 300 miles or 480 kilometers south of Moscow) in August 1943, it was increasingly apparent that the Soviet Union would not only survive the war but would very probably emerge as one of the world's preeminent powers. If the Soviet Union entered the war against Japan, it would obviously play a direct and significant role in the affairs of China and postwar East Asia. Mao also realized that the Soviet Union, like the United States, could help prevent the KMT from launching a war against the CCP prior to Japan's surrender. In spite of, or perhaps because of, the deepening economic, military, and political crisis of the Nationalist regime which developed during 1943, by the middle of that year hard-line KMT anticommunists were arguing for an immediate military showdown with the CCP.[74] Were such a confrontation delayed until the Soviet Union entered the war against Japan, these people argued, the Chinese Communist armies would be in a position to take over north China and Manchuria in the wake of the Red Army's advance.[75]

Just as Chongqing had seized the opportunity of the crisis of 1942 to push the Soviet Union out of Xinjiang, it also took advantage of the Soviet-German war to restrict contacts between the Soviet Union and the Shaan-Gan-Ning region. Prior to late 1942, Chongqing had permitted Soviet aircraft to fly to Yan'an via Dihua and Lanzhou about twice a year in order to supply the Soviet mission at Yan'an. The flights were permitted to carry only Soviet nationals and their personal effects. Although earlier flights had been inspected in Lanzhou by Nationalist authorities to ensure that these regulations were adhered to, by late 1942 these inspections had become extremely meticulous. The inspection of one of the last Soviet aircraft to fly to Yan'an in November 1942 took two full days and resulted in the confiscation of a ton of medical supplies.[76] After this incident, there was apparently only one other, clandestine, Soviet flight to Yan'an during the remainder of the war.

Early in 1943 the KMT began strengthening its blockade of the Shaan-Gan-Ning region and concentrating troops in Gansu and Ningxia provinces to prevent overland communications between the border region and the Mongolian People's Republic.[77] By June, Hu Songnan commanded 500,000 troops and was positioning units for an offensive against the CCP base area. Once Hu's forces were ready, Chongqing demanded the abolition of both the CCP and the Shaan-Gan-Ning special area, citing the abolition of the Comintern as a precedent for such a move.[78] Then, in early July, Hu's forces began an artillery bombardment of CCP-controlled areas.[79]

On 2 August, Zhou Enlai rejected the KMT demand for the dissolution of the CCP. It was not the CCP which should be abolished, Zhou reportedly said, but the fascist special agent organizations of the KMT. The CCP would deal independently with the problems of the Chinese revolution without guidance from the Comintern.[80]

Confronted with what it termed the "Third Anti-Communist High Tide," the CCP sought to check a KMT offensive by mobilizing domestic and international pressure to force the KMT to "maintain unity" and "uphold the united front." Among the international forces mobilized by the CCP was the influence of both the United States and the Soviet Union. According to Vladimirov, in early July 1943 Mao asked him to cable Dimitrov requesting Soviet action to prevent a KMT offensive against the border region. Vladimirov obliged and later reported to Mao that on 13 July the Soviet government had declared to Chongqing that its military assistance to China (*sic*) was aimed at strengthening China's struggle against Japan, not at unleashing civil war.[81] This account was probably apocryphal.[82] It thus appears either than Vladimirov's memoir is inaccurate, or that Moscow falsely informed him that it was protesting to Chongqing. The latter is quite possible. After all, Mao had no way of knowing whether Vladimirov's statement was true, and such a ploy would satisfy the demands of Yan'an and build up some political capital there without alienating Chongqing or rousing American suspicions.

But while the existence of a direct Soviet protest to Chongqing in July is questionable, there clearly were other forms of stepped-up Soviet pressure on Chongqing at this juncture. As was discussed in the last chapter, on 6 August 1943 an article strongly critical of the KMT regime appeared in the Soviet publication *War and the Working Class*. Subsequently, criticism of the Nationalist regime by the Soviet media began to mount. This Soviet media campaign was more closely related to the maneuvering over the terms of postwar relations between the Republic of China and the Soviet Union than it was to CCP–KMT relations. Still, Moscow did have an interest in preventing a KMT–CCP clash and in keeping China in the war against Japan.

In a way it was appropriate that Moscow intervene to check Chongqing since Chongqing used the dissolution of the Comintern as a pretext for its move against the CCP. Implicit in Chongqing's demand for the dissolution of the CCP was the notion that Moscow supported such a move, or at least that it was indifferent to the continued existence of the CCP. Thus, by indicating concern for the CCP via its media polemics, Moscow demonstrated its apparent concern for the CCP. In so doing, Moscow strengthened the "progressive" forces within the KMT who argued that there was a direct linkage between KMT–CCP relations and ROC-USSR relations.

A key dividing line in Chinese politics during the war involved defining how relations between the Soviet Union and the CCP were linked to those between the Soviet Union and the Republic of China. One of the central beliefs which defined "progressivism" in China at that juncture was the notion that the ideological bonds between Moscow and Yan'an were real and strong, and that if the Republic of China wanted friendly and cordial relations with the Soviet Union, China's National Government should deal leniently with, and ultimately cooperate with, the CCP.[83] The United States tended to share this perspective.[84] Chinese "conservatives," on the other hand, believed either that because Moscow was preoccupied in Europe or because it was willing to strike a deal with Chongqing, the National Government could use military force against the CCP without irreparably alienating the Soviet Union. While the differing American "progressive" and Chinese "conservative" views about the nature of Sino-Soviet linkages had a profound impact on Sino-American relations, our concern here is with Sino-Soviet relations. From the latter perspective, the chief political consequence of these clashing "conservative" and "progressive" perspectives was that it made it possible for Yan'an to mobilize American and Chinese "progressive" pressure against Chiang Kai-shek and other "conservatives" by stressing the link between the CCP and Moscow.

Moscow for its part balanced pressure on Chongqing with advice of moderation for the CCP. Dimitrov's cable of 3 January 1944, which was discussed earlier, expressed concern about the poor state of KMT–CCP relations and warned of the ill consequences which would result from a breakdown of the united front. In his response to Dimitrov, Mao politely thanked the former Comintern head for his warning about the inadvisability of a KMT–CCP break. The policy of anti-Japanese unity between the CCP and the KMT remained unchanged, Mao assured Dimitrov.[85]

While Soviet pressure was far less instrumental than American in forcing

Chongqing to abandon its planned move against the CCP in 1943-1944, still Moscow's attitude was an important contributing factor. One reason why the United States forced Chongqing to drop its offensive against the CCP at this point was that American diplomats feared that such a drive would further undermine Soviet-ROC relations. This, in turn, would complicate the future conduct of the war and undermine the postwar peace. By implicitly making public its support for the CCP at this juncture, Moscow reinforced the linkage between KMT–CCP relations and USSR-ROC relations which existed in American minds. As we shall see, Mao was aware of the utility of an apparent Moscow-Yan'an bond in helping induce the United States to restrain the anticommunism of the KMT.

The Grand Alliance and KMT–CCP Relations

Relations between the CCP and the Soviet Union during the last two years of World War II must be viewed from a global perspective. Throughout the war, Stalin perceived important contradictions between his alliance with the United States and Great Britain on the one hand and his role as leader of a international revolutionary movement on the other. Stalin wanted to maintain and manipulate his alliance with the United States in order to ensure the complete destruction of German power, to guarantee postwar Soviet security, and to win concessions from his wartime allies. Continuing Soviet-American amity was endangered, however, by Communist-led revolutions. At the root of Stalin's dilemma was the fact that a whole generation of Marxists had been shaped by the experience of World War I and indoctrinated with the belief that the outbreak of another world war would give rise to a new wave of world revolution which would lead to the demise of capitalism around the world. World War II seemed to be the cataclysm predicted by Marxist-Leninist theory since 1919. Moreover, in many of the Axis-occupied countries, the ruling elites had been tainted by collaboration with the enemy and a deep crisis of legitimacy developed. Many Communist Parties saw the defeat of fascism as the long-awaited opportunity to seize power.[86]

For the sake of his alliance with the Anglo-Americans, Stalin continually tried to staunch such local radicalism and to pressure Communist Parties to come to terms with the nonfascist but bourgeois governments ruling, or claiming the right to rule, their countries. As the war entered its final phase in 1944–1945, with country after country undergoing the crisis of liberation, Moscow's problem became especially acute. The chief method adopted by Moscow for coping with the "insurrectionism" of local Communist Parties was to force those Parties to enter bourgeois-dominated coalition governments. Often a corollary of this was Communist relinquishment of their hard-won arsenals and the disbandment of their paramilitary units.

In Yugoslavia, Greece, France, and Italy there were powerful Communist-led movements which saw the impending collapse of Germany and Italy as the long-awaited opportunity to seize power. In the case of Yugoslavia, Moscow tried valiantly but unsuccessfully to contain the radicalism of Tito's Partisans.[87] The Greek Communists also chafed at Soviet imposed moderation and vacillated between obedience to Moscow and defiance of Soviet orders.[88] In France and Italy, Soviet efforts met with greater success. In April 1944, the Communist Parties of both countries accepted posts in bourgeois governments. Later in the year, the Communist-led resistance in France surrendered its arms to the de Gaulle government under direct orders from Moscow.[89]

Interactions between the Soviet Union and CCP fit into this pattern. Stalin had good reasons for wishing to forestall a CCP uprising. A Communist drive for power in China would make less likely the recognition of Soviet demands by the United States and the Republic of China in Manchuria. Civil war in China would also create chaos on Soviet borders and threaten to draw American troops into China. Finally, as in Greece, France, Italy, and Yugoslavia, it would undermine cooperation with the United States. Mao, on the other hand, was very optimistic about revolutionary prospects in the spring of 1944. KMT armies were disintegrating under Japan's Operation Ichi-go, while the political, moral, and economic crisis of the Nationalist regime deepened. Meanwhile, Communist base areas, armies, and mass organizations were once again expanding rapidly as Japanese forces redeployed from north and central China to south China and the Pacific islands. So advantageous did conditions appear that on 5 June 1944 the Seventh Plenum of the Sixth Central Committee (formally in session from 21 May 1944 to 20 April 1945) ordered preparations for armed insurrections in China's major cities. A special "urban work" committee headed by Peng Zhen was established to plan and organize the seizure of major cities, and cadres and funds were allocated to prepare for urban insurrections. "Unless we occupy big cities and the main lines of communications," said the 5 June resolution on "urban work," "We will not be able to drive the Japs out of China." Previously, "people" had believed that the expulsion of the "Japs" from big cities and the main lines of communication could only be realized by the KMT. Now this view would have to change. Preparations for armed urban insurrection, to be launched in coordination with assaults on big cities by the armies of the CCP, had to begin at once.[90] Vladimirov does not mention the 5 June resolution, but by late 1944 he was very concerned with the CCP's drive for power.

It was the United States rather than the Soviet Union which was the dominant foreign power in China during 1944–1945 (aside, of course, from Japan). Thus, while the focus of our investigation is on Soviet rather than American policy, if we are to understand relations between the Soviet Union and the CCP, we must perforce consider the role of the United States. As we saw in the last chapter, Roosevelt sought to keep China actively in the war against Japan, thereby engaging Japanese troops which might otherwise be used to fight American forces. In terms of the postwar structure of peace in East Asia, Roosevelt sought a united and peaceful China coexisting on friendly terms with both the United States and the Soviet Union. The realization of both Roosevelt's wartime and peacetime objectives necessitated avoidance of a civil war between the KMT and the CCP.

Just as Stalin's attitude toward the CCP was fundamentally conditioned by Soviet-American relations, so was Mao's Soviet policy intertwined with his American policy. Mao, like Chiang, was compelled to maneuver between the United States and the Soviet Union, and like Chiang he attempted to manipulate Soviet-American relations to isolate and crush his Chinese rival. As we saw in the last chapter, Chiang's effort in this regard centered on using American diplomatic mediation to work out a deal with Stalin, the crux of which was Soviet nonsupport for the CCP in exchange for concessions in Manchuria. Mao had less to offer Stalin than did Chiang and, consequently, his efforts to manipulate Soviet-American relations were, unlike those of Chiang, ultimately unsuccessful. Basically, Mao could choose between two options in 1944–1945 regarding relations with the United States. On the one hand, he could agree to peaceful cooperation with the KMT and within this framework attempt to drive a wedge between Washington and Chongqing while winning American support for Yan'an. On the other hand, he could attempt to detach the Soviet Union from the United States, secure Soviet support, and move with Soviet backing against a United States-sponsored KMT regime.[91] The success of the first strategy depended to a considerable degree on the manipulation of American fears of the Soviet Union. The success of the second, on the manipulation of Soviet fears of the United States.

Given the preeminence of American power in non-Japanese-occupied China, it is not surprising that Mao initially pursued the American option. Mao established direct links with the Americans when the U.S. Military Observer's Mission arrived in Yan'an in July 1944. During the second half of 1944 and early 1945, Yan'an assiduously courted the American observers group and tried to assure Washington of its willingness to cooperate militarily and politically with the United States. On 18 August 1944, the Central Committee issued a secret directive instructing CCP cadres how to deal with the personnel of the newly arrived Observers Mission. The arrival of the American mission in Yan'an indicated, the directive said, the beginning of the CCP's diplomatic work. American personnel were to be received modestly but warmly, and military cooperation was to be used to foster cultural and political cooperation. The general purpose of such activity was to win American sympathy and support in order to induce the Untied States to remain neutral in the KMT–CCP confrontation.[92]

One key component of Mao's attempt to cooperate with the United States was the promulgation of a program of coalition government. As will be recalled, the idea of Communist participation in a Nationalist-dominated government had been discussed and rejected by Mao in mid-1938. It had then been superceded in 1940 by a program of New Democracy which the "proletariat" (i.e., the CCP) was to lead. In mid-1944, however, Mao revived the notion of a KMT–CCP coalition government—albeit with the important caveat that this was to be a transition step to the dismantling of the system of political control of the KMT.

Mao proposed a coalition government to John S. Service (whom the CCP leaders identified as the leading political officer attached to the Military Observers Mission) on 23 August 1944 as a way of averting a disastrous civil war. The United States should pressure Chiang, Mao proposed, into convening a multiparty provisional congress which would then establish a coalition government. That coalition government would then democratize China's political system while preparing elections to establish a full-fledged national congress. The United States should flatly demand that Chiang accept this program, Mao said.[93] On 15 September the representative of the CCP at the Political Consultative Conference in Chongqing made public this program of coalition government.[94]

This program of coalition government meshed with the policies of the Soviet Union as well as those of the United States. The lengthy cable Mao received from

Dimitrov on 3 January 1944 had expressed Soviet concern with the tense state of KMT–CPP relations and about the future of the anti-Japanese united front in China. While Vladimirov does not reveal the precise contents of this cable, he does say that it shocked the CCP leadership and was discussed at length by the leadership shortly after its arrival.[95] Given the approach which Moscow was taking toward European Communist Parties at that time, it is highly likely that the 3 January cable proposed a coalition government as a desirable solution to China's disunity. Several months later, Stalin in fact told Hurley that he had already ordered Mao to enter into a coalition government.[96]

The Soviet factor played a subtle but important role in Mao's bid for cooperation with the United States in 1944. In his quest for American support, Mao minimized his Soviet connection to reassure the Americans, while at the same time subtly persuading them that he did have a Soviet option if the U.S. refused to work with the CCP. Mao understood that one reason why the United States might decide to cooperate with the CCP was a desire to keep it from dependency on the Soviet Union in the hope of checking Soviet penetration of China. Stimulating American apprehensions over Soviet intentions combined with indications of CCP willingness to cooperate with the United States was thus useful in prodding Washington toward a more "progressive" policy in China. The existence of an apparent Soviet option for the CCP would also act to help persuade Washington that active intervention by the United States against the CCP was not a viable policy, since such intervention would drive the CCP closer toward Moscow while creating tensions in American-Soviet relations.

CCP leaders frequently introduced these arguments into their discussions with the members of the U.S. military mission. During his 23 August 1944 discussion with John S. Service, for example, Mao skillfully intertwined a vision of a postwar China market opened to American capitalists, the prospect of wartime cooperation against Japanese forces, and a demonstration of the CCP's independence from Moscow. China should not follow the Soviet model of economic development, Mao told Service. Indeed, even the bureaucratic type of industrialization attempted by the KMT was inappropriate for China. China could industrialize only with free enterprise and the assistance of foreign capital. Socialism was impractical for China given its low level of economic development, and this would remain the case for at least the near future. So moderate were the aims of the CCP, Mao said, that it had actually considered dropping the word "Communist" from its name but had decided that this was pointless because its program was so moderate that even the most conservative American businessman would find nothing objectionable in it.[97]

Mao also made it clear to Service that, should the United States cooperate with the CCP, he was prepared to minimize the Soviet role in China. Because of the devastation suffered by the Soviet Union during the war, it could not, Mao told Service, play an important role in China's postwar development. Moreover, for the CCP to seek Soviet assistance would only exacerbate the anti-Soviet sentiments of the KMT leaders, making it even less likely that they would deal with the CCP in a reasonable and "democratic" fashion. Thus, if the United States pursued a correct policy, the Soviet role in China "should be secondary to that of the United States."[98] If, on the other hand, the United States pursued an incorrect policy of one-sidedly supporting Chiang Kai-shek, thereby allowing and perhaps encouraging Chiang to touch off a civil war, then the United States would be confronted with a "major international problem." The Soviet Union would not, Mao assured Service, oppose the interests and policies of the United States in China if they were "constructive and democratic." Mao did not need to draw the conclusion that if the policy of the United States was nonconstructive and undemocratic, then Moscow would oppose it. Service understood Mao's hint. The current desire of the CCP for support from the United States, Service reported to the American embassy on 28 September, "does not preclude their turning back toward Soviet Russia if they are forced to in order to survive [an] American-supported Kuomintang attack."[99]

While marshalling such logical arguments for Service, Communist personnel were careful to conceal from him the extent of direct Soviet presence at Yan'an. In a 23 March 1945 report on the Soviet presence at Yan'an, Service reported the presence of three Soviets, whereas, according to Vladimirov, there were actually five at that point. Service was kept ignorant of the presence of a Soviet liaison officer (Vladimirov), of the existence of a Soviet radio transmitter at Yan'an, and of the visit by a Soviet aircraft to Yan'an in October 1943, stating explicitly that the last visit by a Soviet plane had been in November 1942.[100] Service was also led to believe that none of the Soviets at Yan'an were "on terms of close acquaintance" with the chief CCP leaders, whereas Vladimirov, in fact, met frequently with Mao, Bo Gu, Kang Sheng, and other top leaders.[101] Given that Service was in Yan'an to investigate precisely such matters, and considering that he had extensive contacts with CCP personnel, such a pattern of misinformation was certainly not accidental. Instructions had probably been passed down as to what exactly the Americans should be told about contacts with the Soviet Union, and Kang Sheng's aides probably saw to it that Service was duly misinformed. Service was also allowed to collect a large amount of material dealing with the Zheng Feng campaign; the CCP even obliged by providing English translations of the relevant speeches demonstrating the anti-Soviet nature of that campaign. Service "correctly" concluded from this evidence that the campaign had had an anti-Soviet thrust: "During the past several years an effort [has been made] to get away from slavish attempts to apply Russian communism to China."[102] Even Bo Gu, whom Service identified as a leader of the "pro-Russian clique," was produced to demonstrate to him that even reputedly pro-Soviet Chinese Communists did not want to follow the Soviet path. The CCP would not seek to institute socialism in China for one or two hundred years, Bo told Service.[103] By channeling Service's observations in this fashion the CCP leaders ensured that he reached the "correct" conclusions about relations between the CCP and Moscow.[104]

While bidding for an opening to the United States, Mao acted to reassure Moscow of his unswerving loyalty. Shortly before the arrival of the American Observers Mission in Yan'an, Mao increased his correspondence with Moscow, apparently in an effort to explain away any Soviet apprehensions about this move. Then, in November 1944, after his discussions with Roosevelt's personal representative Patrick Hurley, Mao tried to minimize Soviet suspicions by requesting that Vladimirov radio to Moscow Mao's interpretation of the talks. Shortly after Hurley left Yan'an, Mao sent still another cable to Moscow describing the great strength and good prospects of the CCP. Great changes had occurred in China over the past eight months, Mao reportedly told Stalin, and the influence of the CCP would soon exceed that of the KMT.[105]

Moscow's representative in Yan'an was, in fact, quite suspicious of the CCP's opening to the United States. Vladimirov discussed Yan'an–Washington relations with Mao shortly after the United States Military Observers Mission arrived in Yan'an. Mao stressed the importance of the American role in China and the hopes of the CCP for a rapprochement with the United States. Vladimirov interpreted this as an effort by Mao to use Anglo-American fear of possible Soviet aggression in Manchuria to induce the Western powers to establish relations with Yan'an. Mao wanted to play on American fears of the Soviet Union, Vladimirov felt, to induce Washington to try to entice the CCP away from Moscow.[106]

Vladimirov concluded from what Bo Gu told him of the talks between Mao and Service in August–September 1944 that Mao was using the bogey of a "Soviet threat" to pave the way for a deal between the CCP and the United States. Mao believed, Vladimirov concluded, that the Soviet Union would not enter the Far Eastern war until a late date and that the United States was therefore likely to play an arbiter's role in China. Moreover, Mao hoped to strike an anti-Soviet deal with the United States excluding the Soviet Union from the solution of the Far Eastern question. Mao hoped that by securing American recognition of the Shaan-Gan-Ning special area, he could pit the Soviet Union against the United States.[107] In November, when Vladimirov forwarded Mao's explanation of his talks with Hurley to Moscow, the Soviet officer appended his own view that Mao was now seeking Soviet support because the United States had refused to give him arms. In Vladimirov's view, Mao's more positive attitude toward the Soviet Union which the Soviet officer detected in December 1944 and early 1945 served two tactical purposes. First it was a ploy to hide Mao's anti-Soviet aims from Moscow. Second, it kept the Soviet Union in reserve in case Mao's American option failed. Mao was "playing for safety."[108]

Consistent with his policy of keeping open his options with the Soviet Union, while angling for a deal with the United States, Mao also solicited Soviet aid. Late in September 1944 (after Mao's first round of talks with Service) Mao proposed to Vladimirov that the CCP send 10,000 Eighth Route Army officers to Siberia for training by the Red Army. Once the Soviet Union went to war with Japan, these trained personnel would be able to lead Chinese Communist forces in joint operations with the Red Army.[109] While we have only Vladimirov's account of this bid by Mao for Soviet assistance, upon reflection, it would have been surprising if Mao had not made such a proposal. While Vladimirov interpreted Mao's suggestion as an attempt to exacerbate tensions between the Soviet Union and United States, Mao's bid could have been a more straightforward effort to become a part of the grand antifascist alliance—receiving aid from both the United States and the Soviet Union in the process. In Europe, Moscow had been extremely wary of arming the highly effective Yugoslavian Partisans, but finally did so after Britain and the United States had established the precedent. Mao might have also conceived of Soviet training of CCP forces in Siberia as a balance for the training of KMT forces in India by the United States.

By late 1944–early 1945, CCP leaders closely watched the indications that the

Soviet Union would enter the war against Japan. *Jiefang Ribao* reprinted Stalin's 7 November 1944 speech condemning Japanese "aggression" as well as subsequent articles in the Soviet press attacking Japan. Yan'an, like other interested observers, understood that this mounting Soviet criticism of Japan was political preparation for eventual Soviet entry into the Far Eastern war. According to Vladimirov, an article in *Izvestia* on 2 December 1944 condemning the disunity of anti-Japanese forces in China and warning Chongqing not to unleash a civil war against the CCP, roused great interest in Yan'an. Mao interpreted this article, according to Vladimirov, as proof of Soviet "future activity" in the Far East.[110] On 18 February 1945, another *Izvestia* article reiterated the same themes and endorsed the CCP demand for an end to the KMT "one-party dictatorship" and the establishment of a coalition government.[111]

This mounting Soviet media campaign took place against the backdrop of the Yalta Conference. The CCP welcomed the communiqué of the Yalta Conference, perhaps seeing in its promise of democratic governments chosen by free elections for the liberated countries of Europe an indication that the Allies would pressure Chiang toward democratic reforms.[112] Mao was probably not aware of the Far Eastern provisions of the Yalta agreement, but events shortly after the conference indicated that the Soviet Union would enter the war against Japan. On 13 April Moscow announced that it would not renew its neutrality agreement with Japan.

The possibility of Soviet entry into the war against Japan presented the CCP with new opportunities for cooperation with the Red Army. If the CCP's armies could link up and advance with the Red Army through north China and Manchuria, they might be able to assume administrative authority in the liberated areas while collecting Japanese (and perhaps Soviet) arms. This option became increasingly attractive as it became apparent in April–May 1945 that the "reactionaries" had won the policy debate in the United States.

The reemergence of Soviet interest in the Far East roughly coincided with a increasingly distinct pro-KMT tilt in U.S. policy. In November 1944 the KMT had rejected the plan for a coalition government agreed on by Mao and Roosevelt's envoy Patrick Hurley, and Hurley had then promptly switched positions and endorsed Chiang's program. Rejecting the notion of Communist participation in a coalition government, Chiang and Hurley (who replaced Clarence Gauss as U.S. Ambassador on 17 November) now proposed that some Communists enter the *existing* National Government—after the CCP had relinquished control over its armed forces! The CCP responded to Chiang's hard line and to Hurley's reversal by threatening to formally establish a separate government and then breaking off negotiations on 8 December. Under pressure from the United States, the talks resumed on 24 January, but the deadlock remained. The KMT offered nominal CCP participation in the government in exchange for the CCP giving up control of its armed forces. This was in line with the French model of 1944. The CCP, in turn, insisted that the KMT dismantle its various apparatus of control and share power with the CCP.[113] It was in this context that Mao proposed in January 1945 that he and Zhou Enlai visit Washington for discussions with Roosevelt. By making such an extraordinary trip, Mao hoped to circumvent Hurley who, he had correctly concluded, was blocking Yan'an's efforts at frank and thorough communications with Washington.[114]

Mao kept Vladimirov from learning of this unprecedented proposal by increasing surveillance of the Soviet mission.[115] At the same time Mao began trying to improve his strained relations with Moscow in case Washington rejected his bid. During February Mao sent numerous cables to Moscow. In one, Mao warned that both the United States and Chiang Kai-shek were trying to "win over" the CCP, thereby implying that Yan'an and Moscow should stand together and reject these plots to drive a wedge between them. In another cable Mao warned of Chiang's intentions to use U.S. arms to suppress the CCP.[116]

On 1 March Mao received a simple, one-sentence cable from Stalin replying to an earlier message of greetings from Mao and Zhu De. It was addressed to "Chairman Mao and General Zhu" and read: "I thank you sincerely for your warm congratulations on the 27th anniversary of Red Army Day. Stalin."[117] According to Vladimirov, Mao immediately realized the usefulness of this cable and on receiving it immediately convened the Presidium (i.e., Zhu De, Liu Shaoqi, Ren Bishi, Zhou Enlai, and Mao himself) of the ongoing Seventh Plenum to discuss Stalin's signal. Mao reportedly took the cable as an indication of Soviet support for the CCP and of future Soviet entry into the Far Eastern war. Together with recent pro-CCP commentary in the Soviet press and the collapse of Yan'an's talks with the United States, this demonstration of Stalin's support convinced Mao, according to Vladimirov, that alignment with the Soviet Union was "the only correct course."[118] After receiving permission from the Soviet Union to publicize Stalin's cable, CCP newspapers prominently carried the Soviet leader's greetings to Mao and Zhu, while Yan'an radio began frequent readings of its text.[119] This prominent display of the CCP's Soviet link was a sharp departure from the effort to downplay links with Moscow during 1944. This new tact served several purposes. It reassured Moscow of the CCP's loyalty. It warned Washington not to push the CCP closer to Moscow. A perception of a CCP–Moscow link would also help deter possible American military intervention against the Communists. This latter consideration may have been a major factor. According to Vladimirov, Mao was closely following events in Greece where British troops had just squashed a Communist-led attempt to seize power.[120]

Shortly after publicizing Stalin's cable, Mao again summoned John S. Service. During their talk on 13 March, Mao reiterated his hopes for extensive postwar cooperation with the United States and called on Washington to force Chiang to set up a transitional coalition government, thereby preventing him from launching a civil war. These arguments were presented still once again by Mao, Zhou Enlai, and Zhu De on 1 April just prior to Service's departure for consultations in the United States.[121] At this juncture the CCP leaders did not drop hints about Yan'an's Soviet option. After the publication of Stalin's cable they did not need to. Using the Soviet bogey to influence the United States had to be done subtly. Overplaying this card could backfire by persuading Washington of the pro-Soviet proclivities of the CCP. Thus, in late March Service found the CCP leaders "extremely reluctant" to talk about the possibility of Soviet entry into the war in the Far East.[122]

In March, the policy debate in Washington was resolved in favor of the pro-KMT perspective. Hurley and General Albert Wedemeyer, Joseph Stilwell's replacement, had flown to Washington for discussions with Roosevelt, and at the end of March John Service was also recalled for consultations. The outcome of these proceedings was indicated on 2 April when Hurley addressed a press conference after his talks with

Roosevelt. In his statement Hurley ruled out U.S. assistance to the CCP except in so far as Communist armed forces were amalgamated into the National Government's army. He also endorsed Chiang's proposal for CCP participation in a coalition *cabinet* in lieu of a broader governmental reorganization.[123] Then after his return to China in late April, Hurley began purging the diplomats who opposed his policy of full support for Chiang Kai-shek.[124]

It is ironic that the Soviet factor had exactly the opposite effect than that hoped for by Mao. Soviet policy was a key factor inducing Roosevelt to accept Hurley's hostile approach to the CCP. During their March talks in Washington, Hurley had persuaded Roosevelt that since the Soviet Union had promised in the Yalta agreement not to support the CCP, Yan'an would have no choice but to accept Chiang Kai-shek's terms. Once Yan'an learned that it did not have Soviet support, it would accept the status of a legal, unarmed, minority party within the National Government. In Barbara Tuchman's words,

> Without doubt the primary factor influencing [Roosevelt] was the Russian agreement obtained at Yalta. Both Roosevelt and Hurley believed that the Soviet Union held the key and that its still secret pledge to enter a treaty of alliance with Chiang Kai-shek . . . would in its effect on both sides serve to block the danger of civil war.[125]

But if Hurley was wrong in his estimate of CCP dependence on and subservience to Moscow, at least he was accurate in his evaluation of Soviet intentions. On his way back to China, Hurley stayed over in Moscow to discuss the China situation with Stalin and Molotov. Stalin lauded Chiang Kai-shek as a selfless patriot and said that he hoped to sustain Chiang's preeminent position and avoid a civil war in China. To this end, Stalin said, he had already urged Mao to enter a KMT-dominated coalition government.[126] Overt propaganda supplemented such confidential communications. By early June 1945, the Soviet media was endorsing the formation of a coalition government in China.[127]

The Seventh Congress

By early 1945 the CCP had emerged as the leader of a powerful and dynamic movement. According to the CCP, almost 100 million people lived in CCP base areas, 910,000 soldiers served in its armies, and its nineteen liberated areas counted militia forces of some 2.2 million.[128] While the CCP had reason to exaggerate its strength at this juncture, there is no doubt that it had grown quite powerful. Its opponent had also weakened. Within the KMT areas there were powerful and dynamic antigovernment movements, while the KMT itself was demoralized and factionalized. Yet looming over all was the possibility of intervention by the United States to block a Communist takeover, a possibility heightened by the apparent victory of the "reactionaries" in the policy debate in Washington.

In these circumstances the Seventh Congress of the CCP opened on 23 April, two weeks after Moscow's declaration that it would not renew the 1941 neutrality agreement with Japan. In Vladimirov's opinion, Mao had postponed the congress until he could be sure of eventual Soviet entry into the Far Eastern war.[129] Although it was uncertain just how soon the Red Army would strike (Service reported to Washington that the CCP felt that the Soviet Union might not enter the war until the spring of 1946), the likelihood of eventual Soviet entry into north China and Manchuria meant that Mao needed to strengthen his ties with Moscow. Mao had to position the CCP politically for its armies to link up and advance with the Red Army. As Mao said in his political report to the congress, the CCP should prepare to wage war and recover lost territory "in direct cooperation with allied countries" and independent of the KMT.[130] It was, of course, not certain that the Red Army would cooperate with CCP forces, but the objective of Mao's Soviet policy was to maximize chances that it would.

Mao's attitude toward the United States at the Seventh Congress initially left open the possibility of a change in U.S. policy. As the congress progressed, however, Mao's attitude hardened. In his political report on 24 April, Mao depicted the United States as an antifascist ally, but warned that "in many countries there are still strong reactionary forces which begrudge the people at home and abroad their unity, progress, and liberation." Because of this, there was still the possibility of "serious twists and turns in the course of events."[131] By the time the congress ended on 11 June, Mao took a much more pessimistic view of the United States, condemning its policy in China as brazenly reactionary, counterrevolutionary, and anticommunist. Imperialism was one of the two "mountains" oppressing the Chinese people, Mao declared, and the context of Mao's speech made it clear that the United States was becoming the chief imperialist power in China. Mao also quoted Stalin to the effect that imperialism was the chief enemy of progress throughout the world and asserted that the world's antiimperialist struggles were becoming "more acute and widespread."[132]

While warning Washington, Mao also courted the Soviet Union. In his opening speech to the congress on "China's Two Possible Destinies," Mao lauded the Soviet Union, assigning it primary responsibility for the defeat of Nazi Germany and pointing to "the support of the people of all countries and especially of the Soviet Union" as creating the conditions for the "complete liberation of the Chinese people and building of a new . . . China."[133] In his oral report the next day, heard and recorded by Vladimirov who attended the congress as an observer, Mao was even more forthright in his praise of the Soviet Union: "Political reality and practice demonstrate that in the international arena the Soviet Union is our single and best friend. All the rest are so-called allies."[134] Vladimirov cynically noted the flattery of the Soviet Union by Mao and other speakers at the congress.

Mao also moved to further obfuscate the anti-Soviet nature of the recent Zheng Feng campaign. Many "returned students" who had studied in the Soviet Union gained positions on the Central Committee. Included in this group were, as noted earlier, Wang Ming and Bo Gu.[135] According to Vladimirov, Mao also squelched reports to the congress on the Zheng Feng campaign by Kang Sheng and Ren Bishi because he feared they might inadvertently highlight the anti-Soviet nature of that campaign.[136] Vladimirov's allegation is supported by the remarkable fact that the pivotal, lengthy, tumultuous, and only just concluded Zheng Feng campaign was barely mentioned at the congress. In his political report, Mao mentioned the campaign precisely one time. After spending several paragraphs explaining the need for ideological education to unify thinking, Mao mentioned the campaign but without specifically relating it to those themes.[137] The speeches by Liu Shaoqi and Zhou Enlai likewise barely mentioned the Zheng Feng campaign.[138] Again, this is surprising given the significance of that campaign and indicates prima facie that a decision had been made that rehashing that campaign would not serve current political needs.

Liu Shaoqi's key report on Party history, ideology, and organization— precisely the key issues of the Zheng Feng campaign—demonstrates most clearly the caution with which the campaign was dealt. In his lengthy discussion Liu carefully skirted the Zheng Feng campaign, mentioning it in passing two times. Even when stressing Mao's role in integrating the "universal principles" of Marxism with Chinese practice, Liu found no need to mention the Zheng Feng campaign. He did, however, mention that Mao was a "student" of Marx, Engels, Lenin, and *Stalin*. When recapitulating CCP history to demonstrate Mao's struggle against various left and right deviations, Liu mentioned Chen Duxiu and Li Lisan, but nowhere did he mention Mao's chief opponent and the chief proponent of a non-Chinese variant of Marxism, Wang Ming. Post-1931 "errors" were merely referred to as "later rightist and leftist deviations and capitulationism."[139] Liu clearly intended to avoid embarrassing Moscow.

The central theme of the Seventh Congress was unity. Civil war in China was to be avoided through the creation of a provisional coalition government in which the Communists served as full partners and whose principle objective would be to democratize China's political system. There were a number of reasons why such a demand was useful to Yan'an. It left the door open to rapprochement with the United States. It was popular with China's urban and educated classes. Perhaps most importantly, it placed on Chiang the onus of triggering the upcoming civil war. Since Chiang had explicitly ruled out the idea of a coalition government in a speech on 1 March, the call for such a coalition placed Chiang in the situation of having to defend the "one-party dictatorship of the KMT." For our purposes, however, the most relevant of Mao's considerations had to do with the Soviet Union. Mao's call at the Seventh Congress for a "coalition government" was consistent with Dimitrov's January 1944 directive and with the policies Moscow was then imposing on various European Communist Parties.

But as he had so often done before, Mao again interpreted Soviet directives in a fashion which suited his own needs. He did this by turning the call for a coalition government into a demand for a rapid dismantling of the mechanisms of the KMT power. His "minimum demands" for achieving a coalition government included abolition of the KMT secret police, release of all Communist prisoners, lifting of the KMT military blockade of the Shaan-Gan-Ning district, recognition of the base area governments, and so on. The immediate objective was to end the KMT's "one-party dictatorship" bring Communists into a provisional coalition government, and then convene free and unrestricted elections to form a regular coalition government.[140] Mao's version of coalition government was not a call for Communist power, but it was a call for the abdication of the Nationalists.

The call for coalition government was also a veneer for a program of maximal military expansion and preparation for armed uprising. The Seventh Congress decided that preparations for insurrections to seize major Japanese-occupied cities were to be given equal priority with work in the rural liberated areas. Communist armed forces were to be expanded rapidly and reorganized to wage mobile, rather than guerrilla, war. An additional 100,000 people were to be recruited into the CCP's armies thereby raising Communist forces to 1 million strong. Ten to fifteen divisions were to be reorganized and rearmed to undertake mobile operations and the seizure and defense of large cities.[141] Just as he had done when the Sino-Japanese War began, near that war's end Mao ostensibly accepted Moscow's political formulations while insisting on seizing all opportunities to strengthen revolutionary power. Throughout the summer of 1945 preparations for a showdown with Chiang Kai-shek proceeded apace. This radical approach was brought to an abrupt end, however, by the conclusion of the Sino-Soviet Treaty.

Yan'an and the Treaty of Sino-Soviet Alliance

The terms of the Sino-Soviet Treaty concluded in Moscow on 14 August took Yan'an by surprise. Earlier in 1945 CCP leaders had told John Service that they were confident that the Soviet Union would not demand concessions or special rights in Manchuria as the price for going to war with Japan. "The days of Russian imperialism are over," they told Service.[142] CCP efforts during the summer of 1945 to gauge what sort of deal Moscow and Chongqing were working out were probably without much success.[143] According to members of the United States Observers Mission, Chinese Communist officials were quite shocked once they learned of the Soviet special privileges contained in the treaty.[144]

The CCP already had reason to reflect on Soviet ambitions in Manchuria. During the early 1930s, the CCP organization in that region had been brought steadily under Moscow's control. Finally, in May 1935, the Comintern ordered the CCP Manchurian organization to break contact with the CCP center in China and report directly to the CCP Comintern delegation, that is, to Wang Ming, in Moscow. While this arrangement could be justified on the grounds of difficulties of communication between Manchuria and the CCP center and the need to coordinate anti-Japanese guerrilla operations in Manchuria with Soviet moves to contain Japanese forces, and while this arrangement apparently lost much of its significance when Ren Bishi replaced Wang Ming as head of the CCP Comintern delegation in 1938, still it might have caused Mao to reflect on Soviet aspirations in China's northeastern provinces.[145]

But while Soviet demands on Manchuria may have offended the nationalist sensibilities of CCP leaders, probably more important was the fact that the Soviet Union was now bound to support Chiang Kai-shek's government. This consideration forced a major reorientation of CCP policy. Through early August the CCP had followed a radical line. Talks with Chongqing had been suspended since 9 March, and since June the CCP press had carried strident condemnations of Chiang Kai-shek and American "imperialists" such as Hurley. When it became clear that Japan's surrender was imminent, Yan'an launched an all-out drive to seize Japanese-occupied territory and arms. On 10 August, Zhu De ordered CCP armies to disarm and accept the surrender of Japanese troops. When Chiang attempted to countermand Zhu's order, Mao vetoed this, condemning Chiang as "China's fascist chieftain" and asserting the right of the CCP to disarm defeated Japanese forces. On 13 August, *Jiefang Ribao* openly called for urgent preparations for mobile war and for the seizure of cities.[146] The day before, according to Vladimirov, Mao had requested that the Soviet Union aid the CCP. Such aid would determine, Mao reportedly said, the future course of relations between the CCP and the CPSU.[147]

This radical policy was reversed abruptly once the Sino-Soviet treaty was signed. The day after the treaty was announced, the CCP Central Committee banned all criticism of the KMT and the United States and ordered CCP forces to cooperate with U.S. forces landing in China to help disarm the Japanese. On 16 August, Yan'an issued its first address to the U.S. government, as opposed to the people of the United States, since the end of the Seventh Congress.[148] Then on 22 August Mao informed Chiang that Zhou Enlai would return to Chongqing to resume talks, and two days later Mao informed Chiang that he himself was willing to fly to Chongqing to negotiate. Three days later Mao arrived in Chongqing for talks.

Equally significant, the CCP shelved its plans to seize large cities. This shift was explained at a cadre conference of the North China Bureau on 30 August. While the seizure of large cities was the ultimate goal, a report on the conference by the secretary of the Bureau said, many difficulties presently stood in the way of achieving this goal. First among the "difficulties" enumerated was the attitude of the Soviet Union:

> In order to maintain and consolidate peace in the Far East, the Soviet Union has signed the treaty of friendship with China. This is very advantageous to the people of China and the world and disadvantageous to Japan and all war mongers. But at the same time, in order to fulfill its responsibilities under this treaty, the Soviet Union cannot directly assist us, but is under definite restrictions.[149]

Because of these difficulties, the secretary said, CCP forces should at present seize only small cities, expand the liberated areas, and seize or sever important lines of communication in order to "prepare for the future seizure of big cities." The policy of seizing big cities was "correct" but was not an immediate task.[150]

This turnaround in CCP line was the result of direct Soviet intervention. In Moscow, Foreign Minister Wang Shijie had asked Stalin to encourage Mao to accept Chiang's repeated invitations to go to Chongqing for negotiations and linked this issue to the approval of the Sino-Soviet treaty by the Central Executive Committee of the KMT, the Supreme National Defense Council, and the legislative *Yuan*.[151] Later in August, Moscow rejected Mao's 12 August request for assistance and informed him that the Soviet Union would not interfere in the domestic affairs of China.[152] Apparently there was more to the Soviet message than this. Stalin later told a Yugoslavian Communist leader that "After the war we told [the CCP leaders] that we felt conditions were not ripe for an uprising in China and that they should seek a modus vivendi with Chiang Kai-shek."[153] Mao himself later complained that Stalin had attempted to prevent the CCP from making revolution at this juncture:

> [The Soviet Union] did not permit China to make revolution; that was in 1945. Stalin wanted to prevent China from making revolution, saying that we should not have a civil war and should cooperate with Chiang Kai-shek, otherwise the Chinese nation would perish. But we did not do what he said.[154]

Forty years later, an article in an authoritative CCP journal would characterize Moscow's behavior at this juncture as like an "elder brother" trying to lead the CCP. The Soviet Union in 1945 was like the "bogus foreign devil" in Lu Xun's famous novel who had tried to prevent Ah Q from making revolution.[155]

Moscow's attempt to rein in the CCP was premised on a belief, according to Vladimirov, that Mao Zedong was pursuing a deliberately provocative policy designed to foster friction between the Soviet Union, the KMT, and the United States. Mao was resorting to "tricks" to push the Soviet Union into a fight with the United States.[156] Vladimirov ignores a more embarrassing Soviet concern: lending a hand at restraining the CCP was part of the price Stalin had agreed to pay for his concessions in Manchuria, and the outbreak of a civil war in China would make very problematic the continuing Chinese and American recognition of those privileges.

Although Mao understood that Moscow's new concessions in Manchuria were the quid pro quo for a Soviet guarantee not to support the CCP, he had nothing to gain by criticizing Soviet actions. Thus, CCP media publicly lauded the treaty, while internally a campaign was launched to justify the treaty to skeptical cadres.[157] In spite of his bitterness over Soviet actions, given solid U.S. support for the KMT, Mao had little choice but to continue working with the Soviet Union. In the first instance, CCP forces in Manchuria would find it rough going if they met the active opposition of the Red Army. It was far better to cooperate with the Soviet Union, always trying to push that cooperation a bit further and waiting for a future shift in Soviet policy. It was also possible to use the Soviet desire to avert a Chinese civil war to pressure the KMT. As the report by the secretary of the North China Bureau had pointed out, the fact that both the United States and the Soviet Union did not want a civil war in China might force Chiang to recognize conditionally the position of the CCP.[158] Mao saw such a situation as an unstable transitional stage, but it could be used (as in fact it was) to accelerate work undermining the KMT regime and preparations for the final showdown. Moreover, the very presence of the Red Army in Manchuria made the United States reluctant to send military forces there. This, too, as later CCP publications pointed out, helped the CCP.[159] Mao himself placed the revolutionary role of the Soviet Union in a broader perspective in his speech marking the twenty-eighth anniversary of the founding of the CCP in July 1949 on the eve of nationwide victory:

In the epoch in which imperialism exists, it is impossible for a genuine people's revolution to win victory in any country without various forms of help from the international revolutionary forces. . . . And this is also the case with the present and the future of People's China. Just imagine! If the Soviet Union had not existed, if there had been no victory in the anti-fascist Second World War, if Japanese imperialism had not been defeated, if the People's Democracies had not come into being, if the oppressed nations of the East were not rising in struggle, and if there were no struggle of the masses of the people against their reactionary rulers in the . . . capitalist countries—if not for all these in combination, the international reactionary forces bearing down upon us would certainly be many times greater than now. In such circumstances, could we have won victory? Obviously not.[160]

While Mao's words were influenced by political exigencies of mid-1949, they nonetheless have a ring of truth. The presence of the Red Army in Manchuria did have the effect of greatly limiting the action of the United States there. It also created the political basis for the cooperation between the Soviet Union and the CCP. If and when Soviet policy changed as tensions with the United States increased in the months after Japan's surrender, the CCP might yet be the recipient of that populous and industrialized region.

Notes

1. Sankar Ghose, *Socialism and Communism in India*, Bombay: Allied Publishers, 1971, pp. 314–316.
2. Vladimirov implies that during the spring of 1942 Mao requested immediate and extensive supplies of Soviet weapons. If this report is accurate, one suspects that it was a ploy by Mao to justify his own disregard of Soviet demands. Given Moscow's record of caution, Mao certainly could not have expected Moscow to take such a provocative move at that juncture. In any case, according to Vladimirov, once it became apparent to Mao that the Soviet Union could not meet these demands "because of the war," his attitude toward Moscow began to change. Moscow attempted to placate Mao by providing the CCP, according to Vladimirov, with "substantial sums" of money during 1942– 1943. Peter Pafenovich Vladimirov, *The Vladimirov Diaries, Yenan China: 1942–1945*, Garden City, N.Y.: Doubleday, 1975, pp. 19, 28, 181 (hereafter cited as Vladimirov, *Diaries*).
3. *Cankao Ziliao*, vol. 9, p. 2. Bo Gu was then the chief editor of *Jiefang Ribao*, but the editorial was certainly approved by other top CCP leaders as well.
4. Peng Ming, *Zhong Su Renmin Youyi Jianshi* [Short history of the friendship of the Chinese and Soviet peoples], Beijing: Zhongguo Qingnian Chubanshe, 1955, p. 103.
5. The Japanese debate over joining in the German-Soviet war in 1941–1942 is discussed in George A. Lensen, *The Strange Neutrality, Soviet-Japanese Relations during the Second World War, 1941–1945*, Tallahassee, Fla.: Diplomatic Press, 1972, pp. 21–34.
6. Liu Yixun, "Gongchan Guoji he Sidalin dui Zhongguo kang Ri zhanzheng de taidu he fangzhen" [The attitude and policy of the Comintern and Stalin toward China's war of resistance against Japan], *Dangshi Ziliao Congkan* [Compendium of Materials on Party History], no. 2, 1983, p. 145. Vladimirov, *Diaries*, pp. 37–38. Liu Yixun says that the Comintern and Stalin "demanded" that the CCP attack Japanese forces. Vladimirov says that Moscow "proposed" such attacks. *See also* the broadcast by Moscow radio of 10 May 1970 cited in Richard Thornton, *China, the Struggle for Power, 1917–1972*, Bloomington, Ind.: Indiana University Press, 1973, p. 351. Warren Kuo also cites the 10 May 1970 Soviet broadcast and another to the same effect on 5 May 1970 in *Analytical History of the Chinese Communist Party*, vol. 4, Taibei: Institute of International Relations, 1970, pp. 510–511, 519 (hereafter cited as Kuo, *Analytical History*).
7. Otto Braun, *Comintern Agent in China, 1932–1939*, London: Hurst and Co., 1982, p. 256.
8. Raisa Mirovitskaya and Yuri Semyonov, *The Soviet Union and China: A Brief History of Relations*, Moscow: Novosti Press Agency, 1981, p. 35.
9. The 1970 Moscow broadcast cited by Thornton, for example, says that Mao "openly boycotted" the request (Thornton, *Struggle*, p. 351). The 5 May 1970 Soviet broadcast cited by Kuo says that Mao "promised to give help, but took no action" (*Analytical History*, pp. 510–511). Vladimirov says that the CCP leaders "did not grant" Moscow's request (Vladimirov, *Diaries*, p. 15).
10. Dick Wilson, *When Tigers Fight: The Story of the Sino-Japanese War, 1937–1945*, New York: Viking Press, 1982, pp. 183–185. Chalmers A. Johnson, *Peasant Nationalism and Communist Power: The Emergence of Revolutionary China, 1937–1945*, Stanford, Calif.: Stanford University Press, 1962, pp. 58–59.
11. James Reardon-Anderson, *Yenan and the Great Powers: the Origins of Chinese Communist Foreign Policy, 1944–1946*, New York: Columbia University Press, 1980, p. 15.
12. Vladimirov, *Diaries, Passim*.
13. It makes sense to take some of Vladimirov's account at face value; since there was a Soviet mission in Yan'an, there must have been interactions between it and CCP leaders and between Yan'an and Moscow. In the absence of contrary evidence, either empirical or logical, we can accept Vladimirov's

factual account of these interactions. Regarding broader interpretative issues, we must be more cautious of possible distortion.

14. Vladimirov, *Diaries*, pp. 17, 25, 35.
15. John Costello, *The Pacific War*, New York: Quill, 1981, pp. 263, 281.
16. Vladimirov, *Diaries*, p. 29.
17. Ibid., p. 37.
18. Ibid., pp. 57, 60, 65.
19. Thornton, *Struggle*, p. 132.
20. Vladimirov, *Diaries*, p. 32.
21. A Soviet radio broadcast in 1969 named Zhu, Zhou, Peng, Xiang, and He as "supporters" of the Internationalists. Cited in Huai Yuan, "Wang Ming, Mao Zedong yu Sulian" [Wang Ming, Mao Zedong, and the Soviet Union], in *Feidang Neibu Douzheng Wenti Lunji* [Collection of essays on the internal struggle of the bandit party], Yao Menggan, editor, Taibei: Guoji Guanxi Yanjiusuo, 1975, p. 200. Vladimirov says that Zhang Wentian, Zhou Enlai, and Yang Shangkun supported Wang and Bo, and that Wang Jiaxiang, Chen Yun, and Zhu De all "generally adhered" to the Internationalist position but tended to vacillate (*Diaries*, p. 57). Elsewhere, however, Vladimirov says that Zhu De "supported" the "Moscow group" (*Diaries*, pp. 409, 143–144).
22. *Dangxing Dangfeng Dangji Dawen 250 Ti, Gongchan Dangyuan* [250 Questions and Answers on Party Nature, Party Style, and Party Discipline, Communist Party Member], no. 1, 1982, p. 41. Published by the CCP Publishing House of Liaoning province (hereafter cited as *Dawen 250 Ti*).
23. There is circumstantial evidence that Zhou Enlai differed from Mao at this juncture. This evidence is an article on the Soviet- German war authored by Zhou on 28 June 1941. In this article, Zhou depicted the German attack as a turning point in the war, and asserted that German victory would mean darkness for the entire world, while Soviet victory would mean that the oppressed peoples and nations of the whole world would obtain liberty and liberation. Zhou recognized that it was "very likely" that Japan would join in the attack on the Soviet Union, but contended that first among factors working against this was the fact that the "China problem" remained unsolved. China should, Zhou concluded, unite with all peoples and nations of the Far East to attack Japan (*Cankao Ziliao*, vol. 9, pp. 3–6). This article was written while Zhou was still in Chongqing and, as such, was addressed to public opinion in the Nationalist areas. Nonetheless, assuming that it reflected Zhou's own opinions, such views might easily have brought him into conflict with Mao when he returned to Yan'an.
24. Vladimirov, *Diaries*, p. 20.
25. Yang Yizhou, Lou Feng, and Wang Tianceng, *Tantan Zhongguo Gongchandang de Zheng Dang Zheng Feng* [Discussing Party Rectification and Party Style in the Chinese Communist Party], Fuzhou: Fujian Renmin Chubanshe, 1984, pp. 40–41 (hereafter cited as *Zheng Dang Zheng Feng*).
26. Boyd Compton, *Mao's China: Party Reform Documents, 1942–1944*, Seattle: University of Washington Press, 1952, p. xxxvii.
27. "Pragmatism" and "empiricism" were other key forms of subjectivism.
28. Speech by Mao on 1 February 1942, in Compton, *Mao's China*, p. 64.
29. See Raymond F. Wylie, *The Emergence of Maoism, Mao Tse-tung, Ch'en Po-ta, and the Search for Chinese Theory*, Stanford, Calif.: Stanford University Press., 1980.
30. Wylie, *Emergence of Maoism*, pp. 152–153. *See also Zheng Dang Zheng Feng*, p. 23. *Dawen 250 Ti*, p. 40.
31. Wylie, *Emergence of Maoism*, p. 166.
32. Vladimirov, *Diaries*, p. 156.
33. *Zheng Dang Zheng Feng*, p. 23.
34. *Dawen 250 Ti*, p. 40.
35. Compton, *Mao's China*, p. xxxiv. Yang Shilan, "Deng Fa," in *Zhonggong Dangshi Renwuzhuan* [Biographies of Chinese communist historical personalities], vol. 1, Beijing: Zhongguo Shehui Kexueyuan, p. 363. Kuo, *Analytical History*, vol. 4, p. 595. Peter J. Seybolt, "Terror and Conformity, Counter-espionage Campaigns, Rectification, and Mass Movements," *Modern China*, vol. 12, no. 1 (January 1986), p. 39–73.
36. *Zhongguo Gongchandang Lizi Zhongyao Huiyi Ji* [Historically Important Meetings of the Chinese Communist Party], vol. 1, Shanghai: Renmin Chubanshe, 1982, pp. 222–225.
37. *Zhonggong Dangshi Dashi Nianbiao* [Chronology of CCP History], Nanjing: Jiangsu Renmin Chubanshe, 1981, p. 70.
38. Wylie, *Emergence of Maoism*, p. 227.
39. Ibid., pp. 227–228. *Zheng Dang Zheng Feng*, p. 23.
40. Kuo, *Analytical History*, vol. 4, p. 691.

41. *Zhongguo Gongchandang Lizi Zhongyao Huiyi Ji*, pp. 230–231.
42. Wylie, *Emergence of Maoism*, p. 232.
43. *Zhongguo Gongchandang Lizi Zhongyao Huiyi Ji*, pp. 230-231.
44. Thornton, *Struggle*, pp. 134-135. *Dawen 250 Ti*, p. 40.
45. Wang Ming, Moscow broadcast, 31 March 1969 (Cited in Kuo, *Analytical History*, vol. 4, p. 626). Again there is fragmentary evidence that Zhou Enlai was among those called upon to criticize their earlier support for Wang Ming. Zhou's *Selected Works* contains a report on an investigation of Party history between about 1927 and 1930 which detailed many Comintern-induced errors and Mao's efforts to correct those errors. Zhou played a critical role in those years, and this document may well have been part of his self-criticism. "Guanyu dang de 'liu da' de yanjiu" [Research on the Party's Sixth Congress], *Zhou Enlai Xuanji* [selected works of Zhou Enlai], Beijing: Renmin Chubanshe, 1980, pp. 157–187.
46. Wang Jiaxiang, "Huiyi Mao Zedong tongzhi yu Wang Ming jihui zhuyi luxian de douzheng" [Recollection of comrade Mao Zedong's struggle with Wang Ming's opportunist line], *Renmin Ribao*, [People's Daily], 27 December 1979, p. 2.
47. Vladimirov, *Diaries*, pp. 162–164.
48. Wang Jiaxiang says that Wang Ming relied on "foreign influence" to avoid recognizing his errors (Wang Jiaxiang, "Huiyi Mao Zedong tongzhi yu Wang Ming jihui zhuyi luxian de douzheng").
49. Vladimirov, *Diaries*, p. 185.
50. Compton, *Mao's China*, pp. xl–xli.
51. Mao, "On the Reconstruction of Our Studies" in Compton, *Mao's China*, p. 68.
52. Chen Yun, "How to Be a Communist Party Member," in Compton, *Mao's China*, pp. 88–89.
53. For example, Mao, "In Opposition to Party Formalism," in Compton, *Mao's China*, pp. 40–43.
54. Compton, *Mao's China*, p. xli.
55. Wylie, *Emergence of Maoism*, pp. 190–194, 216.
56. Zhang Pei, *Kang Sheng Ping Zhuan* [Critical Biography of Kang Sheng], Beijing: Hongqi, 1982, p. 84.
57. Ibid., pp. 84–94.
58. The figure given is 20,000. Radio Moscow broadcast, 29 March 1969, cited in Huai Yuan, "Wang Ming, Mao Zedong yu Sulian," p. 200.
59. Seybolt, "Terror and Conformity." According to Vladimirov and Wang Ming himself, Mao, acting through Kang Sheng and Wang Ming's physician, attempted to assassinate Wang Ming in order to get rid of him without antagonizing Moscow. The Soviet doctor assigned to Yan'an reportedly discovered in March 1943 that the medicine prescribed for Wang by his Chinese doctor actually contained small amounts of a substance which would gradually accumulate and decompose in the body, poisoning the person ingesting it. Vladimirov informed Moscow of this episode and insisted that Wang be flown either to Moscow or Chongqing for medical treatment. Mao vetoed such a plan and blocked an investigation of the entire incident (Vladimirov, *Diaries*, pp. 91–92; 106–107; 135–136; 144–145). Wang Ming, *China. Cultural Revolution or Counter-Revolutionary Coup?*, Moscow, Novosti Press Agency, 1969, p. 49. This author knows of no evidence either confirming or contradicting these Soviet accounts of Mao's villainy. Chinese sources indicate only that Wang Ming "claimed to be ill." Wang Jiaxiang, "Huiyi Mao Zedong tongzhi yu Wang Ming jihui zhuyi luxian de douzheng." While lack of evidence forces us to suspend judgment about the alleged assassination of Wang Ming, it is worth noting that such a covert solution, as it were, would have accorded well with Mao's interests. If successful, it would have eliminated, in a fashion which would not alienate Moscow, an unrepentant rival within the Politburo who enjoyed Soviet support and connections. On the other hand, it can be argued that a powerless but living Wang Wing would help Mao placate and mislead Moscow.
60. Vladimirov, *Diaries*, pp. 26, 29, 41, 73.
61. Ibid., pp. 41, 57, 72–73.
62. Ibid., pp. 75, 102, 104.
63. Ibid., pp. 115–116. See also *Zhonggong Dangshi Dashi Nianbiao*, p. 70.
64. A pamphlet printed in Chongqing shortly after the Comintern's public dissolution, for example, presented a realistic appraisal of Moscow's motives. The Soviet Union was under great German pressure, the pamphlet observed. Consequently, Moscow was urging the Anglo-American powers to open a second front in western Europe. Since the successful conclusion of the North African campaign, Moscow feared that London and Washington would postpone a landing in Europe until the Soviet Union and Germany had exhausted each other. Di San Guoji Jiesan Shijian [The disbandment of the Third International], Chongqing: Qingbai Chubanshe, June 1943.
65. Vladimirov, *Diaries*, pp. 115–117.
66. *Zhonggong Dangshi Dashi Nianbiao*, p. 70.

67. Cited in Hu Qiuyuan, *Guanyu Di San Guoji zhi Jiesan yu Mosilini Zhi Xia Tai* (On the dissolution of the Third International and the collapse of Mussolini), Chongqing (?): 1943 (?). No name of publisher given.
68. Wylie, *Emergence of Maoism*, pp. 203–204.
69. Earl Browder was the leader of the Communist Party of the United States who presided over the formal abolition of that Party in May 1944. A pamphlet published by an anticommuniist publishing house, probably in Chongqing, in 1943 asserted that Moscow's dissolution of the Comintern precipitated a sharp debate within the CCP, with Mao's opponents arguing that the CCP should now "alter its attitude" toward the KMT. *Gongchan Guoji Jiesan yu Zhonggong* [The dissolution of the Comintern and the Chinese Communists], Chongqing (?): Tongyi Chubanshe, 1943 (?). Later during his report to the Seventh Congress, Mao mentioned that "some people" had proposed that the CCP change its name, a move Mao felt unnecessary [Steven I. Levine, "Mao Tse-tung's Oral Report to the Seventh Party Congres: Summary Notes," *Chinese Law and Government*, vol. 10, no. 4 (Winter 1977–1978), pp. 16–17]. The KMT did in fact demand the disbandment of the CCP at this juncture, and it is possible that these are the people Mao was referring to in his 1945 speech. Moreover, arguing against a conclusion that Wang supported this idea is the fact that the CCP did not subsequently level this charge against him. But then, the CCP has generally been extremely reticent to talk about its ties with Moscow during the 1941–1945 period. Unfortunately, this is another question which must remain unresolved at present.
70. Vladimirov, *Diaries*, pp. 117, 150–152.
71. Ibid., p. 145.
72. Ibid., pp. 190–194.
73. Ibid., p. 195.
74. Regarding the sharp deterioration of the Nationalist regime in 1943–1944, *see* Lloyd Eastman, *Seeds of Destruction, Nationalist China in War and Revolution, 1937–1949*, Stanford, Calif.: Stanford University Press, 1984, pp. 27–28.
75. Lyman P. Van Slyke, *The Chinese Communist Movement, a Report of the United States War Department, July 1945*, Military Intelligence Division of the War Department (reprint) Stanford, Calif.: Stanford University Press, 1968 (hereafter cited as "War Department Report").
76. Report by John S. Service, in Joseph W. Esherick, *Lost Chance in China, the World War II Despatches of John S. Service*, New York: Random House, 1974, p. 351 (hereafter cited as Esherick, *Lost Chance*).
77. Tetsuya Kataoka, *Resistance and Revolution in China: The Communists and the Second United Front*, Berkeley: University of California Press, 1974, p. 304. *"War Department Report,"* p. 211.
78. *Zhonggong Dangshi Dashi Nianbiao*, p. 70.
79. Ibid.
80. *Zhongguo Gongchandang Lishi Jiangyi* [Lectures on the history of the Chinese Communist Party], Shanghai: Fudan Daxue, 1978, p. 200.
81. Vladimirov, *Diaries*, p. 129.
82. Such a Soviet protest is not contained in the volume on Sino-Soviet relations published by Taibei in 1981, a volume which documents numerous other Soviet attempts to protect the CCP. Nor is there any mention of it in the 1943 volume of *Foreign Relations of the United States*. Nor was Soviet assistance going to China in mid-1943.
83. Thus, Sun Ke protested to American diplomats in 1944 that Chiang Kai-shek had interpreted Molotov's statements to Hurley about the CCP not being genuine Communists to mean that the Soviet Union had no interest in the CCP and that the National Government could deal with them as it pleased. In fact, it was extremely important, Sun explained, that CCP–KMT relations be "adjusted" if friendly relations were to be established between the Republic of China and the Soviet Union. (*FRUS*, 1944, vol. 6, pp. 630–631). *See also* Sun Ke's urging of Ambassador Gauss on 26 July 1944 to tell Roosevelt to pressure Kong Xiangxi that the KMT should seek to improve relations with the Soviet Union by adopting a more conciliatory attitude toward the CCP. *FRUS*, 1944, vol. 6, pp. 135–136.
84. *See*, for example, Vice-President Wallace's comments to Chiang, in Esherick, *Lost Chance*, p. 343. Roosevelt himself, to cite another example, urged precisely the same argument on Kong Xiangxi during their talk at the White house on 15 August 1944 (*FRUS*, 1944, vol 6, p. 142).
85. Vladimirov, *Diaries*, pp. 193-197.
86. William O. McCagg, *Stalin Embattled, 1943–1948*, Detroit: Wayne State University Press, 1978. Nicolai Bukharin's tract, *The ABCs of Communism*, written in 1919, was the classic presentation of the theory that imperialist war gives rise to proletarian revolution.
87. *See* Stephen Clissold, editor, *Yugoslavia and the Soviet Union, 1939–1973: A Documentary Survey*, New York: Oxford University Press, 1975, pp. 143, 145–146, 150, 152. Adam B. Ulam, *Titoism and the Coninform*, Cambridge, Mass.: Harvard University Press, 1952, pp. 73–77.

88. *See* D. George Kousoulas, *Modern Greece, Profile of a Nation*, New York: Charles Scribner's Sons, 1974, pp. 200–215. John O. Iatrides, *Revolt in Athens: The Greek Communist "Second Round", 1944–1945*, Princeton, N.J.: Princeton University Press, 1972, pp. 75, 279. Ulam, *Titoism.* p. 76.

89. McCagg, *Stalin Embattled*, p. 57.

90. *Zhongguo Gongchandang Lizi Zhongyao Huiyi Ji*, pp. 233–234.

91. Reardon-Anderson, *Yenan*, p. 4.

92. "On Diplomatic Work,"" initially published in *Far Eastern Affairs* (Moscow), no. 1, (March 1972), pp. 184–187. Cited in Esherick, *Lost Chance*, pp. 291–292.

93. Esherick, *Lost Chance*, p. 299.

94. *Zhonggong Dangshi Dashi Nianbiao*, p. 75.

95. Vladimirov, *Diaries*, p. 192–194.

96. Michael Schaller, *The U.S. Crusade in China, 1938–1945*, New York: Columbia University Press, 1979, p. 223.

97. Esherick, *Lost Chance*, pp. 306–308; 315–316.

98. Ibid., p. 295.

99. Ibid., p. 309.

100. *See* Vladimirov, *Diaries*, p. 161.

101. Esherick, *Lost Chance*, pp. 351–352.

102. Report of 28 September 1944, in Esherick, *Lost Chance*, p. 309.

103. Ibid. p. 311–312.

104. I do not mean to imply here that Service's basic conclusions in this regard were inaccurate. As this entire book demonstrates, they were in fact quite accurate. What is intended here is rather to show the way in which Mao and his assistants deftly guided Service toward the conclusion they wanted him to reach.

105. Vladimirov, *Diaries*, pp, 311, 315.

106. Ibid., p. 230.

107. Ibid., pp. 254; 256–257; 262–267.

108. Ibid., pp. 290, 292, 311, 315.

109. Ibid., pp. 261–262.

110. Ibid., pp. 346, 311, 315–316.

111. "War Department Report," p. 234.

112. Emily Yaung, *The Impact of the Yalta Agreement on China's Domestic Politics, 1945–1946*, doctoral dissertation, Kent State University, Kent, Ohio, 1979, p. 122.

113. Schaller, *Crusade*, pp. 195–200.

114. Tuchman, "If Mao Had Come to Washington: An Essay in Alternatives," *Foreign Affairs*, October 1972, pp. 44–64.

115. Vladimirov, *Diaries*, p. 326.

116. Ibid., p. 341.

117. 2 March 1945, *Jiefang Ribao* [Liberation Daily], p. 1.

118. Vladimirov, *Diaries*, pp. 361, 365, 385.

119. Ibid., p. 365.

120. Ibid., p. 315.

121. Esherick, *Lost Chance*, pp. 371–378.

122. Ibid., p. 348.

123. *New York Times*, 3 April 1945, p. 4.

124. Tuchman, "If Mao Had Come to Washington," p. 58. Reardon-Anderson, *Yan'an*, pp. 86–87.

125. Tuchman, "If Mao Had Come to Washington," p. 59.

126. Schaller, *Crusade*, p. 223. This was probably a reference to Dimitrov's 3 January 1944 cable.

127. Reardon-Anderson, *Yenan*, pp. 96–97.

128. Ibid., p. 235.

129. Vladimirov, *Diaries*, p. 374.

130. *Zhongguo Gongchandang Lizi Zhongyao Huiyi Ji*, p. 240.

131. Mao Zedong, "On Coalition Government," in *Selected Works, Mao Tse-tung,*, vol. 3, Beijing: Foreign Languages Press 1967, p. 207 [hereafter cited as *Selected Works*].

132. Mao Zedong, "The Foolish Old Man Who Removed the Mountains," in *Selected Works*, vol. 3, p. 273.

133. Mao Zedong, "China's Two Possible Destinies," in *Selected Works*, vol. 3, p. 202.

134. Levine, "Mao Tse-tung's Oral Report," p. 14.

135. Reardon-Andreson, *Yenan*, p. 182.

136. Instead, these sensitive reports were delivered and discussed at the Central Committee plenary session preceding the congress (Vladimirov, *Diaries*, pp. 385–386).

137. Mao, "On Coalition Government," pp. 264–267.

138. Zhou Enlai's speech to the congress is in *Zhou Enlai Xuanji* [Selected works of Zhou Enlai], "Lun Tongyi Zhanxian" [On the united front], Beijing: Renmin chubanshe, 1980, pp. 190–220.
139. Liu Shaoqi, "Lun Dang" [On the party], *Liu Shaoqi Xuanji* [Selected works of Liu Shaoqi], vol. 1, Shanghai: Renmin chubanshe, 1981, pp. 314–372.
140. Mao, "On Coalition Government," pp. 235–242.
141. Levine, "Mao Tse-tung's Oral Report," pp. 19–20. Reardon-Anderson, *Yan'an*, pp. 80–81. Mao, "On Coalition Government," pp. 260–261.
142. Esherick, *Lost Chance*, pp. 345, 349.
143. Guo Morou was in Moscow during the talks and made efforts to learn their content. There is no evidence, however, that these efforts were successful. Wang Jiquan, editor, *Guo Morou Nianbu* [Chronicle of Guo Morou], vol. 1, Nanjing: Jiangsu Renmin Chubanshe, 1983, pp. 496–507.
144. Schaller, *Crusade*, p. 260.
145. Chong-sik Lee, *Revolutionary Struggle in Manchuria: Chinese Communism and Soviet Interest, 1922–1945,* Berkeley: University of California Press, 1983, pp. 220–231, 250–251.
146. Reardon-Anderson, *Yenan*, p. 100.
147. Vladimirov, *Diaries*, p. 496.
148. Reardon-Anderson, *Yenan*, p. 103.
149. Hu Xigui, *Shiju Bianhua he Women de Fangzhen* [Changes in the present situation and our policy]. Secretariat of the North China Bureau of the CCP, 30 August 1945. This document is held by the Bureau of Investigation in Taibei, Taiwan.
150. Ibid.
151. Chien-min Wang, "Zhongguo Gongchandang Shigao" [Draft history of the Chinese Communist Party], Taibei: Xin Ping, 1965, p. 421. Cited in Yaung, *Impact of the Yalta Agreement*, p. 128.
152. Vladimirov, *Diaries*, p. 507.
153. Vladimir Dedijer, *The Battle that Stalin Lost: Memoirs of Yugoslavia, 1948–1953,* New York: Viking Press, 1971, p. 68. *See also* idem, *Tito Speaks, His Self-Portrait and Struggle with Stalin,* London: Weiden, Feld, and Nicolson, 1953. p. 331. Milovan Djilas, *Conversations with Stalin,* New York: Harcourt, Brace, and World, 1963, p. 182.
154. Stuart Schram, editor, *Chairman Mao Talks to the People, Talks and Letters: 1956–1971,* New York: Pantheon Books, 1974, p. 191.
155. Liao Gailong, "Guanyu Gongchan Guoji, Sulian, he Zhongguo Geming" [On the Communist International, the Soviet Union, and the Chinese Revolution], *Dangshi Tongxum* [Party History Bulletin], no. 11–12, 1983, p. 15.
156. Vladimirov, *Diaries*, p. 509.
157. Yaung, *Impact of the Yalta Agreement*, pp. 134–135.
158. Hu Xigui, *Shiju Bianhua he Women de Fangzhen*.
159. Liao Kueilong, "Guanyu Gongchan Guoji, Sulian, he Zhongguo Geming," p. 15.
160. Mao, "On the People's Democratic Dictatorship," *Selected Works*, vol. 4, pp. 416–417.

Chapter IX

Conclusion

Chinese Nationalism and the Soviet Union

Chiang Kai-shek's Soviet policies met with substantial success during the war. He secured large-scale Soviet support for China's war effort, especially during the critical first period when Great Britain, the United States, and (after early 1938) Nazi Germany were unwilling to become involved. Although Chiang did not secure the direct Soviet participation he sought until Japan was on the brink of collapse, except for Moscow's brief flirtation with the Axis bloc in 1940, he generally retained Soviet support. He also succeeded in ousting the Soviet Union from Xinjiang, thereby quite probably retaining that region for the Chinese nation. Although this severely strained relations between the Republic of China and the Soviet Union, Chiang nonetheless proceeded to secure Soviet endorsement of the return to China of Manchuria and Taiwan, its representation first in the Big Four and then in the United Nations Security Council, and the Soviet Union's refusal to support Mao Zedong's revolutionary movement. While not directly related to Sino-Soviet relations, the abolition of the unequal treaties of the nineteenth century further added luster to Chiang's record. And above all, he had led China to victory over Japan against all odds. These were impressive achievements. It seems fair to say that China's rise to great-power status was substantially founded on Chiang's wartime diplomatic accomplishments. The People's Republic of China was heir to an impressive legacy upon which to build.

To what extent were these accomplishment's due to Chiang's skills at diplomatic maneuver as opposed to the intrinsic strengths of the Chinese nation and to a fortuitous coincidence between Chiang's objectives and the objectives of the Soviet Union and the United States? It is clear that Chiang's diplomatic achievements resulted largely from opportunistically responding to events rather than shaping events to his objectives. His efforts to shape relations among the major powers—to precipitate a Soviet-Japanese war, to thwart Soviet-Japanese rapprochement, to foster first Soviet-American cooperation and then a rivalry between them in the Far East—all failed. Yet while unable to influence broader developments, Chiang was a master of utilizing whatever opportunities presented themselves. He seized on growing Soviet-Japanese hostility, on Moscow's desire to cooperate with the West, and on the Soviet fear of a two-front war, to win large-scale Soviet assistance. By striking when the time was right he regained Xinjiang. And by playing on American fears of a Chinese cease-fire with Japan, Chiang was able to persuade Washington to coax Moscow into countenancing China's entry into the Big Four and the restoration of Chinese sovereignty in Manchuria.

Given Chiang's record of diplomatic success, an obvious paradox emerges. If Chiang was substantially successful in achieving the essential international elements of his program of restoring China's national grandeur, why did his regime collapse so rapidly after Japan's surrender? If, as I have argued, nationalism was so powerful a force in wartime and immediate postwar China, how was it that Chiang was repudiated by the Chinese people?

There seem to be both narrow and general answers to this paradox. The narrow answer has to do with the Yalta and Sino-Soviet agreements of 1945 and the popular reaction to them. Those agreements eliminated much of the prestige which Chiang's regime derived from its other diplomatic accomplishments. By granting Moscow special installations and rights in Manchuria and, most important, by recognizing the independence of Outer Mongolia under Soviet and American pressure, Chiang put himself in the position of accepting new "national humiliation" after years of supreme national effort. From a realistic standpoint, it is hard to see how Chiang could have done better. Yet the roused nationalist expectations of the Chinese people were too great. Realpolitik demanded compromise, but nationalist passions were absolutist. Chiang was in a no-win situation. He chose realistic compromise and was condemned by outraged nationalist sentiment.

More generally, Chiang seems to have failed to find a way to translate his diplomatic successes into an organized mass base. In a sense Chiang was, perhaps, not a fully modern leader. His style of control rested not on mass mobilization and mass participation, but on maneuvering and bargaining with various elites. In this he was a master, and it was perhaps not coincidental that high diplomacy is an art which places a premium on just such skills. But aside from his armies, Chiang never developed organizational forms to harness and direct the popular support generated by his diplomatic achievements. While Mao built numerous mass associations and governmental structures designed to make mass participation possible, Chiang either feared or did not understand such populist mechanisms. He was, perhaps, too much of a traditionalist.

Chiang's diplomatic accomplishments may also have obfuscated the dire need for domestic reform and lulled him and his cohorts into a false sense of confidence. It must have been inconceivable to Chiang that, after having led China to victory in a war unparalleled in modern Chinese history, and after having established China as an equal among the world's great powers for the first time in a century, that he could lose popular support. Chiang seems to belong to a class of leaders who enjoy substantial international success but fail as leaders of their own people. Richard Nixon was like this. He too racked up impressive diplomatic achievements—détente with the Soviet Union, the opening to China, ending the war in Vietnam—and yet his presidency collapsed because his domestic policies alienated the American people. If one searches for a commonality among such leaders, it is perhaps that their genuine and impressive diplomatic achievements beguile them and lead them to overestimate both their political skills and their popular support. Those whom the gods would destroy they first make blind.

Another general answer to the paradox of Chiang's career may be that once the war was over and won, foreign policy issues rapidly became less important to the masses than domestic issues. Chiang's failure to solve the "agrarian question," to stabilize the currency, to reform the army, and to satisfy the demands of the middle classes for political rights, ultimately outweighed the merits deriving from diplomatic successes. Perhaps if the CCP had not also had viable nationalist credentials, discontent over the domestic shortcomings of the KMT would not have translated into direct or tacit support for the CCP. But the CCP too *was* credibly nationalist.

The Emancipation of the Chinese Communist Party

The greatest achievement of Mao Zedong's wartime diplomacy, and perhaps of his entire career, lay in his emancipation of the Chinese Communist Party from Moscow's domination. As we have seen, in the heyday of Stalinism this was not an easy accomplishment. The arduous nature of this achievement is obscured by the polycentrism of later international communism and fading memories of the rigors of Comintern control.

The immensity of Mao's achievement in this regard can be illuminated by considering how China might have developed had Mao failed. Modern history is replete with examples of failed revolutionary movements. Had the CCP followed Moscow's bidding during the Sino-Japanese War, it would have sacrificed many more of its cadres in the war against Japan, it would have emerged from the war with a much smaller and weaker territorial-political base in north China, and it might well have surrendered control of its own armed force to the National Government. While Chiang Kai-shek's regime would have faced grave political problems in any case, it is by no means certain that a weakened CCP could have successfully challenged that regime. Rather, the Chinese Communists might have gone the way of the French or the Philippine Communist Parties: permanent opposition or conduct of a protracted but ultimately futile guerrilla insurgency.

Many Soviet-oriented Communist Parties proved unable to capitalize on the profound crises which racked their countries at the end of World War II. In many cases this relative impotence was, in part, a legacy of earlier obedience to Moscow. The French Communist Party, for instance, operated in a country in which the bourgeoisie had been discredited first by the collapse of 1940 and then by frequent collaboration with the Nazi occupiers. The Communists, on the other hand, were able to claim a major role in the Resistance, at least after June 1941. In 1945, the French Communist Party could plausibly argue that during the twentieth century capitalism had brought France the murderous war of 1914–1918, economic collapse during the 1930s, and a humiliating military defeat and foreign occupation in 1940. And France, of course, had a long revolutionary history and a largely Marxist working class. Yet within a few years the French Communist Party was reduced to a position of perpetual opposition. The political consequences of dogged loyalty to Moscow were among the major reasons for this outcome. Too many French men and women had witnessed the French Communists switch overnight in August 1939 from militant antifascism to diligent efforts to undermine France's war effort, and later, to enthusiastic collaboration with German occupation authorities, and then just as abruptly switch back to armed resistance to German power in June 1941. Although the French Communist Party sought power in a quite different society and on very different terms than the CCP, both parties faced a similar problem: how to adjust their political strategies to Soviet needs. They solved that problem in quite different fashions, and these different solutions were one important reason for the differing fates of the French and the Chinese Communist Parties.

It is important to consider, then, the conditions which made possible Mao Zedong's successful emancipation of the CCP from Moscow. It seems possible at the outset to dismiss the notion that Chinese have some sort of uniquely strong sense of nationalism which worked against Soviet efforts at control. Certainly the Spanish and French are no less nationalist in attitude than the Chinese. Yet the Communist Parties of both Spain and France proved servile to Moscow in the 1930s and 1940s. It may also be noted that for its first fourteen years the Chinese Communist Party was an obedient "branch party" of the Comintern; Chinese nationalism was not adequate to prevent Soviet domination during that period.

The great gulf between Chinese Confucian and European cultures may have played a more significant role. Russians were racially and culturally alien in China; this was much less the case in European and European-derived countries. The Chinese language was also more difficult for Russians or other Western Comintern operatives to learn than were European languages. And, of course, the immense philosophical and intellectual differences between China and Europe made it more difficult for Western Comintern apparatchiks to understand just what their Chinese comrades were about. But again this factor can provide only a partial answer: Yugoslavian Communists also proved unwilling to go along with Russian domination, even though both were Slavic peoples.

The opportunity provided by the German invasion of the Soviet Union was clearly a major reason for the final success of Mao's rebellion against Moscow. Extreme Soviet preoccupation with the mortal threat presented by Hitler's armies allowed Mao to extirpate ideologically and organizationally Moscow's influence within the CCP. Prior to 1942 Mao had had to compromise with Stalin. Through the Zheng Feng campaign, Mao, in effect, imposed his own terms and left Stalin to accept them or not. In Yugoslavia, Josip Broz Tito similarly utilized the windfall presented by the German-Soviet war. But the war is also only a partially satisfactory explanation. Many other Communist Parties around the world were similarly offered this opportunity and did not seize it. Mao and Tito did. Why? The answer to this can only lie in the psyches of those two extraordinary men.

Once set on such a course of emancipation from Moscow, the achievement of this objective became a function of Mao's political skills. He sought out and won over other senior CCP leaders who shared his skeptical views of Soviet control (Zhang Wentian, Wang Jiaxiang, Ren Bishi), welded these men into a reliable core, and then relied on them to insulate the CCP to a degree from Comintern control. Mao then slowly expanded his base within the CCP. In late 1937 he won over Zhou Enlai and possibly Chen Yun, and in 1938, Kang Sheng. He began cultivating a cohort of loyal lieutenants, such as Liu Shaoqi and Lin Biao. Occasionally Mao challenged the Internationalists and Moscow, but always he was ready to compromise policy for power when necessary. Mao was also a master of deception. During the eight years of the war, Mao shattered Moscow's mechanisms of control over the CCP and defied Comintern policies and directives repeatedly, all the while presenting a public image of loyalty to Moscow. Mao also excelled at manipulating Chinese cultural symbols to rouse Chinese nationalist sentiments. But it was the interpretation and writing of CCP history that was perhaps Mao's major ideological weapon. Mao spent considerable energy educating his comrades about the failures suffered by the revolutionary movement in China as a result of Soviet interference. The lessons learned from the struggle of the CCP, as told by the Maoist version of history, were very useful to Mao. Many within the CCP rallied to Mao and supported the "bolshevization" of the Party under him because they agreed with his thesis that if the CCP was to succeed in making revolution in China it would have to be prepared to disregard Soviet orders.

The "Lessons" of History

Political leaders often arrive at conclusions regarding the underlying dynamics of events they experience and then use these "lessons" to interpret subsequent phenomena. This is especially the case if the initial learning took place during the formative years of early adulthood. It is therefore appropriate that we consider the possible historical lessons derived by Chinese and Soviets from their tumultuous relations of 1937–1945.

One important "lesson" learned by Chinese has to do with the utility of China in tying down large numbers of foreign invaders. Chiang Kai-shek, and undoubtedly many other astute Chinese as well, understood quite well that Stalin aided China during the pre-1941 period chiefly in order to enhance Soviet security vis-à-vis Japan. They also undoubtedly reflected on the fact that Roosevelt, Hitler, and Churchill, as well as Stalin, all understood the importance of China in this regard, and all tried to utilize China to their advantage: Stalin to keep the war going in order to minimize his two-front threat, Hitler to end the war in order to free Japan's resources for a strike against the British and Americans, and Roosevelt and Churchill to keep China in the war to make feasible their strategy of concentrating on the defeat of Germany before turning their attention to Japan. Chiang realized this basic dynamic quite clearly. Indeed, his diplomacy was founded on it. Stalin, Roosevelt, or Hitler could all play the China card if they wished, but they would have to pay the appropriate diplomatic price. Much of Chiang's wartime diplomacy, in effect, revolved around setting that price.

It is not difficult to find modern legacies of this particular "lesson." A chief characteristic of the diplomacy of the People's Republic of China has been its reluctance to associate too closely with either the Soviet Union or the United States because of a fear of being manipulated. Thus, in 1965, Mao Zedong feared (as he told Edgar Snow) that Moscow was trying to maneuver China into a war with the United States over Vietnam. During the early 1980s, to cite another example, when politicians and commentators in the United States talked glibly about playing the China card against the Soviet Union, Chinese anger and suspicion was roused. There are undoubtedly multiple reasons for this dogged independence and sensitivity to manipulation by other powers. One reason has to do with the memories of wartime experiences.

One of the "lessons" learned by Soviets from the 1937–1945 period is the mirror image of China's fear of manipulation. Until mid-1943, Chiang sought Soviet entry into the war against Japan and spared no effort to achieve this. While some of the more clumsy efforts to provoke a Soviet-Japanese war (e.g., Yang Jie's 1937 efforts and the July 1943 leak of the Soviet transit deal) cannot be attributed to Chiang, they were nonetheless consistent with his policy and, more important for our purposes here, helped shape Soviet perceptions of "China." The avoidance of a two-front war was the *sine qua non* of Stalin's diplomacy and may, indeed, have been the single most important reason for the USSR's survival of the trial of the 1940s. "China," however, worked at cross-purposes to this.

Again, more contemporary reflections of this "lesson" are readily at hand. Nikita Khrushchev suspected that Mao was trying to provoke a Soviet-American nuclear war with his actions in the Formosa Strait in 1958. More generally, he saw Mao's attack on the Soviet policy of peaceful coexistence as an attempt to maneuver the Soviet Union into a confrontation with the United States from which China would benefit. It was for this reason that Khrushchev methodically reduced Soviet support for North Vietnam as Hanoi moved toward a Chinese-backed confrontation with the United States over Indochina in 1963–1964.

Another legacy of the "lessons" learned during the Sino-Japanese War had to do with the frequent contradictions between Soviet ideology and the interests of China's revolutionary movement and regime. When Mao broke with Moscow in the early 1960s, and then moved against "revisionists" within the CCP for the sake of "continuing the revolution under the dictatorship of the proletariat," he probably had in mind his struggle against the CCP's Internationalists during the war. Like Wang Ming, Mao must have believed such revisionists as Peng Dehuai, Luo Ruiqing, and Liu Shaoqi wanted to forego "making revolution" for the sake of "united action" with the Soviet Union. Like the Internationalists of the wartime era, the revisionists of the 1950s and 1960s were, Mao concluded, agents of the Soviet Union who had wormed their way into the CCP and who wanted to prevent China from making revolution in order to conform to Moscow's line. These revisionists were dangerous precisely because, like Wang Ming, they spoke the language of Marxism–Leninism and could therefore "wave the red flag to oppose the red flag." Such a perception was, of course, grossly unfair to such men as Peng, Luo, and Liu. Unlike Wang Ming, they pursued a vision of China's revolution which was not subordinate to the Soviet Union but which sought cooperation with Moscow on grounds of equality and for discrete political objectives. The point is, however, that Mao's protracted struggle against Moscow probably predisposed him to view any pro-Soviet internal Party opposition as lackeys of the Soviet Union. When future historians probe into Mao's psyche in order to explain why he led his nation into the maelstrom of the Cultural Revolution, they will do well to consider the influence of the "lessons" he learned during his long struggle with Stalin from 1937 thru 1945.

It is ironic that both Mao and Chiang were deeply concerned with possible Soviet penetration of China under the guise of Marxist-Leninist ideology. The two men disagreed profoundly, of course, as to just who and what constituted a Soviet agent. They agreed, however, that under the cover of its Marxist-Leninist ideology, Moscow was intervening in China in an attempt to direct its political development along lines compatible with Soviet interests.

Mao must have asked himself what Stalin hoped to do with the CCP if and when he brought it under the control of Wang Ming and his Internationalists. If so, he would have concluded that Stalin could use a compliant CCP in either of two ways. He could use it as an instrument either to pressure greater concessions from Chiang Kai-shek, or to bring part or all of China under Soviet control under the aegis of a compliant CCP. In either case, Soviet aims and methods would differ little from those of capitalist-imperialist powers. Decades later, in the 1960s and 1970s, when Mao concluded that socialist countries may act just as imperialistically as capitalist countries, he reflected on his earlier struggle with Stalin. Mao then concluded that Stalin's "contributions" to the Chinese revolution outweighed his "mistakes." What Mao did not make explicit was that even Stalin's "contributions" came about as a result of a protracted and determined struggle.

There is one final historical "lesson" learned by the Chinese which should be considered: When all was said and done, the Soviet Union accepted and supported China as a united great power. Not that Stalin was above demanding his pound of flesh; Manchuria, Xinjiang, and Outer Mongolia indicate otherwise. But overall, and especially during the critical initial two and the final two years of the war, Moscow endorsed China's essential national demands. As Stalin explained in August 1945, Soviet Russian diplomacy sought a strong and united China to stand alongside Russia against Japan. The experience of 1937–1945 "taught" Chinese that this indeed was the case, at least when China was strong and resolute enough to resist Soviet encroachments. This "lesson" too would influence China's relations with the Soviet Union during the last decades of the twentieth century.

Bibliography

Chinese Language Sources

Many Chinese publications do not give full publication information. Question marks here and in the notes indicate this author's considered guess as to the time and place of publication.

Chen Bulai, *Chen Bulai Huiyilu* [Chen Bulai memoir], Zhuanji Wenxue Congshu, no. 5, Taibei: Zhuanji Wenxue Chubanshe, 1981.

Chen Chongqiao, " 'Jiu yi ba' shibian yu Jiang Jieshi bu dikang zhuyi" [The 18 September Incident and Chiang Kai-shek's policy of nonresistance], *Liaoning Daxue Xuebao* [Liaoning University Journal], no. 5, 1981, p. 61.

Chen Dunzheng, "Wang Pengsheng bu pingfan de yisheng" [The turbulent life of Wang Pengsheng], *Zhuanji Wenxue* [Biographical Literature], Taibei, vol. 35, no. 6 (December 1979), p. 102.

Chen Ruiyun, "Lun kang Ri zhanzheng shiqi jiefangchu de zhengquan jianshe" [On the construction of liberated area regimes during the war of resistance], *Dangxue Yuekan* [Party Studies Monthly], no. 6, 1982, p. 50.

Chen Xiaoceng, "Xian shibian qian Guo Gong liangdang tanpan de pianduan huiyi" [Partial recollection of the KMT–CCP negotiations prior to the Xian Incident], *Dangshi Yanjiu Ziliao* [Research Materials on Party History], Beijing, no. 3, 1981, p. 28.

————, "Xian shibian qian yi nian Guo Gong liangdang guanyu lianhe kang Ri wenti de yi duan jiechu" [KMT–CCP contacts regarding uniting to resist Japan during the year preceding the Xian Incident], *Wenshi Ziliao Xuanji* [Selection of Literary Materials], national edition, vol. 71, n.d., p. 1.

Cheng Tianfang, "Shi De huiyilu" [Memoir of ambassadorship to Germany], *Zhuanji Wenxue* [Biographical Literature], Taibei. Part 1: vol. 4, no. 6 (June 1964), p. 17. Part 2: vol. 5, no. 1 (July 1964), p. 35. Part 3: vol. 5, no. 2 (August 1964), p. 29. Part 4: vol. 5, no. 3 (September 1964), p. 35. Part 5: vol. 6, no. 3 (March 1965), p. 21. Part 6: vol. 7, no. 1 (July 1965), p. 16.

Cheng Yuan, "Guanyu yuandong wenti de huiyi" [Recollection of the Far East problem], *Zhong Su Wenhua* [Sino-Soviet Culture], vol. 1, no. 1 (1 November 1937), p. 35.

Chu Yushen, *Dongtang Zhong de Zhong Su Guanxi* [Sino-Soviet relations in the midst of turmoil], Hankou: Da Gong Bao Chubanshe, 1938.

Dangxing Dangfeng Dangji Dawen 250 Ti, Gongchan Dangyuan [250 Questions and answers on party nature, party style, and party discipline, Communist party member], no. 1, 1982. Published by the CCP Publishing House of Liaoning province.

Dangshi Tongxun [Party History Bulletin], Beijing: Zhonggong Zhongyang Dangshi Yanjiushi.

Dangshi Yanjiu [Research on Party History], Beijing.

Deng Xi, *Taipingyang Jushi zhi Yanbian* [Changes in the Pacific Ocean situation], no. 3, Chongqing (?): Zhenghai Congshu, December 1939.

Di San Guoji Jiesan Shijian [The disbandment of the Third International], Chongqing: Qingbai Chubanshe, June 1943.

Ding Yongnian, "Guanyu di yi ci fangong gaochao de yi xie shishi" [Several facts regarding the first anti-communist high tide], *Dangshi Yanjiu Ziliao* [Research Materials on Party History], no. 12 (20 June 1980), p. 20.

Dongfang Zazhi [Oriental Miscellany], Hong Kong.

Du Yuming, "Zhongguo yuanzhengjun ru Mian dui Ri zuozhan shulie" [General description of the entry into Burma and war against Japan of China's expeditionary army], *Wenshi Ziliao Xuanji* [Selection of Literary Materials], national edition, vol. 8, n.d., p. 1.

Duli Pinglun [Independent commentary], Beijing.

Feng Kufei, "Wosho zhidao de Zhang Qun" [The Zhang Qun I knew], *Wenshi Ziliao Xuanji* [Selection of Literary Materials], national edition, vol. 42, n.d., p. 194.

Feng Yuxiang, *Wosuo Renshi de Jiang Jieshi* [The Chiang Kai-shek I knew], Haerbin (?): Heilungjiang Renmin Chubanshe, 1980.

Fudan Daxüe Lishixi [Fudan University Department of History], *1931–1945, Riben Diguo Zhuyi Duiwai Qinlüe Shiliao Xuanbian* [Collection of historical materials on the foreign aggression of Japanese imperialism, 1931–1945], Shanghai: Renmin Chubanshe, 1983.

Fu Qixue, *Zhongguo Waijiaoshi* [Chinese diplomatic history], Taibei: Shangwu Yinshuguan, 1972.

Fu Yongxun Tailang (transliteration from Japanese), "Riben Guangdongjun dui Guolian diaochatuan jian- xing jiandie huodong" [The spy activities of Japan's Kuantung Army toward the investigation mission of the League of Nations], *Wenshi Ziliao Xuanji* [Selection of Literary Materials], national edition, vol. 76, n.d., p. 125. (Translated from Japanese.)

Gan Sishen, "Huiyi Sanmin Zhuyi Tongzhi Lianhehui" [Recollection of the Three Principles of the People Comrades League], *Jindaishi Yanjiu* [Research on Modern History], vol. 1, 1982, p. 45.

Gao Jun, *Weida de Zhanshi Ren Bishi* [The great warrior Ren Bishi], Beijing: Zhongguo Qingnian Chubanshe, 1980.

Gao Yang, *Chen Guangbo Waizhuan* [Unauthorized biography of Chen Guangbo], Taibei: Nanjing Chuban Gongsi, 1981.

Gongchan Guoji Jiesan yu Zhonggong [The dissolution of the Communist International and the Chinese Communists], Fenduo Congshu di 33 Zhong, Chongqing (?): Tongyi Chubanshe, 1943.

Gu Huimin and Cai Zetong, *Ri Su Xieding yu Zhongguo* [China and the Russo-Japanese agreement], Moscow: Zhenli Chubanshe, May 1941.

Gu Xiaoping, "Kang Ri minzu tongyi zhanxian celüe fangzhen yu di er ci Guo Gong hezuo de xingcheng zong shu" [General description of strategy and direction of the anti-Japanese national united front and the formation of the second KMT–CCP cooperation], *Dangshi Yanjiu* [Research on Party History], no. 2, 1984, p. 77.

Gui Jianshi, "Kang Ri zhanzheng shiqi Jiang Mei goujie de maodun" [Contradictions in the collaboration of Chiang and the Americans during the anti-Japanese war], *Wenshi Ziliao Xuanji* [Selection of Literary Materials], national edition, vol. 57, n.d., p. 187.

Gui Wenhuan, "Kangzhan shiqi zai gongyun wenti shang Liu Shaoqi tongzhi yu Kang Sheng de duozheng" [The struggle between comrade Liu Shaoqi and Kang Sheng over the question of the labor movement during the war of resistance], *Xuzhou Daxue Xuebao* [Xuzhou University Journal], no. 2, 1982, p. 84.

Gui Wuxiang, *Guoji Yuanhua Yundong* [The international movement to aid China], Chongqing: Qingnian Chubanshe, December 1939.

Guo Binwen, "Kangzhan shiqi Ri Yan goujie zhi xinyan ji miyue (san jian)" [Three letters and secret agreements between Yan (Xishan) and Japan during the war of resistance], *Dangshi Yanjiu Ziliao* [Research on Party History], no. 19, 1980, p. 22.

Guo Dequan, "Xianhua liu E wangshi" [Miscellaneous recollections of my stay in Russia], *Zhuanji Wenxue* [Biographical Literature], vol. 29, no. 4 (October 1976), p. 65.

———, *Kangzhan Shiqi Zhu E Wuguan Huiyi Shilu* [True record of service as military attaché to Russia during the war of resistance], Taibei: Guofangbu Shizheng Bianyiju, June 1982.

Guo Xuyin, "Di er ci guonei geming zhangzheng shiqi de Feng Yuxiang" [Feng Yuxiang during the second revolutionary civil war], *Qilu Xuekan* [Shandong Journal], no. 6, 1982, p. 52.

Guofang Zui Gao Weiyuanhui Mishuchu [Secretariat of the Supreme National Defense Council], *Zhong Mei Tungyou Jiekuan Heyue Yijiao Fuxing Gongsi Banli* [Transmission of the Sino-American agreement for a Tung oil loan to the Renaissance Company for implementation], secret letter no. 8994, Guoshi Guan [Academia Historica], Taibei, archive no. 08. 12.

Guo Gong Tewuzhan [Secret agent war of the KMT and CCP], Hong Kong: Yushen Chubanshe, June 1968.

Guoji Fan Qinlüe Yundong Dahui Zhongguo Fenhui [China branch of the assembly of the International Movement against Aggression], *Ozhou Jushi yu Dongya Wenti* [The European situation and the East Asian question], Chongqing, May 1938.

Guomindang Dangshi Weiyuanhui [Committee on party history of the Nationalist Party of China], *Zhonghua Minguo Zhongyao Shiliao Chubian—Dui Ri Kangzhan Shiqi, Di San Bian, Zhanshi Waijiao* [Preliminary compilation of important historical materials of the Republic of China, the period of the war of resistance against Japan, vol. 3, wartime diplomacy], 3 books, Taibei: Guomindang Dangshi Weiyuanhui, 1981. (These are Chiang Kai-shek's archives.)

Guowen Zhoubao [Chinese Weekly], Shanghai, 1935–1937.

Han Yunbu, *Jiji Beizhan de Meiguo* [America actively preparing for war], Chongqing: Guomin Tushu Chubanshe, December 1940.

He Shifen, "Mao Zedong tonghi zai kangzhan chuqi junshi zhanlüe zhuanbian zhong de jiechu gongxian" [The outstanding contributions of comrade Mao Zedong to the changes in military strategy during the early period of the war of resistance], *Dangshi Yanjiu* [Research on Party History], no. 1, 1984, p. 33.

He Yingqin, *He Shangjiang Kangzhan Qijian Baoqao* [Reports of General He during the war of resistance], 2 vols., Zhongguo Xiandai Shiliao Congshu, no. 2, Taibei: Wenxing Shuju, 1962.

Hebei Shehui Kexueyuan [Hebei Academy of Social Sciences], *Huiyi Chen Tanqiu* [Remembering Chen Tanqiu], Wuhan: Huazhong Gongxueyuan Chubanshe, July 1981.

Hongse Zhonghua [Red China], Baoan (?), Shaanxi, 1936–1937. (This was the CCP paper in Shaanxi after the Long March.)

Hu Hua, editor, *Zhonggong Dangshi Renwu Zhuan* [Biographies of Chinese Communist historical personalities], vol. 9 (Chen Tanqiu, p. 1; Mao Zemin, p. 47), Xian (?): Shaanxi Renmin Chubanshe, 1983.

———, *Zhongguo Gemingshi Jiangyi* [Lectures on the history of the Chinese revolution], Beijing: Renmin Daxue Chubanshe, 1979.

Hu Jian, "Miziqi de jianglou" [The fall of the Union Jack], *Xinjiang Wenshi Ziliao Xuanji* [Xinjiang Selection of Literary Materials], vol. 1, n.d., p. 1.

Hu Qingyun, "Kangzhan shengli qianhou Heerli de 'Diaochu' he Sulian de dui Hua zhengce" [Hurley's 'mediation' at the end of the war of resistance and the Soviet Union's policy toward China], *Dangshi Ziliao Congkan* [Compendium of Materials on Party History], no. 2, 1983, p. 148.

Hu Qiuyuan, *Jin Bai Nian Lai Zhong Wai Guanxi* [Relations between China and foreign countries over the past century], 1943. (Republished, Taibei: Zhongwen Tushu Gongsi, 1978.)

———, *Guanyu di San Guoji zhi Jiesan yu Mosilini zhi Xia Tai* [On the dissolution of the Third International and the collapse of Mussolini], Chongqing (?), 1943.

Hu Shi Laiwang Shuxin Xuan [Selected correspondence of Hu Shi], vol. 2, Beijing: Zhongguo Shehui Kexueyuan Jiandaishi Yanjiusuo, May 1979.

Hu Shi Ren Zhu Mei Dashi Qijian Wanglai Diangao [Hu Shi's cable correspondence during the period as ambassador to the United States], Zhonghua Minguoshi Ziliao Zonggao, Zhuanti Ziliao Xuanji, Di San Bian [Compendium of materials on republican Chinese history, selection of special topics, vol. 3], Beijing: Zhongguo Shehui Kexueyuan Jindaishi Yanjiusuo, 1978.

Hu Xigui, *Shiji Bianhua he Women de Fangzhen* [Changes in the present situation and our policy], Report of the secretariat of the North China Bureau of the CCP to cadre conference, 30 August 1945.

Huai Yuan, "Wang Ming, Mao Zedong, yu Sulian" [Wang Ming, Mao Zedong, and the Soviet Union], *Feidang Neibu Duozheng Wenti Lunji* [Collection of essays on the internal struggle of the bandit party], Yao Menggan, editor, Taibei: Guoji Guanxi Yanjiusuo, 1975, pp. 193–214.

Huang Guowen, *Kangzhan Shiqi Woguo Dui Ri Waijiao Molüe, 1937–1945* [Our country's diplomatic strategies toward Japan during the war of resistance, 1937–1945], masters thesis, Political Warfare University, Taibei, 1977.

Huang Kaiyuan, et al., "Wannan shibian dashiji" [Chronology of the Southern Anwei Incident], *Dangshi Ziliao Congkan* [Compendium of Materials on Party History], no. 2, 1981, p. 136.

Huang Yuchuan, editor, *Mao Zedong Shengping Ziliao Jianbian, 1898–1969* [Materials on the life of Mao Zedong, 1898–1969], Hong Kong: Youlian Shubao Gongsi, 1970.

Ji He, "Chen Tanqiu tongzhi zai Xinjiang" [Comrade Chen Tanqiu in Xinjiang], *Xinjiang Wenshi Ziliao Xuanji* [Xinjiang Selection of Literary Materials], no. 8, n.d., pp. 28–33.

Jiang Hong, "Cong wodang yu Gongchan Guoji de guanxi kan duli zizhu de zhongyaoxing" [Viewing the importance of the policy of independence and self-reliance from the perspective of relations between our party and the Communist International], *Neibu Wengao* [Internal documents], 1 November 1983.

Jiang Jieshi, *Zhongguo zhi Mingyun* [China's destiny], Chongqing: Zheng Zhong Shuju, March 1943.

———, *Jiang Zongtong Sixiang Yanlun Ji* [Collected speeches and writings of President Chiang], 15 vols., Taibei.

Jiang Junzhang, "Song Ziwen Mosike tanpan zuiji" [Record of Song Ziwen's negotiations in Moscow], *Zhongguo Yizhou* [China Weekly], no. 100 (24 March 1952), p. 14.

Jiang Tingfu, *Zhongguo Jindaishi Dagang* [Outline of China's modern history], Taibei: Qiming Shuju, n.d. (First published in 1938.)

———, *Jiang Tingfu Huiyilu* [Memoir of Jiang Tingfu], Zhuanji Wenxue Congkan 48, Taibei, March 1979. This is a translation of the English-language memoir held by the Chinese Oral History Collection of Columbia University.

———, *Jiang Tingfu Xuanji* [Selected works of Jiang Tingfu], Zhuanji Wenxue Congshu, no. 81, 6 vols., Taibei: Zhuanji Wenxue Chubanshe, 1978.

Jiang Weiyuanchang Fangwen Yin Yao [Major events in Chairman Chiang's visit to India], Chongqing: Duli Chubanshe, March 1942.

Jiang Yongjing, "Kangzhan chuqi de waijiao yu Guolian yu Deshi zhi tiaoting" [The diplomacy of the early period of the war of resistance and the League of Nations and the mediation of the German ambassador], *Zhongguo Xiandaishi Lunji* [Essays on modern Chinese history], Zhang Yufa, editor, vol. 9, Taibei: Lianjing Chubanshe, 1982, pp. 363–380.

Jiang Zongtong Milu [The secret diary of President Chiang], Taibei: Zhongyang Ribao Chubanshe, 1978.

Material from Chiang Kai-shek's personal diaries made available in 1974 to a team of Japanese reporters from *Sankei Shimbun*.

Jin Hai, "Yimeng shibian de qiyin he Guo Gong liangdang de zhengce" [The causes of the Yimeng Incident and the policies of the KMT and the CCP], *Nei Menggu Daxue Xuebao* [Journal of the University of Inner Mongolia], no. 3, 1983, p. 55.

Jin Shaoxian, "Guomindang fandong shili jinru he tongzhi Xinjiang" [The entry and control of reactionary Kuomintang power in Xinjiang], *Xinjiang Wenshi Ziliao Xuanji* [Xinjiang Selection of Literary Materials], no. 2, n.d., p. 21.

Jin Zehua, *Sulian Shifo Neng Yuanzhu Zhongguo?* [Can the Soviet Union aid China?], Wuhan (?): Feichang Congshu Chubanshe, December 1937.

Jiuguo Bao [National redemption], Paris, 1935–1936.

Jiuguo Shibao [National Salvation News], Paris, 1936.

Junshi Huodong Dashiji [Record of major military events], Beijing: Zhanshi Chubanshe, 1983.

"Kang Ri zhanzheng shiqi Zhongguo Gongchandang zai Xinjiang gemin duozhengshi" [History of the revolutionary struggle of the Chinese Communist Party in Xinjiang during the war of resistance against Japan], *Xinjiang Daxue Xuebao* [Xinjiang University Journal], no. 1, 1981, pp. 44–63.

Kang Ze, "Wo zai Guo Gong di er ci hezuo tanpan zhong de yi duan jingli" [My experiences during one period of the KMT–CCP negotiations over the second period of cooperation], *Wenshi Ziliao Xuanji* [Selection of Literary Materials], national edition, vol. 71, n.d., p. 18.

Kangzhan Wenxian [Documents on the war of resistance], vols. 3, 4. Nanjing: Di er ge Lishi Danganguan. (Clippings file of Chiang Kai-shek's wartime activities held at the Second Historical Archives in Nanjing.)

Kangzhan Zhong Geguo Waijiao Dongxiang [The diplomatic tendencies of various nations in the midst of the war of resistance], no. 2, Chongqing: Zhanshi Zonghe Congshu, December 1939.

Kong Xiangxi, "Xian shibian huiyilu" [Memoir of the Xian Incident], *Zhuanji Wenxue* [Biographical Literature], part 1: vol. 9, no. 6 (December 1966). Part 2: vol. 10, no. 3 (March 1967). Part 3: vol. 10, no. 6 (June 1967).

Lang Daoheng, "Wosuo zhidao de 'Xinjiang wang' Sheng Shicai" [The 'Xinjiang king' Sheng Shicai that I knew], *Xinjiang Wenshi Ziliao Xuanji* [Xinjiang Selection of Literary Materials], vol. 2, n.d., p. 1.

Lang Xung, *Dai Li Zhuan* [Biography of Dai Li], Taibei, Zhuanji Wenxue Congkan, no. 53, Taibei: Zhuanji Wenxue Chubanshe, 1982.

Li Faqing, *Zhongguo Gongchandang zai Kangzhan Qijian zhi Zhengge Yinmo* [The complete plot of the Chinese Communist Party during the period of the war of resistance], May 1940, no publisher or place of publication given. This was the source of the subsequently much quoted statement attributed to Mao that only ten percent of the strength of the CCP should go to fighting Japan.

Li Tianrong, "Wo zai Jiang Jieshi shicongshi gongzuo de pianduan huiyi" [Partial memoir of my work in Chiang Kai-shek's staff office], *Guangzhou Wenshi Ziliao Xuanji* [Guangzhou Selection of Literary Materials], vol. 26, n.d., p. 113.

Li Zhiming and Wang Songguo, "Xi lu jun zai Xinjiang" [The West Route Army in Xinjiang], *Xinjiang Wenshi Ziliao Xuanji* [Xinjiang Selection of Literary Materials], no. 1, n.d., pp. 20–29.

Li Zhongyuan, *Zhong Su Bu Qinfan Tiaoyue yu Ri Su Zhongli Xieding zhi Yanjiu* [Research on the Sino-Soviet Non-Aggression Treaty and the Russo-Japanese Neutrality Agreement], masters thesis, National Cheng-Ch'i University, Taibei, 1980.

Liao Gailong, "Guanyu Gongchan Guoji, Sulian, yu Zhongguo geming" [On the Communist International, the Soviet Union, and the Chinese revolution], *Dangshi Tongxun* [Party History Bulletin], nos. 11–12, 1983, p. 2.

Liu Enmu, et al., "Zhongguo kang Ri zhanzheng ji qi zai di er ci shijie da zhan zhong de diwei yu zuoyong" [The significance and function of China's war of resistance against Japan in the Second World War], *Shijie Lishi* [World History], no. 4, 1980, p. 5.

Liu Guangdan, *Zhongguo Gongchandang Waijiao Lilun de Fenxi* [Analysis of the diplomatic theories of the Chinese Communist party], Chongqing (?): Shengli Chubanshe, 1941.

Liu Shaotang, *Minguo Dashi Rizhi* [Chronicle of major events of the Republic], 2 vols., Taibei: Zhuanji Wenxue Chubanshe, 1978.

Liu Shaoqi, *Liu Shaoqi Xuanji* [Selected works of Liu Shaoqi], Shanghai: Renmen Chubanshe, 1981.

Liu Xining, "Guoji fanqinlüe yundong yu Zhongguo kangzhan" [The international movement against aggression and China's war of resistance], *Zhong Su Wenhua* [Sino-Soviet Culture], vol. 1, nos. 6–7 (16 January 1938), p. 7.

Liu Yixun, "Gongchan Guoji he Sidalin dui Zhongguo kang Ri zhanzheng de taidu he fangzhen" [The attitude and policy of the Comintern and Stalin toward China's war of resistance against Japan], *Dangshi Ziliao Congkan* [Compendium of Materials on Party History], no. 2, 1983, p. 139.

Liu Zhaoai, "Zhongguo Gongchandang zhi nei kang Ri minzu tongyi zhanxian celüe de yanbian" [The changes within the CCP regarding the strategy of the anti-Japanese national united front], *Xiangtan Daxue Xuebao* [Xiangtan University Journal], no. 2, 1982, p. 85.

Liu Zhuguang, "Wo sanjia Chen Jiageng suiling de Nanyang huaqiao huiguo weilaotuan de huiyi" [Memoir of my participation in the overseas Chinese goodwill delegation to China led by Chen Jiageng], *Wenshi Ziliao Xuanji* [Selection of Literary Materials], national edition, vol. 75, n.d., p. 208.

Lo Baoce, "Guoji zhengzhi xin zhongxin yu Zhongguo waijiao" [The new center of international politics and China's diplomacy], *Dongfang Zazhi* [Oriental Miscellany], vol. 36, no. 22 (16 November 1939), p. 5.

Lo Xianglin [Lo Hsiang-lin], *Fu Ping-ch'ang and Modern China* (in Chinese with an English title), Hong Kong: Institute of Chinese Culture, 1973.

——, "Fu Bingchang yu jindai Zhongguo guanxi suozai" [The position of Lo Binchang in modern China's relations], *Zhuanji Wenxue* [Biographical Literature], vol. 20, no. 3 (March 1972), p. 33.

——, "Fu Bingchang xiansheng you Ouzhou fanguo qianhou" [The events surrounding Mr. Fu Bingchang's return from Europe], *Zhuanji Wenxue* [Biographical Literature], vol. 25, no. 2 (August 1974), p. 53.

Lu Lin, *Sulian zai Yuandong de Junshi Jianshe* [Soviet military construction in the Far East], Shanghai: Wenhua Shuju, April 1938.

Lu Zhenxiang, "Guanyu Guomindang gaishupai" [On the KMT's reform faction], *Lishi Jiaoxue* [Teaching History], no. 5, 1981, p. 47.

Lu Zhenyu, "Muqian guoji xingshi de renshi" [Understanding the present international situation], *Zhong Su Wenhua* [Sino-Soviet Culture], vol. 2, no. 2 (1 June 1938), p. 1.

Lun Kang Ri Jiuguo Tongyi Zhanxian [On the united anti-Japanese nation salvation front], Yan'an (?), 1936.

"Lun Zhang Wentian tongzhi Zunyi huiyi de zhuanbian" [On comrade Zhang Wentian's changes at the Zunyi Conference], *Dangshi Yanjiu* [Research on Party History], no. 3, 1983, pp. 13–22.

Ma Qilin, "Kangzhan chuqi de Wang Ming tuoxiang zhuyi luxian zuowu" [The mistakes in line of Wang Ming's capitulationism during the early period of the war of resistance], *Dangshi Ziliao Congkan* [Compendium of Materials on Party History], no. 1, 1981, p. 126.

Mai Chaoshu, "Guanyu Jiang Jieshi Wang Jingwei jinxing xiang Ri huodong de jianwen" [Brief comment on Chiang Kai-shek's and Wang Jingwei's activities with Japan], *Wenshi Ziliao Xuanji* [Selection of Literary Materials], national edition, vol. 22, n.d., p. 53.

Mai Zunde, "Kong Xiangxi yu Rikou goujie huodong de pianduan" [Comment on Kong Xiangxi's collaborationist activities with Japan], *Wenshi Ziliao Xuanji* [Selection of Literary Materials], national edition, vol. 29, n.d., p. 67.

Mao Shaoxian, "Zai Ren Bishi tongzhi de shenbian" [Beside comrade Ren Bishi], *Hongqi Piaopiao* [The Red Flag Waves], no. 5, n.d., p. 257.

Mao Zedong, *Yi jiu si wu Nian de Renwu* [The duties of 1945], Yan'an (?): Yi Lu Yu Shudian, 15 December 1944.

——, *Xin Minzhu Zhuyi Lun* [On new democracy], Yan'an (?), 15 January 1940.

——, *Lun Muqian Guoji Xingshi yu Zhongguo Kangzhan* [On the present international situation and China's war of resistance], Chongqing (?): Xinhua Ribao Chubanshe, December 1939.

——, et al., *Tongyi Zhanxian xia Dangpai Wenti* [The question of parties and factions under the united front], Guangzhou: Xinmin Tushushe, March 1938.

——, *Tongyi Zhanxian yu Kangzhan Qiantu* [The united front and prospects for the war of resistance], Hankou: Ziqiang Chubanshe, February 1938.

——, *Mao Zedong Ji* [Collected works of Mao Zedong], Tokyo: Sososha Company, 1971. This multivolume collection juxtaposes the original versions of Mao's writings with post-1949 alterations.

Nankai Daxue Malie Zhuyi Jiaoyanshi [Marxist–Leninist instructional office of Nankai University], *Huabei Shibian Ziliao Xuanbian* [Selection of materials on the North China Incident], Zhengzhou (?): Henan Renmin Chubanshe, 1983.

Ning Jinan, *Zhang Guotao he "Wo de Huiyi"* [Zhang Guotao and "My Memoir"], Chengdu: Sichuan Renmin Chubanshe, 1982.

Pan Guohua and Lin Dajiao, "Kang Ri zhan shiqi Zhongguo Gongchandang zai sixiang lilun zhanxian shang dui Guomindang wangupai de duozheng" [The Chinese Communist Party's ideological struggle against the Kuomintang die-hards during the war of resistance], *Lishi Jiaoxue* [Teaching History], no. 3, 1982, p. 10.

Peng Dehuai, *Peng Dehuai Zishu* [Peng Dehuai remembers], Beijing: Renmin Chubanshe, 1981.

Peng Ming, *Zhong Su Renmin Youyi Jianshi* [Short history of the friendship of the Chinese and Soviet peoples], Beijing: Zhongguo Qingnian Chubanshe, 1955.

Qian Yishi, *Zhongguo Zenyang Jiangdao Ban Zhimindi?* [How was it that China was reduced to semicolonial status?], Shanghai: Shenghuo Shudian, 1936.

———, *Zhongguo Waijiaoshi* [Diplomatic history of China], Wuhan (?): Shenghuo Shudian, 1938.

Qiu Zongding, "Jiang Jieshi de shicongshi jishi" [Record of Chiang Kai-shek's staff office], *Wenshi Ziliao Xuanji* [Selection of Literary Materials], national edition, vol. 81, n.d., p. 103.

Sai Guoyu, "Kangzhan shiqi Guo Gong jian de junshi shangtan" [Military talks between the KMT–CCP during the war of resistance], *Gongdang Wenti Yanjiu* [Research on the CCP Problem], Taibei, vol. 9, no. 7 (15 July 1983), pp. 48–64.

Shang Mingdong, "Song Qingling yu di er ci Guo Gong hezuo de shixian" [Song Qingling and the realization of the second period of KMT–CCP cooperation], *Renmin Ribao* [People's Daily], 24 January 1983, p. 7.

Shao Lizi, "Chushi Sulian de huiyi" [Memoir of ambassadorship to the Soviet Union], *Wenshi Ziliao Xuanji* [Selection of Literary Materials], national edition, vol. 60, n.d., p. 181. (Shao's memoir was written "before 1966.")

———, "You Zhong Su hubu qinfan tiaoyue dao Zhong Su shangyue" [From the Sino-Soviet treaty of mutual nonaggression to the Sino-Soviet commercial treaty], *Zhong Su Wenhua* [Sino-Soviet Culture], vol. 4, no. 1 (August 1939), p. 1.

Shao Yunrui and Li Wenrong, "Guanyu 'He Mei xieding' de ji ge wenti" [Several matters relating to the 'He-Ozema agreement'], *Jindaishi Yanjiu* [Research on Contemporary History], no. 3, 1979, p. 114.

Shen Qi, *Deguo de Yuandong Liyi yu Yuandong Zhengce* [Germany's Far Eastern interests and foreign policy], Chongqing (?): Zhengzhong Shuju, May 1941. (Translation of German work by Kurt Bloch.)

Shen Zui, *Juntong Neimu* [Secret history of the military police], Beijing: Wenshi Ziliao Chubanshe, February 1980.

Shi Feng, *Fandui Wang Ming Touxiang Zhuyi Luxian de Duozheng* [The struggle against Wang Ming's capitulationist line], Shanghai: Renmin Chubanshe, 1976.

Shi Weifu and Hu Huading, "Shilun dang de bi Jiang kang Ri fangzhen" [Discussing the party's policy of compelling Chiang to resist Japan], *Beijing Shiyuan Xuebao* [Beijing Normal College Journal], no. 2, 1982, p. 91.

Shi Yuanpu, "Xinjiang mimi shenpan weiyuanhui jiepo" [Exposé of the secret investigation committee of Xinjiang], *Xinjiang Wenshi Ziliao* [Xinjiang Selection of Literary Materials], no. 1, n.d., p. 77.

Shi Zhe, "Chen Tanqiu tongzhi zai Mosike" [Comrade Chen Tanqiu in Moscow], in *Huiyi Chen Tanqiu* [Remembering Chen Tanqiu], Central China Engineering College, Wuhan: Hubei Shehui Kexueyuan, July 1981.

Song Enfu, "Dongbei kang Ri lianjun" [The northeastern united anti-Japanese army], *Lishi Zhishi* [Historical Knowledge], no. 5, 1982, p. 4.

Song Ruike, "Dui 'wosuo zhidao de Zhang Qun' yi wen de dingzheng" [Corrections to the article 'the Zhang Qun I knew'], *Wenshi Ziliao Xuanji* [Selection of Literary Materials], national edition, vol. 71, n.d., p. 205.

Sun Ke, "Bashi shulüe" [Summing up at eighty], *Zhuanji Wenxue* [Biographical Literature], part 1: vol. 23, no. 4 (October 1973), p. 7. Part 2: vol. 23, no. 5 (November 1973), p. 11. Part 3: vol. 23, no. 6 (December 1973), p. 64.

———, "Guoji xianshi yu Zhongguo" [The present international situation and China], *Zhong Su Wenhua* [Sino-Soviet Culture], vol. 5, no. 2 (1 February 1940), p. 1.

Sun Wulou, "Gongchan Guoji yu Zhongguo geming guanxi dashiji" [Record of major events in the Communist International's relations with the Chinese revolution], *Dangshi Yanjiu Ziliao* [Research Materials on Party History], no. 21, 1980, p. 26.

Sun Yueji, "Huiyi Shao Lizi xiansheng he wo de guanxi" [Recalling Mr. Shao Lizi's relations with me], *Wenshi Ziliao Xuanji* [Selection of Literary Materials], national edition, vol. 88, n.d., p. 8.

Suo Shihui, "Bai tuan dazhan ying zhongfen kending" [The Hundred Regiments offensive should be substantially upheld], in *Zhonggong Dangshi Yanjiu Lunwen Xuan* [Selection of research essays on CCP history], Zhu Chengya, editor, Changsha: Hunan Renmin Chubanshe, 1984.

Tan Guang, "Wosuo zhidao de Kong Xiangxi" [The H.H. Kung I knew], *Wenshi Ziliao Xuanji* [Selection of Literary Materials], national edition, vol. 25, n.d., p. 213.

———, "Kong Xiangxi yu Guomindang de junhuo maoyi" [H.H. Kung and the Kuomintang's munitions trade], *Wenshi Ziliao Xuanji* [Selection of Literary Materials], national edition, vol. 55, n.d., p. 59.

Tang Baolin, "Jiu an xin kao" [Reexamining old cases], in *Cheng Duxiu Pinglun Xuanbian* [Selection of essays on Chen Duxiu], Wu Shutang, editor, Changsha (?): Hunan Renmin Chubanshe, August 1982.

Tang Manzhen, "Zhongguo Gongchandang shi ruhe datui di yi ci fangong gaochao de" [How it was that the Chinese Communist Party was able to beat back the first anticommunist high tide], *Jiaoxue yu Yanjiu* [Teaching and Research], part 1: no. 3, 1981, p. 14. Part 2: no. 4, 1981, p. 25.

————, "Wang Ming wei 'yiqie jingguo tongyi zhanxian' de zuowu fanan shi tulao de" [It is futile to try to reverse the judgment on Wang Ming's incorrect line of 'everything through the united front'], *Dangshi Yanjiu* [Research on Party History], no. 3, 1983, p. 53.

Tang Shengming, "Wo feng Jiang Jieshi ming sanjia Wang wei zhengquan de jingguo" [The events surrounding my receiving orders from Chiang Kai-shek to participate in Wang's bogus regime], *Wenshi Ziliao Xuanji* [Selection of Literary Materials], national edition, vol. 40, n.d., p. 1.

Tao Zhen, "Sulian heping waijiao de xin jieduan" [A new stage in the Soviet Union's peace diplomacy], *Zhong Su Wenhua* [Sino-Soviet Culture], vol. 4, no. 3 (1 October 1939), p. 15.

Tian Keqin, "Shishu di er ci Guo Gong hezuo de xingcheng" [Factual description of the formation of the second KMT–CCP cooperation], *Dangshi Yanjiu* [Research on Party History], no. 5, 1982, pp. 62–67.

Tian Peng, *Riben Qinzhan Hainan Dao zhi Jiantao* [Brief analysis of Japan's seizure of Hainan Island], no. 6, Chongqing (?): Shishi Baodao Congshu, March 1940.

————, *Su De Guanxi Haozhuan Jingguo Ji Qi Yingxiang* [The process of improvement in Soviet-German relations and its influence], no. 4, Chongqing (?): Shishi Baodao Congshu, December 1939.

Tie Ming, "Wu Jingtong tong Guolian diaochatuan zai Tianjin huiyi de neimu" [The inside story of Wu Jingtong's meeting with the League of Nations' investigation mission in Tianjin], *Wenshi Ziliao Xuanji* [Selection of Literary Materials], national edition, vol. 76, n.d., p. 114.

Tuanjie de Dahui, Shengli de Dahui [A united congress, a victorious congress], Yan'an: Qianjin Chubanshe, July 1945.

Waijiaobu Gongbao [Foreign Ministry Bulletin], National Government of the Republic of China, Nanjing, 1934–1937.

Wang Boyu, "Su jun liang ci ru Xin huanzhu Sheng Shicai shimo" [The full story of the Soviet army's twofold entry into Xinjiang to assist Sheng Shicai], *Zhong Ya Yanjiu Ziliao* [Research Materials on Central Asia], no. 2, 1983, p. 29.

Wang Chonghui, *Wang Chonghui Yizuo* [The works of Wang Chonghui], Taibei: Yuntian Chubanshe, 1970.

————, "Sulian guoqing jinian chengyan" [Sincere words commemorating Soviet national day], *Zhong Su Wenhua* [Sino-Soviet Culture], special issue, November 1940, p. 5.

Wang Jiafu, "Dui 'guanyu Jiang Jieshi Wang Jingwei jinxing xiang Ri huodong de jianwen' de gengzheng" [Additional corrections to the article 'On Chiang Kai-shek's and Wang Jingwei's activities with Japan'], *Wenshi Ziliao Xuanji* [Selection of Literary Materials], national edition, vol. 37, n.d., p. 239.

Wang Jiaxiang, "Huiyi Mao Zedong tongzhi yu Wang Ming jihui zhuyi luxian de duozheng" [Recollection of comrade Mao Zedong's struggle with Wang Ming's opportunist line], *Renmin Ribao* [People's Daily], 27 December 1979, p. 2.

————, "Huiyi Mao zhuxi geming luxian yu Wang Ming jihui zhuyi luxian de duozheng" [Recalling the struggle between Chairman Mao's revolutionary line and Wang Ming's opportunist line], *Hongqi Piaopiao* [The Red Flag Waves], no. 18, n.d., p. 47.

Wang Jingwei Jituan Maiguo Tuodi Pipan Ziliao Xuanbian [Selection of critical materials on the treasonous and capitulationist activities of the Wang Jingwei group], Nanjing: Nanjing Daxue Xuebao Bianjizu, May 1981.

Wang Jiquan and Zhang Weigang, *Guo Morou Nianbu* [Chronology of Guo Morou], Nanjing: Jiangsu Renmin Chubanshe, 1983.

Wang Kunlun, Wang Bingnan, and Chu Wu, "Zhongguo minzu geming tongmeng shilu" [Factual record of the China national revolutionary alliance], *Wenshi Ziliao Xuanji* [Selection of Literary Materials], national edition, vol. 87, n.d., p. 1.

Wang Kaiting, "Wosuo zhidao de Yang Jie jiangjun" [The General Yang Jie I knew], *Kunming Wenshi Ziliao Xuanji* [Kunming Selection of Literary Materials], vol. 1, n.d., p. 20.

Wang Lixi, *Zai Guoji Yuanhua Zhanxian Shang* [In the international united front to aid China], Chongqing: Shenghuo Shudian, March 1939.

Wang Ming (also known as Chen Shao-yu), *Wang Ming Ji* [Collected works of Wang Ming], Tokyo: Ji Gu Shuyuan, 1973.

————, "Sanyue zhengzhiju huiyi de zongjie" [Summary of the March Politburo conference], *Qun Zhong* [The Masses], no. 19 (23 April 1938), p. 322.

————, *Tuopai Zai Zhongguo* [The Trotskyites in China], Zhejiang: Xin Zhongguo Chubanshe, May 1939.

Wang Qi and Wu Rongyi, "Ping kang Ri zhanzheng shiqi Meiguo de dui Hua zhengce" [Critique of American policy toward China during the war of resistance against Japan], *Dangshi Tongxun* [Party History Bulletin], nos. 20–21, 1983, p. 24.

Wang Ruiqing and Lin Wenjun, "Jiantan kangzhan chuqi wojun zhengzhi weiyuan zhidu de chuxiao yu huifu" [Brief discussion of the elimination and reestablishment of the system of political commissars in our army during the early war of resistance], *Dangshi Yanjiu Ziliao* [Research Materials on Party History], no. 3, 1981, p. 19.

Wang Shijie, *Wang Shijie Xiansheng Lunyan Xuanji* [Selected writings of Mr. Wang Shijie], Xiandian: Yutai Gongsi, 1980.

———, unpublished diary of Wang Shijie, 1944–1945.

Wang Shudi, *Chen Duxiu Pinglun Xuanbian* [Selection of essays on Chen Duxiu], vol. 2, Zhengzhou(?): Henan Renmin Chubanshe, 1982.

Wang Yunxue, "Huiyi Tanqiu tongzhi zhanduo zai Xinjiang" [Recalling comrade Tanqiu's struggle in Xinjiang], in *Huiyi Chen Tanqiu* [Recollections of Chen Tanqiu], Central China Engineering College, Wuhan: Renmin Chubanshe, 1981.

Weigesiji (translit. from Russian), editor, *Waijiaoshi* [Diplomatic history], vols. 3–4, Dalian: Dalian Waiyu Xueyuan, 1979. (Translated from Russian. Originally published in Moscow in 1956.)

Wei Ling, "Lun kangzhan zhong de guoji xuanchuan gongzuo" [On international propaganda work during the war of resistance], *Zhong Su Wenhua* [Sino-Soviet Culture], vol. 9, no. 9 (16 March 1938), p. 34.

Wei Zhongxiung, *Ozhou yu Yuandong* [Europe and the Far East], Chongqing: Duli Chubanshe, February 1940.

Wen Feiran, "Sheng Shicai tewu kongzhi xia de Xinjiang" [Xinjiang under the rule of Sheng Shicai's special agents], *Xinjiang Wenshi Ziliao Xuanji* [Xinjiang Selection of Literary Materials], no. 7, n.d., pp. 1–19.

———, "Xinjiang kang Ri minzu tongyi zhanxian de xingcheng yu polie" [The formation and collapse of the anti-Japanese national united front in Xinjiang], *Xinjiang Wenshi Ziliao Xuanji* [Xinjiang Selection of Literary Materials], no. 8, n.d., pp. 1–27.

Wen Huangen, "Gongchan Guoji fan faxice tongyi zhanxian celüe de xingcheng, shishi, jiqi weida shengli" [The formation, implementation, and great victory of the Comintern's strategy of an antifascist united front], *Xibei Daxue Xuebao* [Northwest University Journal], no. 3, 1983, p. 36.

Weng Wenhao, "Yi jiu san qi nian fangwen Ying De He Sulian de huiyi" [Memoir of the missions to England, Germany, Holland and the Soviet Union in 1937], *Wenshi Ziliao Xuanji* [Selection of Literary Materials], national edition, vol. 1, n.d., p. 57.

Wenshi Ziliao Xuanji [Selection of Literary Materials], Beijing: Zhongguo Renmin Zhengzhi Xieshang Huiyi Quanguo Weiyuanhui.

Wu Dakun, "Zai Song Qingling tongzhi lingdao xia gongzuo" [My work under the leadership of Comrade Song Qingling], *Zhongguo Zai Mao Bao* [China Financial and Trade Post], 26 May 1981, p. 1.

Wu Xiangxiang, "Yang Jie yu guofang xinlun" [Yang Jie and the new theory of national defense], *Zhuanji Wenxue* [Biographical Literature], vol. 8, no. 6 (June 1966), p. 28.

———, "Riben tong Wang Pengsheng" [Japan expert Wang Pengsheng], *Zhuanji Wenxue* [Biographical Literature], vol. 8, no. 5 (May 1966), p. 30.

———, "Kangzhan qijian liang guohe zuzi—Hu Shi yu Chen Guangbo" [Two soldiers who never turned back during the war of resistance—Hu Shi and Cheng Guangbo], *Zhuanji Wenxue* [Biographical Literature], vol. 17, no. 5 (November 1970), p. 6.

———, *Di Er Ci Zhong Ri Zhanzhengshi* [History of the second Sino-Japanese War], 2 vols., Taibei: Zonghe Yuekanshe, no year of publication given (1980?).

Wu Xiufeng, "Guoji Lianmeng chuli 'jiu yi ba' shiban qianhou jingguo" [The League of Nations' handling of the 18 September Incident], *Wenshi Ziliao Xuanji* [Selection of Literary Materials], national edition, vol. 76, n.d., p. 95.

Wu Yuzhang, "Wu Yuzhang zizhuan" [Autobiography of Wu Yuzhang], *Lishi Yanjiu* [Historical Research], no. 4, 1981, p. 13.

Wu Zedan, "Ouju yaobian hou de woguo waijiao zhengce" [Our country's diplomacy after the important changes in the European situation], *Dongfang Zazhi* [Oriental Miscellany], vol. 37, no. 17 (1 September 1940), p. 3.

"Wuhan Huizhan" [The battle of Wuhan], *Renmin Ribao* [People's Daily], 18 July 1983, p. 5.

Xia Honggen, "Wang Ming meiyou zai sanyue zhengzhiju huiyi shang zuoguo zongjie" [Wang Ming did not make a summary at the March Politburo conference], *Dangshi Yanjiu* [Research on Party History], vol. 3, 1983, p. 81.

Xia Jinlin, *Wo Wudu Sanjia Waijiao Gongzuo de Huiyi* [Memoir of my fivefold participation in diplomatic work], Taibei: Zhuanji Wenxue, January 1978.

Xia Yanyue, "Di er ci Guo Gong hezuo de jijian shishi" [Several facts regarding the second KMT–CCP cooperation], *Dangshi Yanjiu Ziliao* [Research Materials on Party History], no. 3, 1981, p. 28.

Xiandai Guoji Guanxishi Cankao Ziliao (1933–1939) [Reference materials on the history of modern international relations, 1933–1939], Beijing: Guoji Guanxi Xueyuan, 1958.

Xiang Qing, " 'Ba-yi' xuanyan xingcheng lishi guocheng" [The historical process of the formation of the 1 August manifesto], *Dangshi Ziliao Congkan* [Compendium of Materials on Party History], no. 3, 1982, p. 98.

———, "Gongchan Guoji he Zhongguo Gongchandang guanyu jianli kang Ri minzu tongyi zhanxian de celüe" [The Communist International and the Chinese Communist Party regarding the strategy of forming an anti-Japanese national united front], *Dangshi Tongxun* [Party History Bulletin], nos. 11–12, 1983, p. 16.

Xibaya yu Zhongguo [Spain and China], Zhanshi Congkan, no. 64, Wuhan (?): Zhanshi Chubanshe, 1938 (?).

Xie Mingde, editor, *Huainian Ren Bishi Tongzhi* [Remembering comrade Ren Bishi], Changsha: Hunan Renmin Chubanshe, 1979.

Xing Damo, "Deguo waijiao dangan zhong de Zhong De guanxi, 1928–1938" [Sino-German relations 1928–1938 according to German diplomatic archives], *Zhuanji Wenxue* [Biographical Literature], vol. 41, no. 4 (October 1982), vol. 41, no. 5 (November 1982), vol. 41, no. 6 (December 1982).

Xu Haining, "Lun kang Ri minzu tongyi zhanxian zai xiangchi jieduan zhong de 'zuo' qin zuowu luxian" [On the incorrect leftist line in the anti-Japanese national united front during the period of strategic stalemate in the war of resistance], *Xueshu Yanjiu Congkan* [Compendium of Academic Research], no. 2, 1983, p. 59.

Xu Junji, "Guonei yanjiu Gongchan Guoji he Zhongguo geming wenti xianzhuang" [The current status of domestic research on the problem of the relation of the Communist International to the Chinese revolution], *Dangshi Tongxun* [Party History Bulletin], nos. 11–12, 1983, p. 323.

Xue Qi, "Peng Dehuai tongzhi zai yi jiu san liu nian" [Comrade Peng Dehuai in 1936], *Dangshi Yanjiu* [Research on Party History], no. 1, 1984, p. 72.

Xu Youqun, "Jiang Jieshi yu Deguo faxisi de goujie" [Chiang Kai-shek's collaboration with German fascism], *Zhongguo Xiandaishi* [Chinese Modern History], reprinted in *Fuyin Baokan Ziliao* [Reprint of Journal Materials], 1983, p. K4.

Xu Zehao, "Wang Jiaxiang dui Mao Zedong sixiang de renshi jiqi gongxian" [Wang Jiaxiang's understanding of and contribution to the thought of Mao Zedong], *Dangshi Yanjiu* [Research on Party History], no. 1, 1984, p. 40.

Yan Jingwen, *Zhou Enlai Pingzhuan* [Critical biography of Zhou Enlai], Hong Kong: Powen Shuju, 1974.

Yan Shuheng, "Liu Shaoqi tongzhi dui kang Ri minzu tongyi zhanxian lilun de gongxian" [Comrade Liu Shaoqi's theoretical contribution to the anti-Japanese national united front], *Dongbei Shida Xuebao* [Northeastern Normal University Journal], no. 3, 1983, p. 85.

Yang Chunzhou, "Yang Jie beihai qian de fan Jiang huodong" [The anti-Chiang activities of Yang Jie prior to his assassination], *Yunnan Wenshi Ziliao Xuanji* [Yunnan Selection of Literary Materials], no. 2, n.d., p. 172.

Yang Fangzhi, "Cong Nanjing dao Wuhan" [From Nanjing to Wuhan], in *Xinhua Ribao de Huiyi* [Memoir of the New China Daily], Shi Ximin and Fan Jianhui, eds., Chengdu: Sichuan Renmin Chubanshe, 1983.

Yang Guisong, "Zhongguo Gongchandang kang Ri minzu tongyi zhanxian zhengce de xingcheng yu Gongchan Guoji" [The Communist International and the formation of the Chinese Communist Party's policy of anti-Japanese national united front], *Jindaishi Yanjiu* [Research on Modern History], no. 4, 1980, p. 69.

Yang Shangkun, "Yi beizi zuo haoshi de youyi yu geming" [A lifetime of doing good and helping the revolution], *Renmin Ribao* [People's Daily], 4 April 1984, p. 5.

Yang Shengqing, "Xian shibian qian Guo Gong liangdang de zhongxin jiechu" [The renewal of KMT–CCP contacts prior to the Xian Incident], *Dangshi Tongxun* [Party History Bulletin], no. 2, 1983, p. 9.

Yang Shilan, "Deng Fa," in *Zhonggong Dangshi Renwu Zhuan* [Biographies of Chinese Communist historical personalities], vol. 1, Beijing: Zhongguo Shehui Kexueyuan, p. 347.

Yang Yizhou, Lo Feng, and Wang Tianceng, *Tantan Zhongguo Gongchandangde Zhengdang Zhengfeng* [Discussing party rectification in the Chinese Communist Party], Fuzhou: Fujian Renmin Chubanshe, 1984.

Yang Yuqing, "Wosuo zhidao de Chen Bulay" [The Chen Bulai I Knew], *Wenshi Ziliao Xuanji* [Selection of Literary Materials], national edition, vol. 81. n.d., p. 163.

———, "Guo Taiqi bei Jiang Jieshi mianzhi de neimu" [The inside story of Chiang Kai-shek's firing of Guo Taiqi], *Wenshi Ziliao Xuanji* [Selection of Literary Materials], national edition, vol. 22, n.d., p. 56.

Yao Menggan, *Feidang Neibu Duozheng Wenti Lunji* [Collected essays on the internal struggle of the bandit party], Taibei: Guoji Guanxi Yanjisuo, 1975.

Yu Shaowen, "Yingguo touxie zhengce de qiantu yu Zhongguo kangzhan" [Prospects for England's policy of appeasement and China's war of resistance], *Zhong Su Wenhua* [Sino-Soviet Culture], vol. 2, no. 2 (1 June 1938), p. 4.

Zhang Bofeng,"Guanyu kang Ri zhanzheng shiqi Jiang Jieshi fandong jituan de jizi tuoxiang huodong" [Regarding several instances of the capitulationist and appeasement activities of the reactionary Chiang Kai-shek clique during the war of resistance against Japan], *Jindaishi Yanjiu* [Research on Modern History], no. 2, 1979, p. 215.

Zhang Chong, "Zhu Sulian hongjun jie" [To the Soviet Red Army Day], *Zhong Su Wenhua* [Sino-Soviet Culture], vol. 5, no. 2 (1 February 1940), p. 10.

———, "Zongli yu Zhong Su bangjiao" [The premier and friendly relations between China and the Soviet Union], *Zhong Su Wenhua* [Sino-Soviet Culture], special issue (20 March 1940), p. 26.

Zhang Dalun, "Chen Tanqiu, Mao Zemin lieshi bei Jiang Jieshi, Sheng Shicai goujie mosha de neimu" [The secret story of the collaboration between Chiang Kai-shek and Sheng Shicai to murder the martyrs Chen Tanqiu and Mao Zemin], *Wuhan Wenshi Ziliao Xuanji* [Wuhan Selection of Literary Materials], vol. 3 (June 1981), p. 68.

Zhang Guotao, *Wo de Huiyi* [My memoir], 3 vols., Hong Kong: Ming Bao Chubanshe, 1974.

———, *Kang Ri Minzu Tongyi Zhanxian de Fenxi yu Pipan* [Analysis and criticism of the anti-Japanese national united front], Chongqing (?): Tongyi Chubanshe, May 1942.

Zhang Guoxiang, "Hongjun dongzheng yu Shanxi kang Ri minzu tongyi zhanxian de xingcheng" [The eastern expedition of the Red Army and the formation of the anti-Japan national united front in Shanxi], *Jinyang Xuebao* [Southern Shaanxi Journal], no. 5, 1982, p. 57.

Zhang Pei, *Kang Sheng Ping Zhuan* [Critical biography of Kang Sheng], Beijing: Hongqi Chubanshe, 1982.

Zhang Qi, "Liang shi yi you" [Excellent teacher and good friend], in *Huiyi Chen Tanqiu* [Recollections of Chen Tanqiu], Wuhan: Renmin Chubanshe, 1981.

Zhang Qianhua, "Zhengxuexi zai dongbei jieshou wenti shang de ruyi suanpan" [The foolish dreams of the Political Science clique regarding the recovery of Manchuria], *Wenshi Ziliao Xuanji* [Selection of Literary Materials], national edition, vol. 42, n.d., p. 172.

Zhang Qun, "Yu Riben jiexiale bu jie zhi lu" [Record of the rupture of relations with Japan], *Zhuanji Wenxue* [Biographical Literature], vol. 31, no. 31 (July 1977), p. 53.

———, "Ren waijiaobuchang de huiyi" [Memoir of service as foreign minister], *Zhuanji Wenxue* [Biographical Literature], part 1: vol. 31, no. 6 (December 1977). Part II: vol. 32, no. 1 (January 1978).

Zhang Rixin, "Wang Ming youqin touxiang zhuyi shi heshi xingcheng de" [When did the rightist capitulationist line of Wang Ming materialize?], *Jiangxi Daxue Xuebao* [Jiangxi University Journal], no. 4, 1983, p. 68.

Zhang Ximan, "Jiaqiang Zhong Su youyi yao qingsu hanjian" [To strengthen Sino-Soviet friendship we must purge traitors to the Han race], *Zhong Su Wenhua* [Sino-Soviet Culture], special issue (7 November 1939), p. 26.

Zhang Youyu, "Guanyu buliesete heyue" [On the peace treaty of Brest-Litovsk], *Zhong Su Wenhua* [Sino-Soviet Culture], special issue (7 November 1939), p. 26.

Zhang Zhongdong, *Cong Zhuzhang Heping Dao Zhuzhang Kangzhan de Hu Shi* [Hu Shi, from advocating peace to advocating war of resistance], Taibei: Zhongyang Yanjiuyuan Meiguo Yanjiu Zhongxin, December 1983.

Zhang Zuobin, *Zhang Zuobin Huiyilu* [Memoir of Zhang Zuobin], no. 19, Taibei: Zhuanji Wenxue Congshu, September 1967.

Zhao Kang, "Zhong Su bu qinfan tiaoyue yu Zhong Ri zhanzheng" [The Sino-Soviet non-aggression treaty and the Sino-Japanese War], *Zhong Su Wenhua* [Sino-Soviet Culture], vol. 2, nos. 9–10 (1 October 1937), p. 5.

Zhao Rui, "Yan Xishan gongdi panguo zuixing jiyao" [Major points of the traitorous crimes of public enemy Yan Xishan], *Wenshi Ziliao Xuanji* [Selection of Literary Materials], national edition, vol. 29, n.d., p. 158.

Zheng Xuejia, *Di San Guojishi* [History of the Third International], 2 vols., Taibei: Shangwu Yinshuguan, 1977.

Zhong Su Wenhua [Sino-Soviet Culture], Zhong Su Wenhua Xiehui, Nanjing (1937), Wuhan (1938), Chongqing (1939–1945). This was the publication of the Soviet-Chinese people's friendship association.

Zhong Zhongfa, *De Yi Ri Sanguo Tongmeng* [The German, Italian, Japanese Tripartite Alliance], Chongqing (?): Guomin Tushu Chubanshe, October 1940.

———, *Ying Mei zai Yuandong de Pingxing Xingdong* [The Far Eastern parallel actions of England and America], Chongqing (?): Guomin Tushu Chubanshe, September 1940.

Zhonggong Dangshi Cankao Ziliao [Reference materials on CCP history], Beijing: Zhongguo Renmin Jiefang Jun Zhengzhi Xueyuan Dangshi Jiaoyanshi [The CCP history office of the Political College of the People's Liberation Army], vols. 7–9, no place or date of publication given.

Zhonggong Zhongyang Dangshi Yanjiushi [Party history office of the central committee of the CCP], *Zhonggong Dangshi Dashi Nianbiao* [Chronology of CCP history], Nanjing (?): Jiangsu Renmin Chubanshe, 1981.

Zhonggong Zhongyang Dangxiao Dangshi Jiaoyanshi [Party history instructional office of the party school of the Central Committee of the CCP], *Zhongguo Gongchandang Shigao* [Draft history of the Chinese Communist Party], Beijing: Renmin Chubanshe, 1983.

———, *Zhongguo Gongchandang Lizi Zhongyao Huiyi Ji* [Historically important meetings of the Chinese Communist Party], vol. 2, Shanghai: Renmin Chubanshe, June 1982.

Zhongguo Gongchandang Lishi Jiangyi [Lectures on the history of the Chinese Communist Party], Shanghai: Fudan Daxue, 1978.

"Zhongguo Gongchandang ren zai Xinjiang huodong jishi" [Record of activities of Chinese Communist personnel in Xinjiang], *Xinjiang Wenshi Ziliao Xuanji* [Xinjiang Selection of Literary Materials], no. 1, n.d., pp. 30–36.

Zhongguo Shehui Kexueyuan Jindaishi Yanjiusuo [Institute of Modern History, Chinese Academy of Social Sciences], *Minguo Renwu Zhuan* [Biographies of personnel of the Republic of China], Beijing: Zhonghua Shuju, 1978.

———, *Gongchan Guoji Youguan Zhongguo Geming de Wenxian, 1929–1936* [Documents of the Communist International regarding the Chinese revolution, 1929–1936], vol. 2, Beijing: Zhongguo Shehui Kexueyuan, 1982.

———, *Zhongguo Zhuwai Shiling Nianbiao, 1912–1949* [Yearbook of China's foreign ambassadors and counselors, 1912–1949], Nanjing: Zhongguo Kexueyuan Jiandaishi Yanjiusuo, 1963.

Zhongguo Jindai Duiwai Guanxishi Ziliao Xuanji, 1940–1949 [Selection of materials on China's modern diplomatic history, 1940–1949), vol. 2, book 2, Shanghai: Renmin Chubanshe, September 1977.

Zhongguo Waijiaoshi Ziliao Xuanbian, Di San Ce (1937–1945) [Selection of materials on China's diplomatic history, vol. 3, 1937–1945], Beijing: Waijiao Xueyuan, 1958.

Zhong Su Bu Qinfan Tiaoyue [The Sino-Soviet nonaggression treaty], Taibei: Guoshiguan [Academica Historica], file no. wai 02.1 12.

Zhongyang Diaocha Tongjiju [Statistical office of the Central Investigation Bureau], *Zhongguo Gongchan Zhuyi Tongmeng zhi Zhenzhi Zhuzhang* [The political position of the Chinese Communist League], Chongqing(?), January 1941, no publisher given.

Zhou Enlai, *Zhou Enlai Xuanji* [Selected works of Zhou Enlai], vol. 1, Beijing: Renmin Chubanshe, 1980.

"Zhou Enlai tongzhi kangzhan chuqi zai Wuhan" [Comrade Zhou Enlai in Wuhan during the early period of the war of resistance], *Huazhong Shiyuan Xuebao* [Central China Normal College Journal], no. 2, 1979, p. 1.

Zhou Xicai, *Zhong Su Guanxi Neimu* [The secret history of Sino-Soviet relations], Taibei: Shidai Chuban she, n.d.

Zhou Yawei, "Jiang Jieshi dui Deguo guwen de guoxiang" [Chiang Kai-shek's illusions regarding the German advisors], *Wenshi Ziliao Xuanji* [Selection of Literary Materials], national edition, vol. 19, n.d., p. 190.

Zhou Yingsong, "Chen Shaoguan yu jiu Zhongguo haijun" [Chen Shaoguan and the national redemption navy], *Wenshi Ziliao Xuanji* [Selection of Literary Materials], national edition, vol. 85, n.d., p. 166.

Zhu Chengya, *Zhonggong Dangshi Yanjiu Lunwen Xuan* [Selection of research essays on CCP history], Changsha: Hunan Renmin Chubanshe, 1984.

Zhu Xikang, "Guanyu Guomindang guanliao ziben de jianwen" [Brief description of the KMT's bureaucratic capitalism], *Wenshi Ziliao Xuanji* [Selection of Literary Materials], national edition, vol. 11, n.d., p. 72.

Zhu Xinghua, "Hongjun dongzheng shiwei jianji" [Brief record of the eastern expedition of the Red Army], *Yan'an Daxue Xuebao* [Yan'an University Journal], no. 1, 1983, p. 13.

Zhu Zhenming, "Taipingyang zhanzheng shiqi Riben zhanling xia de Miandian" [Burma under Japanese occupation during the Pacific war], *Dongnanya Ziliao* [Materials on Southeast Asia], no. 1, 1983, p. 1.

Zongtong Jianggong Dashi Changbian Chugao [Preliminary extensive chronology of President Chiang], Taibei: Zhongguo Guomindang Zhongyang Weiyuanhui Dangshi Weiyuanhui, October 1978. (Unpublished compendium of materials dealing with Chiang Kai-shek's life and work. Includes extensive quotes from Chiang's diary. Vols. 3–6 cover the 1934–1945 period.)

Zui Ke Fu, Wa. [Vasilii Chuikov], *Zai Hua Shiming* [Mission to China], Beijing: Xinhua Chubanshe, 1983. (Originally published in Russian in the Soviet journal, *New World*, no. 11/12, 1979.)

Western Language Sources

Angelucci, Enzo, *The Rand McNally Encyclopedia of Military Aircraft, 1914–1980*, New York: The Military Press, 1983.

Appeal of the Finnish Government to the League of Nations, A Summary Based on the Official Documentation, special supplement to the Monthly Summary of the League of Nations, December 1939.

Beloff, Max, *The Foreign Policy of Soviet Russia, 1929–1941*, New York: Oxford University Press, 1949.

———, *Soviet Policy in the Far East, 1944–1951*, New York: Oxford University Press, 1953.

Benton, Gregor, "The 'Second Wang Ming line' (1935–38)," *China Quarterly*, no. 61, pp. 61–94.

Boorman, Howard, editor, *Biographical Dictionary of Republican China*, 3 vols., New York: Columbia University Press, 1967.

Borg, Dorothy, *The United States and the Far Eastern Crisis of 1933–1938*, Cambridge, Mass.: Harvard University Press, 1964.

Borkenau, Franz, *World Communism*, Ann Arbor: University of Michigan Press, 1962.

Bowden, James C., "Soviet Military Aid to Nationalist China, 1923–41," in *Sino-Soviet Military Relations*, Raymond C. Garthoff, editor, New York: Frederick Praeger Press, 1966, pp. 44–56.

Boyle, John Hunter, *China and Japan at War 1937–1945, the Politics of Collaboration*, Stanford, Calif.: Stanford University Press, 1972.

Braun, Otto, *Comintern Agent in China, 1932–1939*, London: Hurst and Co., 1982.

Byrnes, James F., *All in One Lifetime*, New York: Harper and Brothers, 1958.

Carr, E.H., *Twilight of the Comintern, 1930–1935*, New York: Pantheon Books, 1982.

Catell, David T., *Communism and the Spanish Civil War*, Berkeley: University of California Press, 1956.

———, *Soviet Diplomacy and the Spanish Civil War*, Berkeley: University of California Press, 1957.

Chaney, Otto Preston, Jr., *Zhukov*, Norman, Okla.: University of Oklahoma Press, 1971.

Chang Chi-yun, *Record of the Cairo Conference*, Taibei: China Culture Publishing Foundation, 1953.

Chang Chun-ming, *Chiang Kai-shek, His Life and Times* (abridged English translation of *Jiang Zongtong Milu* by *Sankei Shimbun*), New York: St. Johns University Press, 1981.

Cheng Tien-fong, *A History of Sino-Russian Relations*, Washington, D.C.: Public Affairs Press, 1957.

Chi Hsi-sheng, *Nationalist China at War: Military Defeat and Political Collapse, 1937–1945*, Ann Arbor: University of Michigan Press, 1982.

Chiang Kai-shek, *The Collected Wartime Messages of Generalissmo Chiang Kai-shek, 1937–1945*, 2 vols., New York: John Day Co., 1946.

———, *Resistance and Reconstruction: Messages During China's Six Years of War, 1937–1943*, New York: Harper and Brothers, 1943.

China Handbook, 1937–1944, A Comprehensive Survey of Major Developments in Seven Years of War, Taibei: Cheng Wen Publishing Company, 1971. (First published 1944.)

Ch'ien Tuan-sheng, *The Government and Politics of China, 1912–1949*, Stanford, Calif.: Stanford University Press, 1970.

Chudodav, Iu. V., *Soviet Volunteers in China, 1925–1945*, Moscow: Progress Publishing Co., 1980.

Churchill, Winston, *The Second World War*, Boston: Houghton-Mifflin, 1948–1953. I. *The Gathering Storm*, II. *Their Finest Hour*, III. *The Grand Alliance*, IV. *The Hinge of Fate*, V. *Closing of the Ring*, VI. *Triumph and Tragedy*.

Clark, Alan, *Barbarossa, The Russian-German Conflict, 1941–1945*, New York: William Morrow, 1965.

Clements, Diane S., *Yalta*, New York: Oxford University Press, 1970.

Clifford, Nicholas R., *Retreat from China: British Policy in the Far East, 1937–1941*, London: Longmans, Green, 1957.

Clissold, Stephen, editor, *Yugoslavia and the Soviet Union, 1939–1973, A Documentary Survey*, New York: Oxford University Press, 1975.

Clubb, O. Edmund, *China and Russia, the Great Game*, New York: Columbia University Press, 1971.

Cochran, Bert, *Harry Truman and the Crisis Presidency*, New York: Funk and Wagnalls, 1973.

Cohen, Warren I., *America's Response to China: An Interpretive History of Sino-American Relations*, New York: John Wiley, 1971.

———, "American Observers and the Sino-Soviet Friendship Treaty of August 1945," *Pacific Historical Review*, vol. 35 (August 1966), pp. 347–350.

Compton, Boyd, *Mao's China: Party Reform Documents, 1942–1944*, Seattle: University of Washington Press, 1966.

Conquest, Robert, *The Great Terror, Stalin's Purge of the Thirties*, New York: Macmillan, 1973.

Dallin, J. David, *Soviet Russia and the Far East*, New Haven, Conn.: Yale University Press, 1948.

Davies, Joseph E., *Mission to Moscow*, New York: Simon and Schuster, 1941.

Deakin, F.W. and G.R. Storry, *The Case of Richard Sorge*, London: Chatto and Windus, 1966.

Dedijer, Vladimir, *Tito Speaks: His Self-Portrait and Struggle with Stalin*, London: Weiden, Feld, and Nicolson, 1953.

————, *The Battle that Stalin Lost, Memoirs of Yugoslavia, 1948–1953*, New York: Viking Press, 1971.

Deutsch, Harold, *Hitler and His Generals, the Hidden Crisis, January–June 1938*, Minneapolis: University of Minnesota Press, 1974.

Drechsler, Karl, *Deutschland-China-Japan, 1933–1939*, Berlin: Akademie-Verlag, 1964.

Durrence, James Larry, *Ambassador Clarence E. Gauss and United States Relations with China, 1941–1944*, doctoral dissertation, University of Georgia, Athens, January 1972. DAI 32, no. 7.

Eastman, Lloyd E., *Seeds of Destruction, Nationalist China in War and Revolution, 1937–1949*, Stanford, Calif.: Stanford University Press, 1984.

————, *The Abortive Revolution: China Under Nationalist Rule, 1927–1937*, Cambridge, Mass.: Harvard University Press, 1974.

Esherick, Joseph W., editor, *Lost Chance in China, the World War II Despatches of John S. Service*, New York: Random House, 1974.

Feis, Herbert, *The Road to Pearl Harbor*, New York: Atheneum, 1965.

————, *The China Tangle*, Princeton, N.J.: Princeton University Press, 1953.

Fidlon, David, translator, *Soviet Volunteers in China, 1925–1945*, Moscow: Progress Publishing Co., 1980.

Fishel, Wesley, *The End of Extraterritoriality in China*, Berkeley: University of California Press, 1974.

————, "A Japanese Peace Maneuver in 1944," *Far Eastern Quarterly*, no. 13, 1949, pp. 387–397.

Fox, John P., *Germany and the Far Eastern Crisis, 1931–1938*, London: Clarendon Press, 1982.

Garthoff, Raymond, "The Soviet Intervention in Manchuria, 1945–1946," in *Sino-Soviet Military Relations*, Raymond Garthoff, editor, New York: Frederick Praeger, 1966.

Ghose, Sankar, *Socialism and Communism in India*, Bombay: Allied Publishers, 1971.

Gittings, John, *The World and China, 1922–1972*, New York: Harper and Row, 1974.

Goldstein, Steven M., *Yenan's American Policy: 1937–1941*, paper presented to the Conference on Sino-American Relations in the 1940s, sponsored by the Institute of American Culture of Academica Sinica, Taibei, Taiwan, 29–30 December 1982.

Harriman, W. Averell, "Statement of W. Averell Harriman, Special Assistant to the President, Regarding Our Wartime Relations with the Soviet Union, Particularly as They Concern the Agreements Reached at Yalta," *The Military Situation in the Far East*, hearings before the Committee on Armed Services and the Committee on Foreign Relations, United States Senate, 82nd Congress, 1st Session, Part 5, pp. 3328–3342. Washington, D.C.: Government Printing Office, 1951.

Harrison, James P., *The Long March to Power: A History of the Chinese Communist Party*, New York: Frederick Praeger, 1972.

Hauner, Milan, *India in Axis Strategy: Germany, Japan, and Indian Nationalists in the Second World War*, Stuttgart: Klett-Cotta, 1981.

Hildebrand, Klaus, *The Foreign Policy of the Third Reich*, Berkeley: University of California Press, 1970.

Hsu, Immanuel C.Y., *The Rise of Modern China*, New York: Oxford University Press, 1970.

Hsu, Long-hsuen and Ming-kai Chang, *History of the Sino-Japanese War, (1937–1945)*, Taibei: Chung Wu Company, 1971.

Hsu, U.T., *The Invisible Conflict*, Hong Kong: China Viewpoints, 1958.

Hu Chiao-mu, *Thirty Years of the Communist Party of China*, Beijing: Foreign Languages Press, 1959.

Iatrides, John O., *Revolt in Athens, the Greek Communist "Second Round," 1944–1945*, Princeton, N.J.: Princeton University Press, 1972.

Ikle, Frank Y., *German-Japanese Relations, 1936–1940: A Study in Totalitarian Diplomacy*, New York: Bookman Association, 1956.

Isaacs, Harold, *The Tragedy of the Chinese Revolution*, Stanford, Calif.: Stanford University Press, 1961.

Israel, John, *Student Nationalism in China, 1927–1937*, Stanford, Calif.: Hoover Institute Press, 1966.

Japan's Dependence on Foreign Supplies of War Materials, China Reference Series, vol. 1, no. 3 (15 December 1937), Trans-Pacific News Service. (Document presented by China to the Brussels Nine-Power Conference.)

Johnson, Chalmers, *Peasant Nationalism and Communist Power*, Stanford, Calif.: Stanford University Press, 1962.

Kalyagin, Aleksandr Ya. (translated by Steven I. Levine), *Along Alien Roads*, New York: Columbia University, East Asian Institute, 1983.

Katakoa, Tetsuya, *Resistance and Revolution in China, the Communists and the Second United Front*, Berkeley: University of California Press, 1974.

Kimball, Warren F., editor, *Churchill and Roosevelt; the Complete Correspondence*, 3 vols., Princeton, N.J.: Princeton University Press, 1984.

Kirby, William C., *Germany and Republican China*, Stanford, Calif.: Stanford University Press, 1984.

Kitts, Charles R., *An Inside View of the Kuomintang, Chen Li-fu, 1926–1949*, doctoral dissertation, St. Johns University, Jamaica, N.Y., 1978.

Klein, Donald W. and Anne B. Clarke, *Bibliographic Dictionary of Chinese Communism, 1921–1965*, Cambridge, Mass.: Harvard University Press, 1971.

Koo, Wellington, *Reminiscences of Wellington Koo*, Chinese Oral History Project of the East Asian Institute of Columbia University, Rare Book and Manuscript Library, New York.

Kuhfus, Peter M., *Die Risiken der Freundschaft: China und der Jalta-Mythos*, Bochumer Jahrbuch zur Ostasienforschung, no. 7, 1984.

Kukushkin, K.V., "The Comintern and the United National Anti-Japanese Front in China," in R.A. Ulyanovsky, ed., *The Comintern and the East, the Struggle for the Communist Strategy and Tactics in the National Liberation Movements*, Moscow: Progress Publishers, 1979.

Kuo, Thomas C., *Ch'en Tu-hsiu (1879–1942) and the Chinese Communist Movement*, South Orange, N.J.: Seton Hall University Press, 1975.

Kuo, Warren, *Analytical History of the Chinese Communist Party*, Taibei: Institute of International Relations, 1970.

———, "The Conference at Lochuan," *Issues and Studies*, vol. 5, no. 1 (October 1968), pp. 35–56.

———, "The Conflict between Chen Shao-yu and Mao Tse-tung," part 1, *Issues and Studies*, vol. 5, no. 2 (November 1968), pp. 35–45. Part 2, vol. 5, no. 3 (December 1968), pp. 40–54.

———, "The 6th Plenum of the CCP 6th Central Committee," *Issues and Studies*, part 1: vol. 5, no. 6 (March 1969), pp. 34–48. Part 2: vol. 5, no. 5 (April 1969), p. 37.

———, "The CCP after the Government Evacuation of Wuhan," *Issues and Studies*, part 1: vol. 5, no. 8 (May 1969), p. 34. Part 2: vol. 5, no. 9 (June 1969), pp. 41–57.

Lattimore, Owen, *Pivot of Asia*, Boston: Little, Brown, 1950.

———, *The Sinkiang Pivot*, Boston: Little, Brown, 1950.

Lauer, Thomas L., *German Attempts at Mediation of the Sino-Japanese War, 1937–1938*, doctoral dissertation, Stanford University, Stanford, Calif., 1973.

Leahy, William, *I Was There, the personal story of the Chief of Staff to Presidents Roosevelt and Truman*, New York: Whittlesey House, 1950.

Lee, Bradford, *Britain and the Sino-Japanese War, 1937–1939*, Stanford, Calif.: Stanford University Press, 1972.

Lee, Chong-sik, *Revolutionary Struggle in Manchuria: Chinese Communism and Soviet Interest, 1922–1945*, Berkeley: University of California Press, 1983.

Lensen, George A., *The Damned Inheritance: The Soviet Union and the Manchurian Railway Crisis of 1931–1935*, Tallahassee, Fla.: Diplomatic Press, 1974.

———, *Strange Neutrality: Soviet-Japanese Relations During the Second World War, 1941–1945*, Tallahassee, Fla.: Diplomatic Press, 1972.

———, "Yalta and the Far East," in *The Meaning of Yalta*, John L. Snell, editor, Baton Rouge: Louisiana State University Press, 1956.

Levi, Werner, *Modern China's Foreign Policy*, Minneapolis: University of Minnesota, 1953.

Levine, Steven I., "Mao Tse-tung's Oral Report to the Seventh Party Congress, Summary Notes," *Chinese Law and Government*, vol. 10, no. 4 (Winter 1977–1978), p. 16. (This is a portion of Vladimirov's diary which was not included in the standard English translation of that work.)

———, "Comments," in *Nationalist China During the Sino-Japanese War, 1937–1945*, Paul K.T. Sih, editor, Hicksville, N.Y.: Exposition Press, 1977.

———, "Trotsky on China: The Exile Period," *Papers on China*, vol. 18, Cambridge, Mass.: Harvard University East Asia Research Center, December 1964.

Li, Lincoln, *The Japanese Army in North China, 1937–1941*, New York: Oxford University Press, 1975.

Li Tien-min, *Chou En-lai*, Taibei: Institute for International Relations, 1970.

Liang, Chin-jung, "The Sino-Soviet Treaty of Friendship and Alliance of 1945: the Inside Story," in *Nationalist China During the Sino-Japanese War, 1937–1945*, Paul K.T. Sih, editor, Hicksville, N.Y.: Exposition Press, 1977.

Liang, Hsi-huen, *The Sino-German Connection, Alexander von Falkenhausen between China and Germany, 1900–1941*, Amsterdam: Von Gorum, 1978.

Lindsay, Michael, *The Unknown War, North China 1937–1945*, London: Bergstrom and Boyle, 1975.

Lin Hsin-kung, "Settle Accounts with Peng Teh-huai for his Heinous Crimes of Usurping Army Leadership and Opposing the Party," *Peking Review*, no. 36 (1 September 1967), Beijing, p. 12.

Liu, James, *Sino-Japanese Diplomacy during the Appeasement Period, 1933–1937*, doctoral dissertation, University of Pittsburgh, Pa., 1950.

Lo Ruiqing, Lu Zhengcao, and Wang Bingnan, *Zhou Enlai and the Xi'an Incident—An Eyewitness Account*, Beijing: Foreign Languages Press, 1983.

Lowe, Peter, *Great Britain and the Origins of the Pacific War*, London: Clarendon Press, 1977.

Maisky, Ivan, *Memoirs of a Soviet Ambassador, the War 1939–1943*, London: Hutchinson, 1967.

Mao Zedong, *Selected Works of Mao Tse-tung*, Beijing: Foreign Languages Press, 1967.

McCagg, William O., Jr., *Stalin Embattled, 1943–1948*, Detroit: Wayne State University Press, 1978.

McKenzie, Kermit E., *Comintern and World Revolution, 1928–1943, The Shaping of Doctrine*, New York: Columbia University Press, 1964.

McLane, Charles B., *Soviet Policy and the Chinese Communists, 1931–1946*, New York: Columbia University Press, 1958.

Mirovitskaya, Raisa and Yuri Semyomenov, *The Soviet Union and China, a Brief History of Relations*, Moscow: Novosti Press Agency, 1981.

Moore, Harriet L., *Soviet Far Eastern Policy, 1931–1945*, Princeton, N.J.: Princeton University Press, 1945.

Morgenthau Diary (China), Committee on the Judiciary, United States Senate, 89th Congress, 1st session, New York: Da Capo Press, 1974.

Morley, James, editor, *Deterrent Diplomacy: Japan, Germany and the USSR, 1935–1940*, New York: Columbia University Press, 1976.

———, *The China Quagmire: Japan's Expansion on the Asian Continent, 1933–1941*, New York: Columbia University Press, 1983.

———, *The Fateful Choice: Japan's Advance into Southeast Asia, 1939–1941*, New York: Columbia University Press, 1980.

Nagai, Yonosuke and Akira Iriye, *The Origins of the Cold War in Asia*, New York: Columbia University Press, 1977.

Nollau, Gunther, *International Communism and World Revolution, History and Methods*, New York: Frederick Praeger, 1961.

North, Robert C., *Moscow and the Chinese Communists*, Stanford, Calif.: Stanford University Press, 1953.

———, *Kuomintang and Chinese Communist Elites*, Stanford, Calif.: Hoover Institute studies, series B, elite studies, no. 8, July 1952.

On the Question of Stalin, Beijing: Foreign Languages Press, 1963.

Payne, Robert, *Chiang Kai-shek*, New York: Weybright and Talley, 1969.

Pogue, Forest C., "The Big Three and the United Nations," in *The Meaning of Yalta*, John C. Snell, editor, Baton Rouge: Louisiania State University Press, 1956, p. 19.

Pope, Arthur Upham, *Maxim Litvinoff*, New York: L.B. Fisher, 1943.

Reardon-Anderson, James, *Yenan and the Great Powers: the Origins of Chinese Communist Foreign Policy, 1944–1946*, New York: Columbia University Press, 1980.

Roosevelt, Franklin D., *Map Room Messages of President Roosevelt, (1939–1945)*, Frederick, Md.: University Publications of America, 1981. Microfilm, reel 8: communications between President Roosevelt and Generalissmo Chiang Kai-shek, December 29, 1941–January 26, 1945; communications between President Roosevelt and W. Averell Harriman, U.S. Ambassador to Moscow, January 4, 1943–April 12, 1945. The documents in this series are unnumbered.

Rosinger, Lawrence K., *China's Crisis*, New York: Alfred A. Knopf, 1945.

———, *China's Wartime Politics, 1937–1944*, Princeton, N.J.: Princeton University Press, 1944.

Rossi, A. (pseudonym for Angelo Tasca), *A Communist Party in Action, an Account of the Organization and Operations in France*, New Haven, Conn.: Yale University Press, 1949.

———, *The Russo-German Alliance, August 1939–June 1941*, Boston: Beacon Press, 1951.

Rue, John, *Mao Tse-tung in Opposition, 1927–1935*, Stanford, Calif.: Stanford University Press, 1966.

Schaller, Michael, *The U.S. Crusade in China, 1938–1945*, New York: Columbia University Press, 1979.

Schram, Stuart, editor, *Chairman Mao Talks to the People, Talks and Letters: 1956–1971*, New York: Pantheon Books, 1974.

———, *Mao Zedong, A Preliminary Reassessment*, New York: St. Martin's Press, 1983.

———, *The Political Thought of Mao Tse-tung*, New York: Frederick Praeger, 1963.

Schwartz, Benjamin, *Chinese Communism and the Rise of Mao*, Cambridge, Mass.: Harvard University Press, 1951.

Seagrave, Sterling, *The Soong Dynasty*, New York: Harper and Row, 1985.

Seybolt, Peter J., "Terror and Conformity; Counterespionage Campaigns, Rectification, and Mass Movements, 1942–1943," *Modern China*, vol. 12, no. 1 (January 1986), p. 39–73.

Sherwood, Robert, *Roosevelt and Hopkins: An Intimate History*, New York: Harper and Row, 1948.

Shewmaker, Kenneth, *Americans and Chinese Communists, 1927–1945*, Ithaca, N.Y.: Cornell University Press, 1971.

Steenberg, Sven *Vlasov*, New York: Alfred A. Knopf, 1970.

Stettinius, Edward R., *Roosevelt and the Russians, the Yalta Conference*, Garden City, N.Y.: Doubleday, 1949.

Tang Tsou, *America's Failure in China*, 2 vols., Chicago: University of Chicago Press, 1963.

Thomas, Hugh, *The Spanish Civil War*, New York: Harper and Row, 1961.

Thorne, Christopher, *Allies of a Kind: The United States, Great Britain, and the War against Japan, 1941–1945*, New York: Oxford University Press, 1978.

———, *The Limits of Foreign Policy, The West, the League of Nations, and the Far Eastern Crisis of 1931–1932,*, New York: G.P. Putnam's Sons, 1972.

Thornton, Richard C., *China, the Struggle for Power, 1917–1972*, Bloomington, Ind.: Indiana University Press, 1973.

Tong, Hollington K., *China and the World Press*, 1948, no place of publication given.

———, *Chiang Kai-shek, Soldier, Statesman; Authorized Biography*, Shanghai: China Publishing Company, 1937.

Truman, Harry S., *Memoirs*, vol. 1, *Year of Decisions*, Garden City, N.J.: Doubleday, 1955.

Tsiang Ting-fu memoir, Chinese Oral History Project of the East Asia Institute of Columbia University, Rare Book and Manuscript Library, New York.

Tsien Tai, *China and the Nine-Power Conference at Brussels in 1937*, Asia in the Modern World Series, no. 4, New York: St. Johns University Press, 1964.

Tuchman, Barbara, "If Mao had Come to Washington; An Essay in Alternatives," *Foreign Affairs*, October 1972, pp. 44–64.

———, *Stilwell and the American Experience in China, 1911–1945*, New York: Bantam, 1972.

Tung, L. William, *V.K. Wellington Koo and China's Wartime Diplomacy*, Asia in the Modern World Series, no. 17, New York: St. Johns University Press, 1977.

Tuominen, Arvo, *The Bells of the Kremlin, an Experience in Communism*, Hanover, N.H.: University Press of New England, 1983.

Ulam, Adam B., *Titoism and the Cominform*, Cambridge, Mass.: Harvard University Press, 1952.

Ulyanovsky, R.A., editor, *The Comintern and the East, a Critique of the Critique*, Moscow: Progress Publishers, 1979.

United States Department of State, *The Conference at Quebec, 1944*, Washington, D.C.: Government Printing Office, 1972.

———, *The Conference of Berlin (The Potsdam Conference), 1945*, 2 vols., Washington, D.C.: Government Printing Office, 1960.

———, *The Conferences at Cairo and Tehran, 1943*, Washington, D.C.: Government Printing Office, 1961.

———, *The Conferences at Malta and Yalta, 1945*, Washington, D.C.: Government Printing Office, 1955.

———, *The Conferences at Washington, 1941–1942 and Casablanca, 1943*, Washington, D.C.: Government Printing Office, 1968.

———, *The Conferences at Washington and Quebec, 1943*, Washington, D.C.: Government Printing Office, 1970.

———, *Documents on German Foreign Policy, 1918–1945: From the Archives of the German Foreign Ministry, Series D*, 9 vols., Washington, D.C.: 1949–1956.

———, *United States Relations with China*, Washington, D.C.: U.S. Department of State, 1946.

Van Slyke, Lyman, *The Chinese Communist Movement, a Report of the United States War Department, July 1945*, Military Intelligence Division, Stanford, Calif.: Stanford University Press, 1968.

———, *Enemies and Friends: The United Front in Chinese Communist History*, Stanford, Calif.: Stanford University Press, 1967.

Vladimirov, Peter Pafenovich, *The Vladimirov Diaries, Yenan China: 1942–1945*, New York: Doubleday, 1975.

Wang Fan-hsi, *Chinese Revolutionary, Memoirs 1919–1949*, New York: Oxford University Press, 1980.

Wang Ming, *China. Cultural Revolution or Counter-Revolutionary Coup?*, Moscow: Novosti Press Agency, 1969.

Wieczyuski, Joseph L., ed., *The Modern Encylopedia of Russian and Soviet History*, Gulf Breeze, Fla.: Academic International Press, 1978.

Whiting, Allen and Sheng Shih-ts'ai, *Sinkiang: Pawn or Pivot?*, East Lansing: Michigan State University, 1958.

———, *Soviet Policies in China, 1917–1924*, Stanford, Calif.: Stanford University Press, 1954.

Who's Who in Communist China, Hong Kong: Union Research Institute, 1969.

Wilson, Dick, *The Long March, 1935*, London: Hamish Hamilton, 1981.

———, *When Tigers Fight: The Story of Sino-Japanese War, 1937–1945*, New York: Viking Press, 1982.

———, *Zhou Enlai, a biography*, New York: Viking Press, 1984.

Wright, Gordon, *The Ordeal of Total War, 1939–1945*, New York: Harper and Row, 1968.

Wu, Aitchen, *China and the Soviet Union*, New York: Methuen, 1950.

Wu, Tien-wei, *The Sian Incident: A Pivotal Event in Modern Chinese History*, Ann Arbor: University of Michigan, Center for Chinese Studies, 1976.

Wylie, Raymond F., *The Emergence of Maoism, Mao Tse-tung, Ch'en Po-ta, and the Search for Chinese Theory*, Stanford, Calif.: Stanford University Press, 1980.

Yaung, Emily, *The Impact of the Yalta Agreement on China's Domestic Politics, 1945–1946*, doctoral dissertation, Kent State University, Kent, Ohio, 1979.

Young, Arthur N., *China and the Helping Hand, 1937–1945*, Cambridge, Mass.: Harvard University Press, 1963.

Young, C. Kuangson, *The Sino-Japanese Conflict and the League of Nations, 1937: Speeches, Documents, Press Comments*, Geneva: Press Bureau of the Chinese Delegation to the League of Nations, 1937.

Zhukov, Georgii K., *The Memoirs of Marshal Zhukov*, New York: Delacorte Press, 1971.

Index

Ah Q, 264
Altai region, clashes in, 200–202, 203, 206
Argentina, 100
Australia, 192
Atomic bomb, 224, 225

Bai Zhongxi, 146
Bakulin, I.V., 162, 165
Batisky, P.F., 40
Belgium, 22
Benes, Eduard, 35
Bessarabia, 124, 163
Bismark's peace with Austria, 30
Bluecher, Vasilii K., 24, 25, 32, 33
Bo Gu, 11, 58, 70, 80, 241, 244, 247, 248, 255, 265
Bogomolov, Dimitri, 18–20, 21–22, 25, 28, 34
Bohemia, 114
Boxer Rebellion, 3
Braun, Otto, 132, 147, 238
Britain, 6, 22, 24, 26, 153, 164, 168, 177, 205, 271
  anti-Japan front and. *See same listing for* United States
  Communist Party of, 123
  Greece, intervention in, 258
  thalasocracy, 90
Browderism, 248, 268n
Brussels Conference, 22–23, 27
Bukovina, 124, 163
Bulgaria, 100, 114
Burma, 8, 177, 188, 192

Caballero, Largo, 60
Cairo Conference, 192, 196–99, 211
Canada, 155
Casablanca Conference, 192
Changgufeng Hill, battle of, 32–34
Chen Boda, 244
Chen Bulai, 201
Chen Duxiu, 68–69, 86n, 244, 261
Chen Lifu, 18, 51
Chen Tanqiu, 175–76
Chen Yun, 64, 66–67, 274
Cherepanov, A.I., 36, 83
Chiang Kai-shek
  alliance with Soviet Union and, 20, 34, 97–98, 105–106, 112–13, 184–86
  Altai clashes and, 200–202
  China's Destiny, 192–93, 231n
  collective security and, 22–23, 92–95, 106, 184
  as diplomat, 110, 271

Europe First strategy and, 182, 192
German-Soviet war, 183–84, 190–91
nationalism and, 4–5, 30–31, 162–63, 177, 215–16, 228–30, 271–73
New Fourth Army Incident and, 143–44, 146–47
Outer Mongolia and, 216–20, 222, 224–25, 227–30
peace talks with Japan and, 27–28, 30–31, 44, 49, 51, 80, 109–12, 185
second front in Europe and, 196
Sino-Soviet treaty (1937) and, 19–20
Sino-Soviet treaty (1945) and, 212–13, 215
Soviet-CCP relations and, 6, 51–52, 80–81, 131, 143–45, 158, 160, 200–201
Soviet entry into Sino-Japanese war and, 9, 15–16, 22–29, 32–34, 47, 98–99, 106–7, 182–92, 208, 231n
Soviet-Japan partition, 16, 21, 51–52, 97, 103, 115–16, 118, 143–45, 161–64, 200–202
Soviet-Japanese rapprochement and, 94, 96–98, 109, 114–16
Soviet rights in Manchuria and, 198, 211, 213
Soviet Union, European war and, 92
  expulsion from League of Nations and, 102–3
Soviet-U.S. diktat, 195, 209–10, 212, 214
Stalin, rejects meeting with, 197, 208–9
Stilwell, Joseph and, 204–5
Tri-Partite Treaty and, 112, 114, 143–44
U.S. factor in policy toward Soviets, 118, 183, 193–207, 210, 218
Wallace, Henry and, 206
war aims and, 7–8, 80, 110–11, 117–18, 177
Western appeasement of Germany and, 35
Xinjiang and, 153, 156, 162–63, 169–71, 173–74, 176–77
Yalta accords and, 210–214, 222–23, 234n, 235n
Chiang Kai-shek, Madame, 98, 185, 197, 198, 206
China
  anti-Comintern bloc and, 21, 27–28, 30–31, 33, 98, 111
  Big Four and, 193–96, 205, 207–9, 271
  collective security and, 15, 22–24, 35, 51
  declaration of war, 186
  European war and, 91–92
  France, mutual security treaty with, 43
  Germany, severs ties with, 184
  "Incident," 48

China, *cont.*
  international lines of communications and, 39,
      46, 102, 107, 111, 120*n*, 141, 145, 156,
      163, 187–88
  Japan, severs relations with, 29
  national humiliation, 4, 272
  "progressivism," 18, 250
  Soviet-Axis alignment and, 35, 91–92, 271
  Soviet-Japanese treaty (1941), protest of, 116
  Soviet Union, alliance with, 15–16, 18–22, 50
  united front and, 5, 13, 59, 66, 70, 80, 123
  United Nations and, 202–3, 205, 207–9, 228,
      271
  Western sympathy and, 99–100
  World War II and, 183–84, 182, 189
  Xinjiang and, 153, 161, 164–74
Chinese Communist Party
  cities, seizure of, 252, 261–63
  expansion of base areas, 70–72, 75, 79–80,
      136, 138–39, 140, 142, 259
  history, orthodox, 243–44
  Kuomintang pressure and, 82, 143
  military forces of, 61, 72, 79, 140, 142,
      158–59, 259, 263
  North China Bureau, 63, 263–64
  Northwest Bureau, 243
  Politburo Conferences
    December 1937, 65–67
    February 1938, 71–72
    Luochuan Conference, 60–64, 67
  Seventh Congress, 67, 76, 79, 244, 248,
      259–63
  Zheng Feng campaign and, 260–61
  Seventh Plenum of 6th CC, 243, 252, 258
  Sino-Soviet treaty (1945) and, 262–64
  Sixth Congress, 244
  Sixth Plenum of 6th CC, 64, 78–80, 87*n*, 242
  Southeast Bureau, 142
  Soviet assistance and, 134, 139–40, 249
  Soviet-German alignment and, 131–32
  Soviet Union, communications with, 13, 64,
      131, 158, 178*n*, 239, 247, 255, 258.
      See also Comintern: CCP, directives to;
      Mao Zedong: Comintern and; Soviet Union:
      CCP and
  Stalin's purges and, 69–70, 77
  Yalta accords and, 230, 257
  Yangtze River Bureau, 70, 72, 74–75
Chinese Eastern Railway, 8, 16, 162, 215. *See
      also* Manchuria, Soviet special rights in
Chuikov, Vasilii I., 40, 107–8, 131, 137–38,
      145–46
  Chinese efforts to spark Soviet-Japan war and,
      98, 184–85
  recalled to Soviet Union, 231*n*
Churchill, Winston, 186, 215, 275
Clubb, O. Edmund, 173
Comintern (Communist International). *See also*
      Mao Zedong
  CCP, directives to, 65, 77–78, 134–35, 238,
      240, 244–45, 248

  dissolution of, 247–51
  Far Eastern Bureau Chita conference (1940),
      141, 147
  Hundred Regiments Campaign and, 141–42
  international Communist movement, 22, 67
  Mao Zedong, skepticism of, 76, 132, 238–41
  New Democracy and, 123–24, 130–40
  organization of, 10–12, 60, 65, 162, 241, 273
  representatives at Yan'an, 131, 239, 241, 246
  Seventh Congress of, 12, 59
  Soviet-German alignment and, 123–26
  Soviet Union and, 9
Compton, Boyd, 242, 245
Coral Sea, battle of, 240
Currie, Lauchlin, 184
Czechoslovakia, 34–35, 106, 125

Dai Li, 111
de Gaulle, Charles, 7, 252
Dekanozov, Vladimir G., 165–67, 180*n*
Deng Fa, 159
Dimitrov, Georgii, 13, 65, 244–45, 248–50
  coalition government and, 253–54, 261
  endorses Mao Zedong as CCP leader, 77–78
  European War and, 123
  Zhou Enlai talks with (1940), 132–33
Ding Wenyuan, 110
Dogmatism, 242, 246
Dong Daoning, 29
Dumbarton Oaks Conference, 204, 207–9

Eden, Anthony, 189, 194
Eighth Regiment. *See* Xinjiang
Eighth Route Army, 61, 66, 82, 129, 140–43,
      147, 238–40. *See also* Chinese Communist
      Party: military forces of; Hundred
      Regiments Campaign
  proposed operations against Japan, 238–40
  size of, 259
  training of officers in Siberia, 256
  Xinjiang and, 158
Estonia, 124, 163
European War, 35, 91–93, 124–26

Falkenhausen, Alexander von, 32
"Far Eastern Munich," 111, 141. *See also* Chiang
      Kai-shek; Peace talks, China-Japan
  defined, 109–10
Feng Yuxiang, 17
Finland, 106, 124, 162. *See also* Winter War
  Finnish Communist Party, 132
France, 3, 6, 34, 205, 274
  anti-Japan front and, 7, 15, 19, 22, 24, 42, 59,
      99, 139
  Communist Party of, 123–24, 237, 251–52,
      273–74
  Fall of, 90, 111, 139, 141
  mutual security treaty with China and, 43
  Vichy, 144
Franco, Francisco, 59–60, 74
Fu Bingchang, 203

as ambassador to Moscow, 187, 189
Four Power declaration and, 194
Sino-Soviet treaty (1945) and, 214, 227
Yalta accords and, 209

Gandhi, Mohandas, 123, 177
Gao Jun, 132, 134
Gao Songwu, 29
Gauss, Clarence, 173, 257
George VI, King, 25
Germany, 6, 7, 22, 26, 35, 48, 51, 59, 91, 139,
    160, 271
  aid to China and, 28, 32, 42
  Balkans and, 114
  Communist Party of, 9, 12
  Sino-Japan war and, 32–33, 40, 66, 110–11
  Soviet Union, invasion of, 164–66, 170,
    182–83, 237, 240
  Wang Jingwei regime, recognizes, 184
Greece, 100, 114, 242, 251, 258
Guadalcanal, battle of, 240
Guangzhou, fall of, 75
Guo Dequan, 164, 188, 209
Guo Taiqi, 91, 100, 189

Harriman, Averell, 202, 207, 208
  Outer Mongolia and, 217, 218, 220, 222–23
  Sino-Soviet treaty (1945) and, 214, 225
He Lung, 241
He Yaozu, 97, 101–4, 185
He Yingqing, 29, 105, 191, 142–44, 146,
    168–69
He Zuchen, 143
Hirohito, Emperor, 41
Hirota Koki, 29
Hitler, Adolph, 9, 35, 59, 90, 94, 96, 108, 114,
    144, 164, 275
Hopkins, Harry, 189, 192, 208
  talks with Stalin (1945), 210–11, 213, 215,
    223
Hu Shi, 100–101, 104, 155, 185
Hu Songnan, 129–30, 142, 158, 249
Hull, Cordell, 107, 193–94, 201–2, 207
Hundred Regiments Campaign, 140–42, 151n,
    152n, 238
Hurley, Patrick, 197, 208, 214, 262
  appointed ambassador, 257
  delivers Yalta accords to Chiang, 209, 213
  KMT-CCP dispute and, 255, 257–59
  Sino-Soviet talks (1945) and, 218

India, 139, 178n, 188, 256
  Indian Communist Party, 123–24, 237
Insurrectionism, 251
Intelligence operations, 29, 48, 69, 97, 155, 159,
    178n, 183–84, 230n, 241. *See also* Sorge,
    Richard
International Anti-Aggressor Campaign, 22
Internationalism, 79, 83, 237, 238–39, 241, 245
Italy, 22, 26, 59, 139, 184, 185, 187
  Italian Communist Party, 251–52

Japan
  aggression in China, 4, 5, 22, 95, 162
  German-Soviet war and, 177, 238, 240
  military deployments opposite Soviet Union,
    31–32, 50, 110, 117, 238, 240
  Operation Ichi-go, 252
  Three All Extermination policy, 150, 239–40
Jiang Jingguo, 208, 210, 214, 217, 227
Jiang Tingfu, 16, 53n, 189, 155
  Brussels Conference and, 23
  Japan, war with and, 17, 21
  recall as ambassador, 17
  Sino-Soviet treaty (1937) and, 19
  Soviet assistance, negotiations re, 42–47
  Soviet entry into Sino-Japan war and, 17,
    21–22, 24–26, 33
Jiao Fusan, 30

Kai Feng, 243
Kalinin, Mikhail, 214
Kalyagin, Aleksander, 36, 39, 40, 129
Kang Sheng, 64, 66, 69, 241, 246, 248, 255, 260,
    274
Kataoka, Tetsuya, 61–62, 136
Khrushchev, Nikita, 276
Konoe, Fumimaro, 28, 111, 112
Koo, V.K. Wellington
  considered as ambassador to Moscow, 17
  Dumbarton Oaks Conference and, 207–8
  proposes alignment with Allies (1939), 91–92
  Soviet expulsion from League and, 100–101,
    103
Korea, 32, 33
Kung, H.H., 25, 28, 30, 53n, 110
Kuomintang
  crisis of (1943–44), 248–49, 259
  demands disbandment of CCP, 249
  Fifth Plenum of, 81–82, 110, 88n, 129–30, 158
  nationalism and, 3–6
  Seventh Plenum of, 142
Kurile Islands, 212–13, 215
Kursh, battle of, 195, 248
Kusinen, Otto, 124

Latoff, 165
Lattimore, Owen, 184–85
Latvia, 124, 163
League of Nations, 22, 23, 35, 92, 97, 130
  China's role in, 100
  expulsion of Soviet Union, 99–101
Lenin, V.I., 137, 166, 245, 261
Li Lisan, 11, 134, 244, 261
Li Shizeng, 53n
Lin Biao, 274
Lithuania, 124, 163
Litvinov, Maxim M., 53n
  ambassador to U.S., 107, 187
  Brussels Conference and, 23
  replaced by Molotov, 47
  Sino-Soviet treaty (1937) and, 18–19
  Soviet entry into war and, 25

Liu Shaoqi, 63, 243, 244, 258, 274, 276
Lost territories, 8, 117, 153, 177, 193, 195, 197, 232n
Luo Ruiqing, 276
Luo Wengan, 18
Luxun (Port Arthur), 197–99, 204, 211–17

Madrid, defense of, 74
Manchukuo, 5, 8, 16, 115
 Germany recognizes, 32
 Japan insists China recognize, 27
 Xinjiang, equivalent of, 153
Manchuria
 CCP and, 262
 Chiang's 1940 offer of Soviet rights in, 105–7, 120n
 "open door" and, 223, 225
 question of return to China, 8, 116, 195, 197–99, 212–13, 215, 218, 222–30, 271
 Soviet special rights in, 106, 197–98, 204, 211–13, 215, 217–18, 221–22, 225–29, 272
Mao Zedong
 base area regimes and, 70–71
 CCP, position within, 58, 139, 148, 243, 245–56
 Chongqing talks (1945), 263
 coalition government and, 253, 259, 261–62
 Comintern and, 12, 75, 80, 247–48, 250, 255, 273–75
 family, 143, 151n
 German-Soviet war and, 237–43
 global intermediate zone and, 127–28
 guerrilla war and, 62–63, 72–73, 78, 140
 initial wartime program, 60–62
 internationalism and, 79, 83, 237–38, 239
 KMT surrender and, 62, 64, 79, 82–84, 136–39, 150n
 Marxist-Leninist theory and, 13, 76, 238, 245, 276
 nationalism and, 5–6, 9–10, 58, 148, 157, 273–74
 New Democracy and, 126–28
 proletarian leadership of united front and, 64, 78–79, 87n, 126, 131
 revolution and, 6, 12, 58, 73, 128, 136–37, 147, 275
 sinicization of Marxism and, 4, 79–80, 242
 Soviet-German alignment and, 124–26
 Soviet security and, 237–39
 Soviet support for CCP and, 59, 73, 139–40, 147–48, 158, 248–49, 256, 260, 263, 264
 Stalin, endorsed by (1938), 75–79
 Stalin, 1940 compromise with, 148
 U.S. and, 128, 136, 139, 252–62
 Wuhan, defense of and, 73
 Xinjiang and, 157, 160, 163–64, 167, 175–76
Mao Zemin, 132, 175–76
Marco Polo Bridge Incident, 19, 20, 22, 51, 82, 104

Marshall, George C. 202, 211
Marxism-Leninism, 4, 11, 65, 71, 79, 132, 140, 154, 159, 166, 251, 276
May fourth Movement, 4
Midway, battle of, 240
Mif, Pavil, 11, 133, 239, 244
Mikoyan, Anastas, 93, 187, 189
Mobile war, defined, 61–62, 261–63
Molotov, Vyacheslav
 aid to China, suspension of and, 105, 187
 appointed foreign minister, 47
 China as one of Big Four and, 194
 cooperation with Germany and, 90
 League of Nations, Soviet expulsion from and, 101–3
 Sino-Soviet treaty (1945), and 214–27
 Soviet-Japanese treaty, denies reports of, 97
 Winter War and, 101–6, 116
 Xinjiang and, 161, 165–69
 Yalta accords and, 216
Mongolia, Outer, 8, 16, 36, 97, 115, 116, 129, 169, 193, 200, 272, 277. See also Chiang Kai-shek; Harriman, Averell; Roosevelt, Franklin D.; Stalin, Joseph; Truman, Henry
 in 1945 negotiations, 215–20, 222–24, 226-28
 return to China, 197, 204, 212
 significance of cession, 229–30
Morgenthau, Henry, 107
Moscow Foreign Ministers Conference, 194
Mukden Incident, 4, 9, 16, 20
Munich Conference, 34, 35, 109

Nakamura Toyokazu, 30
Nanjing, fall of, 25, 27, 41, 66
Nationalism. See also Chiang Kai-shek; Mao Zedong; Sun Yat-sen
 Chinese politics and, 3–7
 defined, 3
 Marxism-Leninism and, 4
 Outer Mongolia and, 215–17, 223
 united front and, 5
Netherlands, 19, 22, 205
New Camp. See Xinjiang
New Democracy. See Comintern; Mao Zedong
New Fourth Army, 72, 82, 136–37
 Incident, 142–46
New Zealand, 192
Nine Power Conference. See Brussels Conference
Nixon, Richard, 272
NKVD, 11, 60, 67, 133, 155, 165
Nomonhan battle, 35–36, 39, 96
 CCP and, 82–83
Norway, 99

Okamura Neiji, 239

Pacific Island campaign, 192
Paniushkin, Aleksandr S., 94, 103, 146–47, 200–201
 recalled to Moscow, 203–4
 Xinjiang and, 161, 167, 169, 173

Peace talks, China-Japan, 29–30, 50, 109–12. *See also* Chiang Kai-shek
  German mediation effort, 27–29, 50
  Japan's peace terms, 27, 29
Peng Dehuai, 58, 61, 63, 141, 241
Peng Zhen, 252
Petrov, Appolon A., 212–13, 222
Philippines Communist Party, 273
Phony war, 90, 94
Potsdam Conference, 222–24
Pushkin, Grigorii M., 171–72

Quebec Conference, 193

Ren Bishi, 71, 76–78, 132–33, 160, 243–44, 258, 260, 274
  as head of CCP Comintern delegation, 262
Ribbentrop, Joachim von, 32, 108, 113
Roosevelt, Franklin D.
  Altai clashes and, 201–2
  Chiang's proposal for four power alliance and, 184
  China as a great power and, 193, 198, 205, 252
  mediation efforts and, 205–6, 215, 252
  Outer Mongolia and, 197–99, 217, 220
  Soviet desire for warm water ports and, 198
  Stillwell, Joseph and, 204–5
  Yalta accords and, 209, 259
Rossi, A., 124
Rumania, 114
Rykov, A.I., 133
Ryukyu Islands, 197, 232*n*

Sakhalin Island, 96, 114, 201, 212, 213, 215
Sanctions, against Japan, 8, 15, 22–23, 35, 113
Service, John S., 253–54, 257–58, 262
Seybolt, Peter, 246
Shaan-Gan-Ning special district, 64, 145, 243, 248, 256
  Nationalist pressure against, 81–82, 129–30, 158, 239, 242, 249–50
  size of, 89*n*, 139, 140, 142
  Xinjiang and, 157, 159
Shanghai, fall of, 64
Shao Lizi, 116, 183, 145
  appointed ambassador to Moscow, 104–5
  resignation as ambassador, 189
  Sino-Soviet treaty (1937) and, 21
  transit rights negotiations and, 189
  Tri-Partite Treaty and, 112
Sheng Shicai, 131, 222
  breaks with Moscow, 166–67
  CCP/CPSU membership and, 160–62, 166
  removal from Xinjiang post, 203–4, 206
  Xinjiang and, 153–74
Shi Zhe, 134
Singapore, fall of, 240
Slovakia, 114
Smetanin, Konstatin, 186–87
Snow, Edgar, 69, 275

Soong, T.V., 44, 45, 107, 186, 194, 196, 201, 202
  delegation to Moscow and, 203–4, 210
  resignation as foreign minister, 224
  Sino-Soviet treaty (1945) and, 214–22, 224–28
  Yalta accords and, 211, 213
Sorge, Richard, 113, 238, 240
Souritz, 93
Southern Manchurian Railway, 29, 162, 215. *See also* Manchuria, Soviet special rights in
Soviet Union
  Altai clashes, protest of, 201
  assistance to China. *See also* China: international lines of communications and
    advisors, 40–41
    aircraft, types supplied, 39, 105, 120*n*
    aviation assistance, 41, 56*n*, 156
    Chinese repayment, 48, 57*n*
    compared to U.S. aid, 49–50
    corruption and, 42, 49, 50
    final termination of, 187, 204
    Nomonhan battle and third credit agreement, 36
    overall amount of, 37–38, 45, 46, 107–8
    relations with Japan and, 96, 101–8, 115, 185–87
    Southern Anwei Incident and, 145–47
    suspension of, 104–5, 107–8, 111, 120*n*, 129–30, 147
  Brussels Conference and, 23
  Burma road, closing of and, 107
  CCP and, 147, 157–59, 169, 175–76, 203, 213, 215, 220–21, 238, 248–50, 265*n*
  China's alignment with Allies (1939), vetoes, 92
  China's entry into Big Four, opposition to, 194, 207–9
  coalition government and, 259
  collective security and, 19–20, 22–24, 35, 59–60, 66
  entry into Far East war and, 224, 257
  Far Eastern military deployments, 9, 16
  Germany, alignment with, 90–91, 94, 99, 117–18
  Japan, deterrence of and the Sino-Japanese war, 16, 35–36, 50, 77–78, 108, 137–38, 150*n*, 240
  Japan, rapprochement with, 7, 95–99, 207
  League of Nations, expulsion from, 99–102
  Manchuria and, 194–99
  Poland, invasion of, 90–92, 124–25, 138, 163
  Red Army as agent of revolution, 124, 163–64
  second front in Europe and, 196
  summit meeting, proposed Sino-Soviet, 196–7, 208–9
  transit rights for U.S. aid, 187–91
  two-front war and, 15, 24, 26, 96, 108, 114, 117, 147, 186, 275
  U.S., rejects cooperation with in aiding China, 107
  warm water ports and, 8, 198–99, 213, 232*n*

Spain, 16, 39–40, 59–60, 74–75, 125, 144, 274
Stalin, Joseph
 CCP, non-support for, 220–21, 228
 China as ally against Japan, 147, 215, 228
 China's alignment with allies (1939) and, 92
 Chinese charges of Soviet-Japan deal (1944) and, 202
 Chinese revolution and, 58, 83
 Comintern and, 11, 162
 Grand Alliance and revolution, 251–54, 263–64
 Japan's peace terms (1937) and, 28
 Mao Zedong, cable to, 258
 Mao Zedong, endorses as CCP head (1938), 75–78, 148
 Outer Mongolia and, 204, 216–20, 227
 proposes Chinese offensive (1939), 37
 Purges and, 11
 Sino-Japan war and collective security, 26, 35, 51
 Sino-Soviet treaty (1937) and, 19
 Sino-Soviet treaty (1945) and, 214–22, 224–28
 Soviet entry into Sino-Japan war, 24–28, 34, 186
 Soviet security and, 137–38, 148
 Soviet-Western cooperation, rejects Chiang's proposal for, 93–94
 Spanish Republic and, 59–60
 Tri-Partite Treaty and, 113
 U.S. cancellation of 1911 treaty and, 92
 world communist movement, stature in, 12
 Xinjiang and, 153, 156–57, 160–61
 Yalta accords and, 209–10
Stalingrad, battle of, 171–72, 190, 195, 248
Stilwell, Joseph, 204–5, 207–8, 258
Strategic minerals, 38, 48, 57n, 90, 107, 153–54, 156, 170, 172, 189
Sun Ke, 16, 18, 26, 91–92, 96
 negotiations re Soviet aid, 38, 43–47
 Xinjiang and, 156–57, 162–63
Sun Yat-sen, 3–4
Svanidze, Aleksandr S., 154

T-26 tank, 38–39
Taierchuang, battle of, 39
Taiwan, 8, 197, 198, 271
Taiyuan, defense and fall of, 63–64
Tannu Tuva, 197–99, 204
Teheran Conference, 196, 199
Three Principles of the People, 3, 167
Tibet, 8, 97, 168, 216
Timoshenko, Semën, 145–46, 165
Tito, Josip Broz, 10, 251, 274
Tong, Hollington, 24
Togo, Shigenori, 105
Tojo Hideki, 111
Toyoda Teijiro, 186
Trautmann, Oskar, 27–28
Treaties. See also Chiang Kai-shek; Mao Zedong
 Anti-Comintern (1936), 16, 27, 112, 210
 Anti-War, 22
 Brest-Litovsk type, 6, 31, 124

 German-Soviet Non-Aggression (1939), 7, 16, 31, 35, 38, 131
 CCP and, 82, 125
 consequences of on Sino-Soviet relations, 90–94
 impact on German-Japan relations, 95–96
 Nine Power (1922), 22, 23, 27
 non-aggression, defined, 20–21, 96
 Sino-Soviet Commercial (1939), 83
 Sino-Soviet Friendship (1945), 214–28, 236n, 272
 Sino-Soviet Non-Aggression (1937), 15, 18–22, 156, 210
 violated by Soviet-Japan treaty, 115–16
 Soviet-Japan (1944), 201–2, 233n
 Soviet-Japan Neutrality (1941), 7, 96–97, 112, 115–16, 162, 184, 187, 237, 257, 259
 Soviet-Mongolian Mutual Security (1936), 201
 Tri-Partite (1940), 112, 118, 183
 U.S.-Japan Commercial (1911), 93–94
Transit rights via Soviet Union, 187–91, 190, 231n, 276
Trotsky, Leon, 67–68
Trotskyites, 60, 65, 66–70, 133, 160
Truman, Harry
 Outer Mongolia and, 218, 223–24
 U.S. presence at Luxun and, 210–11, 214
 U.S. role in Sino-Soviet talks (1945) and, 224–25
Tsien Tai, 22–23
Tuchman, Barbara, 259
Turkestan-Siberian Railway, 154, 189
Turkey, 103

Ugaki Kazushige, 29, 30
Unconditional surrender, 192
United States. See also Chiang Kai-shek; Mao Zedong; Roosevelt, Franklin D.; Stalin, Joseph; Truman, Harry; Xinjiang
 anti-Japan front and, 7, 15, 19, 22, 23, 24, 25, 26, 30, 35, 37, 42, 49, 51, 59, 60, 66, 74, 90, 91, 93, 94, 95, 96, 99, 100, 101, 103, 106, 107, 109, 112, 114, 116, 117, 136–37, 139, 144, 274
 Communist Party of, 123, 237, 268n
 debate re China policy, 257–59
 Japan, war with and, 182, 184, 185, 187, 188, 192
 Luxun, base at, 211
 mediation of Sino-Soviet relations and, 205–6, 222–25
 military operations in north China and, 211
 Observers Mission to Yan'an, 253
 open door and, 223
 Soviet entry into Far East war and, 223, 235n

Versailles Conference, 4, 182, 210
Vladimirov, Peter, 131, 239, 248, 254, 255, 258, 263
 Mao-Hurley talks and, 256

Seventh CCP Congress and, 260
Zheng Feng campaign and, 246–47
Vlasov, Andrey A., 40, 165
Voroshilov, Kliment E., 24–25, 37, 43–48,
102–4, 161

Wallace, Henry, 206, 207, 208, 233n
Wang Chonghui, 17, 19–20, 98, 115, 192
Cairo Conference and, 208
League of Nations and, 103
peace talks (1939) and, 110
resigns as foreign minister, 189
Wang Jiaxiang, 76–78, 134, 244, 274
Wang Jingwei, 5, 29, 80, 82, 97, 137–38, 144
Wang Ming, 58, 63. See also Trotskyites.
assassination attempt, 267n
base area governments and, 70–71
CCP participation in government and, 72
Chen Duxiu, attack on, 69–70
Comintern powers and, 65, 66, 85n, 133, 247
critique of Mao's program, 65–66, 70–72,
134–35
early ties with Soviet Union, 11
German-Soviet war and, 241–42, 247
Manchuria and, 262
Mao Zedong, defeated by, 139, 148, 245
Marxist-Leninist theory and, 13, 71, 132
military unification and, 66, 75
purges and, 68–70
Qun Zhong and, 72
return to China, 51–52, 64–65, 160
Seventh CCP Congress and, 260–61
Sixth Plenum of CCP Sixth CC, 78–79
Two Lines republication, 134–35, 148
Xinhua Ribao and, 71, 73
Zheng Feng campaign and, 243–44
Wang Shijie, 101
becomes foreign minister, 224
conciliatory approach toward Soviets and,
201–3, 229–30
Henry Wallace and, 206
New Fourth Army Incident and, 144–45
Sino-Soviet treaty (1945) and, 214, 225–27, 263
War and the Working Class, 195, 204
Washington Conference, 193
Wedemeyer, Albert, 258
Wei Daoming, 201, 207, 209, 220
Welles, Sumner, 186
Weng Wenhao, 104, 164, 169, 174, 191
Whiting, Allen S., 154, 160
Winter War, 39–40, 43, 94, 99–102, 104, 111,
124, 130, 138
Wu Guozhen, 173–74
Wu Yuzhang, 53n, 80
Wuhan, battle of, 31–34, 39, 46, 74–75
Madrid and, 74
proposed recapture of, 36–37, 83
strategic significance of, 32

Xian Incident, 5, 18, 77, 166
Xiang Ying, 138, 142–43

Xinjiang. *See also* Mao Zedong; Molotov,
Vyacheslav; Shaan-Gan-Ning special dis-
trict; Sheng Shicai; Stalin, Joseph; Sun Ke
Altai clashes and, 203
Chinese recovery of, 164–74, 176, 197–99,
204, 212
Dihua aircraft factory, 42, 105, 170–74
Dushanze oil facility, 154, 165, 170–74
Eighth Regiment, 156, 158, 163–64, 171–74
independence and, 153, 157, 161, 163, 166,
176–77, 179n
New Camp and, 134, 158–59, 163–64
rebellions and, 176–77,195, 204, 209, 218, 228
Soviet army and, 124, 154, 163–64, 172–74
Soviet-Axis alignment and, 153, 161–64
Soviet interests and, 16, 97, 115, 153–55,
161–63, 165–174, 193, 197, 210, 213, 217
Soviet mining company and, 162–63, 166–67,
171–74
United States and, 164, 168

Yalta accords, 208, 209–15, 222, 229–30, 259,
272. *See also* Chiang Kai-shek; Chinese
Communist Party
Yan Xishan, 17, 70, 129
Yang Hucheng, 13
Yang Jie, 56n, 94, 96–97, 103, 120n
corruption and, 42, 50
negotiations re Soviet aid, 42–48, 50
resignation as ambassador, 43, 101, 104, 189
Soviet entry into Sino-Japan war and, 16–17,
24–26, 31, 33, 47, 276
Yang Shangkun, 58, 63, 241, 244
Yang Song, 64
Yaung, Emily, 229–30
Ye Jianying, 147
Ye Ting, 142–43, 146
Yosuke Matsuoka, 115
Yugoslavia, 100, 114, 251, 256, 263, 274

Zhang Chong, 51, 64, 97, 98, 230n
Zhang Guotao, 58, 61, 63–67, 70, 72, 78
Zhang Jiluan, 33
Zhang Qun, 29–30
Zhang Wentian, 60, 65, 66–68, 71, 241, 244, 274
Zhang Xueliang, 13, 166
Zheng Feng campaign, 241–47, 255, 260–61, 274
Zhou Enlai, 58, 64, 70–71, 139, 142, 144, 175,
249, 258, 274
Chongqing talks (1945), 263
Moscow mission (1940), 131–33, 147
protests KMT move against CCP bases, 82
Wang Ming, possible support for, 61, 63, 241,
244, 266n, 267n
Zhou Xicai, 20, 44, 104
Zhou Zhirou, 105, 174
Zhu De, 58, 61, 63, 77, 143, 241, 258, 262
Zhu Shaoliang, 158, 164, 200
Zhu Shiming, 43
Zhukov, Georgii, 36, 39, 40
Zunyi Conference, 13, 58, 64, 75, 77, 242, 244